Lenin and the Revolutionary Party

Lenin and the Revolutionary Party

Paul Le Blanc

Introduction by Ernest Mandel

Haymarket Books
Chicago, Illinois

This edition published in 2015 by
Haymarket Books
P.O. Box 180165
Chicago, IL 60618
773-583-7884
www.haymarketbooks.org
info@haymarketbooks.org

ISBN: 978-1-60846-464-7

Trade distribution:
In the US, Consortium Book Sales and Distribution, www.cbsd.com
In Canada, Publishers Group Canada, www.pgcbooks.ca
In the UK, Turnaround Publisher Services, www.turnaround-uk.com
All other countries, Publishers Group Worldwide, www.pgw.com

This book was published with the generous support of Lannan Foundation
and Wallace Action Fund.

Cover design by Rachel Cohen. Author photo (cover flap) by Ashtyn Marino.

Printed in Canada by union labor.

Library of Congress Cataloging-in-Publication data is available.

10 9 8 7 6 5 4 3 2 1

Dedicated to the memory of George Breitman (1916–1986),
Gaston Le Blanc (1911–1971),
Shirley Harris Le Blanc (1926–1986)—good people
and dear friends whose lives and commitment to the cause
of labor and socialism inspired me

Contents

Preface

The present study seeks to draw together a great revolutionary's own views on the organizational principles of the revolutionary party, utilizing substantial quotations so that he may speak for himself. Yet it is necessary to go beyond a straightforward presentation or compilation of what Lenin said. Works of that nature too often have contributed to a stilted understanding, if not a gross misunderstanding, of Lenin's views. Lenin's distinctive views on organization were developed within complex and evolving situations, and at first he himself was not even aware that he was creating anything qualitatively different from previous Marxist conceptions of the revolutionary party. An additional complication is that there has been, from the very beginning, a considerable amount of distortion—by pro-Leninists, pseudo-Leninists, and anti-Leninists—of how these principles evolved, why they evolved, and what they actually mean. Therefore, it has been necessary to give significant attention to the following areas: (1) identifying and challenging certain distortions, (2) elaborating on the actual contexts within which Lenin's ideas developed, and (3) critically evaluating problems in Lenin's conception or the Bolshevik organization in one period that resulted in later modifications.

Too often, Lenin's ideas on organization have been abstracted from his commitment to the working class and socialism, from his views on the revolutionary program, and from the vibrancy of Russia's labor and socialist movements. This approach gives a cold and lifeless quality to Lenin's organizational perspectives. I have tried to avoid that difficulty in this study by giving greater attention to the "nonorganizational" matters that must be grasped to appreciate his views on the revolutionary party.

Several serious studies of Lenin's thought take up his views on the party, perhaps the most valuable being Marcel Liebman's *Leninism Under Lenin*, Neil Harding's two-volume *Lenin's Political Thought*, and Tony Cliff's four-volume *Lenin*.

While these deal with the whole range of Lenin's politics, the present contribution attempts to focus more sharply on his organizational thought; in doing this, it also challenges some of their interpretations. There seem to me to be underlying deficiencies in the works by Liebman and Harding, both well-deserved recipients of the Isaac Deutscher Memorial Prize, which result in distortions precisely on the question of the Leninist Party. Harding is inclined to bend the stick too far in his argument that "the 'organizational question' has been given a position of unwarranted importance as the occasion for the Bolshevik/Menshevik dispute"; as a result, he fails to give sufficient attention to the evolving specifics of Lenin's organizational thought. Liebman, on the other hand, recognizes Lenin's passionate determination to defend the revolutionary organization "tooth and nail," but he adds: "That was what in fact he did, indefatigably, the bites and scratches being sometimes distributed to left and right with . . . more generosity and vigor than restraint or scruple."[1] At times, Liebman is so put off by Lenin's fierce polemics on organization that he, too, fails to examine the specifics around which the polemics revolved, giving the benefit of too many doubts to Lenin's critics. Tony Cliff has a more practical-minded (and thus more informative) approach to such questions, despite other deficiencies—such as an ambivalence toward the organizational implications of revolutionary internationalism.

Here I want to indicate briefly the thrust of my own interpretation. Two things are fundamental to Lenin—the political program of revolutionary Marxism and the living movement and struggles of the working class. The function of the revolutionary party for Lenin is to bring these two phenomena together: to develop the program in a way that advances the workers' struggles, and to help advance the workers' struggles in a way that contributes to the realization of the program. This dual commitment is primary for Lenin—everything else is subordinate to it, and any hint of abandoning one or the other is fiercely resisted. Lenin sought to build a cohesive nationwide party, integrated into an international socialist movement, whose members would be working together to realize this dual commitment. His organizational approach, contrary to the assertions of many commentators, was not characterized by personal power-lust or pragmatic opportunism or elitism or authoritarianism. Rather, it involved a dynamic blend of practical-mindedness and profound concern for political principles, and it was essentially democratic in regard both to ends and means. In Lenin's methodological approach there is a great sensitivity to varying and changing contexts; this results in a remarkable flexibility of application within the changing Russian environment and also suggests that Lenin's organizational orientation transcends the specifics of turn-of-the-century Russia. Generally, therefore, Lenin's conception of the party makes sense. It is worth the effort to understand as fully as possible what this conception meant.

As final preparations were being made for the publication of this book, a provocative and valuable work was published in English under the title *Fire in the Americas: Forging a Revolutionary Agenda*, by a U.S. radical named Roger Burbach and a leading Sandinista theorist named Orlando Núñez from Nicaragua. One of the many important passages from that work is so relevant to the concerns of my own contribution that I am moved to reproduce it here:

> This perspective [of revolutions being carried out by small but determined groups of people] was reinforced by the obsession of many political activists in the early 1970s, particularly in the United States, with the role played by Lenin in the Bolshevik revolution. They saw him as a solitary figure who, through his iron will and clear vision, was able to preserve and lead the Bolshevik party to power. Regardless of whether this view of Lenin is correct, it led many revolutionaries to believe that they could adopt a political strategy, and resolutely carry it to completion, no matter what the political realities.
>
> This leads to a broader problem: once a revolutionary political theory has been developed it often tends to limit the imagination of future leaders rather than to guide them. This is not to deny the importance of theory. But it does mean that we have to be constantly on guard to ensure that theory does not become dogma. Each new revolutionary struggle and movement must rethink its premises and its theoretical approach as well as its practice. This is only possible if we apply the Marxist method in the most creative manner, without relying on dogma or letting preconceptions distort our understanding.[2]

The nondogmatic thrust of this passage must be a central component in the outlook of any serious political activist. Genuine revolutions cannot be made by solitary figures who, with "iron will and clear vision," galvanize small groups of followers to seize power. To think otherwise not only will distort our understanding of what is possible in our own time but also will distort our understanding of Lenin and the history of which he was a part and that he helped to shape. An adequate interpretation of Lenin and the revolutionary party he led—an interpretation that guides us rather than blinds us—must be in harmony with the insights of the passage just quoted. A conception of "the Leninist party" that conforms to the caricature sketched by the authors not only will disorient would-be revolutionaries but also will prevent us from understanding what actually happened in history.

The present study attempts to draw together and synthesize a considerable amount of material. It does not claim to be the last word on the subject of Lenin and the revolutionary party, but is offered as a contribution that, I hope, can be of use to those who want to develop an understanding of that subject.[3] Of such people, the most important are those with high ideals who have not lost heart, those who are prepared to struggle against all forms of oppression and human degradation, those who want to commit their lives to creating a decent future in which the free development of each person is the condition for the free development of all. The relevance of this study hinges on the existence of such people.

Acknowledgments

This book would not have been written had it not been for the late George Breit-man, a socialist intellectual-activist of high caliber, whose more than five decades in the revolutionary movement were infused with a rich appreciation of Lenin's thought and example. He urged me to write it, gave me valuable inspiration and encouragement, read and critically responded to an early draft, and set high standards of meticulousness and critical-mindedness, which I have tried to approach. Whatever merit this study has should be considered part of his legacy. I dedicate this book in part to his memory.

Ernest Mandel, whose many writings have contributed to my own Marxist education, read and extensively commented on the manuscript, offering valuable suggestions. Professor William Chase (history) and Professor Jonathan Harris (political science) of the University of Pittsburgh, who were generous with their time and expertise, also deserve my thanks. Others from the University of Pittsburgh's history department who have been especially supportive are Professors Joseph White and Mark McColloch. In addition, I would like to mention two historians who formerly taught at the University of Pittsburgh and greatly contributed to my efforts to understand the history of the labor and socialist movements—David Montgomery and the late Richard N. Hunt.

Michael Löwy, whose Marxist scholarship often stimulated and inspired me, has offered valued criticism and friendship. Pierre Rousset responded with positive words and also searching questions that can receive adequate answers only in future studies (perhaps including those he will carry out). Steve Bloom, who has done some admirable work in his own right, deserves special mention for his critical reading of this study. I was also sustained by the thoughtful reactions and friendship of Tom Twiss, whose studies on the political thought of Leon Trotsky have enriched my own thinking; and by Carol McAllister, a passionate anthropologist, educator, and activist, whose ideas and perceptions have helped me understand more fully the complexities of human culture and experience.

I also appreciate encouragement from Beth Boerger, Janet Melvin, Barney Oursler, Sally Adler, Frank and Sarah Lovell, Dorothea Breitman, Rose and George Brodsky, and others too numerous to name individually—such as the staff, students and supporters of the International Institute for Research and Education. I do want to mention Gabriel Le Blanc and Jonah McAllister-Erickson, who were inclined neither to read nor to discuss with me earlier versions of this work but whose vibrant lives had a profound impact on me as I studied and wrote.

Chapter 7 of this study originally appeared in *Bulletin in Defense of Marxism* (27 Union Square West, Room 208, New York, N.Y. 10003), and portions of chapters 4 and 5 originally appeared in *International Marxist Review* (2 rue Richard Lenoir, 93108 Montreuil, France). I would like to thank both publications for permission to use that material here. Thanks are also due to the staff at Humanities Press—in particular to Judith Camlin, who coordinated the transformation of this work from manuscript to book.

Finally, I would like to dedicate this study to the memory of my father, Gaston Le Blanc, a working-class organizer who told me the first essential truths about V. I. Lenin. I also dedicate it to the memory of my mother, Shirley Harris Le Blanc, whose considerable energies and skills were channeled into the field of social work during labor's "long detour," and who died before I had a chance to share this book with her.

Note to the Haymarket Books Edition

Lenin was tough, and he was for the workers. That's what my father told me as we drove in a car one summer, while I (in my early teens) accompanied him on one of his many trips as a union organizer. I was asking about, and he was explaining, his understanding of how the world was, and the ideas he believed in. When I asked him about Lenin, that is what he said. It stuck with me, and as I have labored to make sense of the things that culminated in *Lenin and the Revolutionary Party*, it seems to me my father's assessment holds up well.

It is immensely gratifying that a new edition of this, my first published book, is being made available to a broader number of readers under the imprint of Haymarket Books. I know that my two mentors and teachers, George Breitman and Ernest Mandel, would have been especially appreciative that this volume would finally be available through the auspices of a substantial and respected revolutionary socialist publisher. As I have explained more than once, Breitman's inspiration and encouragement were decisive for this being written at all. It was he who enlisted Mandel's incredibly meaningful support, which also resulted in Ernest's outstanding introduction to the book, most of which is reproduced here.[*]

It is very good to know that *Lenin and the Revolutionary Party* has been useful (as I have been told innumerable times) for young activists. Such activists have been proliferating in the United States, where a radical ferment has persisted and finally accelerated over the past decade—leading to possibilities that certainly would have intrigued Lenin, but it is also the case globally that, as Bertolt Brecht

---

[*] In the final two pages of his introduction, Ernest included comments dealing with then-recent developments meant to highlight the book's contemporary relevance. If he were alive today, he would most certainly want to revise these now woefully dated comments—but since that is not possible, they are being left out. There are ample examples today of contemporary relevance which will undoubtedly occur to perceptive readers.

once told us, "because things are as they are, they will not stay as they are." As I have traveled to conferences and forums in so many different places since the publication of this book—Australia, Brazil, Britain, Canada, France, Mexico, South Africa, Turkey, China, India—I have had the profound pleasure of connecting with bright, energetic, engaged young militants, precisely the people for whom *Lenin and the Revolutionary Party* was written. Some were not yet born when Breitman and Mandel were encouraging me, as the manuscript was struggling to become a book. I am also pleased that this twenty-five-year-old study harmonizes well (despite one or another interpretive difference) with the rising tide of contributions to Lenin Studies from such scholars (some well-known and some yet-to-be known) as Colin Barker, Eric Blanc, Sandra Bloodworth, Roland Boer, Sebastian Budgen, Kunal Chattopdhyay, Luke Cooper, Paul D'Amato, Alexei Gusev, Tamás Krausz, Ben Lewis, Li Dianlai, Lars Lih, Soma Marik, John Marot, August Nimtz, John Riddell, Alan Shandro, Peter Thomas, Wu Xinwei, and others.

The world of 2015 is quite different from that of 1990—in regard to new scholarship and in regard to ever-changing realities. If I had to identify the Top Five "mustread" works relevant to this book, I would offer the following: Arno J. Mayer's magisterial study *The Furies: Violence and Terror in the French and Russian Revolutions* (Princeton: Princeton University Press, 2000), provides a highly informed, honest, incredibly thoughtful historical contextualization for much that was problematical in the Leninist tradition. There is also Marcel van der Linden's historical survey of Marxists who struggled to make sense of the terrible outcome: *Western Marxism and the Soviet Union: A Critical Survey of Critical Theories and Debates Since 1917* (Chicago: Haymarket Books, 2009). The three more contemporary-focused volumes, highlighting the activist ferment and radical possibilities of our time, would (at this moment) be: Paul Mason, *Why It's Still Kicking Off Everywhere: The New Global Revolutions* (London: Verso, 2013), David Harvey, *Rebel Cities: From the Right to the City to the Urban Revolution* (London: Verso: 2013), and Frances Goldin, Debby Smith, and Michael Steven Smith, eds., *Imagine: Living in a Socialist USA* (New York: Harper-Collins, 2014).

Even in 1994 when the first paperback edition of *Lenin and the Revolutionary Party* came out, I was obsessed with the need to inform readers of important works (many new, a few older) that I had not been able to incorporate into my study—and also to factor in the sudden collapse of the Soviet Union and the meaning of this for the relevance, or presumed lack thereof, of a Vladimir Ilyich Lenin who, in Frederic Jameson's striking phrase, "didn't know he was dead." The result was not only a new four-page introductory note but also an eighteen-page afterword. Rather than expanding upon these in the Haymarket edition, I have chosen to drop them altogether. There are four books I have produced that can take the place of those efforts, all of which refer the reader to new sources, but also do more than that. By referring readers to those books, I can save quite a bit of space in this one.

First came *Marx, Lenin and the Revolutionary Experience: Studies of Communism and Radicalism in the Age of Globalization* (New York: Routledge, 2006), which wrestles, among others things, with the much-vaunted "collapse of Communism" and with the "post-9/11" world (surveying, as well, much radical history of the twentieth century, with some theology blended in) and offers reflections on the continuing relevance, in that new context, of what Lenin represented.

Next came the substantial, multifaceted introduction "Ten Reasons for Not Reading Lenin" to a collection that I edited—V. I. Lenin, *Revolution, Democracy, Socialism, Selected Writings* (London: Pluto Press, 2008), which also includes informative sub-introductions to the various sections of the book plus an overarching documentation of the radical-democratic thrust of Lenin's thought through the course of his life as a revolutionary, as well as suggestions for additional reading.

Third is the collection of my own writings, *Unfinished Leninism: The Rise and Return of a Revolutionary Doctrine* (Chicago: Haymarket Books, 2014). That volume takes up innumerable questions and controversies that have arisen over the past decade-and-a-half regarding ways to comprehend and to utilize (or not utilize) the Leninist tradition. It gives considerable attention as well to what has now become a veritable flood of "Lenin Studies" in our new century, with reflections on the meaning of such a development.

Finally, there is a short biography in the "Critical Lives" series: *Leon Trotsky* (London: Reaktion Books, 2015). Along with the even shorter *Leon Trotsky and the Organizational Principles of the Revolutionary Party* (Chicago: Haymarket Books, 2014), coauthored with Dianne Feeley and Tom Twiss, the Trotsky biography does something to address the only substantial criticism that George Breitman made of *Lenin and the Revolutionary Party*. George felt strongly that there should have been an additional chapter on the heroic struggle of the Left Opposition to defend and advance Lenin's perspectives in the face of the murderous bureaucratic tyranny represented by the regime of Joseph Stalin. I think he was right, but felt unable to do it in 1989 when I completed the manuscript—and I chose not to hold up publication before devoting the additional time and effort to accomplishing that task.

Taken together with the present volume, these offerings constitute what I hope will be a useful contribution for scholars and activists seeking to explore the meaning of Lenin's life and thought as he struggled to help create a society of the free and the equal.

Having produced this additional material also "gets me off the hook" of having to write a revised version of *Lenin and the Revolutionary Party*. A couple of years ago, one friend urged me to do just that. This was in the wake of a substantial controversy with my good friend Lars Lih and others about a conflict between Lenin and other Bolshevik comrades in 1905 and also about whether or not it can be said that a distinctly Bolshevik party was finally established in 1912. The controversy is summarized in an essay in *Unfinished Leninism* entitled "The Great Lenin Debate of 2012."

The fact is that, although I might now add a little more nuance in what I wrote in my old book, I believe that the basic thrust of its major interpretations continue to hold up well. There is nothing *fundamental* in those contested portions of my study that I wish to change. Also, as I've explained elsewhere, I believe Leninism—including the study of Lenin's ideas and experience—is necessarily *unfinished*, regardless of whatever revisions I would choose to make or not to make in this volume. My contributions here can stand as they are, and others will make their own contributions, in this ongoing collective process of making sense of Lenin in all his complexity.

For some years now I have hoped that this volume could come out in an affordable and easily available Haymarket Books edition. I would like to thank my friends Michael Steven Smith (who rendered invaluable legal assistance) and Anthony Arnove (who supplied Haymarket inspiration and push), who together made this possible.

Introduction

I

Paul Le Blanc's book represents an excellent analysis of the development of Lenin's conception of the revolutionary party, from its inception until the immediate aftermath of the October revolution. This conception is dialectically linked with the Marxist conception of the self-activity and self-organization of the working class, which Lenin never abandoned, not even in *What Is to Be Done?*[1]

To be sure, there is a dynamic equilibrium between these two constitutive elements in Lenin's thought. Lenin was not only a great theoretician; he was also an eminently practical political person. Many of his writings had an immediate purpose, often at least partially determined by conjunctural circumstances. The stick was sometimes bent too much in one direction, but as Lenin was, above all, a principled politician, he always bent the stick back in the other direction as soon as a sober balance sheet of the previous stage of debate and activity could be drawn.

This dynamic equilibrium was in turn determined by the ups and downs of mass activity. As Marcel Liebman has convincingly demonstrated, what was typical of Lenin was that in revolutionary situations he went out of his way to emphasize the self-organization of the working class.[2] This is most clearly expressed in *State and Revolution*, centered entirely around the soviets. The "leading role of the party" is not even mentioned once in this book!

Paul Le Blanc correctly and critically examines the roots of Lenin's conception of the revolutionary party. As he indicates in the conclusion of his book, I had already followed a similar analysis.[3] The building of a revolutionary party does not correspond in the first place to an organizational need, to the problem of centralizing local, regional, sectoral, and work-place activities, and grouping them around political objects, although of course that need is very real. Behind the need for organizational centralization there looms a formidable historical problem, both theoretical and practical, to which the adversaries of Lenin's party concept have never been able to give an alternative answer, although ninety years have elapsed since the beginning of the debate. This is the problem of the centralization of living, struggling experience as the basis of the emergence and development of class consciousness.

In other words: the need for the vanguard party results from the de facto, day-to-day fragmentation of the working class as regards its living conditions, its conditions of work, its levels of militancy, its political past, the historical roots and the stages of its formation, and other such factors. The need corresponds to a necessary process of unification and homogenization of self-consciousness of the class. Given the discontinuous character of class *mass* activity, it is illusory to expect unification to occur continuously in mass trade unions or in political parties encompassing a large minority of the class. Only a vanguard will be able to achieve such a unification on the basis of a qualitatively higher level of continuous activity.[4]

But on the other hand, the possibility of making a real proletarian revolution and of building a classless society depends on the capacity of the mass of the workers periodically to reach extraordinary levels of continuous political activity. It follows that the dialectical interrelationship between the revolutionary vanguard party and the capacity for massive self-activity and self-organization of the mass of the wage workers reflects, in the final analysis, precisely that dynamic "tension" between continuous vanguard militancy and discontinuous but no less real mass activity.

II

Except for some general remarks, Paul Le Blanc's book stops after the October revolution. It does not take up the central questions which have been discussed for decades among historians and inside the international labor movement, in the light of subsequent developments in the USSR.

Did Lenin change his view of the interrelationship between the soviets and the vanguard party after 1918, after 1920, after 1921, under pressure from the dramatic conditions that were emerging inside Soviet Russia? Was the gradual emasculation of the soviets rather the inevitable outcome of Lenin's initial conception of the party? Was Lenin at first at least partly unaware of the terrible implications of that emasculation, but did he react later, perhaps too late, yet react indeed, in a consistent way—a reaction that did not lead to any change in Russia's evolution but did conclude Lenin's life in a really tragic way?

This short preface cannot substitute for what should have been at least a couple of additional chapters in Paul Le Blanc's book. We can only advance what we believe should be the general line of the answer to the central question posed in the international debate among historians and socialists/communists.

The economic and cultural backwardness of Russia worsened rapidly from the devastation of the civil war and the foreign imperialist intervention and blockade.[5] A catastrophic decline of the productive forces expressed itself in a no less catastrophic numerical and industrial decline of the working class in 1919–20. This led to a significant decline in the political activity of the proletariat. Basically, the workers were not expelled from the soviets by a Bolshevik conspiracy: they left them in order to fight in the Red Army and to look for potatoes in the countryside.

That negative development was amplified by the retreat of world revolution after 1920. Certainly, the retreat was not a rout nor even a grave defeat, except in Italy, where the fascists came to power. The strength of the British labor movement remained great enough to prevent, through the threat of a general strike, an open intervention by Britain on the side of Poland and France in the war against Russia. The most successful general strike in history broke the German counterrevolutionary coup of Kapp-von Lüttwitz. The chances of revolutionary victory remained objectively open, at least in Germany and Austria. But the perspective of a short-term extension of the revolution to two, three, or four Central European countries, which seemed imminent in 1918–19, now became a medium-term perspective at best.

Under these circumstances, maintaining Soviet power in Russia became for the time being a question of maintaining Bolshevik party power, at least until a change in internal or international conditions would make a political reactivation of the working class objectively possible. Even the Workers Opposition under Shlyapnikov and Kollontai, which tried to oppose its own course to that of the party majority, was dimly aware of this—a fact that puts a question mark over the credibility of its alternative platform.[6]

The "substitutionist" logic of the Bolsheviks—which saw the initiatives of the party cadres as a substitute for the direct action of the working class as a whole—was sketched by Trotsky in a youthful anti-Lenin pamphlet as resulting from Lenin's ideas, but it actually came about as a result of objective conditions and was not opposed by Trotsky himself.[7] In real life, the party or even worse, the party's central "hard core cadre," exercised power in the name of the workers, but in the beginning at least with the more-or-less tacit acceptance of the working class.

III

One can discuss indefinitely whether an alternative course would have been possible at the height of the civil war and of the foreign intervention and the Polish war. In any case, this seems largely an academic debate. When the numerical strength of the working class is reduced by two-thirds and its per capita caloric intake to half the normal level, there is little objective space for direct workers' power.

The real turning point occurred in the year 1921. The civil war was over; the counterrevolution was militarily defeated; the foreign military intervention had been stopped. The decline of the production forces was reversed through the introduction of the New Economic Policy (NEP). Workers' real consumption was rising, and the number of wage workers was rapidly increasing.

At that precise moment, the Bolshevik leadership, including Trotsky, but undoubtedly under the impetus of Lenin, took a decision that, in hindsight, we can only characterize as a tragic mistake, as Isaac Deutscher has already observed.[8] The Bolsheviks should have drawn the conclusion, from a favorable evolution of the social relationship of forces, that a large broadening of soviet and proletarian democracy was now on the agenda, in order to stimulate the political reactivation of the working class. Instead, they decided to narrow democracy in a decisive way, by banning all opposition soviet organizations (Mensheviks, anarchists) and by banning factions inside the Bolshevik party itself, although not banning "tendencies."

The reasoning on which this political regression was based ran roughly along the following lines. Precisely because the civil war had been won and the productive forces were rising again under the NEP (that is, petty commodity production), the danger of the revolution's losing political power was growing and not declining. The proletariat, which had concentrated tremendous energies on the conquering and maintaining of power, but had become *déclassé* under the blows of the decline of the productive forces, would now tend to relax and to defend power much less energetically than in the previous period. Pro-capitalist forces—the NEP men, the kulaks (well-to-do peasants)—would therefore have new opportunities to undermine workers' power. This danger was less obvious than that of open military aggression, and therefore potentially much graver. Against the danger the dictatorship must be strengthened. Under the circumstances, this could happen only through the concentration of power in the party cadre.

This reasoning includes at least three political-theoretical mistakes.

First, it is simply not true that the kulaks were a bigger threat than Kolchak, Wrangel, or Pilsudski for the overthrow of Soviet power. Such an overthrow needs not only a gradual socioeconomic evolution; it also needs an active, organized political force. The kulaks were socially too dispersed and politically too demoralized to be capable of playing such a role, at least in the short term. As to what could happen in a long-term perspective, that depended not only, and even not primarily, on the kulaks. It depended on the political-social correlation of forces between the kulaks and urban pro-bourgeois forces (with foreign help and pressure), on the one hand, and on the urban proletariat, the peasants, on the other hand (again with foreign counter-pressure), the key variable being the capacity of the former con-stellation of forces or the latter constellation to rally into an alliance the majority of the middle peasants.

Second, far from neutralizing or reversing the trend toward "relaxation of en-ergies" (i.e., demobilization and depoliticization) in the working class, all measures limiting soviet and inner-party democracy gravely increased that trend, thereby undermining and weakening workers' power.

Third, the substitutionist identification of workers' power with political power exercised de facto by the party cadre inevitably led to a growing process of bureau-cratization of the party itself. The party apparatus grew by leaps and bounds, from a few hundred full-time functionaries in 1919 to 15,000 in 1922.

To be sure, Stalin's election as party general secretary strongly accelerated that process. But the objective basis of the process has to be understood. Under a one-party regime, the decline of working-class political life unavoidably hits the party and its working-class members as well.[9] De facto exercise of power by paid func-tionaries thereby becomes the most "realistic" stopgap solution, independently of any calculation by unprincipled maneuverers of the Stalin type. The formula "work-ers' power equals party power equals party cadre power equals party leadership power" becomes transformed into "workers' power equals party power equals party leadership power equals party apparatus power equals bureaucracy's power." The party bureaucracy rapidly fuses with the state bureaucracy and identifies itself with it.[10] Far from playing the leading role, the party becomes more and more a tool of the bureaucracy in its totality.[11]

Of course, Lenin, Trotsky, Bukharin; Rykov, Zinoviev, Kamenev, Rakovsky, Pre-obrazhensky, and Piatikov did not want this to happen. They sincerely believed that they ruled for the working class and not for the bureaucracy. They saw the danger—the danger of Thermidor—sooner or later: Lenin starting with 1922; Trotsky a bit later, in 1922–23; Zinoviev in 1925–26; Bukharin in 1927–28. But by the time they recognized the danger—especially as they recognized it in a dis-persed way, without a clear common plan of counteraction—the process of bureau-cratization was already too much advanced to be nipped in the bud. That is the historical balance sheet of the tragic year 1921.

IV

Lenin's impressive stature as a revolutionary theoretician and politician of the working class is enhanced by the rapidity with which he recognized the bureau-cratization process in society, state, and party, and the near desperation with which he reacted to it. One has to discard the mystified picture of the power-hungry character of Lenin, not to say of Trotsky.[12] It is true that Lenin possessed a unique concentration of energy, impressive singleness of purpose, and a tremendous self-confidence that supported that purpose. For a person of that character to use the words "I am greatly guilty in the eyes of the Russian working class" implies a dramatic and extraordinary effort at self-analysis and self-criticism.[13]

In fact, the final two years of Lenin's conscious life convey a tragic image of growing desperation. Lenin was conscious of the process of bureaucratic degeneration in Russia and in the Russian Communist party, but he was increasingly obsessed with a growing sentiment of helplessness, or incapacity to stop the rot. Moshe Lewin has written his well-known book on Lenin's last fight,[14] but in fact it is not only on the Georgian question—in which Lenin struggled against Stalin's bullying tactics toward the Georgian national minority—that Lewin should have concentrated our attention.[15] Lenin's writings and speeches of 1922 and 1923 are full of a constantly growing denunciation of bureaucratization. A book examining and uniting all the successive episodes of that fight is long overdue.

During that fight, Lenin came progressively to conclude that the party apparatus itself was undergoing bureaucratic degeneration. As the sole antidote he saw a much stronger involvement of direct producers—factory workers' cadres and working peasants' cadres—in the central worker-Bolshevik party leadership.[16] One must note, however, that at that moment the capacity of the party apparatus to stifle inner-party democracy and to prevent worker-Bolsheviks from expressing their opinions frankly had already grown to the point where the practicality of Lenin's proposals is at least open to doubt.[17]

The degree of workers' depoliticization and demobilization had strongly increased in 1922–23. The key link between Lenin's conscious insight and his capacity to reverse the wrong party-majority course had been in April 1917 and at the time of the Brest-Litovsk Treaty (1918), when there was an active, broad working-class vanguard, and not solely inside the party. In 1922–23 this link was missing.

Basically, that is the reason why Lenin's 1922–23 fight and Trotsky's 1923 fight against the bureaucratized party leadership were defeated. For that reason Stalin, with the help of Zinoviev, Kamenev, and Bukharin—a help that was literally suicidal—was able to consolidate his hold over the party through the apparatus. Thus he could start on the road toward his bloody dictatorship, which would physically destroy the Bolshevik party.

In the light of these developments, the thesis advanced in recent Soviet publications, that Lenin had consciously embarked on the "self-thermidorization" of the Bolshevik leadership—a thesis based among other things on a sentence that

Jacques Sadoul attributed to Lenin—cannot be seriously defended.[18]

Again, the decisive moment to reverse this process was 1920–21. And the decisive way to achieve that result would have been a broadening and not a restriction of soviet and inner-party democracy. Lenin had no time to consciously formulate a self-criticism in that respect. Bukharin and especially Trotsky had time to do it, and they did it.[19]

Indeed, the emergence of an all-powerful party apparatus had already assumed such proportions in 1922–23 that Lenin himself had become its prisoner in a direct, personal sense of the word. As Neil Harding has described it, "the apparatus now controlled him, dictating his daily regimen, refusing him books and newspapers [even refusing him access to party documents—E.M.], forbidding him to communicate. Lenin was trapped and stifled in the web he himself had spun."[20]

V

Lenin hesitated on the most efficient way to fight the bureaucratic degeneration of the state and party apparatus during the final political battle of his life. To what degree should an appeal to the rank-and-file party members (worker-Bolsheviks) against Stalin's apparatus be linked to appeals to the party leadership to correct its course? To what extent should such an appeal be complemented by appeals, however cautious, to workers outside the party to participate in that struggle? All the successive oppositions inside the Russian Communist party—the "Democratic Centralists" of 1919, the Workers Opposition of 1920–21, Lenin in 1922–23, the "Trotskyite" Left Opposition of 1923, the United Opposition of 1926–27, the Bukharin-Rykov grouping of 1927–30, the Left Opposition from 1927 onward— were faced with the same problem.[21]

What transformed that problem into a real dilemma for Lenin, as it would do later for Bukharin, was his sociological justification of party dictatorship through an analysis of alleged structural long-term deficiencies in the working class. These formulations, which appear frequently in his 1920–21 writings, are in stark opposition to his previous opinions, not only those of the 1917–20 period but also those of 1905–08, and even earlier ones:

> But the dictatorship of the proletariat cannot [sic] be exercised through an organisation embracing the whole of that class, because in all capitalist countries (and not only over here, in one of the most backward) the proletariat is still so divided, so degraded and so corrupted . . . that an organisation taking in the whole proletariat cannot directly exercise proletarian dictatorship. It can be exercised only by the vanguard that has absorbed the revolutionary energy of the class. The whole is like an arrangement of cog wheels. . . . It cannot work without a number of "transmission

belts" running from the vanguard to the mass of the advanced class, and from the latter to the mass of the working people.[22]

Such statements represent an obvious—and theoretically unjustified—telescoping of conjunctural into structural analysis. They fade away from his writings and speeches after 1921, but they were never fully transcended in his thought. As long as the theoretical contradiction was not solved, the political Gordian knot could not be cut.

The problem is very simple, if you reduce it to its inner core. Were the specific déclassé features of the Russian working class in 1920–21 a passing conjunctural result of the exceptional decline of the productive forces in Russia at that moment, in which case they would be gradually overcome by more positive, overarching developments? Or were they rather permanent features of the proletariat, even under conditions of "normal" capitalism, resulting from the past effects of bourgeois society, both objectively and subjectively, on the proletariat's postrevolutionary political behavior? In the latter case, the working class was unfit to exercise "its" dictatorship directly anywhere, anytime, at least in the foreseeable future. The dictatorship could only be exercised by the party.

It is again characteristic of Lenin's tremendous stature as an honest and exceptionally profound revolutionary theoretician that he boldly formulated the problem in this radical, essential way, and groped toward a solution. Stalin, Mao Zedong, and their theoretical offspring never had the courage or honesty to do so. But while Lenin moved away in 1922–23 from his obviously wrong formulation of 1920–21, he never came to a clear counter-position.

It remains the historical merit of Trotsky and the Left Opposition that, starting with 1923, they did find an unambiguous counter-position. Their relentless struggle against Stalin's course, both inside Soviet Russia and inside the Comintern, was based on unshakable confidence in the revolutionary potential of the working class as it actually existed both within Russia and in the rest of the world.

Certainly, that revolutionary potential does not express itself everywhere every day, every month, every year, or even every decade. It passes through ups and downs, periods of reaction and of revolutionary upsurge. But as the upsurges are inevitable, it is the duty of revolutionists to assist in the maturing of the process and to concentrate their efforts on creating the best possible conditions for successive proletarian victories. In terms of Russian party policies, that meant not only political and cultural but also economic and social conditions.

Needless to say, Trotsky's and the Left Opposition's position conformed, in that respect (today totally shared by the Fourth International), with the position of Marx and Engels on the issue. One of the essential specifics of Marx and Engels' thought about capitalism is that in spite of all its negative effects on the proletariat, it develops in the working class an exceptional combination of potential economic and political power and mentalities, including moral values, which give the class a unique superiority compared to any other social force for building a new society. Like the Lenin of *State and Revolution*, the Left Opposition's platform is a "pure" product and application of that essential component of Marxism.

Lenin's wavering on that essential question in 1921–22 of course, had an objective basis. There was a new strengthening of the Russian working class, but to what extent would it rapidly lead to new militancy? A turning point in the "temporary consolidation" of international capitalism was occurring, but to what extent would it lead to short-term revolutionary possibilities?

If Lenin had not suffered his second stroke, and been able to follow all the dramatic developments, especially in Russia and Germany, in 1923, he would probably have arrived at conclusions similar if not identical to those of Trotsky in that year. But Lenin, as both a theoretician and an eminently practical politician, constantly looked at problems through the prism, *What is to be done here and now? What is the next step forward?* In the situation of 1923 the prism deformed his answer.

The bureaucracy was rotten and had to be decisively weakened. The party apparatus was already bureaucratized to the core, unable and unwilling to break the bureaucracy's stranglehold over society. The working class was still at least partially déclassé and demoralized, and was therefore unfit to fight immediately for a new course. The worker-Bolsheviks, at least partly drawn in the same direction of depoliticization and demoralization, could not redress the situation, at least in the short term. So in desperation Lenin turned to the top party leadership as the only tool at history's disposal for a rapid change.

But the central party leadership is composed of individuals, each with their merits and weaknesses. Lenin's *Testament*, while initially posing the problem in sociological terms, ends up with individual assessments and an individual proposal: remove Stalin as general secretary.

There is of course nothing wrong with that approach to the problem. It deals with an essential feature of the ongoing bureaucratization process: Stalin's nearly total grip over the party apparatus and the innumerable consequences of that grip. But it is obvious that this proposal is both insufficient and logically dubious.

If Stalin already had so much power over the party, how could a vote among a few dozen persons break that power? Was not the mobilization of much broader forces indispensable for achieving that result? And there is a very grave and wrong conclusion that could be drawn from concentrating essentially on that line of reasoning: If everything turns around the attitudes and decisions of the central party leadership, the unity of that leadership becomes a key in the fight for conserving Soviet power.

Lenin was definitely not unaware of the evident contradictions of his position. The *Testament* was clearly a letter to the whole party, to the incoming Twelfth Congress. In that sense, if not explicitly, it appealed to the congress delegates against Stalin and the wavering Politburo. When Lenin proposed that several hundred workers and productive peasants be integrated into the Central Committee, he again appealed in fact to forces outside the central party leadership.

But by posing the question of party unity as the central short-term goal in the struggle against the looming Thermidor, Lenin created a conceptual framework that could play a decisive role in the Old Bolsheviks' successive capitulations before Stalin.

This is all the more significant as it completely contradicts the real traditions of Lenin's party and faction before 1921. Top leaders of the Bolsheviks had often appealed to party members against what they considered wrong decisions of the leadership, as Lenin himself did in April 1917, during the Brest-Litovsk debates and on several other occasions. Party leaders never hesitated to publish theoretical positions that were not shared by Lenin and the party majority. In several episodes, they even appealed to the general working-class public against majority political positions which they considered disastrously wrong.

Lenin, admittedly, criticized them, sometimes severely, for these acts.[23] But this never led to inner-party repression, nor did it prevent his comradely, even friendly, collaboration with these leading Bolsheviks. The same is even more true of Lenin's attitude toward Trotsky after the fusion of the latter's "tendency" with the Bolsheviks. Lenin turned to Trotsky to support his fight on the Georgian question early in 1923, in spite of the harsh debate between the two men not long before on the trade-union problem.

So this obsession with keeping the differences bottled up in the central party leadership was inconsistent with the Bolshevik tradition. It was also inconsistent with dialectical logic.

As Trotsky would point out in his *New Course*, in complete conformity with what Lenin himself has stated repeatedly, party unity and the "centralist" component of "democratic centralism" are in the final analysis subordinate to a correct political course of the party leadership (majority).[24]

Once the political decisions of that leadership have such grave consequences for the proletariat, in the living class struggles, that they can lead to real disaster, it becomes totally counterproductive to refuse to fight with all means necessary for redressing that course.[25] A refusal to "undermine party unity" becomes organizational fetishism. It turns the party from an instrument of proletarian emancipation into a goal by itself.

Should revolutionary socialists have refused to question "the unity of the party" when confronted with social democracy's disastrous capitulation before the imperialist war in 1914? Should they have refused to question that "unity" when confronted with Stalin's disastrous agrarian policies of 1926–30? Should they have refused to question that "unity" when confronted with Stalin's and the Comintern's "third period" ultraleftism, which contributed decisively to Hitler's attainment of power in Germany, the worst disaster for the international working class in the twentieth century? The answer is obvious.

In the final analysis, the solution of Lenin's dilemma hinges on the question of the proletariat's revolutionary potential.

If one denies that potential, at least for the foreseeable future,[26] then the unavoidable conclusion is that socialism is unrealizable. To believe that a ruling-party bureaucracy could remain unstained by material privileges, and, despite these privileges, could remain willing to build an egalitarian state and allow it to wither away afterwards—that is, to work consciously toward its own suppression—is to deny the ABC of historical materialism. All evidence points in the opposite direction: party, that is to say, party-apparatus, meaning party-bureaucracy rule, cannot be a long-term substitute for proletarian self-activity and self-organization in the building of socialism. If self-activity and self-organization are not realistic likelihoods, then socialism is not a realistic likelihood. Bukharin, between 1923 and 1927, formulated the opposing theoretical position—"cadres decide everything"—in the most coherent way:

> This transitional period is the time when . . . the working class . . . changes its nature in the most diverse ways, when it pushes forward from its reservoir of forces resolute bands of men, who undergo a transformation that is cultural, ideological, technical, etc., and who emerge from this university in another living form . . . of cadres who are able to govern the entire country with a strong hand, to the extent that the working class places these trusted men into the most diverse posts.[27]

But if one believes that even in periods of steep decline of proletarian militancy this decline remains a temporary and not a definitive phenomenon, then what is on the agenda for the vanguard is a holding operation, in which the struggle against counterrevolutionary dangers must be combined by force with policies that favor a rebirth of working-class militancy. And in that case, the "unity of the party," not to speak of the "unity of the party leadership," must be subordinated to the fight for policies that make the rebirth possible. So Trotsky was right, in his fight against bureaucratic degeneration, when he appealed first to the membership of the Russian Communist party and afterwards to the working class inside and outside the party. Bukharin and the Old Bolsheviks were wrong when they drew back from that decisive step, thereby smoothing the way to Stalin's terrorist dictatorship.[28] Lenin took an intermediary position. Quite rightly he would have adjusted it in the direction of Trotsky's position, had his conscious life extended a bit.

Ernest Mandel

1. Introduction: Authentic Leninism

Vladimir Ilyich Lenin was the foremost leader of the world's first working-class socialist revolution, which swept Russia in 1917 and continues to reverberate down to our own time. People throughout the world—longing for an end to injustice, war, and oppression—have looked hopefully to the example of the Russian Bolsheviks and to the ideas of Lenin as a guide for liberation struggles and social change in their own countries. As another leader of the Bolshevik Revolution, Leon Trotsky, explained: "The main work of Lenin's life was the organization of a party capable of carrying through the October revolution and of directing the construction of Socialism."[1] Because of this, revolutionary-minded men and women have given special attention to Lenin's views on the revolutionary party.

With the triumph of the Bolshevik Revolution, Lenin and his comrades turned their attention to the task of helping revolutionaries in other countries mobilize the workers and the oppressed for the purpose of overthrowing capitalism on a global scale to establish a worldwide cooperative commonwealth in which, as Marx and Engels had written in the *Communist Manifesto*, "the free development of each is the condition for the free development of all."[2] Renaming their own organization the Communist party, the Bolsheviks established the Communist International in 1919 in order to advance this expansive goal.

Millions of people—from a rich variety of cultures, traditions and experiences—responded to the revolutionary appeal of Bolshevism and the Communist International. One of these was James P. Cannon, a veteran of the American Socialist party's left wing and of the militant and colorful Industrial Workers of the World (IWW). Cannon helped to found the American Communist party in 1919, and he was one of its central leaders until his expulsion in 1928 as the Communist International became increasingly bureaucratized. Yet he never abandoned his revolutionary convictions, and in a remarkable essay written in the 1960s continued to affirm:

1

The greatest contribution to the arsenal of Marxism since the death of Engels in 1895 was Lenin's conception of the vanguard party as the organizer and director of the proletarian revolution. That celebrated theory of organization was not, as some contend, simply a product of the special Russian conditions of his time and restricted to them. It is deep-rooted in two of the weightiest realities of the twentieth century: the *actuality* of the workers' struggle for the conquest of power, and the *necessity* of creating a leadership capable of carrying it through to the end.

Recognizing that our epoch was characterized by imperialist wars, proletarian revolutions, and colonial uprisings, Lenin deliberately set out at the beginning of this century to form a party able to turn such cataclysmic events to the advantage of socialism. The triumph of the Bolsheviks in the upheavals of 1917, and the durability of the Soviet Union they established, attested to Lenin's foresight and the merits of his methods of organization. His party stands out as the unsurpassed prototype of what a democratic and centralized leadership of the workers, true to Marxist principles and applying them with courage and skill, can be and do.[3]

These perceptions have been shared by innumerable workers and peasants and students and intellectuals of every continent. They consider themselves Leninists because they are animated by "the categorical imperative to overthrow all conditions in which man is a debased, enslaved, neglected, contemptible being."[4] They are Leninists because they are committed, in a very real and practical way, to replacing the tyranny of capitalism with a socialism in which the immense economic resources of society will be the common property of all people, democratically controlled in order to ensure that the free development of each person can be possible.

1. What Leninism Is Not

Lenin's ideas on the revolutionary party have been greatly distorted by many different kinds of people. It may be useful to survey some of these interpretations.

From the triumph of the Bolshevik Revolution down to the present, liberal and conservative ideologists of the capitalist status quo have utilized immense resources to spread the notion that Lenin and his works—especially his concept of the revolutionary party—constitute a hideous threat to law, order, simple human decency, and Western civilization. One of the clearest expositions of this viewpoint was offered by the late director of the Federal Bureau of Investigation, J. Edgar Hoover. In *Masters of Deceit*, the FBI chief gave this explanation to millions of frightened readers: "Lenin conceived of the Party as a vehicle of revolution. . . . The Party must be a small, tightly controlled, deeply loyal group. Fanaticism, not members, was the key. Members must live, eat, breathe, and dream revolution. They must lie, cheat, and murder if the Party was to be served. Discipline must be rigid. No deviations could be permitted. If an individual falters, he must be ousted. Revolutions cannot be won by clean hands or in white shirts; only by blood, sweat and the burning torch. . . . The skill of Lenin cannot be overestimated. He introduced into human relations a new dimension of evil and depravity not surpassed by Genghis Khan or Attila. His concept of Party supremacy, girded by ruthless and ironclad discipline, gave communism a fanaticism and an immorality that shocked Western civilization."[5]

This basic interpretation is also offered—frequently in a more sophisticated and scholarly form—by many influential academics and intellectuals who are engaged in the defense of "Western civilization." Essential components of that civilization are a myriad of "unavoidable" inequalities and "regrettable" injustices, not to mention the immense power of the big corporations and, of course, the aggressively procapitalist thrust of U.S. foreign policy. Although undoubtedly sincere, many of these ideologists have, like J. Edgar Hoover, been in the pay of the U.S. government or have been conscious participants in government-controlled or corporate-funded operations designed to generate and spread antiradical, antirevolutionary propaganda. They are not objective commentators—they have an axe to grind. And yet their biased interpretations have a substantial impact among many who do not share their particular commitments to U.S. corporate-government power.[6]

Other powerful distortions emanate from a quite different source—the Communist movement itself. Many people drawn to it over the years have absorbed interpretations of Lenin's ideas that have little to do with the experience of the Bolsheviks as, in the years leading up to 1917, they grew into a revolutionary party. Instead, these individuals have been trained in more rigid and stilted conceptions that became dominant particularly after Lenin's death in 1924. Such conceptions gained currency as a rising bureaucratic layer, led by Joseph Stalin, sought to consolidate its control and privileges within the Union of Soviet Socialist Republics from the 1920s onward. The "Leninism" fashioned in this period assumed dominance among revolutionary-minded activists, but it proved to be more useful for enhancing the authority of the new ruling group in the Soviet Union than for duplicating the successes of the Bolsheviks for the peoples of other countries.[7]

A shrewd and somewhat cynical observer in the Soviet Union during this period was *New York Times* correspondent Walter Duranty, who was sympathetic to Stalin—though with a decidedly nonrevolutionary detachment. He noted that a growing number of old Bolsheviks "were showing signs of restiveness, partly because they saw that Stalinism was progressing from Leninism (as Leninism had progressed from Marxism) towards a form and development of its own, partly because they were jealous and alarmed by Stalin's growing predominance." Duranty wrote as follows: "When Lenin died what ignorant mortal could know whether Stalin or Trotsky was the chosen son? Only results could prove that. . . . Stalin rose and Trotsky fell; therefore Stalin, inevitably, was right and Trotsky wrong.... Stalin deserved his victory because he was the strongest, and because his policies were most fitted to the Russian character and folkways in that they established Asiatic absolutism and put the interests of Russian Socialism before those of international Socialism."[8]

Stalin portrayed his "progression from Leninism," however, as nothing more nor less than the most uncompromising defense of Leninist principles. At Lenin's funeral, he religiously intoned: "Leaving us, comrade Lenin enjoined on us to hold high and keep pure the great calling of member of the party. We vow to thee, comrade Lenin, that we will with honor fulfill this thy commandment. Leaving us, comrade Lenin enjoined on us to keep the unity of our party as the apple of our eye. We vow to thee, comrade Lenin, that we will with honor fulfill this thy commandment.... Leaving us, comrade Lenin enjoined on us loyalty to the principles of the Communist International. We vow to thee, comrade Lenin, that we will not spare our lives to strengthen and extend the union of the toilers of the whole world—the Communist International." Instead, Stalin sought to destroy politically (and, eventually, physically) all Communists—including most of Lenin's closest comrades—who challenged his authority, to drive out of the Communist party of the Soviet Union and Communist parties throughout the world all who were unprepared to abandon the "old Leninism" of the Bolsheviks' heroic period, and to subordinate the revolutionary aspirations of parties belonging to the Communist International to narrowly defined foreign policy considerations of the Soviet Union. He went so far as to formally dissolve the Communist International during World War II in order to reassure his wartime capitalist allies. Yet a typical, even obligatory, comment by Communist ideologists while such things were happening was that "the Party is training its cadres in Bolshevik ideological intransigence, is rallying its ranks still more closely around its Leninist Central Committee, around its leader and teacher, Comrade Stalin." Communists throughout the world were lectured that "a study of the history of the Bolshevik Party is impossible without a knowledge of the chief works of its founder and leader, Lenin, and of his best disciple, Stalin, who is continuing his work."[9]

The organizational norms propagated in this period, peppered with fragments from Lenin quoted out of context, stressed "the Bolshevik conception of the Party as a monolithic whole." This was elaborated for the world Communist movement in such works as *Lenin's Teachings About the Party*, by Stalinist ideologist V. Sorin, and circulated widely throughout the Communist International in the early 1930s. Excerpts from that work are quite revealing:

> The Party is governed by leaders. If the Party is the vanguard of the working class then the leaders are the advanced post of this vanguard. The special feature of the

Communist Party is its strictest discipline, i.e., the unconditional and exact observance by all members of the Party of all directives coming from their Party organizations. . . . The Party must be sure that each of its members will do what the Party tells him even if he disagrees with it. . . . Discipline, firm and unrelenting, is necessary not only during the period of underground work and struggle against Tsarism, not only during civil war, but even during peaceful times. . . . The stricter the discipline, the stronger the Party, the more dangerous is it to the capitalists.[10]

Such follow-the-leader conceptions of Leninism helped to overcome the danger of a critical-minded revolutionary membership questioning the policies developed by the Stalinist leadership of the Communist movement. But they had little in common with the organization that actually made the world's first socialist revolution. These conceptions continue to influence would-be Leninists of our own time, however. The pamphlet *Lenin's Teachings About the Party*, for example, was reprinted in the 1970s by former "new left" activists who, influenced by the Chinese and Vietnamese revolutions, believed that "a new communist party is essential for the revolutionary movement in the United States." Revolutionary-minded people throughout the world have mistaken such distortions for genuine Leninism.

Attentive readers may have noticed that the anti-Communist and the Stalinist descriptions of the Leninist party have much in common. Sometimes they are blended together, as in the case of Wolfgang Leonhard, a Stalinist functionary and instructor at the Karl Marx Political Academy of the German Communist party who defected from East Germany in 1949 and became a critical commentator on Communist affairs. Leonhard refrained from adopting the bitterly reactionary orientation of many who went through similar breaks, continuing to identify with what he calls humanist Marxism. Yet he offers the following as an objective description: "Instead of a democratically organized body representing the interests of all workers who engaged in free discussion, Lenin's doctrine of the Party now envisaged an elite led by professional revolutionaries, organized on the principle of democratic centralism, with restricted freedom of discussion, and making great demands on Party members, who must operate in unity and with closed ranks in order to lead the working class."[11] Not surprisingly, many revolutionary-minded people have concluded that if this is Leninism, then Leninism is not for them.

Within the broadly defined socialist movement there is a particularly influential source for the notion that Leninism is basically authoritarian. This is the moderate-socialist current of post-1917 Social Democracy, many of whose spokespersons refer to themselves as "democratic socialists" in order to distinguish themselves from "authoritarian Communism." They tend to perceive democracy as electoral politics within a capitalist framework, to favor the implementation of reform legislation as a means for gradually eliminating the evils of capitalism, and to recognize a kinship with Lenin's moderate-socialist rivals in Russia. In many countries they can boast of mass parties (for example, the Labor party in Britain, the Socialist party in France, the Social Democratic party in Germany), which have sometimes taken office and implemented positive social reforms but have never even attempted to overthrow capitalism. Their current orientation in the United States, as Michael Harrington, of Democratic Socialists of America (DSA), has put it, holds that "the American social democracy" is an "invisible mass movement" consisting of the liberal-labor alliance in the Democratic party with its "ranging program for the democratization of the economy and the society." It is natural that the adherents of this position would find intolerable Lenin's "dogmatic" insistence that it is impossible to peacefully and gradually reform capitalism out of existence. They are inclined to echo, with varying degrees of sophistication, the interpretation articulated for many years within DSA's predecessor, the Socialist Party of America, when it was led by Norman Thomas. Thomas portrayed Leninism as "an authoritarian dogmatism which boasts that it is scientific." In 1931 he explained that Lenin's party was "organized with military discipline, exacting an unquestioning obedience from its members worthy of the order of Jesus." Twenty years later he continued to explain: "In Lenin's theory the Party was to be a dedicated group bent on serving the interests of the workers and the peasants, which it understood better than the masses themselves." Asserting that Stalin's policies were a continuation of the Leninist commitment to "the eventual world-wide triumph of communism," Thomas wrote that Stalin "emphasized Lenin's use of any tactics, including unbounded deceit and violence, to achieve that result."[12] This interpretation of Leninism—remarkably similar, in important ways, to those offered by apologists for Stalinism, on the one hand, and for capitalism, on the other—is widely propagated even by formerly new-left adherents of "democratic socialism" who are not inclined to share Norman Thomas's support for U.S. Cold War policies.

Recently there has evolved another source from which a distorted interpretation of Leninism has arisen. Among new Western scholars studying the history of the Soviet Union, there is an innovative current that, while yielding some valuable new research, has also begun to fashion what Sheila Fitzpatrick has delicately termed "a less judgemental approach" to the Stalin era. Quite similar in temperament and in some of their perceptions to such earlier admirers of Stalin as Walter Duranty, these scholars are also inclined to be somewhat more aloof. "There was a wildly impractical and utopian streak in a great deal of Bolshevik thinking," writes Fitzpatrick. She adds the following, however: "No doubt all successful revolutions have this characteristic: the revolutionaries must always be driven by enthusiasm and irrational hope, since they would otherwise make the commonsense judgement that the risks and costs of revolution outweigh the possible benefits." Fleetingly entertaining the question "of whether in some cosmic sense it was all worthwhile," she draws back with the warning that this is "dangerous ground for historians," who should restrict themselves simply to determining "what seems to have happened and how it fits together."[13]

From this standpoint, Fitzpatrick dispassionately summarizes the Russian Revolution's meaning as "terror, progress and upward mobility." By "upward mobility" she means the many thousands of workers who rose above their class to get relatively good and high-status jobs in the massive postrevolutionary bureaucracy (which she sees as a perversely nuts-and-bolts realization of the revolutionary socialist goal of working-class rule). By "progress" she presumably means the leap forward into industrialization and modernization, the elimination of the backward and inefficient semifeudal and tsarist order, the establishment (despite bureaucratic distortions) of a planned economy, the great strides in spreading education and health care to all, and so forth. And by "terror" she means the disruption and destruction of millions of lives, the violence against and coercion of peasants and workers during the "revolution from above" of collectivization and industrialization under Stalin, the purges and labor camps, and other authoritarian measures. Fitzpatrick asserts that there were "important elements of continuity linking Stalin's revolution with Lenin's," and that one element of this continuity was that "Stalin used Leninist methods against his opponents." (Here one is again reminded of Duranty, who wrote: "Stalin is no less of a Marxist than Lenin, who never allowed his Marxism to blind him to the needs of expediency. . . . When Lenin began a fight, whether the weapons were words or bullets, he showed no mercy to his opponents." Stalin was thus following Lenin in "the brutality of purpose which drove through to its goal regardless of sacrifice and suffering.")[14]

This approach has obvious implications for how one interprets the nature of the Leninist party. Fitzpatrick suggests that "Lenin's dislike of looser mass organizations allowing greater diversity and spontaneity was not purely expedient but reflected a natural authoritarian bent," adding that "Lenin usually insisted on having his own way." She characterizes the Bolshevik party in this way: "It was a party with authoritarian tendencies, one that had always had a strong leader—even, according to Lenin's opponents, a dictatorial one. Party discipline and unity had always been stressed. Before 1917, Bolsheviks who disagreed with Lenin on any important issue usually left the party. In the period 1917–20, Lenin had to deal with dissent and even organized dissident factions within the party, but he seems to have regarded this as an abnormal and irritating situation, and finally took decisive steps to change it."[15]

We will see that this interpretation does not correspond to historical realities. More insightful historians argue that the common thesis of a Lenin–Stalin continuity "rests upon a series of dubious formulations, concepts, and interpretations and ... whatever its insights, it obscures more than it illuminates," as Stephen Cohen has put it.[16] E. H. Carr has attempted to demonstrate the fundamental discontinuity with this argument:

> The Communist Manifesto recognized the role of leadership exercised by Communists as the only full class-conscious members of the proletariat and of proletarian parties. But it was a condition of the proletarian revolution that Communist consciousness should spread to a majority of the workers. ... Lenin's conception of the party as the vanguard of the class contained elitist elements absent from Marx's writings and was the product of a period when political writers were turning their attention more and more to the problem of elites. The party was to lead and inspire the mass of workers; its own membership was to remain small and select. It would, however, be an error to suppose that Lenin regarded the revolution as the work of a minority. The task of leading the masses was not, properly understood, a task of indoctrination, of creating a consciousness that was not there, but of evoking a latent consciousness; and this latent consciousness of the masses was an essential condition of revolution. Lenin emphatically did not believe in revolution from above. ... After Lenin's death, Lenin's successors lacked the capacity or the patience to evoke that measure of mass consciousness and mass support that Lenin had had behind him in the period of the revolution and the Civil War and took the short cut—always the temptation that lies in wait for an elite—of imposing their will, by measures of increasingly naked force, on the mass of the population and on the mass of the party. ... The need, with which Lenin wrestled and which Stalin contemptuously dismissed, of reconciling elite leadership with mass democracy has emerged as a key problem in the Soviet Union today. [17]

This general approach, regardless of imperfections one might find in Carr's specific formulations, captures important aspects of the historical reality that allow a fundamentally different and more perceptive approach to the question of the Bolshevik party's actual organizational structure and functioning. Thus, Moshe Lewin recounts the following:

> Leninism, one of the Russian versions of Marxism, developed by Lenin, was shared by the Bolsheviks who had acquired their ideological formation before the revolution and who maintained an openmindedness, an institutional flexibility in pursuing the struggle of ideas in particular, but not exclusively in the areas of strategy and tactics that made up the core of Leninism. It is important to recall that bolshevism had gone through quite a number of internal debates before 1917, that it had functioned in a multiparty environment, especially after the revolution of 1905, and even after

the takeover of power, until 1920. Starting with the revolution of February 1917, in particular, and until the prohibition of factions by the Tenth Party Congress in March 1921, various wings and tendencies, opposing factions and platforms presented before and during the congresses [of the party], coexisted within the party; these were not only tolerated but were actually used as widely accepted modus operandi [procedure].[18]

This authentic Leninism—qualitatively different from the grotesque distortions of Leninism that are so widely circulated—will be the subject of the present study.

2. A Living Organism and Phases of Development

Like any living organism, the Bolshevik organization was characterized by a particular set of tensions within itself as well as between it and the larger social reality. These tensions gave it a vibrancy and generated growth, causing the organization to go through quite different phases of development. The organization cannot be adequately understood as a revolutionary force unless it is understood in this way. Lenin's views on the revolutionary party, which reflected and were part of this evolution, must likewise not be approached as if they were a finished and self-contained schema. The Leninist conception of the party is animated by certain essential principles and a definite methodological approach; there is an underlying continuity in Lenin's organizational perspectives from the 1890s up to 1917 and beyond. At the same time, there are important shifts in Lenin's thought, flowing from an accumulation of experience and also reflecting changes in the context of the Bolsheviks' activity.

A potential problem, even among revolutionaries who recognize a distinction between authentic Leninism and Stalinism, is a failure to grasp this dialectical aspect of Leninism. Leninist organizational principles are seen as an established organizational schema. This schema typically involves a constricting organizational tightness that supposedly constitutes "Leninist centralism and party discipline." It is something that "Leninist" leaders sometimes attempt to superimpose on the membership, often inflexibly, regardless of the actual situation. This is contrary to Lenin's own method, and it has often had destructive consequences for left-wing groups that glorify an abstract (and therefore non-Leninist) "Leninism." It may be appropriate for the consolidation of a small sectarian group, but it short-circuits the process of building a working-class party capable of leading a successful struggle for socialism. [19]

The present study seeks to recover the actual meaning of Leninist organizational principles by locating them in the specific history of Russia's revolutionary socialist movement. Initially, the organized expression of this movement was the Russian Social Democratic Labor party (RSDLP), and especially its Bolshevik faction from 1903 to 1912; then it was concentrated in the independent Bolshevik party, which became the Russian Communist party after 1917. Within this context, the Leninist organizational perspective can be said to have gone through six phases of development from 1900 to 1923.

1. *1900–1904*. Lenin and other Marxists struggle to establish the RSDLP around the revolutionary program and centralized organizational concepts expounded in the newspaper *Iskra*. The Iskraists and the RSDLP split into bitterly counterposed majority/minority (Bolshevik/Menshevik) factions, with Lenin's Bolsheviks advancing the most consistently centralist and un-compromisingly revolutionary orientation. In this period, however, the RSDLP consists mostly of radicalized intellectuals; it has a small minority of workers and a very weak base in the proletariat.

2. *1905–1906*. The revolutionary upsurge of 1905 catches both Bolshevik and Menshevik factions by surprise. Both factions are swept along by the revolutionary enthusiasm of the workers. Lenin's centralism is tempered by the understanding that looser and more democratic norms can help root the RSDLP in a dramatically radicalizing working class. A convergence of Bolshevik and Menshevik orientations and factions appears to be in process.

3. *1907–1912*. The defeat of the revolutionary wave and a triumphant reaction destroy the RSDLP mass base within Russia. The new situation reverses the convergence of Bolshevik and Menshevik factions as a fundamental programmatic difference, already visible in 1905, pulls the two factions apart. In the struggle to overthrow tsarist absolutism, the Mensheviks put greatest weight on an alliance of the working class with the "progressive" bourgeoisie, while the Bolsheviks counterpose to this a revolutionary alliance of the workers and the peasants. Among the Mensheviks an increasingly strong impulse develops to liquidate the revolutionary workers' party into reformist labor organizations. Among the Bolsheviks an ultraleft sectarian impulse arises, which threatens to draw them into an abstentionist course in the face of opportunities to participate in the actual class struggle. Lenin conducts a bitter war against both liquidators and abstentionists. He drives the latter out of the Bolshevik faction and attempts to drive the former out of the RSDLP altogether. Many nonliquidationist Mensheviks and even some nonabstentionist Bolsheviks fear that Lenin is being too "hard," and they seek "conciliation" with both liquidators and abstentionists in order to preserve the unity of the RSDLP. Lenin forces a decisive organizational split, constituting his faction as a separate party—the Russian Social Democratic Labor party (Bolsheviks).

4. *1912–1914.* The Bolshevik party, unified on the basis of a revolutionary class-struggle program, outstrips the incohesive and squabbling remnants of the non-Bolshevik RSDLP—particularly in the face of a dramatic new wave of working-class militancy.

5. *1914–1917.* The eruption of the First World War diverts the rising wave of militancy into patriotic hysteria and slaughter. The Bolsheviks and the minority of Menshevik-Internationalists vehemently oppose the Russian war effort and are savagely repressed. The reformist and pro-war majority of the Mensheviks are able to assume a dominant position in the workers' movement.

6. *1917–1923.* The devastation of the First World War has a profoundly radicalizing impact on the Russian masses, and the severely weakened tsarist regime is overthrown by a spontaneous revolutionary upsurge. In the new and volatile situation, the reformist and vacillating Mensheviks are once again outstripped by the Bolshevik party, which is able to lead the masses forward to a socialist revolution. The effects of war, civil war, and foreign blockades and interventions result in economic collapse and disintegration of the working class as a political force. The Bolsheviks feel compelled to adopt increasingly restrictive measures, in Russia as a whole and within their own party, while waiting for a revolutionary socialist triumph in the industrially advanced West that will end the desperate isolation of their impoverished and bleeding country.

This highly condensed sketch of the six phases of "Leninism under Lenin" does little more than suggest the shifting contexts within which Lenin's various (and sometimes seemingly contradictory) statements on the organizational question can be understood. There are obvious general points that must be kept in mind regarding the situation in tsarist Russia—the economic backwardness, the predominance in population of the peasantry, the peculiarities of Russian capitalist development, and the repressiveness of tsarist absolutism. This last factor, above all, compelled Russian revolutionaries to develop organizational forms that would be consistent with the realities of underground work and exile politics. There is much in all of this that necessitated the incorporation into the "Leninism of Lenin" of qualities that—at least at this point—have little immediate relevance to the situation of revolutionaries functioning in different contexts (for example, what are sometimes termed "advanced capitalist democracies").

Certain aspects of the Leninist organizational orientation, however, have universal applicability. One is the absolute primacy of the revolutionary program—the principles, general analysis, goals, and strategic and tactical orientation that can lead the class struggle to a revolutionary socialist conclusion. Another is the concept of the revolutionary vanguard party, made up only of activists committed to the revolutionary program. Such a party doesn't attempt to embrace into its ranks the entire working class, but rather seeks to interact with the working class in order to influence it in a revolutionary direction. (Obviously, in order to do this the vanguard party must be predominantly working-class in composition—but these must be revolutionary working-class activists.) Finally, organizational centralism and organizational democracy must be combined in such a way that makes the vanguard party most effective in applying the revolutionary program to living reality. Given the complex, dynamic, and ever-changing character of reality, it is necessary to be flexible in determining the weight to be given to democracy and centralism in different situations and in different periods.

To be true to Lenin's method, revolutionaries must be prepared to apply this orientation creatively to their own specific and changing situations, and to be as innovative as Lenin was from one period to another. In what follows we will concentrate on how this was done in Russia, focusing especially on the years leading up to the working-class victory of 1917.

2. The Context of Lenin's Early Organizational Perspectives

Turn-of-the-century Russia was a vast country in flux and ferment, beset by profound contradictions. The great majority of Russians were peasants with modest land holdings or none at all, who had barely emerged from serfdom and were still oppressed by the powerful landed nobility. At the same time, a dramatic process of industrialization and urbanization was creating a significant and volatile working class, which faced abominable working and living conditions. The new capitalists, while increasingly important, were allowed only the role of junior partners among Russia's quasi-feudal ruling elite. The government of the tsar was frankly autocratic, maintaining an oppressive status quo for workers, peasants, and intellectuals, as well as national and religious minorities. It did this with a repressive apparatus that extended from fierce elite army units of mounted Cossacks to vast networks of spies and secret police, from bureaucratic censorship to Siberian prison camps. Yet the repression could not eliminate the growing tensions that resulted from the combined effects of capitalist modernization and tsarist recalcitrance. One historian has summed it up in this way: "The flux and frustrations in Russian society . . . made it a natural breeding ground for revolutionaries. A volatile combination soon existed: exploited workers, desperate peasants, and angry intellectuals. Only an ideology and an unbending government were needed to set off the explosion. The tsarist system supplied the latter and Karl Marx the former."[1] This didn't happen overnight, however, but was a decades-long process.

In the 1890s, Lenin (whose real name was Vladimir Ilyich Ulyanov) became one of the "angry intellectuals" who were transforming themselves into "professional revolutionaries." Many have seen something ominous in such a label, but Trotsky captured its true meaning in the following description:

A professional revolutionist is a person who completely dedicates himself to the labor movement under conditions of illegality and forced conspiracy. Not everyone is capable of that, and certainly, in any event, not the worst kind of person. The labor movement of the civilized world knows numerous professional officials and professional politicians; the preponderant majority of that caste is noted for its conservatism, egotism and narrow-mindedness, living not for the movement, but at its expense. By comparison with the average labor bureaucrat of Europe or America, the average professional revolutionist of Russia cut an incomparably more attractive figure.

The youth of the revolutionary generation coincided with the youth of the labor movement. It was the epoch of people between the ages of eighteen and thirty. Revolutionists above that age were few in number and seemed old men. The movement was yet utterly devoid of careerism, lived on its faith in the future and on its spirit of self-sacrifice. There were as yet no routine, no set formulae, no theatrical gestures, no ready-made oratorical tricks. The struggle was by nature full of pathos, shy and awkward. The very words "committee," "party" were as yet new, with an aura of vernal freshness, and rang in young ears as a disquieting and alluring melody. Whoever joined an organization knew that prison followed by exile awaited him within the next few months. The measure of ambition was to last as long as possible on the job prior to arrest; to hold oneself steadfast when facing the gendarmes; to ease, as far as possible, the plight of one's comrades; to read, while in prison, as many books as possible; to escape as soon as possible from exile abroad; to acquire wisdom there; and then return to revolutionary activity in Russia.

The professional revolutionists believed what they taught. They could have had no other incentive for taking to the road of Calvary. Solidarity under persecution was no empty word, and it was augmented by contempt for cowardice and desertion. "Turning over in my mind the mass of comrades with whom I had occasion to meet," writes Eugenia Levitskaya concerning the Odessa underground of 1901–1907, "I cannot recall a single reprehensible, contemptible act, a single deception or lie. There was friction. There were factional differences of opinion. But no more than that. Somehow everyone looked after himself morally, became better and more gentle in that friendly family." Odessa was not, of course, an exception. The young men and women who devoted themselves entirely to the revolutionary movement, without demanding anything in return, were not the worst representatives of their generation. The order of "professional revolutionists" cannot suffer by comparison with any other social group.[2]

This was the milieu in which Lenin became active and within which he quickly assumed a position of authority in the period from 1893, when he arrived in St. Petersburg, to 1898, when the Russian Social Democratic Labor party was formed. Lenin's companion, N. K. Krupskaya, has stressed the significance of the time: "This St. Petersburg period of Vladimir Ilyich's work was of great importance, although the work itself was not noteworthy and hardly noticeable.... But it was during this period of his St. Petersburg work that Vladimir Ilyich was moulded as a leader of the working masses."[3] If we abstract Lenin's views on organization from the underlying political grounding established in this early period, it will be impossible to comprehend Lenin's actual perspective on organizational questions. It may be useful, first of all, to consider what Lenin was actually doing in this formative period. Along with this, we should consider the political orientation that he was committed to; we should also have some sense of the working class in which Lenin was investing such profound hopes. Then we will be in a better position to understand the organizational principles that flowed from Lenin's programmatic (practical-political) orientation.

1. Dimensions of Lenin's Activity

Marxist study circles, composed predominantly of students and intellectuals, existed in a number of Russian towns and cities in the early 1890s. By the time Lenin moved to St. Petersburg, at the age of 23, he was already known in revolutionary circles as "a very erudite Marxist." Among the young revolutionaries in the St. Petersburg League of Struggle, Lenin effectively combated a conception of Marxism that Krupskaya later discussed in her memoirs. "The gist of it," she wrote, "was this: the process of social development appeared to the representatives of this trend as something mechanical and schematic. Such an interpretation of social development dismissed completely the role of the masses, the role of the proletariat. Marxism was stripped of its revolutionary dialectics, and only the bare 'phases of development' remained." Lenin considered "this mechanistic view to be the direct opposite of real Marxism." Krupskaya recalled that "in his whole approach one sensed just that live Marxism which takes phenomena in their concrete surroundings and in their development," and that with even a seemingly abstract question "he linked it up with the interests of the masses."[4]

It is worth taking a moment to give a further sense of the quality of Lenin's Marxism. He believed that "by directing socialism towards a fusion with the working-class movement, Karl Marx and Frederick Engels did their greatest service," because the previous "separation of the working-class movement and socialism gave rise to weakness and underdevelopment in each: the theories of the socialists, unfused with the workers' struggle, remained nothing more than utopias, good wishes that had no effect on real life; the working-class movement remained petty, fragmented, and did not acquire political significance, was not enlightened by the advanced science of its time." Consequently, "the task of Social-Democracy is to bring definite socialist ideals to the spontaneous working-class movement, to connect this movement with socialist convictions that should attain the level of contemporary science, to connect it with the regular political struggle for democracy as a means of achieving socialism—in a word, to fuse this spontaneous movement into one indestructible whole with the activity of the *revolutionary party*." Lenin saw Marxism as "the first to transform socialism from a utopia to a science, to lay a firm foundation for this science, and to indicate the path that must be followed in further developing and elaborating it in all its parts. . . . It made clear the real task of a revolutionary socialist party: not to draw up plans for refashioning society, not to preach to the capitalists and their hangers-on about improving the lot of the workers, not to hatch conspiracies, *but to organize the class struggle of the proletariat and to lead this struggle, the ultimate aim of which is the conquest of political power by the proletariat and the organization of a socialist society.*" He added that "to defend such a theory, which to the best of your knowledge you consider to be true, against unfounded attacks and attempts to corrupt it is not to imply that you are an enemy of *all* criticism. We do not regard Marx's theory as something completed and inviolable; on the contrary, we are convinced that it has only laid the foundation stone of the science which socialists *must* develop in all directions if they wish to keep pace with life."[5]

For many Russian intellectuals drawn to socialism in this period, Marxism was viewed—often quite sympathetically—as a fairly rigid "economic determinism." Peter Struve, the most prominent "legal Marxist" intellectual of the 1890s, later recounted: "Socialism, however it be understood, never inspired any *emotions*, still less a passion in me. It was simply by way of reasoning that I became an adept of Socialism, having come to the conclusion that it was an historically inevitable result of the objective process of economic development." George Plekhanov, although considered "the father of Russian Marxism" and offering a more sophisticated interpretation of Marxist methodology and doctrine, did not succeed in eliminating this one-sided view of Marxist "materialism," which was common among would-be Marxists in Russia. As late as 1907, Trotsky felt it necessary to explain to his Marxist readers that "the logic of the class struggle does not exempt us from using our own logic. Whoever is unable to admit initiative, talent, energy, and heroism into the framework of historical necessity, has not grasped the philosophical secret of Marxism."[6]

Lenin's Marxism was of a substantially higher quality than was common among his contemporaries. Because of this, because of his mastery of a rich and complex body of Marx's works (in which, as Trotsky put it, one could "discover under introductory sentences or notes lateral galleries of conclusions"), he was able to give voice to the profoundly nondogmatic expression of Marxism that we have noted. The other side of this was his rejection of attempts to "transcend" Marxism by those who had a more limited grasp of it. In his biography of the young Lenin, Trotsky asserts that he "mastered Marxism as the summation of the previous development of human thought; from this highest level yet attained, he did not wish to descend to a lower one; he fiercely defended what he had thought through to the end and had tested out day after day; and he mistrusted in advance the attempts of self-satisfied ignoramouses and well-read mediocrities to replace Marxism with some other, more portable theory."[7]

At the same time, as Lenin's close comrade and the first editor of his collected works, L.B. Kamenev, once remarked, while "the teachings of Lenin as a whole and in all their ramifications are based on the scientific Socialism of Karl Marx and Frederick Engels," there also is a new element, which "consists in the adaptation of the basic principles and methods of Marxism to a historical setting and period entirely unknown to Marx." Kamenev elaborated: "In the first period of his activities (1890–1914) Lenin, with the help of the methods of Karl Marx, had to solve the problems arising out of the peculiar conditions of a bourgeois-democratic revolution taking place in a backward agrarian country, with a proletariat developed and unified out of all proportion to the general backwardness of the country. This unique situation directed Lenin's attention to that aspect of the teaching of Karl Marx in which the theoretical and practical Marxians of Europe in that period were least interested, and which they studied and understood least of all. Already the 'Marxism' of Lenin differed strikingly from the Marxian shibboleths voiced during the eighties and nineties by the German pupils of Marx."[8]

We must now turn our attention to the manner in which Lenin applied this Marxism to the realities of Russia in the 1890s.

In 1894 Lenin wrote his first major polemical work, *What The "Friends of the People" Are*, directed against the older populist traditions in the Russian revolutionary movement. In this work he sought to define the objectives and the future course of the Russian Marxists, while at the same time conscientiously settling accounts with the older movement, which had greatly influenced the revolutionaries of Russia (including Lenin himself). The populists were inclined to speculate on how Russia could develop an ideal social system, and they did this by closing their eyes to the actual development of capitalism in Russia, a development they hoped Russia would bypass. Lenin complained that "they talk . . . about 'a people's system' and the 'intelligentsia' not only with a serious air but in pretentious, pompous phrases about broad ideals, about presenting problems of life in an ideal manner!" He called for less rhetoric and more serious work: "The socialist intelligentsia can expect to perform fruitful work only when it abandons illusions and begins to seek support in the actual and not the desired development of Russia, in the actual and not the possible social and economic relationships. Moreover, its *theoretical* work should be directed towards *the concrete study of all forms of economic antagonisms in Russia, the study of all their connections and sequence of development.* . . . This theory, based on a detailed study of Russian history and conditions, must meet the requirements of the proletariat—and if it satisfies the requirements of science, then the awakening, protesting thoughts of the proletariat will inevitably guide this thought in the channels of Social-Democracy."[9]

Lenin went on to stress: "By emphasizing the necessity, the importance and immensity of the theoretical work Social Democrats must carry on, I do not in the least wish to suggest that this work must take precedence over *practical* work; still less do I suggest that the latter be postponed until the former is finished. . . . It is impossible to be an ideological leader without performing the above theoretical work, just as it is impossible to be one without directing this work to meet the requirements of the cause, without propagating the deductions drawn from this theory among the workers and helping to organize them." This orientation, Lenin asserted, "will guard Social-Democracy against the defects from which groups of Socialists frequently suffer, *viz.*, dogmatism and sectarianism." He explained this last point: "There can be no dogmatism where the supreme and sole criterion of a doctrine is—whether or not it corresponds to the actual process of social and economic development; there can be no sectarianism when the task undertaken is to assist to organize the proletariat, when, therefore, the role of the 'intelligentsia' is reduced to the task of making special leaders from among the intellectuals unnecessary."[10]

Lenin concluded the polemic by summarizing the central programmatic orientation of revolutionary socialism that guided his work for the next three decades: "It is on the working class that the Social Democrats concentrate all their attention and all their activities. When the advanced representatives of this class will have mastered the ideas of scientific socialism, the idea of the historical role of the Russian worker, when these ideas become widespread and when durable organizations arise among the workers which will transform the present sporadic economic war of the workers into a conscious class struggle—then the Russian *workers* will rise at the head of all the democratic elements, overthrow absolutism and lead the *Russian proletariat* (side by side with the proletariat of *all countries*) *along the straight road of open political struggle towards the victorious communist revolution.*"[11]

The concepts Lenin articulated in this polemic found expression in his own practical activity in this period. The Marxist revolutionaries worked to make contact with workers in a variety of ways, especially through legal adult education classes. Krupskaya, who was a teacher in the Smolenskaya Sunday Evening School for Adults over a three-year period, later commented, "In those days the Sunday Evening School offered an excellent opportunity for studying everyday working-class life, labor conditions and the temper of the masses." Out of such contacts as these, radical workers' study circles were secretly organized. Krupskaya has given this account:

> An intellectual would come to one of the study-circles and read the workers a kind of lecture. A manuscript translation of Engels' *The Origin of the Family, Private Property and the State* circulated among the circles for a long time. Vladimir Ilyich read Marx's *Capital* to the workers and explained it to them. He devoted the second half of the lesson to questioning the workers about their work and conditions of labor, showing them the bearing which their life had on the whole structure of society, and telling them in what way the existing order could be changed. This linking of theory with practice was a feature of Vladimir Ilyich's work in the study-circles. Gradually other members of our circle adopted the same method.[12]

Unexpected problems were sometimes created in the study-circle atmosphere, however. Some participants had a stilted notion of how the revolution would come: "Gradually the number of workers studying Marx will increase; they will draw still more numbers into the circles studying Marx; with time all Russia will be covered with such circles and then we will form a worker's socialist party. What tasks this party was to perform and how it should conduct its struggle remained unclear." Some of the working-class participants, intent upon "self-improvement," disapproved of such "uncultured" activity as strikes and had (according to Julius Martov, one of Lenin's close comrades of this period) "a sort of condescending, contemptuous attitude towards the masses, who one might say were not considered worthy of socialism's teachings."[13]

To counteract this tendency, Lenin and others concentrated on making their Marxism increasingly relevant to the "uncultured" working-class anger and ferment that was promising to generate actual struggles in the factories. Even when teaching classes in the workers' study circles, according to Krupskaya, "Vladimir Ilyich was interested in every little detail that could help him to piece together a picture of the life and condition of the workers, to find some sort of avenue of approach to them in the matter of revolutionary propaganda." In 1895, in an important pamphlet, *On Agitation*, Arkadi Kremer and Julius Martov argued for a focus on immediate economic issues at the factories, in a manner that—compatible with the mass of workers' present level of consciousness—would encourage workers to struggle for their immediate interests: "This very struggle . . . will develop in the working class a degree of stability and endurance, of unity, a sense of independence and class self-confidence, which it will need when it comes face to face with the inevitability of the class struggle in the proper meaning of the word. As it enters this stage, the workers' movement will begin little by little to take on a political tinge."[14]

According to Krupskaya, "The method of agitation based on the workers' everyday needs struck deep root in our Party work." Lenin wrote a pamphlet, *An Explanation of the Law on Fines Imposed on Factory Workers*, "in which he set a brilliant example of how to approach the average worker of that time, and, proceeding from the workers' needs, to lead them step by step to the question of the necessity of political struggle. . . . At that time Vladimir Ilyich had made a thorough study of factory legislation. He believed that explaining these laws to the workers made it much easier to show them the connection that existed between their position and the political regime. Evidences of this study are traceable in quite a number of articles and pamphlets which Ilyich wrote at that time for the workers, notably in the pamphlet *The New Factory Act*, and the articles 'On Strikes,' 'On Industrial Courts' and others."[15]

In addition to pamphlets and articles, Lenin and others wrote and distributed leaflets to factory workers that helped to explain aspects of their oppression and encouraged them to organize unions. One leaflet that Lenin wrote, "To the Working Men and Women of the Thornton Factory," involved several members of the Marxist circle of St. Petersburg in gathering information on which the leaflet was based. "What a thorough knowledge of the subject it shows," Krupskaya recalled. "And what a schooling this was for all the comrades who worked at that time. That was when we really learned 'to give attention to detail.' And how deeply those details have engraved themselves in our minds." Such work as this enabled the Marxists to play a prominent role in the massive strike movement that spontaneously erupted among the workers in 1896–1897.[16]

The full scope of Lenin's orientation is illustrated as we look at three additional aspects of his activity in this period.

In addition to carrying out practical work among factory workers and revolutionary activists, Lenin gave serious attention to Marxist theoretical work. He participated with a number of prominent academics and literary figures influenced by Marxism (who came to be known as the legal Marxists) in publishing a symposium entitled *Materials Characterizing Our Economic Development*.[17] Lenin also contributed to intellectually influential periodicals published by legal Marxists, in some cases to challenge those inclined to dilute one or another aspect of revolutionary Marxism. (The legal Marxists helped to generate an atmosphere that introduced a significant number of students and intellectuals to Marxist ideas; at the same time, they were inclined to be eclectic and to incorporate into their writings other intellectual fashions from the West that were inconsistent with Marxism. Some of the more prominent legal Marxists soon outgrew their radical phase and shifted to liberalism or even further to the political right.)[18] One of Lenin's most substantial achievements in this period was a massive study of the Russian economy, *The Development of Capitalism in Russia*.

Also significant was a trip abroad from May to September of 1895. In Switzerland, Lenin met with the pioneers of Russian Marxism, George Plekhanov, Pavel Axelrod, and Vera Zasulich. In France and Germany he established contacts with such leading personalities of international socialism as Paul Lafargue and Wilhelm Liebknecht, at the same time familiarizing himself with the labor and socialist movements of those countries. Far from being a personal holiday, this trip was designed to strengthen efforts toward establishing a cohesive Marxist organization in Russia that would be integrated into the Second International,[19] the worldwide network of labor and socialist parties.

It should be remembered that most of Lenin's political activities in Russia were considered illegal. He gave particular attention to the development of underground organizational methods to prevent the disruption of socialist activities by the police. "Of all our group Vladimir Ilyich was the most experienced in secrecy methods of work," Krupskaya wrote later. "He knew the through yards, and was a master hand at giving sleuths the slip. He taught us how to use invisible ink and to write messages in books by a dotted code and secret ciphers, and invented all kinds of aliases. One felt that he had been well-schooled in *Narodnaya Volya* methods."[20] Narodnaya Volya (People's Will) was a revolutionary populist current of the 1870s and 1880s that had exercised an important influence on the early Marxists. It was well known for its effective underground methods and highly centralized, disciplined organizational structure, which had been utilized to avoid tsarist repression. Despite Lenin's own underground skills, he and other leaders of the St. Petersburg Marxists were arrested at the end of 1895. Over the next four years, he was confined first to jail and then to Siberian exile. Through the use of underground methods, however, he was able to maintain his involvement in the revolutionary movement.

2. Lenin's Programmatic Orientation

The Russian Social Democratic Labor party was not formally founded until 1898 and would have to wait until 1903 before holding its first truly representative congress. But Lenin naturally gave his attention to what the political orientation and practical activities of such an organization should be. Manuscripts written in 1895–1896 and the end of 1897 provide a clear sense of Lenin's views on what should constitute the program of the revolutionary party. By the late 1890s, in Lenin's opinion, it was necessary to "emphasize the practical side of Social-Democracy, . . . its political program, its methods, its tactics."[21]

Lenin's draft program begins by explaining the dramatic spread of capitalist industry in Russia, stressing the increasing wealth and power of the capitalist class and the increasing oppression of the working class. "Out of the isolated revolts of the workers is growing the struggle of the Russian working class," he wrote, going on to indicate how this would lead to socialism: "This struggle of the working class against the capitalist class is a struggle against all classes who live by the labor of others, and against all exploitation. It can only end in the passage of political power into the hands of the working class, the transfer of all the land, instruments, factories, machines, and mines to the whole of society for the organization of socialist production, under which all that is produced by the workers and all improvements in production must benefit the working people themselves."[22]

The next point Lenin makes is that "the movement of the Russian working class is, according to its character and aims, part of the international (Social-Democratic) movement of the working class of all countries." In his later explanation of this point, he writes the following: "Working-class organization and solidarity is not confined to one country or one nationality: the workers' parties of different countries proclaim aloud the complete identity (solidarity) of interests and aims of the workers of the whole world. They come together at joint congresses, put forward demands to the capitalist class of all countries, have established an international holiday of the entire organized proletariat striving for emancipation (May Day), thus welding the working class of all nationalities and of all countries into one great workers' army. [Here Lenin is referring to the Second International.] The unity of the workers of all countries is a necessity arising out of the fact that the capitalist class, which rules over the workers, does not limit its rule to one country. . . . Capitalist domination is international. That is why the workers' struggle in all countries for their emancipation is only successful if the workers fight jointly against international capital. . . . International capital has already stretched out its hand to Russia. The Russian workers are stretching out their hands to the international labor movement."[23]

Lenin goes on to note that "the main obstacle in the struggle of the Russian working class for its emancipation is the absolutely autocratic government and its irresponsible officials. . . . That is why the struggle of the Russian working class for its emancipation necessarily gives rise to the struggle against the absolute power of the autocratic government." This relates to the belief among Russian Marxists that Russia would have to go through a period of bourgeois democracy and capitalist development before socialism could be realized. Thus, Lenin calls for the struggle "against all the vestiges of serfdom and the social-estate system which hinder free competition" and against "all endeavors to retard the development of capitalism, and consequently the development of the working class." The program therefore concludes with a list of demands that add up to the creation of a democratic republic that includes important social reforms benefiting the workers and the peasants, but not eliminating capitalism. Instead, "the struggle of the Russian working class for its emancipation is a political struggle, and its first aim is to achieve political liberty." In fact, Lenin explains, "the workers' allies are, firstly, all those social strata which oppose the absolute power of the autocratic government. . . . And the Social-Democratic Party proclaims that it will support all strata and grades of the bourgeoisie who oppose the absolute government."[24] Later in this study, we will see how Lenin's thinking on this key question of the democratic revolution (as distinct from the socialist revolution) continued to evolve.

Even at this point, however, Lenin by no means saw the struggle to build a militantly socialist workers' movement as subordinate to the requirements of a broad multiclass democratic movement against tsarism. Quite the opposite. In his *History of the Bolshevik Party*, Gregory Zinoviev correctly observed the following: "All the first phase of the history of our party is nothing other than at first a semi-conscious and then a fully-conscious struggle of proletarian revolutionaries against bourgeois revolutionaries. In so far as it was a case of a struggle against Tsarism we had, I repeat, a united front. But as soon as the struggle to win the masses and the soul of the working class was unleashed, our paths diverged. From this moment the proletarian revolutionaries grappled with the bourgeois revolutionaries, and this struggle filled a number of years which proved to be decisive for the future of Russia." Or, as Lenin put it, "no practical alliances with other groups of revolutionaries can, or should, lead to compromises or concessions on matters of theory, program or banner."[25]

This is evident in Lenin's stress, in his 1895–1896 draft program, of the basic Marxist proposition that "the emancipation of the workers must be the act of the working class itself." He also emphasizes: "The Russian Social-Democratic Party declares that its aim is to assist this struggle of the Russian working class by developing the class-consciousness of the workers, by promoting their organization, and by indicating the aims and objects of the struggle."[26]

What is meant here by "the class-consciousness of the workers," and how are the Social Democrats supposed to "develop" it? Often the term "class-consciousness is used in a relatively uncritical, romanticized, almost mystical fashion. This makes it difficult for socialist activists to come to grips with their own responsibilities. Lenin's approach was different.

"The workers' class-consciousness," Lenin explains, "means the workers' understanding that the only way to improve their conditions and to achieve their emancipation is to conduct a struggle against the capitalist and factory-owner class created by the big factories. Further, the workers' class-consciousness means their understanding that the interests of all the workers of any particular country are identical, that they constitute one class, separate from all the other classes in society. Finally, the class consciousness of the workers means the workers' understanding that to achieve their aims they have to work to influence the affairs of the state, just as the landlords and the capitalists did, and are continuing to do now." Lenin asks a question: "By what means do the workers reach an understanding of all this?" He answers that "they do so by constantly gaining experience from the very struggle that they begin to wage against the employers and that increasingly develops, becomes sharper, and involves larger numbers of workers as big factories grow."[27]

The Social Democrats "develop" working-class consciousness by assisting the workers in this struggle. "The *assistance* which the Social-Democratic Party can render to the class struggle of the workers should be: to develop the workers' class-consciousness by assisting them in the fight for their most vital needs. The second type of *assistance* should consist . . . in promoting the organization of the workers. . . . The third consists in indicating the real aims of the struggle, i.e., in explaining to the workers what the exploitation of labor by capital consists in, what it is based on, how the private ownership of the land and the instruments of labor leads to the poverty of the working masses, compels them to sell their labor to the capitalists and to yield up gratis the entire surplus produced by the worker's labor over and above his keep, in explaining, furthermore, how this exploitation inevitably leads to the class struggle between the workers and the capitalists, what the conditions of this struggle and its ultimate aims are. . . ."[28]

The practical tasks for revolutionary socialists in Russia flow from this general programmatic orientation and involve two spheres—democratic tasks and socialist tasks: "The object of the practical activities of the Social-Democrats is . . . to lead the class struggle of the proletariat and to organize that struggle in both its manifestations: socialist (the fight against the capitalist class aimed at destroying the class system and organizing socialist society), and democratic (the fight against absolutism aimed at winning political liberty in Russia and democratizing the political and social system of Russia)." Lenin stressed that Marxists "have always insisted on the inseparable connection between their socialist and democratic tasks."[29]

Regarding socialist tasks, Lenin made a distinction between propaganda ("spreading . . . the teachings of scientific socialism") and agitation. It is worth taking the time to see how he described the latter term: "Agitation among the workers means that the Social-Democrats take part in all the spontaneous manifestations of the working-class struggle, in all the conflicts between the workers and the capitalists over the working day, wages, working conditions, etc., etc. Our task is to merge our activities with the practical, everyday questions of working-class life, to help the workers understand these questions, to draw the workers' attention to the most important abuses, to help them formulate their demands to the employers more precisely and practically, to develop among the workers consciousness of their solidarity, consciousness of the common interests and common cause of all the Russian workers as a united working class that is part of the international army of the proletariat." For Lenin, this must be blended with propagandistic (that is, socialist educational) work and practical organizational tasks: "To organize study circles among workers, to establish proper and secret connections between them and the central group of Social-Democrats, to publish and distribute working-class literature, to organize the receipt of correspondence from all centers of the working-class movement, to publish agitational leaflets and manifestos and to distribute them, and to train a body of experienced agitators—such, in broad outline, are the manifestations of the socialist activities of Russian Social Democracy."[30]

Into this practical socialist orientation Lenin integrated the democratic tasks of the struggle: "In conducting propaganda among the workers, the Social-Democrats cannot avoid political problems, and they would regard any attempt to avoid them, or even to push them aside, as a profound mistake and a departure from the basic principles of international Social-Democracy. Simultaneously with the dissemination of scientific socialism, Russian Social-Democrats set themselves the task of propagating democratic ideas among the working class masses. . . . In conducting agitation among the workers on their immediate economic demands, the Social-Democrats inseparably link this with agitation on the immediate political needs, the distress and the demands of the working class, agitation against police tyranny, manifested in every strike, in every conflict between workers and capitalists, agitation against the restriction of the rights of the workers as Russian citizens in general and as the class suffering the worst oppression and having the least rights in particular, agitation against every prominent representative and flunkey of absolutism who comes into direct contact with the workers and who clearly reveals to the working class its condition of political slavery." Lenin added: "The Social-Democrats support every revolutionary movement against the present social system, they support all oppressed nationalities, persecuted religions, downtrodden social estates, etc., in their fight for equal rights."[31]

It is profoundly significant, however, that Lenin absolutely refused to subordinate the working-class movement to the broader democratic movement. This was to have decisive repercussions for strategy, tactics, and organizational principles. He insisted that "in the fight against the autocracy, the working class must single itself out, for it is the *only* thoroughly consistent and unreserved enemy of the autocracy, *only* between the working class and the autocracy is no compromise possible, only in the working class can democracy find a champion who makes no reservations, is not irresolute and does not look back." Offering a concise and insightful summary of the inconsistencies of the bourgeoisie, the rural and urban petty bourgeoisie, and of the class divisions among the oppressed nationalities and persecuted religions, he concluded: "The proletariat alone can be the *vanguard fighter* for political liberty and for democratic institutions." He stressed that to the extent that the working class assumed that role, all the other elements in the democratic struggle would be pushed toward "an irrevocable rupture with the whole of the political and social structure of present society."[32]

As Trotsky was later to observe, "the idea of an organized party leadership of the struggle of the proletariat in all its forms and manifestations, which was one of the central ideas of Leninism, is closely connected with the idea of the hegemony of the working class within the democratic movement of the country." Initially, however, this was not by any means the distinctive standpoint of Lenin alone. It was a cardinal principle of Russian Marxist "orthodoxy." In the 1880s, George Plekhanov had written: "I insist upon this important point: the revolutionary movement in Russia will triumph as a *working class movement* or else it will never triumph!" Pavel Axelrod repeated this idea several years later: "If there is no possibility of giving the Russian proletariat an independent, preeminent role in the fight against the tsarist police autocracy and arbitrary rule, then Russian social democracy has no historical right to exist. It becomes, in this event, no longer viable, and its very existence, far from assisting the revolutionary movement, retards it." In the "Manifesto of the Russian Social Democratic Labor Party," written at the founding congress of the RSDLP (independently of Lenin, who was in Siberian exile), we read the following: "The Russian proletariat can only win the political liberty it needs by itself alone. The further to the east of Europe (and Russia, as we know, is the east of Europe) the weaker, more cowardly and baser in its political attitude is the bourgeoisie, and the greater the cultural and political tasks that fall to the proletariat. The Russian working class must and will take upon its strong shoulders the task of winning political freedom."[33] The bulk of the Russian Marxists—including Plekhanov, Axelrod, Martov, and others—drew the same organizational conclusions from this orientation that Lenin drew. One might say that the distinctive trait of Lenin, and the consequent basis of Leninism, was that he (and like-minded thinkers) remained true to the political commitment to, and the organizational implications of, the central tenet of revolutionary Marxism—the leading role of the working class in transforming society.

3. Ferment in the Russian Working Class

It is impossible to grasp the meaning of Lenin's ideas without having some sense of the development of and ferment within the Russian working class that made those ideas relevant. Within the scope of this study we will not be able to examine this question in all of its richness and complexity, but several key points are worth touching on.

In the period we are examining, there was a spectacular increase in urbanization and capitalist industry in Russia. This growth was a focal point of Lenin's *The Development of Capitalism in Russia*. He noted that from 1863 to 1897, the total population increased by 53.5 percent, but that in the rural areas the increase was only 48.5 percent, while in the urban areas it was 97 percent. The number of rural inhabitants migrating to the towns and cities averaged more than 200,000 per year. As Lenin commented, "the diversion of the population from agriculture is expressed, in Russia, in the growth of towns, suburbs, factory and commercial and industrial villages and townships, as well as in non-agricultural migration." The development of capitalism could be gauged by the extent to which wage labor was employed, given that "capitalism is that stage in the development of commodity production in which labor-power, too, becomes a commodity." It was estimated that by the mid-1890s there were 10 million wage workers in European Russia, out of a total population of about 92 million. Lenin, like other Marxists, believed that capitalism was "historically progressive" because it brought about an "increase in the productive forces of social labor, and the socialization of labor." The development of technology and of socially organized labor vastly increased the quantity and quality of goods that could be produced, while at the same time drawing all of society together in new ways: "The very growth of commodity production destroys the scattered condition of small economic units that is characteristic of natural economy and draws together the small local markets into an enormous national (and then world) market. Production for oneself is transformed into production for the whole of society; and the greater the development of capitalism, the stronger becomes the contradiction between the collective character of production and the individual character of appropriation." This last point, involving the tyranny of a capitalist minority over the economy and over all others who contribute to and are dependent on it, underlay much of what Lenin saw as "the negative and dark sides of capitalism, . . . the profound and all-round social contradictions which are inevitably inherent in capitalism, and which reveal the historically transient character of this economic regime." The changes brought about by capitalist development "inevitably lead also to a change in the mentality of the population" and "cannot but lead to a profound change in the very character of the producers."[34]

Lenin recognized that these producers, the growing working class, did not constitute simply an undifferentiated proletarian mass. In *The Development of Capitalism in Russia* he sketched out the following five distinctions: "1) agricultural wage-workers. These number about 3½ million. . . . 2) Factory, mining and railway workers—about 1½ million. . . . Further: 3) building workers—about 1 million. 4) Lumber workers (tree-fellers, log trimmers, rafters, etc.), navvies, railway builders, goods loaders and unloaders, and in general all kinds of 'unskilled' laborers in industrial centers. These number about 2 million. 5) Workers occupied at home for capitalists, and also those working for wages in manufacturing industries not included in 'factory industry.' These number about 2 million." Of these 10 million wage workers, Lenin estimated that one-fourth were women and children.[35] These general estimates, while inexact, were roughly accurate. Yet further distinctions must be highlighted in order to grasp the dynamics of working-class ferment in this period.

Although the industrial work force increased nearly fourfold from 1860 to 1913, it would be a profound error to see all of its members as people who *thought of themselves* as members of a distinctive working class. Many had recently arrived from the countryside and maintained strong ties with the peasant culture from which they came. Characteristics of the peasantry and of these transitional worker-peasants were "servility, individualism, and indifference to public life" (according to Soviet historian Iu. I. Kir'ianov); a strong attachment to relatively narrow religious beliefs; a worshipful attitude toward "our little Father the Tsar"; often a serflike deference to all authority figures; a general acceptance of injustice as God's punishment for sinfulness; a tendency to turn to prayer or vodka instead of rebellion in response to oppressive conditions; and an inclination to place whatever hopes one had for improving one's condition in acquiring and working a little piece of land.[36]

Yet many also began to make an important transition, described in the memoirs of a worker who became a prominent Bolshevik activist, S. I. Kanatchikov: "Two feelings were struggling in my soul. I longed for the village, for the meadows, the brook, the bright country sun, the free clear air of the fields, and for the people who were near and dear to me. Here, in the hostile world of Moscow, I felt lonely, abandoned, needed by no one. While at work in the painting shop, . . . which smelled of paint and turpentine, I would remember pictures of our village life, tears would come to my eyes, and it was only with great effort that I could keep from crying. But there was another, more powerful feeling that gave me courage and steadfastness: my awareness of my independence, my longing to make contact with people, to become independent and proud, to live in accordance with my own wishes, and not by the caprice and will of my father." Kanatchikov goes on to give us a sense of an even profounder shift that was taking place within him, one that caused him to self-consciously embrace the identity of "worker," which is an important first step in the development of class-consciousness. "I began to be gripped by the poetry of the large metal factory, with its mighty metallic roar, the puffing of its steamdriven machines, its columns of high pipes, its rising clouds of black smoke, which sullied the clear blue sky. Unconsciously, I was being drawn to the factory, to the people who worked there, who were becoming my near ones, my family. I had the feeling that I was merging with the factory, with its stern poetry of labor, a poetry that was growing dearer and closer to me than the quiet, peaceful, lazy poetry of our drowsy village life."[37]

The elementary working-class consciousness was even stronger among second- and third-generation workers (about 40 percent of Russia's factory labor force at the end of the nineteenth century), as was an inclination to develop new interests and new values, to become literate and read, and to grapple with ideas and seek answers to a broad range of questions regarding society, the world, and the universe. "In the first decades after the Reform of 1861 [the abolition of serfdom], a tormented search for truth on the part of many progressive workers was accompanied ... by a sincere enthusiasm for religion, which had taken a monopoly on justice," notes Kir'ianov. Yet gradually "their feelings of helplessness and loneliness were supplanted by a sense of collectivism and mutual support and assistance. The proportion increased of second or third generation workers who had lost their ties to the village, where secularization occurred much more slowly than in the cities." As early as the 1870s, growing numbers of urban workers turned, in their "tormented search for truth," to the study of science and history and to the ideas of liberal, radical, and revolutionary intellectuals, spontaneously forming small study circles to read and discuss literature that might provide them with answers. In the 1880s, according to a participant, "'workers' circles were growing more and more. . . . Progressive workers . . . were looking for books and buying them from second hand dealers." These workers would generally find a radical student or intellectual to help guide them through the new realms of knowledge.

Another participant has given a sense of their range of interests: "A good propagandist [educator] must be able to answer such questions as why there is day and night, seasons of the year, eclipses of the sun. He must be able to explain the origin of the universe and the origin of the species, and must therefore know the theories of Kant, Laplace, Darwin, and Lyell. In the program must be included history and the history of culture, political economy, and the history of the working class." The study circles naturally began to gravitate to the works of Marx. "I myself," recalled a worker active in the circles of the 1880s, "had to tear up *Das Kapital* into parts, into chapters, so that it could be read simultaneously in three or four circles."[38]

Participants in these circles then shared their knowledge with fellow workers, often becoming influential figures within the workplace. Historian Reginald Zelnik vividly describes one of these "conscious workers" of the 1890s, a man named Savinov, who worked in a Moscow metal shop: "The stranger's bench soon became the center of jocular chatter, interwoven with serious political and religious discussion, marked by the near absence of the heavy cursing that normally salted workshop banter. . . . It was humor most of all that broke the initial barrier between Savinov and his curious co-workers. . . ."[39] Zelnik describes the knowledge shared with a younger worker named Senka and the others:

> A worker should recognize that his hell was here on earth, which was the paradise of the rich. The pains of hell were nothing more than the strategem of priests whose function it was to obscure the truth from the common people. Then, for the first time, Senka was exposed to quasi-scientific explanations of such phenomena as the origins of the earth and the evolution of man, none the less effective for the simplicity with which they were presented. . . .
>
> Once the initial breakthrough had been made, other openings followed swiftly. Senka began to meet frequently with Savinov, who provided him with a varied, eclectic diet of illegal reading materials. These he devoured greedily, his appetite whetted by curiosity, though an element of fear persisted. Some of the works remained vivid to him decades later: translations of Hauptmann's play *The Weavers* and the Polish radical pamphlet *What Should Every Worker Know and Remember?*; Plekhanov's dramatic recollections of the 1870s *The Russian Worker in the Revolutionary Movement*. All writings that elevated the worker to center stage, these and other motley readings, coupled with Savinov's contradictory mix of militant atheism, vaguely Marxist socialism, and Tolstoyan commitment to non-violent resistance to evil, were not the stuff from which to fashion a well-defined ideological position. But this was of little import. What counted for Senka was his exalted sense of having entered a new road, a dangerous but exhilarating one that led for the first time toward a purposeful life, compared to which his earlier life had been but a dull and empty routine.[40]

Over time, the eclecticism of the conscious workers became somewhat less expansive as different revolutionary currents cohered within Russia. One of the most significant currents consisted of the populists, who looked to "the people" (especially the peasant majority) to liberate Russia from tsarist oppression, who believed that a particularly Russian form of socialism could be achieved through bypassing capitalism altogether, and who were inclined to use individual terrorism against representatives of the autocracy. Adherents of this perspective formed the Socialist Revolutionary party in 1901. While this party attracted some workers (especially among those maintaining ties with the countryside), a majority of conscious workers were drawn to the Marxist program of the Russian Social Democratic Labor party. Zelnik comments: "Although they were familiar with many of the works of Marx and Engels (and, indeed, Lassalle, whom they did not distinguish very sharply from Marx), their sense of what constituted their 'Marxism'—beyond their solidarity with the German movement—was vague but in essence contained two major points: 1) factory workers, rather than peasants, must lead the way to the radical transformation of existing society; and 2) mass organization, rather than acts of individual heroism, . . . must be the primary means of effecting that transformation."[41]

A more significant division, however, was that between radicalized conscious workers and those who were not inclined to share the view that "real life" meant combating human injustice and defending one's ideals. Some of these "non-conscious" workers, while not averse to "mouthing some heretical ideas on the shop floor or in the tavern," were inclined to stay out of trouble and spend their nonworking lives in "the enjoyment of the distractions of city life" or in the quest for personal advancement out of the ranks of the working class.[42]

Such "distracted" workers as these, however, shared with the bulk of the conscious workers the status of skilled workers in the metal shops and semiartisan crafts. Perhaps the greatest division within the working class was between skilled and unskilled workers. One reason for this was that a far greater number of unskilled workers were newly arrived to the ranks of the working class, maintaining many more psychological and cultural and even economic ties to peasant life. The literacy rate among them was substantially lower as well, and a much higher percentage of them were women, whose status (and self-image) was particularly low in patriarchal Russia. "The life of Russia's six million proletarian women," writes Alexandra Kollontai, "was, in those early years of the twentieth-century, one long round of hunger, deprivation and humiliation. The working day lasted twelve hours, or at the very least eleven. The women worked for starvation wages of twelve to thirteen roubles a month and they lived in overcrowded barracks. . . . Even much later, when Marxism had firmly established itself in the Russian workers' movement it was only the occasional proletarian woman who took part in political life. . . . It was only rarely that a factory girl could be persuaded to attend an illegal meeting. Neither did working women visit the Sunday evening classes held on the outskirts of St. Petersburg which were the only 'legal possibilities' in those times, the only way the broad masses could make contact with the ideas of Marxism and revolutionary socialism, presented under the guise of harmless lessons in geography and arithmetic. The working women were still avoiding life and struggle, believing that their destiny was the cooking pot, the washtub and the cradle."[43]

Actually, at least by the late 1890s there *were* female conscious workers participating in socialist study circles—but rarely, and they came largely from the small percentage of women employed in the skilled trades. No less decisive than the gender or the village background of many unskilled workers was the very nature of their work. One observer noted that skilled workers were generally able to earn enough to secure moderately decent living standards (compared with those of unskilled workers), but that in addition the nature of the work itself "must develop in a man the urge toward individuality. Here there must be room for creativity. The worker must think a great deal, reason in the very process of work. And, therefore, the very essence of his work gives him a push toward self-determination." Compare that with the following description of unskilled textile workers: "The weaver and spinner are of a totally different type [from the skilled metalworker]. They are the slaves of the machine. The machine has devoured them with all their essence. It is stubbornly mechanical work. . . . Here the people are numbers. Here, on the faces is written that which is most terrible in a work atmosphere: the hopelessness of labor. People grow dull and go to seed. . . . [There is a total] absence of demand for individual creativity." In another account of women textile workers, this assertion appears: "Exhausted, sick from unhealthy, endless mill work, knowing no peace at home, from morning to night, day in and day out, month after month, the worker mother drudges and knows only need, only worry and grief. Her life passes in gloom, without light."[44]

Not only did such conditions inhibit the intellectual and political development of unskilled workers, but the differences between unskilled and skilled workers created barriers between these two strata of the working class. One worker had the following recollection: "At that time, the difference between metal and textile workers was like the difference between the city and the countryside. . . . Metalworkers considered themselves aristocrats among other workers. Their occupations demanded more training and skill, and therefore they looked down on other workers, such as weavers and the like, as an inferior category, as country bumpkins: today he will be at the mill, but tomorrow he will be poking at the earth with his wooden plough." Yet there were also expansive countertendencies among the politicized skilled workers. One said: "Only a conscious working person can truly respect a human individual, women, cherish a tender child's soul. We will not learn from anyone but ourselves. We, the conscious working people, have no right to be like the bourgeois." Noting the impulse of many conscious workers to reach out to their less-fortunate class brothers and sisters, one observer wrote that "the spiritual process is an active one. Once the voice of the individual has begun to speak in the worker, he can neither sit under a bush . . . nor limit himself to words. . . . The strength of this process is in its dynamism: the upper strata of the proletariat raise up the backward strata to their own level."[45] This process took years before coming to fruition. But even at the turn of the century, networks of Marxist intellectuals and conscious workers (some of whom were themselves being transformed into worker-intellectuals well grounded in Marxist theory) were able to envision this as a goal toward which progress was slowly but surely being made.

Most of the working-class socialists were not yet members of the RSDLP—they did not join on a mass scale until 1905. One problem was that workers harbored suspicions and resentments toward the revolutionary students and intellectuals, whose class origins were so different from theirs. This feeling was heightened by tactlessness and insensitivity that sometimes cropped up among upper-class and petty-bourgeois radicals ("the examples range from patronizing praise to the flaunting of material and cultural advantages," writes Zelnik), but also the suspicion that revolution was "an amusement, a sport" for the youthful radicals who were able to "live off their papas and mamas.... You make a lot of noise, yell, mouth radical phrases when you're young, but then you finish your educational institutions, obtain nice little positions, get married, and become the same kind of exploiters and hard-driving masters as your papas."[46]

Also, among some of the conscious workers who had transformed themselves into worker-intellectuals there was a related irritation: They perceived that many nonworker revolutionaries resisted allowing the workers themselves to have sufficient voice within the underground movement. Lenin and others who were gathered around the underground newspaper *Iskra* (Spark) argued that repressive conditions under the tsar necessarily limited the amount of democracy and openness possible at that time, but they also had a perspective of drawing increasing numbers of workers into central positions within the movement. Despite some impatience with the nonworker revolutionaries, a number of workers found these arguments to be reasonable and rallied around *Iskra*. As one later commented, the relative isolation of a single conscious worker is a difficult thing and "is why for the workers a comradely milieu, an organization, and eventually a party become his family home and hearth, and his comrades in struggle take the place of his brothers, sisters, father and mother. And it is then that the distinctions between him and those who came from another class, but have burned all their bridges behind them, are effaced."[47]

Other workers did not immediately see things this way, and finally drew away from the Social Democratic milieu for a time. Some continued to carry on educational activities of their own while engaging, in some cases, in trade union efforts. The tsarist police were particularly eager to encourage this development and, under the initiative of the imaginative police agent Sergei Zubatov, actually sponsored the establishment of legal nonpolitical trade unions in order to drive a wedge between workers and revolutionaries in the early 1900s. Thousands of workers flooded into these organizations, but soon they became too militant for the tsarist authorities, and the consequent restrictions and repression drove them in a radical direction. Many of the conscious workers involved in these ventures, as well as many who had dropped out of all organized activity, were later drawn into the revolutionary upheaval of 1905, and afterward assumed prominent roles in the labor and socialist movements and membership in the RSDLP. [48]

The labor and socialist movements in Russia were still in their infancy, however, at the turn of the century. Yet the existence and evolution of critical-minded, independently active workers who were coming to Marxism on their own was an essential component for the future success of a revolutionary socialist movement. One participant in the worker's circles of the 1890s later commented: "The mass of workers at that time did not understand the intelligentsia's language. Thanks only to a cadre of translators, so to speak, from the ranks of the semi-intelligentsia workers was activity at all successful."[49]

How could a cohesive organization be built that was capable of "translating" Marxism to the working class in a manner that would draw together the different strata of that class, generating an effective challenge to the power of the tsarist autocracy and the capitalists? What would it take to transform the workers' circles, the embryonic trade unions, the ferment into a force that could overthrow the tsar and pave the way for socialism? Lenin—not content with a fatalistic "Marxism"—concentrated his attention on precisely these questions.

3. Revolutionary Program, Cohesive Organization

In the period 1899–1902, Lenin articulated the essential aspects of his organizational perspective, and spelled out his views on the particular requirements of functioning and surviving under the extremely repressive conditions of tsarist Russia at the turn of the century. These issues are by no means the same, although they are often blurred together. The consequence of this blurring together is a grotesque distortion of Lenin's ideas. To avoid this, we will give separate attention to these two aspects of Lenin's organizational views.

1. Organizational Implications of Revolutionary Program

In 1898, the Russian Social Democratic Labor party had been formally established; but it remained theoretically, programmatically, and organizationally incoherent. This was a problem that Lenin and the great majority of leading Russian Marxists (the old Emancipation of Labor group, led by the exiled Plekhanov, Axelrod, and Zasulich, and the newer network of activists, led by Lenin, Martov, and Alexander Potresov) were committed to overcoming. Between 1899 and 1902, they were in fundamental agreement on how to understand the problem and how to overcome it. This influential current became known as the Iskraists, because in 1900 they founded a monthly underground newspaper called *Iskra* in order to propagate their views in the Russian socialist and labor movements.[1]

"Against us," wrote Lenin, "against the tiny groups of socialists hidden in the expanses of the Russian 'underground,' there stands the huge machine of a most powerful modern state that is exerting all its forces to crush socialism and democracy. We are convinced that we shall, in the end, smash that police state, because all the sound and developing sections of our society are in favor of democracy and socialism; but in order to conduct a systematic struggle against the government, we must raise revolutionary organization, discipline, and the technique of underground work to the highest degree of perfection."[2]

Lenin did not believe that this could be accomplished simply by an act of will, a simple "democratic decision" of the Russian revolutionaries. "To establish and consolidate the Party means to establish and consolidate unity among all Russian Social-Democrats; such unity cannot be decreed, it cannot be brought about by a decision, say, of a meeting of representatives; it must be worked for." First there must be a process of developing programmatic clarification: "We Russian Social-Democrats must unite and direct all our efforts towards the formation of a single, strong party, which must struggle under the banner of a revolutionary Social-Democratic program, which must maintain the continuity of the movement and systematically support its organization."[3]

Time and again, Lenin stressed the central importance of the program. "It goes without saying," he acknowledged, "that 'every step of real movement is more important than a dozen programs,' as Karl Marx said. But neither Marx nor any other theoretician or practical worker in the Social Democratic movement has ever denied the tremendous importance of a program for the consolidation and consistent activity of a political party." His explanation continued:

> At the present time the urgent question of our movement is no longer that of developing the former scattered 'amateur' activities, but of uniting—of organization. This is a step for which a program is a necessity. The program must formulate our basic views; precisely establish our immediate political tasks; point out the immediate demands that must show the area of agitational activity; give unity to the agitational work, expand and deepen it, thus raising it from fragmentary partial agitation for petty, isolated demands to the status of agitation for the sum total of Social-Democratic demands. Today, when Social-Democratic activity has aroused a fairly wide circle of socialist intellectuals and classconscious workers, it is urgently necessary to strengthen connections between them by a program and in this way give all of them a sound basis for further, more extensive activity. Lastly, a program is urgently necessary because Russian public opinion is very often most profoundly mistaken in respect of the real tasks and methods of action of the Russian Social-Democrats: these mistaken views in some cases grow naturally in the morass of political putrefaction that is our real life, in others they are artificially nurtured by the opponents of Social-Democracy. In any case, this is a fact that has to be taken into account. The working-class movement, merging with socialism and with the political struggle, must establish a party that will have to dispel all these misunderstandings, if it is to stand at the head of all the democratic elements in Russian society.[4]

There were some who objected that the attempt to elaborate a program for the RSDLP at that time would, because of differences of opinion, have the actual effect of *disuniting* the Russian Social Democrats, generating an increase of polemics directed at one another. In fact, such polemics had already begun. In Lenin's opinion, "this is another argument *in favor* of the necessity of a program." In explaining this, he also provided a lucid explanation of the value of principled polemics for revolutionaries:

> On the one hand, since the polemic has begun, it is to be hoped that in the discussion of the draft program all views and all shades of views will be afforded expression, that the discussion will be comprehensive. The polemic indicates that the Russian Social-Democrats are showing a revived interest in extensive questions pertaining to the aims of our movement and to its immediate tasks and tactics; precisely such a revival is essential to a discussion of the draft program. On the other hand, if the polemic is not to be fruitless, if it is not to degenerate into personal rivalry, if it is not to lead to a confusion of views, to a confounding of enemies and friends, it is absolutely essential that the question of the program be introduced into the polemic. The polemic will be of benefit only if it makes clear in what the differences actually consist, *how profound they are*, whether they are differences of substance or differences on partial questions, whether or not these differences interfere with common work in the ranks of one and the same party. *Only* the introduction of the program question into the polemic, only a definite statement by the two polemicizing parties on their *programmatic* views, can provide an answer to all these questions, questions that insistently demand an answer.[5]

Lenin was particularly concerned to establish an uncompromisingly revolutionary Marxist program as the basis for the RSDLP. "There can be no strong socialist party without a revolutionary theory which unites all socialists, from which they draw all their convictions, and which they apply in their methods of struggle and means of action." This was a point of contention not only among Russian socialists, but within the international socialist movement: "International Social-Democracy is at present in a state of ideological wavering. Hitherto the doctrines of Marx and Engels were considered to be the firm foundation of revolutionary theory, but voices are now being raised everywhere to proclaim these doctrines inadequate and obsolete." The leading revisionist ideologist was Eduard Bernstein, a prominent theorist in the right wing of the large and influential German Social Democratic Party. As Lenin noted, "Bernsteinism . . . is an attempt to narrow the theory of Marxism, to convert the revolutionary workers' party into a reformist party."[6]

Among the Russian Marxists, this trend was reflected in a current that came to be known as Economism, whose adherents stressed the importance of economic struggles of the workers and argued that the broader political struggle was a diversion. Before examining Lenin's views further, it may be useful to look at the orientation of important elements within this current. One of the most extreme theorists of Economism advanced the following argument: "The fundamental law that can be discerned by studying the working-class movement is that of the line of least resistance." Changing conditions of capitalism had shifted this "line of least resistance," giving rise "in the West to what is now called Bernsteinism, the crisis of Marxism. It is difficult to imagine a more logical course than the period of development of the labor movement from the *Communist Manifesto* to Bernsteinism, and a careful study of this whole process can determine with astronomical exactitude the outcome of this 'crisis.' . . . Intolerant Marxism, negative Marxism, primitive Marxism (whose conception of the class division of society is too schematic) will give way to democratic Marxism, and the social position of the party within modern society must undergo a sharp change." A more "practical" reformist gradualism will thereby gain ascendancy over the "sectarian tasks" of the socialist movement. In Russia, "the line of least resistance will never tend towards political activity" on the part of the actual workers' movement because on that front, "these weak forces are confronted with a wall of political oppression. . . . The economic struggle too is hard, but it is possible to wage it, and it is in fact being waged by the masses themselves. . . . The talk about an independent workers' political party merely results from the transplantation of alien aims and alien achievements to our soil." The bourgeois-democratic liberal elements in Russia were, according to this conception, the logical leaders of the antitsarist struggle. "Our Marxists, forgetting that the working class in the West entered political activity after that field had already been cleared, are much too contemptuous of the radical or liberal opposition activity of all other non-worker strata of society." The Economists proposed a more "practical" orientation: "For the Russian Marxist there is only one course: participation in, i.e., assistance to, the economic struggle of the proletariat, and participation in liberal opposition activity." Many of the Economists rejected the identification of their orientation with Bernstein's revisions of Marxist theory and preferred to consider themselves practical-minded revolutionaries and "orthodox Marxists" rather than reformists. But their practical orientation meshed with this forthright, if extreme, call for a "democratic" and "nonsectarian" Marxism *à la* Bernstein.[7]

"Russian Social-Democracy is passing through a period of vacillation and doubt bordering on self-negation," Lenin commented. "On the one hand, the working-class movement is being sundered from socialism, the workers are being helped to carry on the economic struggle, but nothing, or next to nothing, is done to explain to them the socialist aims and the political tasks of the movement as a whole. On the other hand, socialism is being sundered from the labor movement; Russian socialists are again beginning to talk more and more about the struggle against the government having to be carried on entirely by the intelligentsia because the workers confine themselves to the economic struggle." To the extent that such a course is followed, Lenin warned, "the working-class movement becomes petty and inevitably becomes bourgeois [in ideology]. In waging only the economic struggle, the working class loses its political independence; it becomes the tail of other parties and betrays the great principle: 'The emancipation of the working class must be conquered by the working classes themselves.'"[8]

Lenin, as we saw earlier, defined working-class consciousness in a down-to-earth, practical manner. In criticizing the Economists he defined the term "class struggle" in a similarly nonromanticized way: "We are all agreed that our task is that of the organization of the proletarian class struggle. But what is this class struggle? When the workers of a single factory or of a single branch of industry engage in struggle against their employer or employers, is this class struggle? No, this is only a weak embryo of it. The struggle of the workers becomes a class struggle only when all the foremost representatives of the entire working class of the whole country are conscious of themselves as a single working class and launch a struggle that is directed, not against individual employers, but against the *entire class* of capitalists and against the government that supports that class. Only when the individual worker realizes that he is a member of the entire working class, only when he recognizes the fact that this petty day-to-day struggle against individual employers and individual government officials is against the entire bourgeoisie and the entire government, does his struggle become a class struggle."[9]

The organizational implications of the Economists' orientation was to continue the localized, loosely organized networks, and "to elevate this narrowness to the rank of a special theory." Lenin's orientation required a different conception of organization: "It is the task of the Social-Democrats, by organizing the workers, by conducting propaganda and agitation among them, to *turn* their spontaneous struggle against their oppressors into the struggle for definite political and socialist ideals. This is something that cannot be achieved by local activity alone."[10] He elaborated:

> Our chief drawback, to the overcoming of which we must devote all our energy, is the narrow "amateurish" character of local work. Because of this amateurish character many manifestations of the working-class movement in Russia remain purely local events and lose a great deal of their significance as examples for the whole of Russian Social-Democracy, as a stage of the whole Russian working-class movement. Because of this amateurishness, the consciousness of their community of interests throughout Russia is insufficiently inculcated in the workers, they do not link up sufficiently with the idea of Russian socialism and Russian democracy. Because of this amateurishness the comrades' varying views on theoretical and practical problems are not openly discussed in a central newspaper, they do not serve the purpose of elaborating a common program and devising common tactics for the Party, they are lost in narrow study-

circle life or they lead to the inordinate exaggeration of local and chance peculiarities. Enough of our amateurishness! We have attained sufficient maturity to go over to *common action*, to the elaboration of a common Party program, to the joint discussion of our Party tactics and organization.[11]

Particularly instructive in this passage is the way it indicates the close interrelationship between program, practical tasks, and organization. Similarly instructive is what Lenin had to say in this period on the actual, practical relationship of the revolutionary party to the working class. He anticipated "the attraction of large numbers of *working-class* and intellectual young people to the [socialist] movement," and spoke of the need of "training young socialists and *workers* as able leaders of the revolutionary movement, capable of overcoming all obstacles placed in the way of our work by the tyranny of the autocratic police state and capable of serving all the requirements of the working masses, who are *spontaneously striving towards socialism and political struggle*" (emphasis added).[12] Two aspects of this passage deserve attention here, because they contradict two time-worn distortions of Lenin's thought. First, he believed that workers, not just intellectuals, should be revolutionary leaders. Second, Lenin believed that workers were *spontaneously* striving toward socialism and political struggle. (This second point is the focus of considerable controversy and will be discussed further in the next chapter.)

In Lenin's opinion, the actual experience of workers in struggle would facilitate this political evolution: "The Russian working class is burdened by a double yoke; it is robbed and plundered by the capitalists and the landlords, and to prevent it from fighting them, the police bind it hand and foot, gag it, and every attempt to defend the rights of the people is persecuted. Every strike against a capitalist results in the military and police being let loose on the workers. Every economic struggle necessarily becomes a political struggle. . . ."[13] At the same time, Lenin did not expect all workers consequently to become professional revolutionaries or even stalwarts of the socialist movement. He saw within the working class a stratification that had great relevance for the revolutionary party.

"The history of the working-class movement in all countries," he observed, "shows that the better-situated strata of the working class respond to the ideas of socialism more rapidly and more easily. From among these come, in the main, the advanced workers that every working-class movement brings to the fore, those who can win the confidence of the laboring masses, who devote themselves entirely to the education and organization of the proletariat, who accept socialism consciously, and who even elaborate independent socialist theories." According to Lenin, such a stratum was developing in Russia at the turn of the century. He contrasted this development to the evaporation of the legal Marxist fashions among many academics and writers at that time: "At a time when educated society is losing interest in honest, illegal literature, an impassioned desire for knowledge and for socialism is growing among the workers, real heroes are coming to the fore from amongst the workers, who, despite their wretched living conditions, despite the stultifying penal servitude of factory labor, possess so much character and will-power that they study, study, study, and turn themselves into conscious Social-Democrats—'the working-class intelligentsia.'"[14]

Lenin noted that this stratum of "advanced workers" was numerically small. But in addition, there was "the broad stratum of average workers" who were "absorbed by *local* practical work and interested mainly in the events of the working-class movement"; yet "these workers, too, strive ardently for socialism, participate in workers' study circles, read socialist newspapers and books, participate in agitation, and differ from the preceding stratum only in that they cannot become fully independent leaders of the Social-Democratic working-class movement. The average worker will not understand some of the articles in a newspaper that aims to be the organ of the Party, he will not be able to get a full grasp of an intricate theoretical or practical problem."[15]

Despite the appellation "average workers," however, Lenin did not consider this stratum to be the majority of the working class. He also saw the existence of "the mass that constitutes the lower strata of the proletariat. It is quite possible that a socialist newspaper will be completely or well-nigh incomprehensible to them (even in Western Europe the number of Social-Democratic votes is much larger than the number of readers of Social-Democratic newspapers) ..."[16]

The function of the revolutionary party is to facilitate the interconnection of these different strata of the working class in a way that raises the general level of working-class consciousness and the general level of the class struggle. Therefore, it would be counterproductive for the professional revolutionary to "adapt himself to the lowest level of understanding" in a manner that would "put the 'demands and interests of the given moment' in the foreground and ... push back the broad ideas of socialism and the political struggle." Rather, revolutionaries "must connect socialism and the political struggle with every local and narrow question." Lenin quoted Karl Kautsky approvingly: "Tactics and agitation must not be confused. Agitational methods must be adapted to individual and local conditions. Every agitator must be allowed to select those methods at his disposal.... The agitator must speak so that he will be understood; he must take as a starting-point something well known to his listeners.... One has to talk to cabmen differently than to sailors, and to sailors differently than to printers. *Agitation* must be *individualized*, but our *tactics*, our political *activity* must be *uniform*." The party in Russia must help coor-

dinate diverse efforts so that they are consistent with and help to advance two principles: "1) The essence of Social-Democracy is the organization of the class struggle
of the proletariat for the purpose of winning political power, and of transferring
all means of production to society as a whole, and of replacing capitalist by socialist
economy; 2) the task of Russian Social-Democracy is to organize the Russian revolutionary working-class party which has as its immediate aim the overthrow of
the autocracy and the winning of political liberty."[17]

While Lenin fought for the creation of a party around such a program, he by
no means believed that "party unity" meant a monolithic party. "The elaboration
of a common program for the Party should not, of course, put an end to all
polemics; it will firmly establish those basic views on the character, the aims, and
the tasks of our movement which must serve as the banner of a fighting party, a
party that remains consolidated and united despite partial differences of opinion
among its members on partial questions." It seems that Lenin did not believe that
"differences of substance" (for example, revolutionary versus reformist orientation)
could permanently exist within a single organization—although, as we will see,
there were fluctuations in Lenin's views on this matter. "Differences on partial questions," on the other hand, would arise naturally among revolutionaries and would
be a necessary feature of any healthy revolutionary party.[18]

Lenin also sought a balance between centralized and decentralized functioning:
"How is the need for the complete liberty of local Social-Democratic activity to
be combined with the need for establishing a single—and, consequently a central-
ist-party? Social-Democracy draws its strength from the spontaneous working-
class movement that manifests itself differently and at different times in the various
industrial centers: the activity of the local Social-Democratic organizations is the
basis of all Party activity. If, however, this is to be the activity of isolated 'amateurs,'
then it cannot, strictly speaking, be called Social-Democratic, since it will not be
the organization and leadership of the *class* struggle of the proletariat."[19]

2. Adapting to Russian Conditions

The creation of a revolutionary program and a cohesive organization, Lenin believed,
could be achieved only as a process involving those who would be building the party.
Independent thinking and individual initiative were essential. "We think that an
independent elaboration of Marx's theory is especially essential for Russian socialists;
for this theory provides only general *guiding* principles, which, *in particular*, are applied in England differently than in France, in France differently than in Germany,
and in Germany differently than in Russia. We shall therefore gladly afford space
in our paper for articles on theoretical questions and we invite all comrades openly

to discuss controversial points." Similarly, "the organization and disciplining of the revolutionary forces are impossible without the collective elaboration of certain *forms and rules for the conduct of affairs,* without the establishment—through the central organ—of every Party member's *responsibility* to the entire Party."[20]

Such a process must involve a critical-minded absorption of previous experience and lessons of the revolutionary movement: "The history of socialism and democracy in Western Europe, the history of the Russian revolutionary movement, the experience of our working-class movement—such is the *material* we must master to elaborate a purposeful organization and purposeful tactics for our Party. The analysis of this material must, however, be done independently, since there are no ready-made models to be found anywhere. On the one hand, the Russian working-class movement exists under conditions that are quite different from those of Western Europe. It would be most dangerous to have any illusions on this score. On the other hand, Russian Social-Democracy differs very substantially from former revolutionary parties in Russia, so that the necessity of learning revolutionary technique and secret organization from the old Russian masters . . . does not in any way relieve us of the duty of assessing them critically and elaborating our own organization independently."[21]

The peculiarities of Russia's reality, Lenin believed, necessitated two particular emphases that would not otherwise be as important: a central newspaper "that will appear regularly and be closely connected with all the local groups,"[22] and the development of a more effective and comprehensive underground apparatus and mode of functioning. Both of these emphases, he felt, must shape the organizational structure of the party.

"The necessity to concentrate *all* forces on establishing a regularly appearing and regularly delivered organ," he wrote, "arises out of the peculiar situation of Russian Social-Democracy as compared with that of Social-Democracy in other European countries and with that of the old Russian revolutionary parties. Apart from newspapers, the workers of Germany, France, etc., have numerous other means for the public manifestation of their activity, for organizing the movement—parliamentary activity, election agitation, public meetings, participation in local public bodies (rural and urban), the open conduct of trade unions (professional, guild), etc., etc. *In place of all of that,* yes, *all* of that, we must be served—until we have won political liberty—by a revolutionary newspaper, without which *no* broad organization of the entire working-class movement is possible."[23]

Lenin did not, of course, mean that the revolutionary party in Russia should do nothing but produce a newspaper: "In speaking of the necessity to concentrate *all* Party forces—all literary forces, all organizational abilities, all material resources, etc.—on the foundation and correct conduct of the organ of the whole Party, we do not for a moment think of pushing other forms of activity into the background—e.g., local agitation, demonstrations, boycott, the persecution of spies, the bitter campaigns against individual representatives of the bourgeoisie and the government, protest strikes, etc., etc. On the contrary, we are convinced that all these forms of activity constitute the basis of the Party's activity, but, *without* their unification through an organ of the whole Party, these forms of revolutionary struggle *lose nine-tenths of their significance*; they do not lead to the creation of common Party experience, to the creation of Party traditions and continuity. The Party organ, far from competing with such activity, will exercise tremendous influence on its extension, consolidation, and systematization."[24]

Also crucial for strengthening the party was the improvement of techniques and modes of functioning that would make party activities less susceptible to disruption and party members less susceptible to arrest by the tsarist police. "The improvement of revolutionary organization and discipline, the perfection of our underground technique are an absolute necessity." Lenin returned to this question with increasing frequency in the period we are examining: "In this respect we lag considerably behind the old workers in the Russian revolutionary movement. We must frankly admit this defect and exert all our efforts to devise methods of greater secrecy in our work, to propagate systematically the proper methods of work, the proper methods of deluding the gendarmes and of evading the snares of the police. We must train people who will devote the whole of their lives, not only their spare evenings, to the revolution; we must build up an organization large enough to permit the introduction of a strict division of labor in our work."[25]

We will conclude this section with a more detailed examination of how Lenin integrated this "underground" perspective with his general orientation on organization. His thinking on the question undeniably had a profound impact on what came to be known as Leninism. It must be stressed, however, that he saw these not as generally applicable principles of organization but—and we shall see Lenin himself emphasizing this—as very specialized forms necessitated by the repressive conditions created by the tsarist autocracy. During this period (indeed, until 1914) he seems to have viewed the German Social Democratic party as the appropriate model of socialist organization for countries where relatively democratic conditions prevailed. In this, and in the basic outlines of his organizational thinking, the majority of leading Russian Marxists were in agreement with him.

"We have always protested and will, of course, continue to protest against *confining* the political struggle to conspiracy," Lenin wrote. "But this does not, of course, mean that we deny the need for a strong revolutionary organization. . . . In *form* such a strong revolutionary organization in an autocratic country may be described as 'conspiratorial.'... Secrecy is such a necessary condition for this kind of organization that all the other conditions (number and selection of members, functions, etc.) must be made to conform to it."[26]

Lenin explicitly contrasted the positive model (as he considered it) of German Social Democracy with the harsh organizational necessities imposed by Russian realities. The socialists of Germany had succeeded in establishing an organization, he felt, that was infused with "the broad democratic principle" and was most accessible to the working masses of that country. The Economists, in their newspaper *Rabocheye Dyelo* (Workers' Cause) and elsewhere, argued that this should also be established among the socialists of Russia. Lenin explained his strong disagreement in this way:

Everyone will probably agree that "the broad democratic principle" presupposes the two following conditions: first, full publicity, and secondly, election to all offices. It would be absurd to speak of democracy without publicity, moreover, without a publicity that is not limited to the membership of the organization. We call the German Socialist Party a democratic organization because all its activities are carried out publicly; even its party congresses are held in public. But no one would call an organization democratic that is hidden from everyone but its members by a veil of secrecy. What is the use, then, of advancing 'the *broad* democratic principle' when the fundamental condition for this principle cannot be *fulfilled* by a secret organization? ...

Nor is the situation any better with regard to the second attribute of democracy, the principle of election. In politically free countries, this condition is taken for granted. 'They are members of the Party who accept the principles of the Party program and render the Party all possible support, reads Clause 1 of the Rules of the German Social-Democratic Party. Since the entire political arena is as open to the public view as is a theatre stage to the audience, this acceptance or non-acceptance, support or opposition, is known to all from the press and from public meetings. Everyone knows that a certain political figure began in such and such a way, passed through such and such an evolution, behaved in a trying moment in such and such a manner, and possesses such and such qualities; consequently, *all* party members, knowing all the facts, can elect or refuse to elect this person to a particular party office. The general control (in the literal sense of the term) exercised over every act of a party man in the political field brings into existence an automatically operating mechanism which produced what in biology is called the "survival of the fittest". "Natural selection" by full publicity, election and general control provides the assurance that, in the last analysis, every political figure will be "in his proper place," do the work for which he is best fitted by his powers and abilities, feel the effects of his mistakes on himself, and prove before all the world his ability to recognize mistakes and to avoid them.

Try to fit this picture into the frame of our autocracy! Is it conceivable in Russia

for all "who accept the principles of the Party program and render the Party all possible support" to control every action of the revolutionary working in secret? Is it possible for all to elect one of these revolutionaries to any particular office, when, in the
very interests of the work, the revolutionary *must* conceal his identity from nine out
of ten of these "all"? Reflect somewhat over the real meaning of the high-sounding
phrases to which *Rabocheye Dyelo* gives utterance, and you will realize that "broad
democracy" in Party organization, amidst the gloom of the autocracy and the domination of the gendarmerie, is nothing more than a *useless and harmful toy*. It is a useless
toy because, in point of fact, no revolutionary organization has ever practiced, or could
practice, *broad* democracy, however much it may have desired to do so. It is a harmful
toy because any attempt to practice "the broad democratic principle" will simply facilitate the work of the police in carrying out large-scale raids, will perpetuate the
prevailing primitiveness, and will divert the thoughts of the practical workers from
the serious and pressing task of training themselves to become professional revolutionaries to that of drawing up detailed "paper" rules for election systems.[27]

Given the considerable distortion to which Lenin's actual views have been subjected, by hostile critics and would-be followers alike, it is worth emphasizing some
of the points made in this passage. In politically free countries, Lenin favors socialist
parties in which "the entire political arena" of the party "is as open to the public view
as is a theatre stage to the audience" and in which the entire party membership—
knowing all the facts—is able to set the policies, elect the leadership, and control the
functioning of the party. Because he takes both democracy and revolutionary activity
seriously, however, he refuses to pretend that such a situation is possible "amidst the
gloom of the autocracy and the domination of the gendarmerie."

Lenin makes another point about German Social Democracy that is worthy
of note. He does not view democracy and the membership's control of the leadership as in any way implying that leadership is a negative factor: "Political thinking
is sufficiently developed among the Germans, and they have accumulated sufficient
political experience to understand that without the 'dozen' tried and talented leaders
(and talented men are not born by the hundreds), professionally trained, schooled
by long experience, and working in perfect harmony, no class in modern society
can wage a determined struggle."[28] The accumulated understanding and sustained
work necessary to maintain an organization and a mass movement over a period
of time cannot be dispensed with even in a democratic capitalist country. But this
generalization takes on special meaning in an autocratic country. Lenin develops
this idea in a five-stage argument:

I assert: (1) that no revolutionary movement can endure without a stable organization of leaders maintaining continuity; (2) that the broader the popular mass drawn
spontaneously into the struggle, which forms the basis of the movement and par-

ticipates in it, the more urgent the need for such an organization, and the more solid this organization must be (for it is much easier for all sorts of demagogues to sidetrack the more backward sections of the masses); (3) that such an organization must consist chiefly of the people professionally engaged in revolutionary activity; (4) that in an autocratic state, the more we *confine* the membership of such an organization to people who are professionally engaged in revolutionary activity and who have been professionally trained in the art of combating the political police, the more difficult will it be to unearth the organization; and (5) the *greater* will be the number of people from the working class and from the other social classes who will be able to join the movement and perform active work in it.[29]

Lenin makes a sharp distinction here between the revolutionary organization and the mass movement. He insists that it was impossible "to have a mass *organization* when the maintenance of strict secrecy is essential." At the same time, he argues that "to concentrate all secret functions in the hands of as small a number of professional revolutionaries as possible does not mean that the latter will 'do the thinking for all' and that the rank and file will not take an active part in the *movement*. . . . Centralization of the secret functions of the *organization* by no means implies centralization of all the functions of the *movement*." Lenin elaborates:

> The active and widespread participation of the masses . . . will benefit by the fact that a 'dozen' experienced revolutionaries, trained professionally no less than the police, will centralize all the secret aspects of the work—the drawing up of leaflets, the working out of approximate plans; and the appointing bodies of leaders for each urban district, for each factory district, and for each educational institution, etc. . . . Centralization of the most secret functions in an organization of revolutionaries will not diminish, but rather increase the extent and enhance the quality of the activity of a large number of other organizations, that are intended for a broad public and are therefore as loose and as non-secret as possible, such as workers' trade-unions; workers' self-education circles and circles for reading illegal literature; and socialist, as well as democratic circles among *all* other sections of the population, etc., etc. We must have such circles, trade unions and organizations everywhere in *as large a number as possible* and with the widest variety of functions; but it would be absurd *to confound* them with the organization of *revolutionaries*. . . . [30]

We see here an effort to create a mass socialist workers' movement, on the German model, which would be capable of surviving in the particularly repressive conditions of tsarist Russia. There remains a question, however, as to which of these organizations that Lenin lists would actually constitute the Russian Social Democratic Labor party, as opposed to the broader movement. Lenin answers this question as follows: "Depending on degree of organization in general and of secrecy of organization in particular, roughly the following categories may be distinguished:

1) organizations of revolutionaries; 2) organizations of workers, as broad and as varied as possible (I confine myself to the working class, taking it as self-evident that, under certain conditions, certain elements of other classes will also be included here). These two categories constitute the Party. Further, 3) workers' organizations associated with the Party; 4) workers' organizations not associated with the Party, but actually under its control and direction; 5) unorganized elements of the working class, who in part also come under the direction of the Social-Democratic Party, at any rate during big manifestations of the class struggle."[31]

A question remaining to be answered is how the party itself would function internally. We have seen that, because of Russian conditions, Lenin rejected "broad democracy" (his emphasis), but this does not mean a rejection of *any democracy* or the imposition of some kind of internal dictatorship by a handful of "professionals" within the party. The "Draft Rules of the RSDLP," which Lenin wrote in 1903, establishes the party congress, or convention, as the "supreme organ of the Party." Composed of representatives of all units of the RSDLP, the congress was to meet "not less than once in two years" and was to be responsible for determining party policies and perspectives and for appointing a central committee and an editorial board for the party's central organ (its newspaper). The central committee "coordinates and directs all the practical activities of the Party," while the editorial board "gives ideological guidance." (Lenin also believed, in this period, that the editorial board must function outside of Russia, that the central committee must function inside Russia, and that representatives from each should form a party council to ensure coordination of the two leadership bodies.) The draft rules suggest a balance between democracy and centralization. For example: "Each committee, union [Lenin is referring here to a grouping, not a trade union], organization or group recognized by the Party has charge of affairs relating specifically and exclusively to its particular locality, district or national movement, or to the special function assigned to it, being bound, however, to obey the decisions of the Central Committee and the Central Organ. . . ." On the one hand, "any Party member and any person who has any contact with the Party is entitled to demand that any statements made by him should be transmitted in the original to the Central Committee, the Central Organ, or the Party Congress." On the other hand, "it is the duty of every Party organization to afford both the Central Committee and the editorial board of the Central Organ every opportunity of becoming acquainted with all its activities and its entire composition." Most important, however: "All Party organizations and collegiate bodies decide their affairs by a simple majority vote and have the right of co-optation [that is, the right to take in new members]. A two-thirds majority vote is required for co-optation or expulsion of members."[32]

Despite the democratic nature of these draft rules, however, Lenin was keenly aware of severe limitations on democratic functioning imposed by the necessity of underground work. Yet even with these limitations (and, in a sense, integrated into these limitations), one finds a deeply democratic sensibility in Lenin's orientation:

> The only serious organizational principle for the active workers of our movement should be the strictest secrecy, the strictest selection of members, and the training of professional revolutionaries. Given these qualities, something even more than 'democratism' would be guaranteed to us, namely, complete, comradely, mutual confidence among revolutionaries. This is absolutely essential for us, because there can be no question of replacing it by general democratic control in Russia. It would be a great mistake to believe that the impossibility of establishing real "democratic" control renders the members of the revolutionary organization beyond control altogether. They have not the time to think about toy forms of democratism (democratism within a close and compact body of comrades in which complete, mutual confidence prevails), but they have a lively sense of their *responsibility*, knowing as they do from experience that an organization of real revolutionaries will stop at nothing to rid itself of an unworthy member. Moreover, there is a fairly well-developed public opinion in Russian (and international) revolutionary circles which has a long history behind it, and which sternly and ruthlessly punishes every departure from the duties of comradeship (and "democratism," real and not toy democratism, certainly forms a component part of the conception of comradeship).[33]

Even if one factors out the special underground conditions necessitated by tsarist repression, and even if one keeps in mind that Lenin in this period viewed German Social Democracy as a positive model, one finds in Lenin's early organizational thinking particular emphases and distinctive qualities that were to have an impact in Russia and, ultimately, throughout the world. It is not, as anti-Leninists assert, an elitist-authoritarian orientation. It is something qualitatively different: a serious "organization of real revolutionaries," a "body of comrades in which complete, mutual confidence prevails" and in which all "have a lively sense of their responsibility." For Lenin, the preconditions for this phenomenon are a commitment to a revolutionary Marxist political program and—flowing from that—an effectively, centrally organized party that encourages critical thinking and local initiative; the integration of such thinking and experience into a *partywide* process of development; and, inseparable from all of this, a deeply ingrained democratic sensibility that manifests itself even when unusual conditions preclude the formal observance of democratic procedures. A democratically centralized organization based on a revolutionary program—this was to be the essence of the Leninist conception of organization.

4. The Birth of Leninism

The birth of Leninism is generally traced to the year 1902, when the pamphlet *What Is to Be Done?* appeared. Knowledgeable historians point out that the distinctiveness of Lenin's orientation was not clear to most of his comrades until the tumultuous 1903 congress of the Russian Social Democratic Labor party. All too often, however, the qualitative differences that later developed between Leninism and rival currents among the Russian Marxists are read back into this early period. Elements of these differences certainly can—with benefit of hindsight—be found in the polemics of 1902 and 1903, but the historical evidence also indicates the striking continuity of Lenin's orientation with the mainstream of Russian Marxism up to 1903. When this mainstream divided into Bolshevism and Menshevism, it still seemed to many of the participants (including, at first, Lenin himself) that the two currents remained part of the same general stream and would soon reunite as they flowed onward in the same revolutionary Marxist direction. "Leninism" was not a banner raised by Lenin and his followers, but was a polemical epithet aimed at them by their antagonists in the RSDLP.

The Bolsheviks had no intention, in this period, called "a party of a new type." They saw themselves, simply, as being the *most consistent* defenders of the traditional party perspective held in common by Marxists throughout Russia and the world. The fact remains that concepts and positions advanced in 1902 and 1903 were starting points for what was to evolve into the mature organizational perspectives of the Leninist party. If we can comprehend them within their actual context, without inflating (and thus distorting) them, we can better grasp some of the key aspects of what came to be the Leninist conception of the party.

Many of the ideas of *What Is to Be Done?* were presented in the previous chapter. Here we will explore what have become some of the more controversial aspects of the 1902 polemic. We will then examine the emergence of Bolshevism from the 1903 congress of the RSDLP.

1. *What Is to Be Done?*

Around the newspaper *Iskra* gathered those most dedicated to the creation of a democratically centralized, stable, and cohesive party in Russia, based on a revolutionary Marxist program, providing the kind of leadership to the struggles of the working class that would ensure proletarian hegemony in the fight for democracy, culminating in the triumph of socialism. The ideas of Lenin that we have examined so far were shared by the theorists and activists of the Iskraist current, which was becoming predominant in the RSDLP. These were the ideas that found expression in Lenin's 1902 classic *What Is to Be Done?* This work, Lenin noted several years later, "is a *summary of Iskra* tactics and *Iskra* organizational policy in 1901 and 1902. Precisely a '*summary*,' no more and no less." Theodore Dan, who became one of Lenin's leading Menshevik adversaries (but who in 1902 smuggled the first copies of this work into Russia), has also acknowledged that "the basic objective of *What Is to Be Done?* was the concretization of the organizational ideas formulated in the *Iskra* program," adding that "Potresov expressed the general attitude to Lenin's work of all members of the editorial board and the closest contributors to *Iskra* when he wrote him (22 March 1902): 'I've read your little book twice running and straight through and I can only congratulate its author. The general impression ... is superlative.'"[1]

Despite this and a considerable amount of additional evidence, *What Is to Be Done?* is generally characterized as the most distinctive articulation of the Leninist perspective on the revolutionary party. This perspective has been labeled "the elitist conception of the party," even by so thoughtful and sympathetic a commentator as Marcel Liebman. In the words of the less sympathetic Alfred Meyer, "he created the model on which many other totalitarian parties have been built. Lenin must therefore be considered a pioneer of the totalitarianism of our age."[2]

What are the ideas in *What Is to Be Done?* on which such judgments are based? The perspectives we examined in the previous chapter do not support these judgments, but passages in the pamphlet—particularly in the hands of his critics—appear to provide a basis for saying that Lenin was "elitist," if not "totalitarian." Let us concentrate our attention on the classic section of Lenin's polemic to which his critics habitually allude.

Surveying the history of the Russian labor movement in the last half of the nineteenth century (which first involved strikes accompanied by the spontaneous destruction of machinery), Lenin wrote: "Even the primitive revolts expressed the awakening of consciousness to a certain extent. The workers were losing their age-long faith in the permanence of the system which oppressed them and began ... I shall not say to understand, but to sense the necessity for collective resistance, definitely abandoning their slavish submission to the authorities. But this was, nevertheless, more in the nature of outbursts of desperation and vengeance than of *struggle*. The strikes of the nineties revealed far greater flashes of consciousness; definite demands were advanced, the strike was carefully timed, known cases and instances in other places were discussed, etc. The revolts were simply the resistance of the oppressed, whereas the systematic strikes represented the class struggle in embryo, but only in embryo. Taken by themselves, these strikes were simply trade union struggles, not yet Social-Democratic struggles. They marked the awakening antagonisms between workers and employers; but the workers were not, and could not be, conscious of the irreconcilable antagonism of their interests to the whole of the modern political and social system, i.e., theirs was not yet Social-Democratic consciousness. In this sense, the strikes of the nineties, despite the enormous progress they represented as compared with the 'revolts', remained a purely spontaneous movement."[3]

So far, this may seem to be an unobjectionably objective account. What is significant, however, is the suggestion that the spontaneous movement of the workers "could not be" one that reflected socialist consciousness. Lenin went on to elaborate on precisely this point:

> We have said that *there could not have been* Social-Democratic consciousness among the workers. It would have to be brought to them from without. The history of all countries shows that the working class, exclusively by its own effort, is able to develop only trade union consciousness, i.e., the conviction that it is necessary to combine in unions, fight the employers, and strive to compel the government to pass necessary labor legislation, etc. The theory of socialism, however, grew out of the philosophic, historical, and economic theories elaborated by educated representatives of the propertied classes, by intellectuals. In the very same way, in Russia, the theoretical doctrine of Social-Democracy arose altogether independently of the spontaneous growth of the workingclass movement; it arose as a natural and inevitable outcome of the development of thought among the revolutionary socialist intelligentsia.[4]

Focusing on this passage, numerous critics have offered interpretations in which, as the late Bertram D. Wolfe (ex-Communist ideologist for the U.S. State Department) has written, "Lenin ... proposed that the revolutionary party should be made up of professional revolutionists and that the masses and their wider, more elementary organizations should be directed and controlled by this underground party of professionals." A capable historian, Allan Wildman, has agreed that Lenin was guided by "the imperative to maintain leadership over the workers' movement for the theoretically disciplined Social Democratic elite, the 'professional revolutionary' vanguard." The liberal political scientist Alfred G. Meyer has explained that "according to Leninism, the carriers of proletarian consciousness were bourgeois intellectuals.... The party is therefore to be composed of intellectuals, whatever their background, who . . . have turned into revolutionaries by profession, men whose vocation is to conspire against the existing order and to prepare a proletarian dictatorship." Meyer comments: "Thus the party seems to negate the role attributed to the working class by Marx, that of the chosen people who would destroy the social structure of capitalism and construct a socialist commonwealth." The far-left writer Antonio Carlo agrees: "If a class is unable to elaborate its own consciousness and its own revolutionary organization and must borrow them from other classes, it is subordinate to these other classes and cannot be the subject in the building of a new order. At best, it can only be an instrument in the hands of others." Understanding this, Carlo suggests, "Lenin stressed a strong centralized party, based on the power of 'ten vigorous minds,' which would guide, educate and politicize the masses in the course of the struggle."[5]

This interpretation distorts Lenin's views in several ways. It also glosses over the fact that the points made in *What Is to Be Done?*—including those we have just touched on—come out of the mainstream of Russian Marxism rather than constituting a specific Leninist variant. Although this point has been fully documented, the constant glossing-over necessitates a repetition of some of the key facts.

George Plekhanov, eighteen years before *What Is to Be Done?*, was asserting that "the socialist intelligentsia . . . must become the leader of the working class in the impending emancipation movement, explain to it its political and economic interests and also the interdependence of those interests and must prepare them to play an independent role in the social life of Russia." He stressed that "even the mere possibility of such a purposeful movement of the Russian working class depends in a large degree upon the work referred to above being done by the intelligentsia among the working class," and that the Social Democrats "will bring *consciousness* into the working class and without that it is impossible to begin a serious struggle against capital." Similarly, Pavel Axelrod wrote in 1898 that one of two perspectives exists. One possibility is that "the workers' movement does not leave the narrow course of purely economic clashes of the workers with the employers, and in itself is, on the whole, devoid of political character." The other is that "Social Democracy organizes the Russian proletariat in an independent political party." Axelrod argued for the second option; explaining that "the proletariat, according to the consciousness of the Social Democrats themselves, does not possess a ready-made, historically-elaborated social ideal," and "it goes without saying that these conditions, without the energetic influence of the Social Democrats, may cause our proletariat to remain in its condition as a listless and somnolent force in respect of its political development." All of the Iskraists accepted the idea expressed in the Austrian Social Democratic Hainfeld Program of 1888–1889: "Socialist consciousness is something that is brought into the proletarian class struggle from outside, not something that organically develops out of the class struggle." All agreed with Karl Kautsky, the world's leading interpreter of Marxism at that time, when he argued that "socialism and the class struggle arise side by side and not one out of the other; each arises under different conditions. Modern socialist consciousness can arise only on the basis of profound scientific knowledge." What is more, they were all in agreement with Julius Martov that "in the code of revolutionary behavior the demands of organizational rules and discipline should overrule all personal feelings"; with Plekhanov that "only organized revolutionary forces seriously influenced the course of events"; and with issue number 5 of *Iskra* that "in despotically ruled countries, the socialist groups" must maintain a "rigid and secret conspiratorial organization" and confine themselves to "a small number of members."[6]

It is also important to recognize the dialectical interaction that Lenin perceives between socialist consciousness and the "spontaneous" struggles of the working class. In the previous chapter we saw Lenin referring to "the working class who are spontaneously striving towards socialism and political struggle." In *What Is to Be Done?* he elaborates: "It is often said that the working class *spontaneously* gravitates towards socialism. This is perfectly true in the sense that socialist theory reveals the causes of the misery of the working class more profoundly and more correctly than any other theory, and for that reason the workers are able to assimilate it so easily, *provided* it subordinates spontaneity to itself. Usually this is taken for granted, but it is precisely this which *Rabocheye Dyelo* forgets or distorts. The working class spontaneously gravitates towards socialism: nevertheless, most widespread (and continuously and diversely revived) bourgeois ideology spontaneously imposes itself upon the working class to a still greater degree."[7]

Lenin deals with this question further when he writes: "But why, the reader will ask, does the spontaneous movement, the movement along the line of least resistance, lead to the domination of bourgeois ideology? For the simple reason that bourgeois ideology is far older in origin than socialist ideology, that it is more fully developed, and that it has at its disposal *immeasurably* more means of dissemination. And the younger the socialist movement in any given country, the more vigorously it must struggle against all attempts to entrench non-socialist ideology, and the more resolutely the workers must be warned against the bad counsellors who shout against 'overrating the conscious element', etc." Given the all-pervasive, deeply rooted elements of bourgeois ideology in capitalist society, "the adherents of the 'labor movement pure and simple', ... opponents of any non-worker intelligentsia (even a socialist intelligentsia), are compelled, in order to defend their positions, to resort to the arguments of the *bourgeois* 'pure trade-unionists'.... *All* worship of the spontaneity of the working-class movement, all belittling of the role of 'the conscious element', of the role of Social-Democracy, *means, quite independently of whether he who belittles that role desires it or not, a strengthening of the influence of bourgeois ideology upon the workers.*"[8]

It is worth noting that Lenin is here rejecting the crudely economic-determinist, fatalistic, and romantic-mystical notion that workers will automatically or spontaneously become revolutionary socialists. Rather, workers must be won to socialist ideas not only through their own struggles, but also through the hard work of socialist agitators, educators, and organizers. Lenin is not offering a historical principles or desired ideals. He is not advocating that socialist ideas and analyses originate outside the working class. Instead, he is *describing* a historical situation (with special reference to Russia) in which "we had both the spontaneous awakening of the working masses, their awakening to conscious life and conscious struggle, and a revolutionary youth, armed with Social-Democratic theory and straining towards the workers."[9] It is the transcendence of this reality, not its celebration, that *What Is to Be Done?* was designed to facilitate.

Yet we should return, for a moment, to Lenin's classic formulation: "The history of all countries shows that the working class exclusively by its own effort, is able to develop only trade union consciousness. . . . The theory of socialism, however, grew out of the philosophic, historical, and economic theories elaborated by educated representatives of the propertied classes, by intellectuals." In defending Lenin from those who utilize this formulation to distort his ideas, we should avoid defending too much.

Consider the following comment of Trotsky, writing as the defender of the Bolshevik-Leninist tradition: "According to Lenin's representations, the labor movement, when left to its own devices, was inclined irrevocably toward opportunism; revolutionary class-consciousness was brought to the proletariat from the outside, by Marxist intellectuals. . . . The author of *What Is to Be Done?* himself subsequently acknowledged the biased nature, and there with the erroneousness, of his theory, which he had parenthetically interjected as a battery in the battle against 'Economism' and its deference to the elemental nature of the labor movement. After his break with Lenin, Plekhanov came out with a belated, but all the more severe, criticism of *What Is to Be Done?*"[10] In the polemic to which Trotsky referred, *The Working Class and the Social Democratic Intelligentsia*, Plekhanov wrote: "Excluding socialism from the mass and the mass from socialism, Lenin proclaimed the socialist intelligentsia the demiurge of the socialist revolution." Given earlier assertions of Plekhanov we have seen, it seems unfair of him to tie a tin can to Lenin's tail for this. Yet Plekhanov did go on to offer a more balanced account of the historical interrelationship between the labor movement and the rise of Marxism. Plekhanov's biographer Samuel Baron summarizes: "He adduced evidence that Marx and Engels in the West and he himself in Russia arrived at socialism not independently of the rising labor movement but as a response to their awareness of it and of developing class antagonisms." Plekhanov argued that the workers' experience under capitalism generated not only trade unionism but also anticapitalist sentiments and ideas that made them responsive to the (admittedly necessary) more systematic analyses of socialist intellectuals. In fact, he went so far as to claim that "if the socialist revolution is a necessary consequence of the contradictions of capitalism, then it is clear that at a certain stage of social development the workers of capitalist countries would come to *socialism* even if 'left to themselves.'"[11]

We can afford to set aside the abstract and somewhat fatalistic speculation of this last point. The fact remains that Plekhanov's argument provides an important corrective to the one-sided formulation of Lenin. Of course, Lenin based this on the similarly one-sided formulations of Kautsky and of Plekhanov himself. As late as 1903, when he was defending *What Is to Be Done?*, Plekhanov argued: "Lenin was writing not a treatise on the philosophy of history, but a polemical article against the Economists, who said: we must wait for the working class to catch up, without the help of the 'revolutionary bacillus'. The latter is forbidden to tell the workers anything, precisely because it was a 'revolutionary bacillus', that is because it possessed theoretical consciousness. But if you eliminate the 'bacillus', then you are left with a uniform unconscious mass, into which consciousness has to be injected from without."[12]

Lenin himself, even before the break with Plekhanov, noted: "We all know now that the Economists bent the stick in one direction. In order to straighten the stick it was necessary to bend it in the other direction, and that is what I did." Six years later, he commented: "The basic mistake of those who polemicize against *What Is to Be Done?* today, is that they tear this work completely out of the context of a definite historical milieu, a definite, now already long past period of development of our party." Indicating that he had "exaggerated the idea of the organization of professional revolutionists," he went on to assert that *What Is to Be Done?* polemically corrected Economism, and it is false to consider the contents of the brochure outside of its connection with this task." In 1921, responding to a proposal to translate *What Is to Be Done?* for non-Russian parties, Lenin wrote: "That is not desirable; the translation must at least be issued with good commentaries, which would have to be written by a Russian comrade very well acquainted with the history of the Communist Party of Russia, in order to avoid false application."[13]

Early in 1923, Lenin's comrade Karl Radek recalled that, after the 1917 revolution, "when Vladimir Ilyich once observed me glancing through a collection of his articles in the year 1903, which had just been published, a sly smile crossed his face, and he remarked with a laugh: 'It is very interesting to read what stupid fellows we were!'"[14] Yet this defensiveness should not be allowed to obscure what Lenin was doing in his organizational writings of the early 1900s. He believed, as one later writer has stressed, in the need "to bring together the atomized social-democratic groups and circles into a modern centralized party with a central organ; that at the time was the great next step which had to be taken, it was 'what is to be done.'" The interpretation of this writer, Hal Draper, is worth further consideration:

> [The need to centralize] was key: it had to be pounded home into the consciousness of every militant; everything had to be subordinated to emphasizing it. How do you emphasize it? By repeating it a thousand times, in every conceivable way? Yes. By explaining it patiently over and over? Yes. By piling up argument after argument, seizing every fact, every problem, and converting it into, turning it toward, a lesson on centralization? Yes. But that is not all. The problem is greater centralization, as compared with the present looseness. Then put "Centralization!" on a banner, on a pedestal, emphasize it by raising it to a principle. But the opponents of this elementary need cover their political objections demagogically by yelling "Bureaucratism!" "Lenin wants more bureaucratism, while we are for democracy!"—How does Lenin react? Yes, he replies: *"Bureaucratism versus democracy"*—that is what we need now. He makes perfectly clear what he means, but that is how he seeks to underline, with heavy, thick strokes, the task of the day, by exaggerating in every way *that* side of the problem which points in the direction it is necessary to move *now*. Tomorrow he will recapture the balance, but today that is the way he puts the weight on the side which needs it.

Draper goes on to observe that such a methodology drove home essential points to Lenin's contemporaries, but that it could be a source of confusion to later generations of his readers: "Both the Stalinist and bourgeois falsifiers have naturally found that this gives them all sorts of opportunities to ply their trade; but more important is the fact that it is a pitfall for honest students too."[15]

All of this should not, however, be utilized to shrug off *What Is to Be Done?* as being merely of historical interest. The general arguments it contains—despite polemical exaggerations—remain reasonable and valuable for later periods, including our own.

Even the controversial point about the vital role of intellectuals in developing revolutionary theory involves an important truth. Karl Kautsky's discussion of this, which Lenin quotes, is worth considering. "Modern socialist consciousness," wrote Kautsky, "can arise only on the basis of profound scientific knowledge." One could argue, correctly, that a general class-struggle orientation, an antagonism toward capitalism, and even a socialist vision can be generated more or less spontaneously by the oppressive realities of capitalist society. But is that enough to create a movement capable of actually overturning capitalism and replacing it with a better, socialist society? Such a movement is in need of analyses, approaches, and perspectives that are based on "profound scientific knowledge." Kautsky went on to say: "The vehicle of science is not the proletariat, but the *bourgeois intelligentsia*: it was in the minds of individual members of this stratum that modern socialism originated, and it was they who communicated it to the more intellectually developed proletarians who, in their turn, introduce it into the proletarian class struggle where conditions allow that to be done."[16]

Commenting on this, Lenin added: "This does not mean, of course, that the workers have no part in creating such an ideology. They take part, however, not as workers, but as socialist theoreticians, as Proudhons and Weitlings; in other words, they take part only when they are able, and to the extent that they are able, more or less, to acquire the knowledge of their age and develop that knowledge. But in order that working men *may succeed in this more often*, every effort must be made to raise the level of consciousness of the workers in general; it is necessary that workers do not confine themselves to the artificially restricted limits of '*literature for workers*' but that they learn to an increasing degree to master *general literature*. It would be even truer to say 'are not confined', instead of 'do not confine themselves', because the workers themselves wish to read all that is written for the intelligentsia, and only a few (bad) intellectuals believe that it is enough 'for workers' to be told a few things about factory conditions and to have repeated to them over and over again what has long been known."[17]

Indeed, some workers much *preferred* reading about "broader questions" and shared the feelings of one skilled worker: "When you put in 12 or 15 hours in a row, it makes you sick to even remember your trade, let alone read about it." (On the other hand, one unskilled worker who read newspapers preferred to read "only about our factory . . . accidents and trials . . . or something my husband points out.")[18]

Here Lenin is rejecting both anti-intellectualism and the condescending romanticization of the working class. He insists on "our duty to assist every capable worker to become a *professional* agitator, propagandist, literature distributor, etc." and on the necessity "to place every capable working man in conditions that will enable him to develop and apply his abilities to the fullest." He writes: "As the spontaneous rise of their movement becomes broader and deeper, the working-class masses promote from their ranks not only an increasing number of talented agitators, but also talented organizers, propagandists, and 'practical workers' in the best sense of the term (of whom there are so few among our intellectuals who, for the most part, in the Russian manner, are somewhat careless and sluggish in their habits). When we have forces of specially trained worker-revolutionaries who have gone through extensive preparation . . . , no political police in the world will then be able to contend with them, for these forces, boundlessly devoted to the revolution, will enjoy the boundless confidence of the widest masses of the workers." Such development would be held back by the adaptation by socialists to a romanticized, narrow, "pure and simple" economic orientation among the workers: "We are directly *to blame* for doing too little to 'stimulate' the workers to take this path . . . of professional revolutionary training, and for all too often dragging them back by our silly speeches about what is 'accessible' to the masses of the workers, to the 'average workers', etc."[19]

Related to this notion is Lenin's contention that "working-class consciousness cannot be genuine political consciousness unless the workers are trained to respond to all cases of tyranny, oppression, violence, and abuse, no matter *what* class is affected—unless they are trained, moreover, to respond from a Social-Democratic point of view and no other. The consciousness of the working masses cannot be genuine class-consciousness, unless the workers learn, from concrete and above all from topical political facts and events to observe *every* other social class in *all* the manifestations of its intellectual, ethical and political life; unless they learn to apply in practice the materialist analysis and the materialist estimate of *all* aspects of the life and activity of all classes, strata, and groups of the population. Those who concentrate the attention, observation, and consciousness of the working class exclusively, or even mainly, upon itself alone are not Social-Democrats; for the self-knowledge of the working class is indissolubly bound up, not solely with a clear theoretical understanding—or rather, not so much with the theoretical, as with the practical understanding—of the relationships between *all* the various classes of modern society, acquired through the experience of political life."[20]

Therefore, Lenin insisted, revolutionary socialists must make available to even "average" workers comprehensive political exposures dealing not only with factory conditions and workplace struggles, but also with "the brutal treatment of the people by the police, the persecution of religious sects, the flogging of peasants, the outrageous censorship, the torture of soldiers, the persecution of the most innocent cultural undertakings, etc." He asserted: "When we do that (and we must and can do it), the most backward worker will understand, *or will feel*, that the students and religious sects, the peasants and the authors are being abused and outraged by those same dark forces that are oppressing and crushing him at every step of his life. Feeling that, he will know how to hoot the censors one day, on another day how to demonstrate outside the house of a governor who has brutally suppressed a peasant uprising, on still another day to teach a lesson to the gendarmes in surplices who are doing the work of the Holy Inquisition, etc."[21]

Lenin summed it up by saying that "the Social-Democrat's ideal should not be the trade union secretary, but the *tribune of the people*, who is able to react to every manifestation of tyranny and oppression, no matter where it appears, no matter what stratum or class of people it affects; who is able to generalize all these manifestations and produce a single picture of police violence and capitalist exploitation; who is able to take advantage of every event, however small, in order to set forth *before all* his socialist convictions and democratic demands, in order to clarify for all and everyone the world-historic significance of the struggle for the emancipation of the proletariat." He insisted that "it is not enough to call ourselves the 'vanguard', the advanced contingent; we must act in such a way that all the other contingents recognize and are obliged to admit that we are marching in the vanguard."[22]

The creation of such a revolutionary workers' party, guided by a serious-minded utilization of socialist theory and scientific analysis, drawing increasing numbers of working people into a highly conscious struggle against all forms of oppression—this could not be expected to arise easily or spontaneously. It had to be created through the most persistent, serious, consistent efforts of revolutionary socialists. The working class would not automatically become a force for socialist revolution, but it could develop into such a force with the assistance of a serious revolutionary workers' party. Such a party—making past lessons, the most advanced social theory, and a broad social vision accessible to increasing numbers of workers—would be a vital component in the self-education and self-organization of the working class, helping to develop spontaneous working-class impulses toward democracy and socialism into a cohesive, well-organized, and powerful political force.

In recent years some left-wing writers have felt a need to distance themselves from what Tony Cliff, for example, has called "Lenin's ... mechanical over-emphasis on organization in *What Is to Be Done?*,"[23] but the powerful stress in that work on the *practical implementation* of revolutionary perspectives continues to have an impact after eight decades.

It is worth repeating that Lenin shared this orientation with all those gathered around *Iskra*. Speaking of the upcoming party congress, Martov wrote: "There will be a storm, but from that storm revolutionary social democracy will emerge once more strengthened, and whatever the unpopularity of that small bunch of the 'orthodox', the more popular will become those *ideas* for which they sacrificed their popularity."[24]

As it turned out, however, Lenin was one of the few leaders of the *Iskra* current who was prepared to follow the implications of this orientation through to the end.

2. The Stormy Beginning of Bolshevism

The Second Congress of the Russian Social Democratic Labor party was held in Brussels and London in 1903. The founding First Congress of the RSDLP in 1898 had been a semiabortive affair. There had been only nine delegates, and they were arrested at its conclusion; the loose network of Marxist groups throughout Russia was unable to maintain a cohesive national organization in the following period. The Second Congress was designed to establish precisely such an organization. By the time of the 1903 congress, those adhering to the views expressed in the newspaper *Iskra* were predominant in the embryonic party. Also attending the congress were representatives of the Economist trend, as well as members of the Jewish Bund (which consisted of some, but not all, of the Jewish socialists in Russia). The Economists favored a loose organizational structure, and the Bundists wanted to maintain an autonomous Jewish organization within a loose Russian federation of socialist groups. The Iskraists insisted on the need for a centralized and disciplined national organization based on a revolutionary Marxist program.

What erupted at the 1903 congress was a fierce battle, first of the Economists and Bundists against the Iskraists, and then—unexpectedly among the Iskraists themselves. The Iskraists divided into two factions: "hards," who were led by Lenin and (temporarily) Plekhanov; and "softs," who were led by Martov and Axelrod. The hards had won a majority by the end of the congress, and this gave rise to the factional labels of "Bolsheviks" and "Mensheviks" (derived from Russian words for "majorityites" and "minorityites"). The RSDLP was torn into two ultimately irreconcilable factions.

Many historians have explained this by utilizing what was eventually to become the classic Menshevik interpretation. For example, according to Israel Getzler: "Menshevism had its origins in 1903–04 in the revolt of the large majority of the founders and leaders [of the RSDLP] against Lenin's bid for personal domination of the party and for a hypercentralist scheme of organization which threatened to confine the party to an elite conspiracy of professional revolutionaries. The so-called 'softs' of the Second Congress . . . broke with Lenin in revulsion against the ruthless tactics he had adopted during and after the Congress in order to impose his leadership, and against the organizational concepts set forth in his *What Is to Be Done?* and *A Letter to a Comrade.* They also resented some of Lenin's 'hards,' an aggregation of close personal followers, tough and unscrupulous *Iskra* 'agents,' and young rank-and-filers from the provincial party organizations."[25] Yet this Menshevik bias does violence to the facts.

Even more crudely, Bertram D. Wolfe has described Lenin as "the man who split the *Iskra* editors and *Iskraites* at the Second Congress in 1903 on the niceties of two slightly differing definitions of a member of the party in the first paragraph of the draft statutes, and laid the foundation of a separate party of pure Leninists on that issue."[26] This too is a distortion, but it does identify the issue on which Lenin and Martov first openly opposed each other at the 1903 congress.

A year after the congress, Martov noted that at that time the RSDLP was "by European standards, nothing more than an organization of *leaders* of the proletarian struggle, but not an organization of struggling proletarians." To alter this situation, he proposed that a member of the party be defined as "one who accepts its program and supports it both materially and by regular cooperation under the leadership of one of its organizations." He hoped this relatively loose definition, not requiring members to actually be active in a party organization, would result in an all-embracing mass party. He agreed with the comments of Axelrod, who argued: "First and foremost we are, of course, creating an organization of revolutionaries; but, since we are the party of a class, we must take care not to leave outside the Party ranks people who consciously, though perhaps not very actively, associate themselves with that Party." Martov expanded on this idea: "The more widespread the title of Party member the better. We could only rejoice if every striker, every demonstrator, answering for his actions, could proclaim himself a party member. For me a conspiratorial organization only has meaning when it is enveloped by a broad Social-Democratic working class party."[27]

Lenin disagreed with this conception because "the border-line of the Party remains absolutely vague. . . . What benefit is there in this looseness? A widespread 'title.' Its harm is that it introduces a *disorganizing* idea, the confusing of class and party." Party members, he insisted, must be defined by "personal participation in one of its organizations." Plekhanov agreed with Lenin's proposal: "They talk of persons who do not want to join, or can't join, one of our organizations. But why *can't* they? As someone who has himself taken part in Russian revolutionary organizations, I say that I do not admit the existence of objective conditions constituting an insuperable obstacle to anyone's joining. And as for those gentlemen who *do not want* to join, we have no need for them. " He added that Lenin's formulation would not "shut the door on a lot of workers," because "workers who want to join the Party are not afraid of entering an organization." On the other hand, "many intellectuals, thoroughly imbued with bourgeois individualism, are afraid of joining an organization. But that is a good thing." Lenin's draft would thereby serve as a bulwark against supporters of opportunism and reformism. Lenin elaborated: "In the period of the Party's life which we are now passing through it is just this 'elasticity' [proposed by Martov] that most certainly opens the door to all the elements of confusion, vacillation and opportunism." He stressed the urgency of "safeguarding the firmness of the Party's line and the purity of its principles." In the following year, in his classic *One Step Forward, Two Steps Back*, he explained further: "The stronger our Party organizations, consisting of *real* Social-Democrats, the less wavering there is *within* the Party, the more varied, richer, and more fruitful will be the Party's influence on the elements of the *masses* surrounding it and guided by it. The Party, as the vanguard of the working class, must not be confused, after all, with the entire class."[28]

We have seen how, in *What Is to Be Done?*, Lenin argued that a revolutionary party should be "a close and compact body of comrades" in which all are infused with "a lively sense of their responsibility." At the 1903 congress he argued in a similar vein that "we must not forget that every Party member is responsible for the Party, and that the *Party is responsible for every one of its members*."[29] Such a dynamic interrelationship between the individual members and the party as a whole, he believed, was essential for an organization capable of making a revolution.

Here it may be helpful to step back from this disagreement among Russian revolutionaries in order to gain a greater sense of perspective than even Lenin was capable of at that time. We have seen that all of the Russian Marxists, including Lenin, used the German Social Democratic party as their model. In their own minds, they were simply attempting to adapt this model to very specific and difficult Russian conditions. It may add to our understanding if we look at the German party more closely.

The German Social Democratic party was a mass patty that allowed for a wide range of principles and opinions among its members on a number of basic political questions, despite a formal adherence to a revolutionary socialist program. Created through the unification of a reformist organization founded by Ferdinand Lassalle and a more revolutionary-minded organization led by August Bebel and Wilhelm Liebknecht (who both identified closely with Karl Marx), this party was based on a number of practical compromises devised to preserve working-class unity in a hostile, repressive atmosphere in Germany. As time went on, the German Social Democrats made enormous gains, developing a powerful and comprehensive organizational apparatus. In this same period, economic prosperity and political liberalization grew in Germany. The economic situation—due in part to the growth of German industry, but also to economic expansion overseas and the growth of militarism—created greater opportunities for the workers' movement to achieve material gains, but also was accompanied by sharp class antagonisms in some areas. As a result, divisions occurred between pragmatic reformists inclined to "transcend" Marx's revolutionary doctrines and those who still took Marxist thought seriously; the former were led by Eduard Bernstein, the latter by Karl Kautsky and—even more—Rosa Luxemburg. Because the leadership and the majority of the party, particularly such figures as August Bebel, seemed consistently to reject Bernstein and support Kautsky, Lenin and his comrades in Russia were able to view it as a revolutionary socialist party. But this was an illusion.

Of growing importance in the German party, especially after 1905, was the bu-reaucracy of party functionaries whose task it was to coordinate the movement's activities. There were about 30,000 of these (in a party of about one million), con-stituting an apparatus described as follows by historian Richard Hunt: "Created during a long period of social stability and economic expansion, it was hired to run election campaigns, handle finances, disseminate the press, and do everything pos-sible to attract new members and new voters. It was not expected to mount the barricades or overturn existing society, but only to work within it for the attainment of a socialist majority." Related to the party, and assuming ever-increasing influence in its policy-making, was an even larger conglomerate of trade unions that—under the bureaucratic-conservative leadership of Karl Legien—also operated as a mod-erating influence. Another historian of German Social Democracy, Carl Schorske, has noted that "as the pressure for change came increasingly from the left, the [pro-fessional party] functionary identified himself increasingly with the right." To the extent that a *revolutionary* vanguard continued to exist in the German Social Dem-ocratic party, it was—almost by definition—not in the central party leadership, whose function was to coordinate the movement's activities in such a way as to en-sure internal unity and stable growth. Yet the party leadership's continued lip service to "orthodox Marxism" obscured this reality from most people, including the Russ-ian Marxists.[30]

Lenin's "adaptation" of the German Social Democratic model of organization to Russia actually constituted a qualitatively different kind of organization, a fact that Lenin himself never fully understood before 1914. While the classic Social Democratic party sought to *embrace* the entire working class, the party Lenin was building was designed to *interact* with it, *influence* it. The Social Democratic con-ception of the party involved the absorption of many politically diverse elements, tending to place revolutionary Marxists in the left wing of the party and to place conservative, unity-minded functionaries in the leadership. Lenin's conception of the party, on the other hand, involved nothing more nor less than a collectivity of activists committed to the program of revolutionary Marxism, in which compro-mise on principles or dilution of analysis would be unnecessary and unthought-of and, in fact, self-defeating.

Far from striving for "a party of pure Leninists," Lenin believed that he was, in concert with others committed to the Marxist program, helping to create a Russian section of the international Social Democratic movement. Nor was he prepared to split that party over "the niceties of two slightly differing definitions of a member of the party." It was Martov's definition, not Lenin's, that was adopted by the 1903 congress, by a vote of 28 to 23. (This was an unstable and temporary victory for

Martov. A minority of Iskraists voted for his formulation, but it was also supported by the Economists and Bundists, who soon walked out of the congress after they were defeated by the combined forces of *Iskra* softs and hards on other issues.) Lenin commented: "I by no means consider our difference so vital as to be a matter of life or death for the Party. We shall certainly not perish because of an unfortunate clause in the Rules."[31] Rather than staging a walkout, he continued to participate fully in the congress, utilizing other questions before the delegates in order to win comrades to his organizational perspectives.

Trotsky has written: "Lenin attempted to obtain sharp and explicit boundaries for the Party, a compact composition of the editorial board [of *Iskra*] and severe discipline. Martov and his friends preferred a looser organization, more on the order of a family circle. However, both sides were still merely feeling their way and, despite the sharpness of the conflict, no one yet thought these differences of opinion 'most serious.' According to Lenin's pointed observation of a later day, the struggle at the congress was in the nature of an 'anticipation.'" This last point, however, was hindsight. The fierceness of the debates at the congress, and the consequent tearing apart of the organization, were unexpected, and in the immediate aftermath Lenin did not talk about an "anticipation," but about a "frenzied struggle" and "irrationality" and "madness." He wrote the following words to Potresov, who had sided with Martov: "And so I ask myself: over what, in point of fact, would we be parting company as enemies for life?" He added: "I go over all the events and impressions of the Congress, I realize that I often behaved and acted in a state of frightful irritation, 'frenziedly'; I am quite willing to admit *this fault of mine to anyone*, if that can be called a fault which was a natural product of the atmosphere, the reactions, the interjections, the struggle, etc." Yet he insisted that the substance of his ideas and of the actual differences did not justify a split, which he considered "a piece of inconceivable folly." At least some of the Mensheviks, such as Axelrod, also believed that there were "no clear, defined differences concerning either principles or tactics," and that on the organizational question there was no principled difference regarding "centralism, or democracy, autonomy, etc.," but rather differing opinions regarding the "application or execution of organizational principles . . . we have all accepted."[32]

If the split did not take place over the first clause of the organizational rules that defined membership, then why did the split occur? It is impossible to understand what happened simply on the basis of abstract political principles. Political ideas are held by, and political organizations are composed of, human beings. We cannot afford to lose sight of the interplay between political principles and human dynamics as we attempt to grasp the vibrant reality of an organization's life and development. The 1903 congress of the RSDLP is a classic illustration of this truth.

"We all knew one another," wrote Krupskaya, "not only as Party workers, but in intimate personal life. It was all a tangle of personal sympathies and antipathies. The atmosphere grew tenser as the time for voting approached." In spite of this dynamic, Lenin viewed the congress from the standpoint of a professional revolutionary. Particularly among the leadership of the *Iskra* current (including Plekhanov, Axelrod, Zasulich, Martov, Potresov, and himself—the editorial board of *Iskra*), relations had a "family character" marked by "painful, long-drawn-out, hopeless quarrels . . . which were often repeated, making it impossible for us to work for *months* on end." The idea that personal quarrels would dominate over political considerations and that policies affecting the entire organization would be settled by "arrangements among ourselves" within "the old family editorial board" was intolerable to him. He wanted to ensure that "in the Party, on its formal basis, with subordination of *everything* to the Rules," such a situation would be "absolutely impossible, both judicially and morally." To advance that development, he made it clear that he would call for the *election* at the congress of the *Iskra* editorial board, and also that he would propose the reduction of the board from six to three-Plekhanov, Martov, and himself. These three had done the bulk of the writing and editorial work, and each represented a distinctive element within the RSDLP leadership; the fact that there would be three instead of six also ensured that decision-making deadlocks could be overcome by majority vote. He later explained to Potresov: "I consider this trio the *only* business-like arrangement, the only one capable of being an official institution, instead of a body based on indulgence and slackness, the *only* one to be a real center, each member of which, I repeat, would always state and defend his Party view, *not one grain more*, and irrespective of all personal motives, *all* considerations concerning grievances, resignations, and so on."[33] We can see here that Lenin had no objection to *political* disagreements' arising in the party and among its leaders, that in fact he expected that all comrades would "always state and defend" their particular party viewpoint. But he wanted to see commonly accepted organizational rules that would ensure "business-like" functioning, filtering out "personal motives" as a major factor in party life.

Another aspect of this outlook can be seen in Lenin's attitude toward the party congress, vividly described by Krupskaya: "He always, as long as he lived, attached tremendous importance to Party congresses. He held the Party congress to be the highest authority, where all things personal had to be cast aside, where nothing was to be concealed, and everything was to be open and above board. He always took great pains in preparing for Party congresses, and was particularly careful in thinking out his speeches."[34]

Historian Neil Harding has made an apt observation: "What Lenin failed to take into account was the immense emotional and psychological hurt that this entailed for Axelrod and Zasulich in particular. Earlier in the debate over Article 1 [defining membership], Plekhanov had openly ridiculed Axelrod's objections to Lenin's formulations, pouring public scorn on the man who had, for so long, been his friend and who had been so utterly dependent upon him. Now the final blow was to deprive him of that one mark of prestige which might have given him sorely needed esteem in the eyes of the movement and recognition of a lifetime devoted to it. Much the same would have applied to Zasulich and Potresov.... Martov rallied to their defense, as they had earlier supported him, and categorically refused to serve on the editorial board which was, nonetheless, ratified by the majority."[35]

Trotsky later recalled an example of the reaction of many—the example of himself. "In 1903, the whole point at issue was nothing more than Lenin's desire to get Axelrod and Zasulich off the editorial board. My attitude toward them was full of respect, and there was an element of personal affection as well. Lenin also thought highly of them for what they had done in the past. But he believed that they were becoming an impediment for the future. This led him to conclude that they must be removed from their position of leadership. I could not agree. My whole being seemed to protest against this merciless cutting off of the old ones when they were at last on the threshold of an organized party.... His behavior seemed unpardonable to me, both horrible and outrageous." This statement is corroborated and supplemented by Krupskaya: "Many were inclined to blame Plekhanov's tactlessness, Lenin's 'vehemence' and 'ambition,' Pavlovich's pinpricks, and the unfair treatment of Zasulich and Axelrod—and they sided with those who had a grievance. They missed the substance through looking at personalities. Trotsky was one of them. He became a fierce opponent of Lenin. And the substance was this—that the comrades grouped around Lenin were far more seriously committed to principles, which they wanted to see applied at all cost and pervading all the practical work. The other group had more of the man-in-the-street mentality, were given to compromise and concessions in principle, and had more regard for persons."[36]

After the congress, Lenin wrote to a concerned comrade: "The story goes that the 'praetorians' ousted people because of a slanderous accusation of opportunism, that they cast slurs on and removed people, etc. That is mere idle talk, the fruit of an imaginary grievance, *rien de plus* [nothing more]. No one, absolutely no one had 'slurs' cast upon him or was removed, prevented from taking part in the work. Some one or other was merely removed from the *central body*—is that a matter for offence? Should the Party be torn apart for that? Should a theory of [Lenin's] hypercentralism be constructed on that account? Should there be talk of rule by rod of iron, etc., on that account?"[37]

As the pro-Menshevik historian Israel Getzler has noted, Lenin was perceived and publicly denounced as "an authoritarian seeking solitary power, a man inclined both by temperament and by conviction to think little of party morals or personal loyalties." Almost two years after the Second Congress, the German left-socialist Parvus addressed Martov and Axelrod admonishingly: "Lenin rings all the time in your ears, Leninism sits in your heads and whatever one may say to you, you can only comprehend it in terms of pro or contra Lenin." Getzler has observed that "at the Second Congress, Lenin clearly won. But though he used his slight majority to gain control of the central institutions of the party, Martov was soon in a position to counter-attack, to discredit Lenin considerably, and to deprive him of many of the fruits of his victory.... Martov and his friends had responded to Lenin's victory at the Second Congress by abstaining from voting at the congress and then boycotting the party organs. Martov's supporters refused to become members of the Central Committee, to join the editorial board or even to contribute to *Iskra*."[38]

In the face of this campaign, Plekhanov wavered and then went over to the Mensheviks, among whom were those who had been his oldest friends and comrades. He insisted that the old editors of *Iskra* who had been removed be taken back on to the editorial board. At this point, Lenin wrote, "I resigned from the editorial board, for I considered this modification of the congress under the influence of the rows taking place abroad to be incorrect. But personally, of course, I did not want to prevent peace if peace was possible, and therefore (since *now* I do not consider it possible for me to work in the Six) I withdrew from the editorial board, without, however, refusing to contribute."[39] Two hardened factions—Bolsheviks and Mensheviks—remained.

Writing to Lenin at the beginning of 1904, a worker active in the RSDLP inside Russia complained of this "terrible, crushing blow," and added: "Now, what I cannot understand at all is the fight that's going on now between the majority and the minority, and to a great many of us it seems wrong. Look, comrade, is it a natural state of affairs when all energies are spent on travelling around the committees [in Russia] for the one purpose of talking about the majority and minority? ... I don't mean to say, of course, that the struggle over this issue should be given up altogether, no, only I think it should be of a different kind and should not lead us to forget our principal duty, which is to propagate Social-Democratic ideas among the masses; for if we forget that we shall rob our party of its strength. I don't know if it is fair or not, but when I see people trampling the interests of the work in the mud and completely forgetting them, I call them all political intriguers."[40]

And yet, in this very same letter, the correspondent touched on an important point that was ultimately to cause many of the workers in the RSDLP to go over to Bolshevism: "What's the use of having congresses if their decisions are ignored and everybody does just what he pleases, saying that the Congress decision is wrong, that the Central Committee is ineffectual, and so on. And this is being done by people who before the Congress were always clamoring for centralization, Party discipline, and so on, but who now want to show, it seems, that discipline is only meant for ordinary mortals, and not for them at the top." Lenin responded: "The squabbles abroad among the writers and all the other generals (whom you too harshly and bluntly call intriguers) will cease to be dangerous to the Party only when the leaders of committees in Russia become more independent and capable of firmly demanding the fulfillment of what their delegates decide at the Party congress."[41]

Thirty years later, Trotsky wrote: "At bottom, the separation was of a political nature and merely expressed itself in the realm of organizational methods. I thought of myself as a centralist. But there is no doubt that at that time I did not realize what an intense and imperious centralism the revolutionary party would need to lead millions of people in a war against the old order.... Independently I still could not see Lenin's centralism as the logical conclusion of a clear revolutionary concept."[42]

Two points must be made here, however. First, although we can see with benefit of hindsight a clear link between Lenin's organizational perspective and a consistent attitude toward the revolutionary program (a link discussed in the previous chapter and the next chapter of this study), this connection was to become fully evident, in life, only with the passage of time; at least up to the period following the revolutionary events of 1905, the Bolsheviks and Mensheviks appeared to have a common, and commonly understood, revolutionary program. Second, Lenin's centralism was not of the authoritarian or bureaucratic variety; it was profoundly democratic. And as Neil Harding has pointedly observed: "There is ... no evidence that after 1903 the Mensheviks did in actual practice make the local committees they controlled any more 'democratic', 'open' or 'proletarian' in composition than those of their Bolshevik opponents." In his study of the organizational structure and social composition of the two factions, *The Roots of Russian Communism*, David Lane suggests that "unlike the Menshevik organizational structure, the Bolshevik was more open. The young Bolsheviks were able to advance rapidly to positions of authority—which may help to explain the faction's more radical activity."[43] There were, however, problems and questions that the Bolsheviks had to deal with before they were able to become the revolutionary force they hoped to be.

5. Questions and Problems

Lenin's organizational perspectives contained contradictory elements that reflected the contradictions of the larger realities facing the Russian revolutionaries. This situation resulted in tensions within the Leninist concept of the party that persist to this day, similar to the tensions in any living organism. It also generated problems that were resolved only through the experience of revolutionary struggle, resulting in the further evolution and enrichment of Bolshevism. If we were to restrict our study of the Leninist conception of the party to Lenin's pronouncements of 1902, 1903, and 1904 (a mistake made by too many would-be Leninists, as well as by anti-Leninists), we would have a skewed understanding. To grasp the crucial later developments, however, we must give more attention to certain questions and problems that existed in the aftermath of Bolshevism's birth. First we will examine a critique of Lenin's organizational orientation advanced by Rosa Luxemburg. After sorting out weaknesses and insights of this critique, we will examine an important aspect of its relevance for the early Bolshevik organization. Finally, we will turn our attention to a programmatic divergence between Bolshevism and Menshevism that was to overshadow the early disagreements and problems regarding organization—although, in fact, there was a link between the organizational and programmatic divergences.

1. Luxemburg and Lenin

Perhaps the most important critique of Lenin's views on organization, from a revolutionary Marxist standpoint, was advanced by Rosa Luxemburg. Anyone seriously concerned with Lenin's ideas must come to grips with Luxemburg's 1904 polemic against Lenin. Unfortunately, most commentators have been satisfied with a badly garbled account of the disagreement between these two revolutionaries. Standard interpretations of Luxemburg's critique have her "demonstrate the bureaucratic tendencies inherent in Lenin's conception, speaking prophetically of the inevitable strangling of individual initiative in such an organization, and pointing out clearly that bureaucracy can just as easily work against as for the revolution." This is the interpretation of the ex-Communist Franz Borkenau, who continues: "where Lenin, instead of the belief in the proletarian revolution, had put his hopes in a centralized group under his leadership, Rosa Luxemburg almost alone continued to believe in the proletariat. . . . The masses must not be ordered about by an 'infallible' central committee. They must learn from their own experience, their own mistakes. Revolution must be the result of their increasing political understanding. She believed, in short, in the spontaneity of the proletarian masses."[1] Although Luxemburg raises important questions that we will want to consider, we must also clear away the serious distortions that obscure her actual perspective.

First of all, it should be noted that Luxemburg was not concerned solely with Russia. Her critique of Lenin's *One Step Forward, Two Steps Back*, entitled "Organizational Questions of Russian Social Democracy," appeared in the German theoretical magazine *Neue Zeit* in 1904. It was introduced with the following editorial comment: "The present work deals with Russian conditions, but the organizational questions with which it deals are also important for German Social Democracy. This is true not only because of the great international significance which our Russian brother party has achieved, but also because similar questions of organization presently occupy our own party."[2]

Max Shachtman has insightfully pointed out "that the 'professional revolutionists,' whom Luxemburg encountered in Germany were not, as in Russia, the radical instruments for gathering together loose and scattered local organizations, uniting them into one national party imbued with a firm Marxist ideology and freed from the opportunistic conceptions of pure-and-simple trade unionism. Quite the contrary. In Germany, the 'professionals' were careerists, the conservative trade union bureaucrats, the lords of the ossifying party machine, the reformist parliamentarians, the whole crew who finally succeeded in disemboweling the movement. . . . The 'centralism' of Lenin forged a party that proved able to lead the Russian masses to a victorious revolution; the 'centralism' that Luxemburg saw growing in the German social-democracy became a conservative force and ended in a series of catastrophes for the proletariat."[3] If we fail to recognize the very different context in which Luxemburg's critique was developed, we will not be able to understand what she is actually saying. It is also worth noting that while, in this period, Lenin tended to idealize the German Social Democratic model (even as he unconsciously diverged from it), Luxemburg was already poignantly aware of its deficiencies (even as she was unable to fully transcend them).

Of course, Luxemburg's article has a relevance transcending the German context. The very way in which she frames the problem has had a universal relevance even down to our own time:

> On the one hand, we have the mass; on the other, its historic goal, located outside of existing society. On the one hand, we have the day-to-day struggle; on the other, the social revolution. Such are the terms of the dialectical contradiction through which the socialist movement makes its way.
>
> It follows that this movement can best advance by tacking betwixt and between the two dangers by which it is constantly being threatened. One is the loss of its mass character; the other, the abandonment of its goal. One is the danger of sinking back to the condition of a sect; the other, the danger of becoming a movement of bourgeois social reform.[4]

Luxemburg goes on to criticize Lenin for an "overanxious desire to establish the guardianship of an omniscient and omnipotent Central Committee" in order to protect the Russian workers' movement from opportunism. She argues that "opportunism appears to be a product and an inevitable phase of the historic development of the labor movement," and that it "can be overcome only by the movement itself—certainly with the aid of Marxist theory, but only after the dangers in question have taken tangible form in practice."[5] Compressed into this point is a complex argument that is far richer than such interpreters as Borkenau imply. Certain aspects of this argument, we shall see, are fully compatible with Lenin's views, while others may not be. The fact remains that the entire argument is advanced as a polemic against Lenin's views, and Luxemburg (in 1904) did not fully grasp what these views were—in part because she, like most well-read Marxists outside of Russia, was influenced by what the Mensheviks (who included most of the best-known Russian Marxists) were asserting. Before we examine the substance of Luxemburg's own perspective, it will be necessary to clear away this deadwood of misunderstanding. In doing this, it is useful to refer to Lenin's generally ignored reply to Luxemburg's famous critique.

Luxemburg's writes that *One Step Forward, Two Steps Back* "is a methodical exposition of the ideas of the ultracentralist tendency in the Russian movement. The viewpoint is that of pitiless centralism." Lenin complains that Luxemburg's article "does not acquaint the reader with my book, but with something else.... Comrade Luxemburg says, for example, that my book is a clear and detailed expression of the point of view of 'intransigent centralism'. Comrade Luxemburg thus supposes that I defend one system of organization against another. But actually that is not so. From the first to the last page of my book, I defend the elementary principles of any conceivable system of party organization. My book is not concerned with the difference between one system of organization and another, but with how any system is to be maintained, criticized, and rectified in a manner consistent with the party idea."[6]

According to Luxemburg, "Lenin's thesis is that the party Central Committee should have the privilege of naming all the local committees of the party. . . . It should have the right to impose on all of them its own ready-made rules of conduct." Lenin's reply: "Actually that is not so. What my views on this subject are can be documentarily proved by the draft Rules of Party Organization which I proposed. In that draft there is nothing about any right to organize the local committees. That right was introduced into the Party Rules by the commission elected by the [1903] Party Congress to frame them, and the Congress adopted the commission's text. . . . In this commission which gave the Central Committee the right to organize the local committees, it was my opponents who had the upper hand."[7]

In Luxemburg's view "the two principles on which Lenin's centralism rests are precisely these: (1) The blind subordination, in the smallest detail, of all party organs, to the party center, which alone thinks, guides, and decides for all. (2) The rigorous separation of the organized nucleus of revolutionaries from its social revolutionary surroundings. Such centralism is the mechanical transposition of the organizational principles of Blanquism into the mass movement of the socialist working class." Blanquism, named after the nineteenth-century revolutionary Auguste Blanqui, was a non-Marxist conception of revolution, to be made by conspiracies of a small revolutionary elite instead of by the self-conscious working class. Lenin responds: "She has confused the defense of a specific point relating to a specific clause of the Rules (in that defense I was by no means intransigent, for I did not object at the plenary session to the amendment made by the commission) with the defense of the thesis (truly 'ultra-centralist,' is it not?) that Rules adopted by a Party congress must be adhered to until amended by a subsequent congress. This thesis (a 'purely Blanquist' one, as the reader may readily observe) I did indeed defend in my book quite 'intransigently.' Comrade Luxemburg says that in my view 'the Central Committee is the only active nucleus of the Party.' Actually that is not so. I have never advocated any such view. . . . Our controversy has principally been over whether the Central Committee and Central Organ should represent the trend of the majority of the Party Congress, or whether they should not. About this 'ultra-centralist' and 'purely Blanquist' demand worthy comrade says not a word, she prefers to declaim against mechanical subordination of the part to the whole, against slavish submission, blind obedience, and other such bogeys. I am very grateful to Comrade Luxemburg for explaining the profound idea that slavish submission is very harmful to the Party, but I should like to know: does the comrade consider it normal for supposed party central institutions to be dominated by the minority of the Party Congress?"[8]

According to Luxemburg, Lenin "is convinced that all the conditions necessary for the formation of a powerful and centralized party already exist in Russia." Lenin replies: "The thesis I advanced and advance expresses something else: I insisted, namely, that all the conditions already exist for expecting Party Congress decisions to be observed, and that the time was past when a Party institution could be supplanted by a private circle."[9]

In Luxemburg's words, Lenin "declares that 'it is no longer the proletarians but certain intellectuals in our party who need to be educated in the matters of organization and discipline.' He glorifies the educative influence of the factory, which, he says, accustoms the proletariat to 'discipline and organization.' Saying all this, Lenin seems to demonstrate again that his conception of socialist organization is quite mechanistic. . . . What is there in common between the regulated docility of an oppressed class and the self-discipline and organization of a class struggling for its emancipation?" Lenin protests: "Comrade Luxemburg declares that I glorify the educational influence of the factory. That is not so. It was my opponent, not I, who said that I pictured the Party as a factory. I properly ridiculed him and proved with his own words that he confused two different aspects of factory discipline, which, unfortunately, is the case with Comrade Luxemburg too."[10]

Luxemburg writes: "The social democratic movement is the first in the history of class societies which reckons, in all its phases and through its entire course, on the organization and the direct, independent action of the masses. . . . Lenin seems to slight this fact when he presents in his book the opinion that the revolutionary social democrat is nothing else than 'a Jacobin indissolubly joined to the organization of the proletariat, which has become conscious of its class interests.'" (The Jacobins, also called the Montagnards, were, during the French Revolution of 1789–1795, the radical wing of that bourgeois-democratic revolution, noted for their plebian base and their centralist, at times dictatorial, inclinations; they were opposed by the more moderate Girondists, who were inclined to compromise with the monarchy and aristocracy.) Again Lenin protests: "It was P. Axelrod, not I, who first started talking about Jacobinism. He was the first to liken our Party trends to those of the days of the Great French Revolution. I merely observed that the parallel could only be allowed in the sense that the division of present-day Social Democracy into a revolutionary and an opportunist wing corresponded to some extent to the division into Montagnards and Girondists. The old *Iskra*, which the Party Congress endorsed, often drew such a parallel. Just because it recognized this division, the old *Iskra* fought against the opportunist wing in our Party, against the

Rabocheye Dyelo trend. Rosa Luxemburg here confuses *comparison* of the two revolutionary trends of the eighteenth and the twentieth century with identification of those trends."[11]

Having cleared away these false arguments, we are almost ready to confront the substantive challenge Luxemburg raises. As a prelude, however, we should take note of the common ground shared by Lenin and Luxemburg, which is far more considerable than is generally acknowledged. In fact, much of what Luxemburg has written seems like an elaboration of the "Leninist conception of the party." Even in her 1904 polemic, she stresses the need for "a proletarian vanguard, conscious of its class interests and capable of self-direction in political activity," and this "self-direction" she also calls "social-democratic centralism." She defines this as "the 'self-centralism' of the advanced sectors of the proletariat. It is the rule of the majority within its own party." Far from denigrating organization on behalf of "spontaneity," she insists on the need for a party that "possesses the gift of political mobility, complemented by unflinching loyalty to principles and concern for unity." Two years later, in her classic *The Mass Strike, the Political Party and the Trade Unions*—often interpreted (mistakenly) as a "spontaneist" document—she would write: "The social democrats are the most enlightened, most class-conscious vanguard of the proletariat. They cannot and dare not wait, in a fatalist fashion, with folded arms for the advent of the 'revolutionary situation,' to wait for that which in every spontaneous people's movement, falls from the clouds. On the contrary, they must now, as always, hasten the development of things and endeavor to accelerate events. . . . If the widest proletarian layer should be won for a political mass action of the social democrats, and if, vice versa, the social democrats should seize and maintain the real leadership of a mass movement—should they become, in a *political sense*, the rulers of the whole movement, then they must, with the utmost clearness, consistency and resoluteness, inform the German proletariat of their tactics and aims in the general period of coming struggle."[12]

After the Russian Revolution of 1917, in her sympathetic critique of Bolshevik policy, Luxemburg was to repeat these eminently "vanguardist" assertions, though perhaps even more forcefully: "Thus it is clear that in every revolution, only that party is capable of seizing the leadership and power which has the courage to issue the appropriate watchwords for driving the revolution ahead, and the courage to draw all the necessary conclusions from the situation." Particularly scornful of the Mensheviks, Luxemburg noted that only the Bolsheviks were able to grasp "the true dialectic of revolutions" and to stand the "wisdom of parliamentary moles on its head: not through a majority to revolutionary tactics, but through revolutionary tactics to a majority—that is the way the road runs. Only a party which knows how to lead, that is, to advance things, wins support in stormy times.... Whatever a party could offer of courage, revolutionary far-sightedness and consistency in a historic hour, Lenin, Trotsky and the other comrades have given in good measure."[13]

We are now in a position to examine the substantive disagreement between Luxemburg and Lenin.

Despite the similarity in outlooks, one element in Luxemburg's 1904 critique of Lenin is inconsistent with his fundamental premise that "the Party, as the vanguard of the working class, must not be confused . . . with the entire class." At one point in her polemic, she says precisely the opposite: "The fact is that the social democracy is not *joined* to the organization of the proletariat. It is itself the proletariat." This statement appears to be inconsistent, as well, with the thrust of her own "vanguardist" inclination, which we have just documented. But it is an assertion related to another key point to which she gives particular stress: "The social democratic movement cannot allow the erection of an air-tight partition between the class-conscious nucleus of the proletariat already in the party and its immediate popular environment, the nonparty sections of the proletariat." The attempt to safeguard revolutionary principles by stressing the distinction between the vanguard and the class as a whole, and efforts to establish an organizational structure reinforcing that distinction, can make the party not a living expression of the working class, but a sterile sect. "Stop that natural pulsation of a living organism, and you weaken it, and you diminish its resistance and combative spirit—in this instance, not only against opportunism but also (and that is certainly of great importance) against the existing social order. The proposed means turn against the end they are supposed to serve."[14]

There is a problem, however, with the organizational perspective that Luxemburg appears to be proposing in this criticism of Lenin. She offers no clear alternatives to Lenin's orientation, except the organizational form of German Social Democracy, with its growing bureaucratic-conservatism and opportunism—elements that she was more keenly aware of than Lenin, but that she concluded "arise out of unavoidable social conditions" and "appear to be a product and an inevitable phase of the historic development of the labor movement." The problem would be corrected, she seems to feel, by the crises of capitalist society and by the working-class radicalism and upsurges generated by those crises. "Marxist theory offers us a reliable instrument enabling us to recognize and combat typical manifestations of opportunism," she writes. At the same time, "the working class demands the right to make its mistakes and learn in the dialectic of history."[15]

Yet subsequent developments were to challenge the adequacy of Luxemburg's "solution" to this problem. Luxemburg and her revolutionary comrades found themselves trapped in the left wing of a bureaucratized mass party that, when World War I erupted in 1914, supported the imperialist war effort instead of organizing working-class resistance. In the aftermath of the war, as the working-class radicalization foreseen by Luxemburg gathered momentum, the Social Democratic bureaucracy was able to divert much of the proletarian militancy into "safe" channels; Luxemburg and the most determined revolutionaries were first blocked and finally ejected, left without an adequate revolutionary instrument of their own. That this experience, combined with the 1917 achievement of the Bolsheviks, had an impact on her thinking should be clear from her 1918 comments already quoted. There is also the testimony of those who knew her. For example, Karl Kautsky— her erstwhile comrade turned bitter opponent—noted in 1921 (two years after Luxemburg's death) that "in the course of the war Rosa drew steadily closer to the communist world of thought, so that it is quite correct when Radek says that 'with Rosa Luxemburg there died the greatest and most profound theoretical head of communism.'"[16] Indeed, as early as 1916 one of her closest coworkers complained that her organizational orientation had become "too mechanically centralist," with "too much 'discipline,' too little spontaneity"—an assessment that sounded, as Michael Löwy has commented, like "a distant and paradoxical echo of the criticisms that Rosa herself had made in another context, addressed to Lenin." (Some have argued that even in earlier years Luxemburg favored a highly centralized party in her native Poland.)[17]

To make these observations is by no means to shrug off the many insights in her essay "Organizational Questions of Russian Social Democracy," only some of which have been touched on here. The essence of Luxemburg's 1904 critique, however, is the opposite of that put forward by most latter-day anti-Leninists. She is *not* saying that the kind of party Lenin is building will establish a bureaucratic dictatorship once it makes a revolution. She is saying that such a party is in danger of degenerating into a sect that is *incapable of leading a revolution*. We will see that the tendency to which she directs our attention, while not an iron law, was a very real tendency among Lenin's Bolsheviks, one that Lenin himself was forced to combat time after time. It has been an even stronger tendency among many self-styled "Leninist" organizations and grouplets that have proliferated like mushrooms over the past seven decades.[18] The truth that Luxemburg insists on has, therefore, a great resonance even in our own time.

In the mid-1950s, James P. Cannon, who had been struggling for years to keep alive an American form of Leninism, wrote to another veteran comrade about a particular phrase used by Frederick Engels. "The key to Engels' thought," he commented, "is his striking expression that the conscious socialists should act as a 'leaven' in the instinctive and spontaneous movement of the working class. Those are winged words that every party member should memorize. The leaven can help the dough to rise and eventually become a loaf of bread, but can never be a loaf of bread itself." Cannon stressed the same principle Luxemburg had many years before: "Every tendency, direct or indirect, of a small revolutionary party to construct a world of its own, outside and apart from the real movement of the workers in the class struggle, is sectarian." He saw this as "an everpresent danger to any small organization of revolutionists condemned to isolation by circumstances beyond their control, regardless of their original wishes and intentions. The moment such an organization ceases to think of itself as a part of the working class, which can realize its aims only with and through the working class, and to conduct itself accordingly, it is done for."[19]

This has been a problem in the United States and many other countries where relatively marginalized radicals (largely but not exclusively of student origin) have been inclined, like their counterparts in the early RSDLP, toward intellectualized but impractical organizational constructions. Instead of the "toy democracy" that Lenin warned against in *What Is To Be Done?*, however, there has been a tendency toward creating "toy Bolshevik parties" that, in countries enjoying some degree of bourgeois democracy, are able to perpetuate themselves, in a world of their own, for a considerable period of time before they finally burn themselves out. We will see, however, that a similar tendency—the focus of Luxemburg's critique—threatened the Bolshevik organization in its infancy.

2. Revolutionary Committees Distinct from the Workers

Let us once again consider Luxemburg's non-Leninist assertion: "The fact is that the social democracy is not *joined* to the organization of the proletariat. It is itself the proletariat." This statement suggests the organic growth of a mass socialist movement out of the working class. The conditions existing in tsarist Russia necessitated a different course—the creation of underground revolutionary committees, distinct from the working class, which would facilitate the growth of a mass socialist workers' movement. Bertram D. Wolfe has touched on an important aspect of this question that, while containing serious distortions, is worth considering. Wolfe focuses on full-time functionaries in the Russian and the Western European movements:

> It must be clear that this "professional revolutionary" was something quite different from the full-time paid official of the Western party or trade union. These latter are chosen by and responsible to the rank-and-file. Expertness, a 'machine,' or the passivity and inertia of the rank and file, might give them more or less permanent tenure. But always there remained the possibility of their being overruled, even re-

moved by their membership. Lenin's plan, on the other hand, involved men who were self-chosen, who had chosen themselves as professional revolutionaries and professional leaders of a movement they were to create in their own image. At the top were the self-appointed *Iskra* editors. They, in turn, were to select their agents by careful winnowing and send them into the localities. These in turn, would select their local following with equal care. This organization constructed hierarchically from the top downward would set up or seek to control all broader organizations of actual workingmen, and, in the name of the workingmen, would attempt to assume leadership over the activities of other oppositional classes.[20]

Wolfe's formulations tend to warp one's understanding of the reality. First of all, we should note that in the 1902–1903 period, this general orientation was not simply "Lenin's plan," but was the orientation of all Iskraists, and that it more or less describes the manner in which both Bolsheviks and Mensheviks functioned. (Also, as we have seen, Lenin wanted to alter this plan—for example, by having *Iskra* editors elected by the Party Congress rather than allowing them to be self-appointed.) Furthermore, Wolfe characteristically utilizes words with negative connotations, making reasonable notions seem quite sinister. Thus, "self-chosen" revolutionaries "seek to control" broader workers' organizations, and so forth. More accurately, those who have made a commitment to building a revolutionary socialist movement would seek to win over broader organizations of workers to that goal. There is nothing elitist in trying to win a majority of the working class to the struggle for the most thoroughgoing political and economic democracy.

Wolfe also passes over in silence the internal democracy (modified only by the requirements of underground existence) that was to be part of the organization the Iskraists sought to establish. Moreover, he gives a misleading impression of the possibility that existed for the rank and file of Western Social Democracy to overrule or remove the bureaucratic apparatus of their parties and trade unions: This possibility was realized only under the most unusual circumstances—for example, during the colossal upheaval following World War I. Generally, the full-time paid officialdom, expertly utilizing its bureaucratic machinery within party and trade union, was able to create enough relative passivity among the rank and file to ensure the relative permanence of its own tenure.[21] Particularly after 1914, in Germany and elsewhere, Social Democratic officialdom proved quite capable of utilizing severe repression—sometimes in collaboration with the bourgeois state apparatus—against militant workers and dissident comrades. The growing officialdom of the Social Democratic movement had a significant motivation in maintaining itself that the professional revolutionaries of Russia did not have. As Wolfe acknowledges, the professional revolutionaries' lives were not "as comfortable, or their 'profession' as well-paid, as that of the full-time officials to other European organizations, not to mention the salaries of our American trade union leaders."[22] Often they volunteered their talents and energies to the revolutionary movement while supporting themselves with modest jobs; only small stipends were paid to those able to work full-time for the revolutionary movement.

The fact remains that there is an element of truth in Wolfe's description, which was to create serious problems for the Bolsheviks in the early period. In his *Letter to a Comrade on Our Organizational Tasks* (1902), Lenin endorsed and elaborated on the organizational proposals of an underground organizer in St. Petersburg calling for local committees of professional revolutionaries, answerable only to the central committee of the RSDLP, that would "direct all local work and all the local organizations of the Party."[23] The St. Petersburg organizer, as it turned out, was someone who helped form the Menshevik faction in the following year. The scheme of highly centralized committees, far from being a "Leninist" concoction, was a general product of underground conditions.

Nonetheless, the Bolshevik "committeeman" emerged as a specific type in the early years. As Krupskaya was to write later: "The 'committeeman' was usually a rather self-assured person. He saw what a tremendous influence the work of the committee had on the masses, and as a rule he recognized no inner-Party democracy. 'Inner-Party democracy only leads to trouble with the police. We are connected with the movement as it is,' the 'committeemen' would say. Inwardly they rather despised the Party workers abroad, who, in their opinion, had nothing better to do than squabble among themselves—'they ought to be made to work under Russian conditions.' The 'committeemen' objected to the overruling influence of the Center abroad. At the same time they did not want innovations. They were neither desirous nor capable of adjusting themselves to quickly changing conditions."[24]

Trotsky also recalled that "the habits peculiar to a political machine were already forming in the underground. The young revolutionary bureaucrat was already emerging as a type. The conditions of conspiracy, true enough, offered rather meager scope for such of the formalities of democracy as electiveness, accountability and control. Yet undoubtedly the committeemen narrowed these limitations considerably more than necessity demanded and were far more intransigent and severe with the revolutionary workingmen than with themselves, preferring to domineer even on occasions that called imperatively for lending an attentive ear to the voice of the masses."[25] Polemicizing against this tendency (and, at the same time, unfairly identifying it with Bolshevism as such), the young Trotsky of 1904 decried the conception of a party "which *thinks* for the proletariat, which *substitutes itself* politically for it," calling instead for "a party which politically *educates* and *mobilizes* the proletariat."

He asserted: "The committee has no links to the masses; it does not lead strikes; it no longer calls street demonstrations, or takes the lead in them." He observed that the average committeeman "cannot be described as a tail-ender, lagging behind the masses and bowing to their spontaneous practice. He is not marching at the tail-end, but unfortunately he has no tail behind him! He is gesticulating in empty space. . . . This typical trait is the emancipation of the 'professional revolutionaries' from all obligations, not only of a moral kind ('philistinism!') but also of a political kind ('tail-ending!'), towards the conscious elements of the class to whose service we have decided to devote our lives. The committees have lost the need to base themselves on the workers in so far as they have found a base in the 'principles' of centralism."[26] This youthful polemic finds at least partial confirmation in Krupskaya's later comment that "the 'committeemen' had done a tremendous job during the period of 1904–1905, but many of them found it extremely difficult to adjust themselves to the conditions of increasing legal facilities and methods of open struggle."[27]

One member of a Bolshevik committee in Baku during this period, Cecilia Bobrovskaya, has described a strike in the oil fields in which "a very good agitator" from the Menshevik faction "was never tired at mass meetings of discussing minor questions like the provision of aprons, mitts, etc., by the employers, without touching upon the real significance of the strike." Acknowledging that the local Bolshevik committee "adopted a somewhat academic approach to the working masses," she has offered this account of the workers' reactions to the Bolshevik speakers: "They were often interrupted by uncomplimentary shouts about the Bolsheviks who instead of demanding mitts and aprons demanded the overthrow of the autocracy."[28]

Consequently, when the overthrow of the autocracy became a real issue for Russian workers in 1905, the Bolsheviks were, to a large extent, not in a position to provide leadership. At the beginning of that year, Lenin complained to Bolshevik underground organizers: "Really, I sometimes think nine-tenths of the Bolsheviks are actually formalists. . . . You must be sure to organize, organize, organize *hundreds* of circles, completely pushing into the background the customary, well meant committee (hierarchic) stupidities. . . . Either you create *new*, young, fresh, energetic battle organizations everywhere for revolutionary Social Democratic work of all varieties among all strata, or you will go under wearing the aureole of 'committee' bureaucrats."[29] The upheaval of the 1905 revolution was necessary to transform the Bolshevik faction into an organization capable of breaking free from the sectarian impulse. Even then, as we shall see, this and related impulses were to crop up again in later periods.

In the period leading up to the 1905 revolution, however, a new and more profound divergence began to separate Bolsheviks and Mensheviks. Despite the organizational problems the Bolsheviks had yet to overcome, the distinctive trajectory they maintained in this period would ultimately help to ensure their triumph over Menshevism. It is to this embryonic divergence of trajectories that we must now turn our attention.

3. Was the Bolshevik/Menshevik Split "Unprincipled"?

Sometimes polemics among even small groups of leftists can illuminate problems of earlier periods in the history of the Marxist movement. Thus, a controversy that arose among certain revolutionaries in 1981 brings into focus additional questions of considerable importance regarding the Leninist perspective on organization. It began when Doug Jenness, of the U.S. Socialist Workers party, put forward the view that the political program of Lenin and the Bolsheviks remained the same throughout their history—from the 1903 split in the RSDLP up through (and after) the Bolshevik Revolution of 1917. Challenging this view, the Belgian Marxist Ernest Mandel argued that in "the program of the RSDLP, the Russian Marxists, distinguished *two stages of the Russian revolution*: An immediate stage, which was the democratic (or bourgeois-democratic) revolution, whose goal was the overthrow of the tsarist autocracy and not of capitalism . . . [and] a subsequent stage, that of the social revolution leading to the dictatorship of the proletariat, the overthrow of capitalism, and the construction of a socialist society. . . . The great majority of Russian Marxists—especially Plekhanov, Lenin, Martov, Axelrod, and Trotsky—agreed on that distinction until 1904, despite their differences on the organizational question, which divided them at the Second Congress of the RSDLP in 1903. . . . At first, the differences between Bolsheviks and Mensheviks seemed limited to organizational problems. . . ." Mandel concluded that "Lenin explicitly changed his position" on the nature of the Russian Revolution only in 1917 when he rallied the Bolsheviks around the perspective of making a socialist revolution, not a bourgeois-democratic revolution, in Russia.[30]

Doug Jenness scoffed at this account: "If the reader did not know the outcome of the October 1917 revolution, he or she could quite justifiably conclude, part of the way through Mandel's article, that the Bolsheviks, allegedly educated in an 'erroneous dogma' for at least a dozen years, were going to make a mess of it, that the whole affair would end in disaster." Jenness asked rhetorically: "How could a party so mistrained on such fundamental questions . . . lead this revolution to victory?" He concluded that "the Bolsheviks didn't abandon their strategy, but saw it confirmed and realized by the unfolding revolution."[31] Indeed, there is a compelling quality to Jenness's argument. Would it be possible—and what would be the implications for so-called *scientific* socialists—for an organization built around the *wrong political program* to nevertheless lead a socialist revolution? A secondary, but no less significant, question is this: If the Bolsheviks and Mensheviks had the same basic political program, and were divided only over organizational questions, then how could a split be justified? Did Lenin devote his energies to healing the split, and if not, was he not guilty of participating in an "unprincipled split"?

These questions are especially poignant because, as it turns out, Jenness is simply wrong. He seems to have, quite literally, forgotten *The ABC of Communism*. This can be established by turning to the book of that title, which was written by Bolsheviks Nikolai Bukharin and Eugen Preobrazhensky to explain the new 1919 program of the Bolshevik party. The program opened with the following words: "The November revolution (October 25th, old style; November 7th, new style) in Russia, realized the dictatorship of the proletariat, which began to build the foundations of communist society, with the aid of the poor peasants or the semi-proletariat."[32] Bukharin and Preobrazhensky inform us of the following:

> Our program was adopted by the eighth Party Congress at the end of March, 1919. Prior to this we had not a precise program, written on paper. We had nothing but the old program elaborated at the second Party Congress in the year 1903. When this old program was compiled, the bolsheviks and the mensheviks constituted a single party, and they had a common program. At that date the organization of the working class was only just beginning. . . . The Marxists—the social democrats, subsequently to divide into bolsheviks and mensheviks—supposed . . . that in Russia, as elsewhere, the working class would continue to grow and would constitute the main strength of the revolution. . . . But at the date when the program of the social democrats was elaborated by the second Party Congress (both Lenin and Plekhanov participating in the work), the strength of the Russian working class was extremely small. That is why no one then imagined that it would be possible to undertake the direct overthrow of the bourgeoisie. At that time the best policy seemed: to break the neck of tsardom; to win freedom of association for the workers and peasants in conjunction with all others; to establish the eight-hour day; and to reduce the power of the landowners. No one then dreamed that it would be possible to realize the rule of the workers once and for all, or immediately to dispossess the bourgeoisie of its factories and workshops. Such was our old program of the year 1903.[33]

Does this mean that the Bolsheviks had been "educated in an 'erroneous dogma' for at least a dozen years," as Jenness mockingly puts it? Bukharin and Preobrazhensky attempt to put this question in perspective by suggesting that "circumstances altered profoundly" between 1903 and 1917, and that what was a reasonable proposition at the beginning of that period was transformed by the end into an untenable proposition: "If life has undergone great changes, the program cannot be left as it was."[34] This leads, however, directly into the other question: If the Bolsheviks and Mensheviks shared a common political program in the wake of the 1903 split, did Lenin tenaciously fight for an organizational reunification (and should he not have done so)?

In fact, by the end of 1904 Lenin abandoned the idea of such a reunification. He helped to initiate the establishment of Bolshevik committees in Russia, which held conferences that elected the Bureau of Majority Committees. This hardened Bolshevik faction set up its own newspaper, *Vperyod* (Forward), counterposed to the new Menshevik version of *Iskra*, and it began working for the Third Party Congress, which would be dominated by—and therefore would approve the policies of—the Bolsheviks. Lenin warned that Bolsheviks desiring unity with the Mensheviks would be placing themselves "under the thumb of the Bonapartists of the [Menshevik-controlled] Central Organ and Central Committee." He asserted that "*prior to* the [creation of the Bolshevik] Bureau and *prior to* '*Vperyod*' we did all we could to save loyalty, to save unity, to save formal, i.e., higher methods of settling the conflict." But he had now lost confidence in the revolutionary seriousness of the Mensheviks and therefore insisted that "we bring *the split* into the open, we call the *Vperyod*-ists to a congress, we want to organize a *Vperyod*-ist party, and we break immediately *any and all* connections with the disorganizers." He made it clear that he favored such a course even if it violated the formal statutes of the RSDLP (which he felt the Menshevik "Bonapartists" and "disrupters" had already made a mockery of), and he posed the dilemma to his Bolshevik comrades in the most uncompromising terms: "Either we shall rally all who are out to fight into a really iron-strong organization and with this small but strong party quash that sprawling monster, the new *Iskra* motley elements, or we shall prove by our conduct that we deserve to go under for being contemptible formalists."[35]

Not only did Lenin work to maintain and widen the Bolshevik/Menshevik split, but he argued against the impulse of perhaps a majority of his Bolshevik comrades to heal it. The beginnings of the 1905 revolutionary upsurge caused Bolsheviks and Mensheviks within Russia to work more closely together. Lenin complained: "Our only strength lies in utter frankness, in solidarity, and in determined assault. But people, it seems, have gone soft now that we have a 'revolution'! At a time when organization is needed a hundred times more than ever before they sell out to the disrupters. It is evident from the proposed changes in the draft of the declaration and congress call . . . that 'loyalty' is put on a pedestal."[36] At this point, Lenin felt absolutely no loyalty to a unified RSDLP. He wanted a Bolshevik party. It would be wrong, however, to see this as simply the triumph of petty and narrow factionalism on Lenin's part. Rather, there was the beginning of a programmatic divergence that profoundly influenced his thinking.

Although the Bolsheviks and Mensheviks *formally* adhered to one and the same program, Lenin believed that in practice only the Bolsheviks were advancing that program. The "motley elements" who made up the Menshevik wing of the RSDLP might include genuinely revolutionary-minded activists, but they also included the more reformist-minded Economists. Lenin perceived that, to justify their behavior at the 1903 congress and afterward, an increasing number of Mensheviks were utilizing the same kinds of organizational arguments that had previously been advanced by the Economists against the old Iskraists. The Economist influence, and the overall dynamics among the "motley elements" of Menshevism, Lenin believed, would generate a vacillation on the more substantive aspects of the revolutionary program. And in the autumn of 1904, the Mensheviks did give voice to an orientation that represented a shift away from the 1903 program of the RSDLP.

This view was held not only by Lenin, but also by one of the leading Mensheviks, Theodore Dan, who, "with historical hindsight," thirty-five years later wrote that "the organizational disagreements that, at the second Congress, divided the *Iskra* people into Bolsheviks and Mensheviks were merely the cover for incipient intellectual and political divergences. . . . It was not an organizational but a political divergence that quickly split the Russian Social-Democracy into two factions, which sometimes drew close and then clashed with each other even at a time when they were nominally within the framework of a unitary party." Dan noted that "on the question of the relations between the Party and the laboring masses the Mensheviks had gone a long way towards the organizational ideas of Economism." But he also identified the underlying political divergence: "The basic ideas of the *Iskra* platform were, as we have seen, the primacy of political tasks over the task of leading an economic struggle of the proletariat, and the originating, dominant role of the Social-Democracy, its 'hegemony' in the 'all-national' struggle for political liberation. . . . There is no doubt that Bolshevism carried on this *Iskra* political tradition." The Mensheviks, on the other hand, came to believe in "leaving the dominant role in the solution of the 'all-national' task of the revolution—the task of replacing the Tsarist by a revolutionary government—to non-proletarian, bourgeois social forces that were trying to give the proletariat no more than the role of an influential opposition 'pushing' the bourgeoisie towards political radicalism and compelling it to make substantial socio-economic concessions to the working class. It meant, essentially, liquidating the whole concept of 'hegemony'."[37]

Dan went on to point out that "in theory Menshevism never abandoned this concept and later on appealed to it more than once."[38] Such *verbal* adherence to the idea of working-class political independence and leadership in the revolutionary struggle at the time confused many revolutionary socialists about the actual political trajectory of Menshevism. But Dan identified the point at which the Menshevik leadership tacitly shifted its programmatic focus: It was the autumn of 1904, the period in which Lenin also abandoned the idea of real unity between Bolsheviks and Mensheviks.

The Russo-Japanese War, which had flared up at the beginning of the year, was going badly for the Russian government. Discontent was visibly growing among the major sectors of society—workers, peasants, the intelligentsia, and even sectors of the capitalist class. The tsarist government, losing confidence, began to waver between granting and refusing to grant concessions to those demanding reforms. The bourgeois liberals launched a campaign for political, social, and economic reforms through the local organs of self-government called *Zemstvos*. Pavel Axelrod outlined the Menshevik orientation in this way:

> In the person of the liberal Zemstvos and Dumas we have to deal with the enemies of our enemy, who are not, however, willing or able to go as far in the struggle against him [the tsar] as is required by the interests of the proletariat. But in coming out officially against absolutism and confronting it with demands aimed at its annihilation, by that alone they show themselves to be our allies. . . . Within the limits of the struggle against absolutism, and particularly in its present phase, our attitude towards the liberal bourgeoisie is defined by the task of imbuing it with more courage and impelling it to join in those demands being put forward by the proletariat led by the Social-Democracy. But we should be falling into a fateful blunder if we set as our goal the forcing at this very moment of the Zemstvos or other organs of the bourgeois opposition, by means of energetic measures of intimidation, to make a formal promise, under the influence of panic, to present our demands to the government. Such a tactic would compromise the Social-Democracy, since it would transform our entire political campaign into a lever for the reaction.[39]

Against this, Lenin uncompromisingly insisted on the need for political independence of the working class from the bourgeois politicians, commenting: "the very notion that 'our' demands, the demands of working class democracy, should be presented to the government by the liberal democrats is a queer one. On the one hand, precisely because they are bourgeois democrats, the liberal democrats will never be able to understand 'our' demands and to advocate them sincerely, consistently and resolutely. . . . On the other hand, if we are strong enough to exercise serious influence on bourgeois democrats in general, and on Messieurs the Zemstvo-ists in particular, we are also strong enough to present our demands to the government independently."[40]

Rather than building the confidence of and support for liberals, Lenin asserted that "it is the business of the working class to widen and strengthen its organization among the masses tenfold, to take advantage of every vacillation of the government, . . .

and, pointing to the example of all the halfway 'steps' that were foredoomed to failure from the start, and about which so much fuss is now being made, to explain that insurrection is necessary. It goes without saying that the workers must respond to the Zemstvo petitions by calling meetings, scattering leaflets, organizing demonstrations wherever [there are] sufficient forces to do so, in order to present all the Social-Democratic demands, regardless of the 'panic' of Mr. Trubetskoy [a prominent liberal] and his like, and regardless of the outcry of philistines about a lever of reaction." Lenin called upon revolutionary socialists to make police stations, censorship offices, and jails holding political prisoners the sites for "mass demonstrations (because demonstrations that are not mass demonstrations have no significance whatever)." He called for an orientation in which "the workers will rise still more fearlessly, in still greater numbers, ... to conquer by force for *themselves* that which Messieurs the liberal bourgeoisie promise to give them as charity—the freedom of assembly, the freedom of the workers' press, complete political liberty for the wide and open struggle for the complete victory of socialism."[41] It should be noted that some of the Menshevik-initiated demonstrations turned into militant expressions of working-class consciousness, some of which Lenin himself applauded. Nor was he dogmatically opposed to organizing such demonstrations at the site of the liberals' Zemstvo banquets.[42] What he was concerned with was the growing inclination among the Mensheviks to see bourgeois politicians as the true leaders of the democratic struggle against tsarism.

The incipient divergence in programmatic orientation—the question of whether the workers should rely on bourgeois liberals to lead the democratic struggle or should maintain their own political independence from the bourgeoisie—provided a basis, in Lenin's mind, for two distinct organizations. What is more, the essential element in the Bolshevik orientation, the political independence of the working class and its hegemony in the coming revolution, had an inherent logic that, while not clearly grasped by Lenin until 1917, suggested a flowing over of the democratic revolution into the socialist revolution. This idea of proletarian hegemony was the programmatic key to which the Bolsheviks remained true throughout their history, and it stood them in good stead regardless of the vital questions remaining to be clarified in the future.

Out of the programmatic divergence of Bolshevism and Menshevism, a difference in organizational structure logically suggests itself. If one is inclined to follow the lead of the liberal bourgeoisie in the upcoming democratic revolution, then it makes sense to shift "towards the organizational ideas of Economism," as Theodore Dan puts it. Similarly, if one sees the working class as the driving force and the political vanguard of the democratic revolution, then one may be drawn to what came to be identified as Bolshevik organizational principles. In criticizing "the theoretical position of the Mensheviks . . . who have deviated from revolutionary Social-Democracy towards opportunism," Lenin noted what he viewed as false theories regarding the organizational question: "One such is the organization-as-process theory, which reduces Marxism to an apologia for disorganization and intellectualist anarchism. Another is the reversion to the false ideas concerning the relation of Party to class, which lower the tasks of the Party as vanguard, leader, and organizer of the class." In the words of Theodore Dan, "in contrast to Bolshevik 'discipline', the basic organizational slogan of Menshevism became—workers' initiative."[43] Lenin saw this as a rhetorical cover for a slide into Economism.

In early 1905, Lenin expressed the opinion that "in fact, there are now two Russian Social Democratic Labor Parties." Only the Bolsheviks constituted the *real* revolutionary party, and "adherents of the Party principle have no alternative but to work separately from, and independently of, these [Menshevik] disorganizers," who should "not be admitted to membership in any organization of our Party." But Lenin was, even at the Bolshevik-dominated Third Congress of the RSDLP (which the Mensheviks refused to attend), unable to win a majority of Bolsheviks to this intransigent position. As Theodore Dan remarked, "at that time the political character of the split was far from immediately apparent, not only to the spectators on the sidelines but to the participants in the factional struggle themselves."[44] In adjusting to the Bolshevik sentiment for unity, Lenin reformulated his position after the Third Congress without essentially abandoning it:

> The minority has now severed itself from the Party; this is an accomplished fact. One section of it will probably become convinced by the decisions adopted, and still more so by the minutes of the Congress, of the artlessness of the fables that have been spread about mechanical suppression, etc., it will become convinced that the new rules completely guarantee the rights of the minority in general, that the split is harmful, and it will rejoin the Party. The other section may persist for some time in refusing to recognize the Party Congress. With regard to this section, all we can do is to express the wish that it organize itself as quickly as possible into a united organization with its own tactics and its own rules. The sooner this happens the easier will it be for everybody, for the large mass of Party workers, to understand the causes and the significance of the split, the easier will it be to conclude practical agreements between the Party and the seceded organizations [the Mensheviks] according to the local requirements of work, and the sooner will the way be indicated to the inevitable future restoration of Party unity.[45]

Before such a process could run its course, however, both factions of the RSDLP were to be subjected to severe tests, particularly the test of the 1905 revolutionary upheaval.

6. The Test of Revolution

In late 1904, a growing ferment in the Russian working class found expression outside the framework of the RSDLP. In the course of the following year, this ferment developed into revolutionary storms that dramatically changed the political landscape of Russia and transformed the RSDLP into a mass workers' party. Bolsheviks and Mensheviks alike were forced to adjust to these qualitative changes. Swept up in the insurgent flood and undergoing an invigorating experience of mass struggle, they found that much of what divided them was washed away.

Most relevant for us, the Bolsheviks were compelled to transform their organization in a manner resulting in a more open, *democratically* centralist organization than had been possible during the two previous years. The Mensheviks, too, experienced an organizational transformation and—for a time—also veered away from their programmatic orientation toward the liberal bourgeoisie. By the end of the year, Lenin himself had set aside the view that "there are now two Russian Social Democratic Labor Parties" and instead became a sincere advocate of Bolshevik/Menshevik unity.

After the revolutionary flood receded, giving way to triumphant reaction, the old differences between Bolsheviks and Mensheviks reemerged more sharply than ever. Among the Bolsheviks, the sectarian impulse that we have already noted grew to such proportions that Lenin was forced to use all of his considerable energy to prevent it from overwhelming his organization. More serious than this, however, was the problem that *did* overwhelm the Mensheviks: a fundamental flaw in their programmatic orientation that led to a profound organizational crisis and made it impossible for them, at the decisive moment, to provide revolutionary leadership to the future working-class insurgencies. This backward shift resulted in the revival of factional strife and culminated in a definitive organizational split. In chapter 8 of this study, we will give attention to these post-1905 developments. Here we will concentrate on the manner in which the events of 1905 transformed the Bolshevik organization.

1. The Revolutionary Program

In the period immediately following the 1905 revolution, there was a significant move to heal the rift in the RSDLP. At the Unity Congress held in the spring of 1906, in the words of anti-Leninist historian Leonard Schapiro, "an atmosphere of conciliation prevailed. There was more banter, fewer charges of 'treason' or 'opportunism'. Lenin displayed a greater spirit of conciliation than ever before, or after."[1] This remarkable shift was a direct consequence of the 1905 events and of the changes these events wrought within the Bolshevik and Menshevik factions alike. It is worth dwelling for a moment on Schapiro's description:

> In the course of debate Lenin went out of his way to emphasize that he was 'far from holding the opinion' that bolsheviks and mensheviks could not work together in one party. At the conclusion of the Congress Lenin and a number of other bolsheviks, describing themselves as members of the 'former' bolshevik faction, issued a declaration enumerating those decisions of the Congress which they regarded as mistaken. They declared their determination not to permit another split in the party, but claimed the democratic right, while loyally accepting all decisions of the majority, to propagate their views in 'comradely' debate 'with the aim of winning the majority over to their side. *Time would show how much sincerity there was in these gestures.* (Emphasis added.)[2]

This final editorial comment, suggesting that Lenin was engaged simply in a factional maneuver, constitutes a fundamental but common misunderstanding of the basis of Lenin's organizational orientation. What was essential in a revolutionary party, for Lenin, was not narrow factional advantage but the integrity of the political program. We have seen that it was an incipient but profound programmatic divergence, not simply organizational disagreements, that finally led him to advocate an organizational split beginning in late 1904. This divergence appeared to widen throughout early 1905, but by the end of the year it had been reversed to the extent that Lenin believed unity to be possible. As Theodore Dan put it, "this *rapprochement* was possible because contact with revolutionary realities immediately shook the positions of both factions, which in any case were still inadequately consolidated."[3] Here we shall trace this growing programmatic convergence.

At the Menshevik conference of April–May 1905, the Mensheviks had adopted a resolution stressing the bourgeois-democratic character of the antitsarist struggle and concluded that a successful revolution would result in a provisional government that would "take on itself the task of resolving the problems of what would historically be a bourgeois revolution, [and therefore] it would follow two policies: by regulating the contest between antagonistic classes of the newly liberated nation it would be obliged on the one hand to advance the process of revolution, but on the other to combat those elements which threatened the foundations of the capitalist system." Therefore, the RSDLP "should endeavor to maintain, throughout the course of the revolution, whatever position will best enable it to advance the revolutionary cause, not tying its hands in the struggle with the inconsistent, self-seeking policies of bourgeois parties and not allowing itself to become merged in bourgeois democracy. It follows that the party should not aim to seize power or share it within a Provisional Government, but should remain a party of the extreme revolutionary opposition."[4]

As we shall see, there were contradictory elements in the positions adopted by the Mensheviks at their conference, but this basic idea—*that the working class must not fight for power*—was the element they stressed through the first part of 1905. A. S. Martynov, a former Economist who was now a leading Menshevik, explained this position in his pamphlet *Two Dictatorships*:

> The proletariat cannot win political power in the state, either wholly or in part, until it has made the socialist revolution. . . . But that being the case, it is evident that the coming revolution cannot realize any political forms *against the will of the whole bourgeoisie*, for the latter will be the master of tomorrow. . . . That being the case, the revolutionary struggle of the proletariat, by simply frightening the majority of the bourgeois elements, can have but one result—the restoration of absolutism in its original form. . . .
>
> The struggle to influence the course and outcome of the bourgeois revolution can find expression only in the exertion of revolutionary pressure by the proletariat on the will of the liberal and radical bourgeoisie, and in the compulsion on the part of the more democratic 'lower strata' of society to bring the 'upper strata' into agreement to carry through the bourgeois revolution to its logical conclusion.[5]

Lenin and the Bolsheviks denounced policies through which they believed "the proletariat may be transformed into a mere appendage of bourgeois democracy." This is how they viewed the position voiced by Martynov. It is worth noting first, however, the points of agreement they had with the Mensheviks. The Bolsheviks acknowledged that "under the present social and economic order this democratic revolution in Russia will not weaken but strengthen the domination of the bourgeoisie," that "the democratic reforms in the political system, and the social and economic reforms that have become a necessity for Russia, do not in themselves imply the undermining of capitalism, the undermining of bourgeois rule; on the contrary, they will, for the first time, make it possible for the bourgeoisie to rule as a class." They also agreed with the Mensheviks that "the removal of all the remnants of the old order which hamper the broad, free, and rapid development of capitalism is of absolute *advantage* to the working class." They favored "the democratic revolution which clears the ground for a new class struggle," believing that "to the proletarian the struggle for political liberty and a democratic republic in a bourgeois society is only one of the necessary stages in the struggle for the social revolution which will overthrow the bourgeois system."[6]

They did not, however, agree that leadership of the democratic revolution could be entrusted to the bourgeoisie. Or as Lenin put it: "Shall we be able to make use of the correctness of our Social Democratic doctrine, of our bond with the only thoroughly revolutionary class, the proletariat, to put a proletarian imprint on the revolution, to carry the revolution to a real and decisive victory, not in word but in deed, and to paralyze the instability, half-heartedness, and treachery of the democratic bourgeoisie?" He explained: "The very position the bourgeoisie holds as a class in capitalist society inevitably leads to its inconsistency in a democratic revolution. The very position the proletariat holds as a class compels it to be consistently democratic. The bourgeoisie looks backward in fear of democratic progress which threatens to strengthen the proletariat. The proletariat has nothing to lose but its chains, but with the aid of democratism it has the whole world to win." Lenin warned that the liberals would be attracted to "striking a bargain with tsarism," and that to leave the leadership of the democratic revolution to "the liberal haggling of the landlords and manufacturers" would result "merely in a wretched deal."[7]

The Bolshevik orientation was dramatically different from that of the Mensheviks: "To avoid finding itself with its hands tied in the struggle against the inconsistent bourgeois democracy the proletariat must be class-conscious and strong enough to rouse the peasantry to revolutionary consciousness, guide its assault, and thereby independently pursue the line of consistent proletarian democratism. . . . Only the proletariat can be a consistent fighter for democracy. It can become a victorious fighter for democracy only if the peasant masses join its revolutionary struggle. If the proletariat is not strong enough for this the bourgeoise will be at the lead of the democratic revolution and will impart an inconsistent and self-seeking nature to it. Nothing but a revolutionary-democratic dictatorship of the proletariat and the peasantry can prevent this."[8]

A key aspect of Lenin's innovative conception of the *democratic dictatorship of the proletariat and the peasantry*, of course, was the attention it focused on the Russian peasants, who made up close to 80 percent of the population. This innovation has sometimes been misunderstood. According to George Lichtheim, "the uniqueness of Lenin—and the Bolshevik organization which he founded and held together—lay in the decision to make the agrarian upheaval do the work of the proletarian revolution." This is a gross distortion of Lenin's strategic orientation, which, as we have seen, was rooted in the concept of *working-class hegemony* in the antitsarist struggle. Yet he gave more serious attention than most Russian Marxists to the relationship of the peasantry to the Russian revolution. "Lenin's concept of alliance of the working class and the peasantry," Hamza Alavi has commented, "was a major advance on earlier Marxist propositions; for it was based on a detailed analysis of the transformations that were taking place in the agrarian economy of Russia and the pattern of social forces that was emerging as a result." Even such a severe academic critic of Lenin as Esther Kingston-Mann has acknowledged that "unlike the Mensheviks, Lenin did not use his Western-centered assumptions [Marxism] as a justification for turning his back on the 'would-be' capitalist majority of the population, but attempted instead to bring peasant demands into some sort of constructive relationship to a Marxist economic analysis." She notes that "within the context of his own struggle with a Marxist tradition of condescension toward and contempt for the peasantry, and in the face of hostile criticism from inside and outside the RSDLP, it was evident that Lenin was trying very hard to enlarge the Marxist revolutionary perspective. After 1902 there developed what would become a permanent separation between Lenin and those Marxists who were unsure if Marxist theory permitted them to support revolutionary action by such inappropriate actors as the Russian peasantry." Indeed, the conception of a worker-peasant alliance (counterposed to that of a worker-capitalist alliance) was the red thread running through Lenin's evolving strategic perspective from the early 1900s until his death, and it became a hallmark of Bolshevism. Few Russian Marxists came close to him—Trotsky being the outstanding exception—in grasping the centrality of such an alliance to the coming revolution.[9]

The provisional revolutionary government that the Bolsheviks hoped to see with the overthrow of tsarism, then, was not a bourgeois regime from which the RSDLP would abstain, but rather a radical coalition of workers' and peasants' representatives that would utterly demolish the last vestiges of semifeudal tsarism, establishing a thoroughly democratic republic and initiating sweeping reforms (for instance, equitable redistribution of the land, and institution of the eight-hour day) that would yield meaningful material gains for the masses of Russia's people. Such a "democratic dictatorship" would emerge from the most militant class-struggle orientation and, while neither establishing itself permanently nor overturning capitalism, would create a framework and establish a tradition that would be highly beneficial in the future struggle for a socialist revolution.[10]

Although the thrust of the Bolshevik program seemed sharply counterposed to that of the Mensheviks, there were significant inconsistencies in the Menshevik position in early 1905 that were to contribute to a rapprochement. Thus, in a resolution on armed uprising passed at the 1905 Menshevik conference, it was asserted that "the Social Democratic party will endeavor to bring the rising under its own influence and leadership and use it to serve the interests of the working class." In the resolution on a provisional government already cited, we find the assertion that the Mensheviks' "tactical line of course does not rule out the desirability of a partial, episodic seizure of power and the formation of revolutionary communes in a particular town or area, purely with the object of extending the scope of the rising and disorganizing the [tsarist] government."[11]

On the left fringe of the Menshevik ranks, however, there were voices calling for an orientation similar to that of the Bolsheviks—particularly the voices of Parvus and Trotsky. Parvus was the pen name of Alexander Helphand, a Russian-German left-socialist active in the German Social Democracy but with close ties to the Russian movement. He advanced the following orientation: "A revolutionary overturn in Russia can be accomplished only by the workers. The revolutionary provisional government in Russia will be a government of the workers' democracy. If Social-Democracy heads the revolutionary movement of the Russian proletariat, that government will be Social-Democratic. . . . A Social-Democratic provisional government cannot effect a socialist overturn in Russia, but the very process of liquidating autocracy and establishing a democratic republic will provide a favorable soil for its political work."[12] While Lenin criticized Parvus's failure to relate this orientation to that of a revolutionary alliance with the peasantry, he expressed "warm sympathy" for Parvus's advocacy of "the idea of the revolutionary-democratic dictatorship, the idea that it was the duty of Social-Democrats to take part in the provisional revolutionary government after the overthrow of the autocracy."[13]

Writing in July 1905, Trotsky went as far as Parvus: "A silent national and world conspiracy of the bourgeoisie is putting terrible obstacles in the path of the harsh process of liberation, trying to stop it from going any further than a deal between the property-owning classes and the old order—a deal aimed at holding down the popular masses. Under such conditions, democratic tactics can develop only in the process of struggle against the liberal bourgeoisie." Through the class struggle against the bourgeoisie as well as tsarism, the proletariat would "assume the role of a leading class—if Russia is to be truly re-born as a democratic state." But he went beyond Parvus: "It goes without saying that the proletariat must fulfill its mission, just as the bourgeoisie did in its own time, with the help of the peasantry and petty bourgeoisie. It must lead the countryside, draw it into the movement, make it vitally interested in the success of its plans." Trotsky also went further than Lenin: "But, inevitably, the proletariat remains the leader. This is not the 'dictatorship of the proletariat and the peasantry,' it is the dictatorship of the proletariat supported by the peasantry."[14]

As the Menshevik historian Solomon Schwarz has noted, the radicalization of the Russian workers deepened in the autumn of 1905 and "reshuffled all the cards. *Iskra* closed . . . and was replaced by the Menshevik *Nachalo* . . . , published legally in Petersburg in coalition with Parvus and Trotsky by the former editors of *Iskra* (except for Axelrod and Plekhanov, who were still in Switzerland). Parvus' influence was particularly strong." Theodore Dan later recalled "the 'Trotskyite' themes that began echoing more and more loudly in the utterances and articles of eminent members of the *Iskra* editorial board (first and foremost Martynov and the author of these lines [i.e., Dan himself]) with the manifest approval of a substantial segment of the Mensheviks, especially of the Menshevik workers. The general editorial line of *Nachalo* also began becoming more and more 'Trotskyite.'" A biographer of the Menshevik leader Julius Martov informs us: "The Soviets [mass workers' councils] and the workers' movement were strikingly successful; the liberals and democrats seemed uncertain, unimpressive, or absent; many Mensheviks began to lose faith in the bourgeois revolution. They dismissed the bourgeoisie either as treacherous and counter-revolutionary or as virtually non-existent, and like the Bolsheviks they prepared for a seizure of power and the establishment of a revolutionary provisional government. . . . Martov found himself in a minority on *Nachalo*, . . . which became a propagator of Trotskyism rather than of Menshevism. . . . Thus in the days of freedom Martov had very little influence on his fellow-Mensheviks and his voice was all but unheard. Plekhanov and Axelrod agreed with him but that was small comfort."[15]

Lenin himself, several months later, explained that "the tactics adopted in the period of 'whirlwind' did not further estrange the two wings of the Social-Democratic Party, but brought them closer together. Former disagreements gave way to unity of opinion on the question of armed uprising. Social-Democrats of both factions were active in the Soviets of Workers' Deputies, these peculiar instruments of embryonic revolutionary authority; they drew the soldiers and peasants into these Soviets, they issued revolutionary manifestos jointly with the petty-bourgeois revolutionary parties. Old controversies of the pre-revolutionary period gave way to unanimity on practical questions. . . . In *Severny Golos* [Voice of the North, a legal daily newspaper published jointly by Bolsheviks and Mensheviks in late 1905], the Mensheviks, jointly with the Bolsheviks, called for a general strike and insurrection; and they called upon the workers to continue this struggle until they had captured power. . . . There were arguments only over matters of detail in the appraisal of events: for example, *Nachalo* regarded the Soviets of Workers' Deputies as organs of revolutionary local self-government, while *Novaya Zhizn* [a Bolshevik paper] regarded them as embryonic organs of revolutionary state power that united the proletariat with the revolutionary democrats. *Nachalo* inclined towards the dictatorship of the proletariat. *Novaya Zhizn* advocated the democratic dictatorship of the proletariat and the peasantry. But have not disagreements of this kind been observed at every stage of development of every socialist party in Europe?"[16]

After it became clear that the 1905 revolution had been decisively defeated, the bulk of the Menshevik leadership returned to the earlier conceptions. Martynov, a typical example, bemoaned and dismissed "the fantastic theory of Parvus and Trotsky . . . which enjoyed momentary success among us." In the course of 1906, it was Martov rather than Trotsky who held sway in the Menshevik faction, although Dan notes that it was only by the spring of 1907 "that Menshevism had firmly made up its mind" that the revolutionary moment had decisively passed.[17]

In 1908, Trotsky was denouncing the Menshevik mainstream for "opportunism." His comments are instructive:

It may seem paradoxical to say that the principle psychological feature of opportunism is its *inability to wait*. But that is undoubtedly true. . . . Opportunism, devoured by impatience, looks around for "new" ways and means of putting into effect what history is not yet ready for in practice. Tired of its own inadequacy and unreliability, it goes in search of "allies." It hurls itself avidly upon the dung-heap of liberalism. It implores it, it appeals to it, it invents special formulae for how it could act. . . .

Opportunism does not know how to wait. And that is why great events always catch it unawares. They knock it off its feet, whiz it around like a chip of wood in a whirlpool and sweep it forward, knocking its head now against one bank, now against the other. It tries to resist, but in vain. Then it submits to its fate, pretends to be happy, waves its arms to show that it is swimming, and shouts louder than anyone else. And when the hurricane has passed, it creeps ashore, shakes itself, complains of headache and painful limbs and, in the wretched hangover following its euphoria, spares no harsh words for revolutionary "dreamers."[18]

It was this conservative shift among the Mensheviks—not duplicity on Lenin's part—that generated the renewal of sharp factional struggle, finally leading to the definitive organizational split in the RSDLP. What was primary in Lenin's organizational perspectives was the integrity of the revolutionary program.

2. Revolution Without Bolsheviks?

Earlier we noted that the impulse of sectarianism constitutes a tension within the Bolshevik tradition but that the revolutionary events of 1905 enabled the Bolsheviks to break free from that impulse. This transformation was neither automatic nor easy.

At first the sectarian impulse blocked effective Bolshevik participation in early stages of the revolutionary process—in regard to the immediate economic struggles of the workers, in regard to the mass movement led by Father Georgi Gapon that sparked the 1905 revolution, and in regard to the mass democratic councils of the workers called soviets. Had they persisted in their sectarianism, there would have been a revolution without Bolsheviks. As it was, the Mensheviks were the first to be drawn into these crucial aspects of the revolutionary process. Only the pressure of living class struggle, combined with Lenin's own persistent struggle against sectarianism and organizational conservatism in the Bolsheviks' ranks, compelled the Bolshevik organization to be true to its own revolutionary commitments. Because of this, it was able to grow and to play a heroic role in the events of 1905.

A veteran of the RSDLP from this period has written: "Looking back on the events of 1904–05 and trying to understand their political significance, one is amazed by a paradoxical fact: the Social-Democrats were a considerable force in the country's political life; they were listened to, not only by a great many workers, but also by sizable groups of the intelligentsia and of so-called cultured society; yet the Social-Democratic Party taken as a whole, as the sum total of Social-Democratic organizations, was extremely weak. The weakness of its bonds with the working masses is especially surprising." One of the problems was the Bolshevik/Menshevik split, reflected in this report of Petersburg Bolsheviks regarding the "extremely sorry state" of their committee at the beginning of 1905: "Its ties with the working masses had been utterly disorganized by the Mensheviks. We managed to preserve them, with great effort, only in the City sector (this sector has always held to the Bolshevik viewpoint), on Vasil'ev-Ostrov, and in the Vyborg sector." Although able to maintain contacts among pro-Bolshevik workers in these districts, however, the Bolshevik committee could do little more than circulate the Bolsheviks' views among a not particularly responsive working class: "By that time the Petersburg Committee consisted of a secretary (through him the Committee communicated with the head of the press and with the finances commission [of the Bolshevik organization], a chief writer and editor [responsible for leaflets and for articles sent to *Vperyod*], a chief organizer, an agitator (he was also the student organizer), and four organizers. There was not a single worker among the members of the Committee. The strike at the Putilov plant caught the Committee unprepared. . . . Before January 9, the workers' feelings toward the Committee were extremely hostile."[19]

A Menshevik memoirist later recalled that "during all of 1905—in Kiev, and in Rostov, and in Moscow—I invariably came up against one and the same phenomenon. In the Party organizations were gathered mostly callow youths, hotheaded and resolute but weakly linked to the working masses and uninfluential in the factories. The old Social Democrats among the workers—the real vanguard of advanced workers formed in the period of propagandism [educational circles] and of so-called Economism—these old workers for the most part stood aside. In Kiev, and in Rostov, and in Moscow, and right up to the October [1905] strike, I—and not only I—had to resort to more or less artificial methods to draw the 'oldsters' into active party work. We arranged special meetings and evening parties with them, we reasoned with them, but they went into party work reluctantly and looked upon our organizations and our working methods with distrust."[20]

On the other hand, thousands of workers were flocking in this period into the Assembly of Russian Factory Workers of St. Petersburg, led by Father Georgi Gapon. Gapon was a somewhat muddled pro-Tsar priest who was organizing among Russian workers under the not unsympathetic eye of the tsarist secret police. This organization existed primarily to benefit its members "spiritually and morally as well as materially," to "awaken and strengthen Russian national consciousness in the worker members," and to "form and develop in them responsible views on the obligations and rights of workers." It also sought to encourage "independent activity by the members of the 'Assembly,' conducive to improving the working and living conditions of workers in lawful ways." Among the activities of this organization were the creation of mutual aid funds to assist unemployed workers and the establishment of tearoom—reading rooms that would, according to Solomon Schwarz, "give workers a chance to gather and soberly spend their free time in edifying pursuits. In the early period, . . . every meeting at the first tearoom—reading room 'began and closed with a prayer.' At the official opening of the Assembly on April 11, 1904, after it had received its statute, a religious service was held, 'God Save the Tsar' was sung three times, and the Assembly sent a telegram to the minister of the interior, 'with the respectful request to lay at the feet of His Imperial Majesty the adored Monarch the most submissive feelings of the workers inspired by zealous love for the throne and the fatherland.'"[21]

The Gapon movement was vaguely related to an experiment of the tsarist secret police aiming to build an antirevolutionary workers' movement. This experiment, masterminded by the police official S. V. Zubatov, sought to use apolitical trade unions—set up and financed (secretly) by the autocracy—to draw workers away from the revolutionaries. But these Zubatovite unions soon evolved into militant organizations that were difficult to control and became too threatening for the government to tolerate. They were, eventually, partially repressed and partially absorbed by the rising radical workers' ferment.[22]

A similar fate awaited Gapon's assembly. Schwarz tells us that "the Gapon Assembly was geared to the backward mass, but the need for some kind of cultural intercourse was so great among the more advanced workers that after a while they too began to take notice of the Gapon meetings. Some of them had belonged to the revolutionary 'circles' of the early nineties, had known imprisonment and police surveillance, had eventually withdrawn from revolutionary activities, but retained some intellectual interests and read a great deal." By the end of 1904, Gapon organizations "covered all of Petersburg. The working masses seeking an outlet for their newly awakened social energies were flocking into them, and the Gapon organizations, born as a mongrel police offspring of the labor movement, were turning into far-flung, somewhat diffuse labor organizations reflecting the restive, semirevolutionary mood of the workers."[23]

According to Trotsky, Gapon had "encountered several thousand politically conscious workers who had been through the school of socialism. These men immediately formed an iron ring around him, a ring from which he could not have broken loose even if he had wanted to. But he made no attempt to break loose. Hypnotized by his own success, he let himself be carried by the waves."[24]

By the end of 1904, Gaponite workers were leading a militant strike wave that was sparked at the huge Putilov plant of 140,000 workers. Gapon and his followers called a massive demonstration for January 9, 1905, that would go to the Winter Palace for the purpose of presenting a petition to Tsar Nicholas II. The petition began as follows: "Sire! We, the workers and inhabitants of various ranks of the city of St. Petersburg, our wives and children and our helpless aged parents, have come to you, Sire, in search of justice and protection." Bertram Wolfe has described the demonstration in this way: "Their intention was pacific, even reverential. It was Sunday. Many bore ikons and pictures of the Tsar. . . . As they marched, they sang as only Russian multitudes can sing, and over and over again their song was 'God Save the Tsar.'" The tsar's troops opened fire on the 200,000 unarmed men, women, and children, inflicting at least several hundred casualties and sparking the revolution. After the massacre, Gapon expressed the elemental feelings of millions when he said: "We no longer have a Tsar. A river of blood divides the Tsar from the people. Long live the fight for freedom!"[25]

The Bolsheviks were quite simply not part of this process. As one Bolshevik memoirist later recounted, before January 9 the Petersburg Committee urged its adherents "to penetrate into the factories to the locals of the Gapon society and *oppose* to Gapon's demands the program—minimum of the Party, *exposing* the hopelessness and absurdity of the project of marching to the palace."[26] The leading Bolshevik in Petersburg at this time was S. I. Gusev, a classic example of how rigid and narrow a Bolshevik committeeman could be. We will have cause to note his activities here and also in a later chapter of this study.

The Mensheviks had come into contact with the Gapon movement somewhat earlier than the Bolsheviks had, although their initial reaction was similar. As a Menshevik writer recounted two years afterward, many "strongly insisted that Social Democrats ought to refuse to participate in it in any way. It was shameful and unworthy of Social Democrats, they said, to march to the Winter Palace in a religious procession led by a priest, to beg for compassion and pity for workers, especially as it would end only in shooting and beatings." Yet one experienced woman worker disagreed: "No, better to go to the Gapon organizations, thousands of people go there, people believe in them and put their hope in them. Never mind if they set themselves small goals at present, this cannot last long, and it may depend partly on you to broaden the work over there."[27] At least some of the Mensheviks began to act on these perceptions. Before January 9 they began to exercise enough influence on the Gapon movement to help inject a fairly advanced political content into the petition that was the basis for the mass march.

The Bolshevik committeeman Gusev wrote these words to Lenin: "Exposing and fighting Gapon will be the basis of the agitation we are hurriedly preparing. We have to move all our forces into action, even if we have to squander them all on the [Putilov] strike, for the situation obligates us to save the honor of Social-Democracy." One Bolshevik agitator who, carrying out Gusev's directives, attempted to "expose" Gapon at a meeting of workers was prevented from finishing his remarks by shouts of "Enough, go away, don't interfere," and he was driven out of the meeting hall. By the day of the demonstration the Bolsheviks had decided to participate but were able to pull together a contingent of only fifteen workers.[28]

The orientation of the Petersburg Bolsheviks was significantly different from the orientation of Lenin. Although living in exile, Lenin proved to be far more alive to the dynamics of the struggle. Writing in *Vperyod*, he called the strike begun at the Putilov works "one of the most imposing manifestations of the early working class movement" and "a political event of tremendous importance." He characterized the Gapon movement in this way: "Initiated by the police in the interests of the police, in the interests of supporting the autocracy and demoralizing the political consciousness of the workers, this movement is turning against the autocracy and is becoming an outbreak of the proletarian class struggle. ... We are witnessing one of the great clashes between the developing proletarian class and its enemies, clashes that will leave their mark for many years to come." Noting that "conscious Social-Democratic influence is lacking or is but slightly evident," Lenin asserted that "the primitive character of the socialist views held by some of the leaders of the movement and the tenacity with which some elements of the working class cling to their naive faith in the tsar enhance rather than lessen the significance of the revolutionary instinct now asserting itself among the proletariat. . . . The mobilization of the revolutionary forces of the proletariat in this new and higher form is bringing us gigantic strides nearer to the moment when the proletariat will even more decisively and more consciously join battle with the autocracy."[29]

Contrast this with the account of a Bolshevik historian: "Indeed a vast strike movement was in progress, some unknown tremendous wave was rising, but the Bolshevik Committee [in Petersburg] was living its own segregated life; having once and for all appraised the Gapon movement as Zubatovite, it was not even able to sense that the strike at the Putilov plant was no common strike but a movement linked by the closest ties to all the Gapon locals, to the whole mighty strike movement of the entire Petersburg proletariat."[30]

Before the January 9 march to the Winter Palace, Lenin—in contrast to his comrades in Petersburg—viewed the demonstration positively. After the events of Bloody Sunday he wrote that "the revolutionary education of the proletariat made more progress in one day than it could have made in months and years of drab, humdrum, wretched existence." Referring to the "millions of toiling, exploited people, proletarians and semi-proletarians, suffering every insult and indignity," he wrote that "their feelings and their mood, their level of knowledge and political experience were expressed by Father Georgi Gapon." Noting the existence of "a liberal, reformative movement among certain sections of the young Russian clergy," he remarked that "we cannot, therefore, flatly dismiss the idea that Father Gapon may be a sincere Christian Socialist and that it was Bloody Sunday which converted him to the truly revolutionary path."[31]

Yet even after Bloody Sunday, the Bolshevik organizer Gusev wrote to Lenin that "the workers are also a bit confused (again, under the influence of the Mensheviks' antirevolutionary preachings) and the [proper] attitude to Gapon. Your article . . . depicts the government's role very justly, but you are too lenient with Gapon."[32] In the swirl of revolutionary events, however, Gusev's opinions proved to be irrelevant, and the Bolsheviks in Russia threw themselves into the actual revolutionary struggle.

The sectarian impulse, however, manifested itself in other ways in this period. For example, many Bolsheviks were suspicious of trade unions as competitors of the RSDLP, giving a particularly narrow interpretation to the passage in *What Is to Be Done?* where Lenin asserts that "the *spontaneous* development of the labor movement is trade unionism, . . . and trade unionism means the ideological enslavement of the workers by the bourgeoisie." Wrenched out of context, this statement could be given an extreme interpretation—alien to Lenin's meaning-that (in the words of one Bolshevik in this period) "the trade union struggle . . . makes

bourgeois notions stick to the proletarian's psychology, which obscure his proletarian consciousness or prevent its development." One mid-1905 Bolshevik resolution stated that "in the present period Social-Democracy must not take the
initiative in creating unions." A "compromise" resolution advanced by Gusev
stressed the need "to expose . . . all the illusions about trade unions," to emphasize
"that the most vital, primary task . . . is to prepare immediately for an armed uprising," and "to carry on an energetic ideological struggle against the so-called Mensheviks, who are reverting, on the issue of trade unions, to the narrow, erroneous
viewpoint of the Economists, which demeans the tasks of Social-Democracy and
holds back the thrust of the proletarian movement."[33]

Lenin objected: "We must beware of overstressing the struggle with the Mensheviks over this question. Trade unions are likely to start emerging very soon now.
We must not stand aside from them and above all give no cause to think that one
should stand aside, but try to participate, influence, and so on. . . . It is important
for Russian Social-Democracy to strike the right note about unions from the very
beginning, to create from the first a tradition of Social-Democratic initiative in
this matter, of Social-Democratic participation, Social-Democratic leadership."[34]

Yet even such prominent Bolsheviks as Alexander Bogdanov and Anatoly Lunacharsky were inclined to belittle trade union activity in this period. "A spontaneous
strike over individual economic demands," Lunacharsky asserted, "is a weapon in the
class struggle of a still backward proletariat, and no theories of stages can make us
view such a strike as some sort of perfection." He counterposed to this "a political
mass strike . . . in conjunction with an armed uprising." Bogdanov dismissed the
spontaneous strikes sparked by Bloody Sunday as "anarchic striking" and stressed
"the importance of discipline for saving and concentrating the revolutionary forces."
According to Solomon Schwarz, who was a Bolshevik agitator in this period: "This
wary attitude to the growing strike movement prevailed among the leading Bolsheviks right up to the general strike of October. It was not, however, a hostile attitude.
In the climate of 1905, a hostile attitude was psychologically impossible for a revolutionary party. In many places the Bolsheviks found themselves drawn into strikes
and playing an active part in them despite themselves, as it were—especially where
they made up most of the Party organizations, as, for instance, in central Russia."[35]

A similar trajectory can be traced in regard to the Bolsheviks' attitude toward
the workers' soviets that sprang up in Petersburg and elsewhere.

As Trotsky, the most influential spokesman of the Petersburg soviet, has commented, "this purely class-founded, proletarian organization was the organization
of the revolution as such. The Soviet was the axis of all events, every thread ran towards it, every call to action emanated from it." The RSDLP as such was not able

to play this role. In Petersburg it had, by the autumn of 1905, only a few hundred members and several thousand supporters. Trotsky notes that the RSDLP "was able to speak for the masses by illuminating their immediate experience with the lightning of political thought; but it was not able to create a *living* organizational link with these masses, if only because it had always done the principle part of its work in clandestinity, concealed from the eyes of the masses." There was also the fact that the RSDLP was divided into two competing public factions, and that both of those were in competition with other radical groups, the most prominent being the populist-terrorist Socialist Revolutionary Party. All of this "rendered the creation of *non-party* organization absolutely essential. In order to have authority in the eyes of the masses on the very day it came into being, such an organization had to be based on the broadest representation." It came into being as a body to coordinate the workers' activities during the October general strike, with delegates elected from the various workplaces of the city. But it became more than a strike committee. "With the Soviet we have the first appearance of democratic power in modern Russian history," Trotsky wrote. "The Soviet is the organized power of the mass itself over its separate parts. It constitutes authentic democracy, without a lower and an upper chamber, without a professional bureaucracy, but with the voters' right to recall their deputies at any moment. Through its members—deputies directly elected by the workers—the Soviet exercises direct leadership over all social manifestations of the proletariat as a whole and of its individual groups, organizes its actions and provides them with a slogan and a banner."[36] The soviet took on various governmental functions, forced the tsarist regime to negotiate with it, and mobilized the working class and its allies in the struggle against the autocracy.

The Bolsheviks initially viewed the soviets mistrustfully as a Menshevik maneuver, then decided to participate in them but saw them as "politically amorphous and socialistically immature workers' organizations created by the spontaneous revolutionary movement of the proletariat." Years later, Trotsky recalled that "the Petersburg contingent, led by Bogdanov, of the Bolshevik Central Committee resolutely opposed the creation of an elective non-party workers' organization. The negative attitude of the Bolshevik summit in Petersburg continued until Comrade Lenin's arrival in Russia [in mid-November].... Bogdanov proposed the following plan: Put before the Soviet, in the name of the Bolshevik faction, the proposal to accept the Social-Democratic program and the general leadership of the Party; [and] if the Soviet decided against it, leave the Soviet."[37] When the Bolshevik proposal was rejected, however, the Bolsheviks decided to remain within it.

When Lenin returned to Russia, he articulated a conception of the soviets that, as Solomon Schwarz points out, "came close to Trotsky's variant of the Menshevik viewpoint." Lenin wrote: "It seems to me that Comrade Radin is wrong in raising the question . . . the Soviet of Workers' Deputies or the Party? I think that . . . the decision must *certainly* be: *both* the Soviet of Workers' Deputies and the Party. . . . It seems to me that the Soviet of Workers' Deputies, as an organization representing all occupations, should *strive* to include deputies from all industrial, professional and office workers, domestic servants, farm laborers, etc., from *all* who want and are able to fight in common for a better life for the whole working people, from *all* who have at least an elementary degree of political honesty, from all but the Black Hundreds." (The Black Hundreds were reactionary, anti-Semitic gangs of lower-class thugs organized by the tsarist police.) Lenin therefore found it "inadvisable to demand that the Soviet of Workers' Deputies should accept the Social-Democratic program and join the Russian Social Democratic Labor Party." In sharp contrast to his comrades who believed the soviets should be confined to being simply temporary strike committees, Lenin suggested "that politically the Soviet of Workers' Deputies should be regarded as the embryo of a *provisional revolutionary government.*"[38]

Lenin was unable to win the Bolshevik organization as a whole to this outlook until after the defeat of the 1905 revolution, but his position helped to diminish his comrades' sectarian hostility to the soviets. In the last months of 1905 this enabled the Bolsheviks to play a more effective role in the desperate but heroic armed resistance that took place as the tsarist forces moved to crush the revolution.

3. The Party Broadens

The radical upsurge in the Russian working class and, in the face of mass pressure, the partial "liberalization" of the tsarist regime—involving a dramatic expansion of such democratic rights as freedom of speech and press, legalization of many kinds of organizations, and so on—created a qualitatively new situation for the socialist movement. The Mensheviks were the first to adjust. Eva Broido, a Menshevik organizer in Baku and Petersburg during this period, describes how she helped win over workers who had been following the Bolsheviks:

> Several districts and factory groups came over to us. The ease with which we won them was, however, at least partly due to the fact that the workers involved had little understanding of the factional conflicts and differences. They came over to us simply because they were dissatisfied with the conditions in this particular Bolshevik organization. But, of course, the structure of the Bolshevik party with its elite of professional revolutionaries demanding absolute obedience from the rank and file accorded badly with the spirit of a mass movement, particularly at that time. The fact that the Bolshevik "Baku committee" did not allow democratic elections only weakened its influence. And the exaggerated and quite unnecessary secretiveness in which it shrouded itself was also a mistake. . . . Whenever one of the members of

the Bolshevik "Baku committee", usually well-informed and intelligent men, had to work side by side with one of our members, however ordinary, our man invariably had a considerably greater influence with the workers, simply because we were well known to them and worked in the open.[39]

Lenin quickly perceived the need for a shift. Writing to S. I. Gusev in February 1905, he complained of the Bolsheviks' organizational stagnation: "Be sure to put us in *direct* touch with new forces, with the youth, with newly formed circles.... So far *not one* of the St. Petersburgers (shame on them) has given us a single new connection.... It's a scandal, our undoing, our ruin! Take a lesson from the Mensheviks, for Christ's sake." In a letter to Gusev and Bogdanov, he insisted on "completely pushing into the background the customary, well meant committee hierarchic stupidities."[40] In March he wrote as follows in the pages of *Vperyod*:

We must reckon with the growing movement, which has increased a hundredfold, with the new tempo of the work, with the freer atmosphere and the wider field of activity. The work must be given an entirely different scope.... Young fighters should be recruited more boldly, widely, and rapidly into the ranks of *all and every kind* of our organizations. *Hundreds* of new organizations should be set up for the purpose without delay. Yes, hundreds; this is no hyperbole, and let no one tell me that it is 'too late' now to tackle such a broad organizational job. No, it is never too late to organize. We must use the freedom we are getting by law and the freedom we are taking despite the law to strengthen and multiply the number of Party organizations of all varieties. Whatever the course or the outcome of the revolution may be, however early it may be checked by one or other circumstance, all its real gains will be rendered secure and reliable only insofar as the proletariat is organized.... If we fail to show bold initiative in setting up new organizations, we shall have to give up as groundless all pretensions to the role of vanguard. If we stop helplessly at the achieved boundaries, forms and confines of the committees, groups, meetings and circles, we shall merely prove our own incapacity.[41]

Later in the year, Lenin wrote that it was "absolutely necessary to create ... new legal and semi-legal organizations," noting that "our Party has stagnated while working underground." While by no means under the illusion that it would be possible to eliminate the underground apparatus, he insisted that "the new form of organization, or rather the new form of the basic organizational nucleus of the worker's party, must be definitely much broader than were the old circles. Apart from this, the new nucleus will most likely have to be a less rigid, more 'free,' more 'loose' organization." Far from seeing the elective principle as the "useless and harmful toy" it had been "amidst the gloom of the autocracy" in 1902, he favored "a decisive step towards the full application of the democratic principle in Party organization" and stressed "the general importance of the elective principle in the Party." In "building up a genuinely proletarian Social-Democratic Party on new lines," the clandestine committees of professional revolutionaries would necessarily find their roles changing. Lenin suggested that "our committees must show great tact: previous formal prerogatives inevitably lose their significance at the present time." It was also now necessary to proletarianize the committees in a way that had not been possible before: "At the Third Congress of the Party I suggested that there be about eight workers to every two intellectuals in the Party committees. How obsolete that suggestion seems today! Now we must wish for the new Party organizations to have one Social-Democratic intellectual to several hundred Social-Democratic workers." What is more, it was now becoming important that professional revolutionaries "not hang about uselessly where the movement has already stood up on its feet and can, so to speak, shift for itself." Rather, they should be sent among sectors "where the conditions are most difficult, where the need for experienced and well-informed people is greater, where the sources of light are fewer, and where the heartbeat of political life is weaker."[42]

At the Third Congress, in April 1905, the Bolshevik committeemen had revolted against such ideas and defeated a proposal offered by Lenin and Bogdanov reflecting this new orientation. (At one point during that congress, to both booing and applause, Lenin declared that "the inertness of the committeemen has to be overcome." At another point he exclaimed, "I could hardly keep my seat when it was said here that there are no workers fit to sit on the committees. . . . Obviously there is something the matter with the Party. Workers must be given places on the committees."[43]) But— as with the sectarian impulses we noted earlier regarding various political questions— the pressure of events vindicated Lenin's more open and flexible approach.

By the close of 1905, the Bolsheviks had about 8,400 members (over 60 percent of whom were factory workers and more than 27 percent of whom were office and shop workers). By April 1906 they had 13,000 members, and the Mensheviks had 18,000. By October of that year it was estimated that there were 33,000 Bolsheviks and 43,000 Mensheviks. By 1907, the RSDLP had 150,000 members; over 46,000 were Bolsheviks, and over 38,000 were Mensheviks (the others were in the Jewish Bund and in the Polish and Latvian sections of the party). Furthermore, as Lenin observed in the spring of 1906, "the whole Party organization is now built on a *democratic* basis. This means that *all* the Party members discuss and decide questions concerning the political campaigns of the proletariat, and that all the Party members *determine* the line of tactics of the Party organizations."[44]

Some of the Bolsheviks had been concerned that such developments would mean that "the Party would be dissolved among the masses, it would cease to be the conscious vanguard of the class." Lenin explained the factors he believed would ensure revolutionary continuity: "We Bolsheviks ... have demanded class-consciousness from those joining the Party, we have insisted on the tremendous importance of continuity in the Party's development, we have preached discipline and demanded that *every* Party member be trained in one or other of the Party organizations. We have a firmly established Party program which is officially recognized by all Social-Democrats and the fundamental propositions of which have not given rise to any criticism (criticism of individual points and formulations is quite legitimate and necessary in any live party). We have resolutions on tactics which were consistently and systematically worked out at the Second and Third Congress and in the course of many years' work of the Social-Democratic press. We also have some organizational experience and an actual organization...."[45] Such factors as these enabled the Bolsheviks to absorb the influx of new members in a way that strengthened the organization.

Lenin believed that the RSDLP must broaden itself in yet another way: "It is high time, furthermore, to take steps to established local economic strong points, so to speak, for the workers' Social-Democratic organizations—in the form of restaurants, tea-rooms, beer-halls, libraries, reading-rooms, shooting galleries, etc., etc." Marcel Liebman has observed that "in St. Petersburg and also in the provinces there appeared 'political associations' and 'workers' clubs', in the formation of which the Mensheviks usually took the initiative, but which the Bolsheviks also helped to form. A new phenomenon in Russian political life, they translated into reality the Party's desire to open itself to the masses."[46] Eva Broido's vivid description of the Petersburg workers' clubs of the RSDLP is worth quoting at length:

> The most important centers of party work were our clubs. In them we concentrated all our propaganda activities: our propaganda was distributed from them, and there the workers came to hear lectures on current affairs. There, too, our members in the *Duma* [the limited, quasi-parliament which the autocracy agreed to establish] came to report to us on their work. Virtually all the organizational work was centered on these clubs—general and special party meetings were held there, party publications were distributed from there, there were the "addresses" of the local district and sub-district branches, there all local news was collected, from there speakers were sent to factory meetings. And these were also the places where enlightened workers—men and women—could meet for friendly exchange of ideas and to read books and newspapers. All clubs aimed above all at having good libraries. And eventually they also encouraged art, there were music and song groups and the like.
>
> At first clubs were exclusively political, but soon their character changed. Propaganda meetings gave place to lectures and discussions of a more general nature, the clubs became "colleges" of Marxism. Representatives of all club committees combined to work out systematic courses of lectures, to provide and distribute the nec-

essary books and to supply book catalogues. And already in the winter of 1906–7 the programs included physics, mathematics and technology alongside economics, historical materialism and the history of socialism and the labor movement. . . .

Apart from their educational functions—varied and important as these were—the clubs provided the workers with their first training ground in practical politics. This was their main value for the future and for the historical development of the Russian proletariat. Built from the very start on democratic principles, the clubs taught the workers the techniques of elections—how to elect and be elected, to accept and exercise responsibility, to organize and lead the movement. It was in the clubs and in the trade unions that the elite of the Russian proletariat was trained. . . .

All in all, the clubs can fairly be described as the pioneers of the new proletarian culture. In the past, after a century under the yoke of absolutism, workers had no place to meet in their leisure hours except the tavern. But now new and better ways of life were being created in the clubs, and this explains the devotion that the workers brought to them.[47]

Lenin also stressed other aspects of the broadening process. "We must not forget," he wrote, "that so far we have had to deal too often only with revolutionaries coming from a particular social stratum, whereas now we shall have to deal with typical representatives of the masses." He called for a change "in the methods of propaganda and agitation and a more popular style, ability to present a question, to explain the basic truths of socialism in the simplest, clearest and most convincing manner." While saying that he did not want "in the least [to] belittle the great role played by consciousness in the working-class movement" nor "in any way [to] detract from the tremendous importance of Marxist theory and Marxist principles," Lenin suggested that "the relation between the functions of the intellectuals and of the proletariat (workers) in the Social-Democratic working-class movement can probably be expressed, with a fair degree of accuracy, by the following general formula: the intelligentsia is good at solving problems 'in principle', good at drawing up plans, good at reasoning about the need for action—while the workers act, and transform drab theory into living reality." He added: "We have 'theorized' for so long (sometimes—why not admit it?—to no use) in the unhealthy atmosphere of political exile, that it will really not be amiss if we now 'bend the bow' slightly, just a little, 'the other way' and put practice a little more in the forefront." Lenin himself "bent the stick back" away from one of his formulations of 1902, writing now that "the working class is instinctively, spontaneously Social-Democratic, and more than ten years of work put in by Social-Democracy has done a great deal to transform this spontaneity into consciousness."[48]

Lenin forcefully raised two practical questions in the context of the 1905 revolution—the united front and the armed struggle.

The term "united front" did not exist in this period, but Lenin clearly advanced the concept in February in response to Father Gapon's appeal to "all the socialist parties of Russia to enter immediately into an agreement among themselves and to proceed to the armed uprising against tsarism." Lenin wrote: "We consider that the 'agreement'... is possible, useful, and essential. We welcome the fact that Gapon speaks explicitly of an 'agreement', since only through the preservation of complete independence by each separate party on points of principle and organization can the efforts at a fighting unity of these parties rest on hope. We must be very careful, in making these endeavors, not to spoil things by vainly trying to lump together heterogeneous elements. We shall inevitably have to . . . march separately, but we can . . . strike together more than once and particularly now." He added that "it would be desirable, from our point of view, to have this agreement embrace the *revolutionary* as well as the socialist parties, for there is nothing socialistic in the immediate aim of the struggle, and we must not confound or allow anyone ever to confound the immediate democratic aims with our ultimate aims of socialist revolution." He also stressed that "complete clarity and definiteness in the relations between parties, trends, and shades are absolutely necessary if a temporary agreement among them is to be in any way successful." Lenin elaborated on this idea: "In the interests of the revolution our ideal should by no means be that all parties, all trends and shades of opinion fuse in a revolutionary chaos. On the contrary, the growth and spread of the revolutionary movement, its constantly deeper penetration among the various classes and strata of the people, will inevitably give rise (all to the good) to constantly newer trends and shades. Only full clarity and definiteness in their mutual relations and in their attitude towards the position of the revolutionary proletariat can guarantee maximum success for the revolutionary movement. Only full clarity in mutual relations can guarantee the success of an agreement to achieve a common immediate aim."[49]

At the Third Congress, Lenin noted that "the entire history of the past year proved that we underestimated the significance and the inevitability of the uprising. Attention must be paid to the practical aspect of the uprising." The Bolsheviks went on to pass a resolution stressing "the necessity of an armed uprising" and that the workers' "participation will decide the destiny of the revolution in Russia." This meant that the Bolsheviks would have to devote considerable energy to explaining to the workers "not only the political significance, but the practical organizational aspect of the impending armed uprising," and "to take the most energetic steps towards arming the proletariat." While some Mensheviks were critical of this Bolshevik "fixation" on the armed struggle, Lenin—noting the rising violence against the revolution on the part of the infamous Black Hundreds—made this observation: "In fact, civil war is being forced on the population by the government itself. It is a fact that 'tramps, rowdies, and hawkers' are being taken into government service." Furthermore, he went on, "the masses, who stand farthest from all 'conspiracies', began to be drawn into an insurrection because of the misdeeds of the Black Hundreds."[50]

Trotsky has explained: "To look on passively would have meant, for the Tsarist government, to let itself be scrapped. That much was clear. What, then, could it do? It had to fight the political self-determination of the people with its last forces, with every means at its disposal. The ignorant army, the Black Hundreds, the secret police, the corrupt press, all had to be sent into action. To set people against one another, to cover the streets in blood, to loot, rape, burn, create panic, lie, cheat and slander, that is what the old criminal power had to do." Speaking of the orientation of the Petersburg Soviet, Trotsky asserted: "To prepare for an inevitable insurrection . . . meant to us, first and foremost, enlightening the people, explaining to them that open conflict was inevitable, that all that had been given to them [as concessions from the autocracy] would be taken away again, that only might can defend right, that a powerful organization of the working masses was necessary, that the enemy had to be met head on, that the struggle had to be continued to the end, that there was no other way."[51]

As late as mid-October, Lenin was urgently complaining to his comrades: "It horrifies me . . . to find that there has been talk about bombs for *over six months*, yet not one has been made! . . . Form fighting squads *at once* everywhere, among the students, and *especially among the workers*, etc., etc. Let groups be at once organized of three, ten, thirty, etc., persons. Let them arm themselves at once as best they can, be it with a revolver, a knife, a rag soaked in kerosene for starting fires, etc. . . . You must proceed to propaganda on a wide scale. Let five or ten people make the round of *hundreds* of workers' and students' study circles in a week, penetrate wherever they can, and everywhere propose a clear, brief, direct, and simple plan: organize combat groups immediately, arm yourselves as best as you can, and work with all your might; we will help you in every way we can, but *do not wait for our help*; act for yourselves."[52]

In his classic history *1905*, Trotsky describes how militarily organized armed detachments from the revolutionary organizations not only helped to combat or even prevent the pogroms of the Black Hundreds, but also were essential in winning over some sections of the army to the revolution: "Only when the soldiers become convinced that the people have come out into the streets for a life-and-death struggle—not to demonstrate against the government but to overthrow it—does it become psychologically possible for them to 'cross over to the side of the people.'"

Unfortunately, not enough of the Tsar's military forces were won over to bring about a revolutionary victory. But the armed groups were the key to galvanizing popular resistance in the final phase of the struggle, in December 1905. "The whole city [of Moscow] with its streets, houses, walls, and gates entered into a conspiracy against the government troops. The million-strong population formed a living wall between the guerillas and the government troops. . . . The people surrounded the armed revolutionaries with an atmosphere of active sympathy, foiling the government's plans wherever they could."[53]

As Zinoviev later wrote, "the culminating point of this movement was the December rising at Presnya in Moscow. The leading organizational role in it belonged to Bolsheviks and their committee. . . . The Moscow armed rising, which had an enormous historical significance, was smashed and drowned in the workers' blood." Krupskaya tells us: "Vladimir Ilyich felt the Moscow defeat very keenly. It was clear that the workers had been poorly armed, and that the organization was weak. Even the link between St. Petersburg and Moscow was poor." Lenin himself wrote: "The heroic proletariat of Moscow has shown that an active struggle is possible, and has drawn into this struggle a large body of people from strata of the urban population hitherto considered politically indifferent, if not reactionary. . . . The new form of action was confronted with gigantic problems which, of course, could not be solved all at once. But these problems are now confronting the whole people in a clear and definite way; the movement has been raised to a higher level, consolidated and tempered. No power on earth can wrest these gains from the revolution. . . . We are now confronted with the new task of studying and utilizing the experience of the latest forms of struggle, the task of training and organizing forces in the most important centers of the movement."[54] The Moscow uprising of 1905 was to become an important part of Bolshevism's legacy, a vital component of its growth as a revolutionary organization.

Despite the existence of a number of unresolved questions for the Bolsheviks, we can see that their organization was changed in important ways by the 1905 events. The most important factor was the creative and largely self-generated mass action of the workers and their allies, which—as historian Laura Engelstein aptly noted—"frightened the tsarist regime into making the first constitutional concessions in its history," but which also "pressured the socialist parties into altering their own expectations and strategies." And yet, the interaction of workers and revolutionaries involved a profound mutual influence. There was certainly no question about either RSDLP faction being in command of the proletarian upsurge. "The masses were learning how to think under party tutelage," the editors of *Iskra* pointed out, "but they would not listen to the party's instructions on how to act." The role of a revolutionary vanguard, however, is in large measure to teach the masses of people, especially working people, how to think about things from a revolutionary socialist standpoint. "At the least," according to Engelstein, "they had been exposed to a set of ideas that, however meaningless or threatening they had seemed at the time, would later offer them a framework for interpreting the political developments of the fall [of 1905]."[55] When this happened, the revolutionaries were able for the first time to provide practical and organizational leadership in a revolutionary situation. Despite the defeat of 1905, the revolutionaries no less than the working class received a political education—a qualitative broadening of their experience and understanding—that would have an effect on their future activity.

At the same time, this process would have to be extended through a difficult period—the years of reaction form 1907 to 1912—before Bolshevism could emerge as a mature revolutionary force.

7. The Meaning of Democratic Centralism

Few terms have been so endowed with almost magical connotations, and have been so grotesquely distorted by commentators from almost all points on the political spectrum, as the term that is sometimes said to be the essence of Leninism—democratic centralism.

According to the liberal anti-Communist scholar Alfred Meyer, for the Leninist model of organization "decision-making . . . presents organizational problems. . . . The formula Lenin found for the resolution of the problems has become famous. It is the 'principle of democratic centralism.'" Suggesting that "the synthesis of such opposites might seem almost impossible," Meyer assures us that "the whole setup functioned pretty well, while the party was commanded by a strong leader who ruled it with an iron grip." He writes: "Lenin liked to speak of the party as a genuinely collectivist organization, consciously, and joyfully submitting to the leadership imposed on it by the senior members."[1]

In his classic *The Communist Party, A Manual on Organization* (1935), Stalinist ideologist J. Peters describes the party in this way: "The Communist Party is organized in such a way as to guarantee, first, complete inner unity of outlook, and, second, combination of the strictest discipline with the widest initiative and independent activity of the Party membership. Both of these conditions are guaranteed because the Party is organized on the basis of democratic centralism. . . . On the basis of democratic centralism, all lower Party organizations are subordinated to the higher bodies: District organizations are subordinated to the Central Committee; Section organizations are subordinated to the District committee; Party Units (shop, street and town) are subordinated to the Section Committees." Sociologist Philip Selznick, offering an unfriendly elaboration of this definition, writes that democratic centralism "refers to the pattern of a hierarchy of party organizations and committees, each of which is elected by the next lower body, but once elected the higher bodies exercise executive authority over the lower ones. Typically, it is the latter aspect which is stressed, elections becoming ratifications of choices made by the permanent leadership."[2]

Not surprisingly, many critical-minded activists have reacted to such conceptions by deciding that they want nothing to do with "democratic centralism." Yet these conceptions have little to do with the Bolshevik organization that was developing into a force capable of providing leadership for the Russian Revolution. Recent scholarship has done much to undermine this mythology, even compelling Leonard Schapiro to add this demystifying footnote to the revised edition of his anti-Leninist history *The Communist Party of the Soviet Union*: "It will be recalled that, in the Russian context, the phrase was of menshevik origin. Historically, the phrase originated in the German Social Democratic Movement, and was first used in 1865 by J. B. Schweitzer, one of the principal followers of Lassalle."[3]

Considerable light will be shed on the meaning of this term if we examine the manner in which it was defined by those who began to utilize it within the RSDLP.

1. Democratic Centralism in the RSDLP

The term "democratic centralism" was first put forward and adopted at the Mensheviks' All-Russian Conference on November 20, 1905. The Menshevik resolution "On the Organization of the Party" included these statements:

> The RSDLP must be organized according to the principle of democratic centralism.
>
> All party members take part in the election of party institutions.
>
> All party institutions are elected for a [specified] period, are subject to recall and obligated to account for their actions both periodically and at any time upon demand of the organization which elected them.
>
> Decisions of the guiding collectives are binding on the members of those organizations of which the collective is the organ. Actions affecting the organization as a whole (i.e., congresses, reorganizations) must be decided upon by all of the members of the organization. Decisions of lower-level organizations are not to be implemented if they contradict decisions of higher organizations.[4]

The term surfaced in the Bolshevik Conference of December 12–17, 1905, in the resolution "On Party Reorganization":

> Recognizing as indisputable the principle of democratic centralism, the Conference considers the broad implementation of the elective principle necessary; and, while granting elected centers full powers in matters of ideological and practical leadership, they are at the same time subject to recall, their actions are given broad publicity, and they are to be strictly accountable for these activities.[5]

As has already been noted, the Bolshevik/Menshevik convergence seemed to be taking place on a deeper level than simply organizational terminology. In the wake of the 1905 revolution, Menshevik leader Pavel Axelrod asserted that "on the whole, the Menshevik tactics have hardly differed from the Bolshevik. I am not even sure that they differed from them at all." Trotsky put it more eloquently: "The differences of opinion between our factions are so insignificant, so uncertain, so minute, that they seem like chance wrinkles on the great brow of the revolution." Nor did Lenin disagree: "The tactics adopted in the period of 'whirlwind' did not further estrange the two wings of the Social Democratic Party, but brought them closer together. . . . The upsurge of the revolutionary tide pushed aside disagreements, compelling Social Democrats to adopt militant tactics."[6]

At the RSDLP Unity Congress of Bolsheviks and Mensheviks on April 25, 1906, therefore, it did not seem surprising that such "Leninist" organizational rules as these were adopted without controversy:

1. A member of the party is one who accepts the party program, supports the party financially, and belongs to some party organization.

2. All party organizations are built on the principles of democratic centralism.

3. All party organizations are autonomous with respect to their internal activities. Every approved party organization has the right to issue party literature in its own name. . . .

7. The Central Committee and the editorial board of the Central Organ are elected at the [party] congress. [It should be noted here that the Bolsheviks had pushed unsuccessfully to make the editorial board of the central party publication subordinate to the Central Committee.] The Central Committee represents the party in relations with other parties; it organizes various party institutions and guides their activities; it organizes and conducts undertakings of significance for the party as a whole; it allocates party personnel and funds, and has charge of the central party treasury; it settles conflicts between and within various party institutions and it generally coordinates all the activity of the party. . . .

8. The congress is the supreme organ of the party. Regular congresses are summoned annually by the Central Committee. An extraordinary congress must be called within two months upon the demand of not less than one-half of the party membership. . . . All approved party organizations are represented at the congress. . . . Elections to a congress are conducted on democratic principles. . . .[7]

With relatively minor variations, these remained the fundamental organizational principles of Bolshevism up to and beyond the Bolshevik Revolution.

Interestingly, the report of the commission that drafted these statutes was given by a Menshevik, Zagorsky-Krokhmal, who informed the delegates at the Unity

Congress that "the disagreements which once divided us on this question (of membership) have disappeared, and we accepted the formula for membership unanimously." Thus, the old dispute that first divided Lenin and Martov at the 1903 congress was finally resolved unanimously in Lenin's favor. Zagorsky-Krokhmal continued: "We must say the same for the second paragraph. The principle of democratic centralism is now acknowledged by all. As for the details of applying this principle, the commission did not think it necessary to work them out, since it found that it would be better for people to work it out on the spot."[8]

In fact, the application of the principle of democratic centralism by the Bolsheviks was to vary significantly, depending on the specific circumstances they faced.

Almost immediately after the adoption of these rules in 1906, Lenin offered this clarification:

> In a revolutionary epoch like the present, all theoretical errors and tactical deviations of the Party are most ruthlessly criticized by experience itself, which enlightens and educates the working class with unprecedented rapidity. At such a time, the duty of every Social Democrat is to strive to ensure that the ideological struggle within the Party on questions of theory and tactics is conducted as openly, widely and freely as possible, but that on no account does it disturb or hamper the unity of revolutionary action of the Social-Democratic proletariat. . . .
>
> We are profoundly convinced that the workers' Social-Democratic organizations must be united, but in these united organizations there must be wide and free discussion of Party questions, free comradely criticism and assessment of events in Party life.
>
> . . . We were all agreed on the principles of democratic centralism, guarantees for the rights of all minorities and for all loyal opposition, on the autonomy of every Party organization, on recognizing that all Party functionaries must be elected, accountable to the Party and subject to recall.[9]

Not long afterwards, Lenin published some additional thoughts on the meaning of democratic centralism. The central committee of the RSDLP had proposed "limits within which the decisions of Party congresses may be criticized." It assured "full freedom to express personal opinions and to advocate individual views" in the party press and at party meetings, but not at public meetings. Lenin complained that this was too restrictive. He wrote: "The principle of democratic centralism and autonomy for local Party organizations implies universal and full *freedom to criticize* so long as this does not disturb the unity *of a definite action*; it rules out *all* criticism which disrupts or makes difficult the *unity* of an action decided on by the Party." Lenin argued that "the Central Commitee has defined freedom to criticize inaccurately and too narrowly, and unity of action inaccurately and too broadly." He insisted that "criticism within the limits of the *principles* of the Party Program must be quite free . . . , not only at Party meetings, but also at public meetings."[10]

It is worth remembering that on the eve of the Unity Congress, Lenin, who was not confident that the Mensheviks would prove to be consistent partisans of the revolutionary program, confided to A. V. Lunacharsky: "If we have a majority in the Central Commitee we will demand strictest discipline. We will insist that the Mensheviks submit to party unity." And if the Bolsheviks were a minority? "We won't permit the idea of unity to tie a noose around our necks," Lenin replied, "and we shall under no circumstances permit the Mensheviks to lead us by the rope."[11] As it turned out, the central committee emerging from the Unity Congress had a Menshevik majority. This may help explain why Lenin favored giving significantly greater weight to the democratic component of democratic centralism at this time.

Yet Lenin's formulations are hardly a cynical maneuver. First of all, it is clear that at all times his touchstone is the revolutionary program. In his comments to Lunacharsky it is that program that Lenin is talking about safeguarding from the Menshevik tendency to rely upon the liberal bourgeoisie. In his most elastic formulation of democratic centralism, the limits he sets are "the principles of the Party Program." Indeed, it was the apparent leftward shift, in words and practice, among the Mensheviks in 1905 that had been the basis for the healing of the factional split in the RSDLP. It should also be remembered that the 1905 upsurge had loosened the repressive grip of tsarism and had brought a massive working-class influx into the RSDLP, creating conditions that Lenin felt necessitated greater openness in the party. (Despite the defeat by the end of 1905, many of the liberal reforms granted in that year remained intact throughout 1906.) Lenin believed that a dramatic increase in party democracy would help to "enlighten and educate the working-class," particularly the new cadres, the only limit being that this should not "hamper the unity of revolutionary action of the Social-Democratic proletariat."

Lenin put it succinctly: "Freedom of discussion, unity of action—this is what we must strive to achieve." This principle was consistent, he felt, with the need to "wage a most determined, open and ruthless ideological struggle" against certain Menshevik positions through the "widest possible discussion of the decisions of the [Party] congress . . . in the press, at meetings, in circles and at group meetings." Yet in regard to RSDLP participation in the 1906 Duma elections, decided upon over Bolshevik objections, Lenin asserted: "The Congress has decided: we will *all* take part in elections, wherever they take place. During the elections there must be no criticism of participation in elections. *Action* by the proletariat must be united." Another example would be an insurrection: "Here unity of action in the midst of the struggle is absolutely essential. In the heat of battle, when the proletarian army is straining every nerve, *no* criticism *whatever* can be permitted in its ranks. But before the call for action is issued, there should be the broadest and freest discussion and appraisal of the resolution, of its arguments and its various propositions."[12]

An essential component of democratic centralism for Lenin was that the organization would be under the control of its membership: "The Russian Social-Democratic Labor Party is organized on democratic lines. This means that all the affairs of the Party are conducted, either directly, or though representatives, by all the members of the Party, all of whom without exception have equal rights; moreover, all officials, all leading bodies, and all institutions of the Party are subject to election, are responsible to their constituents, and are subject to recall." He also stressed that when the party was dealing with significant disputes, *all* the members of the organization should have an opportunity to "expess their opinion on the point at issue before the whole organization."[13]

Related to this was the need "to work tirelessly to make the local organizations the principal organizational units of the Party in fact, and not merely in name," a point Lenin stressed more than once. "The Rules of our Party very definitely establish the democratic organization of the Party," he wrote. "The whole organization is built from below upwards, on an elective basis. The Party Rules declare that the local organizations are independent (autonomous) in their local activities." While "the Central Committee coordinates and directs all the work of the Party," Lenin insisted that "it has no right to interfere" with local activities that are consistent with the basic decisions of the party congress.[14]

Marcel Liebman, in his useful and influential study *Leninism Under Lenin*, sees 1905–1906 as the golden age of Leninism, when "the river that during the dry season had been only mud was ... once more flowing broad and full of life." Liebman contrasts this to the period of 1907–1912, in which it all once again turned to mud. "One could go on indefinitely," he writes mournfully, "accumulating examples of the invective indulged in by Lenin in his pursuit of what he himself called an 'implacable campaign.'" Liebman describes the period this way:

> It was in a party such as this, turned in upon itself for a long time by force of circumstances, cut off from its working-class hinterland, often reduced to the sluggish conditions of exile, enfeebled, split and scattered, that sectarian tendencies developed which were destined to set their imprint upon the subsequent history of Communism. Among these must be mentioned first and foremost a deliberate striving to transform the Party into a monolithic bloc. This resulted from an attitude of strictness on two fronts—against Menshevism, and against those tendencies within Lenin's organization whose strategy, or merely tactics, conflicted with Lenin's own ideas.[15]

Liebman's error here is one that we must avoid. He has found Lenin quotes that he likes from 1905–1906, and has elevated them to fashion a "good Leninism," counterposed to a "bad Leninism" based on nastier quotes from other periods. (Another variant would be to see the 1905–1906 quotes as "authentic Leninism" and pretend that the nastier quotes do not exist.)[16] Despite Liebman's superficial references to the historical context, however, this is an ahistorical approach that badly mutilates the Leninist organizational perspective. What Lenin did in the muddy years of 1907–1912 is central to the whole meaning of Leninism. Only by comprehending this will we be able to grasp the revolutionary organizational principles that are vitally relevant for our own time.

In chapter 8 we will examine the evolution of Leninism and the Bolshevik organization in the years over which Liebman renders his somber judgment. But it may be worth skipping ahead to get some sense of the flexibility as well as the continuity in the Bolshevik application of democratic centralism.

2. Democratic Centralism in the Bolshevik Party

In 1912 the Bolsheviks split totally from the Mensheviks and other elements of the RSDLP by establishing their own party—the Russian Social Democratic Labor party (Bolsheviks). They did this by calling a congress of the RSDLP and—on their own—organizing it in such a manner that their opponents in the party refused to recognize the congress's legitimacy or participate in it. The Bolsheviks then declared the bulk of these opponents to be outside of the party. All of this constituted, obviously, a departure from the *normal* functioning of the democratic centralist principle. The Bolsheviks justified their actions by referring to programmatic resolutions adopted in 1908 and 1910 by congresses of the RSDLP as a whole, that, however, the Mensheviks and others had been systematically violating. (These resolutions condemned RSDLP members who were working to liquidate the underground party apparatus and establish a purely legal workers' movement. Lenin believed that this was no mere tactical difference, but involved a "disagreement concerning the very existence of the party."[17] He labeled as "liquidators" those who were condemned by the 1908 and 1910 resolutions, as well as those willing to shield such elements within the RSDLP. Details on this controversy will be found in the next chapter.)

After a year and a half of existence as an independent party, the Bolsheviks were pressured by the prestigious world federation of socialist parties, the Second International, in conjunction with various Russian socialists, to reunify with the other elements of what had once been the RSDLP. In response, Lenin acknowledged that "the workers do need unity," but he added that "unity cannot be 'promised'—that would be vain boasting, self-deception; unity cannot be 'created' out of 'agreements' between intellectualist groups. To think so is a profoundly sad, naive, and ignorant delusion." He went on to refer to the principle of democratic centralism: "Unity without organization is impossible. Organization is impossible unless the minority bows to the majority."[18]

By 1914, Lenin went on to emphasize, the majority of class-conscious workers in Russia (measured by adding up members of workers' groups supporting either the Bolshevik or Menshevik newspaper) were identifying with the Bolshevik RSDLP. He insisted, "It is for this unity, for submission to this four-fifths majority of the workers, that we must go on fighting. *There is not, nor can there be*, any other way to unity. The workers are not infants to believe that this four-fifths majority will allow the minority of one-fifth, or intellectuals who have no workers' backing at all, to *flout the will* of the majority of the workers!" Lenin also stressed the importance of party program: "The decisions of 1903, 1908 and 1910 were adopted *prior to any splits* between the Marxists and the liquidators. These decisions are the banner of all Marxists. If any agreement between the Russian Social-Democratic Labor group and the 'Social-Democratic group' is at all possible, then it is of course possible only on the basis of the unqualified recognition of these decisions, which were adopted before the split."[19]

It should be noted that of these two points—majority support of the workers and the revolutionary Marxist program—Lenin viewed the latter as more decisive. "If, for example, the Socialist-Revolutionary Party (left Narodniks), whose program and tactics differ from ours, were to win over the majority of workers in Russia," he said, "that would not in the least induce us to depart from our line." Lenin added that the Bolsheviks themselves would not abandon their views on the need for an underground apparatus under tsarism (a position with profound programmatic implications) even if the liquidators had won a majority of workers to such a position. He commented that "certain Social Democratic groups and some liquidators assert that there are no irreconcilable disagreements on principle between us. We are obliged to point out their inconsistency to these groups and individuals, when they refuse to submit to the majority."[20] Obviously, he believed that it would be necessary and possible to win a working-class majority to a correct revolutionary program, which precluded any compromise on basic political principles; the Bolsheviks were in the process of accomplishing precisely that in 1914. But more is implied in Lenin's argument. The logic of his comment is that the existence of principled programmatic differences necessarily makes the principle of democratic centralism inoperable. The logic of Lenin's actions indicate that in such a situation, two separate organizations should exist, rather than two irreconcilably opposed political currents attempting to coexist (in perpetual factional conflict, compromising themselves, and making a mockery of the principle of democratic centralism) within a single party.

Lenin made an additional comment on the connection between political program and majority support that is of interest: "We have been convinced of the correctness of our line on tactics and organization primarily by our long years of acquaintance with the workers' Social-Democratic movement in Russia, and by our participation in it, as well as by our theoretical Marxist convictions. But we are of the opinion that the practical experience of the *mass* working-class movement is no less important than theory, and that this experience alone can serve as a serious *test* of our principles. 'Theory, my friend, is grey, but the tree of life is eternally green' (Faust). Therefore, the fact that, after two-and-a-half years of struggle against liquidationism and its allies, four-fifths of the class-conscious workers have expressed themselves in favor of Pravdism [*Pravda* was the Bolshevik paper of that period], strengthens our convictions that our line is correct and makes this conviction unshakeable."[21] This statement conveys, with almost telegraphic brevity, the dynamic tension which exists in Lenin's view of the interplay between the revolutionary program and the movement and struggle of the working class. There are, inevitably, ambiguities here that can be resolved only with reference to specific situations. Similarly, democratic centralism is a living reality only in its necessarily varied application in specific contexts.

At this time Lenin articulated requirements for party membership and democratic centralism designed to preserve the Bolshevik party and to sharply delineate it from the liquidators and those inclined to compromise with the liquidators. Not surprisingly, then, these seem considerably more restrictive than his formulations of 1906. In the intervening eight years, of course, much had changed. The political divergence between Bolsheviks and Mensheviks had deepened and widened dramatically; through years of discussion and debate, a number of major issues had been clarified within the workers' movement; substantial numbers of working-class activists had been won to Bolshevism; and the Mensheviks had conclusively demonstrated their unwillingness to abide by majority decisions with which they disagreed. Now a cohesive mass organization, adhering to a revolutionary program, existed in the form of a distinct Bolshevik party, and Lenin was determined to prevent its dissolution into a heterogeneous tangle of squabbling factions.

Thus a number of positions were "deemed deserving of condemnation and .. not [to] be tolerated in the ranks of illegal RSDLP." This included deprecating the role and importance of the underground, failing to devote all efforts to promoting the development of the illegal press and illegal leaflets, supporting the creation of a purely legal workers' party in tsarist Russia, opposing revolutionary mass strikes and demonstrations, denigrating the slogans of a democratic republic and confiscation of landed estates, entering into unauthorized alliances with non-Social Democratic parties, advancing positions on the question of oppressed nationalities at variance with the 1903 congress decisions of the RSDLP, and the advancing of positions in the trade unions and other broad workers' organizations at variance with positions of the RSDLP.[22]

Lenin also insisted that "the principle of federation, or of equality for all 'trends' shall be unreservedly rejected, and the only principle to be recognized shall be that of loyal submission of the minority to the majority." He added that "the minority shall have the right to discuss before the whole Party, disagreements on program, tactics and organization in a discussion journal especially published for the purpose, but shall not have the right to publish, in a rival newspaper, pronouncements disruptive of the actions and decisions of the majority."[23]

Absent from all of this is the almost unlimited openness and freewheeling tone that seems to characterize Lenin's discussion of democratic centralism in 1906. At the same time, there is an essential continuity between the principle he advocated for the unified party of 1906, in which Bolshevik and Menshevik factions were to coexist, and for the uncompromisingly Bolshevik party established in 1912. And, although the term "democratic centralism" was apparently absent from Lenin's vocabulary before 1906, the same principle runs through his thinking on organization from the 1890s onward.

At this point we can fruitfully summarize Lenin's organizational perspective:

1. The workers' party must, first of all, be based on a revolutionary Marxist program and must exist to apply that program to reality in a way that will advance the struggle for socialism.

2. The members of that party must be activists who agree with the basic program, who are committed to collectively developing and implementing the program, and who collectively control the organization as a whole.

3. To the extent that it is possible (given tsarist repression), the party should function openly and democratically, with the elective principle operating from top to bottom.

4. The highest decision-making body of the party is the party congress, made up of delegates democratically elected by each party unit. The congress should meet at least every two years and should be preceded by a full discussion throughout the party of all questions that party members deem important.

5. Between congresses, a central committee (elected by and answerable to the congress) should ensure the cohesion and coordinate the work of the party on the basis of the party program and the decisions of the congress. In addition, the central committee has a responsibility to keep all local units of the

party informed of all party experiences and activities, while the local committees have a responsibility to keep the central committee informed of their individual experiences and activities. Under conditions of severe political
repression and in the midst of major struggles, the authority of the central
party leadership may assume much greater weight than at other times; yet
that leadership is always bound by the revolutionary Marxist program of the
party, by the decisions of the party congress, and by a responsibility (and accountability) to the membership as a whole.

6. It is assumed that within the general framework of the revolutionary program
there will be shades of difference on various programmatic, tactical, and practical questions. These should be openly discussed and debated, particularly
(but not necessarily exclusively) before party congresses. Within limits—
which vary depending on time, place, and circumstance—such differences can
be aired publicly. All members should be encouraged to participate in this discussion process and should have an opportunity to make their views known to
the party as a whole. It is assumed that at times, groupings will form around
one or another viewpoint or even around a full-fledged platform that certain
members believe the party should adopt. This—as opposed to groupings based
on personal likes and dislikes, and ill-defined moods and biases—provides a
basis for ongoing political clarity and programmatic development, which are
essential to the health and growth of the party.

7. All questions should be decided on the basis of democratic vote (majority
rule), after which the minority is expected to function loyally in the party,
and particularly, to in no way undermine the specific actions decided on.

8. Local units of the party must operate within the framework of the party program and of the decisions of the party as a whole, but within that framework
they must operate under the autonomous and democratic control of the local
membership.

This list describes an organization functioning according to the principle of
democratic centralism. It also describes the way in which Lenin thought an organization should function—in 1900, in 1906, as well as in 1914 and afterward.
The manner in which democratic centralism could or should be applied would vary
depending on the specific circumstances. But the Bolshevik party functioned according to the democratic centralist principle from 1912 until well after the Bolshevik Revolution of 1917.

3. Lenin's "Iron Grip"

We have noted Alfred Meyer's view that democratic centralism operated successfully only "while the party was commanded by a strong leader who ruled it with an iron grip." As we can see, such a notion is inconsistent with the democratic centralist principle. But what about the actual practice? Lenin was the central leader of the Bolsheviks from 1903 until his illness and death in 1923–1924. Why was this the case? Does it indicate an element of truth in Meyer's assertion? Perhaps democratic centralism applied equally to all, but Lenin was "more equal than others." It is worth asking if in some sense he operated above the democratic centralist principle, or somehow ensured that it was applied in a manner that guaranteed his rule over the organization. Scholars such as Robert V. Daniels have asserted that "despite Lenin's verbal obeisance to democratic principles, his centralist conceptions when consistently applied rendered the democratic ideal an empty illusion." The problem was that "Lenin was a man who could bow to no contrary will."[24]

Actually, Lenin continually faced disagreements and opposition from his comrades. We have seen that he by no means called the shots in the Bolshevik faction of 1905, but was compelled—despite his leadership role—to operate as part of a dynamic collectie in which his opinions do not always prevail. Far from establishing the line of the Bolsheviks in the pages of *Vperyod*, he sometimes found his articles rejected by the editors of this Bolshevik organ. (The same was true with later Bolshevik periodicals, such as *Proletary*, *Social Democrat*, and *Pravda*—much to Lenin's chagrin.) Far from ruling the Bolshevik organization with an iron grip, he often found himself in a minority. This was true not only in 1905, but also initially in an internal struggle among the Bolsheviks in 1907–1909; it was the case immediately *after* Lenin won this particular struggle, and in the period leading up to the founding of the Bolshevik party in 1912. It was also the case in the spring of 1917 when Lenin concluded that Russia needed a socialist (not simply a bourgeois-democratic) revolution, and in the autumn of 1917 regarding certain tactics of the Bolshevik insurrection. In the period immediately following the Bolshevik Revolution, Lenin's views aroused fierce opposition among Bolsheviks first with regard to the manner in which Russia should withdraw from the First World War and then with regard to a number of other issues. His authority was always considerable, but his positions were questioned by his comrades time and again throughout his political career, and it was not uncommon for Lenin to find himself outvoted.

More often than not, after initial defeats Lenin eventually was able to win majorities to his positions. In some cases—when he believed that questions of fundamental principle or life-and-death tactics were involved—he was prepared to openly break with his comrades rather than submit to majority decisions. Aside from such exceptional cases, he was fully prepared to test what he felt to be a mistaken majority line while patiently working to win his comrades to his own views within a democratic centralist framework.

At the same time, it is undeniable that Lenin's stature among the Bolsheviks was unequaled. Several qualities contributed to his status.

Certain of these qualities were noted by the late Menshevik historian and archivist B. I. Nicolaevsky, who had an opportunity to observe Lenin closely over an extended period. One of Nicolaevsky's colleagues has recounted: "Boris Ivanovich also admired Lenin as a good *khorziain* or party manager. With the exception of V. N. Krokhmal, Boris Ivanovich felt that among the Mensheviks there was no good *Iskra* type of organizer. The Mensheviks were more in the tradition of *Rabocheye Dyelo*, that is, they knew how to start a movement but not how to weld together the kind of organization that gave the party strength in underground conditions." A related aspect of Lenin's character helped play a role in the cohesion of the Bolshevik organization: "Boris Ivanovich often wistfully reminisced about how skillfully Lenin generated loyalties by showing, in little things, that he cared for and remembered the services of party activists. For instance, Krupskaya would write a letter to an exile to which Lenin would add a short note, thus forging a lasting bond between the exile and the party leader who remembered him. Nobody ever received such notes from Martov or Dan." In addition to Lenin's skills as a party manager and his comradely warmth, there was what Lunacharsky has called "his astonishing vitality. Life bubbles and sparkles within him."[25]

While such qualities naturally made Lenin attractive to revolutionary activists, they were hardly enough to give him the influence and authority he attained in the revolutionary movement. Historian M. N. Pokrovsky, who was also a Bolshevik activist, mentions "his immense erudition in theory," but adds that this was "not so much the quality of Vladimir Ilyich himself as an indispensable quality of every political leader." What was essential was the way Lenin utilized his mastery of Marxist theory, which Lunacharsky referred to in describing his "extremely firm, extremely forceful will capable of concentrating itself on the most immediate task but which yet never strayed beyond the radius traced out by his powerful intellect and which assigned every individual problem its place as a link in a huge, world-wide political chain." Trotsky also referred to this: "It was Lenin's peculiar gift, which he possessed to the highest degree, that with his intense revolutionary gaze, he could see and point out to others what was most important, most necessary, and most essential. Those comrades who, like myself, were given the chance to observe Lenin's activity and the working of his mind at close quarters could not help but enthusiastically admire ... the perspicacity, the acuteness of his thought which rejected all that was external, accidental, superficial, and reached to the heart of the matter and grasped the essential methods of action.

The working class learns to value only those leaders who, having opened new paths, go forward with determination even if the proletariat's own prejudices temporarily hinder their progress."[26]

Related to this is the comment of Pokrovsky that "the essential quality of Ilyich, when you look back at the past, is his colossal political courage.... The characteristic trait of Ilyich was that he was not afraid to assume the responsibility for political decisions of any size. In this respect he did not retreat in the face of any risk; he took upon himself the responsibility for steps on which hung the fate not only of his own person or of his party, but that of the whole country and to some extent of the world revolution. Because this was such an unusual phenomenon, Ilyich always launched all his actions with a very small group, in as much as there were very few people to be found who were bold enough to follow him."[27] By this Pokrovsky was referring especially to Lenin's capacity, when he believed he was right, to forthrightly take a stand and follow it through to the end, in the face of the great external pressures exerted by comrades and opponents and awesome (but transient) external events.

Pokrovsky added: "But, of course, that alone was not enough. Here it is necessary to speak of those qualities which supplemented the first.... First of all, his colossal insight, which towards the end filled me with certain superstitious feelings. I often quarreled with him about practical matters, got into a mess each time, and after this operation was repeated about seven times, I stopped arguing and submitted to Ilyich, even when logic was telling me you must not act that way—but, I thought, he understands better. He sees three *arshin* deep in the ground and I cannot.... He reached depths that none of us ever had occasion to reach."[28]

Such qualities as these helped to ensure Lenin's unique position of leadership within the Bolshevik organization. Yet rather than attempting to secure his own "iron grip" over the organization, Lenin sought to establish ever more securely the principle of democratic centralism, grounded in the revolutionary Marxist program. He seemed convinced that only this could ensure the health and growth of an effective revolutionary organization that would be best able to utilize his own remarkable abilities and those of his comrades. Democratic centralism meant majority rule, freedom of discussion, unity in action.

8. Preparing for Revolution

The revolutionary veteran Eva Broido has described the situation created by the 1905 revolution and its aftermath in the following manner: "The masses had woken up to political life. . . . And in all these activities of the workers the leadership was firmly in the hands of the Social-Democracy. Later, from about the middle of 1907, the pendulum began to swing back. The fighting spirit of the workers subsided, while disillusionment and apathy increased. Tsarism tried to regain the positions it had lost to the workers during their years of relative ascendancy. . . . There followed an economic crisis with its usual psychological concomitants; the disillusionment and political apathy among the workers, such as usually follows in the wake of a failed revolution, were intensified. On the Bolshevik side some very dubious adventures were undertaken—this was the period of bank, mail, and spirit-shop robberies or 'appropriations', which were meant to provide funds for a revival of party activities. Some of the Mensheviks, on the other hand, reacted in exactly the opposite manner—they lost all interest in underground party work and, intent on holding on to the few legal conquests of recent years, worked only within the narrow legal limits."[1]

This aptly characterizes the problems confronting Lenin and his comrades in the period following 1905: demoralization of the working class, the intensification of tsarist reaction, the disintegration of the RSDLP in Russia, an ultraleftist drift among the Bolsheviks, opportunist deterioration among the Mensheviks. It was in confronting and ultimately overcoming these problems that the Bolshevik organization was tempered so that it became the revolutionary force capable of meeting the demands of 1917. This was not commonly understood by Lenin's contemporaries, nor has it been comprehended by many historians. Lenin's clash with leading members of his own faction over tactics and philosophy, resulting in an organizational split among the Bolsheviks themselves, is often portrayed as a classic example of the Bolshevik leader's presumed authoritarianism and intolerance running rampant. His supposed utilization of philosophy as a weapon against his dissident comrades is especially seen either as a manifestation of irrational factionalism or as a case of intellectual narrowness and of a totalitarian inclination to establish party controls over all realms of thought. Similarly, the decisive decision of the Leninist Bolsheviks to split the RSDLP in order to establish a purely Bolshevik party is seen as a culmination of Lenin's many years of antidemocratic and sectarian intrigues. The present chapter will be devoted to these factional battles of the 1907–1912 period, and it will frankly challenge the standard anti-Leninist interpretation.

First we will trace the deepening tactical differences among the Bolsheviks that ultimately resulted in a split. Then we will focus on the philosophical dispute that was related to this split. We will describe the distinctive orientation of Alexander Bogdanov and contrast it with that of Lenin, and suggest how these counterposed philosophies relate to practical politics. Finally, we will examine the five-year dispute of Lenin and his cothinkers with the Mensheviks that led to the Bolshevik organization's establishing itself as a distinct party. What will be argued here is that, in each case, the general thrust of Lenin's position made sense, being consistent with the principled revolutionary politics of democratic centralism and of Marxism to which he was committed. More than this, the developments of 1907–1912 contributed significantly to the capacity of the Bolsheviks to grow into a party deeply rooted in the most revolutionary sections of the working class and with majority influence among the masses of Russian workers. This last point will be demonstrated in the three subsequent chapters of this study.

1. Overcoming Ultraleftism

The activities of the Bolshevik organization in 1905–1907 were overseen by the troika of Lenin, Alexander Bogdanov, and Leonid Krasin. Lenin was the foremost political leader, the primary analyst of social and political events, the theorist creatively focusing on strategy, tactics, and organization. With the assistance of N. K. Krupskaya, he was involved in the overall direction of Bolshevik activities—but as an émigré functioning abroad. Bogdanov coordinated the Bolshevik's practical work inside Russia itself, and he also directed the work of the Bolshevik deputies elected to the Second Duma, a quasi-parliament set up by the tsarist regime in 1906. Krasin, an engineer by training, had been won to Bolshevism by Bogdanov. Before his conversion to Bolshevism he had been the only member of the RSDLP central committee inside Russia who had not been arrested, and when he threw his support to the Bolshevik Third Congress of 1905, he gave it a certain legitimacy it would not have had otherwise. As part of the troika, Krasin assumed responsibility for procuring funds (through a variety of legal, quasi-legal, and illegal methods) to support Bolshevik activities, was in charge of coordinating the Bolsheviks' armed fighting groups, and was centrally involved in the technical work of producing and distributing Bolshevik newspapers.[2]

In the aftermath of the 1905 revolution, the Bolshevik organization became divided over a growing number of political questions; an outright split occurred in 1909. The foremost protagonists were Lenin and Bogdanov.

Years later, the prominent Bolshevik Nikolai Bukharin noted that Bogdanov had "played an enormous role in the development of our party and in the development of social thought in Russia."[3] He was indeed an extremely interesting figure. In addition to his outstanding practical work as a revolutionary, he was a medical doctor with a keen and wide-ranging interest in the natural sciences, wrote an influential treatise on Marxist economics, produced significant works in sociology and, especially, philosophy—and also wrote science fiction. Through his prestige and hard work, he helped win to Bolshevism an impressive group of revolutionary intellectuals, such as Anatoly V. Lunacharsky, Mikhail N. Pokrovsky, Vladimir A. Bazarov, Maxim Gorky, and others.

Although George Plekhanov was considered Russia's foremost Marxist philosopher, his blending of Hegelianism and philosophical materialism was not accepted by many of these newly won intellectuals. Many came to Marxism by way of positivist currents that were prevalent among the Russian intelligentsia. The intellectual historian James D. White has made this observation: "Typical of early Russian Marxism was its tendency to eclecticism. Above all, Marxism seen in terms of previous positivist thought was held to be fatalistic and deterministic, and in this was seen its great virtue as a truly scientific doctrine. . . . Since Marxism was regarded as 'economic materialism', a deterministic and even fatalistic doctrine·, it became clear that it was incapable of producing any cogent system of epistemology [philosophical theory of knowledge]. The solution had to be found somewhere outside Marxism." Bogdanov and many others drew on the positivist-empiricist philosophies of the Viennese physicist Ernst Mach and the Swiss experimental psychologist Richard Avenarius, developing an original synthesis in which, as White notes, they "spoke of positivism and Marxism as [being] virtually synonymous."[4] Although Lenin's own theoretical education had been influenced by Plekhanov's interpretation of Marxism, his organizational and programmatic perspectives were embraced by Bogdanov and others like him, and an uneasy philosophical truce was maintained— until the fissure opened up around practical-political questions. (In the next section of this chapter we will say more about these philosophical differences.)

Gorky has described Bogdanov as "an extremely attractive person, gentle, and very fond of Lenin, but rather proud." In 1907 Bogdanov himself characterized Lenin as "exclusively a man of struggle and revolution," and "indispensable to the struggle," but added that "he is a man of iron, and men of iron are not flexible. They also have a strong measure of inborn conservatism." Already this "inborn conservatism" was beginning to manifest itself in the realms of philosophy and political tactics. Within two years, however, the differences had deepened to the point where Bogdanov was denouncing his former comrade as being basically authoritarian, as betraying Bolshevik principles and adopting a Menshevik orientation, and finally (though privately) as being on a trajectory that would lead to bourgeois-liberal or even bourgeois-monarchist politics. The split exacted a great toll on all concerned. "For about three years prior to this we had been working with Bogdanov and the Bogdanovites hand in hand, and not just working, but fighting side by side. Fighting for a common cause draws people together more than anything." This was the comment of Krupskaya, who added: "The conflict within the [Bolshevik] group was a nerve-wracking business. I remember Ilyich once coming home after having words with the [ultraleftists]. He looked awful, and even his tongue seemed to have turned grey."[5]

The break between Bogdanov and Lenin was not simply a personal rupture, but had a profound significance for Bolshevism and the Leninist conception of the party. It also transformed the composition of the Bolshevik leadership and shifted the political axis of the Bolshevik organization, not totally but in significant ways. Bolshevism could not have become the decisive revolutionary force that it came to be without this wrenching struggle. Just as the contributions of Bogdanov were important for the survival and growth of Bolshevism in the period of 1903–1906, so did the later struggle against him prove to be essential for its survival and growth in the subsequent period.

Since Bogdanov's view of the 1905 revolution and its aftermath was commonly held among the Bolsheviks, it may be useful to examine the way he described it in 1907.

"The excitement of battle quickly spread throughout the masses," wrote Bogdanov of the revolutionary upsurge. "Souls opened selflessly to welcome the future as the present dissolved in a rosy mist and the past receded somewhere into the distance and disappeared." Yet the past was not so easily overcome: "The revolution had developed fitfully and had dragged on over a frustratingly long period. The working class was the first to attack, and the swift offensive resulted in significant early victories. Lacking the support of the peasant masses at the critical moment, however, it subsequently suffered a resounding defeat at the hands of the united reactionary forces."[6]

Analyzing class forces in the aftermath of the defeat, Bogdanov asserted that "the proletariat was gathering strength for new battles and waiting for the peasant rearguard." He added that "the peasant masses were in a thoroughly revolutionary frame of mind, and as they slowly gained political experience the flames of countless burning manor houses illuminated their path to higher forms of struggle." By themselves the peasant uprisings could not dislodge tsarism, but neither could tsarism quell the ferment in the countryside: "Besides bloodily repressing the peasantry, the old regime also attempted to bribe part of it by selling plots of land, but the whole scheme was managed so idiotically and on such a petty scale that nothing came of it." Meanwhile, "the bourgeoisie, exhausted by the storms of revolution and intimidated by the independence and energy of the first offensives of the proletariat, drifted further and further to the right."[7]

The analysis up to this point was shared by all Bolsheviks. But on the question of what to do next, differences began to emerge. Bogdanov observed that "the landowners and bourgeoisie entered into negotiations with the government, haggling to settle their internal differences so as to be able to crush the revolution once and for all. Disguised in the form of a parliamentary comedy these attempts repeatedly ran aground against the uncompromising attitude of the reactionary feudal landlords. Puppet parliaments were convened and brutally dissolved one after the other." These "puppet parliaments" were called Dumas. The First Duma had been promised during the tumultuous events of 1905, and the revolutionary parties—not inclined to compromise with tsarism—had declared a boycott of the March 1906 Duma elections. As a consequence, the new bourgeois-liberal Constitutional Democrat party (known as the Kadets) became the dominant force in the First Duma. The Kadets soon came into conflict with the tsar over the issue of land reform, and the Duma was dissolved. When the Second Duma was constituted later in the year, the reunified RSDLP decided to participate in the elections, although there was dissatisfaction among the Bolsheviks over this policy. In 1907, the Second Duma was dissolved and replaced by the Third Duma, based on a more restricted franchise that guaranteed that the majority of its deputies would be rightwing, pro-tsarist elements. Sharp differences arose among the Bolsheviks over whether to participate in the Duma elections. A majority favored a boycott. At the same time, as Zinoviev later commented, the "party's work in the trade unions had been insufficiently successful" because "the upper hand was gained by people who said: Why go into trade unions? Our concern is the party. We will go underground and work there and as far as the trade unions are concerned the Mensheviks can sit tight."[8]

Bogdanov seemed to attach greater significance to insurrectionary activities "led by bands of partisans or other groups," which—he asserted—"multiplied day by day." He believed that "we were clearly on our way toward new and decisive battles," that "it was obviously impossible to maintain a balance between reaction and terror. A new upsurge was inevitable and near at hand."[9] This viewpoint coincided with the impulses of the Bolshevik majority at that time.

In the latter part of 1905 and into the first months of 1906, Lenin had also given great stress to insurrectionary activity, believing that the 1905 upsurge had not been decisively defeated and—as Bogdanov put it—that a new upsurge was near at hand. Lecturing a Menshevik worker at the Unity Congress of 1906 (when Bolshevik/Menshevik differences were beginning to reemerge), he admonished: "Your friends want to sit in Parliament, while we are convinced that the working class has got to prepare for battle."[10] In the autumn of 1905, he had urgently written the following to his comrades:

> Squads must *at once* begin military trainning by launching operations immediately, at once. Some may at once undertake to kill a spy or blow up a police station, others to raid a bank to confiscate funds for the insurrection, others again may drill or prepare plans of localities, etc. But the essential thing is to begin at once to learn from actual practice: have no fear of these trial attacks. They may, of course, degenerate into extremes, but that is an evil of the morrow, whereas the evil today is our inertness, our doctrinaire spirit, our learned immobility, and our senile fear of initiative. Let every group learn, if it is only by beating up policemen: a score or so victims will be more than compensated for by the fact that this will train hundreds of experienced fighters, who tomorrow will be leading hundreds of thousands.[11]

That the Bolsheviks should think in such terms is hardly surprising, given the context. The regime they were up against was prepared to shoot down hundreds of unarmed men, women, and children of the working class engaged in peaceful protest, as Bloody Sunday had shown. It was similarly inclined to organize the goon squad/death squad networks of the Black Hundreds, to unleash vicious and lethal pogroms against the Jews and other scapegoats, and to engage in massacres among the rebellious peasantry. (A directive from the tsar's minister of home affairs stated: "Rioters to be exterminated immediately by force of arms, their dwellings to be burned down in the event of resistance. Arbitrary self-rule must be eradicated once and for all-now. Arrests would not serve any purpose at present and anyway it is impossible to try hundreds and thousands of persons. It is essential that the troops should fully understand the above instructions.")[12] Only through the most relentless armed struggle could such a murderous tyranny be vanquished, and the opportunity seemed to exist in 1905. The working-class poet Evgeny Tarasov expressed a common sentiment of radicalized workers, particularly the younger militants swept up in the 1905 upheaval, when he wrote: "Only what is taken by force/Will live, will be holy,/Will be taken forever."[13]

For the following year and a half, Lenin continued to support the organization and activity of the armed groups. One of the most controversial aspects of their activity were the "expropriations"—armed robberies to finance Bolshevik activities. The Mensheviks in particular were horrified by this policy and created a scandal to discredit the Bolsheviks. But even among the Bolsheviks themselves there was opposition. Cecilia Bobravskaya, a veteran Bolshevik underground worker, later wrote: "In the summer of 1906 our armed workers' units, which had played such a militant role in the October–December days in 1905, although formally connected with our Party organization, began gradually to drift away from it and finally broke up into disorganized groups of *boyeviki* [fighters], independently becoming 'expropriators,' and bringing the poison of decay into our ranks." Another veteran Bolshevik, Mikhail Olminsky, recalled that "not a few of the fine youth perished on the gibbet; others degenerated; still others were disappointed in the revolution. At the same time people at large began to confound revolutionists with ordinary bandits." Bobrovskaya added: "In the autumn of 1906 the Ivanovo Committee issued a leaflet in which it disclaimed all connection with the *boyeviki* or their 'expropriation' activities which had degenerated into mere robbery and even murder. In order to give a political color to their misdeeds the *boyeviki* offered part of their spoils to our organization, but we refused to touch their money under any circumstances."[14]

For a time Lenin did not share this attitude. As Trotsky later noted, "The Bolsheviks, in direct contact with the fighting detachments, had extremely convincing observations of their own, which Lenin, again an emigrant, did not have. Without corrections from below, the leader of the greatest genius is bound to make crude errors." Yet as early as the autumn of 1906, comments Geoffrey Swain, Lenin "was becoming worried by the independence of the 'fighting groups' from party control, especially since Krasin had his own secretariat for military affairs, although Lenin's wife, Krupskaya, acted as secretary in all political matters. All too easily, Krasin's units seemed to get involved in 'adventures' or go to 'extremes'." Nonetheless, Krasin "spent much time and money during 1906 in gun-running and buying explosives so that the 'fighting groups' were well armed." By late 1907, as Trotsky later wrote, "Lenin changed front and came out more resolutely than ever against the tactic of expropriations, which for a time became the heritage of the 'Left' Wing among the Bolsheviks."[15]

This coincided with Lenin's conclusion, after the tsar's dissolution of the Second Duma (and the absence of a mass response), that the revolutionary wave of 1905 had receded for the foreseeable future. He had always, as we have seen, had misgivings about the impulse among many of his comrades to abstain from what were perceived as "unrevolutionary" activities of the masses of the workers. Now he dramatically broke with them over the question of participation in the Duma. The July 1907 Fourth Congress of the RSDLP provided the occasion for this confrontation, around the issue of what to do regarding the Third Duma. The Mensheviks favored participation, a Bolshevik majority favored Bogdanov's position of boycott. The Menshevik resolution was defeated by the Bolshevik majority at the congress, but then Lenin crossed over to vote with the Mensheviks in order to defeat Bogdanov's resolution. "Then," notes Swain, "Lenin's own proposal that the Party should take part in the Duma in a revolutionary way was passed with Menshevik support. The divisions had now come into the open."[16]

M. N. Pokrovsky later recalled the reaction of many Bolsheviks: "Thus, the man who had sounded the call for armed revolt began to urge us to read the newspaper *Russia* (*Rossia*), which printed stenographic reports on the sessions of the State Duma. What a hail of ridicule this called forth on Lenin—this time not from the bourgeoisie but from our midst! Who did not jeer at him? Who did not bait him? The man had lost his fire, nothing of the revolutionary was left in him. The faction had to be recalled, the Duma faction liquidated; an armed revolt had to be called immediately."[17] Not the least of his comrades' shock was that Lenin had openly broken ranks with his own faction. The only justification for doing so (aside from the view that Lenin was abandoning the revolutionary standpoint) was that this was necessary to defend the survival of the revolutionary Marxist movement. And this was precisely his motivation.

Lenin's tactical orientation was related to his vision of the kind of revolutionary party that was now required, which he explained as having "outgrown the narrow framework of the 'circles' of 1902–05," in which "close-knit, exclusive" committees of "professional revolutionaries" had constituted the RSDLP. "Undoubtedly, the present leaders of the present workers movement in Russia will have to break with many of the circle traditions . . . so as to concentrate on the tasks of Social-Democracy in the present period. Only the broadening of the Party by enlisting proletarian elements can, in conjunction with open mass activity, eradicate all the residue of the circle spirit." He added that "the transition to a democratically organized workers' party, proclaimed by the Bolsheviks in . . . November 1905, . . . was virtually an irrevocable break with the old circle ways that had outlived their day." Zinoviev later noted: "Comrade Lenin's main idea was that we had to remain with the working class and be a mass party and not to coop ourselves up exclusively in the underground and turn into a narrow circle. If the workers are in the trade unions then we must be there too; if we can send just one man into the Tsar's Duma then we shall: let him tell the workers the truth and we can publish his speeches as leaflets. If something can be done for the workers in the workers' clubs then we shall be there. We have to use every legal opportunity, so as not to divorce ourselves from the masses...."[18]

Bogdanov and like-minded thinkers, on the other hand, saw the three principal tasks of the party as being cultivation of the illegal organization of the party, extension of socialist information and propaganda, and theoretical and practical military preparations for the oncoming revolution. As Geoffrey Swain observes, also, Bogdanov and Krasin "diverted party funds into revolutionary partisan operations and vigorously opposed Bolshevik participation in the new parliament." By the summer of 1908, the Bogdanovites were preparing to found a school for party activists at Maxim Gorky's summer mansion at Capri; they hoped this would provide a center around which non-Leninist Bolsheviks could organize themselves and thereby achieve the "revitalization" of Bolshevism.[19]

N. K. Krupskaya later wrote the following: "A Bolshevik, they declared, should be hard and unyielding. Lenin considered this view fallacious. It would mean giving up all practical work, standing aside from the masses instead of organizing them on real-life issues. Prior to the Revolution of 1905 the Bolsheviks showed themselves capable of making good use of every legal possibility, of forging ahead and rallying the masses behind them under the most adverse conditions. Step by step, beginning with the campaign for tea service and ventilation, they had led the masses up to the national armed insurrection. The ability to adjust oneself to the most adverse conditions and at the same time to stand out and maintain one's high-principled positions—such were the traditions of Leninism."[20]

Bogdanov and his cothinkers called themselves Forwardists, after the Bolshevik journal *Vperyod* (Forward) of 1904–1905. They believed it was they who were defending "true Bolshevism" (centralized committees of professional revolutionaries, a refusal to compromise with the tsarist autocracy by participating in its "puppet parliament," and an unswerving commitment to armed struggle and a revolutionary uprising) against what they hoped would be the temporary vacillations of Lenin. Bogdanov later explained that Lenin and others "have come to the conclusion that we must radically change the previous Bolshevik evaluation of the present historical moment and hold a course not toward a new revolutionary wave, but toward a long period of peaceful, constitutional development. This brings them close to the right wing of our party, the Menshevik comrades. . . . Bolshevism continues to exist as before. . . . Comrades, a glorious cause—political, cultural, social—stands before us. It would be shameful for us if leaders who have outlived their times, overcome by adversity, should prevent us from fulfilling it. . . . We will proceed on our way according to the old slogan—with our leaders, if they wish; without them if they do not; against them, if they oppose us."[21]

Lenin, however, insisted that the new period required a shift: "During the (1905) revolution we learned to 'speak French,' i.e., to introduce into the movement the greatest number of rousing slogans, to raise the energy of the direct struggle of the masses and extend its scope. Now, in this time of stagnation, reaction and disintegration, we must learn to 'speak German', i.e., to work slowly (there is nothing else for it, until things revive), systematically, steadily, advancing step by step, winning inch by inch. Whoever finds this work tedious, whoever does not understand the need for preserving and developing the revolutionary principles of Social-Democratic tactics *in this phase too, on this bend* of the road, is taking the name of Marxist in vain."[22]

It is worth pausing for a moment over the question of who represented the traditions of, and who represented a divergence from, "true Bolshevism." If one counts Bolshevism's beginnings simply from the 1903 split in the RSDLP, one can argue that Bogdanov was being true to the major positions and dominant impulses of what was seen as Bolshevism. But the Bolshevism of Lenin, as we have tried to indicate throughout this study, involved more than that. One must examine the underlying orientation of Lenin that evolved in the 1890s—a commitment to relating the revolutionary program to the actual, ongoing experiences and struggles and consciousness of working people (real working people, not revolutionary-romantic idealizations) and a determination to create an internally democratic mass workers' party based on the revolutionary Marxist program—in order to grasp what Krupskaya calls the traditions of Leninism. We have seen how, in the course of 1905, tensions developed on a number of questions between Lenin and many of his comrades who had a less flexible, more sectarian "storm-the-barricades" approach to the revolutionary struggle. This is documented, interestingly, in Solomon Schwarz's *The Russian Revolution of 1905*. Schwarz had been a Bolshevik until 1906, then switched over to Menshevism for the rest of his life. He argues that Lenin's more rounded approach to building the revolutionary workers' movement was never really assimilated into the actual practice of the Bolshevik organization.[23] *This is true for the period in which Schwarz himself was a Bolshevik*. But it was precisely this fact that in 1907 set the stage for the fierce struggle over what "true Bolshevism" really meant.

Lenin believed that the ultraleftists constituted only "a caricature of Bolshevism." They asserted that "Russia . . . is moving towards a new revolutionary upswing." Lenin responded: "Quite right! She is only *moving towards* an upswing, i.e., there is no upswing yet that is what this means, both in logic and grammar! It appears, however, that this still non-existing upswing is 'characterized by a sharp conflict', etc. The result is utter nonsense." The ultraleftists, he concluded, "are incapable of characterizing the present. They 'characterize' the future, which we are 'moving towards', in order to cover up failure to understand the present."[24]

Taken separately, the differing positions of Bogdanov and Lenin could be termed merely tactical differences. Taken together, they eventually constituted a sharp strategic, practical-programmatic divergence, which also found expression in the realm of theory and philosophy.

The divergence within the Bolsheviks' leading troika (Lenin–Bogdanov–Krasin) affected the entire Bolshevik organization, necessitating the creation by mid-1907 of a more broadly representative "Bolshevik center" to coordinate the faction's activities. Bogdanov had considerable authority, and a majority or near-majority of Bolshevik groups in Russia were first inclined to support him. Soon the balance began to shift. Among those rallying to Lenin's orientation were activists inside Russia who were to become some of Bolshevism's foremost leaders, such as Gregory Zinoviev, Lev Kamenev, Alexei Rykov, and Mikhail Tomsky. While their opponents and unsympathetic historians have been inclined to dismiss them as Lenin's yes-men, they proved to be talented, capable, and independent-minded revolutionary leaders who were fully prepared to disagree with Lenin on a variety of issues. But they happened to disagree with Bogdanov's basic orientation even more. At the beginning of 1909, they concurred with Lenin on the need to expel Bogdanov and Krasin from the Bolshevik center (though not from the faction). It should be remembered that these two were channeling Bolshevik funds into maintaining the armed groups, into preparing their own school at Capri, and into other activities not supported by the Bolshevik organization as a whole.[25]

Bogdanov demanded a general conference of the Bolshevik faction, convinced that he would be able to win a majority, overturn the decisions and authority of the Bolshevik center, and save Bolshevism from Lenin's "semi-Menshevik" orientation. Instead, Lenin and a majority of the Bolshevik center decided to conclude the eighteen-month struggle inside the Bolshevik faction by engineering a conference of the extended editorial board of the Bolshevik newspaper *Proletary*. This conference "stated in its resolutions that tendencies were beginning to appear within the Bolshevik section which run counter to Bolshevism with its specific tactical principles," and which disassociated the Bolshevik faction from the ultraleft positions of Bogdanov and those sharing his views. When Bogdanov declared that he would refuse to accept the decisions of this rather irregular conference, he was expelled from the Bolshevik faction. When he again demanded a more authoritative conference of the Bolshevik faction, Lenin and the remaining Bolshevik leaders refused to comply. Lenin stated, "The Bolsheviks have to lead the Party. To do so they must know their course, they must stop hesitating, they must stop wasting time on persuading waverers, and fighting dissidents in their own ranks."[26] He elaborated as follows:

In our Party Bolshevism is represented by the Bolshevik *section*. [Here "section" means what we would call a *faction*.] But a section is not a party. A party can contain a whole gamut of opinions and shades of opinion, the extremes of which may be sharply contradictory. . . . That is not the case with a section. A section in a party is a group of *like-minded persons* formed for the purpose primarily of influencing the party in a definite direction, for the purpose of securing acceptance for their principles in the party in the purest possible form. For this, real *unanimity of opinion* is necessary. The different standards we set for *party* unity and *sectional* unity must be grasped by everyone who wants to know how the question of the internal discord in the Bolshevik section really stands.[27]

Some historians (for example, Geoffrey Swain) have asserted that at the *Proletary* meeting Bogdanov and his followers were "presumptuously expelled from the party by Lenin," but as we can see, this is false. As Lenin explained to Maxim Gorky, the separation of the two Bolshevik currents *within* the RSDLP framework would "show the workers clearly, directly and definitely two ways out. The Social-Democratic workers will make their choice easily and swiftly, for the tactics of preserving (in storage cans) the revolutionary *words* of 1905–06 instead of applying the revolutionary *method* to a new, different situation, to a changed epoch, which demands different methods and different forms of organization—these tactics are dead. The proletariat is moving towards revolution and will come to it, but *not in the way* it did prior to 1905." Lenin emphasized that Bogdanov and his followers were distinct from Lenin's faction but not outside the party: "The divergence resulting from this is, undoubtedly, deep enough to make a split—at least abroad—inevitable. But it does not come anywhere near the split between the Bolsheviks and Mensheviks, if one is to speak of the depth of the split in the Party, in Social Democracy, among Marxists."[28]

Regardless of the insights one might gain from this, one should not fail to recognize that Lenin's mode of operation within the Bolshevik faction at this point-utilizing an expanded conference of the *Proletary* editorial board rather than a broader and more representative conference of the faction as a whole in order to defeat Bogdanov—appears to contradict the principles of democratic centralism. This is precisely the kind of "muddy" problem that Marcel Liebman referred to when criticizing Lenin's "implacable campaign" against opponents in the RSDLP. A hostile historian of Leninism, Bertram D. Wolfe (who, however, had benefited from two decades of Leninist and quasi-Leninist experience before losing the faith), has grappled with this question in a more skillful manner than Liebman, and what he says merits attention:

The question arises: why did Lenin choose to expel such subjectively loyal revolutionists, in place of taking his chances on persuading them, or persuading his faction against them, while permitting them to remain within it? The answer to this we find in Lenin's temperament, in the 'orthodoxy-heresy' atmosphere of Russian political thought, in the bitterness of the years of reaction, *in Lenin's conception of the nature of a faction, and, above all, in his fear that they might capture the group machinery or get in the way of its proper functioning.* They were the more dangerous to him because the type of instinctively rebellious workers to whom Bolshevism appealed was easily influenced by this one-sided, romantic extension of a major aspect of that in Lenin which appealed to them most. [Emphases added.][29]

The point should be made that the separation from the ultraleft was not simply the result of an organizational maneuver, but was the conclusion of a thoroughgoing ideological dispute in which counterposed perspectives were openly laid out. Lenin explained: "We did everything possible, we left nothing untried, to persuade dissenting comrades: we were at it for over eighteen months. But as a wing, i.e., a union of like-minded people in the Party, we cannot work without unanimity on fundamental issues."[30] It must be realized also that this was an extraordinarily difficult period. Truly extraordinary measures were required to preserve an organization capable of advancing the revolutionary program to which Lenin was committed.

We saw in the 1905–1906 period how flexible was Lenin's conception of democratic centralism. In the 1907–1909 period, as we have seen, Lenin was prepared to vote with the Mensheviks against the majority of his own faction, to refuse to bring together a general conference of his own faction for democratically resolving internal problems in the faction, and to subordinate democratic centralist norms to the defense of the revolutionary program. His actions, although extreme, clearly illustrate his priorities and indicate how seriously he felt the Bolsheviks were threatened by Bogdanov's orientation: He was not inclined to risk the Bolsheviks' veering away from the revolutionary program, toward becoming an ultraleft sect, for the sake of organizational abstractions. The subsequent history of the Forwardists suggests that Lenin's fears were not groundless.

Although they were graced with an array of talented intellectuals, a significant treasury, and full faction rights in the RSDLP, the Forwardists did not survive for long as a distinctive political force. One problem was that, as one contemporary Bolshevik document noted, they became "cut off from the workers' movement, occupied with the dead work of practical military preparations." In a perceptive essay, Kendall Bailes has suggested another weakness of Bogdanov's approach to problems in politics, which flowed from his "conception of truth as ultimately a group consensus." This "implied more hesitation, discussion, and persuasion before a course could be undertaken. Lenin, on the contrary, tended to trust his own views and undertake action first, even with a minimum of support and often in opposition to the opinion of Social Democrats at large, or even a majority of his own faction, believing that his own insight and force of leadership [and also the impact of *objective realities*] would prove the validity of his ideas and gain acceptance by the rank and file." As the Bolshevik-Leninists were moving toward the conception of a purely Bolshevik party, the Forwardists were becoming more inclined toward a notion of RSDLP unity on the basis of ideological polycentrism; yet differences among the Forwardists themselves finally resulted in the disintegration of their faction.[31]

Gorky records a sad and regretful comment of Lenin's after the split: "Such clever and talented people, who have done a great deal for the Party, and could do ten times more—and they will not go with us! They cannot. And scores, hundreds of such people are ruined and mutilated by this criminal regime."[32]

Yet by this point, according to Gorky, Lenin had become "firm . . . inflexible," manifesting "a calm, rather cold and satirical mood" in regard to the Forwardists. He recounts that Lenin challenged Bogdanov: "Schopenhauer said that 'clear thinking means clear speaking' and I think he never said a truer word. You don't explain yourself clearly, Comrade Bogdanov. Explain to me in a few words what your [philosophical] 'substitution' will give to the working class, and why Machism is more revolutionary than Marxism." According to Gorky, "Bogdanov tried to explain but he really did speak in a confused and wordy fashion." Lenin brutally advised: "Drop it."[33]

The philosophical debate between Lenin and Bogdanov had been an important dimension of the split, one that also sheds light on Lenin's organizational orientation. We should not "drop it," therefore, but give it some attention—particularly since the philosophical debate (like the tactical debate) has found echoes in the later history of the revolutionary movement and quite conceivably could be repeated in some form in the future.

2. Philosophy and Revolutionary Program

There has been a considerable amount of confusion over the meaning of the fierce philosophical dispute that erupted in the Bolshevik organization in 1908–1909. Some commentators (for example, Carmen Sirianni) have seen Lenin's "long philosophical diatribe against Bogdanov on the nature of materialism" as simply one of many examples of "the enormous time and energy he put into sectarian squabbles." Others (such as Leonard Schapiro) have tagged it "a smokescreen of philosophy" used to veil a grubbier conflict over who would rule the Bolshevik organization. Still others (Richard Stites, for one) would argue that "the break which ensued was, in the last analysis, caused by a fundamental difference between an increasingly rigid and ideologically authoritarian Lenin and a Bogdanov whose encyclopedic knowledge of the sciences and whose personal proclivities toward revolutionary action could not be reconciled to the views of a self-appointed and self-righteous leader."[34]

Such interpretations as these pose a serious challenge to the characterization of Leninist organizational principles sketched in the present study. But a closer examination of the polemics on philosophy will demonstrate the seriousness of the philosophical differences between Bogdanov and his followers on the one hand, and those Leninists committed to the ideas of Marx and Engels on the other. And the philosophical divergence, as we shall see, had programmatic implications no less significant than the tactical differences we have just examined.

Bogdanov and his cothinkers blended the ideas of Marx and Engels with the "empiriocriticism" of Ernst Mach and Richard Avenarius. A. V. Lunacharsky later explained: "We were all deeply interested in the philosophical side of Marxism and we were anxious to strengthen its epistemological, ethical and aesthetical aspects, independently of Kantianism . . . and without falling into the narrow French encyclopaedist [materialist] orthodoxy on which Plekhanov was seeking to base Marxism." According to Bogdanov, "the philosophy of the proletariat needs further elaboration, not only because Marx and Engels did not succeed in formulating it fully enough, but also because of the new accumulation of new scientific material which philosophy must take into account." Such an approach was by itself guaranteed to generate controversy. Bogdanov called his synthesis "empiriomonism" and asserted that it corresponded to "the philosophy of the proletariat."[35]

Lenin was hardly the only Russian Marxist to attack Bogdanov's philosophy, nor were his criticisms nastier than those of the other critics. Menshevik theoreticians devoted considerable time and energy to such efforts, and no one was more scathing than Plekhanov, whose open letters to Bogdanov contained such passages as these: "That you are outside the confines of Marxism is clear for all those who know that the whole edifice of this teaching rests upon *dialectical materialism*, and who realize that you, as a convinced Machist, do not and cannot hold the materialist viewpoint. . . .

"While not a Marxist yourself, you would like nothing better than that we Marxists should accept you as our *comrade*. . . . You are not only very far from 'being a good Marxist,' but you are fated to acquire the unenviable bliss of attracting all those who, while claiming the title of Marxist, want to adapt their outlook to suit the palate of our contemporary little bourgeois supermen."[36]

Compare this with Lenin's *Materialism and Empirio-Criticism*, where Lenin asserts: "Let Bogdanov, accepting in the best sense and with the best intentions *all the conclusions* of Marx, preach [the empiriomonist notion of] the 'identity' of social being and social consciousness; we shall say: Bogdanov *minus* 'empiriomonism' (or rather, *minus* Machism) is a Marxist."[37]

Lenin had been aware of Bogdanov's distinctive views since at least 1902, and at least since 1904 he had been convinced that the blend of Marxism and empiriocriticism posed a serious challenge to what he viewed as the scientific and dialectical materialist foundations of Marxism. It was precisely this question that had led to a serious rupture with one of his adherents, Nikolay Valentinov, well before the start of the internal struggle in the Bolshevik faction. But Lenin later offered this explanation to Maxim Gorky: "In the summer and autumn of 1904 Bogdanov and I joined each other finally as Bolsheviks, and formed that tacit bloc which tacitly excluded philosophy as neutral ground. The bloc lasted throughout the entire time of the [1905] Revolution and gave us the possibility of introducing together those tactics of revolutionary socialism (bolshevism) which, according to my deepest conviction, were the only correct ones." He added that "a certain amount of conflict among the Bolsheviks on the philosophical question is, I think, unavoidable," but that "we must carry on our scrap with each other about philosophy" in a way that would not "hamper the cause of carrying out the tactics of revolutionary Social Democracy in the Party."[38]

Historian Geoffrey Swain has suggested that after the emergence of sharp tactical differences between Lenin and Bogdanov, Lenin came to feel that Bogdanov's tactical views "resulted from the un-Marxist philosophy that he propounded. His errors, therefore, could not be confined to this one issue [of recalling RSDLP deputies from the Duma] but would recur over and over again." This seems to be a reasonable proposition, but the issue is complex. Aside from vague references to "the cycle of ideas of boycottism," Lenin seems to have refrained from drawing a bold, straight line from the tactics of Bogdanov to the philosophy of Bogdanov. At the same time, there did appear to be such a correlation in the minds of the disputants.[39]

"Dialectical materialism" is a term, like "democratic centralism," that has suffered from considerable mystification on the part of friend and foe alike. Its critics sometimes liken it to what George Orwell calls "double-think" in *1984* ("the power of holding two contradictory beliefs in one's mind simultaneously, and accepting both of them"), and some of its alleged partisans utilize it in such mind-bending ways as to make such a definition seem plausible. But dialectical materialism is actually less mystifying and more interesting than this. While the term gained currency after the deaths of Marx and Engels, it signifies a general philosophical orientation, an approach to reality and a methodology, that was first systematically articulated in Engels's classic *Herr Eugen Dühring's Revolution in Science* (*Anti-Dühring*), written in 1878 with some input from Marx. It is an approach that blends the methodology of the philosopher Hegel with the philosophical materialism of the French Enlightenment. Although many commentators were later to argue that Engels's popularization seriously distorts Marx's own approach, David Riazanov has aptly commented that "for the dissemination of Marxism as a special method and a special system, no book except *Capital* itself has done as much as *Anti-Dühring*. All the young Marxists who entered the public arena in the early eighties . . . were brought up on this book." Marx himself, in an 1873 preface to the second edition of *Capital*, described his materialist recasting of dialectics: "My dialectical method is, in its foundations, not only different from the Hegelian, but exactly opposite to it. For Hegel, the process of thinking . . . is the creator of the real world, and the real world is only the external appearance of the idea. With me the reverse is true; the ideal is nothing but the material world reflected in the mind of man, and translated into forms of thought. . . . In its rational form . . . [dialectics] includes in its positive understanding of what exists a simultaneous recognition of its negation, its inevitable destruction; because it regards every historically developed form as being in a fluid state, in motion, and therefore grasps its transient aspect as well; and because it does not let itself be impressed by anything, being in its very essence critical and revolutionary." Engels elaborates on all of this in *Anti-Dühring* (discussing such dialectical "laws of motion" as the interpenetration of opposites, the transformation of quantity into quality, the negation of the negation), but the basic worldview is the same: "Everything is and also is not, for everything is in *flux*, is constantly changing, constantly coming into being and passing away." He argues that "dialectics . . . grasps things and their images, ideas, essentially in their interconnection, in their sequence, their movement, their birth and death." Such an approach is fruitful not only for the study of human history and society, but also for the study of nature; in fact, "Nature is the test of dialectics" because "in the last analysis Nature's process is dialectical."[40] Bogdanov and his philosophical co-thinkers rejected this approach to reality.

The belief that a correlation existed between dialectical materialism and consistent revolutionary politics—and the counterposed belief that Bogdanov's orientation was the only genuine "philosophy of the proletariat"—necessarily gave the philosophical dispute a depth and ferocity that cannot be explained by the petty causes some commentators project onto it.

Yet, some of Lenin's contemporaries did not see the point of it all. M. N. Pokrovsky, the Bolshevik historian who was aligned with Bogdanov's faction at this time, later recalled the consternation created in Bolshevik ranks when Lenin shifted the dispute among Bolsheviks to the realm of philosophy: "I might cite for you how he quarreled with Bogdanov after discovering that a pile of husks, thought to be utterly unrelated to politics, contained a political kernel. . . . When Ilyich began to quarrel with Bogdanov on the issue of *empiriomonism*, we threw up our hands and decided Lenin had gone slightly out of his mind. The moment was critical. The revolution was subsiding. We were confronted by the need for a radical change in our tactics; yet, at that time Ilyich immersed himself in the Bibliothéque Nationale [in Paris], sitting there for whole days, and wrote a philosophical book as a result. The scoffing was endless."[41]

If the debate was a sterile "squabble" of no programmatic significance, or if it was simply a "smokescreen" for a power struggle, the question arises of how seriously Leninist organizational principles should be taken, when such foolishness or dishonesty on the part of Lenin himself can gain the upper hand. Yet Pokrovsky's judgment sixteen years after the dispute was that "Ilyich turned out to be right" and that "one had to have insight to do this."[42] A careful examination suggests that this judgment has merit. While it will be impossible to do justice to the philosophical dispute, a sense of the actual differences and of their practical implications—suggested in the remainder of this section—may help us understand why this abstract dispute became an issue for Lenin.

The dispute seems very abstract indeed. Frederick Engels had argued that a distinction must be made between "things and their mental images," that the fundamental principles of knowledge "can never be created and derived by thought out of itself, but only from the external world ... the principles are not the starting point of the investigation, but its final result; they are not applied to nature and human history, but abstracted from them; it is not nature and the realm of humanity which conform to these principles, but the principles are only valid in so far as they are in conformity with nature and history. That is the materialistic conception of matter."[43] Bogdanov, on the other hand, was influenced by Ernst Mach, who argued, "Sensations are not 'symbols of things.' The 'thing' is rather a mental symbol for a complex of sensations of relative stability. Not the things (bodies) but colors, sounds, pressures, spaces, times (what we usually call sensations) are the real *elements* of the world." Following Mach, Bogdanov asserted that *matter* does not exist as a "thing-in-itself" but rather is inseparable from human sensations, that matter, the material world, objective reality are only concepts constructed on the basis of human sensations or experience, and do not exist "beyond experience." Engels believed that "truth" could be grasped only through the disciplined study of objective reality. Against this, Bogdanov asserted that "truth is by no means a simple copy of the facts, not a petty representation of them; it is an instrument for domination over them."[44]

Bogdanov insisted that this outlook, while conflicting with Engels's assertion, was in harmony with Marx's views: "Marx, for the first time, understood that objectivity does not possess absolute significance but rather a *social-practical* significance. He first indicated this in the notes on Feuerbach. . . . There he suggested one should understand reality, . . . the objective world as human practice and thus, as social practice." The idea that a fundamental difference existed in the worldview of Marx and that of Engels, while a commonplace of later currents in "Western Marxism," was in itself a disturbing piece of revisionism for those in the Russian Marxist mainstream. But Bogdanov sought to demonstrate that his interpretation was more in harmony with the revolutionary proletarian-socialist values of Marxism: "The basis of 'objectivity' must lie in the sphere of *collective* experience. . . . The agreement in collective experience which is expressed in this 'objectivity' can only appear as the result of the progressive concordance of the experience of different people as they express themselves to each other. . . . In general the physical world is this: socially agreed-upon, socially harmonized, in a word, *socially organized* experience."[45]

Proceeding from this standpoint, Bogdanov wrote: "Physical experience is the experience of *something*, namely of all mankind in its development. This is a world of strict, constructed, worked-out, regular, determined, precise correlates; the well-organized world where all the theories of geometry, all the formulae of mechanics, physics, astronomy, etc. operate. How could one understand *this* world, *this* system of experience independent of mankind? How could one say that it existed before him?" A sympathetic latter-day expositor of Bogdanov's viewpoint, Michael Boll, explains that Bogdanov was not really denying that the world existed before mankind: "Of course the world existed before man; such a view was entirely consistent with twentieth-century socially-organized knowledge. 'Before' and 'prior to', however, had to be understood as formal constructs which evolved through man's active pursuit of knowledge. They were not meaningful in some abstract or absolute sense, but as reflecting the stage of man's ceaseless interaction with his reality. Perhaps one day even these notions would change, would evolve further. Perhaps it would be determined *by man* that time was not a separate form of organization but rather a derived form of space or energy. At that moment the notion of the world 'existing' before man would take on an entirely new meaning consistent with the changing forms of socially-organized knowledge."[46]

Bogdanov was critical not only of the traditional Marxist view of materialism, but also of the standard view of dialectics as advanced by Engels. Defining dialectics as "an organizational process proceeding by the path of contradiction," Bogdanov denied that this "placid scheme" could "fit the harsh struggle of elementary, spiritless forces of the universe." His own approach to reality involved him in no such "placidity" as this. Boll comments on this admiringly: "Bogdanov's historical analysis provided a basis for understanding the interrelatedness of the physical and mental constellations through the historical interactions of group praxis." On the other hand, Bogdanov himself recognized a difficulty in the logic of his own perspective: "For a wide circle of backward Russian peasants, spirits and goblins represent a living reality which is understood as a phenomenon of the physical world.... If there were, perhaps, no other groups besides the backward peasants, then the spirits and goblins would even now possess 'objectivity', would be socially harmoniously related to experience."[47]

Of course, the world consisted of more than backward peasants. It included scientifically inclined revolutionary socialists (such as Bogdanov and his followers) who were determined to organize the workers around broader conceptions of reality, to help them organize their "experience" and "energy" in a manner that would make humanity's "fragmented existence whole." This determination to overcome such fragmentation was related to the exuberant stress that Bogdanov and his co-thinkers placed on human sensations. V. A . Bazarov asserted: "That man is not free who is afraid of himself, who does not dare to acknowledge that each of his sensations is in principle of equal value, [and who does not] seek in them, in the testimony of direct feeling, the norms of his life. The demand for an absolute non-empirical norm ["matter as a thing-in-itself"] is psychological slavery." Proletarian collectivism would naturally generate a tendency of all cognition "towards a harmoniously integral system" in which everything "from the most primitive cosmic complex of elements to artistic creativity . . . will be explained and harmoniously united by the conclusions of the formalized, organized experience of mankind."[48]

As the intellectual historian Aileen Kelly points out, such Marxists as Bogdanov, Bazarov, and Lunacharsky were convinced that "historical determinism, narrowly interpreted by party theorists, had destroyed the revolutionary enthusiasm of socialism and turned its poetry into dull prose." But she also offers the interesting comment that their revision of Marxism "was designed to fulfill a need that was emotional as much as intellectual. Its proponents had an immediate practical goal: to sustain and increase the intelligentsia's revolutionary enthusiasm by allowing it to justify and defend its voluntarism, traditionally expressed in the idea of the integral personality, against the encroachments of the 'integral world view' of orthodox marxism."[49]

The philosophical orientation of Bogdanov also had a profound appeal for many newly radicalized young workers with an intellectual bent and was in harmony with the psychology of a number of militant Bolshevik committeemen. It would be an error to think that those commonly considered to be Bolshevik hards automatically lined up behind Lenin or simply scoffed at philosophical discussions. One well-known Bolshevik committeeman, Joseph Stalin, wrote from a Baku jail in 1908 in praise of the "good sides" of Ernst Mach's philosophy and urged that

Marxism be developed and revised "in the spirit of J. Dietzgen" (an earlier socialist philosopher who was influential among Bogdanov's cothinkers). Stalin also favored what he called "a deviation from strict bolshevism"—the recall of RSDLP deputies from the Duma. Seeing Bogdanov's group as an impressive alternative to "the other part ('orthodox') of our fraction, headed by Ilyich," he praised Bogdanov's latest writings for indicating "individual blunders of Ilyich." Even in late 1909 Stalin was criticizing the earlier removal of Bogdanov from the *Proletary* editorial board and accused Lenin of "schismatic tactics." It was not until 1910, after the consolidation of a Bolshevik majority around Lenin, that Stalin expressed appreciation of his "wisdom."[50]

Although there were some Mensheviks among the supporters of empirio-criticism, the Menshevik leaders were inclined to see this as an essentially Bolshevik philosophy and agreed with Theodore Dan that it represented "the impotent revolt of 'the personality' against 'the environment' which it could not control." One of Plekhanov's disciples, A. M. Deborin, elaborated the "orthodox" Menshevik standpoint in this manner: "The stamp of 'subjectivism' and 'voluntarism' lies on all the tactics of so-called Bolshevism, the philosophical expression of which is Machism. . . . Our Machist-shaped Marxists are conscious Bolsheviks, who 'give meaning' to the practice and tactics of the latter."[51]

It is hardly surprising that Lenin was eager to engage in a sharp public polemic to demonstrate that "only utter ignorance of the nature of philosophical materialism generally and of the nature of Marx's and Engels' dialectical method can lead one to speak of a 'union' of empirio-criticism and Marxism." Lenin quoted Bogdanov's proposition that "social being and social consciousness are, in the exact meaning of these terms, identical," and responded that—to the contrary—"the fundamental principle of historical materialism [is that] social consciousness *reflects* social being." He saw Bogdanov's outlook as a form of philosophical idealism "disguised in Marxist terminology and decked out in Marxist words. 'Socially organized experience,' 'collective labor process,' and so forth are Marxist words, but they are *only words*, concealing an idealist philosophy that declares things to be complexes of 'elements,' of sensations, the external world to be 'experience,' or an 'empiro-symbol' of mankind, physical nature to be a 'product' of the 'psychical,' and so on and so forth. An ever subtler falsification of Marxism, an ever subtler presentation of anti-materialist doctrines under the guise of Marxism—this is the characteristic of modern revisionism in political economy, in questions of tactics and in philosophy generally, both in epistemology and in sociology."[52]

It was Lenin's belief that the defense of materialism "is *always* connected 'by an organic real bond' with 'the Marxist socio-political movement'—otherwise the latter would be neither Marxist, nor socio-political, nor a movement." Yet as historian David Joravsky has commented, Lenin's "reply to the Menshevik correlation of Bolshevism and 'Machism' was contemptuously to ignore it, and to show by example how philosophical issues should be separated from factional politics." In his writings of this period, Lenin sometimes polemicizes against philosophical revisionism, and he sometimes polemicizes around the questions of tactics and strategy, but invariably keeps the issues separate. In *Materialism and Empirio-Criticism* there is no attempt to demonstrate any one-to-one linkage between philosophy and political tactics, nor is there even a mention of the ultraleftism of Bogdanov and others. Joravsky makes the interesting comment that Lenin "*had* a political aim in writing the book, but it was not to join the philosophical and political issues that Russian Marxists were arguing about; it was to separate them. The Mensheviks were trying to join them, in order to picture the Bolsheviks as philosophical no less than political revisionists, and Lenin's chief political hope in working up his book was, as he wrote to Gorky, that 'the Mensheviks will be reduced to politics, and that is death for them.'"[53] The significance of this approach for the revolutionary party will be examined shortly.

Given the controversy surrounding the philosophical "respectability" of Lenin's *Materialism and Empirio-Criticism*, it is interesting to note a comment of Bertram D. Wolfe, the ex-Communist who carried on what E. H. Carr once called a "lifelong love-hate affair with Lenin."[54] While spending considerable time denigrating Lenin's polemic, Wolfe also writes that "its primary concerns are to defend orthodox Marxism . . . but over and above this, the work has a more ambitious aim: to expound afresh the basic philosophical position of Marx and Engels, and to evaluate from its standpoint the main philosophical currents and scientific discoveries of Lenin's day. . . . In the midst of all the anti-rationalism that surrounds him in the post-1905 reaction, and that surrounds us in our own day, Lenin's plea for a rational, experimental approach to nature and society . . . represents an important contribution."[55] The existence of an "objective world" that is "knowable" is a prerequisite for testing and advancing human knowledge. Lenin put it as follows: "For the materialist the 'success' of human practice proves the correspondence between our ideas and the objective nature of the things we perceive." He endorsed Engels's view that "freedom does not consist in the dream of independence of natural laws, but in the knowledge of these laws, and in the possibility of making them work towards definite ends." Lenin commented that "Engels takes the knowledge and will of man, on the one hand, and the necessity of nature, on the other, and . . . says that the necessity of nature is primary, and human will and mind secondary." He insists that those who deny this "will inevitably arrive at subjectivism."[56]

This comment suggests that for Lenin there *is* an important interrelationship between philosophy and practical politics. He is not trying simply to establish his credentials as a good Marxist nor, as David Joravsky tends to argue, simply to make philosophy a "nonissue" in the Bolshevik/Menshevik dispute. Krupskaya recalls that he "took the struggle in the philosophic front very much to heart" and felt that "philosophy was a weapon in the struggle, organically bound up with the question of evaluating all phenomena from the point of view of dialectic materialism, with the questions of the practical struggle in all directions." In his 1910 critique of the Forwardist group's political platform, one can see his counterposition of the limitations imposed by objective realities to the Bogdanovite blurring of reality with subjective desire. "The revolution must again strive for and achieve the overthrow of tsarism—say the authors of the new platform. Quite right. But that is not all that a *present day* revolutionary Social Democrat must know and bear in mind. He must be able to comprehend that this revolution is coming to us in a new way and that we must march towards it in a new way (in a different way than hitherto; not only in the way we did before; not only with those weapons and means of struggle we used before); that the autocracy itself is not the same as it was before." In his careful analysis, Lenin held that there had been a mutual adaptation of tsarism and capitalism in Russia, creating a new stabilization, a transition period between the 1905 revolution and a future revolutionary upsurge. "In order to prepare for the second revolution we must master the peculiarities of this transition, we must be able to adapt our tactics and organization to this difficult, hard, obscure transition forced on us." Acknowledging that this was "devoid of outward glamor" to be found in the Forwardists' stirring statements, Lenin insisted that objective realities—quite independently of revolutionary desires—necessitated "humble methods of struggle" designed to "prepare and rally the [revolutionary] forces, and not to bring them into immediate and decisive actions."[57]

The interrelationship of philosophy and practical politics is too complex to allow for easy generalizations. Lenin's philosophical orientation coincided with that of certain leading Mensheviks who remained consistent political opponents. Yet it is undeniable that Bogdanov's political orientation was not able to assist the Forwardist Bolsheviks in surviving as a political force, while the distinctive approach to party building advanced by Lenin contributed substantially to the survival and ultimate triumph of Bolshevism. Perhaps no iron law precluded Bogdanov's development of a sounder political orientation. The fact remains that such an orientation was the fruit of *Lenin's* political analysis, and of his analytical method, which was grounded in a philosophical approach rejected by Bogdanov. Lenin's basic commitment to dialectical materialism- articulated in *Materialism and Empirio-Criticism* and substantially refined through his philosophical studies in 1914–1916—placed a significant role in the development and elaboration of the Bolsheviks' revolutionary program, both its general outlines and its specific application.

By the 1930s, dialectical materialism had been transformed into a rather schematic set of ideological principles. These were utilized by the Stalin leadership in the world Communist movement to justify various pragmatically developed policies and to consolidate a rigid intellectual "orthodoxy" that would facilitate the leadership's control over the thinking of its adherents. This vulgarization of dialectical materialism—or diamat, as it came to be known in some circles—had little to do with Lenin's approach to the relationship between philosophy and party program. He utilized and propagated a dialectical materialist approach to reality but refrained from the kind of assertion that Stalin made in 1938: "Dialectical materialism is the world outlook of the Marxist-Leninist party."[58]

We have seen that Lenin and Bogdanov agreed that philosophy would be a neutral issue for the Bolshevik faction as a whole. At the beginning of 1908, David Joravsky has pointed out, this was formalized by a resolution that *Proletary*, "the faction's illegal, official newspaper, was to publish no articles on philosophy of any sort. In legal publications philosophical articles could be printed, on condition that orthodox dialectical materialism and 'Machism' were to have equal space." After Bogdanov's expulsion, a new position was adopted: "If philosophical questions should come up in the [Party's] Central Organ, the representatives of [*Proletary's*] extended editorial board in the Central Committee [of the RSDLP] should take the definite position of Marx-Engels dialectical materialism." Yet Lenin firmly opposed a formal condemnation of Bogdanov's philosophy. He wanted to be in a position neither of calling into question the 1908 resolution on philosophical neutrality nor of contradicting his own argument in *Materialism and Empirio-Criticism* that philosophical issues transcended factional politics in the RSDLP. Nor was he inclined to urge the establishment of a philosophical line mandatory for all Bolsheviks, or to suggest the desirability of any ongoing supervision of philosophical inquiry and discussion on the part of some central committee. "Ironically," Joravsky comments, "some of the Marxists who accused him of authoritarianism came somewhat closer to the narrow concept of partyness [ideological control of party leaders over philosophy, art, and scholarship] than he did: Plekhanov and his disciples by arguing a one-to-one correlation between philosophical and political trends, Bogdanov and the *Vperyodists* by demanding a clearly defined Bolshevik line in philosophy." Lenin—although determined to defend and utilize dialectical materialism and to prevent the association of Bogdanov's empiriomonism with Bolshevism as such—was not inclined to impose a rigid philosophical orthodoxy on the members of the revolutionary party.[59]

3. The Bolsheviks Become a Party

So far in this chapter we have focused on Lenin's battle and break with ultraleftist elements within the Bolshevik faction. No less important, however, was the battle he carried on at the same time against the Mensheviks. This conflict ultimately meant an even more significant kind of break.

The period spanning 1907–1912 culminated in the transformation of the Bolshevik faction into a separate political party—which meant a rupture with all other distinctive currents in the RSDLP. It also meant a very serious struggle with many moderate members of Lenin's faction who were committed to the traditional and quite popular concept of unity within the RSDLP. We have seen that in late 1904 and early 1905 Lenin had favored an uncompromising organizational split from the Mensheviks and the creation of an exclusively Bolshevik party; this was because of what he perceived as a growing programmatic divergence. By the end of 1905 he had reversed himself on the basis of a reversal of this divergence. Even when some of the differences reemerged, Lenin did not at first give up on the idea of RSDLP unity. Krupskaya notes that in 1906, "although the Mensheviks had shown themselves in their true colors . . . , Ilyich still hoped that the new wave of the revolution, of whose rise he had no doubt, would sweep them along with it and reconcile them to the Bolshevik line."[60] As we have seen, however, the expected new wave of revolution was delayed, and the Mensheviks continued to evolve in a direction of seeking greater collaboration with the liberal bourgeoisie and, in some cases, of significant compromise with the tsarist order. When he became convinced that revolutionary events would not once again heal the rift, Lenin reverted to the split perspective, which he believed was necessary for the future effectiveness of a genuinely revolutionary vanguard.

This split perspective constituted a veering away from the classic example of German Social Democracy, in a manner more profound than any of the formulations in *What Is to Be Done?* or *One Step Forward, Two Steps Back*. The German Social Democratic party contained within it revolutionary and antirevolutionary currents and was held together, particularly from 1905 onward, largely by balancing "orthodox" theory with reformist practice. The realities of the German situation were not commonly understood, however. Particularly from Russia, it seemed that the "orthodox Marxists" were firmly in control of the German party.

Lenin and other Russian Marxists did not believe in the ideal of an all-inclusive party in which revolutionaries and reformists were permanently balanced off, nor did they view German Social Democracy as such a party. We have seen that in the 1890s and early 1900s Lenin appears to have questioned whether such "substantive differences" could permanently coexist in the same organization, although in 1906 he did express the idea that "right up to the social revolution there will inevitably always be an opportunist wing and revolutionary wing of Social Democracy." The hegemony of the Marxist "orthodoxy" represented by Bebel and Kautsky in Germany was something he sought to duplicate within Russian Social Democracy, although as early as 1907 he may have had some at least half-formed reservations about the German reality. The American socialist William English Walling reported, after an interview with Lenin, that "he sharply differentiates his Socialism from that prevailing in Germany, whence the leaders of the opposite faction [the Mensheviks] have taken bodily nearly all their ideas. The German movement, he finds, has been too anxious to be legal." It is possible that Walling oversimplified Lenin's position by blurring together the "orthodox Marxist" and revisionist elements in German Social Democracy. (On the other hand, the Bolshevik Piatnitsky vividly recalls Lenin's "skepticism" about the German party at least by 1912.)[61]

In much of his writing, Lenin seems to have viewed the rise of revisionism and reformism in the socialist movement not as something to be fatalistically accepted, but as a serious problem, one that must be resolutely fought and decisively overcome. His goal was a relatively homogeneous party in the sense that all elements, whatever their differences, would be firmly committed to a revolutionary Marxist program. But Lenin's determined effort to do all that was necessary to establish such a party, his single-mindedness and increasing refusal to compromise, his willingness to actually split the RSDLP to achieve that goal, meant going farther than most Russian Marxists (and almost all German Marxists) considered acceptable.

Given all of this, it is hardly surprising that by 1912 almost the entire RSDLP—the different elements among the Mensheviks, the nonfaction party members such as Trotsky, the remnants of Bogdanov's Forwardists, and even a significant "conciliator" wing of the Bolshevik faction itself—could be found indignantly and furiously opposing the Leninist Bolsheviks as irresponsible splitters and sectarians within the workers' movement.

Joining in the chorus of critics have been later historians—from the sour ex-Communist Bertram D. Wolfe, to the more balanced Leninist sympathizer Marcel Liebman, to a younger socialist historian such as Geoffrey Swain in his recent study *Russian Social Democracy and the Legal Labor Movement: 1906–14*. Swain tells us that he began his study as "a good Leninist," believing that "Lenin's tactical genius" in this period was not appreciated "because he was surrounded by fools and traitors." Swain had expected to write a "hymn of praise" to the founder of Bolshevism. "Instead, like so many other academics, I end by sniping at Lenin. The problem is that Lenin's ideas, so cogent and convincing on paper just do not tally with the reality of what was happening in the labor movement in Russia." Actually, Swain goes further than this, and further than his evidence will provide support for, by arguing that Lenin rigidly "thought in terms of a hierarchy of committees, of military discipline, of committees being disbanded if they fell out of line." Swain terms this "a party organization that excluded every revolutionary worth his salt," and he adds that "nothing could persuade him that his vision of a centralized structure of hierarchically organized cells, with tentacles stretching into every section of the labor movement, was an empty abstraction."[62] While this view corresponds to the judgments of Lenin's critics (many of whom were neither "fools" nor "traitors") in the period of the final split, it provides little understanding of how and why the Leninist Bolsheviks, and not their critics, were able to triumph as an effective revolutionary force.

In the immediate aftermath of the 1905 defeat, the working class and the RSDLP were able to take advantage of the liberalization of the tsarist regime that had been forced by the revolutionary upsurge. The regime had not yet regained sufficient confidence to eliminate the relatively broad civil liberties, trade union rights, and so forth that had been conceded when it had been forced to its knees. At the Unity Congress of 1906, the RSDLP recorded 148,639 members; the trade unions were larger and in some ways stronger in that year than at any time before or after (until the overthrow of tsarism); a legal press and an array of legal workers' organizations continued to flourish. With 1907, however, the regime began a devastating counteroffensive that—while never completely eliminating the gains—succeeded in driving them back dramatically.

The survival of elements of the legal labor movement, despite the periodic closing down or smashing of unions and social-educational clubs by the authorities, was an important step forward from the pre-1905 period. Thus, although only 500 activists remained in the RSDLP's underground cells of Petersburg, for example, there were 2,500 members of the legal labor movement who considered themselves Social Democrats in that city during 1907. At the same time, the existence of these two components of the socialist workers' movement created new tensions within the party. This was deepened as the tsarist repression became more severe.[63]

The repression took an especially severe toll on the RSDLP as a nationally organized entity. Zinoviev notes: "In retrospect we can say quite unhesitatingly that in those hard times the party as such did not exist: it had disintegrated into tiny individual circles which differed from the circles of the 1880s and early 1890s in that, following the cruel defeat that had been inflicted upon the revolution, their general atmosphere was extremely depressed." By 1910, the party had perhaps 10,000 members. Martov observed that it had "collapsed like a deck of cards." Krupskaya wrote that "we have no people at all." Trotsky commented that "formal organizations on the local level are the exception rather than the rule." A Moscow activist reported that "since the mass arrests and exiling of our most active comrades in January 1909, organizational work has been almost completely disrupted. The sick and the weak remain—work is temporarily suspended." The situation was the same in Petersburg, where a party member reported that "beginning with 1907 things have gone from bad to worse, temporarily recovering and then deteriorating again."[64] The same was true throughout Russia up to 1912.

Within the working class as a whole, the impact of defeat and repression created a situation later summed up by Trotsky as follows: "Factories which two or three years ago would strike unanimously over some single arbitrary police action, today have completely lost their revolutionary color, and accept the most monstrous crimes of the authorities without resistance. Great defeats discourage people for a long time. The consciously revolutionary elements lose their power over the masses. Prejudices and superstitions not yet burned out come back to life. Grey immigrants from the village during these times dilute the workers' ranks. Skeptics ironically shake their heads." Looking ahead, Trotsky immediately adds: "But molecular processes in the masses are healing the psychological wounds of defeat. A new turn of events, or an underlying economic impulse, opens a new political cycle. The revolutionary elements again find their audience. The struggle reopens on a higher level."[65] This resurgence, however, was in the vague future, while the utter disintegration of the revolutionary workers' movement was a vivid, poignantly felt, immediate reality.

According to Menshevik A. N. Potresov, in a letter to Axelrod in October 1907, "We are undergoing complete disintegration and utter demoralization.... There is not only no organization, but not even the elements for it. And this non-existence is even extolled as a principle...." Trotsky later commented: "This extolling of dis-integration as a principle soon became the task of most leaders of Menshevism, including Potresov himself. They declared the illegal Party liquidated once and for all, and the aim to restore it-a reactionary utopia. ... Entrenching themselves in trade unions, educational clubs and insurance societies, they carried on their work as cultural propagandists, not as revolutionists. To safeguard their jobs in the legal organizations, the officials from among the workers began to resort to protective coloration. They avoided the strike struggle, so as not to compromise the scarcely tolerated trade unions. In practice, legality at any price meant outright repudiation of revolutionary methods."[66]

In 1910 Potresov responded to such charges by asking, "Can there exist in sober reality, and not merely as the figment of a diseased imagination, a school of thought that advocates liquidating what has ceased to be an organic whole?" He likened the concerns of his critics to "playing with toy soldiers in the face of tragedy," and predicted that a "new" and "wider" workers' movement would "in its own good time" transcend the shambles of the old.[67]

It is worth dwelling on this phenomenon, which would ultimately guarantee the final split in the RSDLP. According to historian Leopold Haimson, it arose in "a period of relative labor tranquility, as in a context of economic stagnation the masses of the Russian working class relapsed into apathy, after the defeat of their great expectations of 1905." Haimson, a capable historian sympathetic to Menshevism, offers a more positively worded description than Trotsky's of the liquidator sentiment:

> It was in this ultimately deceptive setting of labor peace, and of the futile and increasingly degrading spectacle of the Bolsheviks' collapsing underground struggle (this was the classic period of Bolshevik "expropriations"), that the leaders of the Menshevik faction began to articulate the philosophy and programs of an open labor party and labor movement. The current task of Social Democracy, they insisted, was not to pursue in the underground, under the leadership of a handful of intelligentsia conspirators, now clearly unattainable maximalist objectives. It was to outline for the labor movement goals, tactics, and organizational forms which, even within the narrow confines of the existing political framework, would enable the masses of the working class to struggle, day by day, for tangible improvements in their lives and to become through the experience of this struggle "conscious" and responsible actors— capable of making their own independent contribution to the vision of a free and equitable society. Not only did the Menshevik "Liquidators" articulate this vision of an open labor party and labor movement during these years but they appeared to be making progress in erecting the scaffolding of the institutions through which the vision was to be realized. They were seeking to organize open trade unions, cooperatives, workers' societies of self-improvement and self-education, and workers' insurance funds: organs intended not only to help the worker but also to enable him to take his life into his own hands.[68]

Trotsky tells us that "the Liquidators were in the forefront during the most desolate years," and veteran Bolshevik Mikhail Olminsky later recalled that "they suffered less from police persecution. They had many of the writers, a good part of the lecturers and on the whole most of the intellectuals. They were the cocks of the walk and they crowed about it."[69] Yet there was an important element of demoralization associated with this current. This comes through clearly in the reminiscences of the old Menshevik Boris I. Nicolaevsky (who himself had for some years been a full-time professional revolutionary), conveyed by one of his colleagues: "Lenin possessed qualities which Boris Ivanovich appreciated and admired and which he would have liked to see in Menshevik leaders. One such quality was total devotion to the cause of revolution. . . . It pained him to see how in the post-1905 era the ranks of the professional revolutionaries began to thin rapidly, especially among the Mensheviks.

Everyone was preoccupied with his own affairs, he recalled; revolutionaries were talking about such things as planning marriage and a family, about getting out of the revolutionary movement—temporarily, they claimed—in order to finish school or find a job. Even among the more educated and intelligent workers, precisely those who were most needed in the movement, there was a tendency to desert the ranks of the proletariat, to take up teaching or some other white-collar job in order to achieve a more promising personal career and life. The intellectuals within the party, too, often turned to more lucrative types of writing and other intellectual pursuits not directly related to the revolutionary movement."[70]

Among some of the Menshevik leaders, there was a growing anxiety over the rise of this mood. Martov complained of "the fragmented, differentiated and small-craft-like practical activity of the Mensheviks at present," of "moods which negated the old Menshevism," and of possibilities of a "real liquidation of our traditions, real legalism raised to a principle, a fundamental break with our past."[71] Yet Martov expressed such anxieties privately, while publicly associating himself with the liquidators. Lenin, on the other hand, defended the old revolutionary perspective openly:

> The flight of some people from the underground could have been the result of their fatigue and dispiritedness. Such individuals may only be pitied; they should be helped because their dispiritedness will pass and there will again appear an urge to get away from philistinism, away from the liberals and the liberal-labor policy, to the working-class underground. But when the fatigued and dispirited use journalism as their platform and announce that their flight is not a manifestation of fatigue, or weakness, or intellectual wooliness, but that it is to their credit and then put the blame on the "ineffective", "worthless", "moribund", etc., underground, these runaways then become disgusting renegades, apostates. These runaways then become the worst advisors for the working-class movement and therefore its dangerous enemies.[72]

Indeed, Lenin saw the liquidationist trend as being no less dangerous for the RSDLP as a whole than ultraleftism. His determination to carry on an uncompromtsmg struggle on both fronts was clearly articulated most clearly in 1909:

> Our immediate task is to preserve and consolidate the Russian Social Democratic Labor Party. The very fulfillment of this great task involves one extremely important element: the combating of both varieties of *liquidationism*—liquidationism on the right and liquidationism on the left. The liquidators on the right say that no illegal RSDLP is needed, that the Social-Democratic activities should be centered exclusively on legal opportunities. The liquidators on the left go to the other extreme: legal avenues of Party work do not exist for them, illegality at any price is their "be all and end all." Both, in approximately equal degree, are liquidators of the RSDLP, for without methodical judicious *combination* of legal and illegal work in the present

situation that history has imposed on us, the "preservation and consolidation of the RSDLP" is inconceivable. . . . The Bolshevik section as a definite ideological trend in the Party must exist as before. But one thing must be borne firmly in mind: the responsibility of 'preserving and consolidating' the RSDLP . . . now rests primarily, if not entirely, on the Bolshevik section.[73]

This last sentence essentially amounts to a declaration of war on the other currents in the RSDLP, the logic of which culminated in the creation of the Bolshevik party in 1912. Indeed, according to Gregory Zinoviev: "After the 1908 conference, and more especially after the 1910 plenum, we Leninist Bolsheviks said to ourselves that we would not work together with the liquidator Mensheviks and that we were only awaiting a convenient moment to break finally from them and form our own independent organization based upon the resurgent workers' movement. Our group decided such a moment had arrived at the beginning of 1912. . . ."[74]

Such a split perspective has often been attributed to "the hothouse atmosphere of emigre life" in which Lenin found himself after the 1905 defeat and the reaction of 1907. Lenin referred to Paris as the "foreign Petersburg" because it teemed with 80,000 Russians who had been forced into exile. As he wrote to Gorky, "emigre life is now a hundred times more difficult than it was before 1905." Historian Ralph Carter Elwood has expressed the common opinion that "it is not surprising that this artificial and isolated life in western Europe engendered a renewal of the personality clashes, ideological debates and organizational schisms which rent the party hierarchy after the Second Congress [of 1903]."[75] Indeed, it would be strange if even Lenin had not been affected by this strained and bitter atmosphere, and the tone of some of his polemics indicates that he was.

Many are inclined to ignore the fact that the impulse to lash out was not peculiar to Lenin. Among the Mensheviks, factional knives were being sharpened for the purpose of cutting down the Bolsheviks. In 1907 Pavel Axelrod was raising the question with Martov, "How can we remain with them in one party?" Martov outspokenly favored a complete break. One of the more "moderate" of the anti-Leninists, Theodore Dan, favored a "tactic of preservation of 'unity' at all costs," but his reasoning included elements that are quite instructive. First of all, the Menshevik organization in Russia was in a shambles: "There are no money, no people, no [interest in party] work. . . . Menshevism as an organization simply does not exist in Russia, and to assemble it once again by mechanical means is impossible." A split with the Leninists might therefore give them clear hegemony over the remnants of the RSDLP inside Russia. Instead it was necessary to "fight all these nasty people and slime" within a unified RSDLP while working to win control of the party. Yet Dan was fully committed—as were all the dominant Mensheviks—to the goal (as Axelrod put it) of rooting out the "moral-political depravity . . . and ideological chaos that the Bolsheviks introduced into our movement."[76]

Although the Mensheviks decided to bide their time, they proved fully prepared to maneuver organizationally and declaim polemically for the purpose of crushing the Bolsheviks in the RSDLP. Perhaps the most infamous example was Martov's 1911 diatribe *Saviors or Destroyers?* There he castigated the Bolsheviks for their erstwhile "expropriation" adventures of 1906–1907. Accusing the Bolsheviks of a "Nechayev type policy" of "criminal activities" and "systematic corruption of the party" (Nechayev was a fanatical revolutionary of the nineteenth century who utilized corrupt and murderous tactics against others in the revolutionary movement), Martov declaimed against "the war which the party Jacobins are waging against the Social Democratic movement." As Martov's biographer comments, "the moral and news value of the revelations was insignificant so many years after the scandals had broken and more than a year after the Bolsheviks had reformed" through the break with ultraleftism. He also takes note of Plekhanov's evaluation of the pamphlet's purpose. At this time, Plekhanov was fiercely critical of the liquidationist trends among the Mensheviks and shocked by Martov's pamphlet: "Plekhanov advised Kautsky that the Mensheviks, being a minority in the party, strove to destroy it in the hope that 'once the party is destroyed, they could call a conference for the organization of a new one' and thus become a majority." Isaac Deutscher has shrewdly summarized the evidence: The Menshevik leaders "were no less determined than Lenin to carry the schism through to the end. The main difference was that while Lenin openly avowed his intention and almost shouted it from the housetops, Martov, Axelrod, and Dan kept their design to themselves and sought to put it into effect through a subtle tactical game." While convinced that "the split was both inevitable and desirable," however, they hoped to place "the odium of the schism on Lenin."[77]

It would be a mistake to see all of this as simply senseless factional squabbling among frustrated political exiles. The polemics and maneuvers flowed from profound programmatic disagreements that were becoming too significant to contain within a single political party—assuming that the party hoped to provide leadership for the working class. At the RSDLP conference of 1908, a Bolshevik majority succeeded in passing a resolution condemning liquidationism as "the attempts of a certain section of the Party intellectuals to liquidate the existing organization of the . . . Party and substitute for it an amorphous association within the limits of legality at all costs, even if this legality is to be attained at the price of an open renunciation of the program, tactics and traditions of the Party." The political implications of the liquidators' proposed organizational "reform"—given the realities of tsarist repression, which required workers' organizations to be nonpolitical in order to be legal—ensured the sharpening of the factional struggle in the RSDLP. "Naturally, repudiation of the 'underground' goes hand in hand with the repudiation of revolutionary tactics and advocacy of reformism," Lenin commented. He believed that the liquidators were bending to the bourgeois liberals "who advocate only 'reforms' and spread among the masses the highly pernicious idea that reform is *compatible* with the present tsarist monarchy."[78]

An interesting minor example of the practical effects of divisions in the RSDLP can be found in the case of a legal workers' educational society in Petersburg: The Bolsheviks hoped to use it for the instruction and recruitment of party members, while the liquidators tried to forbid all Social Democratic activity within it; the Forwardists, for their part, wanted to force the withdrawal of Social Democratic instructors in order to "destroy from within" what they saw as an institution that would conjure legalist illusions among the workers.[79]

Significantly, the actual experience of the workers who were active in the legal labor movement generated support for the Bolsheviks' position. In 1908, Trotsky wrote in his influential bimonthly newspaper *Pravda* (this "nonfactional" paper, not to be confused with the later Bolshevik daily, was the most popular illegal paper circulating among Russian workers): "Advanced workers are abandoning the hope of holding their ground in the open field of activity and are taking up the task of reforming the illegal Social Democratic organization. They have now become convinced that without such an organization it is now impossible to advance a step in either the economic or political sphere." Historian Geoffrey Swain reports: "An agent for Trotsky's *Pravda* noted the new mood among workers when he toured Russia during [1909]. On the same trip the previous year, union leaders had been wary of the author; they saw him as an 'illegal', an outlaw, now he was positively welcomed." In the same year, the following declaration came out of a meeting of nonfaction party trade unionists in Petersburg: "So that the individual Social Democrats scattered among the various trades ... should become a solid mass, and not act separately but according to a definite plan in contact with one another, an illegal organization should be formed, into which can go and should go only 'experienced workers who have gone through political school', old workers, who by joining an illegal organization will take on themselves the exclusive leadership of political life and the movement of the working masses."[80]

Such sentiment resulted in a unanimous vote (including liquidators) at the January 1910 RSDLP plenum for the following resolution: "The historical situation of the Social-Democratic movement in the period of the bourgeois counter-revolution inevitably gives rise, as a manifestation of the bourgeois influence over the proletariat, on the one hand, to the renunciation of the illegal Social-Democratic Party, the debasement of its role and importance, the attempts to curtail the program and tactical tasks and slogans of consistent Social-Democracy, etc.; on the other hand, it gives rise to the renunciation of the Duma work of Social-Democracy and of the utilization of the legal possibilities, the failure to understand the importance of either, the inability to adapt consistent Social-Democratic tactics to the peculiar historical conditions of the present moment, etc. An integral part of the Social-Democratic tactics under such conditions is the overcoming of both deviations by broadening and deepening the Social-Democratic work in all spheres of the class struggle of the proletariat and by explaining the danger of such deviations."[81]

Although this would seem to have resolved the question in Lenin's favor, such was not the case. Lenin described the 1910 plenum in a letter as "three weeks of agony" in which there was "a mood of 'conciliation in general' (without any clear idea with who, for what, and how); hatred of the Bolshevik Center for its implacable ideological struggle; squabbling on the part of the Mensheviks, who were spoiling for a fight. . . . " The Bolsheviks (who at this point were split between conciliators, or party Bolsheviks, and an irreconcilable grouping of what came to be known as Bolshevik Leninists) felt compelled to make a number of organizational concessions. "Ilyich believed that the utmost concession should be made on organizational issues," wrote Krupskaya, "without yielding an inch on fundamental issues." But paper resolutions were not capable of resolving the fundamental issues. Although the Mensheviks had formally taken an antiliquidationist stand, they were not prepared to carry it out, because doing so would have torn apart the Menshevik group. Tony Cliff has pointed out that "Martov made it clear a little later that he had not even intended to carry out this commitment and that he had agreed to the 'unity' in the plenum only because the Mensheviks were too weak to risk an immediate break." The most open of the liquidators even refused to serve on the central committee of the underground RSDLP. And as Lenin later commented, "it was precisely after the Plenum Meeting of 1910 that the . . . chief publications of the liquidators, *Nasha Zarya* and *Dyelo Zhizni*, definitely turned to liquidationism all along the line, not only 'belittling the importance of the illegal Party', but openly renouncing it, declaring that the Party was 'extinct', that the Party was already liquidated, that the idea of reviving the illegal party was 'a reactionary utopia', using the columns of legally published magazines to heap slander and abuse on the illegal Party, calling upon the workers to regard the nuclei of the Party and its hierarchy as 'dead', etc."[82]

Krupskaya summarizes the conviction that was hardening among Lenin and his cothinkers: "The thing was to have a united Party center, around which the Social-

Democratic workers masses could rally. The struggle in 1910 was a struggle waged for the very existence of the Party, for exercising influence on the workers through the medium of the Party. Vladimir Ilyich never doubted that within the Party the Bolsheviks would be in the majority, that in the end the Party would follow the Bolshevik path, but it would have to be a Party and not a group. . . . Not a group, but a Party pursuing a Bolshevik line. Naturally, there was no room in such a Party for Liquidators, against whom forces were being rallied. Obviously, there could be no room in the Party for people who made up their minds beforehand that they would not abide by the Party decisions."[83]

There were, however, a significant number of RSDLP members who favored the combination of legal and illegal tactics, who maintained a revolutionary class-struggle orientation, but who were unalterably opposed to a split in the RSDLP. "With some comrades," Krupskaya later wrote, "the struggle for the Party assumed the form of conciliation; they lost sight of the aim of unity and relapsed into a man-of-the-street striving to unite all and everyone, no matter what they stood for." Initially this conciliatory outlook was the standpoint of a majority of Bolsheviks. It was also the position articulated by Trotsky in *Pravda* and was an attitude common among many working-class activists. One such activist from Vologda commented, "The workers are opposed to the factional fight. Many understand the issues but nevertheless cannot bear the polemics which they view as mainly personal affairs which disrupt comradely solidarity." Another complained that "as workers we thirsted for active work but were forced to waste our energies on endless and useless polemics . . . about whether Lenin said this or Martov said that. . . . In between this and that argument it is forgotten that the first and essential condition of the struggle—of the victorious struggle—is the absence of any discord and unity. Thus I, like many others . . . am not a Bolshevik, I am not a Menshevik, I am not an Otzovist [ultraleftist], I am not a Liquidator—I am only a Social Democrat." Even a Bolshevik organizer complained about "the tempest in a teapot abroad," adding that "in general the workers are beginning to look disdainfully at the emigration: 'let them crawl on the wall as much as their hearts desire; but as for us, whoever values the interests of the movement—work, the rest will take care of itself.' I think that is for the best." (The author of these lines was Joseph Stalin.) This was precisely the sentiment that the conciliators—whether nonfaction Social Democrats aligned with Trotsky or party Bolsheviks—responded to and hoped to mobilize. Lenin observed that "Trotsky expressed conciliationism more consistently than anyone else" and "was probably the only one who attempted to give the trend a theoretical foundation." Trotsky himself later summarized this position: "As long as the revolutionary intellectuals were dominant among the Bolsheviks as well as among the Mensheviks and as long as both factions did not venture beyond the bourgeois democratic revolution, there was no justification for a split between them; in the new revolution, under the pressure of the laboring masses, both factions would in any case be compelled to assume an identical revolutionary position, as they did in 1905."[84]

Geoffrey Swain has recently argued that Trotsky was right: If Lenin had not embarked upon the "farce" of a separate Bolshevik party, then the unity of the RSDLP would have been preserved, and within that context the Bolsheviks—working with Trotsky and other revolutionaries, and in light of the leftward shift of the Russian workers that was already beginning—could have established a revolutionary socialist majority. Of course, as Krupskaya related, "Ilyich simply could not stand this diffuse, unprincipled conciliationism, conciliationism with anyone and everyone, which was tantamount to surrendering one's positions at the height of the struggle." But Swain sees this as a serious flaw, concluding severely: "To Lenin, it was not only safer, but far more principled to split the party and cock a snook at those dreamers like Trotsky who tried to suggest that 'wallowing in the swamp' was really the cut and thrust of running a democratic party."[85]

Yet consider Trotsky's later critique of his own position: "Certain critics of Bolshevism to this day regard my old conciliationism as the voice of wisdom. Yet its profound erroneousness had been long ago demonstrated both in theory and practice. A simple conciliation of factions is possible only along some sort of 'middle' line. But where is the guarantee that this artificially drawn diagonal line will coincide with the needs of objective development? The task of scientific politics is to deduce a program and a tactic from an analysis of the struggle of classes, not from the ever-shifting parallelogram of such secondary and transitory forces as political factions."[86]

This was precisely the point that Lenin made over and over again in his fiercely uncompromising polemics with Trotsky, the party Bolsheviks, and others. He characterized their views on party unity as seeking to "place in the forefront the 'reconciliation' of 'given persons, groups and institutions.' The identity of their views on Party work, on the policy of that work, is a matter of secondary importance. Differences of opinion must be hushed up, their causes, their significance, their objective conditions should not be elucidated. The principal thing is to 'reconcile' persons and groups. If they do not agree upon the carrying out of a common policy, that policy must be interpreted in such a way as to be acceptable to all. Live and let live."[87]

Against this, Lenin projected a revolutionary perspective on party unity: "From this point of view the unification of the Party may proceed slowly, with difficulties, vacillations, waverings, relapses, but it cannot but proceed. From this point of view the process of unification does not necessarily take place among the '*given persons, groups and institutions*,' but irrespective of the given persons, subordinating them to itself, rejecting those of the 'given' persons who do not understand or who do not want to understand the requirements of objective development, putting forward and attracting new persons, who do not belong to the 'given' set, effecting changes, reshufflings and regroupings within the old factions, tendencies, divisions. From this point of view, unity is inseparable from its ideological foundation, it can grow only on the basis of an ideological *rapprochement.* . . . "[88]

Utilizing the Russian Organizing Committee, which enjoyed the full support of perhaps one-fifth of the RSDLP, Lenin and his closest comrades convened the predominantly Bolshevik All-Russian Conference of the RSDLP in Prague in January 1912. The Forwardists (who were moving significantly away from ultraleftism), Trotsky and his followers, and the antiliquidator "party Mensheviks" who had grouped around Plekhanov were invited. All refused to attend, with the exception of two party Mensheviks. The liquidator and semiliquidator components of the Mensheviks were not invited at all. The conference assumed for itself the authority of a regular RSDLP congress, declared the liquidators to be outside of the party, passed a number of major resolutions, and elected a new central committee. As Zinoviev notes, "The conference at Prague consisted in effect of a handful of delegates (some 20 to 25 in number) led by Comrade Lenin, and took upon itself the presumption to proclaim itself to be the party and to break once and forever from all other groups and sub-groups." Geoffrey Swain documents that even among these delegates there was no clear agreement on the idea of such a breathtaking split and that "to the Russian delegates at least, Prague remained a provisional gathering."[89] Yet Krupskaya indicates that its actual accomplishments were more far-reaching:

> The Prague Conference was the first conference with Party workers from Russia which we succeeded in calling after 1908 and at which we were able in a businesslike manner to discuss questions relating to the work in Russia and frame a clear line for this work. Resolutions were adopted on the issues of the moment and the tasks of the Party, on the elections to the Fourth Duma, on the Social-Democratic group in the Duma, on the character and organizational forms of Party work, on the tasks of the Social Democrats in the anti-famine campaign, on the attitude toward the State Insurance for Workers' bill before the Duma, and on the petition campaign [calling for freedom of trade union organization, assembly, and strikes]. The results of the Prague Conference were a clearly defined Party line on questions of work in Russia, and real leadership of *practical* work. . . . A unity was achieved on the [Central Committee] without which it would have been impossible to carry on the work at such a difficult time.[90]

Many who were inclined to adhere to such a Bolshevized RSDLP were hesitant to turn their backs on the other elements of the old party. But these other elements—enraged by Lenin's "sectarian arrogance" (or what the historian Pokrovsky later termed his "political courage")—were quick to denounce the Bolshevik "usurpers." Trotsky initiated a countermove, the convocation of a unity conference of all other components of the RSDLP: his own nonfaction adherents, Menshevik liquidators and antiliquidator party Mensheviks, Forwardists, the Jewish Labor Bund, and even remnants of the conciliationist party Bolsheviks. This conference met in Vienna in August 1912, and its participants were termed the "August bloc." One of the left-wing participants, David Riazanov, gloomily observed that "only personal hatred for the scoundrel Lenin keep together most of the Mensheviks, Bundists, and Trotsky." The Forwardist representatives had walked out of the conference as soon as it became clear that the liquidator and semiliquidator Mensheviks would dominate the framing of the political resolutions. Trotsky himself found it impossible to remain in the August bloc for very long. It took less than a year for the bloc to disintegrate altogether.[91] Lenin did not hesitate to chide his conciliator critics as he pointed out the lesson of their experience, a theme he repeatedly returned to in the subsequent period. Writing in 1914, for example, he made the following remarks:

> You consider that it is the 'Leninists' who were the splitters? Very well, let us assume that you are right. But if you are, why have not all the other sections and groups proved that unity is possible with the liquidators *without* the "Leninists", and *against* the "splitters"? ... If we are splitters, why have not you, uniters, united among yourselves, and with the liquidators? ... If disagreements are only invented, or exaggerated, and so forth, by the "Leninists", and if unity between the liquidators, Plekhanovites, Vperyodists [Forwardists], Trotskyists, and so forth, is really *possible*, why have you not proved this during the past two years by *your* own example?[92]

The Bolshevik party was hardly monolithic, but it was cohesive and was able to rebuild a revolutionary workers' organization inside Russia through the combination of legal and illegal methods. Lenin's description of what this looked like is worth considering:

> The exceptional and unique feature of our position ... is that our illegal Social-Democratic Labor Party consists of *illegal* workers' organizations (often called 'cells') which are surrounded by a more or less dense network of *legal* workers' associations (such as sick insurance societies, trade unions, educational associations, athletic clubs, temperance societies, and so forth). Most of these legal associations exist in the metropolis; in many parts of the provinces there are none at all. Some of the illegal organizations are fairly large, others are quite small and in some cases they consist only of "trusted agents.[93]

These "trusted agents" were leading workers chosen to maintain contact between the central committee and the local Social Democratic groups and to create flexible forms of leadership for local activities in the large centers of the labor movement.

The interrelationship of legal and illegal forms was extremely important: "The legal associations serve to some extent as a *screen* for the illegal organizations and for the extensive, legal advocacy of the idea of working-class solidarity among the masses. Nation-wide contacts between the leading working-class organizations, the maintenance of a center (the Central Committee) and the passing of precise Party resolutions on all questions—all these are of course carried out quite illegally and call for the utmost secrecy and trustworthiness on the part of advanced and tested workers.... We make use of every reform (insurance, for example) and of every legal society. But we use them to develop the revolutionary consciousness and the revolutionary struggle of the masses."[94]

In order to advance this goal, Lenin stressed, the workers should be encouraged to conduct political strikes, meetings, and street demonstrations for the purpose of drawing in more forces to push forward the workers' interests and challenge established authority. This necessitated the publication and circulation of revolutionary leaflets and an illegal newspaper. He added: "The ideological unification of all these propaganda and agitation activities among the masses is achieved by the slogans adopted by the supreme bodies of our Party, namely: (1) an eight-hour day; (2) confiscation of the landed estates, and (3) a democratic republic." These demands were incessantly put forward and popularized by the Bolshevik party and came to be known as the three whales of Bolshevism. (This phrase derives from a fable in which the world was balanced on the backs of three whales.) Lenin stressed that "in the present situation in Russia, where absolute tyranny and despotism prevail and where all laws are suppressed by the tsarist monarchy, *only* these slogans can effectively unite and direct the entire propaganda and agitation of the Party aimed at effectually sustaining the revolutionary working-class movement."[95]

The underground RSDLP, under Bolshevik leadership, began to revive dramatically on the basis of this orientation. "The sudden growth of the illegal Bolshevik nuclei," Theodore Dan later recalled, "was an unpleasant surprise for those Mensheviks who regarded these nuclei as a product of the disintegration of the old prerevolutionary Party organization and doomed to inevitable extinction." In comparing the fortunes of the Bolsheviks and Mensheviks in the difficult period of 1907–1912, Dan was forced to conclude that "while the Bolshevik section of the party transformed itself into a battle-phalanx, held together by iron discipline and cohesive guiding resolution, the ranks of the Menshevik section were ever more seriously disorganized by dissension and apathy."[96]

9. The Almost-Revolution

Events in the period of 1912–1914 seem to have vindicated the orientation for which Lenin fought in the period just examined. The programmatic clarity and tactical flexibility facilitated an organizational cohesion and effectiveness that enabled the Bolsheviks to make substantial gains in their efforts to build an expanded membership and sphere of influence among the Russian working class. It would be a mistake to view "organizational cohesion" as being synonymous with any kind of rigid centralism, however. Rather, centralism was necessarily blended with local autonomy and a democratic internal life without which the Bolshevik organization could not have functioned effectively, particularly because many of the veteran committeemen and intellectuals so central to the organizational apparatus had faded away, and their functions had to be taken over by rank-and-file activists who arose from and were directly tied to the local working-class organizations. This was the period in which the worker-Bolshevik became the predominant party type. Two interrelated processes—the "proletarianization" of the Bolsheviks and the Bolshevization of the "conscious workers"—accelerated in these years.

These developments were related to the internal struggles of preceding years discussed earlier, but also to a dramatic radicalization that was beginning to sweep through the working class as a whole. In some ways the radical upsurge was comparable to that of 1905. In certain respects, the situation was even more advanced, as workers struck and took to the streets in the summer of 1914. Lenin noted that instead of raising banners and following a Father Gapon, as they had in 1905, the workers now used barricades and the illegal RSDLP as their starting points.[1] How far the workers' militancy could have gone is a point of controversy, but some historians argue that only the eruption of the First World War decisively broke the revolutionary wave that might otherwise have washed away tsarism in 1914.

The developments in this period of "almost-revolution" were to add important new components to the Bolshevik party as it went into the storms of war and revolution. The way in which the Bolsheviks were affected by (and in turn affected) these later storms will be explored in chapters 10 and 11. Here we will give our attention to the essential prologue: the rise of the worker-Bolsheviks, and the role they played in the almost-revolution.

1. Worker–Bolsheviks

The proletarianization of the Bolshevik organization had taken a qualitative leap forward with the massive working-class influx into the RSDLP during the 1905 revolution. Following the defeat of the revolution, particularly in the period of 1907–1912, membership in the party declined no less dramatically. Yet the proportion of workers in and around the RSDLP may have been higher than ever in this period. This was because of the rightward shift of the Russian intelligentsia in general, and because of the exodus of intellectuals from the RSDLP. Historian Ralph C. Elwood has explained:

> The revolution of 1905 ... drastically changed the perspective of the Russian intelligentsia. Many were arrested and sent into prison or exile since they represented the leadership of the revolutionary party. The irrational anarchy, pogroms and insurrections unleashed by the revolution frightened others whose rational commitment to a revolutionary ideal had somehow precluded violence. Then came the failure of the revolution and the realization that the party would once again be forced to go underground. To a majority of the disillusioned intelligentsia, the sacrifices required could not be justified by the indefinitely postponed revolution.[2]

Some of them sought to maintain links to their old ideals by finding jobs in the newly legalized trade unions and other institutions of the legal labor movement—or, as one Bolshevik activist complained, "at the first convenient opportunity, [the intellectuals] retire into trade unions as secretaries, clerks, etc." According to Elwood, "at first, they made a pretense of retaining their Social Democratic identity but gradually these 'small deeds' intelligentsia dissociated themselves from the illegal apparatus."[3]

There were other revolutionary intellectuals who shifted their energies from political activity to purely intellectual or literary efforts. One example, a Bolshevik named George Denicke who dropped away from political work after 1907, has been described by Leopold Haimson as being "attracted by the broader intellectual and social vistas that seemed to open despite, or perhaps because of, the 'political stagnation' of the Stolypin years. [Peter Stolypin was the reactionary tsarist prime minister who maintained a particularly repressive regime while also pushing modernizing reforms, from 1907 to 1911.] He felt the need to refurbish his intellectual baggage, now that his fundamental assumptions about Russian society had been repudiated by events. He also felt very deeply the sense of revulsion that affected so many of his contemporaries against their earlier life in the underground—with the blunting of emotions, the psychological distance in human relations, indeed the dulling of all perceptions which this life had caused."[4] Many of these people returned to political life during the later upsurges in the class struggle (some joining the Bolsheviks, others—such as Denicke—the Mensheviks), but their absence from the revolutionary movement for an extended period was keenly felt.

One party activist from the industrial city of Ekaterinoslav wrote a typical complaint to *Proletary* in the autumn of 1907: "The chief weakness of the Ekaterinoslav organization is the absence of party workers [full-time activists, professional revolutionaries]. We have neither agitators nor propagandists, nor organizers." The same problem existed even in Petersburg, as one correspondent wrote to the party organ *Social Democrat* in early 1909: "The general flight of the intelligentsia has had an especially serious effect. Individual workers are incapable of conducting independent work well." Another complaint from Petersburg: "We need organizers and propagandists; if we had them things would move." The same lament came from Ekaterinoslav: "Even if only one experienced comrade took on the work here of implementing political leadership, arranging leaflets, contacting surrounding organizations [then] . . . one would be sure that the influence of our party would be quickly restored."[5]

While this situation severely damaged the RSDLP, it also resulted in "the unplanned tranfer of local leadership from the intelligentsia to the younger workers," as Ralph C. Elwood has documented. Slowly, often painfully, working-class revolutionaries learned to carry out the tasks necessary for maintaining their party. As one émigré Bolshevik concluded, "the activity of every worker-agitator, worker-propagandist and worker-organizer [is] now more than ever repaid 100-fold." Lenin was particularly heartened by the development of the new "Bolshevik mass worker" and believed that the RSDLP was being immensely strengthened because "work on the local level has passed to a remarkable degree into new hands: into the hands of a new generation of party workers."[6] One of the foremost worker-Bolsheviks, Alexander Shlyapnikov, vividly summed up the phenomenon:

A typical feature of the pre-war period of party work was its lack of intellectuals. The exodus of intellectuals that had begun in 1906 and 1907 meant that party workers, full-time staff and so on were workers. There was so little of the intelligentsia left that it barely sufficed to meet the needs of the Duma faction and the daily paper. The place of the petty-bourgeois intellectuals and student youth was taken up by the intellectual proletarian with calloused hands and highly developed head who had not lost contact with the masses. A very favorable impression was made by our insurance organizers G. I. Osipov, C. M. Shkapin, N. I. Ilyin, Dmitriev, and others, and also the trade-union activists such as the metalworkers Kiselev, Murkin, Schmidt and others.

Working in the shops and being often at comrades' houses I met a few outstanding workers who were more highly developed than many famous European workers I had known well abroad. Bitter struggle, exile and prison crippled thousands, but they reared individuals incomparably better than the 'peaceful' struggle in the west.[7]

These developments, however, took place not only in the Bolshevik organization but also among the Mensheviks. Given the Mensheviks' particular emphasis of, and immersion in, the legal labor movement, and the common working-class distaste for splits and polemics, one might assume that their own working-class activists would have won support from the majority of Russian workers. In fact, the opposite was the case. The period 1912–1914, years of rapidly accelerating working-class activity, saw the Bolsheviks quickly become the dominant force within the Russian labor movement.

An early harbinger was the election campaign for the Fourth Duma in the autumn of 1912. There was a two-tier election system in tsarist Russia at this time: The voters elected representatives of electoral colleges, or curiae, who then elected deputies to the Duma. Thirteen Social Democrats were elected to the Duma in this way. Of those, nine were elected from overwhelmingly working class curiae, six of these representing Russia's major industrial areas. These six deputies all identified with the Bolsheviks. They represented a million workers, while the seven Menshevik deputies represented only 250,000 workers. Martov complained in a letter to Potresov: "The failure of the Mensheviks in the labor curiae . . . shows once more that Menshevism caught on too late to the reviving danger of Leninism and overestimated the significance of its temporary wholesale disappearance." Another indicator can be found in the circulation in 1912–1914 of the two legal newspapers—the Menshevik *Luch* (Ray) and the Bolshevik *Pravda* (Truth). In 1914 an investigation by the International Socialist Bureau of the Second International determined that the weekly circulation of *Pravda* was 240,000, as opposed to 96,000 for *Luch*.[8]

Some historians have argued that in 1913 "Lenin overplayed his hand" when the "Bolshevik six" deputies in the Duma separated publicly from the "Menshevik seven." According to Leonard Schapiro, "it caused a profound shock . . . and many of the workers were bewildered and outraged." He adds that "the circulation of *Pravda* had fallen dramatically under the impact of the split in the Duma fraction," citing reports of late 1913 and early 1914 indicating a decline in circulation from 40,000 daily to 20,000 or 25,000.[9] There are two major problems with this inter-

pretation—what it fails to say about *Pravda* and what it fails to say about the Bol-
shevik/Menshevik split in the Duma fraction. When we examine such issues, the
truth comes close to being the opposite of Schapiro's assertions.

The circulation of *Pravda* fluctuated from one point to another. It began with
a daily readership of 60,000. This may have been in part because unity-minded
workers appreciated the attitude expressed in its first editorial (written by Stalin)
that "*Pravda* will call, first and foremost, for unity in the proletarian class struggle,
for unity at all costs." Yet the daily circulation soon fell to 20,000. Lenin, who had
been frustrated by the conciliatory tone of the paper, warned that the fall in circulation was related to the tone: "You complain about monotony. . . . By avoiding
'painful questions,' *Pravda* and *Zvezda* [another Bolshevik publication] *make themselves* dry, monotonous, uninteresting, uncombative organs. A socialist organ *must*
conduct polemics." In a later letter he added: "You will spoil everything and provoke
protests from the workers *on the left*, if you keep silent about this. The Liquidators
must be rebuffed." At the beginning of 1913, the central committee determined
that *Pravda* was "insufficiently firm in its party spirit" and initiated a reorganization
of the paper under the capable leadership of Iakov Sverdlov. Although Sverdlov
was soon arrested, the orientation changed significantly. With a more combative
tone, the daily circulation rose to 32,000.[10]

By the late summer, however, a Bolshevik named Chernomazov assumed editorial responsibilities. Chernomazov utilized dictatorial methods within the *Pravda*
staff and insisted on printing such provocative material in the paper that the tsarist
Press Commission often closed down its offices and confiscated an increasing number of issues. From July through September, 80 percent of the issues were seized
by the tsarist censor. Because of its irregular appearance, *Pravda's* circulation fell
to 18,000 in the autumn of 1913. Lenin urged the editor that "it is necessary to
strive for legality, to be able to pass the censor. This can and must be achieved. Otherwise you are destroying, for no purpose at all, the work you have undertaken."
But Chernomazov paid no heed, because—as it later turned out—he was in the
pay of tsarist secret police. Nor was he the only police agent in the Bolsheviks'
higher circles; the most infamous was Roman Malinovsky, a union leader and Bolshevik deputy in the Duma. While able to do considerable damage, however, such
agents were never able to overcome the capacity of the Bolshevik organization to
generate "anti-bodies" within itself to counter the infection of provocateurs.[11]

By early 1914 Chernomazov was removed through the democratic decision
of his comrades and replaced by one of the most experienced Bolshevik publicists,
Lev Kamenev. Under Kamenev's experienced hand, the number of permanent
subscribers doubled, the daily circulation rose to 40,000 (and then to 130,000 for

Pravda's second anniversary), while the Mensheviks' *Luch* averaged only 16,000 in the same period. Ralph Elwood sums it up in this way: "The paper had acquired a national audience, being distributed to some 9444 cities in Imperial Russia. Its columns about workers' problems and interests undoubtedly gave a sense of class identity and solidarity to its readers. Its accounts of economic abuses and of successful strikes helped spread social and economic unrest. By constantly harping on the correctness of the six Bolshevik Duma deputies and championing Bolshevik candidates in trade union and insurance elections, it promoted factional identification which had been conspicuously absent before 1912. *Pravda*, for all its difficulties, provided a degree of political coordination and leadership that had been lacking since 1905. . . . As a result of two and a half years' work, the majority of the Social Democratic workers in Russia now apparently identified themselves as *Pravda*ists."[12]

If it was affected at all, this situation seems to have been *enhanced* by the split in the Duma fraction. The Bolshevik deputy Badayev later pointed out about the period leading up to this rupture: "With every month that passed it became more clear that the unity of the Social-Democratic fraction was only a formal unity, and that it was bound to collapse sooner or later. . . . The Bolshevik and Menshevik deputies, while formally bound by the existence of a united fraction, were in daily conflict on a whole series of questions concerning the revolutionary movement. The divergences between the Bolshevik 'six' and the Menshevik 'seven' were rooted in the very conception of the course of the Russian revolution." The Mensheviks attempted to use their one-vote majority to hobble their Bolshevik rivals in the Duma fraction. Finally, in the autumn of 1913, the Bolshevik deputies issued an open ultimatum, explaining their situation to the readers of *Pravda* and demanding of the Menshevik deputies that all disagreements between the two components of the Duma fraction be worked out on the basis of consensus. The split occurred when the Mensheviks rejected this demand. An intense discussion within the working class was generated by these events and by the ensuing polemics. Not surprisingly, significant numbers of workers were dismayed by the split. But—again, not surprisingly—many workers were inclined to defend the actions of the Bolshevik deputies who represented their districts. (Even Plekhanov was moved to comment that "the differences of opinion which have existed within the Russian Social Democratic Labor Party during the last few years have now led to the division of our Duma fraction into two competing groups. This split occurred as the result of certain regrettable decisions taken by our Liquidationist comrades, who chanced to be in a majority of seven against six.") According to Badayev, "During their struggle against the seven deputies, the Bolsheviks had carried new positions

and considerably widened and deepened their influence among the workers. . . .
The split in the fraction and the creation of an independent Bolshevik fraction was
discussed by thousands of workers, who until then had no clear notion of the
essence of the Party differences and, inclined towards the Menshevik-Liquidators,
joined the Bolsheviks as the result of the information gained during this period."[13]

Alexander Shlyapnikov has offered a similar description of this period: "The
spring and summer of 1914 was the high point of our party's struggle against liquidationism. The polemics between *Pravda* and *Luch* had developed such acrimony
that workers at the grass roots from both warring factions began to talk of the need
for some control over their papers. A gathering of serious-minded workers from
Ericsson and Lessner factories was held in the allotment nearest the works, where
we started a discussion not about the tone but about the essence of the differences,
and the '*Pravda*-ites' did not have much difficulty in demonstrating to the 'Menshevik' workers the whole hypocrisy of the '*Luch*-ites', the liquidators of the party's
revolutionary traditions, who had clad themselves in the shining armor of the 'unity
of the workers' party.'"[14]

By early 1914, the Menshevik deputy Chkhenkeli complained that the Menshevik fraction "had lost all influence, deserted the political life of the country, broken its connections with the workers and finally forced the most active members
to leave the fraction and consequently brought the work of the fraction to a standstill." Another of the Menshevik deputies, Tulyakov, offered a similar judgment:
"The fraction calls itself Social-Democratic but it does not reflect the life and aspirations of the workers either in the State Duma or in the press. The fraction has,
for political, police and ethical considerations, abandoned the workers and landed
itself in a state of 'splended isolation.'" Shortly afterward, one of the deputies left
the Menshevik fraction to adopt an independent position midway between the
Bolsheviks and Mensheviks; in addition, the Mensheviks felt compelled to expel
another deputy from the fraction because he was taking positions that were too
right-wing. "Thus while the Mensheviks disintegrated and lost the confidence of
the workers," Badayev later reminisced, "the influence of our 'six' increased and we
were enthusiastically supported by the revolutionary proletariat."[15]

This interpretation of growing working-class support for *Pravda* and for the
distinct Bolshevik fraction in the Duma is corroborated by other information we
have on shifts taking place in the political consciousness of the Russian workers. A
report of the tsarist police, whose spies honeycombed the workers' movement, noted
that "the most energetic and audacious element, ready for tireless struggle, for resistance and continual organization, is that element, those organizations, and those
people who are concentrated around Lenin." This energetic core proved to be an

intense pole of attraction for masses of workers in the period after 1911, when there was, as Trotsky put it, a "healing of the psychological wounds of defeat."[16] Shifts within the legal labor movement demonstrated a decisive tilt from Menshevism to Bolshevism among the most active elements within the working class.

Most dramatic was the loss in 1913 and 1914 of Menshevik control of the trade unions (with some exceptions, such as in the printers and railway workers unions) and the labor insurance movement, which the Mensheviks had initiated, to the Bolsheviks. By the summer of 1914, the Bolsheviks controlled fourteen and one-half out of eighteen governing boards of trade unions in Petersburg and ten out of thirteen in Moscow. Martov wrote to Potresov in the autumn of 1913: "I am dejected by the story of the Unions of Metalworkers which exposes our weakness even more than we are used to. It is altogether likely that in the course of this season our positions in Petersburg will be squeezed back even further. But that is not what is awful. What is worse is that from an organizational point of view, Menshevism—despite the newspaper, despite everything that has been done for the past two years—remains a weak little circle."[17]

The Menshevik explanation of this development is interesting. According to one prominent liquidator, the Bolsheviks were appealing to the newly arrived influx of ex-peasants who had not yet adjusted to the factory environment and urban life, and who were therefore "driven by instincts and feelings rather than consciousness and calculation." The rebelliousness of these new workers was creating a militancy that had little patience for partial reforms and introduced a "disorganized, primitive, elemental character" into working-class life. Martov wrote of "the swilling mixture of anarchist and syndicalist tendencies with remnants of peasants urges and utopias" among the new workers, adding that "as they face the hardships, the darkness of city life, they hold onto their dream of returning to a patch of land with their cow and chickens . . . and they respond to the slogans of those who promise them the fulfillment of this dream." Therefore—in the words of Theodore Bulkin, a Menshevik "practical" who had been voted off of the Metalworkers' Union governing board—"the masses which have recently been drawn into the trade union movement are incapable of appreciating its great significance for the proletariat. Led by the Bolsheviks, they have chased the Liquidators, those valuable workers, out of all leading institutions. . . . Bolshevism—*intelligenskii*, narrowly factional, Jacobin—has found its support in the masses' state of mind."[18]

Many anti-Leninist scholars have utilized this interpretation to explain the Bolshevik success not only in the pre-World War I period, but also in 1917. Recent scholarship has conclusively established, however, that the Menshevik interpretation was as faulty as the Mensheviks' general orientation. In saying this, we should acknowledge an element of truth in the Menshevik perception. The period of 1912–1914 saw a great new surge of industrialization, during which thousands of the rural poor were continually flooding into the labor force of Petersburg and Moscow. Between January 1910 and July 1914, the industrial work force had risen from 1,793,000 to 2,400,000—an increase of more than 30 percent. Victoria Bonnell comments that "these new workers, concentrated in some of the largest Petersburg and Moscow factories, rarely joined the trade unions, which recruited mainly experienced, skilled, and urbanized workers." This fact punctures the Menshevik rationalization. Only members of a union could vote for a replacement of Mensheviks with Bolsheviks on the union's governing board. On the other hand, this was a period of dramatically increased strike activity, and for a strike to be successfully conducted (and as militant as those of Russia in 1912–1914), nonunion workers must be actively involved. Bonnell points out that "the young volatile workers did contribute to the general atmosphere of 'elemental rebelliousness.' The mixture of militance and desperation that characterized the work stoppages in this period affected the environment in which unions recruited their membership and the way in which organized workers responded to political appeals." Reginald Zelnik adds that the consciousness of "the typical worker" may best be characterized "as a uniquely volatile and dynamic *mixed* consciousness that combined peasant resentment against the vestiges of Russian 'feudalism' (i.e. serfdom) with a proletarian resentment against capitalist exploitation in the factories." This may be an overgeneralization, however, if there is any truth to Leopold Haimson's reference to the "unskilled workers who have just come . . . from the countryside to try to make some quick money, and not get into trouble."[19] In either case, the Menshevik rationalization does not hold up. Nor is it in harmony with what is known about the social composition of Bolshevism at this time.

The Bolshevik party was not simply a fusion of elitist intellectuals and inexperienced workers. Haimson records that despite waves of arrests that ravaged the Bolshevik organizations in this period, "the Bolshevik Party apparatus managed to survive, to retain some old and recruit some new members: younger workers, but also older workers, with a background of participation in the revolutionary underground, who in many cases had left the party during the years of reaction but were now returning to the fold. . . ." Statistics on the Moscow Bolsheviks indicate that about 60 percent were workers, that over 49 percent of their leadership cadres were also workers, and that the overwhelming majority of these were either second-generation workers or urbanized and proletarianized first-generation workers. Also significant was the fact that they included substantial percentages of general industrial workers and textile workers, as well as more skilled metalworkers and printers. Haimson summarizes: "The Bolshevik Party cadres were now able to play a significant catalytic role. They succeeded . . . in chasing the Menshevik 'Liquidators' out of the existing open labor organizations. They transformed these organizations into 'fronts' through which they managed to absorb, if not control, the young workers who headed the Petersburg strike movement. Through the pages of *Pravda*, through the verbal appeals of their deputies in the Duma, by leaflet and by word of mouth, they managed to stir up and exploit the workers' embittered mood. Thus, it seems fair to say that by the outbreak of war [August 1914] the Bolshevik center in Petersburg, and particularly its open organizations, had developed an organism whose arms, while still very slender and vulnerable, were beginning to extend into many corners of the life of the working class."[20]

2. The Upsurge

We should give more attention to the questions of *why* and *how* the Bolsheviks were able to establish such authority among the Russian working class as a whole, from the most inexperienced militants to the most mature stalwarts.

The question of why has to do with two interrelated realities that characterized the Russian scene in this period: the inherent repressiveness of the tsarist order, and the rightward shift of the bourgeoisie. One liberal writer warned in 1906 that the political inflexibility of the major sectors of the bourgeoisie and their support for tsarist repression as a bulwark against working-class militancy would "teach the workers that the workers would only obtain what they grabbed by force, that is, they were being taught to seize power, and this is penetrating to the very heart of the broad masses." The following years saw a deepening of the polarization between workers and the members of educated, privileged society. This polarization was greatly intensified by government and employer labor policies that allowed only limited trade union rights, policies marked by systematic harassment and periodic repression designed to prevent workers from using the legal unions to function in a manner that would result in tangible benefits. "Trade unionists were faced with an unprecedented situation," writes Victoria Bonnell, "On the one hand, they had acquired the opportunity to establish legal mass-membership organizations. On the other hand, they were prevented from expanding the size and scope of these organizations and exercising their major functions, such as collective bargaining." She observes that "organized workers grew enraged at their inability to achieve redress for their grievances, their militance was fortified by an appreciation of the potential for collective action, while their indignation was fueled by violations of what they conceived to be their moral and legal rights." Little wonder that there was an evaporation of "their willingness to pursue a gradualist approach," which had been advocated by the Menshevik liquidators. The militancy of the "spontaneous" legal labor movement, the movement the Mensheviks had counted on to supersede the old revolutionary underground, was increasingly directed against all existing authority, including the liberal bourgeois elements whom the Mensheviks hoped would provide leadership in the democratic struggle to overthrow tsarism. "While the Mensheviks reacted helplessly to this fundamental challenge to their faith in the orderly pattern of spontaneity," writes Reginald Zelnik, "it was the Bolsheviks who, unfettered by any sentimental vision of the Party's dissolving itself in the spontaneous labor movement, exploited their position of independence with the utmost flexibility."[21]

Leopold Haimson has also remarked on the Bolsheviks' flexibility in this period, their ability "to strike a note of militance, and yet seemingly a note of realism; to appeal to anger, and also to make its expression appear eminently reasonable, if not practical. And it is because of this multiplicity of the notes they strike, and the varying ways in which they harmonize them, that Bolshevik propaganda and agitation prove so successful by the eve of the war, not only among the explosive strata of the Petersburg working class, but also among the 'less advanced' workers of the more isolated industrial towns and villages." Haimson's elaboration on this point brings to mind the Bolsheviks' fierce internal polemics of the period leading up to 1912, polemics that resulted in a cohesive organization based on a clear revolutionary program: "By 1914 the Bolshevik platform variously offers the workers the promise of the eventual overthrow of the bourgeoisie and establishment of a proletarian dictatorship; the more ambiguous, if less distant, promise of the establishment of a 'firm democratic regime,' in which the masses of workers and peasants will already hold the upper hand over the privileged elements of 'census' society; and most literally the political objective of a democratic republic, under which the workers will gain civic and political rights equal to those of more privileged elements, as well as a better opportunity to pursue their struggle against their employers. Even more strikingly, Bolshevik slogans emphasize the need for workers to unite, not only in pursuit of these (varyingly distant) political objectives, but also to achieve more immediate improvements in their lives. And even the definition of these ostensibly more tangible objectives, particularly in the workers' economic struggle with their employers, are subtly adjusted to the differences in the mood and expectations of the various working class groups to which they are presented."[22]

Without an uncompromising dual struggle against the ultraleft and the liquidators, without an uncompromising struggle against the conciliators who sought to maintain a "unified" party with such profoundly divergent forces, without an independent party based on the Bolshevik program, the Bolsheviks could not have functioned as effectively as historians and contemporaries have reported they did.

One key sector of the working class to which the Bolsheviks began to give special attention in this period were women workers, who made up roughly one-third of the labor force. While both factions of the RSDLP had always formally adhered to the Marxist position favoring equal rights for women, many of the male party members, imbued with the patriarchal attitudes of their culture, did not see women as equals in their daily lives, let alone in the class struggle. Even leading Bolsheviks (male and female) were suspicious of feminism as a bourgeois current that would blunt class consciousness, and they initially resisted the idea of setting up special organizations for working women. Some of these had been created, however, as early as 1909. At the Fifth Congress of the RSDLP (1907), fifteen of the female delegates were Bolsheviks and four were Mensheviks. On the other hand, no female delegates were elected to the Prague conference of 1912 that established the Bolshevik party. This reflected a situation the Bolsheviks evidently hoped to reverse. *Pravda* began a special women's section in 1913. In that same year, the Bolsheviks began publishing the journal *Rabotnitsa* (Working Woman), which, according to historian Anne Bobroff, carried articles embracing "a wide range of women's concerns: maternity insurance, female labor (including a demand for female factory inspectors), child care centers, hygiene information, the problems of working women and the family, children's stories, Women's Day, electoral rights for women." The journal explained its position in its first issue: "The 'women's question' for working men and women—this question is about how to involve the backward masses of working women in organization, how better to make clear to them their interests, how to make them comrades in the common struggle quickly. The solidarity between working men and women, the common cause, the common goals, and the common path to those goals. Such is the settlement of the 'women's' question in the workers' midst." Even this position, however, was secured only after some years of resistance in the ranks and among the leadership of both Bolsheviks and Mensheviks. "Much passive resistance," reminisced Alexandra Kollontai, "little understanding, and even less interest for this aim, over and over again, lay as an obstacle in the path. It was not until 1914, shortly after the outbreak of the World War, that finally both factions—the Mensheviks and the Bolsheviks—took up the question in an earnest and practical way...." While even the Bolsheviks' improved understanding of women's liberation may seem limited by present-day standards, it represented a major advance in the context of tsarist Russia and had a significant impact among women workers awakening to political consciousness.[23]

In this and in other important ways, the Bolsheviks sought to spread, broaden, and deepen what Iu. I. Kir'ianov has aptly referred to as a "new proletarian morality," a phenomenon that Leopold Haimson has also vividly described in his discussion of the intensifying revolutionary working-class consciousness of this period. Such consciousness was hardly an alien worldview that was somehow inserted into working-class heads by Bolshevik propagandists. It was latent within large numbers of workers and was already developing under the impact of experience—to some extent it was the accumulated and shared experience of many years, to some extent it was recent experience laden with new shocks and revelations (for example, the massacre of protesting workers in the Lena goldfields, which set off a massive strike wave in 1912). But the educational and agitational efforts of the Bolsheviks drew this consciousness out in a way that added new dimensions and gave it a new edge. Haimson makes this point in the following way: "If Petersburg workers displayed greater revolutionary explosiveness, and especially greater responsiveness to Bolshevik appeals, than the workers of Donbas, it was undoubtedly in part because of the Petersburg workers' greater exposure to Bolshevik propaganda and agitation. Similarly, if the workers in the metalworking industry were so much more agitated politically than the workers in other industries, it was partly because the labor force in the metalworking industry consisted of a peculiar combination of skilled and unskilled, experienced and inexperienced workers—the older and more skilled workers contributing in their contacts with the young and unskilled a long-standing exposure to revolutionary, and specifically Bolshevik, indoctrination."[24]

There was nothing mechanistic or alien about such "revolutionary indoctrination" among the workers. It was not a case of the central committee's handing down directives that were parroted by platoons of glib agitators to gullible masses. The dynamic within the factories was described this way in the memoirs of a conscious worker who belonged to the Socialist Revolutionary party, V. Buzinov: "There were few socialist workers [party members] and they were supported by the conscious workers. The latter were ten times more numerous as the socialists. . . . Each was, in a way, 'juridically reasoning individual' capable of understanding all that surrounded him." This is worth noting—the worker-Bolshevik functioned in a milieu in which respect and authority were not guaranteed but instead would have to be earned. At the very least, his or her articulation of the party program and positions would have to make sense to experienced and critical-minded "conscious workers," whose support would be crucial in gaining a general and sympathetic hearing. Buzinov continues: "They all, to a greater or lesser degree, understood the situation of the workers and their relations with the factory owners. Life itself transformed them into the vanguard of the worker masses. Their native keen wit and worker sensitivity did not fail them when they exposed the hidden ends behind this or that maneuver of management. And they were no longer silent. Somehow in their midst, a special type of agitator was created, a man always hammering away at the same point—I would say—of class isolation from the exploiters. In the persons of these agitators life had hammered a wedge between workers and owners that no party agitator, not so closely tied to the masses as they, could have done. . . . This self-made agitator spoke of that which each worker had in his head but, being less developed, was unable to verbalize. After each of his words, the workers would exclaim: 'That's it! That's just what I wanted to say!'"[25]

This has important implications for the functioning of the revolutionary party. To be effective in such a context, a party member would have to develop a capacity to think critically, to show initiative, to act independently in a complex and volatile situation. The basic framework and priorities for party activity might be established by a party congress and overseen by a central committee, and special campaigns could be initiated and coordinated on a national level. But such a party could not thrive if its members did not have the confidence to speak up and show leadership in the swirl of radicalization and spontaneous action, without feeling a compulsion to obtain prior approval or instructions from some central authority. As Trotsky later commented, "the will to struggle is not stored up in advance, and is not dictated from above—it has on every occasion to be independently renewed and tempered." More than this, "a Bolshevik is not merely a disciplined person; he is a person who in each case and on each question forges a firm opinion of his own and defends it courageously and independently, not only against his enemies, but inside his own party."[26]

As this statement implies, in some situations the party ranks were most sensitive to shifts in moods and struggles of the working class and were sometimes compelled to interpret and carry out party policies in new ways while at the same time internally challenging and attempting to correct less-informed judgments of party leaders. (We will see a striking example of this in 1917.) Such divergences would have to be resolved through further discussion and the test of events, not through the imposition of mechanical discipline and expulsions. The cadres of worker-Bolsheviks were tempered by the experience of learning and growing and proving themselves in the living class struggle.

The role and temperament of revolutionary youths were certainly an important component of Bolshevism's internal chemistry. Although there had been efforts to create a Social Democratic youth group by such Bolshevik students as Bukharin and Sokolinkov in 1907, they did not survive tsarist repression and were not repeated before 1917. Nonetheless, Krupskaya's views on youth organizations, summarized by historian Pierre Broué, have relevance: "Lenin's companion in fact hoped to see an organization of young revolutionaries directed by the youths themselves, that could risk committing its own errors, which she saw as preferable to seeing it strangled under the tutelage of well-intentioned 'adults.'"[27] As it turned out, however, young revolutionaries actually were assimilated into Bolshevism's "iron guard" of professional revolutionaries. Broue's discussion of this point is interesting:

> A Mikhail Tomsky, lithographer, who enters the party at twenty-five years of age, is an exceptional figure, despite his earlier years passed as a non-party fighter. At his age, in fact, the majority of the others have behind them years of political militancy. The student Piatakov, son of a great bourgeois family in the Ukraine, becomes a Bolshevik at twenty, previously having been an anarchist militant. The student Rosenfeld, whose party name was Kamenev, is nineteen when he joins, as is the metalworker Schmidt and the skilled mechanic I. N. Smirnov. It is at the age of eighteen that there enter into the party the metalworker Bakaiev, the students Bukharin and Krestinski, the shoemaker Kaganovitch. The clerk Zinoviev, the metalworkers Serebriakov and Lutovinov are Bolsheviks at seventeen. Sverdlov works in a pharmacists' shop when he enters the struggle at sixteen, as does the student Kuibyshev. The shoemaker Drobnis and the student Smilga enter the party at fifteen and Piatnitski at fourteen. These young men haven't left the age of adolescence when they are already old militants and cadres. Sverdlov, at the age of seventeen, directs the Social Democratic organization in Sormovo, and the tsarist police look for him under the nickname "Tiny." Sokolnikov is eighteen when he is secretary of one of the Moscow districts. Rykov is twenty-four when, as a spokesman for the "committeemen," he enters the Central Committee in London [at the conference of 1905]. Zinoviev is already known as a leading Petersburg Bolshevik and writer for *Proletary* when at the age of twenty-four he begins his residence on the Central Committee. Kamenev is twenty-two when he is a delegate to London, Sverdlov twenty at the Tammerfours conference [1906]. Serebriakov is the organizer and one of the delegates of the Russian underground organizations, at the age of twenty, at the Prague conference of 1912.[28]

It is hardly the case that the Bolsheviks or their working-class base were exclusively young, but the fact that young revolutionaries were so integrated into the Bolshevik organization was a special advantage as the party related to the working-class upsurge in which young workers were such a vital component.

The dramatic rise in working-class militancy and radicalization on the eve of World War I resulted in "an unprecedented swell of both political and economic strikes" that was comparable to the revolutionary upsurge of 1905. Haimson writes: "By the beginning of the summer of 1914, contemporary descriptions of the labor scene forcibly suggest, the workers, especially in Petersburg, were displaying a growing spirit of *buntarstvo*—of violent if still diffuse opposition to all authority—and an instinctive sense of class solidarity, as they encountered the repressive measures of state power and what appeared to them the indifference of privileged society."[29] The seasoned worker-Bolshevik Alexander Shlyapnikov describes this ferment in a manner that also illuminates the Bolshevik orientation of combining legal with illegal work:

> Propaganda was done in the plants and shops on an individual basis. There were also discussion circles, but they were joined only by the most conscious workers. Legal meetings took place on matters concerning the insurance funds, but this activity was skillfully integrated into the general struggle for the liberation of the working class. Illegal meetings were arranged fairly often in the plants during the summer of my stay in Petersburg. This was usually done on the spur of the moment but in an organized way, during the lunch or evening break in front of the exit, in the yard or, in establishments with several floors, on the stairs. The most alert workers would form a 'plug' in the doorway, and the whole mass piled up in the exit. An agitator would get up right there on the spot. Management would contact the police on the telephone, but the speeches would have already been made and the necessary decision taken by the time they arrived. Frequently clashes with the police would ensue, in which the latter would put its "herrings" [clubs] into action and the workers nuts and cobblestones. Mass rallies took place all round Petersburg. The Vyborg district gathered mainly at Ozerki, Shuvalov and Grazhdanka. Holidays brought crowds of visitors to these villages on the outskirts. This made it easier for workers to get to the mass meetings.
>
> In the spring of 1914 the atmosphere in the factory districts was tense in the extreme. Every conflict, small or large, irrespective of its origin, provoked a protest strike or walk-out. Political meetings and skirmishes with the police were everyday occurrences. The workers began to make contacts among the soldiers at the nearby barracks. Revolutionary propaganda was also carried out in the army camps. An extremely active part in propaganda work was taken by women workers, the weavers and mill-girls: some of the soldiers were from the same villages as the women workers, but for the most part the young people came together on the basis of "interests of the heart", and thus kinship relations were established between barracks and factory. It was totally impossible to turn such troops against the workers.[30]

Some historians have suggested that in this period, all the elements of a revolutionary situation were beginning to take shape—a rising crescendo of working-class consciousness and militant activity, a sharpening polarization between the working class and the forces of the bourgeois-tsarist order, and growing malaise and divisions within "respectable" society itself. This is a particularly important question, given the common view that only the devastation of World War I could have shaken the tsarist order sufficiently to allow a revolution. Leopold Haimson has argued, to the contrary, that "what the war years would do was not to conceive, but to accelerate substantially, the two broad forces of polarization that had already been at work in Russian national life during the immediate prewar period." He suggests "a set of hypothetical circumstances under which Russia might have undergone—even in the absence of the specific strains induced by the war, though maybe under the immediate stimulus of some other, purely domestic crisis—the kind of radical overturn on which Lenin was already gambling by late 1913—early 1914 and which Russia actually experienced with the October Revolution."[31]

If this revolution actually erupted, it would differ from that of 1905 in many ways. The working class now had many fewer illusions, a considerably greater amount of experience, a higher level of organization, a more revolutionary consciousness. Also the Bolsheviks themselves were far more numerous, experienced, influential, and rooted in the working class. At the same time, there was a danger that the spontaneous upsurge could rapidly overwhelm the revolutionary and working-class organizations and yet be too diffuse, that the moment of the revolutionary "final conflict" would come too soon, that the revolutionary forces—insufficiently prepared, as in 1905—would be crushed by the still-considerable repressive forces of a desperate autocracy. Lenin's concern about this possibility is reflected in a report of the tsarist secret police regarding one of his communications with a Bolshevik deputy to the Duma in April 1914.

Defining the state of affairs at the present moment, Lenin expressed himself as follows:

> Our victory, i.e., the victory of revolutionary Marxism, is great. The press, the insurance campaign, the trade unions, and the societies of the enlightenment [worker's clubs], all this is ours. But this victory has its limits. . . . If we want to hold our positions and not allow the strengthening labor movement to escape the party's sway and strike out in an archaic, diffuse movement, of which there are some signs, we must strengthen, come what may, our underground organizations. [We] can give up a portion of the work in the State Duma which we have conducted so successfully to date, but it is imperative that we put to right the work outside the Duma.[32]

Three months later, however, international events profoundly altered the situation, when the First World War began.

10. Party and War

The outbreak of the First World War, in August 1914, disrupted the combined revolutionary and Bolshevik upswing in Russia. It also provided a new and severe test for all revolutionary currents in that country throughout the world. The result was both the devastation and the transformation of the international socialist movement, generating a revolution within Marxism of which Lenin became the foremost proponent. Out of this upheaval came the Bolshevik Revolution, which became the inspiring beacon for those who would change the world.

Some writers have overstated the theoretical shifts entailed by this revolution within Marxism. The young Antonio Gramsci, the "early" Georg Lukacs, Karl Korsch, and others identified as "praxis theorists" or "Western Marxists" were inclined to invoke Lenin's authority to justify their own innovative (often idealist and voluntaristic) reinterpretations of Marxism. Perhaps the most extreme example was Gramsci's suggestion that "the Bolshevik Revolution ... is the revolution against Karl Marx's *Capital*.... Events have exploded the critical schema determining how the history of Russia would unfold according to the canons of historical materialism." Although they soon became aware that this distorted Lenin's Marxism (offering initial formulations in some ways closer to the Bolshevism of Bogdanov than to that of Lenin), later writers have been influenced by their early views.[1] Some have seen almost an "epistemological break" in 1914 that divides Lenin's thought more fundamentally than he himself would have accepted. It has even been argued recently, by the late Steve Zeluck, that the Leninist conception of the party came into existence only with World War I, which yielded Lenin's "theory of monopoly capital, imperialism, and the presumed theory of a labor aristocracy." Zeluck asserts that only then was "the theoretical basis ... laid for Lenin to emerge from his Kautskian shell both politically and organizationally, and break with the Mensheviks of all varieties and nationalities on principle."[2] As we have seen in previous chapters, this is not the case. At least for Russia itself, the essential components of the Leninist party had become fully developed theoretically in the years 1903 to 1914.

Nonetheless, in the 1914–1917 period Lenin's thinking underwent a profound reorientation. The eruption of World War I and the collapse of the Second International forced him to deepen his understanding of Marxism in order to develop a better analysis of capitalist reality and a more sharply focused revolutionary strategy. In his *Philosophical Notebooks* he labored to attain a surer grasp of the dialectical philosophy of Hegel, which had been an essential source of the Marxist method. He developed a critique of the vulgarization of Marxist theory and the abandonment of revolutionary politics that had come to characterize the "orthodox" center of the Second International. He found it necessary to study more closely new trends in the world economy, producing *Imperialism, the Highest Stage of Capitalism*. Related to this, he sharpened his understanding of nationalism and produced a more advanced Marxist approach to this thorny question. And he pioneered in the development of a deeper comprehension of the Marxist theory of the state and of revolutionary strategic and tactical perspectives, which was reflected in his classic *The State and Revolution* and in a wealth of other writings during 1917 that—among other results—advanced the working-class socialist revolution in Russia as an immediate goal.[3]

We should not make the mistake of assuming that the ideas, analyses, and perspectives of Lenin simply were translated into Bolshevik policy or even reflected the theoretical understanding of a majority of the Bolsheviks. Yet the Bolshevik party was certainly altered by the experience of the war. One of the most important developments was a heightening of the revolutionary internationalism that, while always a component of Bolshevism, took on greater meaning and assumed a more dynamic function in the Bolshevik program. Given the profound repercussions of this development, it will make sense for us to give it significant attention. As we will see in this chapter, it was not simply a product of Lenin's thought, but was part of a broader internationalist revitalization taking place in the leftwing of the world socialist movement. After examining this revitalization, we will take up the question of whether or not there was a fatal illusion built into this vibrant internationalism that became so crucial to Bolshevik perspectives. Finally, we will turn our attention to how the Bolshevik organization functioned in this complex and stressful period, touching both on the role it played in the larger Russian and world movements and also on its internal functioning inside and outside of Russia.

The wartime evolution and experience of Lenin's party, in the realms of program and organization and class-party interaction, were a vital prelude preparing it for the great events of 1917.

1. Revolutionary Internationalism

We have seen that the Bolshevik program was grounded in a revolutionary-internationalist orientation. The Bolsheviks were loyal and committed partisans of the Second International, looking for inspiration especially to the German Social Democratic party—particularly to what they considered its "orthodox Marxist" majority, represented theoretically by Karl Kautsky. They consistently sought to learn from and contribute to the theoretical and practical work of this world federation of working-class socialist organizations, embracing close to 25 million workers. The Bolsheviks found nothing abstract about this internationalism, because they were convinced that the struggle of workers in other countries would strengthen the revolutionary movement in Russia and that advances of the Russian workers' movement would bring closer the possibilities of socialist revolution in the West. It was their conviction in 1905 that the overthrow of tsarism through a working-class upsurge with peasant support could lead to a similar upsurge in Western and Central Europe that would overturn capitalism; that Western revolution would then be decisive both for the thoroughgoing triumph of Russia's own bourgeois-democratic revolution and for a relatively rapid transition to socialist revolution in Russia. Since capitalism was an international system, the dynamics of class oppression and proletarian insurgency were also international; the struggle to overthrow it would therefore have to unfold on a world scale, and socialism could come into being only as a world system.

Beginning in the latter part of the nineteenth century, tensions began to increase among capitalist nations, generated by the competition for world markets and raw materials and by the national drive of capitalist economies to expand and seek new investment opportunities in other countries. There was a marked increase in militarism and national chauvinism, in new alliances and counteralliances among the most powerful nations. The possibility of a destructive world war began to loom over Europe.

From the center to the left end of opinion in the Second International, there tended to be a general consensus around the remarks Frederick Engels had made in 1892: "No Socialist of whatever nationality can wish the triumph of the present German Government in the war, nor that of the bourgeois French Republic, and least of all that of the Tsar, which would be equivalent to the subjection of Europe, and therefore the Socialists of all countries are for peace. But if it comes to war nonetheless, just one thing is certain—this war in which fifteen or twenty million men will slaughter one another, and all Europe will be laid to waste as never before—this war must either bring the immediate victory of Socialism, or it must upset the old order of things from head to foot and leave such heaps of ruins behind that the old capitalistic society will be more impossible than ever, and the social revolution, though put off until ten of fifteen years later, will surely conquer after that time all the more rapidly and all the more thoroughly."[4]

August Bebel, the aging leader of the German Social Democrats, commented at the 1907 Congress of the Second International, "We do not wish for such a dreadful means of reaching our goals. However, if those who have the greatest stake in maintaining bourgeois society cannot perceive that such a war would uproot it, then we cannot object. Then I say; 'Just keep right at it, we shall be your heirs.' If the ruling class had not known this, we would long ago have had a Europe-wide war. Only the fear of Social Democracy has prevented it so far. If such a war breaks out, then much more will be at stake than mere trifles like insurrection and mass strike. Then the entire civilized world will change, from the ground up. . . . Never before in the history of the civilized world has a movement embraced the masses as profoundly as does the Socialist movement. Never before has a movement given the despised masses such an insight into the nature of our society. Never have there been so many who knew what they wanted from the state and society. Let us keep our eyes open and our heads clear, so that we are prepared for the moment, when it comes."[5]

At this same congress, a manifesto was adopted (including key amendments submitted collectively by Lenin, Martov, and Rosa Luxemburg) that concluded: "If a war threatens to break out, it is the duty of the working classes and their parliamentary representatives in the countries involved, supported by the coordinating activity of the International Socialist Bureau, to exert every effort in order to prevent its outbreak. . . . In case war should break out anyway, it is their duty to intervene for its speedy termination and to strive with all their power to utilize the economic and political crisis created by the war to rouse the masses and thereby hasten the downfall of capitalist rule."[6]

Nevertheless, serious differences remained, dividing revolutionary socialists from those inclined toward reformism, and there were also differences dividing those adhering to a revolutionary standpoint. The resulting debates contributed substantially to the enrichment of the Bolshevik program.

By and large, the reformists in the Second International favored imperialism. Hendrick van Kol of the Netherlands argued that without capitalist expansion into the colonized areas of Asia and Africa, "the native peoples there would today still be living in the most backward social conditions." Eduard Bernstein asserted: "We must get away from the utopian notion of simply abandoning the colonies. . . . The colonies are there; we must come to terms with that. Socialists too should acknowledge the need for civilized peoples to act somewhat like guardians of the uncivilized. . . . Our economies are based, in large measure, on the extraction from the colonies of products that the native peoples had no idea how to use." Another right-wing German Social Democrat, Eduard David, similarly warned against the demand "to abolish colonies as such, [because] it would mean giving them back to their native peoples. What then would occur in the colonies? They would not experience humane rule but a return to barbarism. . . . The colonies as well must go through a stage of capitalist development. There too you cannot simply leap from savagery to socialism. Nowhere is humanity spared the painful passage through capitalism. The scientific outlook of Karl Marx makes very clear that this stage is a precondition for the socialist organization of society."[7]

Lenin's view was that colonialism represented "the downright enslavement of primitive populations. The bourgeoisie was actually introducing slavery in the colonies and subjecting the native populations to unprecedented outrages and acts of violence, 'civilizing' them by the spread of liquor and syphilis."[8] Rosa Luxemburg also took a dim view of capitalism's "civilizing mission," expressing herself in terms that continue to illuminate:

> Capitalist desire for imperialist expansion, as the expression of its highest maturity in the last period of its life, has the tendency to change the whole world into capitalistically producing nations, to sweep away all superannuated, precapitalistic methods of production and society, to subjugate all the riches of the earth and all means of production to capital, to turn the laboring masses of the peoples of all zones into wage slaves. In Africa and in Asia, from the most northern regions to the southernmost point of South America and in the South Seas, the remnants of old communistic social groups, of feudal society, of patriarchal systems, and of ancient handicraft production are destroyed and stamped out by capitalism. Whole peoples are destroyed, ancient civilizations are levelled to the ground, and in their place profiteering in its most modern forms is being established.
>
> This brutal triumphant procession of capitalism through the world, accompanied by all means of force, of robbery and of infamy, has one bright phase: it has created the premises for its own final overthrow, it has established the capitalist world rule upon which, alone, the socialist revolution can follow. This is the only cultural and progressive aspect of the great so-called works of culture that were brought to the primitive countries. To capitalist economists and politicians, railroads, matches, sewerage systems and warehouses are progress and culture. Of themselves such works, grafted upon primitive conditions, are neither culture nor progress, for they are too dearly paid for with the sudden economic and cultural ruin of the peoples who must drink down the bitter cup 'of misery and horror of two social orders, of traditional agricultural landlordism, of supermodern, super-refined capitalist exploitation, at one and the same time. Only as the material conditions for the destruction of capitalism and the abolition of class society can the effects of the capitalist triumphal march

through the world bear the stamp of progress in a historical sense. In this sense imperialism, too, is working in our interest.[9]

Revolutionary Marxists argued, as the Dutch socialist Herman Gorter put it, that "it makes no difference to the working class as a whole whether England or another country possesses a greater part of the world. . . . They should oppose capitalistic colonial policies, because they aim at a better society than this capitalistic one, a society that needs no colonies to exploit. . . . The colonial program of revolutionary social-democracy is as follows: (1) Protesting against colonial usurpation and extortion. (2) Attempting to protect and liberate the natives so long as they themselves are too weak for revolutionary action. (3) Supporting every revolutionary act of the natives and demanding their political and national independence, as soon as they begin revolutionary activity for themselves." Lenin noted the following in regard to the growing anticolonial struggle: "Hundreds of millions of the downtrodden and benighted have awakened . . . to a new life and are rising to fight for elementary human rights and democracy. The workers of the advanced countries follow with interest and inspiration this powerful growth of the liberation movement, in all its various forms, in every part of the world. . . . The awakening of Asia and the beginning of the struggle for power by the advanced proletariat of Europe are a symbol of the new phase in world history that began early in this century."[10]

And yet imperialism was a relatively new phenomenon, the dynamics and implications of which Marxists were still laboring to understand in the early years of the twentieth century. As late as 1907, Lenin commented that imperialism provides in certain advanced capitalist countries "the material and economic basis for infecting the proletariat with colonial chauvinism. Of course, this may be only a temporary phenomenon, but the evil must nonetheless be clearly realized and its causes understood in order to be able to rally the proletariat of all countries for the struggle against such opportunism. This struggle is bound to be victorious, since the 'privileged' nations are a diminishing faction of the capitalist nations."[11] This optimistic view, shared by such "orthodox" thinkers as Kautsky, proved to be woefully inadequate. But the first substantial Marxist theoretical work to analyze imperialism, Rudolf Hilferding's *Finance Capital*, appeared only in 1910. Rosa Luxemburg's study *The Accumulation of Capital* appeared in the following year, generating a fierce controversy over how best to comprehend this new phenomenon. The major Bolshevik works on imperialism were written only after the eruption of World War I—Nikolai Bukharin's theoretical treatise *Imperialism and the World Economy* (1915) and Lenin's popular outline *Imperialism, the Highest Stage of Capitalism* (1916).[12]

A failure to integrate a thoroughgoing analysis of imperialism into a general strategic orientation was common throughout the Second International and helped to politically disarm many in the face of the oncoming war. In previous Marxist thinking on war and international affairs, aside from a general and somewhat vague opposition to capitalist wars, various notions had influenced Social Democrats: a belief that socialists of different countries should support "defensive wars" to protect their homeland; a bias toward more industrially advanced countries with democratic-republican governments, as opposed to economically backward nations under autocratic regimes; and a belief that Russian tsarism was the "bulwark of reaction" in Europe that must be resisted and—in case of military aggression—defeated by all possible means. But what of a situation in which England, France, and Russia were aligned against Germany and Austria-Hungary, a situation in which "who was responsible" for the onset of hostilities was obscured by secret diplomatic maneuvers and massive propaganda, and in which complex and long-term economic and geopolitical trends formed the background for an explosive world conflict? For this eventuality, the "common wisdom" of the socialist movement offered no clear guidelines. This was precisely the situation, however, when World War I began. ·

Massive socialist antiwar demonstrations throughout Europe in July 1914 were followed by ineffectual hand-wringing consultations among Second International leaders of the various parties. When war was declared, in the name of "defending the nation" against one or another allegedly aggressive act, "everywhere the masses and the Socialist organizations rallied to support their governments," as Karl Kautsky noted. He added: "Taking sides in a war according to your national point of view clearly endangers the International. This is not because such a course violates our principles. We certainly can rally behind a war fought to fend off enemy invasion. . . . Proletarian internationalism would be in a grievous state if it were not compatible with national defense. . . . [But] the International is not an effective tool in wartime; in essence it is an instrument of peace. Only in peacetime can it develop its full strength, and in so far as it is able to bring this strength to bear, it always works for peace." This apology for the collapse of the Second International and rationalization for prowar socialists permanently placed Kautsky on the opposite side of the barricades from those continuing to adhere to a revolutionary Marxism. Their approach to the war and their method of analysis were qualitatively different. Yet even among the Bolsheviks there was some initial confusion. Krupskaya later recalled that "people were not clear on the question, and spoke mostly about which side was the attacking side."[13]

Lenin expressed what came to be the viewpoint of all revolutionary internationalists in sharply distinguishing between "national wars" of the late eighteenth and nineteenth centuries and the modern imperialist war. The old national wars were struggles "for the self-determination of the nation, for its independence, for the freedom of its language, for popular representation [through] the creation of national states, which were, at a certain stage of capitalism, indispensable soil for the growth of productive forces." On the other hand, he wrote, "it is imperialism that lends the present war an entirely different imprint; it is imperialism that distinguishes it from all past wars. Only when we observe this war in its peculiar historical surroundings . . . can we determine our attitude towards it. Else we would be manipulating with old terms, with arguments fitting old and different surroundings. Among such antiquated terms is the term fatherland and the . . . distinction between defensive and aggressive wars. . . . The historic era of national wars is past. We are now confronted with an imperialist war, and it is the task of Socialists to turn the 'national' war into civil war [a revolutionary struggle to overthrow the capitalist government]. . . . This being the case, it is unimportant who has made the attack. Everybody was prepared for the war; the attack was made by one who considered it most auspicious for himself at a given moment."[14]

Even Lenin, however, had not yet entirely broken free from the "old terms" of nineteenth-century socialist analysis. Continuing to see tsarism as the "bulwark of reaction" in Europe, he argued that "by far the lesser evil would be the defeat of the Tsar's armies and the Tsar's monarchy" in the world war. This was the initial basis for Lenin's controversial slogan of "revolutionary defeatism"—a desire to see the Tsar's armies defeated by the opposing side. Within a fairly short period, however, it became clear that the already weakened tsarist autocracy was no longer capable of playing as powerful a reactionary role in Europe as it had assumed in the nineteenth century; also, the special revolutionary defeatist position with regard to Russia left an opening for prowar German socialists to justify their own orientation. The slogan then became generalized by Lenin for all combatant nations and came to be understood as a call for the workers of all countries to advance the class struggle of the workers in spite of the war effort, and to work uncompromisingly for the overthrow of their own capitalist governments rather than supporting "defense of the fatherland."[15]

Lenin's orientation in regard to imperialism was related to the position he developed on nationalism. Some revolutionaries, such as Rosa Luxemburg and even some Bolsheviks, were inclined to argue that in the new imperialist epoch, all forms of nationalism were incompatible with working-class internationalism. Lenin, on the other hand, made a sharp distinction between the nationalism of the imperialist nations and the nationalism of those countries oppressed by imperialism. "The Socialists cannot reach their great aim without fighting against every form of national oppression. They must therefore unequivocally demand that the Social Democrats of the *oppressing* countries (of the so-called 'great' nations in particular) should recognize and defend the right of the *oppressed* nations to self-determination in the political sense of the word, i.e., the right to political separation. A Socialist of a great nation or a nation possessing colonies who does not defend this right is a chauvinist.... Imperialism is the period of an increasing oppression of the nations of the whole world by a handful of 'great' nations; the struggle for a Socialist international revolution against imperialism is therefore impossible without the recognition of the right of nations to self-determination."[16]

2. The Actuality of World Revolution

As always, a central theme of Bolshevik education and agitation in this period was something that Georg Lukács had identified as an element at the core of Lenin's thought—*the actuality of revolution*. Comparing Lenin to what he called the "vulgar Marxists" of the Second International, Lukács commented that "the average man first sees the proletarian revolution when the working masses are already fighting on the barricades, and—if he happened also to have enjoyed a vulgar-Marxist education—not even then. For to a vulgar Marxist, the foundations of bourgeois society are so unshakeable that, even when they are most visibly shaking, he only hopes and prays for a return to 'normality', sees its crises as temporary episodes, and regards a struggle even at such times as an irrational and irresponsible rebellion against the ever-invincible capitalist system." In 1920 the poet Valery Bruisov observed, "Now, for example, there is talk of travel to other planets, but few of us hope to see them. That is exactly how far away the Russian Revolution seemed to us then. To foresee that the Revolution was not so far away and that now was the time to be moving towards it—this was possible only for a man of colossal wisdom. And this is what astonishes me most of all in Lenin." Lukács points out: "On the one hand neither Marx nor Lenin ever thought of the actuality of the proletarian revolution and its aims as being readily realizable at any given moment. On the other hand, however, it was through this actuality that both gained a sure touchstone for evaluating all questions of the day. The actuality of the revolution provides the key-note of a whole epoch." So it was with Lenin's orientation during the First World War.[17]

"War inflicts horrible sufferings on the people, but we must not, and we have no reason at all, to despair of the future," Lenin insisted in early 1916. "The millions of victims who will fall in the war, and as a consequence of the war, will not have died in vain. The millions who are starving, the millions who are sacrificing their lives in the trenches, are not only suffering, they are also gathering strength; they are pondering over the real causes of the war; they are becoming more determined and are acquiring a clearer revolutionary understanding. In *all* countries of the world there is growing discontent among the masses and greater ferment; there are strikes, demonstrations and protests against the war. *This is an earnest of the proletarian revolution against capitalism that is bound to follow the European war.*" Gregory Zinoviev similarly gave voice to the revolutionary internationalism that underlay the Bolshevik orientation: "The imperialist World War has indissolubly bound the revolutionary crisis in our country to the growing proletarian socialist revolution in the West. Even ten years ago revolutionary Russian Social Democracy conceived of the democratic revolution in Russia as the prologue to the socialist revolution in the West. Developments have taken a strong step forward. The time of the prologue is approaching that of the epilogue. The tie between the democratic revolution in Russia and the socialist revolution in the West has become closer still."[18]

Ultimately, the shock of the First World War did not shake the Bolsheviks' internationalism but, if anything, deepened it.

Before examining the relationship of the revolutionary-internationalist orientation to the functioning of the Bolshevik organization in 1914–1917, we should give some attention to the argument of some commentators that this programmatic fundamental of Bolshevism was based on an absurd or tragic illusion.

From the left end of the political spectrum, perhaps the most succinct expression of this view has been offered by Fritz Sternberg. "The period of capitalist imperialist development which culminated in the outbreak of the first world war," he writes, "was not characterized—as many socialists, including Lenin and Rosa Luxemburg, thought—by a simultaneous increase of both social and foreign-political tension. . . . The truth was that the period immediately before the first world war was marked by a lessening of social tension and by a rise in living standards for all sections of the population in the highly developed imperialist States, though this had been brought about by capitalist and imperialist expansion all over the world, and this expansion necessarily aggravated foreign-political antagonisms and finally led to war." Sternberg suggests that imperialism brought about only a "temporary decline of social tension," but stresses that the revolutionary Marxists "refused to see that the repercussions of this outward expansion of capitalism had raised living standards for the whole of the working class in the highly-developed industrial countries, and had done so not for a short time only, but for years, even whole generations, in succession. The result of this blindness was that the Left wing of the working-class movement believed that if a world war did break out it would end comparatively swiftly in the overthrow of capitalism." In the period leading up to World War I, "there was no fear of social revolutionary developments," nor could the war "lead to social revolutionary actions on any dangerous scale in the big European industrial countries. . . ."[19] To the extent that this analysis is accurate, the program of the revolutionary Marxists—the Bolsheviks most of all—was fatally flawed. This has been the judgment of many scholars, conservatives, liberals, and moderate socialists. As one moderate socialist, George Lichtheim, put it, the Russian Revolution was to spring from "a unique constellation of events," and therefore Western Europe and North America came to "represent a reality against which revolutionary movements inspired by Russian example would beat in vain."[20]

Yet this seemingly hardheaded analysis suffers from a crude economic determinism that leaves out so many essential factors as to make it almost valueless. Its reduction of social stability to a generalized "rise of living standards" limits its usefulness for any social scientist wishing simply to *understand* the world, let alone for a revolutionary intent upon *changing* it. Even the non-Marxist social historian Peter Stearns has felt the need to point out that in prewar Western Europe "there was discontent, although it was not strong enough to shake the foundation of society. The massive agitation of workers could not be ignored. Sometimes it had revolutionary overtones; certainly it sought major change. Nowhere was the social question solved in the period, although welfare measures and collective bargaining satisfied some. In countries where economic conditions deteriorated significantly for the working class, notably Britain and Belgium, discontent grew to alarming proportions." Stearns's picture of "the nonindustrial areas of Europe" indicates even more that "a clearly revolutionary mood prevailed at the end of the century. Peasants were everywhere restive because they suffered from the pressures of agricultural crisis, overpopulation, and, often, the dominance of large landowners. . . . Urban workers were also discontent. Their numbers were not yet large, but they could dominate the cities. Socialist and anarchist doctrines spread, and the harsh working conditions and brutal police repression gave a revolutionary cast to strikes and riots in Catalonia, Sicily, and Russia. Unlike most strikes in western Europe, these often raised direct questions about the nature of the political regime." In a comparative analysis of pre-1914 Germany and Britain, Michael R. Gordon goes somewhat further: "Each nation experienced an alarming wave of unsettling events, resulting in social strife, economic dislocation, and left-right polarization. In both a constitutional crisis was emerging and with it the prospect of large-scale violence."[21]

If we focus on highly industrialized and prosperous Germany, we find the rising living standards to which Sternberg refers: The index of annual real income for industrial and commercial workers, standing at 100 points in 1895, rose to 114 by 1905 and to 125 by 1913. Yet as German historian Volker R. Berghahn points out, "the material benefits of industrial growth were very unevenly distributed." In Prussia, the second-largest state in the German Reich, more than half of the 15.7 million taxpayers were in the lowest income category. "Fluctuations of the economy tended to affect many workers very immediately, and it appears that living conditions experienced a deterioration shortly before the First World War. This implies that working-class families, most of whom fell into this low-income category, still found it extremely difficult to make ends meet, and relative improvements were often achieved only because several family members went out to work." Illness and layoffs, not uncommon phenomena, could send such families tumbling into poverty, and about 30 percent of all family households, writes Berghahn, "lived in destitution and abject misery. Yet even those whose income was sufficient and who kept it above the rate of inflation did not enjoy a particularly comfortable life. Over half the weekly wage packet was spent on food, with bread being the main item in the diet. What more than anything else made their daily existence so arduous were not only the ten to twelve working hours, often in very unhealthy conditions, for six days of the week, but also their housing conditions. . . ."[22]

Little wonder, then, that the Russian working-class upsurge of 1905 had struck a responsive chord in the West. In 1906, Rosa Luxemburg offered to her comrades a pioneering analysis, *The Mass Strike, the Political Party and the Trade Unions*, that—drawing from her rich knowledge of the Polish and Russian movements— demonstrated the relevance of the Russian upsurge for the German workers' movement. Enumerating whole sections of the German working class that had not been drawn into the organizations of the Social Democratic party and its trade union affiliates—among the unorganized sectors were mine workers, textile and clothing workers, electricity workers, railway and postal employees, agricultural workers— she argued that the party could encourage the development of spontaneous or semi-spontaneous mass actions and mass strikes in which "the living revolutionary class feeling, capable of action, [would] affect the widest and deepest layers of the proletariat in Germany," suggesting that "when conditions in Germany have reached the critical stage for such a period, the sections which are today unorganized and backward will, in the struggle, prove themselves the most radical, the most impetuous element, and not one that will have to be dragged along." The Russian events had demonstrated that "six months of a revolutionary period will complete the work of the training of these as yet unorganized masses which ten years of public demonstrations and distribution of leaflets would be unable to do."[23]

This was not simply the reaction of one revolutionary enthusiast. "On 23 January 1905 the first reports of Bloody Sunday and the outbreak of revolution in Russia reached Berlin," notes historian Robert C. Williams. "In the following months the SPD [Social Democratic Party] and the German labor unions responded to the fresh wind from the East that revitalized the forces of radicalism against those of reformism within the movement. Over 500,000 German workers were involved in work stoppages, strikes and lockouts in 1905—more than the total for the previous five years. For all of 1905 and into 1906 German socialists followed the news from Russia with great interest through a daily column in *Vorwarts*. The SPD collected some 350,000 Marks to aid Russian revolutionaries inside Russia and abroad. The fact that the ideological justification of the new radicalism, Rosa Luxemburg's *Mass Strike, Party and Trade Unions*, had been written by an 'easterner' was not lost on German [conservative] opinion. The very enthusiasm of German socialists for the Russian revolution and the discovery of Russian revolutionaries within the SPD heightened the fears of similar violence in Germany."[24]

Despite the fact that moderate, reformist, bureaucratic elements in the Social Democratic party quickly and successfully moved to check this sentiment and redirect it into safely "disciplined" parliamentary and conservative trade union channels, the situation was by no means stable. "After 1909 class conflicts had again become more intense," notes Wolfgang J. Mommsen. "The employers tried to check the rise of the trade unions by the use of effective counterorganizations; and they used all their means of influencing public opinion to bring a stop to 'Sozialpolitik.' On the other hand, real wages, after a period of almost continuous rise, had again become almost stagnant, largely as a result of rising food prices." According to Michael R. Gordon, "The SPD's revisionism did little to assuage the fears of . . . the forces of order. On the contrary, the most moderate proposals for electoral and fiscal reforms were denounced as though tantamount to revolution. And, indeed, in a sense they were: for the Bismarckian system, fabricated for a traditional social order, could hardly accommodate strong bourgeois participation—let alone that of the working class. Following the SPD advances in the 1912 Reichstag elections, a precarious situation, latent for years, was thus pushing to the surface. The more the forces of change pressed for reforms, the more the forces of order took fright. Hence the alarming wave of fanatical chauvinism, mass demagogy, and crude racism that enveloped the nation from the right in the years before the war. Hence, too, the revived interest in coup d'état schemes. The whole interrelated but untenable system of power and privilege was moving toward crisis and probable breakdown."[25]

It was this context that gave Rosa Luxemburg's perspective a particular vibrancy. She ridiculed the conception, articulated by her moderate critics, of some "apocalyptic mass strike in which the stoutest oaks crack, the earth bursts asunder and the graves open." Surveying the proliferation of actual mass mobilizations among the workers of Western Europe, she commented: "None of the mass strikes known till now was a 'final' struggle 'to the death'; none led to the total victory of the workers, but none 'smashed the totality of organizations and the entire strength' of the proletariat 'for years on end.' Success was mostly a partial and indirect one." They contained, she believed, "a developing sense of the proletariat's power in which the fighters steel their strength and sense of responsibility, and the ruling classes become conscious of their adversary's might." Despite the moderation of the party leadership, she was convinced that "it is just because we in Germany have 'a half century of socialist enlightenment and political freedom' behind us, that as soon as the situation has so ripened that the masses take to the field, the action of the proletariat set in motion will roll together all ancient reckonings against private and state exploitation, and unite the political with an economic mass struggle." The powerful bureaucratic-conservative tendencies in the SPD would, by themselves, prove incapable of providing a permanent brake on the radicalizing dynamics of the class struggle.[26]

Indeed, a recognition of this danger was a contributing factor in the thinking of political and economic decision makers to pursue policies resulting in World War I. In more than one way, "German imperialism . . . was essentially a defensive strategy of the upper and middle classes against the Social Democrats and, in a wider sense, against the democratic tendencies of the age in general," as Mommsen has commented. The advance of capitalist modernization and industrialization, on which rising profits and living standards were dependent, required further economic expansion beyond German borders, and this in itself was a prerequisite for the prosperity capable of turning back the revolutionary threat. But there was an additional concern among those who made and influenced German foreign policy—the desire "to divert the internal struggle to the *foreign sphere*," because as the Prussian minister of finance stated, "in foreign affairs the sentiments of the nation could usually be united." A German banker was more candid in an informal conversation soon after World War I erupted: "This war had to come. If it had not come this year it would have come next year. The military program in Germany had reached the ultimate. Its maintenance for five years more meant a possible revolution and overturning Prussian militarism; perhaps the downfall of the Hohenzollerns [the German monarchy]. By that time the appeal to patriotism and the war spirit might not overcome the rising democratic trend. Thus it would be better for the present monarchy to bring on the war now, unite factions in the cry of 'Fatherland' and thus discredit the Social Democratic movement in the eyes of the whole civilized world. True, it might mean a defeat by the Allies, but even the worst probable defeat would not be so bad, from the monarchy's standpoint, as a possible social revolution which, within a few years, might overthrow the autocracy forever."[27]

The kaiser's government was prepared to discredit the Social Democrats not simply through propaganda measures, but also through elaborate plans to suppress them politically and physically—a fact of which the Social Democratic party leaders had been well aware. But a majority of them proved unwilling to endure either fate, allowing themselves instead to be persuaded that the kaiser's war effort merited socialist support.[28] As we have noted, a similar dynamic became manifest in almost all of the major parties affiliated with the Second International.

Yet the triumphant "patriotic" impulse did bring another kind of discredit to the party, dramatically identified by Rosa Luxemburg: "If the stand taken by the German [Social Democratic] Reichstag group on the fourth of August was correct, then the death sentence of the proletarian International has been spoken, not only for this war but forever. For the first time since the modern labor movement exists, there yawns an abyss between the commandments of international solidarity of the proletariat of the world and the interests of freedom and nationalist existence of the people; for the first time we discover that the independence and liberty of the nations command that working men kill and destroy each other.... It was left to the present world war and to the Social Democratic Reichstag group to uncover, for the first time, the terrible dilemma: either you are for national liberty—or for international socialism."[29]

Similarly, a terrible blow was, in fact, delivered to the organizations and cadres of the socialist movement. Once again, it was vividly described by Luxemburg: "It is the mass destruction of the European proletariat.... Millions of human lives were destroyed in the Vosges, in the Ardennes, in Belgium, in Poland, in the Carpathians and on the Save; millions have been hopelessly crippled. But nine-tenths of those millions come from the ranks of the working class of the cities and the farms. It is our strength, our hope that was mowed down there, day after day, before the scythe of death. They were the best, the most intelligent, the most thoroughly schooled forces of international socialism, the bearers of the holiest traditions, of the highest heroism, the modern labor movement, the vanguard of the whole world proletariat, the workers of England, France, Belgium, Germany and Russia who are being gagged and butchered.... For the advance and victory of socialism we need a strong, educated, ready proletariat, masses whose strength lies in knowledge as well as in numbers. And these very masses are being decimated all over the world. The flower of our youthful strength, hundreds of thousands whose socialist education in England, in France, in Belgium, in Germany and in Russia was the product of decades of education and propaganda, other hundreds of thousands who were ready to receive the lessons of socialism have fallen, and are rotting upon the battlefields. The fruit of the sacrifices and toil of generations is destroyed in a few short weeks, the choicest troops of the international proletariat are torn out by the life roots." She added: "Another such war, and the hope of socialism will be buried under the ruins of imperialistic barbarism."[30]

Luxemburg and her comrades in Germany, in the face of this horror and in the teeth of fierce repression, labored to organize a revolutionary socialist opposition to the war and called for the creation of a new and disciplined revolutionary International of the working class, whose first principle would be: "The class struggle against the ruling classes within the boundaries of the bourgeois states, and international solidarity of all countries, are the two rules of life, inherent in the working class in struggle and of world-historic importance to it for its emancipation. There is no socialism without international proletarian solidarity, and there is no socialism without class struggle."[31] Similar revolutionary-internationalist groupings came together throughout Europe. The most substantial of these consisted of the revolutionaries of Russia, among whom the Bolsheviks were the most cohesive force.

In addition, the war created a new revolutionary dynamic in Russia that enabled the Bolsheviks to play the magnificent role for which they had been preparing for a decade and a half.

3. How the Party Functioned

The development of Lenin's views during the war, and his immense efforts to advance a clear, effective revolutionary orientation within the international current of antiwar socialists deserve a separate and detailed study. In his excellent history of Russian revolutionaries living in Switzerland from 1914 to 1917, Alfred Senn has summed up important aspects of Lenin's orientation: "Among the emigres, only Lenin responded to the new conditions of wartime with a comprehensive program of action. To be sure, at first he worked just to consolidate his own party ranks: he made little effort to appeal to Western Europeans in the first months of the war. Nevertheless, by the winter and spring of 1915 he had developed a clear pattern: unyielding criticism of other [Russian non-Bolshevik] socialist leaders and violent denunciation of the Second International, combined with a more flexible attitude toward dissident members of foreign socialist parties." The Bolshevik orientation—forcefully advanced at international conferences of antiwar socialists at Zimmerwald (1915) and Kienthal (1916) in Switzerland—linked an antiwar position to a perspective of intensifying class struggle and working-class revolution. Lenin insisted on a thoroughgoing split of genuinely revolutionary socialists away from the opportunistic and prowar socialists of the Second International, arguing that "a new International must arise again, which can only be born of the revolutionary class struggle of the proletarian masses in the most important capitalist countries."[32]

The Bolsheviks became notorious for their uncompromising attitude, but this was to be a pole of attraction as the bankruptcy of the Second International came to be more widely recognized among antiwar socialists. "The section of Central Committee members which was abroad," Zinoviev later recounted, "began to work on uniting internationalists on an international scale. We took part in the Zimmerwald conference where we constituted a weak minority and organized the Zimmerwald left which in fact served as the first nucleus of the future Third International." Alfred Senn's account gives an even greater sense of dramatic shifts taking place: "Now, for the first time, Lenin began to collect an international following. 'No matter that we are so few,' he declared, 'we shall have millions with us.' He considered his work 'already different, closer to action.' In contrast, other Russian internationalists proved incapable of developing strong organizations, and a drift into Lenin's camp was already visible in the spring of 1915."[33]

The impact of the war on the workers' movement and the Bolsheviks inside Russia was complex. As discussed in the previous chapter, the period of 1912–1914 saw a crescendo of working-class radicalization and militant struggle, in which the Bolsheviks became the hegemonic force among the workers. In July 1914, this culminated in mass strikes and street fighting in Petersburg that were reminiscent of the early 1905 events. At this point, according to the Bolshevik A. E. Badayev, "the tsarist government did not let anything stand in the way of their endeavors to crush the incipient revolution. The series of lockouts had struck at the economic conditions of the workers and mass arrests and deportations weakened the political organization of the working class." Different leading Bolsheviks who had been on the scene later looked back on this period with different estimates. From his vantage point as Bolshevik deputy in the Duma, Badayev tells us that "the proletariat required a certain time to recover, to collect its forces for fresh onslaughts on tsarism." On the other hand, from his vantage point as prominent underground activist functioning in the factories, Alexander Shlyapnikov asserted that "the mood of workers was very buoyant, in spite of the orgy of repression, the lack of newspapers and the fortnight's unemployment. Everyone was overjoyed and encouraged by the recent strike which had united a large army of labor in one vivid upsurge of anger. . . . Everyone felt that a decisive and nationwide battle was just around the corner."[34] In any event, the outbreak of the world war prevented the realization of either the "time to recover" or the "decisive nationwide battle."

"Events developed so rapidly that organized workers were caught off guard," noted Shlyapnikov. Badayev recalls: "the declaration of war was a signal for the blackest reactionary forces to redouble their attacks on the working class movement. In the atmosphere of rabid chauvinism and artificial jingoism, the tsarist government savagely repressed all legal and illegal working-class organizations." Added to this was the political disorientation brought on by the collapse of the Second International and especially the betrayal of German Social Democracy. "Workers showered us with questions as to the meaning of the behavior of the German socialists," writes Shlyapnikov, "whom we had always presented as models for our-selves. Where was all that world solidarity? . . . 'Burying the German leaders' did not come easily to us, as in the broad circles of workers supporting social democracy the idea emerged of 'if the Germans have done it, we might as well too.' It took a lot of effort to explain to thinking workers that betrayal by some must not lead to universal betrayal, as only the capitalists would stand to gain from that. It was vital to restore international contact between workers over the heads of the leaders."[35]

Shlyapnikov describes a meeting between the Bolshevik deputies to the Duma and a few key working-class activists, who gathered in an attempt "to find a key to the Germans' conduct. Several expressed the sentiment that the deciding factor was probably the threat of tsarism, and it was common knowledge that even Engels had, in his day, wished for a war against tsarist Russia. But whatever the reasons, it all amounted to one thing only: such behavior was a betrayal of all the precepts of revolutionary socialism. At the crucial moment the German social democrats had felt that they were closer to their own bourgeoisie than to the workers of other countries. Nationalism had proved stronger than socialism."[36] Independently of the exiled Lenin (from whom they were cut off at the outset of the war), these Bol-shevik stalwarts were determined to remain true to the revolutionary internation-alism that was an essential component of their program.

Despite such sentiments, the revolutionary workers' movement was overwhelmed by the tidal wave of war. Trotsky summarizes: "The more active layers of the workers were mobilized [by the regime into the army]. The revolutionary elements were thrown from the factories to the front. Severe penalties were imposed for striking. The workers' press was swept away. Trade unions were strangled. Hundreds of thou-sands of women, boys, peasants, poured into the workshops. The war—combined with the wreck of the International—greatly disoriented the workers politically, and made it possible for the factory administration, then just lifting its head, to speak patriotically in the name of the factories, carrying with it a considerable part of the workers, and compelling the more bold and resolute to keep still and wait. The rev-olutionary ideas were barely kept glowing in small hushed circles. In the factories in those days nobody dared to call himself a 'Bolshevik' for fear not only of arrest, but of a beating from the backward workers. . . . It seemed as though the war had pro-duced a new working class. To a considerable extent this was the fact: in Petrograd the personnel of the workers had been renewed almost forty percent."[37]

Political repression hit the Bolsheviks harder than the Mensheviks. All five Bolshevik deputies in the Duma (there were only five after the defection of the police-spy Malinovsky) were arrested, while the Menshevik deputies remained at liberty. The Bolshevik organization was especially hard hit by repression, while those elements among the Mensheviks who, with various rationalizations, supported the war effort were able to assume prominent positions in what was left of the workers' movement. The Bolshevik daily *Pravda* was quickly closed down completely, while "patriotic" labor papers continued to appear. On the other hand, as historian Ronald Suny has commented, "while the war years demonstrated the fragility of the Bolsheviks' newly conquered positions within the working class and arrests and patriotism ate into their influence, the potential for a renewal of militance remained intact."[38]

The Mensheviks made particularly significant gains in the network of war industry committees set up in 1915 "to bring more closely together the industrialists, the workers and the government, and thus to encourage greater effort in production for war needs." The Bolsheviks opposed participation, as did the most consistent of the Menshevik-Internationalists outside of Russia, such as Martov. Yet according to Leonard Schapiro, "unlike the more disciplined Bolsheviks, the Mensheviks were disinclined to accept such leadership as emanated from the 'Secretariat in Exile'" (this was true especially, though not exclusively, of the "pro-defense" liquidators); consequently, they "immediately welcomed the new opportunity for concrete social democratic activity" in these government-sponsored bodies. This enabled them to regain much of the ground they had lost to the Bolsheviks in the 1912–1914 period. And yet David Mandel remarks that among certain strata of the workers there was "a fundamental internationalism . . . both in relation to ethnic groups within Russia and towards the war and the struggles of oppressed peoples abroad. . . . Even the initial patriotic wave that swept up broad strata of workers throughout Russia found only a weak and relatively short-lived echo in Petrograd, and, according to the police, little remained of it by the autumn of 1915. N. I. Potresov, a right-wing Menshevik and defencist . . . bitterly lamented in 1915 the fact that the 'German invasion' had 'aroused nothing in the proletarian masses', no response worthy of the 'most revolutionary class of today's society.'"[39] These realities set the stage for Bolshevik resurgence.

The Bolsheviks' orientation in Russia was not dictated from abroad by Lenin. For one thing, underground communications with him were initially disrupted by war and repression. When Lenin's theses on war were finally transmitted, according to Shlyapnikov, "they responded to the mood of party workers at the time, but the question of 'defeatism' did cause perplexity. Comrades did not want to link their tactics to the army's strategic situation, but at the same time nobody wished Nicholas II the smallest victory, as it was clear that a victory would strengthen the vilest reaction."[40] The Bolsheviks' outlook was summed up in inscriptions that appeared first on factory walls and ultimately on banners carried by factory workers:

Comrades: we won't be any better off if Russia wins—they'll squash us even harder.[41]

We swear to achieve the brotherhood of all peoples. Long live the Russian Revolution as the prologue to the Social Revolution in Europe.[42]

It bears remembering that after the February–March revolution of 1917—particularly after Lenin's return to Russia—Lenin himself dropped the "revolutionary defeatism" slogan, which had been his trademark in polemics he had conducted from his Swiss exile. "We Bolsheviks are in the habit of adopting a maximum of revolutionism," he commented. "But this is not enough. We must study the situation." The situation during his exile, from 1914 through 1916, when he was attempting to "bend the stick" far to the left in order to consolidate an international revolutionary socialist current completely free from conciliation with prowar and moderate Social Democrats had been one thing. The situation among war-weary soldiers and peasants and workers in Russia was something else again. "There is no doubt that, as a class, the proletariat and semi-proletariat are not interested in the war," he remarked in a speech on the political situation in early 1917. "They are still influenced by tradition and deception. They still lack political experience. Therefore, our task is that of patiently explaining. Our principles remain intact, we do not make the slightest compromise; yet we cannot approach those masses as we approach the social-chauvinists [the prowar socialists]."[43] The new slogan he favored in regard to the war was now simpler—*peace*, linked with demands advancing the rights of the workers and peasants. And this approach had, despite some vacillations, characterized the Bolshevik approach in Russia during the war.

The divergence between Lenin and his comrades inside Russia before 1917 should not be overstated, although among certain currents in the party it seemed to go deeper than simply a choice of different slogans. The Bolshevik deputies to the Duma and *Pravda* editor Kamenev had equivocated in the direction of patriotic sentiment. A joint statement of Bolshevik and Menshevik deputies, although denouncing the war as resulting from imperialist politics, nonetheless contained the ambiguous assertion that "the proletariat, permanent defender of freedom and the interests of the people, will carry out its own duty at all times and will defend the cultural welfare of the people from all kinds of encroachments, wherever they come from—either from inside or outside." This statement was mitigated by the walkout of the RSDLP deputies when the Duma was about to vote on war credits, but during the later trial of the Bolshevik deputies and Kamenev, the defendants explicitly disassociated themselves from Lenin's "revolutionary defeatism" and presented the Bolshevik opposition to the war in muted tones. This caused some consternation among the Bolsheviks, and historian Tsuyoshi Hasegawa finds that "it was the rank-and-file activists who accepted Lenin's radical position quickly." Lenin's intransigent theses on the war, in the words of one underground worker, "gave us a fresh spirit, vindicated and inspired us, fired our hearts with an irresistible desire to go further, not stopping at anything." Some took bold initiatives independently of the more cautious leaders inside Russia, publishing an illegal workers' paper with a clear antiwar stand and producing leaflets with such messages as this: "The Russian proletariat will find a method against the war. And there is only one method: to strengthen its class organizations by oral and printed propaganda among the troops of the active army and among the workers and the peasants against militarism with the appeal for a general insurrection for a democratic republic." These became the dominant themes of Bolshevism inside Russia, and they had growing impact as the war's devastating effects were felt among the workers.[44]

Despite the gains that particularly the prowar reformist wing of the Mensheviks was able to make in wartime Russia, it was noted by many that the Bolsheviks were, in Leonard Schapiro's words, "somewhat better organized, and the more united" and that they were "attracting the more vigorous elements among the workers." The strongest and most dynamic organization of worker-Bolsheviks was concentrated in the solidly proletarian Vyborg district of Petersburg. While not yet able to win the majority of workers to their banner, the Bolsheviks maintained an impressive underground network based in the factories and were capable of exercising increasing influence despite unremitting tsarist repression.[45]

Both inside and outside Russia, the Bolsheviks' political and organizational achievement was a powerful pole of attraction for revolutionary-minded activists, including many who had previously remained aloof from Lenin's party. In the pages of Trotsky's paper *Nashe Slovo* at the beginning of 1916, one writer expressed the growing conviction of many: "One ought not to and one need not share the sectarian narrow-mindedness of [Lenin's group] . . . but it cannot be denied that . . . in Russia, in the thick of political action, so-called Leninism is freeing itself from its sectarian features . . . and that the workers' groups connected with *Social Democrat* (Lenin's paper) are now in Russia the only active and consistently internationalist force. . . . For those internationalists who belong to no faction there is no way out but to merge with the Leninists, which in most cases means joining the Leninist organization."[46] Many such activists ultimately concluded that much of "the sectarian narrow-mindedness" they had found so offensive in fact reflected a realistic appraisal of the necessary tasks at hand (as well as of the actual bankruptcy of the bulk of the Mensheviks, and of the moderates of the Second International)— an appraisal that was a key component of the Bolsheviks' ability to become "the only active and consistently internationalist force," and genuinely revolutionary party, in Russia.

A minor indication of the antiwar militancy of Bolsheviks inside Russia is that when the autocracy changed the name of Petersburg to the more Russian-sounding name of Petrograd after the war began, the Petersburg committee of the Bolsheviks remained the *Petersburg* committee. Tsuyoshi Hasegawa offers this illuminating description of the internal functioning of the Petrograd Bolsheviks during this period: "The central leadership could not and did not extend a strong control over the local organizations. The Russian Bureau of the Central Committee did not exist most of the time during the war, and when it finally came into existence, it was too weak and its means too limited to assume effective leadership. The Petersburg Committee assumed virtual leadership over the Bolshevik organizations in Petrograd, but its members were subject to constant police repression, and the turnover rate of its membership was high. Thus, most of the day-to-day operations was left to the discretion of the local organizations. The rank-and-file activists freely exchanged opinions, unafraid of challenging directives from the center. It was thanks to such independent but dedicated party activists—united by a common repudiation of the war and hatred against the regime, and motivated only by their desire for revolution—that the Bolshevik party endured the trials and tribulations of the war."[47]

These independent-minded and resourceful militants, Hasegawa points out, were the key to the Bolshevik party's maintaining contact with the working class, and they were the first to rebuild the party organizations in the wake of the repression. "They met clandestinely, organized an illegal network of party organizations, recruited [to the party], recruited sympathizers, set up illegal printing presses . . . in their apartments, printed leaflets, and distributed them among the workers. They lived under constant peril of arrest, court martial and exile." The Bolsheviks had had almost 6,000 members in Petrograd immediately before the war. The disruptive effects of repression left them with about 100 by December 1914. The membership climbed to 1,200 by the end of 1915 then to 2,000 in the autumn of 1916, and 3,000 in the beginning of 1917. And they were predominantly young, as the then thirty-two-year-old Shlyapnikov later recalled: "The red banner of the workers' movement passed out of the weakening hands of the old men to a younger and more energetic generation of workers." Of the Petersburg committee in 1917, only one member was over forty, five were in their thirties, and nine were in their twenties. "Despite their youth," Hasegawa comments, "the Petersburg Committee members had been arrested a total of forty-four times and exiled eleven times—proof that they were experienced revolutionary leaders." A majority were workers. This was also true of the Bolshevik party as a whole—by early 1917, the organization throughout Russia had about 24,000 members, over 60 percent of whom were workers.[48]

As we have seen, Lenin was able to exert little direct influence over the daily internal functioning of his comrades inside Russia. It is worth noting how he operated in contexts within which he *could* have direct influence. Among the Bolsheviks living abroad, many immediately agreed with his opposition to the war, but some were uncertain. Lenin did not attempt to ram his position through. Krupskaya writes: "Vladimir Ilyich realized how important it was at such a serious moment for every Bolshevik to have a clear understanding of the significance of events. A comradely exchange of opinions was necessary: it was inadvisable to fix all shades of opinion right away until the matter had been threshed out."[49] Such "threshing out" was essential for the Bolshevik unity that was achieved during the war years. Yet such unity did not extend to all questions.

Sharp differences flared up particularly between Lenin and a group that gathered around the young theoretician Nikolai Bukharin. Lenin respected Bukharin's intellectual abilities, but also viewed him as somewhat immature, unstable, and ultraleftist. Bukharin had been influenced in earlier years by Alexander Bogdanov, and during the war years by the Dutch left Marxists around Anton Pannekoek. His group included Nikolai Krylenko, Elena Rozmirovoch and, later, G. L. Piatakov and Yevgenia Bosch; these last two (influenced by Rosa Luxemburg and Karl Radek) sharply disagreed with Lenin's support of self-determination for oppressed nationalities, counterposing to it a somewhat abstract proletarian internationalism. Not only did Bukharin share this position, but in this period he dismissed the peasantry as a significant ally of the working class, and he also disagreed with Lenin's strong emphasis on the importance of democratic demands (as opposed to specifically socialist ones). It could be strongly argued that, on all of these questions, Lenin's position was subsequently vindicated. There were other points of disagreement on which Lenin was ultimately to shift somewhat in Bukharin's direction. For example, Bukharin disagreed with Lenin's initial position of labeling Russia's defeat in the war a "lesser evil" (rather than damning all the imperialist powers equally). He disagreed with Lenin's inclination to sweepingly exclude "peace slogans appealing to broader anti-war sentiment," something that could not be done by calling for "revolutionary defeatism" or "turning the imperialist war into a civil war." Also, he believed that, as Stephen Cohen expresses it, the future Third International "should include all anti-war social democrats, including left-wing Mensheviks around Lev Trotsky whom Lenin was ostracizing. Bukharin and his friends simply wanted the new organization to be as broad as possible." (Not *all* antiwar socialists rallied to the new International, but those around Trotsky certainly did.) Finally, Bukharin was developing an interpretation of the Marxist theory of the state that Lenin at first dismissed as "semi-anarchism"; by 1917, however, he was to conclude that Bukharin's interpretation had merit. It would coincide with much of Lenin's classic study, *The State and Revolution*.[50]

Apart from the question of who was right or wrong on particular issues, however, was the question of how such disagreements should be handled in the Bolshevik party. Even before it was clear that there were differences, in early 1915, Bukharin and some like-minded thinkers decided to publish their own newspaper. According to Krupskaya, they "went about it with such precipitancy that they did not even arrange the matter with the Central Organ. . . . Such a publication would hardly have been expedient in any case. There was no money with which to publish the Central Organ, and although there were no differences so far, they might easily arise. An unguarded phrase might be pounced upon by opponents and exaggerated in every way. We had to keep step together. It was such a time." Bukharin hastened to offer the assurance that the new periodical was conceived "*not as an opposition . . . but as a supplement. . . .* What can you have against another party newspaper which in the very first editorial states that it stands on the viewpoint of the Central Organ?" The Bolshevik Central Committee Bureau explained that such initiatives should be decided "collectively" and "not by just several comrades." There was no attempt, however, to apply "disciplinary" measures. Rather, a special Bolshevik conference in Switzerland, convened to deal with wartime policies, was at the last minute lengthened to enable Bukharin and his cothinkers to attend and participate in the discussions and decision making. Bukharin was able to influence some of the formulations of the Bolsheviks' positions. At the same time, he and his comrades agreed to drop their plan for a separate periodical.[51]

Not long afterward, Lenin agreed to participate as a contributor and on the editorial board of a theoretical magazine, *Kommunist*, initiated by Bukharin, Piatakov, and Bosch. It was seen as a publication of the Bolshevik central committee, which contributed significant resources, although the dissident comrades would assume major editorial responsibility. Lenin was uneasy with this "abnormal" arrangement, but he went along with it for practical reasons (which included the fact that the three had acquired money to publish the magazine). As it turned out, however, Bukharin, Piatakov, and Bosch were not inclined to collaborate closely with the party leadership in this venture. Instead, they moved to open the magazine's pages to non-Bolshevik currents within the Zimmerwald left and to initiate a discussion presenting their own views on the national question. A furious Lenin withdrew from the editorial board, and the central committee ruled that *Kommunist* was no longer a Bolshevik publication. "We cannot contribute and shall be compelled to fight it," Lenin wrote to the three editors, "since we find your attitude to the Party's Program . . . to be not only wrong and harmful, but frivolous. . . . Your arguments for a 'free' journal (free from the Party Program? from the central bodies of the Party?) are just as frivolous, if not worse—anti-Party." He added: "If you wish to persist in the theses, we (1) are prepared to publish them and (2) we are bound to give our opinion; publish them yourselves (if you do not want us to do it) and furnish them with a discussion pamphlet in which all three of you could make clear to the Party your motives." A new theoretical magazine was established under the control of the central committee. Lenin also made it clear that he had no desire to muzzle the dissidents: "The young contributors want freedom of opinion *for themselves*—freedom of discussion—that is legitimate." But he denounced their attempt to use *Kommunist*: "If you ... want to help disorganize our Party, do it on *your own* responsibility. Your purse is full. Go ahead and ... then the *Russian* workers will see at once that you are intriguers and will kick you out. But you want to *play* this trick *under cover* of a 'collective board'. Sorry, but I won't accept this and will expose you." He proposed instead that the Bolshevik leadership and dissidents publish either a "miscellany" (essentially, a public discussion bulletin) on the national question, open only to Bolshevik contributors, or a separate pamphlet with a debate between Bukharin and Lenin.[52]

As it turned out, Bukharin and his sympathizers backed off, and *Kommunist* went out of existence. On the other hand, Bukharin felt free to submit articles expressing his own distinctive views to non-Bolshevik publications (and Lenin felt free to criticize them in Bolshevik publications). Despite the great strain in relations, Bukharin remained in the Bolshevik party. And the revolutionary upsurge of 1917 was to draw him and Lenin much closer together than seemed possible in 1915–1916.[53]

Inside Russia throughout 1915–1916, a profound radicalization developed within the working class, which was reflected in a dramatic proliferation of strikes. Along with this, the ineptness and corruption of the tsarist autocracy was increasingly exposed under the pressures of the war. Hasegawa summarizes: "The workers in Petrograd were the fundamental source of instability in Russian politics during the war. The patriotism at the outbreak of the war was quickly dissipated as wartime reality hit. Excluded from the established order of society and deprived of legal organizations to air their grievances, yet asked to continue their sacrifices for 'national honor and pride,' the workers became receptive to the agitators' call for radical action." Objective conditions blended with revolutionary agitation and organizing to create a general mood of proletarian insurgency.[54]

The Bolsheviks were central to this process. In the course of the war, there had been a realignment of socialist organizations in Russia. Gradually, a loose alliance of antiwar, internationalist forces came into being—the Bolsheviks, radical

Menshevik-Internationalists (who became known as the initiative group), the *Mezhraointsy* (Interdistrict Group—left-wing nonfaction Social Democrats, whose standpoint coincided with Trotsky's positions), and the left wing of the Socialist Revolutionaries. The non-Bolshevik components of this alliance were extremely important, but Hasegawa notes: "There is no question that the Bolsheviks were the dominant force among the internationalist groups, with their organizational strength, ideological unity, and tactical militancy." Counterposed to the internationalists were the "defensist" and "semidefensist" moderates—predominantly Mensheviks and right-wing Social Revolutionaries who were committed to a proletarian-bourgeois alliance against tsarism and for the fatherland. The key formation in this moderate-socialist axis was what became known as the Workers' Group, a Menshevik current coordinating involvement of the workers in the war industry committees. Its moderation enabled it to function legally and thereby gain influence among workers. And yet, as Hasegawa writes, "by the fall of 1916, the workers' group was obviously losing ground to the Bolsheviks and to regain its lost influence among the workers, the workers' group turned leftward in December 1916, sharpening its attack on the government and advocating a decisive offensive for its overthrow." Hasegawa concludes that "the conflict between the two groups [revolutionary internationalists and moderate defensists] did not hinder, but rather hastened the development of the revolutionary crisis."[55]

In other words, the Bolsheviks were having an impact not only among revolutionary socialists but also upon the moderates. And this influence—in part a result of the Bolsheviks' legendary intransigence and organizational seriousness—was helping to bring on the revolution.

Throughout this study it has been necessary, in examining the Leninist conception of the party, to take up nonorganizational questions in order to grasp the meaning of Lenin's organizational thought. In the present chapter in particular, it has been necessary to go rather far afield to examine the revolutionary internationalist foundations of the Bolshevik-Leninist orientation and the world realities of 1914–1916, in order to understand elements of the Bolshevik program (and also the beginnings of a programmatic evolution) that had profound political and organizational implications both in Russia and beyond. This helps explain the final phase of Bolshevism's development as a force capable of leading the Russian Revolution of 1917 and founding the Communist International in 1919.

11. Party and Revolution

The Bolshevik Revolution of 1917 was in large measure the triumph of the organizational perspective that has been the focus of this study, combined with the political perspective which held that revolutionary Marxists would have to lead the working-class and peasant masses toward the creation of proletarian rule in Russia. Much can be learned from the examination of the reasons why the Bolshevik party was able to play a decisive role in Russia's revolution and the manner in which it did so. The story of the Bolshevik triumph has been told and retold in great detail. One of the best eyewitness accounts is John Reed's *Ten Days That Shook the World*, written one year after the event. One of the most profound was offered fifteen years later in Trotsky's *History of the Russian Revolution*. Sixty years after the event, one of the most scholarly accounts, Alexander Rabinowitch's *The Bolsheviks Come to Power*, was published. Each of these classics—corroborating the others in all fundamentals—provides a clear outline and rich detail for any interested reader. In addition, recent studies by a new wave of historians have greatly added to our understanding of this inspiring chapter in the history of the labor and socialist movements.[1]

Still powerfully influential, however, is the slant offered by historians who see the Bolshevik triumph as a historical disaster. George Katkov is one of many to suggest that the working-class strikes and demonstrations that toppled tsarism were, in fact, instigated by agents of the German kaiser as a wartime maneuver; although Lenin was (we are told) afflicted by a brain disease that resulted in "very peculiar thinking" on his part, a vast influx of German money was sufficient to promote the decisive effectiveness of Bolshevik propaganda in these confusing times.[2]

Such respected historians as Leonard Schapiro and Robert V. Daniels have similarly given credence to the myth of German gold in Bolshevik coffers, but they are inclined to take Lenin's "peculiar thinking" (minus the brain disease) more seriously.[3] So does Bertram D. Wolfe, who characterizes the Bolshevik leader as a "virtuoso of organization and total power" who had a remarkable "ability to mobilize, manipulate, and organize discontent and hatred." John Keep agrees that Lenin's achievement was "less a matter of mobilizing 'class conscious proletarians' than of harnessing elemental energies and hatreds of all segments of society." This interpretation has implications for Lenin's conception of organization that these historians have not hesitated to point out. For Lenin, Keep tells us, "the active catalyst of change is a body of professional revolutionaries, bound together by close ties of loyalty to their leader, so homogeneous as to reduce to a minimum the likelihood of dissent or indiscipline." Wolfe has taken it further: "The first peculiarity that strikes one in Lenin's organizational doctrine is his centralism, and his extreme distrust not only of whole classes (the intelligentsia, the petty bourgeoisie, the peasantry, the working class itself), but even of the rank and file of his own Party, his own local organizations." According to Robert V. Daniels, "Lenin insisted that the proletarian revolution had to be accomplished by the deliberate action of a tightly organized conspiratorial party. He did not trust spontaneous mass movements, and at several crucial moments—in 1905 and in July 1917—opposed the 'adventurism' of Bolsheviks who wanted to exploit a popular outburst. In the fall of 1917, when it seemed as though the proletarian revolution might roll to victory almost as spontaneously as the bourgeois revolution of February, Lenin was beside himself. He was desperate then to demand that his party impose itself by force, to prove its own necessity and keep alive for himself the chance of ruling alone."[4]

If such an organization is what made the revolution, this has implications for how one understands the revolutionary process and the nature of the working class. We find, as Diane Koenker has aptly noted, "an image among Western historians of these masses as irrational, easily swayed, and prey to the machinations of political leaders. They are acted upon, they do not act."[5] This is the outlook not only of prominent anti-Communist ideologists, but also—despite a twist of romanticization—of some left-wing sects that would like to "duplicate" this elitist scenario.

The question is this: Can an organization with such an approach win enough support to lead a revolution? This would seem doubtful, because such an understanding of the working class has little to do with real working people, particularly—as the new historians have demonstrated—the Russian working class in 1917. Recent works of scholarship have confirmed the judgment Trotsky offered more than fifty years ago: "The swift changes of mass views and moods in an epoch of revolution thus derive, not from the flexibility and mobility of man's mind, but just the opposite, from its deep conservatism. The chronic lag of ideas and relations behind new objective conditions, right up to the moment when the latter crash over people in the form of a catastrophe, is what creates in a period of revolution that leaping movement of ideas and passions which seems to the police mind a mere result of the activities of 'demagogues.'... The fundamental political process of the revolution thus consists in the gradual comprehension by a class of the problems arising from the social crisis—the active orientation of the masses by a method of successive approximations."[6] Irrationality certainly comes into play in such complex situations, but all is not simply "elemental energies and hatreds." In 1917 large numbers of working people in Russia thought long and hard about what they were experiencing, discussed and debated a number of options before them, and—although not without deep passion—made reasoned choices about what to do next.

It is within this context that the Bolshevik party operated in 1917. The ideals and ideas and proposals it articulated, the plans of action it offered, could become relevant only to the extent that the party won the respect and confidence and agreement of the masses of increasingly critical-minded and energetic individuals who constituted the most experienced and active layers of the Russian working class. What is more, the Bolsheviks had articulate rivals with comparable or greater material resources, who attempted to win the support of the working class for quite different programs. But within eight months after the tsar was overthrown, the Bolsheviks outstripped all rivals and won majority support for a socialist revolution.

For detailed examinations of the Russian Revolution, the reader is urged to begin with the works mentioned earlier in this chapter. In what follows, we will focus on the dynamic interaction between the Bolshevik party and the insurgent masses as revolutionary events unfolded, on the crucial programmatic shift that enhanced the Bolsheviks' capacity to play a decisive role, and on the manner in which the Bolshevik organization functioned internally in this stormy period.

1. Overthrowing Tsarism but Not Taking Power

In February–March 1917 there was a working-class revolution in Petrograd that overthrew tsarism, but that also stopped short of transferring power to the workers themselves. An examination of the causes and dynamics both of this proletarian initiative and of proletarian hesitation suggests much regarding the role of the revolutionary party.

As many contemporaries and historians have commented, there had been no plan to make a revolution on this date, and no one had guessed beforehand how close was this event nor how quickly and easily it would finally take place. At the same time, however, this point has been so overstated by some that it has assumed the character of a myth. "In retrospect," Robert V. Daniels writes, repeating the conventional wisdom, "it is easy to see that Russia was ripe for revolt, though no one realized it at the time, not even the Bolsheviks. Lenin, spinning theories of world revolution against imperialism while he fretted in his Swiss exile, said as late as January, 1917, 'We of the older generation may not live to see the decisive battles of this revolution.'" Yet as the Soviet historian and dissident Roy Medvedev notes, the widely quoted comment of Lenin that Daniels cites "was only a rhetorical device" utilized to make an important point (the need to have a "long view" of history if one is a revolutionary) in "a particular context" (an educational talk to a group of young Swiss workers). Medvedev documents that "Lenin actually felt a great certainty that the revolution was not far off," and that "the world war would end in a revolution in most of the countries of Europe, but he could not of course predict the exact course of events, either political or military." One can find many statements in the period immediately preceding the February revolution that "the revolution is growing," that "Europe is pregnant with revolution," that "*our* day will come." As Krupskaya writes: "Never before had Vladimir Ilyich been in such an uncompromising mood as he was during the last months of 1916 and the early months of 1917. He was positively certain that the revolution was imminent." A careful analysis of Lenin's writings in this period will disclose that, while he obviously could have no idea of the specific date or details of the uprising, there was no question in his mind that Russia "was ripe for revolt." Nor did one need to be a political genius to understand that the radicalization process was again in motion.[7]

The new wave of working-class radicalization was part of a general collapse of the tsarist system and of an even deeper crisis that was overtaking Russian society under the impact of the First World War, which had greatly intensified the immense problems already generated by the processes of industrialization and modernization. Many millions of people were displaced by the war—15 million were mobilized into the army, millions were drawn into the factories and cities to keep the economy running, millions more became refugees from the war zones. The absolute destructiveness of the war—6 million Russian soldiers killed, wounded, or captured; the loss of one-fourth of the Russian Empire's richest lands to the German forces; and so forth—was matched by the breakdown of much of the Russian economy: prices rising far above wages, deteriorating transportation and distribution systems, food and fuel shortages, dramatically worsening living conditions. The faith of the most loyal of Tsar Nicholas's "lowly" subjects began to turn into its opposite as they asked, "If the tsar were a good tsar, why could he not save Russia and its people?" Scandalous corruption and ineptness in the highest circles—topped by the amoral intrigues and escapades of the tsar's favorite holy man, Gregory Rasputin—undermined the confidence of even the most conservative elements of Russia's ruling classes in tsarism's capacity to endure.[8]

Another important factor was the profound weakening of tsarism's repressive forces, particularly the army. Allan Wildman writes that "the soldiers felt they were being used and recklessly expended by the rich and powerful, of whom their officers were the most visible, immediate representatives." Roy Medvedev adds: "By drafting millions of peasants and workers into the army and training them to handle weapons, the tsarist regime, without intending to, provided military and technical training. . . . The likely allies of the working class, the peasants, were armed and organized in military garrisons in every major city, with especially large garrisons in Moscow and Petrograd."[9]

William Henry Chamberlin once commented that "the collapse of the Romanov autocracy in March 1917 was one of the most leaderless, spontaneous, anonymous revolutions of all time." This is both true and false—a paradox that sheds much light on the role of the revolutionary party. John M. Thompson aptly notes that "war-weariness, despair, and hatred of the old system became dominant throughout all levels of Russian society. The people's only hope seemed to lie in victory [in the war]—which seemed increasingly illusory—or in a radical change, some sudden liberation from their bonds and burdens."[10] These moods and feelings and beliefs, "spontaneously" generated by objective conditions, were certainly the source of the uprising, but the revolutionary parties played an essential role in offering coherent conceptual alternatives to the status quo. Only the organized socialists—defensists as well as internationalists—articulated such alternatives, and their appeals were generating an increasingly visible response among the Russian workers as 1916 faded into 1917.

It is important to recognize that the Bolsheviks were not the only group playing this crucial role. "The active members of the revolutionary parties combined constituted no more than 2 percent of the total number of Petrograd workers," writes Tsuyoshi Hasegawa, "but with the indifference of the vast majority of workers to the doctrinal differences separating the parties, they found it significant that both camps [defensists and internationalists] stood for overthrow of the regime. The differences assumed practical importance only after the February Revolution, not before." Of course, not all of the different currents were doing their work in the same manner. The Menshevik moderates and their allies were concentrating their efforts in the war industries committees and in caucusing with elements of the bourgeois-liberal opposition. The 24,000 Bolsheviks (including 2,000 in Petrograd and 600 in Moscow) were, according to the Menshevik-Internationalist Sukhanov, "buried in a completely different kind of work, keeping the equipment of the movement in repair, forcing the pace for a decisive clash with the tsarist regime, organizing propaganda and the underground press."[11]

Yet according to Gregory Zinoviev, "The February revolution found our Central Committee in part abroad and in part in jail or exile. The party appeared not to exist, it was dispersed and broken. . . . It did not play a decisive role in the February revolution. . . ."There is an important element of truth in this, but also a serious distortion, which is perhaps not surprising, given Zinoviev's own inclinations toward interpreting Bolshevik organizational norms in a mechanistic and bureaucratic elitist manner. He overlooks the remarkable initiative of the local Bolshevik organizations. Trotsky has described how "conscious and tempered workers educated for the most part by the party of Lenin" played an essential role: "In every factory, in each guild, in each company, in each tavern, in the military hospital, at the transfer stations, even in the depopulated villages, the molecular work of revolutionary thought was in progress. Everywhere were to be found the interpreters of events, chiefly from among the workers, from whom one inquired, 'What's the news?' and from whom one awaited the needed words. These leaders had often been left to themselves, and nourished themselves upon fragments of revolutionary generalizations arriving in their hands by various routes, had studied out by themselves between the lines of the liberal papers what they needed. Their class instinct was refined by a political criterion, and though they did not think all their ideas through to the end, nevertheless their thought ceaselessly and stubbornly worked its way in a single direction."[12] Recent scholarship has corroborated this imaginative insight.

On the other hand, the local Bolsheviks and their sympathizers were hardly in control of events. The overthrow of tsarism involved a far more interesting dynamic.

The Petrograd Bolsheviks were intending to make May 1, the international workers' holiday, the time for massive demonstrations and a general strike that they hoped would culminate in the overthrow of the autocracy. Yet International Women's Day (March 9, or February 23 of the old Russian calendar) was also a day observed by the workers' movement. It took place amid rising prices, bread lines, and the disappearance of bread from some bakeries, on top of a lockout and militant strike at the massive Putilov works. According to David Mandel "the mood of the women workers was very militant." He continues: "The day began with meetings featuring anti-war speeches, but no other actions were planned. Among the Bolsheviks, who tended to be the most militant, the strategy was to conserve energy for a decisive general strike on May Day. Nevertheless, in the Vyborg District the women workers of several textile mills quit work and, gathering outside the nearby metalworking factories, easily persuaded the men to join them."[13] Earlier in this study we noted the relative political "backwardness" and passivity of unskilled workers—such as female textile workers—throughout the early history of the workers' movement, as well as the determination of the more conscious workers (such as those predominating in the heavily Bolshevik-influenced metal trades) to reach out to them and draw them into the struggle. Consider the recollection of one Bolshevik machinist:

> On the morning of February 23 one could hear women's voices in the lane which the windows of our department overlooked: "Down with the war: Down with high prices! Down with hunger! Bread for the workers!" Myself and several comrades were at the windows in a flash. . . . The gates of No. 1 Bol'shaya Sampsio'evskaya Manufaktura were wide open. Masses of women workers filled the lane, and their mood was militant. Those who caught sight of us began to wave their arms, shouting: "Come out! Quit work!" Snowballs flew through the window. We decided to join the demonstration. . . . A brief meeting took place outside the main office near the gates, and we poured out into the street. . . . The comrades in front were seized by the arms amidst the shouts of "Hurray!", and we set off with them down Bol'shoi Sampsion'evskii Prospekt.[14]

Such scenes took place at numerous factories. Some Bolsheviks were anxious or even indignant that the "undisciplined" workers were not heeding their advice to stay calm and conserve their energy for future battles. But the Bolshevik rank and file threw itself into the actual struggle that was erupting around it. On the following day demonstrations and strikes spread throughout Petrograd. A police informant reported on the scene: "Since the military units did not hinder the crowd and in individual cases even took measures to paralyze the initiative of the police, the masses have acquired a sense of certainty that they will go unpunished, and now after two days of unhindered marching about the streets, when revolutionary circles have put forward the slogans 'down with the war' and 'down with the government', the people have become convinced that the revolution has begun, that success is with the masses, that the government is powerless to suppress the movement since the military units are not on its side, that victory is close since the military units will soon cross over to the revolutionary forces."[15]

The day after this street fighting broke out, the police attempted to take the offensive and fired into the crowds. But the workers persisted wth growing confidence. As a general strike paralyzed the city, the overwhelming majority of the working class demonstrated that it shared the views of the agitator who proclaimed: "We cannot live like this any longer. We are human beings, not animals."[16] By the fourth day of the insurgency the troops were disobeying the commands of tsarist officers, openly joining the workers in massive numbers, firing on the police stations, helping to free all political prisoners. The tsarist autocracy collapsed. The revolution was triumphant. The insurgents went on to establish soviets, democratic councils, through which the workers and their most loyal allies confronted and gradually developed responses to their difficult situation. We will touch on these later developments in the final section of this chapter.

At this point we must take a closer look at the dynamic between the Bolshevik party and the revolutionary masses during the February–March events. Tsuyoshi Hasegawa, summarizing the historical data, stresses "the importance of the middle-echelon activists of the Bolshevik Party in the February Revolution. . . . A group located between the top revolutionary leaders and the rank and file often played a crucial role in providing the masses with direct, immediate leadership, channeling their diffused discontent into specific actions, and communicating their sentiment to the revolutionary leaders. In the case of the February Revolution the radical orientation of the mass movement came precisely from this group."[17] To understand what happened, we must examine the structure and internal functioning of the Bolshevik organization in Petrograd at this time.

The party in Petrograd consisted essentially of factory cells, which were coordinated by district committees; the committees were coordinated by the Petersburg committee. In addition, at the highest level inside Russia, there was the recently reconstituted Russian Bureau of the Central Committee, made up of V. M. Molotov, P. A. Zalutsky, and the experienced underground activist and worker-Bolshevik Alexander Shlyapnikov (the most authoritative of the three). Trotsky comments that this "central Bolshevik staff . . . was amazing in its helplessness and lack of initiative."[18] This assessment brings to mind the limitations of the Bolshevik leadership in the beginning of 1905, although the caliber of Shlyapnikov as a working-class leader was certainly higher than that of the 1905 committeeman S. I. Gusev. Yet Shlyapnikov, who had seen the workers' movement ebb and flow time and again over the years, later admitted that he had no idea that "this would be the last and decisive battle against tsarism." On the third day of the upsurge he said to one of the militants of the Vyborg district committee: "What revolution is happening here?! Give the workers a loaf of bread, and the movement would be gone." His primary concern was to counter the spread of revolutionary illusions, to prevent unnecessary and fruitless bloodshed, and to conserve Bolshevik and working-class energies and organizations for the struggles of the future. The Bolshevik rank and file, particularly the confident working-class activists of the Vyborg district, were openly dissatisfied with the orientation provided by their "leaders" of the Russian Bureau of the Central Committee. They attempted to pressure Shlyapnikov into providing revolutionary leadership—then despairing of this—ignored his advice and defied his directives, took initiatives on their own, issued their own leaflets, and made their own decisions on how they would function in the struggle. In their own district organizations and partially through the Petersburg committee, which they temporarily dominated, the radicals sought to co-ordinate Bolshevik activity without being impeded by those who, according to party rules, had greater authority. At certain points even the Petersburg committee seemed too cautious and conservative for the embattled rank-and-file militants. On the other hand, when the Petersburg committee was wiped out by arrests, the radical Vyborg district committee assumed its functions. Regardless of who was formally supposed to be "leading" the work, however, the real struggle was a higher priority for them than were the formalities of party discipline.[19]

"A colossal role was played by the revolutionary party members, organically connected with the crowds," a working-class member of the Socialist Revolution-aries later recalled. "They were internal, moral inspiration, led the masses, and ex-perienced all the peripeteia of the movement with them. Only the workers and a handful of intelligentsia integrally connected with the workers could be such lead-ers." Soviet historian E. N. Burdzhalov has noted that the party affiliations of these key activists faded in the heat of the struggle: "In the streets of Petrograd, the Men-sheviks, SRs, and nonparty workers fought together with the Bolshevik workers. In the course of this struggle the unity of their aims took shape and the unity of their action was formed."[20]

The limitations of rank-and-file initiative, however, quickly became evident. As the fighting was still raging, the moderate Menshevik and right-wing Socialist Revolutionary leadership was taking bold steps to channel the victory in a "proper" direction. Among the insurgent workers, the idea had begun to circulate that, as in 1905, a soviet was necessary to coordinate the workers' activities throughout Pet-rograd. The moderate socialists, particularly the Menshevik deputies to the Duma, utilized this sentiment to rally the workers around a widely publicized proposal for the workers and soldiers to quickly select representatives for a soviet to meet at the Tauride Palace, the seat of the Duma. The moderates dubbed themselves the Provisional Executive Committee of the Soviet of Workers Deputies. Convinced that the liberal bourgeoisie must assume leadership of the bourgeois-democratic revolution, they intended through the creation of the soviet to draw the revolu-tionary movement into support for a bourgeois-liberal provisional government to be created through the Duma. Elements among the Bolsheviks, the Mezhraiontsy, and the left Socialist Revolutionaries wanted to see the soviet itself become the provisional government, but they were not sufficiently organized to communicate this notion as a coherent and reasonable alternative to the revolutionary workers who were overturning tsarism. The moderate leaders—although not involved in the strike movement or insurrection in the way that the semileaderless Bolsheviks were—had the capacity and the resources to articulate effectively a course of action.

A very important additional factor has been noted by David Mandel: "It was one thing to overthrow the government in the capital! but quite another to obtain the allegiance of peasants and soldiers throughout the country and to set the state and economic machines working effectively. The workers did not feel prepared to attempt this on their own. They needed the authority that the Duma presumably enjoyed outside the capital and especially within educated society."[21]

Thus, the working-class revolution of February–March did not transfer power to the workers themselves. Instead, there was the creation of a "dual power". On the one hand there were the soviets of workers' and soldiers' deputies, the political expression of the socialist working class and its allies. On the other hand there was the provisional government, whose outstanding liberal member, Kadet party leader P. N. Miliukov, expressed the sentiment of its bourgeois members in this statement: "We did not want this revolution. We did not wish particularly that it would come at the time of the war. And we had desperately struggled so that this would not happen." One of Miliukov's colleagues, V. V. Shulgin, commented that "if we do not take power, others will take it for us, those rotters who have already elected all sorts of scoundrels in the factories." The most radical of the provisional government liberals, N. V. Nekrasov, expressed the hope that the government could achieve "the avoidance of social revolution through social reform." The reluctant bourgeois "leaders" of the provisional government enjoyed (if one can use the term) the support of the revolutionary soviets that were proliferating throughout Russia. Shlyapnikov remarked with surprise "how easily the worker masses were taken in by the trap of national unity and the unity of revolutionary democracy, in which the capitalists were included." The logic of this "trap" was, as we have seen, a fear that the working class—a minority class in Russia—would be isolated and crushed (as had happened to the Paris Commune of 1871 and, in a different and less-definitive way, to the Russian workers' uprising of 1905). It was a complex situation, and the "common-sense" solution for even many of the more militant workers seemed to be precisely "the unity of revolutionary democracy, in which the capitalists were included."[22]

Tony Cliff's judgment also seems well taken: "Although the revolution was led by class-conscious workers who were mostly Bolsheviks, it was not led by the Bolshevik Party. Furthermore the number of class-conscious workers active in the revolution could be counted in thousands, or tens of thousands, while the number who were aroused by the revolution was measured in millions. No wonder the leadership of the rank-and-file Bolsheviks in the February revolution, although able to achieve the victory of the insurrection, could not secure political power for the working class or the Bolshevik Party." The Mensheviks, however, felt that the revolution was a vindication of their own perspective: "Our revolution is a political one. We destroy the bastions of political authority, but the bases of capitalism remain in place. A battle on two fronts—against the Tsar and against capital—is beyond the forces of the proletariat."[23]

The Mensheviks' article of "Marxist" faith, of course, had been that the bourgeois-democratic revolution must have a bourgeois leadership. Yet blended with this was an outlook that soon became characteristic of modern Social Democracy. Marcel Liebman has described it well: "The men who at that moment held the country's fate in their hands belonged to the variant of European socialism which, although concerned for the interests of the proletariat and sincerely devoted to its cause, had never believed in the possibility of entrusting political power to this class. Such a development seemed to them to be conceivable only after a long period of preparation and education. The sentiments of these Social Democrats in relation to the bourgeoisie were a mixture of hostility and respect, in which respect often outweighed hostility. The Menshevik Potresov expressed a belief common to many socialists in Russia and the West when he declared that, 'at the moment of the bourgeois revolution, the [class] best prepared, socially and psychologically, to solve national problems, is [the] bourgeoisie.' In reality, despite all proclamations of faith in socialism, many socialists believed that the bourgeoisie would continue, for an indefinite period, to be the necessary and almost natural wielder of political and social authority. As for the proletariat, if Sukhanov was to be believed, 'isolated as it was from other classes, [it] could create only fighting organizations which, while representing a real force in the class struggle, were not a genuine element of state power.'"[24]

Such a perspective, however, rather than being boldly stated, was muted and glossed over amid revolutionary euphoria and rhetoric. The insurgent masses of workers who were newly drawn into the struggle did not distinguish clearly among the variety of revolutionary and moderate socialists who seemed equally opposed to tsarist oppression and in favor of democracy and social justice. The system of dual power seemed a reasonable way to consolidate their victory, and only a militant minority was inclined to question the decision of the newly established soviet to give power to the predominantly bourgeois provisional government.

Yet the alliance of the soviets and the provisional government, which combined working-class power and capitalist authority, was necessarily unstable and temporary. Given the nature of the situation, the gains of the workers' revolution could not be preserved and extended by relying on the liberal capitalist politicians. The clear-sighted revolutionary minority realized, as historian David A. Longley has expressed it, that "the Russian bourgeoisie, through its involvement in the war, was tied very closely to the capitalists of Britain and France. . . . The Russian bourgeoisie, caught between fear of its own workers and peasants and pressure from its allies in Britain and France, was incapable of implementing any real reforms. On the contrary, they would only attempt to curtail those freedoms that the workers and soldier-peasants had won."[25] Over the next seven months a working-class majority became convinced of the need to transfer power from the Provisional government to their own soviets. The Bolshevik party was to play an essential role in this process, but not before its programmatic orientation underwent a crucial shift.

2. Reorientation

We have already noted a key tension in the Bolshevik orientation—an uncompromising class-struggle attitude that rejected proletarian subordination to the liberal bourgeoisie in the antitsarist struggle, and yet adherence to the traditional assumption that Russia would have to undergo a period of capitalist development before being ready for a socialist revolution. This tension became explicit in 1917 and created profound strains that were overcome only through a process of programmatic reorientation.

Even before this reorientation, major shifts were taking place in Lenin's thinking. "By 1915–1916 Vladimir Ilyich had gone deep into the question of democracy," Krupskaya recalled, "which he examined in the light of socialist construction." She draws our attention to a particular passage that "strikingly expresses the thoughts which had occupied Ilyich's mind at the end of 1915 and during 1916, thoughts which tinctured all his subsequent utterances."[26] It is worth turning our attention to this passage, which occurs in a polemic with Karl Radek on the national question:

> The proletariat can win only through democracy, i.e., through putting into effect full democracy and linking up every step of its progress with democratic demands in their most emphatic wording. It is absurd to *offset* the socialist revolution and the revolutionary struggle against capitalism by *one* of the questions of democracy, in this case the national question. We must *combine* the revolutionary struggle against capitalism with a revolutionary program and tactics in respect of *all* democratic demands, including a republic, a militia, election of government officials by the people, equal rights for women, self-determination of nations, etc. So long as capitalism exists all these demands are capable of realization only as an exception, and in incomplete, distorted form. Basing ourselves on democracy as already achieved, and showing up its deficiency under capitalism, we demand the overthrow of capitalism and expropriation of the bourgeoisie as an essential basis both for abolishing the poverty of the masses and for *fully* and *thoroughly* implementing *all* democratic transformations. Some of those transformations will be started before the overthrow of the bourgeoisie, others *in the course* of this overthrow, and still others after it. The social revolution is not a single battle but an epoch of a series of battles on all and every problem of economic and democratic transformations, whose completion will be effected only with the ex-

propriation of the bourgeoisie. It is for the sake of this ultimate goal that we must formulate *every one* of our democratic demands in a consistently revolutionary manner. It is quite conceivable that the workers of a given country may overthrow the bourgeoisie *before* any single cardinal democratic transformation has been fully implemented. But it is quite inconceivable that the proletariat, as an historical class, will be able to defeat the bourgeoisie unless it has been prepared for it by being educated in a spirit of the most consistent and determined revolutionary democratism.[27]

This vision of the democratic revolution's flowing over into the socialist revolution brings to mind Trotsky's conception of *permanent revolution*. It is unlikely—given Lenin's antipathy toward Trotsky in 1915, and given indications that he had never read Trotsky's *Results and Prospects* or *1905*—that Trotsky was Lenin's source. On the other hand, there are indications that the two were influenced by a common source: the writings of Marx and Engels in 1850, especially the two "Addresses of the Central Committee to the Communist League." According to David Riazanov, "Lenin, who knew them by heart, used to delight in quoting them."[28] Marx and Engels had written as follows:

The relation of the revolutionary workers' party to the petty-bourgeois democrats is this: it marches together with them against the [reactionary-monarchist] faction which it aims at overthrowing, it opposes them in everything whereby they seek to consolidate their position in their own interests. . . .

While the democratic petty-bourgeois wish to bring the revolution to a conclusion as quickly as possible, and with the achievement, at most, of the above [democratic] demands, it is our interest to make the revolution permanent, until the proletariat has conquered state power, and the association of proletarians, not only in one country but in all the dominant countries of the world, has advanced so far that competition among the proletarians has ceased and that at least the decisive productive forces are concentrated in the hands of the proletarians.[29]

The First World War convinced Lenin that such an orientation had new relevance throughout the world: "Imperialism forces the masses into this struggle by sharpening class contradictions on a tremendous scale, by worsening the conditions of the masses both economically—trusts, high cost of living—and politically—the growth of militarism, more frequent wars, more powerful reaction, the intensification and expansion of national oppression and colonial plunder. . . . It would be a mistake to think that the struggle for democracy was capable of diverting the proletariat from the socialist revolution or of hiding it, overshadowing it, etc. On the contrary, in the same way as there can be no victorious socialism that does not practice full democracy, so the proletariat cannot prepare for its victory over the bourgeoisie without an all-around, consistent and revolutionary struggle for democracy."[30]

This was the orientation Lenin brought to the situation created by the over-throw of the tsar. "The imperialist war was bound, with objective inevitability, im-mensely to accelerate and intensify to an unprecedented degree the class struggle of the proletariat against the bourgeoisie; it was bound to turn into a civil war be-tween hostile classes," he wrote in his *Letters from Afar*. "This *transformation has been started* by the February–March Revolution of 1917, the first stage of which has been marked, firstly, by a joint blow at tsarism struck by two forces: one, the whole of bourgeois and landlord Russia with all her unconscious hangers-on and all her conscious leaders, the British and French ambassadors and capitalists, and the other, the *Soviet of Workers' Deputies*, which has begun to win over the soldiers' and peasants' deputies."[31] To the Mensheviks' attitude toward the bourgeois pro-visional government, Lenin counterposed a profoundly different perspective:

> Ours is a bourgeois revolution, *therefore*, the workers must support the bourgeoisie, say the Potresovs, Gvozdyovs and Chkeidzes, as Plekhanov said yesterday.
>
> Ours is a bourgeois revolution, we Marxists say, *therefore* the workers must open the eyes of the people to the deception practised by the bourgeois politicians, teach them to put no faith in words, to depend entirely on their *own* strength, their *own* organization, their *own* unity, and their *own* weapons.[32]

Stressing that "the only *guarantee* of freedom and of the complete destruction of tsarism lies in *arming the proletariat*, in strengthening, extending and developing the role, significance and power of the Soviet of Workers' Deputies," Lenin argued for "a *transition* from the first stage of the revolution to the second." He argued that the Russian workers had two allies in the second revolution: "the broad masses of the semi-proletarian and partly also of the small-peasant population, who num-ber scores of millions and constitute the overwhelming majority of the population of Russia," and also "the proletariat of all the belligerent countries and of all coun-tries in general."[33]

In his "Farewell Letter to Swiss Workers," Lenin expressed the revolutionary internationalist dimension of his orientation with special clarity:

> It was not our impatience nor our desire, but *the objective conditions* created by the imperialist war that brought the whole of humanity to an impasse, and faced it with the dilemma of either permitting the extermination of more millions of lives and the complete extinction of European civilization, or handing over the power to the rev-olutionary proletariat and achieving the socialist revolution in *all* civilized countries.
>
> To the Russian proletariat has fallen the great honor of *initiating* the series of revolutions which are arising from the imperialist war with objective inevitability. . . .
>
> The Russian proletariat single-handed cannot successfully *complete* the socialist revolution. But it can lend such a sweep to the Russian revolution as would create

the most favorable conditions for a socialist revolution, and, in a sense, *start that revolution*. It can render more favorable the conditions under which its *most important*, most trustworthy and most reliable coadjutor, the *European* and the American *socialist* proletariat will undertake its decisive battles. . . .

The objective conditions of the imperialist war make it certain that the revolution will not be limited to the *first stage* of the Russian revolution, that the revolution will *not* be limited to Russia.[34]

In the fifth installment of *Letters from Afar*, Lenin focused on the specific forms that would be taken by the struggle for democracy's flowing over into the struggle for workers' power, a workers' state:

> The workers, guided by their class instinct, have realized that in revolutionary times they need an entirely different organization, of a type above the ordinary. They have taken the right attitude suggested by the experience of our revolution of 1905 and by the Paris Commune of 1871: they have created a *Soviet of Workers' Deputies*, they have set out to develop it, widen and strengthen it, by attracting to it representatives of the soldiers and no doubt of the hired agricultural workers, as well as (in one form or another) of the entire poor section of the peasantry. . . .
>
> The question, then, is: What is to be the work of the Soviets of Workers' Deputies? We repeat what we once said in No. 47 of the Geneva *Social-Democrat* (October 13, 1915): "They must be regarded as organs of insurrection, as organs of revolutionary power."
>
> This theoretical formula, derived from the experience of the Commune of 1871 and of the Russian Revolution of 1905, must be elucidated and concretely developed on the basis of the practical experience gained at this very stage of this very revolution in Russia.
>
> We need revolutionary *power*, we need (for a certain period of transition) the *state*. . . . We need the state, but not the kind needed by the bourgeoisie, with organs of power in the form of police, army, bureaucracy, distinct from and opposed to the people. All bourgeois revolutions have merely perfected this government apparatus, have merely transferred it from one party to another.
>
> The proletariat, however, if it wants to preserve the gains of the present revolution and to proceed further to win peace, bread, and freedom, must "*destroy*," to use Marx's word, this "ready-made" state machinery, and must replace it by another one, *merging* the police, the army, and the bureaucracy *with the universally armed people*. Advancing along the road indicated by the experience of the Paris Commune of 1871 and the Russian Revolution of 1905, the proletariat must organize and arm *all* the poorest and most exploited sections of the population, so that they *themselves* may take into their own hands all the organs of state power, that they *themselves* may constitute these organs.[35]

Careful scholars have provided us with a detailed picture of how the Bolshevik party responded to Lenin's orientation. We have noted that the party—whose cadres were made up of seasoned and independent-minded militants—had been divided over how to respond to the revolutionary upsurge of February 1917. In the period leading up to Lenin's return to Russia in early April, new divisions and discussions opened up. One Bolshevik veteran, Vladimir Bonch-Bruyevich, later recalled: "When the February revolution broke out to so speedily topple the monarchy of Nicholas II, we Petrograd Bolsheviks, who were undoubtedly in the minority in all institutions that appeared, nevertheless participated most vigorously, and strove to consolidate the new order and pursue our own policy wherever possible. Nevertheless we felt the absence of one common will, one common leadership in all this extremely responsible work in a situation that changed with kaleidoscopic rapidity and was marked by madly racing political developments. Everyone felt the absence of Vladimir Ilyich Lenin."[36] In fact, there were four distinct tendencies, during the month of March, that crystallized within the Bolshevik party's center in Petrograd: one represented by the influential Vyborg district committee; one represented by the citywide Petersburg committee; one represented by the Russian Bureau of the Central Committee (which had expanded to fifteen members under Alexander Shlyapnikov's leadership); and one represented by a newly returned leadership group headed by Kamenev, Stalin, and the former Duma deputy M. K. Muranov (which had minority adherents in each of the other three bodies and which took control of the resurrected daily *Pravda*). Yet when Lenin arrived, the positions he advanced were questioned by each of these tendencies, in some cases arousing fierce opposition. Historian Alexander Rabinowitch has effectively challenged as "vastly exaggerated" the "organizational unity and discipline" commonly attributed to the Bolsheviks. While acknowledging that they were "doubtless more unified than any of their rivals for power," Rabinowitch finds the Bolshevik organization to have had an "internally relatively democratic, tolerant, and decentralized structure and method of operation, as well as [an] essentially open and mass character."[37] Lenin was in no position to simply call the shots upon his return.

The open and mass character of the Bolshevik party is shown by the fact that it grew from 24,000 in February to 80,000 in April, 240,000 in July, and 350,000 in October. Of the entire Russian working class, it is estimated that over 5 percent had enrolled in the Bolshevik party by October; in Petrograd 7 percent of all industrial workers were Bolsheviks. Workers represented 61 percent of the Bolshevik membership. Bolshevik influence was, of course, considerably broader than its membership, and the influence of the insurgent working class was also powerfully felt—as we have seen—in Bolshevik ranks. Rabinowitch has identified another important aspect of the Bolsheviks' openness: "within the Bolshevik Petrograd organization at all levels in 1917 there was continuing free and lively discussion and debate over the most basic theoretical and tactical issues. Leaders who differed with the majority were at liberty to fight for their views, and not infrequently Lenin was the loser in these struggles."[38]

Initially, Lenin was the loser when he articulated his position on the course to be followed after the overthrow of tsarism. N. N. Sukhanov has referred to his "complete intellectual isolation, not only among Social Democrats in general but also among his own disciples."[39] The only prominent party leader to endorse his new orientation from the beginning was Alexandra Kollontai, a recent convert to Bolshevism. In order to understand Lenin's minority status—and how the situation was reversed within a month—it is necessary to consider at least briefly the positions of the existing tendencies in the party before his arrival: The Vyborg district committee; the Petersburg committee; the Russian Bureau of the Central Committee; and the newly-arrived team of Kamenev, Stalin, and Muranov.

The Vyborg district committee, as we have seen, was directly in touch with the most militant sectors of the Petrograd working class and had played a leadership role in the February uprising. While reflecting the uncompromising class-struggle militancy of its contituency, however, it was not capable of projecting the sweeping vision Lenin had developed, and it feared that if the revolution became too radical, "the workers of the cities would be cut off from the peasants and . . . 1917 would merely repeat the events of the Paris Commune of 1871," when an isolated working-class uprising established "a proletarian state" that was quickly drowned in blood. Nonetheless, the committee thoroughly distrusted the provisional government and wanted the soviets to constitute themselves as a provisional revolutionary government to replace it. This soviet provisional government would oversee the establishment of the Constituent Assembly, a democratic republic, which would become a permanent government.[40]

After the February revolution, the Petersburg committee was reconstituted in its majority with members who had "gone into prison at a very low moment in the party's fortunes, . . . had virtually no contact with the outside world, and [had] come out to find the revolution over." As one of them later acknowledged, they were not "psychologically prepared" for the new situation and could not share the militancy of their Vyborg comrades. A majority of them resolved to "not oppose the power of the Provisional Government *in so far as* its activities correspond to the interests of the proletariat and of the broad democratic masses of the people." This attitude slid over into one of conditional support for the provisional government not dissimilar to that of the Mensheviks and the Socialist Revolutionaries.[41]

The Russian Bureau of the Central Committee initially called for the replacement of the provisional government by a new provisional revolutionary government made up of the parties represented in the soviets. Unlike the Vyborg Bolsheviks, however, the bureau hoped to bring this about not through militant actions but through negotiations with the other soviet parties—a hope that soon proved utopian. The bureau then developed a perspective that envisioned the soviets themselves—not some future Constituent Assembly—as becoming the new state power, which should keep a careful check on the provisional government while preparing to replace it. The soviets, according to this perspective, should consolidate themselves and deepen the revolution by working to arm the masses of the people and by creating an independent red guard. Yet even this current, seemingly the most radical in the party, declared in the days when it was setting the editorial line in *Pravda*: "Of course there is no question among us of the downfall of the rule of capital, but only of the downfall of the rule of autocracy and feudalism." Nonetheless, as historian David Longley asserts, the majority of the members of the bureau, while not anticipating "Lenin's full program, . . . were moving towards a similar position before he returned." The Russian Bureau's effectiveness was undercut by the fact that the majority of the Vyborg Bolsheviks and of the Petersburg committee—although from different vantage points—viewed it as too removed from the practical struggle to offer more than "academic" and unrealistic generalizations.[42]

The Russian Bureau's authority was even more profoundly undercut by the positions and activities of Kamenev, Stalin, and Muranov, who—according to Shlyapnikov—introduced "into the leading bodies of the party disagreements and deep organizational frictions." Through their insistence on pushing through their own vision of the "correct line" despite majority decisions and rank-and-file protests, Shlyapnikov tells us, "disorder continued inside the party. Breaches of Bolshevik policy were committed in many areas and the example for all this was given by comrades whom we had grown accustomed to regard as leaders in tsarist times." As is generally the case, the high-handed attitude in regard to organizational norms was inseparable from a deeper political difference. Kamenev and his co-thinkers were convinced that the bourgeois-democratic revolution would have to be completed before the working class could think of taking power. They followed this notion to its logical conclusion. The provisional government, precisely because it was a political reflection of the bourgeoisie, had a progressive role to play and should be supported by Marxists "not from fear, but from conscience." What is more, the new revolutionary government and the gains won by the workers must be defended from all enemies, including German imperialism. Therefore—and here Kamenev and his cothinkers were sharply at variance with the other Bolshevik tendencies—the character of the Russian war effort had changed and should be supported by all revolutionaries, with the proviso, of course, that any imperialist or annexationist goals should be repudiated.[43] These positions were in harmony with radical public opinion (that is, majority views among the Mensheviks and Socialist Revolutionaries, and their sympathizers) and corresponded with the views of many workers. But they also had a coherence and internal consistency that, before the arrival of Lenin, seemed difficult to challenge.

This current was not, however, embraced by the party as a whole. The Russian Bureau majority was furious, a sentiment that continued to reverberate in Shlyapnikov's memoirs several years later: "Comrades Kamenev, Stalin, and Muranov decided to take over *Pravda* and give it 'their' line. . . . On the basis of their formal rights they completely took into their hands the editing of the regular issue No. 9, of March 15, employing their majority and formal prerogatives to prevail over the representative of the Central Committee Bureau, Comrade V. Molotov." Angry protests were raised in the Vyborg and other working-class districts over the moderation and "defensism" of the new leadership, and there were even demands that Kamenev, Stalin, and Muranov be expelled from the party. Trotsky reports: "The same thing was to be observed in the provinces. Almost everywhere there were left Bolsheviks accused of maximalism, even of anarchism. These worker-revolutionists only lacked the theoretical resources to defend their position. But they were ready to respond to the first clear call."[44]

Yet before April there was no such "clear call." The problem can be traced to a fundamental theoretical-programmatic limitation of Bolshevism. It was commonly assumed that there would be an interval, perhaps of decades, between the democratic revolution and the socialist revolution, and many Bolsheviks, as Stalin later expressed it, had an "inadequate theoretical preparation" for grasping Lenin's deepening conviction that the bourgeois-democratic revolution would grow into a proletarian-socialist one.[45] Zinoviev noted, similarly, that while the Bolshevik demand for a democratic republic had been put forward often, "we did have some lack of agreement and confusion over this question in 1915–1917," and that "some of us (including myself) for too long upheld the idea that in our peasant country we could not pass straight on to the socialist revolution, but merely hope that if our revolution coincided with the start of the international proletarian one it could become its overture."[46] The veteran Bolshevik publicist Mikhail S. Olminsky suggested in 1921 that one problem was that the old "democratic dictatorship" perspective, despite its profoundly radical thrust, was based on the view that "the coming revolution must be only a bourgeois revolution. . . . That was an obligatory premise for every member of the party, the official opinion of the party, its continual and unchanging slogan right up to the February revolution of 1917, and even some time after." In mid-April, as the debate initiated by Lenin was generating a "complete revolution in the thinking of the Party's leaders" (as the Bolshevik Raskolnikov termed it), one of the leading women Bolsheviks, Ludmila Stahl, commented: "All the comrades before the arrival of Lenin were wandering in the dark. We knew only the formulas of 1905. Seeing the independent creative work of the people, we could not teach them."[47] Even the most radical opponents of the Kamenev-Stalin-Muranov line had found themselves trapped in the bourgeois-democratic framework that justified that line. There had been a muted contradiction in the old "democratic dictatorship" formula—on the one hand radical working-class tactics, involving a worker-peasant alliance that was counterposed to the bourgeoisie; on the other hand, a rejection of creating a workers' state of the Paris Commune type because first the bourgeois-democratic revolution would have to run its course. The contradiction became manifest with the overthrow of tsarism: The party began to fragment, with one wing holding firm to the militant tactical orientation and another wing insisting that the bourgeois-democratic limitations of Russia's revolution necessitated the Bolsheviks' (and the workers') coming to terms with the undeniably bourgeois-democratic provisional government.

In the end of March and beginning of April, a conference of Bolshevik representatives from all of Russia met in Petrograd to thrash out the differences and forge a more unified policy for the complex situation. Kamenev and Stalin adjusted their formulations in order to mollify their more militant comrades. Sharp differences continued to be voiced at the conference, but a synthesis of the different positions seemed to be evolving. Stalin gave a report, "On the Attitude to the Provisional Government," designed to help bridge the gaps between the positions of the different Bolshevik tendencies, in which he commented: "The question of support—let us even allow that support is not permissible. In so far as the Provisional Government fortifies the steps of the revolution, to that extent we must support it; but in so far as it is counterrevolutionary, support to the Provisional Government is not permissible. Many comrades who have arrived from the provinces ask whether we shouldn't immediately pose the question of the seizure of power. But it is untimely to pose the question now."[48]

At the same time, there was a strong pull toward Bolshevik/Menshevik unity at the conference. The meeting was interrupted for a joint session with several Menshevik spokesmen to discuss the possibility of a common statement on the war. One of these spokesmen noted: "At the present time, in many places in the provinces there is taking place the spontaneous unification of the masses of Bolsheviks and Mensheviks. Every time that party activity is revived, such a unification takes place.

I consider this to be a sign of a healthy instinct on the part of the working class masses who strive with all their might for the creation of a *united* social democratic party." In a later session of the resumed Bolshevik conference, Stalin expressed his agreement that at least those supporting the broad antiwar resolutions of the Zimmerwald and Kienthal conferences should join together in a common party. The Menshevik Tseretelli had proposed a meeting to discuss unification. "We should go," argued Stalin. "It is necessary to define our proposals as to the terms of unification."[49]

Members of the Russian Bureau argued against this perspective. Molotov remarked that "Tseretelli wants to unite heterogeneous elements. Tseretelli calls himself a Zimmerwaldist and a Kienthalist, and for this reason unification along these lines is incorrect both politically and organizationally. It would be more correct to advance a definite internationalist socialist platform. We will unite a compact minority." Zalutsky elaborated: "If we enter into negotiations with the Mensheviks, we must put forward our own views. We proceed from a definite position. Only a petty bourgeois and not a social democrat can proceed from a mere desire for unification. There is disagreement between us on the following questions: 1) the attitude to war; 2) the evaluation and role of the capitalist forces in the revolution. If we now slur over them, we will have a split in a week just the same. It is impossible to unite on the basis of a superficial Zimmerwald-Kienthal token.... He is a poor social democrat who will allow himself to become dissolved in the mass. It is necessary to lead the masses behind us. It is necessary to advance a definite program."[50]

This impulse of the Russian Bureau majority—and especially the reasoning of Zalutsky on the primacy of the revolutionary program—was consistent with the entire history of Bolshevism, particularly with the thrust of Lenin's thinking. Yet we have noted that there was a lack of programmatic clarity even among the members of the Russian Bureau. They did not offer a framework that was clearly distinct from that of Stalin. Only one maverick Bolshevik, Krassikov, ventured even to suggest a clear alternative framework: "If we recognize the Soviets of Workers' Deputies as the organs that express the will of the people, then the question before us is not the consideration of what concrete measures must be taken on this or that issue. If we think the time has now come to realize the dictatorship of the proletariat, then we ought to pose the question that way. We unquestionably have the physical force for a seizure of power." But Krassikov was ruled out of order (the chairman of the meeting admonished him that "the question under discussion involves the practical steps for today"), and no one defended his point or raised it again. Krassikov himself seems to have raised it to demonstrate the necessity of taking "steps in relation to the Provisional Government" that would be conciliatory, as the Mensheviks were doing.[51]

One delegate in favor of a unity orientation, Luganovsky, argued that "the Kharkov Committee is carrying on negotiations precisely along these lines. . . . Many disagreements have been outlived. It is out of place to underscore tactical differences. We can have a joint [party] Congress with the Mensheviks, the Zimmerwaldists and Kienthalists." Stalin added: "There is no use running ahead and anticipating disagreements. There is no party life without disagreements. We will live down trivial disagreements within the party. . . . We will have a single party with those who agree on Zimmerwald and Kienthal. . . ."[52] A majority of the delegates voted in favor of entering negotiations with the Mensheviks on this basis. Given the shared conceptual framework regarding the nature of the Russian Revolution, there was a logic to all of this. In the new situation, Bolshevism could not maintain itself as a distinct current (or, one might say, Bolshevism could not remain true to itself) unless the old "orthodox" framework was transcended.

It was precisely the transcendence of the old "orthodoxy" in the Bolshevik program that Lenin's position represented. Lenin himself recognized this quite clearly and called for the "immediate convocation of a Party congress" and the "alteration of the Party Program," particularly:

(1)   On the question of imperialism and the imperialist war;
(2)   On our attitude toward the state and *our* demand for a 'commune state';
(3)   Amendment of our out-of-date minimum program.[53]

We see, then, that Lenin—convinced of the need for major revisions in the party program—did not try to camouflage the changes or sneak them through. Instead he responsibly indicated that the only way this could fruitfully be accomplished was with a frank and democratic discussion in the party, followed by clear-minded decision-making by the party's most authoritative body, a party congress. Such a discussion was in fact opened, although a broad party conference at the end of April had to suffice for deciding upon the new orientation.

Yet at first Lenin's position proved too radical for the majority of his comrades. When he presented the new perspective in his "April Theses," first at the end of the Bolshevik conference of late March and early April, then immediately afterward at a joint meeting of Bolsheviks and Mensheviks, it was received with shock and embarrassment by his own comrades. The Petersburg committee voted against Lenin's position by a vote of 13 to 2, with one abstention; the Bolshevik committees of Moscow and Kiev also formally rejected it. *Pravda* published the "April Theses" with this editorial comment: "As for the general scheme of Comrade Lenin, it seems to us unacceptable in that it starts from the assumption that the bourgeois-democratic revolution is ended, and counts upon an immediate transformation of this revolution into a socialist revolution." A debate was opened in which leading

Bolsheviks sharply criticized the proposed revisions. Kamenev argued forcefully: "Lenin is wrong when he says that the bourgeois-democratic revolution is finished. . . . The classical relics of feudalism, the landed estates, are not yet liquidated. . . . The state is not transformed into a democratic society. . . . It is early to say that the bourgeois democracy has exhausted all its possibilities." Bolshevik trade union leader Mikhail Tomsky insisted on the continued relevance of the orientation Lenin himself had developed in 1905: "The democratic dictatorship is our foundation stone. We ought to organize the power of the proletariat and the peasants, and we ought to distinguish this from the Commune, since that means the power of the proletariat alone." The veteran underground organizer Alexei Rykov asserted that "gigantic revolutionary tasks stand before us, but the fulfillment of these tasks does not carry us beyond the framework of the bourgeois regime."[54]

It is important to note that Lenin did not favor an *immediate* seizure of power and initiation of the socialist revolution. The reason for this, however, had nothing to do with an alleged "bourgeois-democratic stage" of the revolution, but stemmed purely from the present level of consciousness of the Russian working class. In his "April Theses" he stated this explicitly: "We must explain to the masses that the Soviet of Workers' Deputies is the *only possible form* of revolutionary government; and that, therefore, our task is, while this [Soviet] Government is submitting to the influence of the bourgeoisie [by supporting the Provisional Government], a patient, systematic and persistent *explanation* to the masses of the error of their tactics, an explanation especially adapted to the practical needs of the masses. So long as we remain in the minority, we carry on the work of criticism and of explaining errors, advocating all along the necessity of transferring the entire state power to the Soviets of Workers' Deputies, so that the masses may learn from experience how to rid themselves of their errors." Responding to his comrades' criticisms in his *Letter on Tactics*, Lenin stressed that "it is not possible to establish even a 'commune state' (i.e., a state organized on the type of the Paris Commune) in Russia 'immediately,' since that would require that the *majority* of the deputies in all (or in most of) the Soviets should recognize the utter erroneousness and perniciousness of the tactics and policy of the Socialist-Revolutionaries, [and of the Mensheviks] Chkeidze, Tseretelli, Steklov, etc. And I explicitly declared that in this respect I calculate only on 'patient' explanation. . . ."[55]

Lenin found it necessary to "patiently explain" to his own comrades that "the Bolshevik slogans and ideas *in general* have been fully corroborated by history; but *concretely*, things have turned out *differently*," and in particular that the "revolutionary-democratic dictatorship of the proletariat and the peasantry" had become a formula that "is already antiquated. . . . Whoever speaks *now* of a 'revolutionary-democratic dictatorship of the proletariat and peasantry' only is behind the times, has consequently in effect *gone over* to the side of the petty bourgeoisie and is against the proletarian class struggle. He deserves to be consigned to the archive of 'Bolshevik' prerevolutionary antiques (which might be called the archive of 'old Bolsheviks')."[56] Many of his comrades were offended. For example, Mikhail Kalinin—who had been part of the radical Russian Bureau—responded: "I belong to the old Bolshevik Lenin- ists, and I consider that the old Leninism has not by any means proved good-for- nothing in the present peculiar moment, and I am astonished at the declaration of Comrade Lenin that the old Bolsheviks have become an obstacle at the present mo- ment."[57] But Lenin was unyielding: "One must know how to adapt schemes to facts, rather than repeat words regarding a 'dictatorship of the proletariat and peasantry' *in general,* words which have become meaningless. . . . No, that formula is antiquated. It is worthless. It is dead. And all attempts to revive it will be in vain."[58]

The new framework and vision that Lenin projected to guide the work of the Bolsheviks transcended the contradiction that had, under the impact of new events, begun to pull the party into the Mensheviks' orbit. Internationally, the time was ripe for the spread of working-class socialist revolutions. These could be initiated by the rapid transition of the Russian Revolution from the bourgeois-democratic stage to the proletarian stage. There was a need for militant class-struggle tactics on the part of the Russian workers—in alliance with the poor peasants and op- pressed nationalities—to realize democratic rights, immediate and pressing eco- nomic needs, and the withdrawal of bleeding Russia from the imperialist war. The bourgeois-democratic provisional government stood as an obstacle to all of this and, despite its democratic trappings, was a dictatorship of the bourgeoisie—that is, it was a state form that kept political power in the hands of the capitalist class. The soviets, on the other hand, not only were organs of struggle through which the workers and the oppressed could fight for their interests, but also were embry- onic forms of an alternative kind of state, the radically democratic "Paris Commune type state." (At various points, Lenin was to make it clear that he considered this to be the *dictatorship of the proletariat,* referring to the Paris Commune as "a new type of state, a proletarian state" and as a "proletarian dictatorship."[59] While this new state form could not immediately bring socialism to Russia, it could give power to the working class and the oppressed that would enable them to deal effectively with the problems facing them and would involve taking introductory steps toward socialism. In turn, this proletarian revolution in Russia would help inspire and gen- erate working-class socialist revolutions in more industrially developed countries that, when victorious, would be able to assist in Russia's socialist development. A majority of Bolsheviks soon embraced this orientation.

Later Mikhail Olminsky asked, "How did it happen that the party, from its leaders to its rank-and-file members, so suddenly renounced everything that it had regarded as fixed truth for almost two decades?" Part of the answer can be found in the fact that, as Trotsky commented, "Lenin was relying against the old formula upon the living tradition of the party—its irreconcilable hostility to all half-way measures." We have seen that over the two-year period preceding the outbreak of World War I, this "living tradition" became rooted in a layer of worker-Bolsheviks. "It was on this stratum of workers, decisively risen to their feet during the upward years of 1912–14, that Lenin was now banking." Trotsky has also pointed out that despite the similarities in the formal program of the Bolsheviks and Mensheviks in early 1917, the tactical orientation characteristic of each current tended to be quite different: "The worker-Bolsheviks immediately after the revolution took the initiative in the struggle for the eight-hour day; the Mensheviks declared this demand untimely. The Bolsheviks took the lead in arresting the tsarist officials; the Mensheviks opposed 'excesses.' The Bolsheviks energetically undertook the creation of a workers' militia; the Mensheviks delayed the arming of the workers, not wishing to quarrel with the bourgeoisie. Although not yet overstepping the bounds of bourgeois democracy, the Bolsheviks acted, or strove to act—however confused by their leadership—like uncompromising revolutionists. The Mensheviks sacrificed their democratic program at every step in the interests of a coalition with the liberals."[60]

Olminsky's succinct comment is quite apt: "We (or at least many of us) were unconsciously steering a course toward proletarian revolution, although thinking we were steering a course toward a bourgeois-democratic revolution."[61] Another factor facilitating the rapid adoption of Lenin's perspective was the provisional government's failure to satisfy the needs and win the continued loyalty of the workers. "In Petrograd," according to Alexander Rabinowitch, "mass disenchantment with the revolution, partly a consequence of continued economic hardship, was just starting to set in." A citywide meeting of the Petrograd Bolsheviks in mid-April, where Lenin and Kamenev debated their perspectives, saw an overwhelming majority vote for Lenin's perspective. Given the central importance of Petrograd and the fact that it now contained 15,000 Bolsheviks, this was extremely significant. But similar shifts were taking place elsewhere. At the end of April a conference of 151 delegates representing 80,000 Bolsheviks from all over Russia also carefully considered the contending perspectives of party leaders and then adopted Lenin's basic position. Lenin did not have his way on all questions, however, as Rabinowitch has pointed out. "Taken as a whole, however, the resolutions of the April conference were a summons to prepare for a socialist revolution and thus constituted a great personal triumph for Lenin."[62] His authority in Bolshevik ranks increased phenomenally. One conference participant later recalled: "When V. I. Lenin appeared in the hall all of us delegates were overwhelmed by an undescribable delight. The conference ardently acclaimed Lenin as leader of our Party and of the revolution. In those days such acclamation and tumultuous applause were a novelty in the Party. What particularly struck us at the time in Lenin was his combination of highly scholarly approach to the analysis of events, fearless thought and the mastery of a revolutionary leader who never carried his head in the clouds."[63] Such "mastery" was related to the fact that Lenin's orientation was in harmony with the experience and mood of a growing majority of party members. Lenin's triumph and the party's reorientation were the culmination of—and could not have been achieved without—a thoroughly democratic process in which the party ranks had an opportunity to hear, debate, and vote on alternative perspectives regarding what to do next.

3. Diversity and Discipline

John Basil, in his recent study *The Mensheviks in the Revolution of 1917*, has described the dilemma of the Menshevik organization: "Divisiveness within the party was rife and organizational unity, although sought, was never found. Individuals or small groups firmly convinced of the correctness of their own opinions prevented the Mensheviks from enjoying the advantages of unified action. During the events of 1917 internal controversy frustrated attempts to create a cohesive political party and divided the Mensheviks during their efforts to present a consistent program to the Provisional Government; it easily kept the party divided in its relations with the Bolsheviks and the west European socialists. . . . Disagreement might also have been less harmful if large numbers of industrial workers had been lured into the ranks of the movement, but they were not present in sufficient force to coax the Mensheviks onto the path of unity. As a result, the Mensheviks were always prevented from acting in unison, and often their strongest weapons were rendered useless simply because party members disagreed on how to aim them." Basil, like many other historians sympathetic to Menshevism, argues that there were virtues embedded in these weaknesses: "They brought independence to party members, freeing them from the narrow and tyrannical leadership of one figure. They brought a well-founded confidence and an ability to judge events by one's own standards."[64] Here he is obviously using Lenin and the Bolsheviks as a negative contrast.

As we have seen throughout this study, however, Lenin had no iron grip over the Bolshevik organization, which was composed of confident activists who also judged events with critical minds and who consequently formed a spectrum of diverse shades of opinion within the Bolshevik party. This has been documented for the period spanning late 1904 through April 1917. The victory of Lenin's "April

Theses" in no way reversed this dynamic, but, if anything, heightened it. "To gauge the importance of this tolerance of differences of opinion and ongoing give-and-take," writes Alexander Rabinowitch, "it is enough to recall that throughout 1917 many of the Bolsheviks' most important resolutions and public statements were influenced as much by the outlook of right Bolsheviks as by that of Lenin. In addition, more moderate Bolsheviks like Kamenev, Zinoviev, Lunacharsky, and Riazanov were among the party's most articulate and respected spokesmen in key public institutions such as the soviets and the trade unions."[65] Rabinowitch elaborates on this in a passage that deserves to be quoted at length:

> In 1917 subordinate party bodies like the Petersburg Committee and the Military Organization were permitted considerable independence and initiative, and their views and criticism were taken into account in the formation of policy at the highest levels. Most important, these lower bodies were able to tailor their tactics and appeals to suit their own particular constituencies amid rapidly changing conditions. Vast numbers of new members were recruited into the party, and they too played a significant role in shaping the Bolsheviks' behavior. Among these newcomers were many of the leading figures in the October revolution, among them Trotsky, Antonov-Ovseenko, Lunacharsky, and Chudnovsky. The newcomers included tens of thousands of workers and soldiers from among the most impatient and dissatisfied elements in the factories and garrison who knew little, if anything, about Marxism and cared nothing about party discipline. This caused extreme difficulties in July when leaders of the Military Organization and Petersburg Committee, responsive to their militant constituencies, encouraged an insurrection, against the wishes of the Central Committee. But during the period of reaction that followed the July uprising, in the course of the fight against Kornilov, and again during the October revolution, the Bolsheviks' extensive, carefully cultivated connections in factories, local workers' organizations, and units of the Petrograd garrison and the Baltic Fleet were to be a significant source of the party's durability and strength.[66]

The difference between the Bolsheviks and the Mensheviks, as we can see, did not lie in the existence of openness and democracy in the latter and their absence in the former. This does not mean that there were no organizational differences, however. The Bolsheviks traditionally enjoyed a higher degree of internal cohesion than could be found among the Mensheviks, in part because of Bolshevik loyalty to the notion that majority decisions must be respected by dissenting minorities. Under normal circumstances, neither factions nor tendencies nor prestigious individuals could disregard decisions they did not like. We have seen that this sometimes happened, nonetheless, within the Bolshevik organization. When it did, there was neither the shrugging off of the violated decisions on the one hand nor mechanical expulsions on the other; instead, a democratic process of political clarification—

often accompanied by incisive polemics and fierce factional conflict—would be initiated. Ultimately, the cohesion of democratic-centralist norms would again reassert itself around the clarified political positions.

Another essential element helps to explain this cohesion and also helps us to understand the dynamic growth and final triumph of Bolshevism in 1917: the fact that the Bolsheviks were organized around a revolutionary program. Proletarian independence and hegemony in the struggle for democracy, as well as militant class-struggle and mass action tactics to advance the workers' interests, were always central to this program; in April 1917 this evolved into a commitment to replace the capitalist state with a workers' state. The Mensheviks, on the other hand, were profoundly disoriented by a fatal contradiction in the heart of their own programmatic perspective. John Basil has termed it a "clumsy strategic position" of seeing the democratic revolution as "a socialist-liberal alliance (with the liberals running up front)" while at the same time seeing the liberals as "natural enemies" because "they were the representatives of capitalism," which the Mensheviks hoped to overthrow in the long run: "At the root of the Menshevik dilemma was the incompatibility of their liberal-socialist alliance scheme and their radical mentality encouraged by doctrinaire Marxism." This contradiction generated a disunity of diverging standpoints— some giving greater weight to the liberal-socialist alliance, some remaining closer to the principles of what Basil terms "doctrinaire Marxism." But all were united in the debilitating contradiction. Basil concludes: "The presence of Russian liberals was essential for the full operation and understanding of Menshevism. The Mensheviks were part of that group in the Russian socialist intelligentsia that saw the revolution against tsarist Russia as a cooperative effort [of the bourgeoisie and proletariat], even when their anti-liberal strain was playing an influential role in the day-to-day political combat. Menshevism as a viable revolutionary program ceased to exist once the Kadets were driven from Russian politics and Tseretelli, Martov and Dan were left without their foil."[67] The Bolsheviks' programmatic orientation for the most part generated internal cohesion and political effectiveness, even with all of the tumult and diversity that characterized 1917.

An important contribution to Bolshevik cohesion was, in fact, made by the vitality of inner-party democracy. Marcel Liebman points out that "all the major choices and great decisions that the Party had to take in 1917 were always subjected to discussion and a vote." He adds: "All these votes showed that a strong minority, the numbers of which fluctuated but which was always there, existed among the Party cadres, and there was never any question of excluding this minority from the *executive* organs of the Party. The idea that these organs must, for reasons of efficiency, be marked by strict political homogeneity and therefore composed exclusively of members of the majority, had not yet entered into Communist practice. Whenever the Bolsheviks had to elect their leading bodies, a more or less proportional representation of the different tendencies was guaranteed.... This desire to associate the minority with the deciding and application of Party policy is to be seen in other ways: the presence of 'minority' members in the Bolshevik press organs, and the practice of providing for a 'minority report', giving a representative of the 'opposition' an opportunity of expounding the latter's view in thorough fashion at important Party meetings."[68]

Although Liebman has done much to challenge anti-Leninist myths, he has also tended to concede too much to Lenin's critics. Thus he writes of "the challenging within his own organization of the leader who had been thought unchallengeable," asserting that "Lenin had sought, when it became an independent formation (1912), to exclude every factor of division" from the Bolshevik organization. Alluding to Trotsky's reference in the spring of 1917 to "a de-Bolshevized party," he elaborates that "if Bolshevism in its original form meant, above all, on the organizational plane, centralism, discipline and the 'Party spirit', then the formula of 'de-Bolshevization', whatever its shortcomings, does indeed illuminate the process of genuine transformation that Lenin's Party underwent in the great revolutionary period opening with the fall of Tsardom in February 1917.... Lenin understood that *this* Bolshevik Party was profoundly different from the Bolshevik organization as it had existed before the revolution. He understood it so well that he called, on his return to Russia, for a change in the Party's name, for it to abandon the title 'Social-Democrat' and become the 'Communist Party', thus cutting the terminological cord that bound it to the past."[69]

This is all quite misleading. Lenin had hardly been "unchallengeable" before 1917, nor had he ever sought the elimination of "every factor of division." Lenin *did* seek to change the name of the Russian Social Democratic Labor Party (Bolsheviks) to the Russian Communist Party—a change finally made in 1918—but it is well known that this change was meant to signify a decisive break with the bankrupt Social Democratic movement of the Second International, which had failed the tests of war and revolution so miserably, *not* to signify the existence of greater openness and democracy than had existed in the old Bolshevik organization. It is certainly the case that the Bolshevik party experienced a profound transformation in 1917, but far from throwing into question the pre-1917 experience of Bolshevism, this transformation vindicated that experience. Historian Pierre Broué has put it this way: "The Bolshevik party of 1917, the revolutionary party that Lenin called upon to form around the 'better elements of Bolshevism,' was born from the heart of the Bolshevik current coming together with independent revolutionary currents which constituted the Interdistrict Group [the Mezhraiontsy associated with Trotsky, with 4,000 members in Petrograd] and numerous organizations of Social-Democratic internationalists [associated with Menshevism's left wing] that until then had remained outside of Lenin's party. Thus the conception of the party which he had defended for years was solidified: the Bolshevik faction succeeded in making prevail, in the way that he'd hoped it would, his conception of a workers' party, and rallying other revolutionaries to it."[70] The result hardly conformed to the monolithic and authoritarian organization that has in later years passed for the Leninist party, but Lenin had never been such a "Leninist."

Although there was, in these months of ferment and fluidity, a continual tendency for party groupings and activists to assume initiative in a manner that sometimes overstepped the normal bounds of "discipline," Lenin seems to have accepted this as an inevitable and acceptable element of party life—with certain crucial exceptions. It is worth taking note of what he viewed as acceptable and unacceptable in this period of revolutionary turmoil.

Vladimir Bonch-Bruyevich describes accompanying Lenin to a mass rally where various left-wing speakers were haranguing the crowds. "Suddenly one extremely nervous almost hysterical comrade spoke and began frantically to urge the crowd to rise up at once, and spewed forth interminable utterly unrealistic anarchistic phrases." Lenin asked someone for his name, and "with a wry grin" asked also if he was a Bolshevik (which he was). "Meanwhile the man, as if wishing to capture everyone's fancy, brandished his arms with all his might, shouted at the top of his voice, bent, twisted, turned and bellowed one slogan after another as he exhorted the throng." An exasperated Lenin remarked: "No, that's impossible. He has to be checked at once. That's some sort of leftist tommy rot."[71] But under the circumstances described, it was hardly possible to oversee and control the utterances and actions of every Bolshevik orator and militant. Lenin had stressed the need of "patiently explaining" the necessity of a proletarian revolution and of not attempting to initiate one until the majority of the workers had become disillusioned with the moderate orientation of the Mensheviks and Socialist Revolutionaries. But the radicalization of the working class, proceeding unevenly, soon swept important sections of the workers, soldiers, and sailors far to the left of the class as a whole; important sections of the Bolshevik party—such as the reorganized Petersburg committee and the Military Organization (set up to conduct revolutionary work among soldiers garrisoned in Petrograd and sailors at the Kronstadt naval base)—assumed a militantly radical orientation. There was a growing impatience with the "firemen" of the central committee (Lenin included), who sought to dampen the fiery moods of the more revolutionary elements among the masses until their class sisters and brothers could catch up. In May, June, and especially July, this extreme left wing again and again pulled ahead of the party as a whole, more than once directly challenging the authority and disregarding the decisions of the party leadership. Especially in early July, this contributed to serious difficulties, when armed mass demonstrations of workers, soldiers, and sailors— carried away by their impatience and revolutionary fervor—provoked violent repression by the provisional government. Although the Bolshevik Central Committee had issued directives instructing party members to work for restraint, Petersburg committee member M. I. Kalinin later admitted that "the majority of Communists in the districts took upon themselves an active role" in the aggressive militancy. But the provisional government still enjoyed the support of many workers and soldiers. The radicalized sectors found themselves isolated, temporarily discredited, and demoralized. Many were arrested and the Bolsheviks were forced partially underground. Within the organization itself, it was proposed that a party trial be organized for some of the undisciplined leftist comrades. While Lenin would obviously have preferred a greater degree of "revolutionary patience" among the Bolsheviks and was concerned about the centrifugal tendencies that might undermine the party's effectiveness, he opposed bringing anyone up on charges or expelling anyone to set an example.[72]

Other instances can be cited of the party's lower bodies refusing to subordinate themselves to the higher bodies. For example, in May the Petersburg committee decided to set up a newspaper that would be independent of the organ of the central committee, *Pravda*, which it felt was too moderate. Opposing this as "wasteful and harmful," Lenin proposed that a compromise resolution be adopted providing other guarantees of freedom of expression for the Petrograd organization. This idea was rejected by the militants, but Lenin insisted that "the decision of the Petrograd Committee's Executive to establish a *special* newspaper in Petrograd is utterly wrong and undesirable." Nonetheless, a conference of Petrograd Bolsheviks decided by a substantial majority to go ahead with the plan. By August, the central committee decided that "for the moment" the Petersburg committee could not have a "separate organ," but the Petersburg committee then made it clear that it still intended to put out its own paper. Only the October Revolution swept aside this controversy. Similarly, an attempt by the central committee to end the virtual autonomy of the Military Organization's paper, *Soldatskaya Pravda* (Soldier's Truth), ran into intransigent opposition, although Stalin made it clear to the Military Organization that, once arrived at, a central committee decision "must be carried out without discussion." Terming this "unacceptable," the Military Organization forced a discussion that resulted in a compromise. There was also the case of a handful of Bolshevik writers who regularly contributed to Maxim Gorky's paper, *Novaya Zhizn*, which occupied a position between Bolshevism and Menshevism and was often critical of Bolshevik policy. The central committee decided to "order these Party members to inform the editorial board of their refusal to continue writing" for Gorky's paper, but their resistance also forced a compromise. In none of these cases, as Russia moved rapidly toward socialist revolution, were disciplinary measures taken.[73]

In most of these cases, it should be noted, the "delinquents" were guilty of running ahead of a general revolutionary trajectory of the party, with which they were in harmony. Also they were challenging certain proposals or interpretations of the central committee, not violating the basic decisions or program of a party congress or conference.

There is the well-known case, however, of Lenin's demanding the expulsion of two outstanding veterans of the Bolshevik leadership, Lev Kamenev and Gregory Zinoviev. This occurred in October, on the eve the Bolshevik insurrection. An expanded meeting of the central committee—to which members of the Petersburg committee's executive, the Military Organization, and leading Bolsheviks in the Petrograd soviet, the trade unions, and the factory committees were invited—there was a full discussion of the proposal for the Bolshevik party to begin preparations for an armed uprising to overthrow the provisional government. After a number of reports and a thorough debate, with Kamenev and Zinoviev arguing forcefully against, the proposal received a decisive majority of the votes. Lenin was enraged not by the opposition of the two dissidents, but by what they did after the vote was taken.

As the party began to move toward the implementation of this decision, Kamenev and Zinoviev—"deeply convinced that to proclaim an armed insurrection now is to put at stake not only the fate of our Party but also the Russian and international revolution"—insisted that the Bolsheviks would, by "assuming the initiative for a rising in the present circumstances, [be] putting the proletariat under attack from the whole unified counterrevolution, supported by the petty-bourgeois democrats" (the non-Bolshevik left), and "it is against this fatal policy [that] we raise our voice in warning." Each had denounced the proposal as "adventurism" at the expanded central committee meeting. After they lost the vote, they withdrew from activity on the central committee (Kamenev formally resigning), and they continued working against the proposed uprising, in a manner that caused information about the dispute—including hints that preparations for the insurrection were under way, and an indication of what the timetable might be—to leak out to the Bolsheviks' opponents. Kamenev, in his efforts to force the party to draw back from this "adventurism," went so far as to write for Gorky's *Novaya Zhizn* that "not only comrade Zinoviev and I but also a number of comrades with experience in the field consider it would be inadmissible, and fatal for the proletariat and the revolution, for us to initiate an armed insurrection at the present moment," although he also asserted (dishonestly) that "I am not aware of any decisions by our Party which fix a rising of any sort for this or any other date."[74]

In the face of objections against their campaign to reverse the decision, Zinoviev pointed out that Lenin had felt free to do campaigning of his own, circulating letters in the party arguing for an insurrection "before decisions of any kind were taken." Lenin responded: "Is it really so difficult to understand that *before* the [party] center has come to a decision on the question of a strike, there can be agitation both for and against, but *after* a decision in favor of a strike (and after an additional decision to conceal this from the enemy), to campaign against the strike after that is strike-breaking? Any worker will understand it. The question of an armed insurrection has been discussed in the center since September. That is when Zinoviev and Kamenev could and should have put their view in writing so that *everyone*, seeing their arguments, . . . could judge their confusion. To conceal your views from the Party for a whole month *before* a decision is taken and to circulate a dissenting opinion after the decision—that makes you a strikebreaker." Condemning those who would "campaign in the lower bodies against the decision" after it had been made by the central committee, Lenin stressed that "until the Party congress, the CC takes the decisions" and that "any kind of dispute after the decision has been taken is *inadmissible*. . . . To come out *against* a 'decisive' resolution of the Party in a newspaper which, on this particular issue, is of one mind with the whole bourgeoisie [is inadmissible]. If this is tolerated, there can be no Party, the Party will be destroyed." Lenin added: "Kamenev's and Zinoviev's statement in the non-Party press was particularly despicable, too, because the Party cannot publicly refute their *slanderous* lie: I know of no decisions about a date, writes Kamenev, publishing it in his own name and that of Zinoviev. . . . How can the CC refute this? We cannot tell the truth in front of the capitalists, that is, we have decided on a strike and *have decided* to *keep its timing secret*." On the basis of all this, he drew his harsh conclusion: "It is not easy for me to write this about people who were once close comrades but it would seem to me a crime to hesitate here, for a party of revolutionaries which did not punish prominent strike-breakers would *perish*. . . . The more '*prominent*' the strike-breakers, the greater the obligation to punish them instantly by expulsion."[75]

Lenin is not arguing here that challenging or campaigning against any central committee decision should be seen as grounds for expulsion, although clearly he views such activity on the part of party leaders as inadmissible. But we have seen that others had challenged or even flouted central committee decisions without his proposing expulsions. Rather, his demand for the expulsion of Kamenev and Zinoviev flows from the view that this is a measure to be used against those who become strike-breakers, those willing to undermine class-struggle *actions* of the workers' movement, whether a strike or a working-class uprising, giving aid to the bourgeoisie to the detriment of the organizations of the working class.

Lenin was not able to attend the central committee meeting that considered the problem of Zinoviev and Kamenev. It is worth considering the thinking of other central committee members. Interestingly, Stalin hoped that "the matter may be considered closed" (without any disciplinary measures), because he believed that "Kamenev and Zinoviev will submit to CC decisions," and because "what is needed is to preserve Party unity." He felt that despite "the sharp tone" of Lenin's proposals, this did "not change the fact that, fundamentally, we [the central committee, *including* Zinoviev and Kamenev] remain of one mind." This appears to have been a minority opinion, however. Adolph Joffe, for example, suggested that "it be announced that Zinoviev and Kamenev are not members of the CC and that a resolution be passed that not a single Party member may come out against Party decisions, otherwise things will run wild in the Party." Sverdlov, one of the most conscientious of Bolsheviks on organizational matters, considered that "nothing can justify the behavior" of Kamenev, "but the CC does not have the right of expulsion from the Party." However, he urged the acceptance of Kamenev's resignation from the central committee. Trotsky, agreeing with this proposal, argued "that the situation which has been created is completely intolerable" and that conciliatory gestures were "inadmissible." While Kamenev and Zinoviev were not expelled, Kamenev's, resignation from the central committee was accepted, the committee agreed formally to warn Kamenev and Zinoviev that they must "refrain from any statements against the decisions of the CC and its projected line of work," and it agreed formally "that not a single member of the CC should have the right to come out against decisions passed by the CC."[76] As it turned out, Kamenev and Zinoviev drew back from their undisciplined actions and soon resumed (and were allowed to resume) leadership responsibilities in the party. Two obvious lessons can be drawn from this. First, once again, simply because Lenin forcefully demanded something, his comrades did not feel obligated to agree, and he could be outvoted; second, the Bolshevik central committee did not have a rigid or mechanistic attitude regarding party discipline and disciplinary measures.

Some independent-minded commentators on the left, seeking to fashion a "libertarian Leninism," have been inclined to celebrate the great organizational difficulties of 1917 Bolshevism, creating an idealized model out of the contradictions and compromises that proliferated in that tumultuous period. Often they have done this to underscore the differences between Leninism and Stalinism, yet sometimes also as a means of harmonizing a rather amorphous "anything-goes" organizational practice with a sentimental attachment to the Bolshevik tradition. The celebration of the 1917 party is often combined with a rejection or blurring of pre-1917 Bolshevism. This kind of "libertarian Leninism," however, differs profoundly from the real, historical Leninism of Lenin and his comrades, and it obscures the revolutionary process of 1917.

A careful examination of the reaction of Lenin and other Bolshevik leaders to the many challenges of 1917 hardly suggests the abandonment of pre-1917 organizational perspectives. Rather, there is a dynamic tension, one element of which is the tenacious commitment to the preservation of the old democratic-centralist norms, in order to avoid "things running wild in the Party." Without the maintenance of a coherence and discipline in the organization (which was not achieved without mistakes and compromises and adaptations, but which *was achieved*), it is questionable whether the Bolshevik party would have been capable of being a pole of attraction and—at the decisive moment—of providing effective revolutionary leadership to the working class of 1917 Russia. The tension between diversity and discipline, between local or individual initiative and centralism, was mediated through the common commitment to the revolutionary program and through the dynamic of inner-party democracy.

Looking back on this period, Trotsky commented on "how much a revolutionary party has need of internal democracy. The will to struggle is not stored up in advance, and is not dictated from above—it has on every occasion to be independently renewed and tempered." Expanding upon this, he explained the interplay between diversity and discipline that characterized Bolshevism in 1917: "And, indeed, how could a genuinely revolutionary organization, setting itself the task of overthrowing the world and uniting under its banner the most audacious iconoclasts, fighters and insurgents, live and develop without intellectual conflicts, without groupings and temporary faction formations? . . . The Central Committee relied upon this seething democratic support. From this it derived the audacity to make decisions and give orders. The obvious correctness of the leadership at all critical stages gave it that high authority which is the priceless capital of centralism."[77]

4. Party and Masses in the Workers' Revolution

In the 1960s, the radical sociologist C. Wright Mills, not unsympathetic to the Bolshevik Revolution, expressed the commonly held notion that "whatever 'orthodox marxism' may reasonably be taken to mean, it does not include bolshevik practice." Acknowledging that the Bolsheviks claimed to be guided by Marx in everything they did, Mills insisted that "the doing was not in line with his theory or with his political orientation." Rather, "taken as a whole, bolshevism is a distinct theory and has a quite different political orientation." Two essential components of Bolshevik ideology, he felt, made this so: "1. A socialist revolution can occur in a backward country which has a weak capitalist development," and "2. A disciplined, tightly organized party of professional revolutionaries . . . 'represents' (or replaces) the proletariat as the spontaneous historical agency of this revolution."[78] Yet this second point especially, which is central to Mills's (and others') whole argument, is not in harmony with what happened in 1917.

Less than a year after the Bolshevik Revolution, in one of the more perceptive, if underrated, eyewitness accounts, Louise Bryant wrote: "In Russia, where the proletariat is armed, the proletariat becomes the only real influential body. *The Bolsheviks are in power because they bow to the will of the masses.*" Another eyewitness, John Reed, offered a similar picture: "Not by compromise with the propertied classes, or with other political leaders; not by conciliating the old government mechanism, did the Bolsheviki conquer the power. Nor by the organized violence of a small clique. If the masses all over Russia had not been ready for insurrection it must have failed. The only reason for Bolshevik success lay in their accomplishing the vast and simple desires of the most profound strata of the people, calling them to the work of tearing down and destroying the old, and afterward, in the smoke of falling ruins, cooperating with them to erect the framework of the new."[79]

This coincides with the way Lenin viewed the revolution. In a speech he gave to the Third Congress of the Communist International in 1921 he polemicized against a strong ultraleft current that *did* believe, to use Mills's formulation, that tightly organized Communist parties could "replace the proletariat as the spontaneous historical agency" of revolution. Lenin argued: "He who fails to understand that in Europe—where nearly all the proletarians are organized—we must win over the majority of the working class is lost to the Communist movement. If such a person has not yet learned this in the course of the three years of a great revolution, he will never learn anything. . . . We achieved victory in Russia, not only because we had the undoubted majority of the working class on our side (during the elections in 1917 the overwhelming majority of the workers voted for us and against the Mensheviks), but also because half the army—immediately after we seized power—and nine-tenths of the masses of the peasantry—within the course of a few weeks—came over to our side."[80]

The fact remains, however, that the Bolshevik Revolution of October–November 1917 was not a spontaneous uprising of the working class as a whole in the way that the February–March uprising had been. It was decided upon, planned, and led by the Bolshevik party. Trotsky has pointed out that it was this—"the conscious preparation of an overturn, the plan, the conspiracy"—that is offensive to democratic liberals and post-1917 Social Democrats who are able to sympathize with spontaneous uprisings.[81] Since Trotsky has offered the clearest discussion of the revolutionary party/mass dynamic from the Bolshevik standpoint, it may be useful to give attention to his argument.

First of all, an insurrection such as that organized by the Bolsheviks cannot be successful if there is no revolutionary situation. "People do not make revolution eagerly any more than they do war. There is this difference, however, that in war compulsion plays the decisive role, in revolution there is no compulsion except that of circumstances. A revolution takes place only when there is no other way out. And the insurrection, which rises above a revolution like a peak in the mountain chain of its events, can no more be evoked at will than the revolution as a whole." At the same time, Trotsky argues, a *spontaneous* insurrection cannot transcend the framework of capitalism. "To overthrow the old power is one thing; to take the power in one's own hands is another. The bourgeoisie may win the power in a revolution not because it is revolutionary, but because it is bourgeois. It has in its possession property, education, the press, a network of strategic positions, a hierarchy of institutions. Quite otherwise with the proletariat. Deprived in the nature of things of all social advantages, an insurrectionary proletariat can count only on its numbers, its solidarity, its cadres, its official staff." Only if these working-class resources are consciously mobilized in a particular way can the framework of capitalism be transcended. The working class, a vast and complex social formation composed of individuals with diverse experiences and inclinations, cannot spontaneously—as if with a single mind and will—formulate such a plan of action. "If a referendum could have been taken on the question of insurrection, it would have given extremely contradictory and uncertain results. An inner readiness to support a revolution is far from identical with an ability clearly to formulate the necessity of it." Yet such clear formulation is essential: "The proletariat can become imbued with the confidence necessary for a governmental overthrow only if a clear prospect opens before it, only if it has had an opportunity to test out in action a correlation of forces which is changing to its advantage, only if it feels above it a far-sighted, firm and confident leadership. This brings us to the last premise—by no means the last in importance—of the conquest of power: the revolutionary party as a tightly welded and tempered vanguard of the class."[82]

It could be argued that the working class had an adequate revolutionary instrument in the form of its own democratic councils, the soviets. Had Lenin and Trotsky themselves not held up these institutions as *the* revolutionary formations through which the workers should shape their own destiny? Trotsky responds: "However, the soviets by themselves do not settle the question. They may serve different goals according to program and leadership." Until late August 1917, it was the program and leadership of the Mensheviks and Socialist Revolutionaries that were predominant within the soviets, the Bolsheviks being only an increasingly influential minority; by September the Bolsheviks were able to win decisive majorities. "The soviets receive their program and leadership from the party. Whereas the soviets in revolutionary conditions—and apart from revolution they are impossible—comprise the whole class with the exception of its altogether backward, inert or demobilized strata, the revolutionary party represents the brain of the class. The problem of conquering the power can be solved only by a definite combination of party with soviets—or with other mass organizations more or less equivalent to soviets." For the final revolutionary triumph, however, it is necessary to go beyond the counting up of absolute majorities, because under the circumstances we have been discussing— as Rosa Luxemburg put it—the road to victory runs not from achieving a majority *in order to* make a revolution, but rather from winning a majority *through the act* of making a revolution. According to Trotsky: "The difference in level and mood of the different layers of the people is overcome in action. The advance layers bring after them the wavering and isolate the opposing. The majority is not counted up, but won over. Insurrection comes into being at exactly that moment when direct action alone offers a way out of the contradictions." This was true for the working class as a whole, but also for the other insurgent layers of society. "Although lacking the power to draw by themselves the necessary political inferences from their war against the landlords, the peasants had by the very fact of agrarian insurrection already adhered to the insurrection of the cities, had evoked it and were demanding it. . . . Within those limits in which the support of the peasantry was necessary for the establishment of a soviet dictatorship, the support was already at hand. . . . In order that the soldiers, peasants and oppressed nationalities, floundering in the snow storm of an elective ballot [for the Constituent Assembly], should recognize the Bolsheviks in action, it was necessary that the Bolsheviks seize the power."[83] In short, the question of the insurrection dramatizes the need for a party to provide effective revolutionary leadership; at the same time, this would have to be the kind of leadership that insurgent masses would be willing to accept.

The whole history of Bolshevism can be seen as a process through which such a revolutionary party was forged: the development of the revolutionary program (through study and research, through practical experience, through polemics and factional disputes); the immersion in and growth of influence through effective involvement in the actual struggles of the working class and the oppressed; the accumulation of cadres and the building up of a political culture—internal thinking and operating—that could sustain and ensure the development of the vital revolutionary activists who would be capable of influencing the consciousness and activity of the working class; the maintenance of an organizational structure that would enable these revolutionary activists to collectively analyze complex, often rapidly changing situations and formulate revolutionary yet practical perspectives to offer the masses of workers and the oppressed. Ultimately, the adequacy of such a party would be demonstrated by the manner in which the working class and its allies responded to the perspectives and proposals the party advanced. "Studying the aspirations of factory workers, soldiers, and sailors as expressed in contemporary documents," writes Alexander Rabinowitch, "I find that these concerns corresponded closely to the program of political, economic, and social reform put forth by the Bolsheviks at a time when all other major political parties were widely discredited because of their failure to press hard enough for meaningful internal changes and an immediate end to Russia's participation in the war. As a result, in October the goals of the Bolsheviks, as the masses understood them, had strong popular support."[84]

Still influential cold war "scholarship" about the "elitist Bolshevik coup" enfolds the Bolshevik Revolution in thick layers, making it difficult for even some who are sympathetic to revolutionary socialist ideas to see this event without distortion. Yet a growing body of careful research by a new wave of social historians peels away these polemical layers to reveal the revolution's true nature. In what follows, an attempt will be made to summarize their findings.

In February–March the uprising of the workers smashed the power of the tsar, and in the course of this struggle the soviets came into being once again. Yet there was a general spirit of national-democratic unity in which the soviets, while continuing to exist and develop their own authority, handed much of their power over to a predominantly bourgeois provisional government, under the liberal former monarchist Prince Lvov, creating a situation of dual power. The provisional government was empowered to create a framework for setting up a democratic parliament, the Constituent Assembly, and to govern the country in the interim. The revolutionary masses hoped that the provisional government would initiate far-reaching social reforms, and although they wanted to defend their revolution from any possible assault by German imperialism, they also hoped that the provisional government would begin to initiate a Russian withdrawal from the First World War. The soviets, now organized on a national scale (the First All-Russian Congress of Soviets of Workers' and Soldiers' Deputies was held in April), with a Menshevik-Socialist Revolutionary majority, stood for all of these things.

It soon became clear, however, that the provisional government was reluctant to go too far or too fast with the hoped-for reforms, and Pavel Miliukov, Kadet party leader who was minister of foreign affairs, made it clear that the government remained committed to the war effort. The consequent popular anger and mass demonstrations forced a reshuffling within the regime, with Miliukov and others resigning, as Mensheviks and Socialist Revolutionaries agreed to assume six ministerial posts in a new coalition government. A polarization began to set in: the bourgeois-liberal Kadets shifted further to the right, while even more reactionary elements became involved in counterrevolutionary plotting; on the other end of the spectrum, growing numbers of workers were enthusiastic about Bolshevik proposals for a Menshevik-Socialist Revolutionary provisional government without any capitalist participation, and for the transfer of all political power to the soviets. The working-class ferment rose to a peak in July. Some of the most militant sectors in Petrograd insisted on organizing a revolutionary armed demonstration. The Bolshevik leaders found it impossible to defuse the volatile situation but also chose not to draw back from their ties with the impatient sectors of the working class that were attempting to push the revolution forward. This was used as a pretext for government repression against the Bolsheviks in the wake of the violent suppression of the armed demonstration. For their part, the Bolsheviks withdrew their call for "all power to the soviets," which under Menshevik-Socialist Revolutionary leadership seemed, in Lenin's words, to be acting "like sheep brought to the slaughterhouse."[85]

Yet working-class discontent remained as strong as ever, and the failure of a new Russian military offensive generated deepened opposition to the war. The soviets were becoming restive. The pressures of the situation resulted in another governmental reshuffling, with Prince Lvov stepping aside for the moderately radical lawyer Alexander Kerensky. The tensions of the dual power situation mounted, however, and Kerensky appointed military strongman General Kornilov as commander-in-chief of the army. With this move he hoped to counter the pressure of the "unreasonable" workers, who since February had been establishing militant trade unions, setting up aggressive factory committees for workers' control (though not takeovers) of the workplaces, and even organizing their own "red guard" paramilitary groups to help maintain public order and guard against reactionary violence and counterrevolutionary attempts. Although Kerensky was disturbed by such radicalism, right wingers such as General Kornilov found moderates like Kerensky just as distasteful. Thus in August, Kornilov decided to march his troops to Petrograd in order to establish a military dictatorship of his own. A frightened Kerensky appealed to the workers' organizations (including the Bolsheviks, who were again granted full legality) to rally to the defense of the revolution. The Bolsheviks played an especially aggressive role in mobilizing against the counterrevolutionary attempt, and their authority in the working class soared. In the face of the determined working-class mobilization, and through the efforts of revolutionary agitators who made contact with the soldiers under Kornilov's command, the right-wing military offensive simply disintegrated before reaching Petrograd.

While the Bolsheviks were willing to form a united front against Kornilov, they gave no political support to Kerensky, and once again they raised the demand for "all power to the soviets." Meanwhile, throughout the summer, disorder had been escalating across the countryside as the rural poor—impatient with government promises of a future land reform that would redistribute agricultural holdings more equitably—on their own began to take over and divide up the great landed estates. Urban discontent was also rising as food shortages hit the cities. Lenin was now convinced that the overthrow of the provisional government was a practical possibility, especially as Bolsheviks began to win majorities in the soviets. Bolshevik demands for "peace, bread, land" clearly had majority support throughout the country, but it was clear too that the provisional government was incapable of satisfying them. The Socialist Revolutionary party split, with a sizable group of leftists supporting Bolshevik proposals. Elements from the Mensheviks also were drawn to the Bolshevik orientation, despite the rigid opposition of their leaders. Lenin was now eager to see the revolutionary insurrection carried out as soon as possible and therefore urged that it be done by the Bolshevik party in its own name. Other Bolshevik leaders, closer to the scene, believed that this could be done more effectively through the soviets. They proved to be right.

The Petrograd soviet established a military revolutionary committee to coordinate defense of the city against possible German attacks and counterrevolutionary attempts. Under Trotsky's direction, it began covertly to prepare for the overthrow of the provisional government. It gained control over government troops in the city when representatives of military units agreed to obey only orders that the soviet confirmed. The provisional government made repressive moves against both the committee and the Bolshevik party, and it ordered the transfer of loyal troops to Petrograd. In response, the forces of the committee took over the city, storming the Winter Palace, where they arrested most of the provisional government's ministers. On the same day, the Second All-Russian Congress of Soviets of Workers' and Soldiers' Deputies began. By an overwhelming majority, it approved the Bolshevik-led actions and formed a new government. Similar events in Moscow and other cities consolidated the power of the new workers' state, which began as a coalition of Bolsheviks and Left Socialist Revolutionaries.

Diane Koenker's detailed study of Moscow workers in this period provides important insights into the dynamics of the revolution. "First of all," she writes, "the view that the workers are one uniform mass must be rejected. Urbanized workers possessed different values from those of workers recently migrated from the countryside; workers in small shops faced organizational constraints different from those confronted by workers in large plants; workers living in purely working-class neighborhoods formed different attitudes from those of workers living in socially-mixed neighborhoods." She notes that the eight-month period from the February to the October revolutions provided a complex and rich experience that "helped to educate workers and to develop their political as well as their class consciousness." Observing the initial differences between the more conscious skilled workers (such as metalworkers) and less-conscious unskilled workers (such as textile workers), Koenker demonstrates the existence "of a leading, politically experienced segment of the working class uniting over time with other varying but less mature segments, plus the existence of a dynamic revolutionary process [suggesting] new approaches to the familiar and important problems of radicalization, Bolshevization, class consciousness, and organization." She finds "overwhelming evidence not of workers' notoriously irrational militancy but in fact of its opposite. The behavior of Moscow's workers in 1917 suggests a working class that was both highly rational and extremely patient as well. . . . Radicalization was an incremental process, which took place in response to specific economic and political pressures, and it reflected the political maturation of an increasing number of workers." She finds it natural that the Bolsheviks would enjoy only minority support within the working class in the first few months of the revolution, when the prevailing sentiment was for national unity and thus ran counter to the Bolsheviks' class-focused perspective. But gradually this situation changed: "Capitalists began to behave as Marx said they would: no concessions to the workers, no compromise on the rights of factory owners. Mensheviks and SRs tried to straddle both sides of the class split; this appeal can be seen in the mixed social composition of their supporters. The Bolsheviks, however, had offered the most consistent class interpretation of the revolution, and by late summer their interpretation appeared more and more to correspond to reality."[86]

David Mandel's detailed study of Petrograd workers yields similar findings. He documents, also, a demoralization afflicting major sectors of the working class in the autumn of 1917, and writes: "In these circumstances, the presence of a resolute minority willing and able to take the initiative was critical. All that was required was for them to begin, to force the issue, to inject a new dynamism into the movement and to make it impossible to procrastinate further. The others would rally. . . . But without this initiative, the very powerful, commonly shared yearning for revolutionary change would have had little real impact. Political stagnation and economic misery would have completely demoralized the workers, paving the way for the counterrevolution." Mandel finds that "the great majority of Petrograd's workers greeted the news of the insurrection unconditionally. Resolutions supporting the action came from every type of factory—from long-time supporters of soviet power in the machine—construction plants of the Vyborg District to the relatively recent converts in the textile mills, the Nevskii District and even a significant number of printing plants [which were Menshevik strongholds]." He notes: "Many writers hostile to the October Revolution are unable to reconcile themselves to the absence of the outer trappings of a popular rising. Yet the October Insurrection, perhaps best of all, shows that a planned, military-like operation can be a popular insurrection in the sense that it was embraced by the masses as a whole even if their direct participation was not called for." He quotes the Menshevik Sukhanov, who pointed out that the broad masses "had nothing to do on the streets. They did not have an enemy which demanded their mass action, their armed forces, battles and barricades. . . . This was an especially happy circumstance of our October Revolution, for which it is still being slandered as a military rising and almost a palace coup. It would be better if they asked: Did the Petrograd proletariat sympathize or did it not with the organizers of the October insurrection? . . . There are no two answers here. Yes, the Bolsheviks acted on the mandate of the Petrograd workers and soldiers."[87]

Rex A. Wade—who has studied the red guards and workers' militias, which ultimately encompassed about 200,000 activists throughout Russia—has focused on "the issue of spontaneity versus leadership in the Revolution." He finds that out of the militant rank and file of local soviets and factories, there was a spontaneous tendency toward forming such armed groups with two broad purposes: "first, the defense of public order and personal security, especially among workers; and second, the defense of the Revolution, and especially worker interests." Noting that they "remained basically local in orientation and organization down to the October Revolution," he stressed that "their essential characteristics remained more those of self-assertion, self-organization and spontaneity rather than those of leadership, discipline and direction from above. " Yet there was a dynamic that went beyond this: "The armed bands were a complex combination of spontaneity, voluntaristic action, and initiative from below interacting with ideas derived from outside ideologies and attempts at control or influence by political parties." Wade writes that the insurgent masses "looked for leadership and direction" from the larger working-class institutions and parties, "yet they also clung to their own autonomy." As early as April, the Menshevik leadership's "position on the Red Guard was an early example of a broader attitude of distrust about where spontaneous activity by the masses might lead and of an insensitivity to worker concerns and fears that would result four months later in their [the Mensheviks'] loss of control of the Petrograd Soviet." Distrust of both the Bolsheviks and the working class was clear in the Menshevik leaders' commentary about armed workers' groups in their own newspaper: "As always in such situations, the workers, revolutionary-minded but insufficiently politically educated, follow revolutionary slogans rather than the voice of reason." Wade concludes: "The impulse toward a more class-oriented, disciplined, aggressive armed workers' force was a fundamental urge among the workers in 1917, emerging time and again as one of their most deeply felt needs. One could debate whether they should have arms, or whether they could use them effectively, but this missed the essential point: they felt that they must have them. . . . Only the Bolsheviks made arming the workers an integral part of their party posture, and only they 'legitimized' the workers' desire for arms." The Bolshevik Shlyapnikov pointed out in May 1917, "No kind of essay, no kind of resolution, can force the revolutionary workers and people to refrain from arming themselves." The dynamic between spontaneity and leadership that Wade has traced meant, ultimately, that "the Red Guards were important in providing both armed force and psychological and moral force for the establishment of soviet power in late 1917."[88]

Ronald Suny summarizes the recent scholarship as follows: "As historians have shifted their attention away from the political elites that formerly dominated explanations of the Russian Revolution and to the people in the streets, the victorious Bolsheviks have appeared less like Machiavellian manipulators or willful conspirators and more like alert politicians with an acute sensitivity to popular moods and desires." He points out that a "heightened feeling of class was forged in the actual experience of 1917 and contained both social hostilities bred over many years and intensified under wartime and revolutionary conditions and a new political understanding that perceived government by soviets as a preferable alternative to sharing power with the discredited upper classes. The Bolsheviks had since April been advocating such a government by the lower classes. With the failure of the coalition [provisional government] and its supporters to deliver on the promise of the revolution, the party of Lenin and Trotsky took power with little resistance and with the acquiescence of the majority of the people of Petrograd. The Bolsheviks came to power not because they were superior manipulators or cynical opportunists but because their policies as formulated by Lenin in April and shaped by the events of the following months placed them at the head of a genuinely popular movement."[89]

Such scholarship tells us much about the nature of the October–November revolution and the party that led it. So do the statements of the triumphant Bolsheviks themselves. It shines through in such proclamations as this one from Lenin to the people of Russia:

Comrades workers, soldiers, peasants—all toilers!

The Workers' and Peasants' Revolution has won at Petrograd, at Moscow. . . . From the Front and the villages arrive every day, every hour, greetings to the new Government . . . . The victory of the Revolution . . . is assured, seeing that it is sustained by the majority of the people. . . .

Comrades workers! Remember that you yourselves direct the government. No one will help you unless you organize yourselves and take into your own hands the affairs of the State. Your Soviets are now the organs of governmental power. . . .

Comrades workers, soldiers, peasants-all toilers!

Take immediately all local power into your hands . . . . Little by little, with the consent of the majority of peasants, we shall march firmly and unhesitatingly toward the victory of Socialism, which will fortify the advance-guards of the working class of the most civilized countries, and give to the peoples an enduring peace, and free them from every slavery and every exploitation.[90]

12. After Taking Power

We have, in the foregoing chapters, accomplished the primary task we set for ourselves: to trace the manner in which the Bolshevik organization transformed itself into a revolutionary mass-vanguard party capable of leading a working-class socialist revolution, and to examine Lenin's ideas on the organization of the revolutionary party within that framework. This lengthy account has hardly exhausted the subject, but it provides a basis from which we can begin to draw some conclusions. Before doing this, however, it will be necessary to give at least minimal attention to developments that took place after the Bolshevik seizure of power. To do this in a satisfactory way would require a work at least as lengthy as the previous chapters. That will not be possible here. But it will be necessary to address these developments because the profoundly inspiring vision Lenin articulated in 1917, which guided Bolshevik efforts from the beginning, was not realized. Instead, a bureaucratic and authoritarian regime was established in the name of Leninism. That regime has been dubbed Stalinism, but it is impossible not to recognize that this was the culmination of a transitional period that began while Lenin was still the leader of the Bolshevik party and in which that party dominated the new Soviet Republic. Many commentators have argued that Leninism, and particularly the nature of the Leninist party, cannot be understood and evaluated without coming to grips with this later period.[1]

In this chapter it will be argued that there was not some underlying authoritarian essence in Lenin's perspective that led to the rise of a bureaucratic dictatorship. In fact, we can find the beginnings of a realization of the Bolsheviks' libertarian vision in the first months of the new regime. Yet none of this survived the crisis that overwhelmed the Russian workers' state; the Bolshevik party itself—upon taking power, and particularly as it struggled to maintain power—was transformed into an institution quite different from the organization that led the revolution. The Third International, or the Communist International, which the Bolsheviks helped form to coordinate revolutionary socialist efforts on a world scale, transmitted many of the positive lessons that were part of the Bolshevik heritage—yet even in its early years it began to reflect some of the problems affecting Bolshevism in power. Here we will offer some material on these questions. We will, finally, touch on further developments occurring after Lenin's death.

1. State, Revolution, and Socialist Democracy

Richard N. Hunt, in his valuable work *The Political Ideas of Marx and Engels*, discusses and documents conclusively the profoundly democratic orientation of "scientific socialism's" founders, but he contrasts this to what he perceives as an elitism inherent in Leninism. He seeks to illustrate this elitism with the following passage from Lenin's *State and Revolution*:

> The proletariat needs state power, the centralized organization of violence, both for the purpose of crushing the resistance of the exploiters and for the purpose of *guiding* the great mass of the population—the peasantry, the petty-bourgeoisie, the semi-proletarians—in the work of organizing Socialist economy.
>
> By educating a workers' party, Marxism educates the vanguard of the proletariat, capable of assuming power and of *leading the whole people* to Socialism, of directing and organizing the new order, of being the teacher, guide and leader of all the toiling and exploited in the task of building up their social life without the bourgeoisie and against the bourgeoisie.

Hunt comments: "Here, in a whole series of tutorial relationships, the great mass of the population would be 'guided' by Russia's small proletariat, which in turn would be 'led' by a still smaller vanguard of the proletariat, and this vanguard would be 'educated' by 'Marxism,' that is, the doctrines disseminated by party intellectuals like Lenin himself."[2] This runs counter to the injunction of Marx and Engels, argues Hunt, that the working class must reject all "condescending saviors" and *emancipate itself*, learning from its own mistakes, and shaping through its own self-activity (i.e., activity initiated and directed by the working class itself) the socialist reconstruction of society. Lenin's elitist perspective is related to a "totalitarian-democratic" (as opposed to a genuinely democratic) tradition that goes as far back as Rousseau, Hunt asserts, but that was emphatically rejected by Marx and Engels themselves. He suggests that this element, embedded in Lenin's conception of a vanguard party, logically resulted in a bureaucratic dictatorship. Hunt's argument, of course, is hardly new, but it stands as one of the clearest expressions of a very common and influential view.

There are serious problems with this interpretation. A practical problem is that those revolutionary-minded socialists who advance it have failed to articulate a serious alternative orientation for Marxist activists. Consequently, they are subject to deactivization, or to absorption into political phenomena that do not lead in a socialist direction (such as adaptation to welfare-state capitalism and to liberal capitalist parties). Only Marxists who accept the concept of the revolutionary vanguard have been able to avoid such a fate. This holds not only for Leninists but also for revolutionary socialists not commonly associated with the Leninist tradition. We saw earlier in this study that Rosa Luxemburg was one such revolutionary, but she is not unique.

We should note that there is a historical current among revolutionary socialists—associated with Anton Pannekoek, Herman Gorter, the older Karl Korsch, Arthur Rosenberg, Paul Mattick, Noam Chomsky, and others—known as council communism, in which the rejection of Leninism is an article of faith. Yet even within this alternative tradition, when it was a force within the workers' movement, we find Pannekoek stating: "The function of a revolutionary party lies in propagating clear understanding in advance, so that throughout the masses there will be elements who know what must be done and are capable of judging the situation for themselves. And in the course of revolution the party has to raise the program, slogans and directives which the spontaneously acting masses recognize as correct because they find that they express their own aims in their most adequate form and hence achieve greater clarity of purpose; it is thus that the party comes to lead the struggle." Gorter elaborates on this by noting that "the great majority of the proletariat is badly fed, badly housed, overworked and has no free time for self-education. It is badly brought up, very poorly informed, and is in such a state of mental dependence from birth onwards, and has been so as a class for centuries, that not only does it not see the road to liberation, it does not dare think of it." Yet "not *all* proletarians are insufficiently well informed. In the German proletariat particularly there are many who are genuine revolutionaries not only in sentiment, but also have a broad and deep understanding of politics and economics. Marx and Engels, Mehring, Bebel, Luxemburg and others did not live among them for nothing." According to Gorter, it is necessary "to unite this section of the proletariat within one organization" that "is revolutionary not only in heart, but also in mind. It can therefore lead in word and deed. It takes the lead in both if it is the true party." It should not be surprising that such "vanguardist" notions are articulated by any revolutionary current that hopes to be relevant in the workers' struggles. Any organized group that has a definite perspective it feels is superior to others, and that seriously attempts to win large numbers of working-class activists (not to mention the majority of the working class) to that perspective, is open to charges of "vanguardism." The abandonment of such an orientation can lead only to inactivity (or the elevation of contemplation and commentary to the status of "revolutionary praxis") or, in the best of cases, to individualistic political acts. This became the fate of the council communist current itself once it abandoned the project of building a revolutionary party.[3]

There is also an interpretive problem with the argument that Hunt articulates. His reading of the passage in *State and Revolution* is obviously related to later authoritarian developments in the Soviet Union, but different readings are possible—including one more in harmony with the libertarian thrust of that work, with Lenin's other writings, with the experience of Bolshevism, and with the realities of 1917.[4] In order to discuss the alternate interpretation, however, it will be necessary to complete the second paragraph in the passage Hunt cites. In addition to the long sentence he quotes there is a second long sentence. Here they are together:

> By educating the workers' party. Marxism educates the vanguard of the proletariat, capable of assuming power and *leading the whole people* to socialism, of directing and organizing the new system, of being the teacher, the guide, the leader of all the working and exploited people in organizing their social life without the bourgeoisie and against the bourgeoisie. By contrast, the opportunism now prevailing trains the members of the workers' party to be the representatives of the better-paid workers, who lose touch with the masses, 'get along' fairly well under capitalism, and sell their birthright for a mess of pottage, i.e., renounce their role as revolutionary leaders of the people against the bourgeoisie.[5]

By "the opportunism now prevailing" Lenin is referring to the dilution and distortion of Marxism within the Second International: "The proletariat needs the state—this is repeated by all the opportunists, social-chauvinists and Kautskyites, who assure us that this is what Marx taught. But they '*forget*' to add that, in the first place, according to Marx, the proletariat needs only a state which is withering away, i.e., a state so constituted that it begins to wither away immediately, and cannot but wither away. And secondly, the working people need a 'state, i.e., the proletariat organized as the ruling class.'"[6] These are points Lenin makes as he leads up to the passage quoted by Hunt.

We have seen that Lenin's experience with "the better-paid workers" in Russia was that, by and large, they constituted the more conscious workers and were the heart of the revolutionary vanguard sector of the working class. Imbued with Marxism, they had *not* renounced "their role as revolutionary leaders of the people against the bourgeoisie." Marxism had made them "capable of assuming power and *leading the whole people* . . . , of directing and organizing . . . , of being the teacher, the guide, the leader of all working and exploited people. . . ." Lenin is not simply laying out an abstract schema, but is describing the dynamic between Marxism and the more advanced sections (that is, the vanguard) of the working class, a dynamic that had evolved over a half-century—resulting in the Russian Revolution—and that Lenin has projected into the future socialist reconstruction of Russia. In the passage under discussion, he is contrasting this education in Marxism and this commitment to establishing a socialist democracy with what had taken place elsewhere: the education of workers' parties and advanced sections of the working class in a pseudo-Marxian reformist and opportunist orientation that is incapable of transcending the framework of bourgeois democracy and allows these better-paid workers to "'get along' fairly well under capitalism," at least in contrast to the masses with whom they have lost touch. In other words, the passage under examination comes close to having the opposite meaning of that invested in it by Hunt and others. (Interestingly, Lenin's line of reasoning here is related to such early works as *What Is to Be Done?* and such later writings as *Imperialism, the Highest Stage of Capitalism*, discussed in Eric Hobsbawm's useful essay "Lenin and the 'Aristocracy of Labor.'"[7]) The vanguard sections of the working class must not elevate themselves above the less conscious workers and other oppressed groups, but instead should fight for them and, more than this, should strive to raise their consciousness to a level equaling their own so that they can join in the struggle for their common liberation (or self-emancipation).

Of course, the Communist party of the Soviet Union and other such organizations have over the years presented themselves as "the teacher, guide and leader of all the toiling masses," but often this description is used to veil a system of extreme compulsion: The party "patiently explains" things to the masses, which they are then expected to go along with—or else. But a one-party dictatorship was neither projected nor established by the Bolshevik Revolution. (This came later, as we shall see.) Rather, there was a vital working-class democracy in which paternalism and authoritarianism had little ground in which to sink root.

We have seen how Lenin, in numerous writings, gave expression to the belief that socialism and democracy are inseparable, but that socialist democracy would have to go beyond the liberal democracy of capitalism. This is a central theme of *State and Revolution*: "Marx grasped the *essence* of capitalist democracy splendidly when, in analyzing the experience of the Commune, he said that the oppressed are allowed once every few years to decide which particular representatives of the oppressing class shall represent and repress them in parliament." Against this, Lenin advanced a genuine democracy that would exist under the political rule of the proletariat: "The dictatorship of the proletariat, the period of transition to communism, will for the first time create democracy for the people, the majority, along with the necessary suppression of the exploiters, the minority. . . . At a certain stage in the development of democracy, it first welds together the class that wages a revolutionary struggle against capitalism—the proletariat, and enables it to crush, smash to atoms, wipe off the face of the earth the bourgeois, even the republican-bourgeois, state machine, the standing army, the police and the bureaucracy and to substitute for them a more democratic state machine, but a state machine nevertheless, in the shape of armed workers who proceed to form a militia involving the entire population."[8]

These were not simply Lenin's ideas, but were written into the new program of the Russian Communist Party (Bolsheviks) in 1919: "A bourgeois republic, however democratic, . . . inevitably expresses . . . the dictatorship of the bourgeoisie, of a machine for the exploitation and oppression of the immense majority of the workers by the capitalist clique. In contrast with this, proletarian or soviet democracy transforms the mass organizations of those who are oppressed by the capitalist class, . . . that is to say, of the immense majority of the population, into the permanent and unified foundation of the entire State apparatus, local and central, from the bottom to the top. Thereby the Soviet State realizes, among other things, in an immeasurably wider form than ever before, local self-government, without any sort of authority imposed from above. It is the task of our party to work indefatigably on behalf of the complete inauguration of that higher type of democracy which needs for its right functioning the continuous uplifting of the level of culture, organization, and initiative power of the masses." While arguing that certain "limitations . . . imposed on freedom, are necessary only as temporary measures to cope with the attempts of the exploiters to regain their privileges," the program promised that "with the disappearance of the objective possibility of the exploitation of man by man, there will likewise disappear the need for these temporary measures, and our party will aim at their restriction and ultimately at their complete abolition." The program linked restrictions on freedom of expression for the bourgeoisie with an expansion of free expression for the working class: "The Soviet Power confiscates the possessions of the bourgeoisie, i.e., its printing presses, stores of paper, etc., in order to place them entirely at the disposal of the workers and their organizations. The Russian Communist Party must induce wider and yet wider masses of the working population to avail themselves of the democratic rights and freedoms, and it must enlarge the material possibilities in this direction." In addition to freedom of expression, the program insisted on the existence of institutional guarantees of grass-roots control over the new governing bodies of society: "The Soviet Power secures for the working masses, to an incomparably greater extent than was secured for them under bourgeois democracy and parliamentarism, the power of carrying on the election and recall of delegates [to the soviets]; this is made easy and accessible for the benefit of the workers and peasants."[9]

Nor was this simply rhetoric. While there were certain initial restrictions on freedom of the press following the October–November insurrection, these were carefully and explicitly limited and, as the Petrograd soviet declared at the beginning of 1918, "no special permission is required for publishing any kind of printed work." Regarding the same period, Louise Bryant commented: "While the Soviets declared a temporary suppression of the press, they never at any time tried to interfere with public speaking or with theatrical performances which ridiculed them or the revolution. I have often watched a crowd of rich bourgeoisie bullying sailor guards in front of the City Duma and marvelled at the patience of the sailors. Street talks were common. Red Guards would stand quietly listening to a speaker berate them without getting the least bit ruffled; they often seemed deeply interested in the arguments put up by their opponents."[10] It was not only the "rich bourgeoisie" who voiced criticisms, however. Mensheviks, Socialist Revolutionaries, anarchists, and independent socialists like Maxim Gorky expressed their views not only verbally but also in print. Moreover, they themselves were able to secure representation in the soviets.

As we will see, this "left-wing pluralism" was to be severely curtailed with the onset of the brutalizing civil war, and fateful precedents were to be established that would be used to justify the consolidation of the bureaucratic dictatorship in the Stalin period. And yet up until 1921 opposition parties and Menshevik and anarchist newspapers functioned legally; and mass demonstrations organized by these groups were held at the funerals of Plekhanov and Kropotkin, and other activities took place that were to become unthinkable in the Soviet Union not only under Stalin but also in the 1980s. Even after the formal banning of oppositional soviet parties, many non-Bolshevik socialists and scholars could continue, in the 1920s, to produce freely "nonconformist" (today one would say "dissident") publications— pamphlets, books, magazines. And until the 1930s, they involved themselves in many scientific, historiographical, and cultural controversies (which were often de facto political). The early policies of the Bolsheviks indicate that—far from planning to eliminate such pluralism—they assumed it would flourish. The welter of anti-Bolshevik opinion to the contrary, however, requires that we provide a more thorough examination.

In January 1918 the Third All-Russian Congress of Soviets of Workers' and Soldiers' Deputies opened, merging with the All-Russian Congress of Peasants' Deputies, and proceeded to adopt an initial constitution for he new Soviet Republic, as well as a number of other important resolutions. Slightly more than half of the delegates were Bolsheviks: the second-largest group was composed of their Left Socialist Revolutionary allies. At the conclusion, they elected a new All-Russian Central

Executive Committee, the legislative committee operating between congresses, with 306 members: 160 Bolsheviks, 125 Left Socialist Revolutionaries, two Menshevik-Internationalists (the group led by Martov and Dan), three Anarcho-Communists, seven Socialist Revolutionary-Maximalists, seven Right Socialist Revolutionaries, and two Menshevik-Defensists. As Roy Medvedev comments: "The Bolsheviks obviously recognized the rights of many political minorities at that time and proceeded on a pluralist basis in the representative Soviet bodies."[11]

Those who argue that the Bolsheviks even at this time opposed such a pluralism of working-class currents and genuine democracy often point to two facts that allegedly demonstrate early Bolshevik authoritarian inclinations: the Bolsheviks' decision to dissolve the Constituent Assembly, and their decision—forced by Lenin, Trotsky, and Sverdlov against the initial reluctance of the central committee majority of the Bolshevik party—*not* to form a coalition government with the moderate socialist parties. Brief attention should be given to these two points.

The nationwide Constituent Assembly elections, organized before the Bolshevik insurrection but held shortly afterward, gave Lenin's party only 25 percent of the vote; the lion's share went to the Socialist Revolutionaries, who received 58 percent, while the Mensheviks won only 4 percent. The Kadets and others like them got 13 percent in all. Yet this was rather deceptive. The Bolsheviks won overwhelmingly in the decisive urban areas, especially among the working class and among soldiers in the major urban centers. The Socialist Revolutionary slate—made up *before* that party split, at which point its large leftwing allied itself with the Bolsheviks—represented a party that no longer existed by the time the voting took place, and the large number of peasant votes it received were cast largely for its traditional program of agrarian reform, which the Bolsheviks themselves had adopted. When the Constituent Assembly convened in January 1918, the great majority of its members turned out to be hostile to soviet power (which by this time was clearly supported by a majority of the population) and was committed instead to a bourgeois-democratic republic. By an overwhelming majority, the All-Russian Congress of Soviets concurred with the Bolshevik proposal to dissolve this body as not being truly representative of the great majority of the Russian people and as threatening to provide cover for a "bourgeois counterrevolution" that would attempt "to crush the power of the Soviets." There was little protest over this action from the majority sectors of the population, the workers and peasants, who already had a government of their own in the form of the soviets.[12]

A coalition government of all socialist parties within the soviets had been advocated, after the insurrection, by what was at first a majority of the Bolshevik party's central committee, against the dogged opposition of Lenin, Trotsky, and

Sverdlov. The implementation of the proposal would have meant dividing up posts in the Council of People's Commissars, the leading executive body set up by the Second All-Russian Congress of Soviets. Lenin was convinced that a coalition with moderate socialists who had demonstrated their hostility to the Bolshevik Revolution would not be viable. This position, which finally won a bare majority of the central committee after a fierce debate, is often interpreted as a determination to establish a *one-party dictatorship*. But if this term is defined as is commonly understood, then the interpretation is flawed. If the Conservative party or Labour party in England, or the Democratic party or Republican party in the United States, refuses to share cabinet posts and executive authority with its opponents after an election, then similar logic could condemn them for setting up a dictatorship. There was, at this time, no proposal by Lenin to ban opposition parties of the left or to throw them out of the soviets, but simply a determination not to bring them into the Council of People's Commissars. (For a brief period in early 1918, representatives of the Left Socialist Revolutionaries were in fact taken into this body.) As Roy Medvedev indicates, in this early period Lenin favored a multiparty democracy within the framework of the soviets.[13]

As early as September 1917, before the Bolshevik Revolution but after the Bolsheviks had won control of the Petrograd soviet, Trotsky—as the soviet's new president—told his opponents: "We are all party people, and we shall have to cross swords more than once. But we shall guide the work of the Petersburg Soviet in a spirit of justice and complete independence for all fractions; the hand of the praesidium will never oppress the minority." In the same month, Lenin was describing what soviet democracy would look like, with special reference to freedom of the press: "State power in the shape of the Soviets takes *all* the printing presses and *all* the newsprint and distributes them *equitably*: the state should come first— in the interests of the majority of the people, the majority of the poor, particularly the majority of the peasants, who for centuries have been tormented, crushed and stultified by the landowners and capitalists." His next point makes it clear that, as Bertram Wolfe noted in 1947, "Lenin had no idea of outlawing all other parties and creating a one-party system." Rather, Lenin argued: "The big parties should come second—say, those that have polled one or two hundred thousand votes in both capitals [Petrograd and Moscow]. The smaller parties should come third, and then any group of citizens which has a certain number of members or has collected a certain number of signatures."[14]

Four weeks after the insurrection, Lenin demonstrated his continued commitment to soviet democracy in drafting for the Council of People's Commissars a resolution stating that "no elective institution or representative assembly can be regarded as being truly democratic and really representative of the people's will unless the electors' right to recall those elected is accepted and exercised. This fundamental principle of true democracy applies to all representative assemblies without exception." Explaining this statement in the All-Russian Central Executive Committee of Soviets, he provided this significant line of reasoning: "Various parties have played a dominant role among us. The last time, the passage of influence from one party to another was accompanied by an overturn, whereas a simple vote would have sufficed had we the right to recall. . . . The right of recall must be granted the Soviets, which are the most perfect carrier of the state idea, of coercion. Then the passage of power from one party to another will proceed without bloodshed, by means of simple new elections." Early in the following year he was still emphasizing the role of political pluralism in soviet democracy: "If the working people are dissatisfied with their party they can elect other delegates, hand power to another power and change the government without any revolution at all."[15]

In the spring of 1918, commented Victor Serge, the soviet congress reflected "a whole system of inner democracy. The dictatorship of the proletariat is not the dictatorship of a party, or of a Central Committee, or of certain individuals. . . . Lenin himself is obliged to follow strict rules. He has to convince a majority in the Central Committee of his party, then discuss with the Communist fraction in the Vee-Tsik [the All-Russia Central Executive Committee of the Soviets] and then, in the Vee-Tsik itself, brave the fire of the Left SRs, anarchists and International Social-Democrats, all doubtful allies, and of the Right SRs and Mensheviks, irreducible enemies. All the decrees are debated during sessions which are often of tremendous interest. Here the enemies of the regime enjoy free speech with a more than parliamentary latitude."[16]

The Bolsheviks looked to more than simply the soviets as an instrument of proletarian democracy. Although late in appreciating the spontaneously developing factory committees and the demand for workers' control of the workplace, they embraced them more enthusiastically than most other left-wing groups (an exception being the anarchists); in the months leading up to the October–November revolution, worker-Bolsheviks became the leading cadres of the factory committee movement, and Lenin argued: "Vital creativity of the masses—that is the fundamental factor in the new society. Let the workers take on the creation of workers' control in their works and factories, let them supply the countryside with manufactured goods in exchange for bread. . . . Socialism is not created by orders from on high. Its spirit is alien to state-bureaucratic automatism. Socialism is vital and creative, it is the creation of the popular masses themselves." Historian S. A. Smith, in his detailed study of the Petrograd factory committees, terms as "fundamentally misguided" the common assertion of anti-Leninist scholars that this was simply a cynical ploy of the Bolsheviks to use the committees in order to seize power for themselves. He does argue that Lenin failed to "satisfactorily theorize the relationship between grass-roots workers' control of production and state-wide regulation of the economy," and that "he was intoxicated by the spectacle of workers, soldiers and peasants taking power into their own hands, and profoundly optimistic about the potential inherent in such self-activity." After 1917 there certainly developed much confusion and debate among Bolsheviks regarding the proper function of the factory committees, resolved in a tragic manner amid the chaos of the civil war period. Nonetheless, in the early period of the Bolshevik regime Lenin was constantly making such points as this: "One of the most crucial tasks at present, if not the most crucial, is to develop the independent initiatives of the workers and toilers and exploited generally in the sphere of creative, organizational work. At all costs, we must destroy that old, absurd, savage, vile and loathsome prejudice that only the so-called 'upper classes' can run the state."[17]

In this period trade unions continued to be an important factor in working-class life as well. Although many were led by Bolsheviks, some were under Menshevik control. Not surprisingly, however, there was considerable confusion over the respective roles and authority of unions, factory committees, and soviets in economic decision making (not to mention over how much authority the remaining capitalists should have in the large sectors of the economy that were not yet nationalized). All too often debates and efforts to overcome this confusion are simplistically interpreted by latter-day historians as sinister Bolshevik attempts to undermine one or another working-class organization.[18]

The full range of freedom of expression and workers' democracy in the earliest period of the Soviet Republic requires an examination that is beyond the scope of the present study.[19] But the evidence suggests that the Bolsheviks initially had no intention of establishing their party as a paternalistic oligarchy. Their words and actions instead reveal a continuity with the profoundly democratic nature of the Bolshevik program throughout its previous history. This was in harmony, similarly, with the internal structure and workings of the Bolshevik party that we have traced in this study. The situation in Russia and within the Russian Communist party was soon fundamentally reversed. But as Moshe Lewin has argued, "Leninist doctrine did not originally envisage a monolithic state, nor even a strictly monolithic party; the dictatorship of the Party over the proletariat was never part of Lenin's plans, it was the completely unforeseen culmination of a series of unforeseen circumstances."[20]

2. Crisis of Bolshevism

The disintegration of soviet democracy, and the related transformation of the Russian Communist party into an increasingly undemocratic entity, cannot be examined in detail here, but it will be possible to indicate some of the dynamics that have relevance for our study. A combination of factors, arising after the Bolsheviks took power, fundamentally changed the context and milieu within which they had traditionally operated. Also fundamentally changed were the basic tasks they faced. Consequently, the very nature of the organization changed radically over the next five years. And in the period from 1922 to 1937, the Russian Communist party (renamed the Communist party of the Soviet Union) experienced further metamorphoses that in many ways made it the opposite of what it had been in the years leading to the Bolshevik triumph.

In examining the crisis of Bolshevik Russia, many commentators present the tragic escalation of violence and authoritarian measures of the "red terror" as if they were part of some totalitarian master plan, abstracted from the actual context. In one of the most severe yet lucid critiques of Bolshevism as it was in 1920, however, eyewitness Bertrand Russell felt it necessary to make this acknowledgment: "It is, of course, evident that in these measures the Bolsheviks have been compelled to travel a long way from the ideals which originally inspired the revolution." He added: "I recognize to the full the reasons for the bad state of affairs, in the past history of Russia and the recent policy of the Entente [the wartime coalition of Britain, France, and the United States, which was economically blockading and militarily intervening to overturn the revolutionary regime]. But I have thought it better to record impressions frankly, trusting the readers to remember that the Bolsheviks have only a very limited share of responsibility for the evils from which Russia is suffering." He was of the opinion that the Bolshevik regime "represents what is most efficient in Russia, and does more to prevent chaos than any possible alternative government would do," and noted that Maxim Gorky (one of the sharpest left-wing critics of the Bolsheviks at this time) "supports the Government—as I should do, if I were a Russian—not because he thinks it faultless, but because the possible alternatives are worse." Russell also felt compelled to point out that "it seems evident, from the attitude of the capitalist world to Soviet Russia, of the Entente to the Central Empires, and of England to Ireland and India, that there is no depth of cruelty, perfidy or brutality from which the present [capitalist] holders of power will shrink when they feel themselves threatened."[21]

We have seen that a fundamental component of the Bolshevik program was revolutionary internationalism, and that the perspective of the Russian workers seizing power in 1917 was based in large measure on the expectation that socialist revolutions were on the order of the day in at least some of the more advanced capitalist countries. In April 1918 Lenin told the Moscow soviet: "We shall perish unless we can hold out until we receive powerful support from workers in revolt in other countries." Indeed, this was a commonplace articulated openly and frequently by all of the leading Bolsheviks. Yet Lenin had been confident that "the objective conditions of the imperialist war make it certain . . . that the revolution will not be limited to Russia," and that "the *European* and the American *socialist* proletariat will undertake its decisive battles."[22] This may seem a vain hope to those who, with benefit of hindsight, know that such "decisive battles" did not yield capitalism's overturn in Western Europe, not to mention the United States. Yet it is worth considering Bertram Wolfe's recollections of 1919, when the American Communist movement was born:

> The opportunities for American radicalism of all varieties seemed immense in that year of interregnum between all-out war and what was supposed to be all-out peace. Millions of soldiers were being demobilized and hundreds of thousands of those who had risked their lives at the front were finding that there were no jobs waiting for them at home. Europe was in turmoil: crowns were tumbling and ancient empires falling; there were revolutions, still not defined in their nature, in Russia, Germany, Austria-Hungary, then a Communist revolution in Hungary itself and another in Bavaria; soldiers were carrying their arms from the front and imposing their will insofar as they knew what they willed. A strike wave unprecedented in our history swept through America: the Seattle General Strike grew out of a protest at the closing down of the shipyards; the Lawrence Textile Strike; the national coal strike; and, wonder of wonders, the Boston police strike; the great steel strike involving 350,000; the battles of the workers in many industries to keep wages abreast of the high cost of living, and of the employers to end the wartime gains of the labor movement [and] to establish or restore the [non-union] open shop. Not until the Great Depression [of the 1930s] would the labor movement again show so much militancy.[23]

The reality turned out to be not that the Bolsheviks were wrong about the revolutionary upsurge outside of Russia, but that the workers' movements in other countries were unable to provide revolutionary leadership. One problem was identified by Rosa Luxemburg: "The flower of our youthful strength, hundreds of thousands whose socialist education . . . was the product of decades of education and propaganda, other hundreds of thousands who were ready to receive the lessons of socialism have fallen, and are rotting upon the battlefields."[24] Another problem was that much of the surviving socialist workers' movement had yet to shake loose from the sway of the established reformist leaderships. Those elements that were prepared to follow the example of the Bolshevik Revolution were badly disorganized, in many cases lacking in the immense experience and authority the Bolshevik organization had built up in Russia. Revolutionary sentiment and upsurges without revolutionary leadership failed to bring into existence new socialist republics. Even when power was seized, in Hungary and Bavaria, it could not be held for long. In 1919, the Bolsheviks and a scattering of militant socialists from other countries established a revolutionary Third International to strengthen these insurgent efforts, but already it was clear that it would take longer than expected to end the isolation of the Soviet Republic.

"From this period on," writes Moshe Lewin, "the hope of being towed along in the wake of a victorious revolution in the West began to fade. Bolshevik power, then, was about to find itself all alone, in an underdeveloped country, left with no forces but its own to count on—and these seemed far too meager for the task at hand."[25] Lenin and his comrades gave up neither on the world revolution nor on the survival of the Russian Revolution. But there was a new note of desperate detemination in their statements:

An extraordinarily difficult, complex and dangerous situation in international affairs; the necessity of maneuvering and retreating; a period of waiting for new outbreaks of the revolution which is maturing in the West at a painfully slow pace; within the country a period of slow construction and ruthless 'tightening up,' of prolonged and persistent struggle waged by stern proletarian discipline against the menacing element of petty-bourgeois laxity and anarchy—these in brief are the distinguishing features of the special stage of the socialist revolution in which we are now living. This is the link in the historical chain of events which we must at present grasp with all our might in order to prove equal to the tasks that confront us before passing to the next links to which we are drawn by a special brightness, the brightness of the victories of the international socialist revolution.[26]

Lenin had hoped to bring about a rapid Russian withdrawal from the First World War. He also had hoped to reach an understanding with certain sectors of the Russian capitalist class in order to establish a mixed economy supervised by the proletarian dictatorship, so that at least a modicum of political and economic stability could be temporarily achieved.

Both of these policies generated fierce debate among Russian revolutionaries. German imperialism demanded immense concessions, and when Bolshevik peace negotiators hesitated, a German offensive ripped away a massive piece of agriculturally rich Russian territory. The Left Socialist Revolutionaries and "Left Communists" in the Bolshevik party itself demanded that the Soviet Republic launch a "revolutionary war" to smash the imperialists, but a more realistic Lenin forced through a peace settlement at Brest-Litovsk. The "Left Communists" publicly denounced this settlement, as well as the moderate economic policies. The Left Socialist Revolutionaries furiously abandoned the coalition government and initiated uprisings, as well as assassination attempts—some successful—against German diplomats and Bolshevik leaders. (It should be noted, however, that some Left Socialist Revolutionaries preferred a different orientation and actually joined the Bolshevik party.) Meanwhile, the Western "democracies" that were allied in the fight against Germany, enraged over the Russian withdrawal from the war and fearful of the "bad example" of the Bolshevik Revolution, hoped to overturn the Soviet Republic by setting up an economic blockade, which was supplemented by military intervention designed to assist anti-Bolshevik forces (monarchists, Kadets, Right Socialist Revolutionaries, and sections of the Menshevik party) that were beginning a bloody civil war in the Russian countryside. This generated fierce repression of the opposition political parties. When it became clear that the Russian capitalists were also working to sabotage the economy, a policy of rapid nationalizations was initiated. "This expropriation of industry," according to Victor Serge, "verging ever closer to a total nationalization, placed an increasingly numerous population of workers within the responsibility of the Socialist State, and compelled it hastily to establish a body of functionaries, managers and administrators who could not be recruited straight away from among the working class. The bureaucracy was born, and was rapidly becoming a threat."[27] The sweeping nationalizations established what became known as war communism, and there was at the time a tendency among Communists to romanticize this period, which undoubtedly was characterized by considerable idealism and heroism. Stephen Cohen provides this stark summary of its negative features:

> The experience of civil war and war communism profoundly altered both the party and the emerging political system. The party's democratic norms of 1917, as well as its almost libertarian and reformist profile of early 1918, gave way to a ruthless fanaticism, rigid authoritarianism, and pervasive "militarization" of life on every level. Victimized was not only internal party democracy, but also the decentralized forms of popular control created throughout the country in 1917—from local soviets to factory committees. Bolsheviks professed to see no choice because, as Bukharin declared, "The republic is an armed camp." As part of this process, the party's attitude toward its political rivals changed, moving from reluctant tolerance at the outset, to expulsion of other socialist parties from the soviets in June 1918, and finally an outburst of terror following the assassination of several Bolsheviks and an attempt on Lenin's life on August 30, 1918. Repression by the security police, the Cheka, added a new dimension to Soviet political life.[28]

Lenin's earlier assertion that there should be means for voting Bolsheviks out of power took on a grim meaning when—under civil war conditions in Baku—conscientious Bolsheviks who agreed to step down after being outvoted in local soviet elections were subsequently shot by their enemies. Karl Radek pointed out that "it must have been evident not only to the Russian Mensheviks [opposed to Bolshevik rule], but to their stupid Western imitators, that if the Russian workers' dictatorship with its [Red] Terror collapsed, its place would be taken, not by democracy, but by the White Terror of [reactionary Generals] Kolchak and Denikin."[29]

Despite the ferocity of the civil war, however, the ban on left-wing opposition parties was not yet complete or permanent. Those not engaged in activity to overturn the regime by force and violence were allowed to maintain a precarious legal existence and even to seek election to the soviets. Yet by the end of 1919, Lev Kamenev observed that "the soviet plenary sessions as political organizations often waste away, the people busy themselves with purely mechanical chores.... General soviet sessions are seldom called, and when the deputies meet, it is only to accept a report, listen to a speech, and the like."[30]

This political reality was in large measure the reflection of an even greater socioeconomic calamity. The economy had collapsed, and hunger tightened its hands around the entire country. The vital social force that had made the revolution ceased to be an active political factor. As Lenin explained, "an industrial proletariat ... in our country, owing to the war and the desperate poverty and ruin, has become declassed, i.e., dislodged from its class groove, and has ceased to be a proletariat.... Since large-scale capitalist industry has been destroyed, since the factories and works are still at a standstill, the proletariat has disappeared. Sometimes it was considered to exist officially, but it was not bound together by economic roots." Many working-class Bolsheviks were not only forced to abandon idle factories but were also drawn into the new Red Army and the growing state apparatus, where so much desperately needed to be done. Thus, what was left of the working class no longer contained the vast numbers of politically experienced conscious workers who had been so crucial to the functioning of the class as a self-conscious and self-acting political force. This was reflected in the changing composition of the Bolshevik party: In 1917, 60 percent were engaged in manual occupations, but by 1923 only 15 percent were.[31]

It was in this period that "dictatorship of the proletariat" came to be equated with the dictatorship of the Communist party, not only in fact but also in official statements of the Bolshevik leadership. By 1921 Lenin was saying: "Ruin, want and the hard conditions of life give rise to vacillation: one day for the bourgeoisie, the next, for the proletariat. Only the steeled proletarian vanguard is capable of withstanding and overcoming this vacillation."[32] In the same year Trotsky offered the following elaboration:

It is only with the aid of the party, which rests upon the whole history of its past, which foresees theoretically the path of development, all its stages, and which extracts from it the necessary formula of action, that the proletariat frees itself from the need of always recommencing its history: its hesitations, its lack of decision, its mistakes. . . .

Under the form of the "struggle against despotic centralism" and against "stifling" discipline, a fight takes place for the self-preservation of various groups and subgroupings of the working class, for their petty interests, with their petty ward leaders and their local oracles. The entire working class, while preserving its cultural originality and its political nuances, can act methodically and firmly without remaining in the tow of events and directing each time its mortal blows against the weak sectors of its enemies, on the condition that a.t its head, above the wards, the districts, the groups, there is an apparatus which is centralized and bound together by iron discipline.[33]

In 1921 new developments profoundly contributed to the further drift of the Communist party away from its earlier character. Until then, it had maintained an intensely democratic internal life. If anything, the crises of the Soviet Republic had generated fiercer disagreements and debates within it than ever before, with factions known as the Left Communists, the Democratic Centralists, and the Workers' Opposition of Alexander Shlyapnikov and Alexandra Kollontai. These factional groupings openly and sharply challenged—sometimes with pamphlets and periodicals—the party leadership and its government policies. In January, Lenin voiced concern that the "fever" of factionalism was becoming "chronic and dangerous." Particularly anxious about what he perceived as (under the circumstances) romantically utopian demands for working-class control of decision making being advanced by the Workers' Opposition, he initiated measures to limit this faction's influence. Yet he continued to support the right of party members to form inner-party groups: "To form ourselves into different groups (especially before a congress), is of course permissible (and so is to canvass for votes). But it must be done within the limits of communism (and not syndicalism) and in such a way as not to provoke laughter." (The "syndicalism" and "laughter" references are aimed at the Workers' Opposition.) Expressing the hope that "the Party is learning not to blow up its disagreements," he approvingly quoted Trotsky's suggestion that "ideological struggle within the Party does not mean mutual ostracism but mutual influence."[34] Within a few weeks, however, the situation changed drastically.

Two developments coincided in March, as the Tenth Party Congress was convening, to push the Bolsheviks in a less-democratic direction than ever: the decision to initiate the New Economic Policy, and the Kronstadt uprising. The economic chaos and bottlenecks, created in large measure by the bungling of the inexperienced bureaucracy as a result of the rapid and sweeping nationalizations, had convinced a majority of the Bolshevik leaders of the need to retreat. This took the form of reestablishing market relationships, encouraging the revival of widespread petty capitalism in the cities and especially the countryside, and completely dropping all pretenses—which had flourished during the civil war—that Russia had somehow developed a new shortcut to communism. This would involve favoring the peasants and urban petty bourgeoisie at the expense of the urban laborers, but would begin to generate agricultural surpluses that, with the help of market relationships, would find their way into the cities. It would constitute a retreat nonetheless, which the Bolsheviks feared would turn into a rout if panic was sown among prorevolutionary sectors and if anticommunist elements were encouraged to view the regime as vacillating and unstable. As party members were beginning to consider and debate this proposal, however, sailors, soldiers, and workers at the Kronstadt naval base—impatient with economic shortages and dictatorial restrictions—rose up, arms in hand, calling on the workers and peasants of Russia to carry out a new revolution that would reestablish soviet democracy, which some interpreted as "soviets without Communists." They were able to count on Menshevik, Socialist Revolutionary, and anarchist support— and anticommunist forces and governments watched expectantly from abroad. The uprising was brutally suppressed, but the Bolsheviks were deeply shocked by such a visible erosion of their popular support and by how close they seemed—after winning the decisive battles of the civil war—to the abyss of counterrevolution.[35]

The Tenth Congress, convinced that the revolution's survival depended on a firm demonstration of intransigent determination and unity, adopted an orientation that definitively banned all opposition parties. It also banned any factions within the Communist party. Years later, Trotsky was to write: "Not until the Tenth Party Congress, held under conditions of blockade and famine, growing peasant unrest, and the first stages of NEP—which had unleashed petty bourgeois tendencies— was consideration given to the possibility of resorting to such an exceptional measure as the banning of factions. It is possible to regard the decision of the Tenth Congress as a grave necessity. But in the light of later events, one thing is absolutely clear: The banning of factions brought the heroic history of Bolshevism to an end and made way for its bureaucratic degeneration."[36] The delegates to the Tenth Congress, however, were eager to prevent this development and therefore wrote into the resolution banning factions a lengthy section on the need for the party to "fight with all the means at its disposal against the evils of bureaucracy" and "for the extension of democracy and initiative." Because "criticism of the party's shortcomings" was "absolutely necessary," according to the resolution, a periodical discussion bulletin and other such avenues were promised for expressing these criticisms. What is more, leaders of the banned factions were included on the newly elected central committee.[37]

It is worth looking at Lenin's statements during the discussion of this question. He argued that the 1921 crisis of the Soviet Republic "undoubtedly demands of the ruling party of Communists and of the leading revolutionary elements of the proletariat a different attitude to the one we have time and again displayed over the past year. It is a danger that undoubtedly calls for much greater unity and discipline; it undoubtedly requires that we should pull hard together. Otherwise we shall not cope with the dangers that have fallen to our lot." In the ensuing debate, he reemphasized the temporary and emergency nature of the measure: "Comrades this is no time to have an opposition. Either you are on this side, or on the other, but then your weapon must be a gun. This follows from the objective situation and you must not blame us for it. Comrades, let's not have an opposition just now."[38] At the same time, the crisis had stirred some Bolsheviks to advance proposals that would tighten up the party even more. For example, David Riazanov put forward an amendment that would forbid any future elections to the central committee on the basis of different platforms submitted to the party congress. Lenin responded:

> I think that the desire of Comrade Riazanov is unfortunately not realizable. If fundamental disagreements exist on a question, we cannot deprive members of the Central Committee of the right to address themselves to the party. I cannot imagine how we can do this. The present congress can in no way and in no form engage the elections to the next congress. And if, for example, questions like the Brest-Litovsk peace arise? Can we guarantee that such questions will not arise? It cannot be guaranteed. It is possible that it will be necessary to elect by platform. That's quite clear. . . . I do not think we have the power to prohibit this. If we are united by our resolution on unity, and, of course, the development of the revolution, there will be no repetition of elections according to platforms. The lesson we have learned at this Congress will not be forgotten. But if circumstances should give rise to fundamental disagreements, can we prohibit them from being brought before the judgment of the whole Party? No we cannot. This is an excessive desire, which is impracticable, and I move that we reject it."[39]

More than this, the Tenth Congress voted not for prohibition of tendency groupings in the party, but for "the complete prohibition of all factionalism," defined as "the formation of groups with separate platforms, striving to a certain degree to segregate and create their own group discipline." The classic, though perhaps the most extreme, example of this had been the existence of Bolshevik and Menshevik factions within the pre-1912 Russian Social Democratic Labor party. It was this that had to be prevented. E. H. Carr comments: "Thus 'groups' were not in themselves illegitimate; 'factions' were." On the other hand, as a recent Communist commentator, Bernie Taft, has pointed out, "a distorted version of the 10th Congress decision became the 'norm' later. In Stalin's days, the tendency grew to treat all opposition, all differences of view, all groupings however transitory, fluid and open, as factions."[40] Yet even under Lenin, the tightening up was beginning to transform "disciplined" quantity into authoritarian quality. Victor Serge later recalled:

> "Totalitarianism" did not yet exist as a word; as an actuality it began to press hard on us, even without our being aware of it.... What with the political monopoly, the Cheka, and the Red Army, all that now existed of the "Commune-State" of our dreams was a theoretical myth. The war, the internal measures against counter-revolution, and the famine (which had created a bureaucratic rationing-apparatus) had killed off Soviet democracy. How could it revive and when? The Party lived in the certain knowledge that the slightest relaxation of its authority could give the day to reaction.[41]

Serge also pinpointed a related problem: "The state of siege had now entered the Party itself, which was increasingly run from the top, by the Secretaries. We were at a loss to find a remedy for this bureaucratization: we knew that the party had been invaded by careerist, adventurist and mercenary elements who came over in swarms to the side that had the power. Within the Party the sole remedy of this evil had to be, and in fact was, the discreet dictatorship of the old, honest, and incorruptible members, in other words the Old Guard."[42] Yet even elements of this "old guard" were not immune from the corrupting influences of bureaucratic power and opportunistic impulses, the inclination to adapt to their environment or even to seek personal power and material comforts at the expense of revolutionary principle. Victor Serge and Natalia Sedova, both of whom were in a position to observe Lenin at fairly close range, later summarized how he responded to the growth of this new crisis of Bolshevism, which was also very much his own crisis:

> Lenin's speeches and writings of 1921-2, while still self-assured and authoritative, did not conceal his uneasiness and occasional bitterness. Reminiscences by his con-temporaries show that Vladimir Ilyich was, like so many people he attacked, highly critical of the conduct and outlook of those Party leaders who favored a bureaucratic dictatorship. At times, Lenin was brutally frank in his defense of the people—a bru-tality that no doubt reflected his anguish. "What mistakes we have made!" he said repeatedly. "It would be criminal to deny that we have exceeded all bounds ..." Or again: "Our attempt to implement socialism here and now has failed.... The dicta-torship shows that never before has the proletariat been in such a desperate situation ..." We must "abandon the construction of socialism and fall back on state capitalism in many economic spheres." We are "uncouth"; we live in "administrative chaos", in "waves of illegality". He coined words like *Kom-chvantso* and *Kom-vranio* (com-

conceit and com-deceit, where 'com' was an abbreviation for communist); he compared some Party leaders to those brutal satraps of the old regime who had been dubbed *derzhimordas*, after the repulsive bully in Gogol's satire.[43]

Lenin did more than figuratively wring his hands over this situation, however. He energetically looked for ways to counteract it, proposing a variety of government reforms, and finally—while seriously ill, in the period just before his death—forming a covert alliance with Trotsky to wage a struggle against what he viewed as dangerously bureaucratic policies represented in the top party leadership by the increasingly dominant triumvirate of Stalin, Zinoviev, and Kamenev. In his last written statement to the party, dictated when he was almost totally incapacitated, he went so far as to denounce Stalin for being "disloyal" to the party and to urge his removal from the powerful position of general secretary. When he died, in early 1924, however, it became clear that he had failed to reverse the situation.[44] This failure was shared by those, like Trotsky (and later, to an extent, even Zinoviev and Kamenev, as well as Krupskaya and other leading Bolshevik veterans), who attempted to combat the phenomenon that came to be known as Stalinism.

Yet it was not possible to overcome this darkening crisis within the borders of a bleeding and devastated Russia. It could be dispelled only by what Lenin had called "a special brightness, the brightness of the victories of the international proletarian revolution."[45] The Communist International had been established precisely to help bring this about. And it was through this body that revolutionaries throughout the world were educated in what came to be known as the principles of the Leninist party. We must therefore turn our attention, at least briefly, to an examination of the principles—which in fact were a blend of distilled Bolshevik wisdom and a reflection of the Bolshevik crisis—in which these revolutionaries were educated.

3. Communist International

Even a modest history of the Third International under Lenin would require a separate study. There already exist several works, of varying quality, that deal with this topic.[46] In the several pages that follow, however, it will be possible only to touch on several limited points having to do with the nature of the "Leninism" that was transmitted to the newly organized world Communist movement.

Bertram Wolfe, who saw the rising movement as something "new, malleable, fresh, spontaneous, and open," later described the impact that Bolshevism had inspired among revolutionaries, old survivors and young converts alike: "From all lands men and women turned in the midst of the darkness of universal war toward the beacon of hope they thought they saw shining from the Kremlin towers. . . . They had been shocked to their inmost depths by the failure of all their institutions from the churches of the Prince of Peace to the Socialist International. Socialists looked toward Moscow for the redemption of the sullied honor of their movement. Impatient rebels . . . had long fretted at the slowness with which the nineteenth and twentieth century had been realizing their dreams, and . . . were now shocked by the speed with which the civilized world had relapsed into brutality. . . . In his first decree Lenin had called to the world for peace and world revolution simultaneously. . . . From all the ends of the earth, across mountains and seas, through shell-torn battlefields and past sentries, they found their way to answer Lenin's call." Victor Serge, one of the "impatient rebels" who was in the center of the Communist International in its earliest years, recalls: "The first days of the International were days of heroic camaraderie. We lived in boundless hope. There were rumblings of revolution in the whole of Europe. . . . The Third International of the early days, for which [people] fought and many died, which filled the prisons with martyrs, was in reality a great moral and political force, not only because following the war the workers' revolution was on the ascendant in Europe and was very nearly victorious in several countries, but because it brought together a multitude of passionate, sincere, devoted minds determined to live and die for communism."[47]

In early 1919, the founding congress adopted the "Manifesto of the Communist International to the Workers of the World," drafted by Trotsky; this document clearly established the revolutionary-internationalist basis for the new organization:

> Seventy-two years ago the Communist Party proclaimed its program to the world in the form of a Manifesto written by the greatest heralds of the proletarian revolution, Karl Marx and Frederick Engels. . . . The epoch of final; decisive struggle has come later than the apostles of the socialist revolution had expected and hoped. But it has come. We Communists, the representatives of the revolutionary proletariat of the various countries of Europe, America and Asia who have gathered in Soviet Moscow, feel and consider ourselves to be the heirs and consummators of the cause whose program was affirmed 72 years ago. Our task is to generalize the revolutionary experience of the working class, to purge the movement of the corroding admixture of opportunism and social-patriotism, to unify the efforts of all genuinely revolutionary parties of the world proletariat and thereby facilitate and hasten the victory of the Communist revolution throughout the world. . . . If the First International presaged the future course of development and indicated its paths; if the Second International gathered and organized millions of workers; then the Third International is the International of open mass action, the International of revolutionary realization, the International of the deed. . . . We summon the men and women of all countries to unite under the Communist banner which is already the banner of the first great victories.[48]

At the Second Congress, in 1920, Lenin presented a draft for "Statutes of the Communist International," which underscored key aspects of this orientation: "The

Communist International once and for all breaks with the tradition of the Second International, which recognized only white-skinned peoples. The aim of the Communist International is the liberation of the working people of the *whole* world. In its ranks the Communist International unites white, yellow, and black-skinned working people in brotherhood. . . . The Communist International knows that in order to hasten victory. . . , [it] must have a strongly centralized organization. In reality and in action the Communist International must be a single universal Communist Party, the Parties in each country acting as its sections. The organizational apparatus of the Communist International must guarantee the working people of every country the opportunity to receive maximum assistance at any time from the organized proletarians of other countries."[49]

Many different elements are combined and compressed in these statements, which were developed and elaborated in the numerous debates, theses, resolutions, and manifestos of the Communist International's first four congresses. Reading through these and related materials, one finds an incredibly rich pooling of experience, analyses and insights—almost breathtaking in their historical and geographical sweep, and impressive in their great attention to detail. Not surprisingly, there were contradictory elements, troubling ambiguities, and grave limitations as well. Focusing on these, many commentators have conveyed the impression that there is little of enduring merit in all of these documents, that even from its earliest period the Third International was at best a fiasco, if not a diabolical plot of the Bolsheviks to dupe millions of idealists for the purpose of establishing a totalitarian empire. We need not blind ourselves to the International's inevitable shortcomings in order to see the utter falseness of this interpretation. Reviewing the immense work of this body led by Lenin and the Bolsheviks, revolutionaries of our own time can find much that remains vibrant and relevant.

Much of the International's work involved the effort to communicate the decades of accumulated Bolshevik experience and to apply these lessons on a world scale in the new context in which revolutionaries of 1919–1922 found themselves. We can find the insistence that a revolutionary vanguard must split away from reformist and even vacillating "centrist" forces, establishing a distinct and cohesive party around the revolutionary Marxist program. At the same time, there is considerable stress on the need for such a vanguard to be organically rooted in the working class, which often meant participating in nonrevolutionary organizations and institutions, whether "reformist" trade unions or bourgeois-democratic parliaments, as well as being willing to form united fronts with moderate Social Democratic parties and others in the immediate and daily struggles of the working class. In addition to a rejection of "economism" and narrow "workerism," there is an insistence that the struggles of oppressed groups, such as women, national minorities, and poor peasants, be embraced by Communist parties; that the struggle against imperialism and war be central to the work of the revolutionary vanguard; that a lively sense of solidarity with the workers and oppressed of all other countries animate the life of each section of the Communist International. And of course there is the underlying assumption, frequently made explicit, that all of this can be done in such a way—with sensitivity to national peculiarities and practical possibilities, with a blending of organizational discipline and the creative initiatives of party members—as to generate widespread socialist consciousness and mass actions capable of putting revolution on the agenda.

On the other hand, in a serious examination of the Third International's early history, one also finds the development of problems. In 1915, Lenin and Zinoviev had written in their pamphlet *Socialism and War* that "it is perfectly obvious that to create an *international* Marxist organization, there must be a readiness to form independent Marxist parties in the *various* countries.... The immediate future will show whether the conditions are mature for the formation of a new and Marxist International. If they are, our party will gladly join such a Third International, purged of opportunism and chauvinism. If they are not, then that will show a more or less protracted period of evolution is needed for that purging to be effected." By 1919, however, the Bolsheviks no longer felt able to wait for "a more or less protracted period of evolution."[50] They decided it was absolutely necessary to force the pace, and while the Bolshevik Revolution gave them the authority and material resources required, the organic developments that could result in "independent Marxist parties" (of the nature that had resulted in the Bolshevik party itself) were not always present in each country.

This situation was exacerbated by the point we have seen Lenin making in 1920, about how "the Communist International must be a single universal Communist Party, the Parties in each country acting as its sections." Lenin's impulse was egalitarian—he referred to the International as "an alliance of the parties which are leading the most revolutionary movement in the world"—but the degree of centralization dramatically exceeded that of the First and Second Internationals. The "international alliance of parties" was supposed to meet yearly at the World Congress, which was the supreme decision-making body and which was to elect and oversee the work of an executive committee. Yet "the Executive Committee directs the entire work of the Communist International from one Congress to another, ... [and] when necessary publishes appeals in the name of the Communist International and issues instructions which are binding on all parties and organizations affiliated to the Communist International." This executive committee had the right to demand that parties "expel groups or individuals who violate international discipline," to expel entire parties, and to set up "technical and other auxiliary departments," answerable only to the committee, in the various countries.[51]

Such a situation would not necessarily lead to disastrous situations, assuming that the Executive Committee of the Communist International (ECCI) and its staff had a high level of political sensitivity, understanding, and maturity. Yet this was not always the case. The most capable people in the Russian party as well as in the parties of other countries often could not be spared for full-time work with the ECCI. Of course, Zinoviev, Radek, and Bukharin—assigned from the Russian party to direct its work—were certainly extremely talented. As one American representative to the ECCI, James P. Cannon, later wrote: "They were the veterans who were schooled in the doctrine and knew the world movement, especially the European section of it, from study and first-hand experience in their years of exile. In addition, they had the commanding moral authority which accrues by right to the leaders of a victorious revolution." But for every capable person there were others like Bela Kun, Josef Pogany, and Matyas Rakosi, refugees from the failed Hungarian revolution who more often than not blurred together their own mistaken views and methods with the principles of Bolshevism. Among the Russians assuming responsible positions in the work of the ECCI, most had risen dramatically from quite humble roles in the Russian revolutionary movement. Even Gregory Zinoviev, the International's president, while in many ways immensely capable, energetic, and brilliant, tended to veil his own limitations with extreme arrogance and high-handedness. The bulk of those working under him, according to Pierre Broué, were people whose "experience . . . was limited, if not rudimentary, and leftist tendencies were rife among them. They did not know the workers' movement in western Europe well and were instead permeated by a belief in the superiority of the Russian experience, of which they enjoyed the results." The capable leader of the German Communist party, Paul Levi, was moved to complain that "to our knowledge, in virtually every country in which such [ECCI] emissaries are at work the dissatisfaction with them is the same. . . . They never work with, but always behind the backs of, and quite frequently against, the domestic party's central committee. Moscow listens only to them." Levi's judgment may contain exaggeration, but there are ample cases—especially in Germany itself—that confirm it at least in part.[52]

Even some of the less negative aspects of the ECCI's interventions had negative consequences. By itself, for example, the German Communist party could have afforded to maintain only four periodicals and a paid staff of twelve people. Thanks to financial assistance from the International, the German Communists published twenty-seven daily newspapers and paid 200 full-time personnel. Heinrich Brandler, then a leader of the organization, later commented: "Without the financial help of the Comintern we would have been developing in a much healthier manner. Before, we were publishing a few newspapers with pennies contributed by workers. We were dependent on workers, we had to be in constant touch with them, and we could not have embarked on enterprises which were above our real political strength. All this changed from the moment we received money from the Comintern. . . . Our financial means were all the time greater than our political possibilities, and we began to judge our strength and importance according to the length of our purse and not according to the support of the workers. This was bound to lead to disaster."[53]

In more ways than one, the German Communist party was severely damaged by the policies of the ECCI under Zinoviev's leadership. One of the most serious problems was that the party's course was determined less by the actual situation inside Germany than by the policies of the ECCI. Many see this situation as demonstrating that the principles developed by Lenin in Russia are inapplicable for a more advanced country, like Germany. After all, in his polemic with Karl Kautsky, Lenin had asserted that "Bolshevism *has created* the ideological and tactical foundations of the Third International" and that "Bolshevism *can serve as a model of tactics for all*."[54] The German Communist party obviously failed to make a revolution; therefore Lenin's claims are seen to be invalidated. Yet it should be clear that the German party in fact did not function according to the actual, historical Bolshevik model. The Russian party grew organically out of the Russian experience, and did not develop on the basis of directives and financial aid from abroad. We see in these negative policies of the ECCI *not* an application of the Bolshevik model, but rather a reflection of the post-1917 crisis of Bolshevism and the Soviet Republic. Unfortunately for the Soviet Republic, Zinoviev was not able to command or buy a German revolution into existence. The policies he promoted undermined the organization that might ultimately have been able to lead such a revolution.[55] They also helped introduce a profound distortion into what came to be known as Leninism within the world Communist movement.

If we examine how the Communist International sometimes defined the term "*democratic centralism*," we find a similar problem. As historian S. A. Smith notes, this principle was not a distinctly Bolshevik one, but in Russia "was accepted by the labor movement as a whole. . . . 'Democratic centralism' did not represent a coherent set of organizational rules; it was rather a vague principle of democratic decision-making, combined with centralized execution of decisions taken." We have seen that it was embraced by Bolsheviks and Mensheviks alike, and even a trade union conference before the Bolshevik Revolution could assert that the trade unions should function according to democratic centralism in order to ensure "the partic-ipation of every member in the affairs of the union and, at the same time, unity in the leadership of the struggle." Yet in 1920, in a document drafted by Zinoviev for the Second Congress of the Communist International, the term is defined in a man-ner that has little in common with this traditional usage but is more in line with the desperate situation that developed after 1917. As one Bolshevik commentator later recounted, "in the period of the civil war and of war communism the whole of the Bolshevik Party was converted into a military camp, and frequently the decisions of the Central Committee were carried out as military orders." Reflecting this, the relevant passage in Zinoviev's draft reads as follows: "The Communist Party must be organized on the basis of democratic centralism. The main principles of demo-cratic centralism are that higher bodies are elected by lower bodies, all directives of higher bodies are absolutely binding on subordinate bodies and a powerful Party center exists whose authority between congresses is unquestioned by all leaders of the Party."[56]

In the following year, however, the Third Congress attempted to provide a better definition: "The democratic centralism of the Communist Party organization should be a real synthesis, a fusion of centralism and proletarian democracy. This fusion can be achieved only when the Party organization *works* and *struggles* at all times together, as a united whole." This was contrasted to "formal, mechanical cen-tralization," with the explanation that "formal or mechanical centralization would mean the centralization of 'power' in the hands of the Party bureaucracy, allowing it *to dominate* the other members of the Party or the proletarian masses which are outside the Party." This mechanical centralization was unambiguously rejected. Also rejected was a formal kind of democracy that divided an organization "into the ac-tive functionaries and the passive masses." Democratic centralism was supposed to mean "*centralization of Communist activity*, i.e., the creation of a leadership that is strong and effective and at the same time flexible," as well as "the active participa-tion of working people."[57]

Yet Lenin expressed misgivings about the 1921 resolution. "I am prepared to subscribe to every one of its fifty or more points," he commented at the Fourth Congress, in 1922. "But we have not learned how to present our Russian experience to foreigners." He suggested that "the foreign comrades have signed without read-ing and understanding" the resolution, yet he expressed the thought that "they can-not be content with hanging it in a corner like an icon and praying to it. Nothing can be achieved that way." Elaborating, Lenin argued that "the resolution is an ex-cellent one, but it is almost entirely Russian, that is to say, everything in it is based on Russian conditions. That is its good point, but it is also its failing." Even if the foreign comrades read the lengthy document, it would be extremely difficult to understand it. "And . . . if by way of exception some foreigner does understand it, he cannot carry it out." Arguing that, nonetheless, the other Communists of the world "must assimilate part of the Russian experience," Lenin confessed: "Just how that will be done, I do not know." He thought that they might ultimately accomplish this on the basis of their own experience, but added that "we Russians must also find ways and means of explaining the principles of this resolution to the foreigners. Unless we do that, it will be absolutely impossible for them to carry it out."[58] In all of this anguished groping, it seems clear that Lenin—convinced that Bolshevism could not be transmitted through commands or idolization—felt that an understanding of texts on organization can be achieved only if their organic relationship to specific social and political contexts is understood; this understanding must then be translated into one's own specific cultural, social, and political environment. If one was to follow the Bolshevik model, one would have to do more than vote for and worship lengthy theses of the Communist International, loyally but blindly endorsing the ideas of the Russian Communists. Rather, it would be necessary to develop a native variant of Bolshevism—through one's own experience and struggles—that could duplicate the Russian model by being as rooted in one's own traditions and one's own working class as had been Lenin's party.

Lenin had made a similar point earlier: "It is now essential that communists in every country should quite consciously take into account . . . the *concrete features* which [the] struggle assumes and must invariably assume in each country, in conformity with the special character of its economics, politics, culture, and national composition. . . ."[59] As we can see, however, it was not a simple thing for loyal Communists to achieve the kind of balanced approach Lenin sought to convey.

Many attempted to do this. One of these was described many years later by Harry Braverman: "He spoke to us in the accents of the Russian revolution and of the Leninism which had gone forth from the Soviet Union in the twenties and the thirties. But there was in his voice something more which attracted us. And that was the echoes of the [American] radicalism of the pre-World War I years, the popular radicalism of Debs, Haywood and John Reed. And he spoke with great force and passion."[60] This was James P. Cannon, one of the founders of American Communism—one of many who, as he himself put it, "learned to do away forever with the idea that a revolutionary movement, aiming at power, can be led by people who practice socialism as an avocation. . . . Lenin, Trotsky, Zinoviev, Radek, Bukharin—these were our teachers. We began to be educated in an entirely different spirit from the old lackadaisical Socialist Party—in the spirit of revolutionists who take ideas and program very seriously." Moreover, in Cannon's opinion, "the honest and capable help we got from Lenin, Trotsky and the whole Comintern in 1921 and 1922 on the trade union question, and on the underground and legal questions, enabled us to solve the problems and liquidate the old factional fights." There was another vital question on which, Cannon has argued, the influence of the Communist International was highly beneficial: "Even before the First World War and the Russian Revolution, Lenin and the Bolsheviks were distinguished from all other tendencies in the international socialist and labor movement by their concern with the problems of oppressed nations and national minorities, and affirmative support of their struggles for freedom, independence and the right of self-determination.... After November 1917 this new doctrine— with special emphasis on the Negroes—began to be transmitted to the American communist movement with the authority of the Russian Revolution behind it. The Russians in the Comintern started on the American communists with the harsh, insistent demand that they shake off their own unspoken prejudices, pay attention to the special problems and grievances of the American Negroes, go to work among them, and champion their cause in the white community." Cannon sums up the early influence of the Communist International in this way: "The power the Russians exerted over the American movement in that early time was ideological, not administrative. They changed and reshaped the thinking of the young American communists by explanation and persuasion, not by command; and the effect was clarifying and enlightening, and altogether beneficent for the provincial American movement."[61]

It could be argued that, since he remained a Leninist until the day he died, Cannon was tailoring reality to his ideological preferences. Yet his account of the early experience of American Communists coincides, in large measure, with what one can cull from the posthumously published memoirs of his erstwhile comrade Bertram D. Wolfe, who became a professional anti-Leninist for the last three decades of his life. According to Wolfe, before 1925 it was not the case that "all important decisions for the American Communist Party were being made in Moscow." In fact, in the early 1920s, "the first decisions made in Moscow were salutary and beneficial." He continues: "I rejoiced that the Communist International had pressured us to end our factionalism and set up an open, legal, unified party." He also explains: "However much we were inspired by Lenin's success in Russia and by the revolutionary movements that seemed to be sweeping through Central Europe, we had no thought of becoming a mere adjunct and agency of the Russian Communist party.... Even though we were beginning to get peremptory notes from Zinoviev and not too knowledgeable, but forceful and didactic, letters from Lenin, ... I still believed that they were intended only as helpful suggestions, often exciting ones, and as successful examples to imitate after adapting them to American conditions, but not as categorical commands."[62]

The fact remains that the dominance of the Russian party within the Communist International was unquestioned. Lenin himself was quite explicit about this, although he sought to articulate it with a distinctly nonauthoritarian balance: "Leadership in the revolutionary proletarian International has passed for a time— for a short time, it goes without saying—to the Russians, just as at various periods of the nineteenth century it was in the hands of the British, then of the French, then of the Germans." Zinoviev made a similar point to a young foreign Communist who had come to Moscow to work on the staff of the ECCI: "Abroad there is frequent talk about a Moscow dictatorship over the Comintern. You will see for yourself that we would be overly happy if the foreigners would take upon their shoulders part of this dictatorship. It is too bad that they do so little of it. I hope some day we will be able to transfer the entire dictatorship to you foreigners, and shift the Executive Committee from Moscow to Berlin or Paris." Typically, however, he linked this with the emphasis on the central authority of the ECCI. On the fifth anniversary of the Third International he stressed the need "to work still more consciously and methodically at the strengthening of international discipline within our ranks and at converting the Comintern into a really unified international Communist Party, guided by one center—for the time being—'for a very short time,' from Moscow, such a center being transferred to a country with a more numerous proletariat upon the first decisive victory over the bourgeoisie."[63]

It seems clear that Zinoviev sincerely hoped that such prophecies would come to pass, and that he had a genuine concern for the success of revolutionary movements and struggles in other countries. "It is painful to blunder within one's own party," he wrote shortly after Lenin's death, "but still more fearful was Lenin of making mistakes that would affect the workers of other countries. He first of all imparted to us this feeling of devoutness to the affairs of the International. He taught us to approach the questions which affect the German peasants and the Chinese coolies, the American negroes and the French workers with a warm heart and a cool head. Look long before you jump, for it is the sacred cause of the working classes of the whole world—this is what he taught us."[64] In the mid-1920s, when it became clear that Stalin was determined to subordinate revolutionary internationalism to the bureaucratically defined national interests of the Soviet Union, Zinoviev became a leading oppositionist. From shortly before Lenin's death until 1925, however, he and Stalin were closely allied and shared authoritarian organizational impulses.

Thus Zinoviev played a mixed role in the life of the International of which he was president. Increasingly, he gave "Leninism" an authoritarian twist, as we have seen from his definition of democratic centralism. "It will be of great benefit for the parties of all countries," he commented, "if they acquire a fear of the Communist International." On another occasion he asserted that "the chief conclusion of the proletarian revolution is the need for an iron, organized and monolithic party." In his discussion of Lenin and the party at the time of Lenin's death, Zinoviev chose to underscore that "the party should be built from above," with "unlimited iron discipline" and "relentless iron discipline." According to Trotsky, Lenin had been a moderating influence on the "centralist predilections" of Zinoviev and others in the ECCI, but "when Lenin ceased working, the ultra-centralist manner of handling questions was the one which triumphed." Victor Serge, who worked under Zinoviev, later recalled that "in the International he was a man of shady little schemes; at home the exponent of repression. Into ideological struggles, he introduces intrigue and trickery in increasing doses; by gradual steps he introduces repression in the party...." Another who worked under Zinoviev in the International, Alfred Rosmer, wrote in his memoirs of "the 'Zinovievite Bolshevization' undertaken immediately after Lenin's death," through which "communism itself was reduced to the level of maneuver." All too often, practices that had little to do with the successful development of Bolshevism up through 1917—but that were now deemed to be expedient—were elevated to the rank of "principle" and incorporated into what came to be known throughout the world as Leninism.[65]

An additional element also assumed central importance in this period, which would have fateful and ultimately fatal consequences for the Communist International. It was expressed as early as 1924 in an article entitled "Under the Leadership of Russia," by the Finnish Communist and Comintern functionary O. W. Kuusinen. "Renegades and enemies repeatedly accused the Communist International of aiding the foreign policy of Soviet Russia," wrote Kuusinen. "To us as Communists it would be a matter of joy to be able to render efficient aid to the Socialist power of the Soviets." He also emphasized that "the Communist International possesses in the Russian leadership, in the person of its chairman and of the Russian delegation as well as of the Central Committee of the R. C. P., and accumulated stock of far-reaching revolutionary experience, of Marxian leadership and of proven ability, which are requisite to the historic tasks of the Communist International."[66] Yet what if the Russian leadership, while maintaining revolutionary Marxist pretenses, would become cynical about revolutionary movements in other countries and make foreign policy decisions simply on the basis of narrowly perceived national self-interest?

Throughout the latter half of the 1920s, internal factional fights in the Russian Communist party were to have devastating repercussions throughout the Communist International, particularly as the triumphant Stalin faction imposed its own authoritarian interpretation of Marxist-Leninist orthodoxy. By the 1930s many revolutionaries who did not believe that healthy and indigenous Communist parties could develop by blindly following commands from Moscow, like James P. Cannon and Bertram D. Wolfe, found themselves expelled. Some, like Wolfe, became bitterly disillusioned, grew to hate the movement to which they had devoted "the whole of their lives," and began identifying Bolshevism with the totalitarian order they perceived as developing under Stalin; they ultimately transferred their loyalties and energies to combating the "Communist threat" through such bulwarks of "Western democracy" as the U.S. State Department and the Central Intelligence Agency. Others, like Cannon, remained true to the revolutionary commitments of their youth, laboring to retrieve the historic lessons of Bolshevism and the fundamental principles that guided Lenin; in this way they hoped to help advance the struggle for workers' democracy and socialism.

For the millions of revolutionary-minded people, on the other hand, who remained loyal to a Communist International "under the leadership of Russia," the understanding of what constituted genuine principles of Leninist organization assumed a form that was qualitatively different from the principles that had guided the Bolsheviks in their own revolutionary struggle.

4. A Note on Lenin's Authority

Here it may be useful to take up once again a question we addressed earlier, though now on a broader scale: the nature of Lenin's authority in the Russian Communist party, which also came to be felt in the world Communist movement as well as throughout Russia. There is little to suggest that Lenin was motivated by the desire "to rule alone" as Robert V. Daniels has put it, or that he placed himself above democratic centralist norms after his party came to power. Yet his ideas and personality had immense influence.

Even the reminiscences of ex-Communists confirm Theodore Draper's comment that "Lenin's personal influence was one of Communism's most important assets" in the early period following the Bolshevik Revolution. Observing Lenin at the Fourth Congress of the Communist International, in 1922, Max Eastman was moved to describe him as "the most powerful man I ever saw on the platform. I do not know how to define the nature of his power, except to say that he is a granite mountain of sincerity. . . . You feel that he is all there for you—you are receiving the whole man." Years later, although an ardent anti-Communist, Eastman continued to feel that it was as though Lenin were "taking us inside his mind and showing us how the truth looks. . . . He was as selfless as any of the saints. Every act and every judgment of his was directed toward that goal that, as a Marxist, he believed would free the world from its age-old miseries."[67]

Another ex-Communist, writing under the pseudonym Ypsilon, recalled that "he has the ability to destroy the ideas of a man without touching the man himself. He himself does not hesitate to admit a blunder that he has committed, with complete frankness. There is no trace of personal vanity in him." Writing of Lenin as he was in 1921, at the Third Congress of the Communist International, he offers these impressions: "What is the measure of this man's greatness? I believe it is the complete fusion of his own individual self with his historical task that has raised him above all others. This required the ability to solve the stupendous contradictions between the duties of a revolutionary statesman and the desires and dreams of a revolutionary idealist. In fact this ability had become second nature. At the same time, however, Lenin had to guard against setting himself apart from his revolutionary comrades, and had to master the art of acting as a 'first among equals.' This calls for continuous incessant self-control, a daily victory over the temptations of power."[68]

Robert C. Tucker writes that "events in the revolutionary period so often vindicated Lenin's political judgment that a saying became common in leading party circles: 'Vote with Ilyich and you won't be wrong.'" Yet Lenin refused to accept this dynamic, which could seriously weaken the revolutionary fiber of his party. When one leading Bolshevik sent him a note that included the comment "the Central Committee—c'est vous," Lenin felt compelled to object, pointing out: "On organizational and personal questions I have been in the minority countless times. You yourself saw many instances when you were a Central Committee member." Tucker comments that Lenin's authority "in the final analysis . . . derived from his extraordinary qualities as a revolutionary leader and political personality." Lenin believed that revolutionary leadership could be preserved "not by force of power but by force of authority, by force of energy, by greater experience, greater versatility, and greater talentedness" (as he himself put it in 1902). Tucker comments: "Formally, he was on a par with the other full members [of the Central Committee]; his vote counted for no more than theirs. . . . The acceptance of Lenin's authority did not mean that the other leaders were indisposed to disagree with him on specific policy questions. . . . Automatic acquiescence in his position was not expected; the whole previous history of Bolshevik leadership politics militated against any such dictatorial relationship of the leader to his followers."[69]

And yet a growing element of adulation spontaneously arose after the Bolshevik Revolution. Ypsilon recalled that "Lenin always concluded his speeches in a logical, never a rhetorical way. . . . But whatever the ending, the ovations never ended, and unfailingly Lenin suffered the same painful embarrassment each time. Quickly he would gather his papers together. Eyes lowered, face closed, he would disappear as fast as possible from sight. . . . When he leaves the hall, all eyes follow him as if afraid to lose sight of his slight figure. . . ." Deeply disturbed by this and similar developments, Lenin discreetly took steps to curb it. "It's shameful," he commented to a trusted comrade. "They write about me, that I am like this and that and so on, exaggerating everything, calling me a genius, a kind of extraordinary man—there is an element of mysticism in all of this. . . . All our lives we fought against exalting the individual, against the elevation of the single person . . . and here it comes up again: the glorification of one personality. This is not good at all. I am just like everybody else. . . . This is superfluous and harmful, and goes against our conviction and our view on the role of personality."[70]

After his death in early 1924, Lenin was converted into a kind of deity. His "successor," Joseph Stalin, willingly assumed deification while still alive and—under the mantle of "Lenin's most devoted pupil"—really did establish an "an iron grip" over the party apparatus. Although all of this has been graced with the "Leninist" label, it has little in common with the thought and practice of Lenin himself. Respect for Lenin's ideas and impressive human qualities preclude transforming him into an icon.

Genuine democratic centralism did not prevent those with greater experience and talent from earning an authority that made them "first among equals," but under Lenin there was no place for those who were "more equal than others." Leaders were also members of a party whose democratic norms applied to all. Tragically, this tradition was being undermined in Lenin's last years as the Bolsheviks were entangled in the mounting crisis overwhelming the Soviet Republic. His final illness and death removed an important obstacle to the further degeneration of Bolshevism.

5. Bureaucratization After Lenin

The bureaucratic degeneration of the Communist party of the Soviet Union cannot be understood if we attempt to tease it out of the particular ideas on organization that Lenin presented in 1902. Something more can be gained, however, if we turn to an even earlier text from Marx, *The German Ideology* (1845), where it is argued that for communism the "development of productive forces . . . is an absolutely necessary practical premise because without it *want* is merely made general, and with *destitution* the struggle for necessities and all the old filthy business would necessarily be reproduced. . . ." Ninety years later, Trotsky utilized this insight and explained that "the basis of bureaucratic rule is the poverty of society in objects of consumption, with the resulting struggle of each against all. When there is enough goods in a store, the purchasers can come whenever they want to. When there is little goods, the purchasers are compelled to stand in line. When the lines are very long, it is necessary to appoint a policeman to keep order. Such is the starting point of the power of the Soviet bureaucracy."[71] The "policemen/bureaucrats" naturally made sure that their own needs were met first of all, and soon their function came to be not merely to keep order in the face of poverty, but also to defend their own material privileges. Although a ceiling was initially imposed on the earnings of Communists working in the state and party apparatus, this party maximum, as it was called, was gradually made more elastic, especially with the inauguration of the New Economic Policy. A veteran of the Communist International, Joseph Berger, recalls that "as long as Lenin was alive something more than lip service was paid to it. . . . The change came with Stalin and his high material rewards to his supporters. In preparation for the final struggle with the Opposition, the struggle against privilege was finally given up."[72]

The opposition to which Berger refers was formed in 1926, containing such people as Trotsky, Zinoviev, Kamenev, and Krupskaya. They opposed policies advanced by Stalin—who had support from much of the party and state apparatus—that subordinated revolutionary internationalism to the notion of creating socialism in one country (the Union of Soviet Socialist Republics); they also advocated a more conscientious plan for creating an industrial basis for the country's economic development, while improving the conditions of the workers and expanding their role in decision making. More than this, they denounced "the bureaucratic perversion of the Party apparatus," warning that "the methods of mechanical adjudication are preparing new splits and cleavages, new removals, new expulsions, new pressures with respect to the party as a whole. This system inevitably constricts the leading summit, reduces its authority and compels it to replace its ideological authority with doubled and tripled pressure. . . . Genuine discipline is shaken apart and replaced by subordination to the influential figures in the apparatus." This opposition engaged in a series of fights for the defense or revival of a genuinely Leninist party; while many oppositionists finally capitulated in the face of immense pressures, thousands of heroic people endured hardship and ultimately death because they continued to resist.[73]

Stalin's temporary ally in the fight against the oppositionists, Nikolai Bukharin, argued that their very existence as an opposition was intolerable because "the party is *unitary* in its structure, that is, represents a structure excluding any independent and autonomous groups, functions, organized currents, etc." The opposition was crushed, with many being pressured into renouncing their views and the others being sent to prison camps. When Bukharin himself came into opposition against new policies of Stalin (a badly organized plan for rapid industrialization and for collectivization of the land, which constituted a violent and authoritarian "revolution from above"), Stalin suppressed him, with the reminder that "freedom for factional squabbling among groups of intellectuals is not inner-party democracy." After engineering Bukharin's defeat, Stalin declared: "When 99 percent of our Party vote for the Party and against the opposition, that is real, genuine proletarian unity as there has not been in our Party before."[74]

Leopold Trepper, a dedicated Communist who was to organize the heroic anti-Nazi espionage network known as the Red Orchestra during World War II, lived in Moscow during this transitional period. His later reminiscences are worthy of note:

> During Lenin's lifetime, political life among the Bolsheviks was always very animated. At the congresses, in the plenums, at the meetings of the Central Committee, militants said frankly what they thought. This democratic and often bitter clash of opinions gave the party its cohesion and vitality. From the moment Stalin extended his power over the party machine, however, even old Bolsheviks no longer dared to oppose his decisions or even discuss them. Some kept silent and suffered inwardly; others withdrew from active political life. Worse, many militants publicly supported Stalin's positions although they did not approve of them. This terrible hypocrisy accelerated the inner demoralization of the party....
>
> Along with the cult of Stalin there developed the cult of the party.... The party cannot be wrong, the party never makes a mistake; you cannot be right if you oppose the party. The party is sacred. Whatever the party says—through the mouth of its secretary general—is the gospel truth. To question it is sacrilege. There is no salvation outside the party: and if you are not with the party, you are against it. These were the unspoken truths that were beaten into the heads of skeptics; as for heretics, they were doomed to excommunication.[75]

In 1938 Max Shachtman made an interesting point: "In the days of illegality and thin purses, under Tsarist despotism the Russian party nevertheless held four regular congresses between July 1903 and May 1907. (Of party conferences under Tsarism, there were eight, from the Tammerfors meeting in 1905 to the Provino meeting in 1913). In the revolutionary period, between the overthrow of the Tsar and the death of Lenin, the party held eight regular party congresses (and seven conferences).... Under the Stalinist bureaucracy, the Bolshevik party (if it may be called that) has been allowed to meet in congress (again, if it may be called that) only four times in more than thirteen years. The party met more often under the Tsar!"[76]

In terms of program, morale, and internal organizational norms and activity, the party of Lenin had—under the banner of "Leninism"—passed out of existence. But the Communist party of the Soviet Union was to be de-Bolshevized in more ways than these. The extreme stresses of industrialization and the degree of violence with which the peasantry was repressed during the collectivization process created a dynamic resulting in a massive purge of the party, accompanied by arrests, executions, and imprisonment for perhaps half a million party members. Although 40 percent of the delegates to the Seventeenth Party Congress, in 1934, had been Bolsheviks in 1917, this figure had dropped to 5 percent at the 1939 Eighteenth Party Congress. Of all the members of the Bolshevik central committee of 1917, only Stalin remained in the party leadership after the purges.[77]

New studies are beginning to appear on this period that deserve close attention. J. Arch Getty, in a challenging interpretation of the Great Purges of the 1930s, has suggested that they were "often populist, even subversive," constituting "a radical, even hysterical *reaction* to bureaucracy. The entrenched officeholders were destroyed from above and below in a chaotic wave of voluntarism and revolutionary puritanism." There are serious problems with this view. Not *all* "entrenched officeholders" were destroyed—those "above" (Stalin and his closest circle) eliminated real and imagined rivals with the enthusiastic assistance and sometimes even over-zealous initiative of ambitious bureaucrats "from below," with considerable populist, radical, and even Marxist rhetoric, to be sure. On the other hand, Getty raises interesting questions about whether "an untrained and uneducated bureaucracy in a huge, developing peasant country somehow functioned and obeyed well enough to be termed totalitarian." He suggests that "the party in the 1930s was inefficient, fragmented, . . . split several ways by internal conflict . . . [with] organizational relationships [that] seem more primitive than totalitarian."[78] If "totalitarian" means something akin to what is described in Orwell's *1984* or the inhumanly efficient apparatus of evil described by cold war ideologists, then Getty has a point here; but if we define it as attempting to subjugate to the state all functions of the country's social, political, and ideological life and crushing the slightest manifestations of criticism and independent opinion (regardless of clumsiness and inefficiency on the part of those who would do the crushing), Getty's argument is overstated.

Getty tells us that "the party in the thirties was neither monolithic or disciplined." Here too, it depends on one's frame of reference. Surely the Communist party was more monolithic in 1938 than it was in 1918, despite the nuances and tensions and divergences that one can find among adherents of the obligatory orthodoxy of Stalinized "Marxism-Leninism." Discipline, too, surely had a more unyielding character once the "correct line" was handed down from above, regardless of the infractions and ambiguities that can be documented. At the same time, however, we can find valuable insights as Getty develops his point: "Its upper ranks were divided, and its lower organizations were disorganized, chaotic, undisciplined. Moscow leaders were divided on policy issues, and central leaders were at odds with territorial secretaries whose organizations suffered from internal disorder and conflict. A bloated party membership containing political illiterates and apolitical opportunists plus a lazy and unresponsive regional leadership was hardly the formula for a Leninist party. Such a clumsy and unwieldy organization could not have been an efficient and satisfying instrument for Moscow's purposes." Having little sympathy for Leon Trotsky, he nonetheless is struck by the great revolutionary's "particularly lucid analysis of Stalin's role. . . . Trotsky noted that Stalin was the front man, the symbol of the bureaucracy. In Trotsky's view, Stalin did not create the bureaucracy but vice versa. Stalin was a manifestation of a bureaucratic phenomenon: 'Stalin is the personification of the bureaucracy. That is the substance of the political personality.'" Getty argues that "Stalin did not initiate or control everything that happened in the party and country. The number of hours in the day, divided by the number of things for which he was responsible, suggests that his role in many areas could have been little more than occasional intervention, prodding, threatening, or correcting. . . . He was an executive, and reality forced him to delegate most of his authority to his subordinates, each of whom had his own opinions, client groups, and interests." Getty concludes: "It is not necessary for us to put Stalin in day-to-day control of events to judge him. A chaotic local bureaucracy, a quasi-feudal network of politicians accustomed to arresting people, and a set of perhaps insoluble political and social problems created an atmosphere conducive to violence. All it took from Stalin were catalytic and probably ad hoc interventions . . . to spark an uncontrolled explosion."[79]

Yet the results of all this were proclaimed—by pro-Stalin Communists and fierce opponents of communism alike—a triumph of genuine Leninism and a model of how an efficient revolutionary party deals with internal dangers. This naturally affected the manner in which millions of people throughout the world were to understand the Leninist conception of the party.

6. The Fate of the Comintern

George Orwell once made an interesting observation: "In abbreviating a name one narrowed and subtly altered its meaning, by cutting out most of the associations that would otherwise cling to it. The words *Communist International*, for instance, call up a composite picture of universal brotherhood, red flags, barricades, Karl Marx, and the Paris Commune. The word *Comintern*, on the other hand, suggests merely a tightly knit organization and a well-defined body of doctrine. It refers to something almost as easily recognized, and as limited in purpose, as a chair or table. *Comintern* is a word that can be uttered almost without taking thought, whereas *Communist International* is a phrase over which one is obliged to linger at least momentarily."[80]

Orwell captures something here of the transformation experienced by the Third International from 1919 to the 1930s. Of course, the abbreviation had currency before Stalin's triumph and continued to be utilized by many dissident Communists who remained loyal to the original ideals of the Bolshevik Revolution. Nor were the ranks of the mainstream of the world Communist movement devoid of sincere supporters of Stalin who were, nontheless, profoundly idealistic and heroic fighters for social justice.[81] But the movement to which they had committed their loyalties and energies had norms and an orientation that had changed dramatically since the time of Lenin. There was an essential element of critical thinking, a vital revolutionary consistency that passed out of existence with the transition from Lenin to Stalin. As Trotsky protested as early as 1928, "the living, active parties" were being "subordinated to the control of the 'revolutionary order' of an irremovable governmental bureaucracy," and "theory, ceasing to be an instrument of foresight and knowledge, has become an administrative technical tool." There was in the Comintern a substitution of "strictly administrative measures for independent activity, for self-criticism, for the capacity of self-orientation."[82]

In 1932 a leading spokesman for the Comintern perspective in the United States, William Z. Foster, explained that "the Communist Party of the United States ... is the American section of the Communist International. ... The Communist International is a disciplined world party: only such a party can defeat world imperialism. Its leading party, by virtue of its great revolutionary experience, is the Russian Communist party. In its general work it applies the principles of democratic centralism, even as its affiliated parties do in their respective countries. That is, the policies of the International are worked out jointly with the several parties and then applied in the usual disciplined Communist way." The Italian Communist leader Palmiro Togliatti, however, had pointed out six years before: "Of course, we have the statutes of the International which guarantee certain rights to certain comrades, but there is something else which is not contained in these statutes. That is the position of the Russian party in the International, its leading function—that goes beyond the limits of the statutes."[83]

This had certain implications in the 1920s, as the Stalin leadership assumed dominance within the Comintern. Communist parties around the world experienced a "Bolshevization" campaign, initiated in Moscow, to recast them in a more "Leninist" mold—as defined by the Stalin leadership.[84] As a result, there were shakeups and ultimately expulsions in all sections of the Comintern. One example we will touch on here brings us back to a person discussed in an earlier chapter— S. I. Gusev, the leading Bolshevik committeeman in Petersburg during the early days of 1905—who assumed a responsible position in the Comintern apparatus and was sent (clandestinely) as the Comintern representative to the United States in 1925.

In the American Communist party of that period, a factional rift had developed between a current led by Charles Ruthenberg and dominated by a group of bright and energetic politicos headed by Jay Lovestone, and a current more oriented to indigenous labor-radical traditions, whose leading personalities were William Z. Foster and James P. Cannon. The Foster-Cannon bloc had a majority and seemed more inclined toward developing a homegrown left-wing orientation. Gusev, then "a soft-spoken, roly-poly man in his fifties," arrived on the scene with the authority not only of his present position, but also of having been among the original old Bolsheviks who had worked closely with Lenin. Theodore Draper writes that he "spoke sparingly in a slow, methodical English or German, and ended all discussions with a finality that precluded further disagreement." It was widely assumed that Gusev would use his authority and experience to help break down the faction walls in the American Party, in order to unify it, with Foster, Ruthenberg, Cannon, and Lovestone being transformed into a dynamic leadership team. Cannon later recalled: "I was then a convinced 'Comternist.' I had faith in the wisdom and also in the fairness of the Russian leaders." At the time, none of the American Communists were aware that Stalin's influence was being consolidated within the Comintern. Gusev's arrival in the United States, as Theodore Draper has shown, was "one of Stalin's first moves to wrest control of the International from Zinoviev." Bertram Wolfe, then a member of the Lovestone faction who knew Gusev quite well, later recalled that "in the faction fight going on in the Russian party he was a supporter of Stalin, and, because of certain experiences in the Red Army during the civil war, a bitter enemy of Trotsky.... Gusev was ... sent to spread the Russian fight to the American Party and to weaken the Foster faction because it contained a number of people, including one of its leaders, James P. Cannon, who were inclined to Trotsky. He was going to the American Party to deepen the fight, strengthen the Lovestone-Ruthenberg faction, and weaken, even destroy, the strength of the Foster-Cannon faction."[85]

At the 1925 party convention, Gusev presented a telegram from Moscow noting that "it has finally become clear that the Ruthenberg Group is more loyal to decisions of the Communist International and stands closer to its views." It demanded an equal division of the leadership between the majority and minority, concluding that "those who refuse to submit will be expelled." Although Foster almost openly rebelled, he was restrained by those, like Cannon, who had greater faith in the Comintern. After this 50–50 parity between majority and minority was accepted, Gusev informed the American comrades that as Comintern representative, he would be a voting member of the political committee and would throw his vote to the "minority" because it was "more loyal" to the Comintern.[86]

Wolfe, who shared in the rejoicing of the Ruthenberg-Lovestone group over their victory, did have inner qualms, but he expressed them only much later:

> This is no way to win a majority. If we get a majority because the Comintern says we are more loyal to the Communist International and closer to its views, some day it might send the same message concerning another group, call it more loyal, etc., and then our majority would be lost. The only majority that counts is the one you get by winning the conviction of every individual member on the merits of your arguments, your actions, and your views.[87]

But that is not how the new Lovestone "majority" functioned. It sought to display its loyalty to the Stalinized Comintern in numerous ways, and Wolfe himself misused his knowledge of Russian-language sources to produce a classic of polemical dishonesty, *The Trotsky Opposition*, and to make—as he put it—"my own contribution to this Stalin cult." In 1928 Lovestone and Wolfe presided over the expulsion of Cannon and others on charges of "Trotskyism." Yet before the decade was over, the Lovestone leadership itself was in disagreement with the Stalin leadership on the question of tactics in the United States—and it was quickly transformed into a minority and expelled. Years later, Lovestone commented: "I reaped a harvest of my own sowing. I was largely responsible for that mechanical concept of loyalty to the Communist International, and it came home to roost with its claws in my eyes." And Cannon remembered that the experience of the 1920s was difficult to live through "without sliding into cynicism as did so many others—good companions in earlier endeavors."[88]

The Comintern interventions, and the cynicism they generated, did little to help the American Communists develop according to the actual model of Bolshevism. Some of the victims, such as Lovestone and Wolfe, gradually gravitated toward professional anticommunism. Others kept their faith in communism intact by becoming uncritical admirers of Stalin and believing that a healthy socialist society was being built in the Soviet Union. They went along with other interventions by Stalin in their party, including, in 1930, the elevation to the party leadership of an underling in Foster's shattered faction, Earl Browder, and Browder's dramatic demotion and expulsion fifteen years later. The general line of the American Communist party was also determined from outside. From 1928 to 1934, the Comintern leadership maintained an extreme ultraleft and sectarian orientation apparently designed, bureaucratically, to force revolutionary breakthroughs that would end Russian isolation. By 1935, however, the line shifted, as the Stalin leadership began to place hopes in the possibility of establishing friendly ties with liberal capitalist governments through an alliance opposing Nazi Germany. The task of Comintern affiliates was no longer to lead socialist revolutions but to defend democratic capitalist regimes. "Now the toiling masses in a number of capitalist countries are faced with the necessity of making a *definite* choice," stated Comintern spokesman Georgi Dimitroff, "and of making it today, not between proletarian dictatorship and bourgeois democracy, but between bourgeois democracy and fascism.[89]

Even after the formal dissolution of the Comintern in 1943 (to satisfy the Soviet Union's capitalist allies during World War II), the Stalinist dynamics within the world Communist movement remained intact. For innumerable revolutionary militants operating in this context, it became almost impossible to maintain a clear and coherent understanding of actual Leninist principles. After Stalin died, in 1953, and after dramatic changes (such as the Yugoslav and Chinese revolutions) began to affect the world Communist movement, the legacy of Stalinism continued to have a profound influence. When Nikita Khrushchev exposed many of Stalin's crimes in 1956, a central component of many Communists' faith was shattered. Yet much of the Stalinist tradition and the bureaucratic dynamics underlying it remain intact to this day, continuing to affect how "Leninism" is understood.[90]

Our study of what kind of party actually led the working class to victory in 1917, however, indicates that there is a considerable difference between bureaucratized "Leninism" and the Bolshevik-Leninist current of 1903–1923.

13. Conclusion

"Marxism will go through many vicissitudes of fortune, perhaps even eclipses. Its power, conditioned by the course of history, none the less appears to be inexhaustible. For its base is knowledge integrated with the necessity for revolution."

—Victor Serge[1]

"The Bolsheviks are not unjustified in claiming Marx as their own. Do you know? Marx had a strong Bolshevik streak in him!"

—Eduard Bernstein[2]

"Read Lenin again (be careful)."

—C. Wright Mills[3]

In 1920 Lenin reviewed the history of the Bolsheviks for the benefit of revolutionaries in other countries who sought lessons from the Russian experience that might be useful in their own situations. "As a current of political thought and as a political party, Bolshevism has existed since 1903," Lenin wrote, but he immediately added: "Only the history of Bolshevism during the *entire* period of its existence can satisfactorily explain why it has been able to build up and maintain, under the most difficult conditions, the iron discipline needed for the victory of the proletariat." Many sympathetic and hostile commentators have sought the golden key to Bolshevism's success in the study of the organizational structure that supposedly generated such discipline. But Lenin warns that without certain conditions, "all attempts to establish discipline inevitably fall flat and end up in phrasemongering and clowning."[4] This has certainly proved to be the case for many would-be Leninist organizations.

Lenin enumerates three prerequisites of the discipline needed for the revolutionary victory: the class-consciousness and devotion to revolution of significant elements of the working class (whom Lenin terms the revolutionary vanguard); the ability of this proletarian vanguard to link up "and—if you wish—merge in a certain measure, with the broadest masses of working people"; the correctness of the political leadership of the revolutionary vanguard, and the understanding of this by the broad masses on the basis of their own experience. "Without these conditions," Lenin writes, "discipline in a revolutionary party really capable of being the party of the advanced class, whose mission is to overthrow the bourgeoisie and transform the whole of society, cannot be achieved .... On the other hand, these conditions cannot emerge at once. They are created only by prolonged effort and hard-won experience. Their creation is facilitated by a correct revolutionary theory, which, in turn, is not a dogma, but assumes final shape only in close connection with the practical activity of a truly mass and truly revolutionary movement."[5]

It is worth reflecting on this. First of all, we should consider the word "discipline," which Lenin stresses. It can be defined in two very different ways, according to Webster's *New World Dictionary*. On the one hand, it can mean "training that develops self-control, character, or orderliness and efficiency." On the other hand, it can mean "submission to authority or control" and "treatment that corrects or punishes." The kind of discipline Lenin is talking about—the very way in which he describes its possibility—has little to do with blind "submission to authority," but rather requires a kind of training that enhances self-control, character, efficiency. A revolutionary vanguard cannot simply *proclaim* its existence and expect people to submit to its dictates. It must *prove* itself by growing into what it aspires to be. It must, through "prolonged effort and hard-won experience," transform itself into a truly relevant and revolutionary political force. It can do so only by utilizing "a correct revolutionary theory" not as a dogma but as a body of thought that "assumes final shape" in the context of mass movements and revolutionary struggles.

The vision Lenin offers us is not of a self-righteous and authoritarian sect. It is the vision of a determined, principled—but also open and evolving—collectivity in which the knowledge, self-control and character of its members grow through their collectively (democratically) directed effort and their common pool of accumulated experience. Such a collectivity must grow in a way that is true to (and capable of developing and refining) serious revolutionary theory, thereby enabling it to light up paths for successful struggles; it must grow in a way that is integrated into the life and experiences and struggles of working people and the oppressed. Only then will it have proved to be a revolutionary vanguard. It may be added that this two-pronged proviso also indicates the two essential dimensions of the revolutionary program.

Ultimately, the hard-won authority of such a vanguard can result in the coordination of nationwide efforts that can match and overcome the power and efficiency of reactionary and capitalist forces. This is "the iron discipline needed for the victory of the proletariat"—a fundamentally democratic and popular discipline in which self-control and self-initiative, efficiency, and creativity, are blended on a massive scale.

This cannot be achieved easily, but can be realized only through a long and difficult process. The very structure, the internal norms, the operational mode of the revolutionary organization—summed up in the elastic concept of democratic centralism—must be designed to facilitate that process. What must be encouraged is neither a loose federation of radical circles and freelance activists nor a monolithic entity in which all members attempt to transform themselves into interchangeable parts, simply carrying out the political line and campaigns dictated by all-knowing leaders. Rather, the revolutionary organization must be a cohesive whole, with a variety of critical minded individuals who are committed to working together for a common goal.

There will inevitably be—and must be—different shades of opinion, some of which will cohere around one or another view on how the organization should proceed. The formation of principled groups and tendencies is sometimes necessary for the organization to achieve political clarity, to test one or another perspective, and to move forward. All of the different groups and tendencies in the organization will then be able to learn from the experience gained, which may lead to a reshuffling or dissolution of the groupings in the organization. It is also possible that the differences will sharpen. Sometimes differences will involve such a divergence in orientation, or will cover such a breadth of issues, that they will assume the quality of a programmatic divergence, necessitating the need for a *factional* struggle and perhaps a split in the organization. At times, the consequent experience gained will narrow the differences and yield a convergence of separate organizations into one. All of this can be found in the history of Bolshevism and Lenin's conception of the organizational principles of the revolutionary party.

It is worth recalling that democratic centralism was not a distinctly Leninist concept, but was embraced by the bulk of those in the revolutionary workers' movement in Russia. It was fully consistent, however, with the serious and principled attitude toward organizational norms (the structuring and coordination of revolutionary activity) that Lenin, more than most Marxists, displayed with remarkable consistency from the 1890s to the 1920s. There was a great flexibility in the way this principle was applied in various situations. But, from the early period of study circles and networks of activist committees, to the later period of a mass working-class vanguard party, Lenin believed that revolutionary socialists must be committed to organizational forms and principles that involve democratically deciding what should be done and then actually implementing the democratically made decisions. Those who have objected that such notions are "authoritarian," and more recently those who have argued that such "Leninism" is appropriate only in revolutionary periods, seem to place a question mark over the very idea of *an activist organization of revolutionary socialists working together to advance the struggle of the working class*.[6] For those who want to get together with other socialists simply for educational discussion purposes, while being free to do whatever practical political work they please (or not to do any such work at all), this shrugging-off of Leninism is a reasonable stance. But for those prepared to engage in serious efforts to build a genuinely revolutionary movement, it is difficult to imagine a coherent alternative to the basic orientation that guided Lenin for three decades.

We can conclude from our study that Lenin's organizational perspective was fundamentally democratic in its basic principles, in its goals, and in its application. It was consistent as well both with the proletarian-democratic principles and with the "scientific socialist" and practical revolutionary framework that characterize the political thought of Karl Marx and Frederick Engels. Only in the final years of Bolshevism under Lenin, from 1918 to 1924, do serious ambiguities and contradictions crop up in the Leninist perspective. Yet these flow from problems inherent in the desperate Russian conditions, and in a sense also in Marxism and twentieth-century reality, rather than from any authoritarian problematic in the distinct organizational concepts of Lenin himself.[7] Many thus conclude that the Bolshevik tradition, Marxism, socialism, or twentieth-century humanity face a crisis to which there are no solutions. Others would argue, to the contrary, that the solutions simply remain to be created by people like ourselves, and that there is much of value in the Leninist experience for understanding and overcoming the problems with which humanity is confronted.

It is difficult to disagree with C. Wright Mills's suggestion to the "new left" in the early 1960s to "read Lenin again (be careful)." But the words in parentheses have often been translated into something like "take it with a grain of salt" or "avoid becoming a Leninist." For critical minded revolutionaries, however, they can have a less superficial meaning.

Lev Kamenev, in discussing Lenin's collected works, once commented "Lenin did not write and could not have written a textbook of Leninism. I am even afraid that every attempt to expound the teaching of Lenin in paragraphs, divisions and sub-divisions, to create any kind of a 'Handbook' of Leninism, a collection of formulae applicable to all questions at any time—will certainly fail. Nothing would be more foreign to Lenin in his work than any tendency to catechism." He added that each of Lenin's writings "is permeated through and through with the anxieties and lessons of a particular historical situation . . . written under great pressure and . . . concerned with a given situation. This is why we can only approach the real science of Lenin through a consideration of his *complete works* in the light of contemporary events."[8] There is a minor ambiguity in this insightful comment: Does Kamenev mean relating Lenin's works to events contemporary to Lenin or to ourselves? Perhaps the most fruitful answer would be—*both*. This would compel us to consider similarities and differences between Lenin's situation and our own.

Despite the risks indicated by Kamenev, many intelligent writers have sought to identify essential principles and elements of Lenin's organizational perspective. It may be useful to consider some of the more thoughtful of these, and then to conclude with some suggestions on the relevance of all this for countries such as the United States.

1. Reflections on the Leninist Party

In her reminiscences of the heroic but confused early days of German Communism, the veteran militant Rosa Leviné-Meyer makes a number of assertions that may seem unfashionable for many radicals of our own time. "The role of the revolutionary leader in history is both over- and underestimated," she writes, "but its importance cannot be undervalued. True, the leader cannot create the national conditions which enable him to influence the course of history. On the other hand, the most favorable conditions can peter out without the so-called 'personal factor.' Lenin warned that no difficulty was too complex for the ruling class to tackle and overcome, 'if we let them.' In other words, without a party and a set of well-trained, able leaders, the world could not achieve its emancipation."[9]

A commonplace of Marxism is that "the emancipation of the working classes must be conquered by the working classes themselves." Another is Marx and Engels's assertion that "the Communists do not form a separate party opposed to other working-class parties. . . . They do not set up any sectarian principles of their own, by which to shape and mould the movement." These notions are often counterposed to the kinds of points that Leviné-Meyer makes, and to a fundamental assumption of Leninism. That assumption involves a "conception of the way in which the proletariat will really gain its own class-consciousness and be able to master and fully appreciate it," as Georg Lukács has put it. "This does not happen of itself, either through the mechanical evolution of the economic forces of capitalism or through the simple organic growth of mass spontaneity." According to Lukács, the Leninist party is "the tangible embodiment of proletarian class-consciousness." Of course, here "class-consciousness" is being defined not simply as the actually existing ideas and outlooks of all working people, but rather as an understanding of the nature and total situation of the working class, combined with "the immediate aim of . . . the formation [self-conscious organization] of the proletariat into a class, overthrow of the bourgeois supremacy, conquest of political power by the proletariat." The last passage is from the *Communist Manifesto*, and Marx and Engels write that this is also the immediate aim "of all the other proletarian parties." One can only assume that if other parties claiming to be proletarian *rejected* this aim, then—because "the Communists disdain to conceal their views and aims," according to Marx and Engels—the two revolutionaries would *favor* Communists' forming a separate party.[10] In fact, Lukács suggests the proper understanding of "the relationship between the revolutionary party of the proletariat and the class as a whole" by quoting the following passage from the *Manifesto*:

> The Communists are distinguished from the other working-class parties by this only: 1. In the national struggles of the proletarians of the different countries, they point out and bring to the front the common interests of the entire proletariat, independently of all nationality. 2. In the various stages of development which the struggle of the working class against the bourgeoisie has to pass through, they always and everywhere represent the interests of the movement as a whole.
>
> The Communists, therefore, are on the one hand, practically, the most advanced and resolute section which pushes forward all others; on the other hand, theoretically, they have over the great mass of the proletariat the advantage of clearly understanding the line of march, the conditions, and the ultimate general results of the proletarian movement.[11]

One suspects that Marx and Engels did not believe such consciousness would come to the working class as a whole spontaneously, given their belief that "the most advanced section" of the workers would have to organize under the Communist banner and lead (or "push forward") all others, and also given the lifelong effort of the two men to help transmit such consciousness to the labor movement.

Lukács offers this summary: "The party's role is to foresee the trajectory of the objective economic forces and to forecast what the appropriate actions of the working class must be in the situation so created. In keeping with this foresight, it must do as much as possible to prepare the proletarian masses intellectually, materially, and organizationally both for what lies ahead and how their interests relate to it."[12]

Rosa Leviné-Meyer attempted to convey more vividly a sense of what this means:

> Politics according to Lenin became a science, and "without revolutionary theory no revolutionary practice." A leader of a modern revolution is therefore remote from the image of a daredevil with a mysterious capacity for inspiring blind obedience in

"the mob." The leader must be some steps ahead of the people, and this demands a broad outlook, the ability to draw historical parallels and a thorough acquaintance with world affairs, both past and present. Lenin demanded knowledge of the essential events in history and public life of *every* party member. As to the leaders, he insisted that to "beat" their counterparts they must absorb not only political and economic knowledge but the existing bourgeois culture as well. They can qualify for their role only by making politics their profession to the exclusion of any other striving. But knowledge, and even oratorical and literary talents must be regarded as mere accessories. The essential feature is dedication to the cause and readiness to pledge one's life to its service. . . . Moreover, the leaders who lived up to these standards regarded their share as a privilege, preferable to all the temptations of a conventional life.[13]

Turning his attention to a detailed analysis of the specific underlying components of the Leninist theory of organization (the "science" that Leviné-Meyer refers to), Ernest Mandel has identified what he considers to be "a dialectical unity of three elements," which he compresses into the following passage: "a theory of the actuality of revolution for the underdeveloped countries in the imperialist epoch (which was later expanded to apply to the entire world in the epoch of the general crisis of capitalism); a theory of the discontinuous and contradictory development of proletarian class consciousness and of its most important stages, which should be differentiated from one another; and a theory of the essence of Marxist theory and its specific relationship to science on the one hand and to the proletarian class struggle on the other."[14]

It may be useful to relate the elements identified by Mandel to what we have found in the present study. A sense of *the actuality of revolution*, we have seen, contributed to the vibrancy of Lenin's Marxism from the beginning, giving it a distinctively sharp edge in the early 1900s, making him more alive than most of his comrades to the possibilities of 1905, infusing the Bolshevik party with a special dynamism in the years 1912–1914, and then dramatically deepening and expanding with the eruption of World War I, thereby contributing decisively to the triumph of 1917. It would be remarkable if Lenin's specific organizational perspectives were not profoundly affected by this kind of Marxism, and in fact they were thoroughly imbued with it even in the difficult years of 1907–1912 (giving a meaning to the polemics and factional struggles of that "muddy" period often missed by latter-day commentators).

Similarly, the understanding of the *uneven and contradictory* development of *proletarian class consciousness* is there in Lenin's thought from the 1890s onward. His contact with the early workers' movement revealed that some workers were "conscious," some only partly so, some hardly at all. The development of such consciousness was neither simple nor automatic, and it required careful and determined efforts on the part of revolutionaries—of both proletarian and nonproletarian origin—to advance this development. Objective conditions and events played a crucial, but not exclusive, role. Ultimately, the hard work of conscious elements in certain sectors of the working class could not only advance the level of their own sector but help to influence and raise up other sectors as well. We have seen that this describes the history of the Russian labor movement, and it too was central to the orientation of the Bolsheviks.

Finally, *the special relation of Marxist theory to science and to the class struggle*, again stressed in Lenin's writings and activity from the earliest days, is certainly fundamental to his organizational perspectives. Its fruits can be found in Lenin's own research and theoretical productions: *The Development of Capitalism in Russia; Materialism and Empiro-Criticism* and the *Philosophical Notebooks; Imperialism, the Highest Stage of Capitalism;* and *The State and Revolution.* There are other such contributions by his comrades as well, and at the same time an infusion of this knowledge into the polemics and popularizations and practical activities of the movement. Mandel's comment on this is quite apt: " . . . the Leninist concept of the party is [in part] based upon the premise of *a certain degree of autonomy of scientific analysis*, and especially of Marxist theory. This theory, though conditioned by the unfolding of the proletarian class struggle and the first embryonic beginnings of the proletarian revolution, should not be seen as the mechanically inevitable product of the class struggle but as the result of a theoretical practice (or 'theoretical production') which is able to link up and unite with the class struggle only through a prolonged struggle."[15]

And yet, as Rosa Leviné-Meyer commented, "a revolutionary party cannot stand aloof and revel in its cleverness and foresight. It must give a positive answer to the problem: where do we go from here?" And it must offer comprehensive and practical answers to that question for the working class in particular. This was the point that Lukács sought to emphasize in such labored prose as this: "But the masses can only learn through action; they can only become aware of their interests through struggle. . . . The vanguard party of the proletariat can only fulfil its destiny in this conflict if it is *always a step in front* of the struggling masses, to show them the way. But only one step in front so that it always remains leader of *their* struggle. Its theoretical clarity is therefore only valuable if it does not stop at a general— merely theoretical—level, but always culminates in the concrete analysis of a concrete situation; in other words, if its theoretical correctness always expresses the sense of the concrete situation." James P. Cannon expressed it more matter-of-factly: "The conscious socialists should act as a 'leaven' in the instinctive and spontaneous movement of the working class. . . . The leaven can help the dough to rise and eventually become a loaf of bread, but can never be a loaf of bread itself. . . . Every tendency, direct or indirect, of a small revolutionary party to construct a world of its own, outside and apart from the real movement of the workers in the class struggle, is sectarian."[16] One might add that there are different varieties of sectarianism—ones that use crude "Marxist" jargon and fiercely polemicize against anything that moves in the living class struggle, but others that employ the most sophisticated concepts and highly intellectualized terminology, which remain impenetrable for most people and are equally divorced from living struggles. All of this was alien to Lenin's political practice.

There are important connections between the political orientation we have been examining and the organizational forms associated with Leninism. "Revolutionary Marxists stand for democratic centralism," writes Ernest Mandel. "But the word centralization is not to be taken in the first place as an organizational dimension, and in no way whatsoever is it essentially an administrative one. It is political. What does 'centralization' mean? It means *centralization of experience, centralization of knowledge, centralization of conclusions* drawn out of actual militancy. Here again, we see a tremendous danger for the working class and labor movement if there is no such centralization of experience: this is the danger of sectoralization and fragmentation which does not enable anyone to draw adequate conclusions for action." Mandel also argues: "Mistakes in themselves are *unavoidable*. As Comrade Lenin said, the key for a revolutionary is not that he avoids making mistakes (nobody avoids making mistakes) but how he goes about correcting them. Without internal party democracy, . . . without the nonbanning of factions . . . , without free public debate, you have great obstacles in correcting mistakes and you will pay a heavy price for this. So we are absolutely in favor of the right to different tendencies, full internal democracy, and the non-banning of factions . . . I do not say the right to factions, because . . . factions are a sign of illness in a party. In a healthy party you have no factions; a healthy party from the point of view of both the political line and the internal regime. But the right not to be thrown out of the party if you create a faction is a lesser evil than being thrown out, and stifling the internal life of a party through excessive forbidding of internal debate."[17]

In 1924 the internal process that led to the Bolsheviks' triumph was perceptively discussed by the great Italian Communist Antonio Gramsci: "Did the Bolshevik Party become the leading party of the Russian nation by chance? The selection process lasted thirty years; it was extremely arduous; it often assumed what appeared to be the strangest and most absurd forms. It took place, in the international field, in contact with the most advanced capitalist civilizations of central and western Europe in the struggle of the parties and factions which made up the Second

International before the War. It continued within the minority of international socialism which remained at least partially immune from the social-patriotic conta-
gion. It was renewed in Russia in the struggle to win the majority of the proletariat;
in the struggle to understand and interpret the needs of a numberless peasant class,
scattered over an immense territory.... This selection process was a struggle of factions and small groups; it was also an individual struggle; it meant splits and fusions,
arrest, exile, prison, assassination attempts; it meant suffering hunger while having
millions in gold available; it meant preserving the spirit of a simple worker on the
throne of the Tsars; it meant not despairing even when all seemed lost, but starting
again, patiently and tenaciously ..."[18]

This remarkable passage sums up admirably the sweep of history and the quality
of the process we have examined in this study. It gives an essential sense of perspective on what is required for the evolution of an organization that aspires to
play a vanguard role in the struggle for socialist revolution. Such an organization,
undergoing a decades-long internal process, must be not simply grounded in Marxist theory and in tune with international developments, but also rooted in the particular national experience and culture of its own working class.

All of this applies not simply to the history of Bolshevism, but to that of other
revolutionary movements. Gramsci himself attempted to do this for his own country (and with implications for other nations that were considerably more industrially advanced than tsarist Russia had been.)[19] On the other hand, the modern-day
Sandinistas of Nicaragua have blended Marxism with popular national traditions
in an underdeveloped country, and according to Norma Stoltz Chinchilla, their
organization, the FSLN, evolved as "a variation on the classical Leninist conception
of the vanguard as a party of the working class and peasantry, formed as a precondition for taking power."[20]

One of the Sandinista theorists, Orlando Núñez, has admirably discussed this in
a manner largely in harmony with the underlying perspectives which we've noted in
the development of the Bolsheviks: "In our countries [in the "third world"], all forms
of struggle are necessary; all the sectors involved can be brought together in practice;
all the experiences can be built upon. We are faced in our countries by great historic
and cultural limitations. The objective conditions are not at the same level as the proj-
ects we dream of; and in the beginning stages of the struggle, the proletariat does not
present itself as the social force for transformation *par excellance*. Furthermore, the
doctrinaire parties have not been able to become the political nucleus of a revolutionary organization. Given these conditions, revolutionary 'purism' must cede to the
concrete possibilities for a coherent struggle led by that revolutionary organization
which dedicates itself to the destruction by force of the apparatus of power of the es-

tablished order. The politics of the unity of the Sandinista revolution meant the utilization of all the forms of struggle-legal, clandestine, unionist, subversive. It signified politics based on alliances with [proletarian] hegemony guaranteed by the FSLN. That is to say, the FSLN guaranteed the hegemony of an armed organization, ensuring the development of the struggle in favor of the working classes. . . ."[21]

Some would-be Leninists—admiring the accomplishments of the Bolsheviks, the Sandinistas, or others—have failed to translate the successful models into the political-cultural realities of their own specific national situations. This is in stark contrast to the actual method of the successful revolutionaries, and quickly results in or reinforces the marginalization of a would-be revolutionary group. Sometimes, as James P. Cannon observed in regard to the United States, such a group will consequently "abandon its struggle for a social revolution in this country, as the realistic perspective of our epoch, and degrade itself to the role of sympathizer of revolutions in other countries." Cannon goes on to argue: "I firmly believe that American revolutionists should indeed sympathize with revolutions in other lands, and try to help them in every way they can. But the best way to do that is to build a party with a confident perspective of a revolution in this country."[22] Of course, there is also much to learn from the revolutions of the Bolsheviks and others, but one of the primary lessons— to be absorbed in a self-reflective manner—is how they translated general revolutionary principles and perspectives into their unique, culturally specific situations.

This relates to another point that Cannon stressed. "The fate of every political group-whether it is to live and grow or degenerate and die—is decided in its first experiences by the way in which it answers two decisive questions. The first is the adoption of a correct political program. But that alone does not guarantee victory. The second is that the group decide correctly what shall be the nature of its activities, and what tasks it shall set itself, given the size and capacity of the group, the period of the development of the class struggle, the relation of forces in the political movement, and so on." A similar insight is offered by Rosa Leviné-Meyer: "Attention to detail and precision of terms is no less important than 'major policy.' In fact, it is the only guarantee of a successful 'major' action. It safeguards at least against what Lenin regarded as 'one of the gravest sins against the revolution: the substitution of the abstract for the concrete.'" As Cannon explained, "if the group misunderstands the tasks set for it by the conditions of the day, if it does not know how to answer the most important of all questions in politics—that is, the question of what to do next—then the group, no matter what its merits may otherwise be, can wear itself out in misdirected efforts and futile activities and come to grief."[23]

We have found the Bolsheviks grappling with such questions as these over the course of their evolution: sometimes with only partial or belated success, as in 1905;

sometimes amid tremendous disagreement, as in 1907–1912 (with a consequent payoff for the correct choices made); and ultimately—in 1917—in a manner that resulted in the world's first socialist revolution.

2. Problems of Leninism

In chapter 5, we noted that certain tensions are inherent in the Leninist conception of organization. There is potential, in this organizational form for the development of sectarian arrogance and elitism, which can contribute not only to its degeneration into a bureaucratic dictatorship after capitalism is overthrown, but even more to its degeneration beforehand into a sect that isolates itself from living social struggles. We also saw that important early criticisms articulated by Rosa Luxemburg, often portrayed as a refutation of Lenin's organizational orientation, can be better appreciated and more fruitfully utilized if incorporated into a Leninist framework.

The same holds for some more recent critiques of Leninism, or to be more accurate, critiques of what has passed for Leninism since the 1920s. Many critiques are, of course, quite worthless, being the work of anticommunists who are hostile to socialist goals, or of academics who have no sense of real political movements and struggles and are therefore quite incapable of understanding what they are criticizing. Far more valuable are the critiques—in some cases somewhat subjective, in many cases rather fragmentary—of those who are (or have been) revolutionary—minded activists and who have firsthand experience in an organization that was (or claimed to be) organized along Leninist lines. Even if these critiques are one-sided and far from satisfactory, they often identify genuine problems and yield important insights.

One of the more influential of these critiques in radical circles was offered by the British socialist-feminist historian Sheila Rowbotham, who had been a member of a group first known as the International Socialists, then as the British Socialist Workers party. This group had its origins as a split-off from the Trotskyist Fourth International and had a reputation as being one of the more open and democratic organizations on what has been called the Leninist left. Her experience with democratic centralism has led her to conclude that "there has been something very funny indeed about it in practice." She writes that "it is a curious fact that the hard core of the leaderships of these [Leninist] groups . . . manage to tuck themselves into the [party] center [or national office] into perpetuity," where they can comfortably nourish egotistical images of themselves as great revolutionary leaders. Unencumbered by the "routinism" of the daily organizational life lived by the rank and file, they every so often "leap out towards 'the class' to knock the members into shape. Whoosh—Superman. Poor old members, they look on with awe. Some get a bit grumpy. Why isn't democratic centralism binding on the leadership? Because the leaders know best. How else could they possibly be leaders?" The democracy is undermined by the centralism: The ensconced leaders "have a permanent advantage against all incipient oppositions because they are at the hub of communication and can organize to forestall resistance quicker than people who are scattered in different branches and districts. Also they are known. . . . They are further legitimated by the respect in Leninism due to leaders and by the assumption that, just as the members know better than the non-members, leaders know better than opposing members. The factions can stand up democratically and be counted. They can thus be rapidly isolated."[24]

Rowbotham raises another problem—the relationship between the party and the broader social movements and nonparty organizations in which its members function (trade unions, community organizations, women's liberation groups, antiwar groups, and so forth). She writes: "The individual member will face a split loyalty between a commitment to an autonomous group and the [Leninist] organization. The theory says the Party must be more important. The choice is either to get out of the organization (which seems from within to be leaving socialist politics itself), to ignore the center (in which case democratic centralism has proved unworkable), or to accept the line [of the Leninist organization even if you feel it would harm the autonomous group]. So however unsectarian this socialist may be, he or she has very stark choices and a political ideology which sanctions accepting party discipline more than helping to develop the self-activity of other people." She adds: "If you accept a high degree of centralization and define yourselves as professionals concentrating above everything upon the central task of seizing power you necessarily diminish the development of the self-activity and self-confidence of most of the people involved." Rowbotham suggests that the problems exist even with an ideal Leninist party, but that "if we descend from the ideal Party in the sky to more earthly groups and parties the prospect is even more gloomy."[25]

It is difficult to assess the merit of Rowbotham's specific grievances against the British Socialist Workers party's organizational functioning, particularly since the underlying political differences she seems to have remain somewhat hazy in her essay. The fact remains that the kinds of questions she is raising transcend such specifics. The most serious limitations of her position, however, are that her focus on Leninism obscures a more fundamental problem, while her alternative to Leninism remains extremely vague. "The structures of thought and feeling inherent in Leninism continually brake our consciousness of alternatives," she complains. But surely this is too narrow. The elitism, arrogance, hierarchy, bureaucratism, "mind trips," insensitivity, and so on that she attributes to Leninism can be found throughout our society, including in trade unions, feminist organizations, peace organizations, and political parties and groups with impeccably non-Leninist credentials. Her conclusion is this: "I don't see the way through this as devising an ideal model of a non-authoritarian organization but as a collective awakening to a constant awareness about how we see ourselves as socialists, a willingness to trust as well as criticize what we have done, a recognition of creativity in diversity and a persistent quest for open types of relationships to one another and to ideas as part of the process of making socialism."[26]

None of this should be shrugged off or devalued. But neither can it be counterposed to the Leninist conception of organization. In a sense, Rowbotham herself seems to recognize this: "The versions of Leninism current on the left ... are difficult to counter because at their most superficial they have a surface coherence, they argue about brass tacks and hard facts. They claim history and sport their own insignia and regalia of position. They fight dirty—with a quick sneer and the certainty of correct ideas. *At their most thoughtful intensity they provide a passionate and complex cultural tradition of revolutionary theory and practice on which we must certainly draw.* Socialist ideas can be pre-Leninist or anti-Leninist. But there is no clear post-Leninist revolutionary tradition yet. Leninism is alive still, whatever dogmatic accoutrements it has acquired."[27] (Emphasis added.) What this statement suggests is that Leninism's "dogmatic accoutrements" must be shed, and that new insights and experience should be integrated into this "passionate and complex tradition" that "is alive still."

Rowbotham instead questions "the extent of [Leninism's] usefulness for making socialism now"[28] and, presumably, for building an effective socialist movement in our own time. In the United States, too, a majority of those who became politically active in the 1960s and considered themselves Leninists in the 1970s have concluded in the 1980s that a Leninist organization is not what U.S. socialists should be trying to build.

The history of Leninism in the United States is certainly not a happy one. The pioneer American Leninists came out of a rich tradition represented by the left wing of the Socialist party and the IWW and had roots in significant sections of the "conscious" working class. Yet their organization, after what were difficult but then promising beginnings in the early 1920s, underwent a bureaucratizing "Bolshevization" process fostered by the Communist International under Stalin. Zigzagging from ultraleftism to reformism under the influence of the ruling bureaucracy in the Soviet Union, the American Communist party failed to develop a durable working-class base around a coherent revolutionary program of its own, despite the often heroic efforts and sometimes impressive successes of its cadres. One of the most enduring contributions was helping to organize millions of industrial workers into the unions of the CIO, yet for the most part the dedicated Communist party organizers in this effort organized workers *politically* not as socialists, but as part of a left-liberal wing of the Democratic party. Cold War anticommunist persecution, followed by Khrushchev's revelations of Stalin's crimes, left the American Communist party shattered and discredited in the eyes of many. While it persists as a force on the left, its commitment to the "Leninist" leadership of the Soviet Union has failed to win the confidence of many radical activists.[29] The numerous "Leninist" splinter groups that flourished in the 1930s, on the other hand, left behind little more than a notorious reputation for often comical sectarianism and pretentiousness.[30] The one serious Leninist alternative, the U.S. Trotskyists of the Socialist Workers party, was able to have a major impact on the intellectual life of the left, and also to play a significant part in the class struggle (for example, in the Minneapolis teamsters' strikes). The Trotskyists, however, never were able to accumulate more than 2,000 members; although their growing numbers and influence in the 1960s and 1970s seemed to indicate an impressive vitality and a promising future, the organization was wracked by a devastating political and organizational crisis in 1979–1983. The party's new leadership fundamentally changed the party program by fiat, grotesquely tightened organizational norms, and expelled scores of dissidents. While the Socialist Workers party may not be dead as a potentially revolutionary force, its recent experience has done little to inspire confidence in the "Leninism" it raises as its own banner.[31]

A majority of the young radicalizing activists of the 1960s' "new left," however, came to Leninism by a different path. Impressed by the Chinese Revolution of 1949 and by what appeared to be the Chinese Communist leadership's radical stance in world politics beginning in the early 1960s, and inspired by the seemingly egalitarian ideals and commitments of the Great Proletarian Cultural Revolution, launched by Mao Zedong in 1966, they were drawn to the Maoist variant of the Stalinist tradition. A proliferation of groups—the Progressive Labor party, the Communist party (Marxist-Leninist), the Revolutionary Communist party, the Black Workers Congress, the Communist Labor party, the Revolutionary Workers Headquarters, the League for Revolutionary Struggle, and many others—came into being during the 1960s and, especially, the early 1970s[32] "The major efforts," according to one participant, Mel Rothenberg, "simply took the self-description of the Communist Party of China, added a few slogans from Mao and Stalin, added the practical experiences of their older cadre from the [American Communist party] . . . and projected this stew as the party they were going to build." Another, Carl Davidson, later commented: "What experience did we really have? We had the experience of the things we went through in the 1960s, an experience of having become revolutionaries in a period of upsurge and upheaval, and involvement in the youth movement that gave a certain one-sidedness to our experience. When the 1970s happened we had a period of ebb, we really lacked the maturity to be able to deal with it and clung to one-sided conceptions that had developed in a different period. . . . We believed that tens of thousands of advanced workers were standing on our doorsteps." Another veteran of this experience, Bruce Bodner, remembers: "There was a lot of frustration in the organization at the slow progress made in carrying out our partybuilding line in the working class." John Trinkl, a staff writer for the *Guardian*, the radical newsweekly, which had enthusiastically supported the efforts to build a Marxist-Leninist-Maoist party, reflects: "An overall ultraleftism led to dogmatism and sectarianism in practice. Harmful contradictions emerged between the party-building movement and the 'new social movements,' particularly the women's movement, between party building and the working class, and between the leadership and membership of party-building organizations and parties." There was also a disillusionment with Chinese Communism stemming from the collapse of the Cultural Revolution with all of its irrationality and abuses, the persistence of bureaucracy, the rightward shift in foreign policy, and other such factors.

By the early 1980s, this "new communist" party-building effort had almost completely disintegrated; most of the new organizations had passed out of existence, and the bulk of those involved had concluded, as John Trinkl put it, "that a Leninist party as it was understood by 1970s activists is not appropriate for current U.S. conditions," although a significant number had even more fundamental reservations about Leninism in general. Some of these drifted into the openly reformist Democratic Socialists of America or the reform wing of the Democratic party. Others have concentrated on important but more narrowly focused political work in the efforts of the antiwar, third world solidarity, women's liberation, antinuclear, trade union, and unemployed movements. Some have turned away from radical politics altogether, although a large percentage, as Bruce Bodner has observed, while "reeling from their experiences in the 1970s," are "sort of waiting and hoping that something will happen. There are thousands of them."

Thus, a very big question mark has been placed over the future of Leninism in countries such as the United States, at least in the minds of many radical activists whose commitment and energies might be expected to make Leninism a living reality. Some of the more thoughtful of those activists would agree with Marxist historian Dan Cohen that "we have to have some way of talking to each other about developing some kind of strategy. Some kind of organization—whether it's called a party or not—that helps coordinate struggles will be necessary." This could be a Leninist organization, but not necessarily. Another activist, Phil Hill, argues, "We ought to be issue-oriented rather than ideology-oriented."

Such an organization might duplicate the experience of the leading new-left group of the 1960s, Students for a Democratic Society (SDS). Starting as a relatively loose and pragmatically issue-oriented organization of radicals, SDS initially had strong ties to the reformist Social Democracy; as the youth radicalization mushroomed, SDS was overwhelmed and chaotically moved in an ultraleftist, quasi-anarchistic direction, with members inclined to "do their own thing," which often meant expressing themselves through ill-conceived confrontations with the "power structure"; as the need for greater ideological and organizational coherence became clear, SDS was drawn to Maoism, then exploded into a variety of increasingly rigid, dogmatic sects (discussed above), whose energy and commitment did not prevent them from being burned out.[33] It is quite possible, however, that a new organization will be more stable and cohesive than this. A number of questions arise: Which issues would be prioritized? What kind of strategy would be developed? How would struggles be coordinated? It would be naive to assume that strong ideological currents would not profoundly influence how the members of an organization (no matter how "issue-oriented") would answer these questions. What ideology or ideologies would come into play? For the new-left socialists of the New American Movement in the early 1970s, the ideology that finally cohered was a leftish variant of modern Social Democracy, culminating in an organizational merger that yielded the Democratic Socialists of America.[34] We see, then, that the new-left radical organizations that consciously rejected the ideologies of the "old left" ended up eventually gravitating to variants of what had come to be the two dominant ideologies of the old left—Social Democracy and Stalinism. Would a new organization also gradually evolve in such directions? Or would it be something else? If something else, what and how?

In contrast to SDS and the New American Movement, Lenin was convinced that a coming-together of socialist ideas and the working class was possible and necessary, that it would transform each and create a force capable of bringing revolutionary change, *but that a serious, democratic, and cohesive organization guided by a critical-minded and revolutionary Marxism was necessary to accomplish this.* The underlying assumption of the present study is that in the United States a new, specifically American variant of Leninism makes sense. It must be new in the sense that it incorporates the following: (1) a deeper understanding of the experience of the Bolsheviks themselves (the focus of this book); (2) an understanding of the experience of revolutionary and would-be revolutionary movements since the 1920s; (3) a serious-minded analysis of recent developments in the world capitalist system; (4) a critical-minded (and self-critical) shaping of organizational norms and political functioning of the organization in light of such understanding and analysis.

And for Americans it must, above all, be "American"—grounded in our own specific radical traditions; integrated with the actual experience, struggles, needs, and
idiom of the working people of our own country; related to and learning from, and
helping to advance the world revolutionary process, but in a manner that facilitates
the forward movement of the real, actually existing working class in the United
States. Nothing like this exists or has existed in our country on a significant scale.
Nor can a genuine revolutionary party exist simply because a small band of relatively intelligent and dedicated people decide that it must exist; that is a necessary
condition for the existence of such a party, but by itself it is not sufficient. This has
not been understood by many would-be Leninists in our history who claimed for
themselves a historic right—leadership of the workers' struggle—without earning
it. Ernest Mandel once made this point quite well:

> There is a real contradiction in the relationship between a vanguard organization
> and the broad masses. There is a real dialectical tension, if we can call it that, and we
> have to address ourselves to that tension. First of all, I used the words "vanguard or-
> ganizations"; I did not use the words "vanguard parties." This is a conceptual dis-
> tinction I introduce on purpose. I do not believe in self-proclaimed parties. I do not
> believe in fifty people or a hundred people standing in Market Square beating their
> breasts and saying, "We are the vanguard party." Perhaps they are in their own con-
> sciousness, but if the rest of society does not give a damn about them, they will be
> shouting in that marketplace for a long time without this having any result in prac-
> tical life, or worse, they will try to impose their convictions on an unreceptive mass
> through violence. A vanguard party has to be constructed, has to be built through a
> long process. One of the characteristics of its existence is that it becomes recognized
> as such by at least a substantial minority of the class itself. You cannot have a van-
> guard party which has no following in the class.
>
> A vanguard organization becomes a vanguard party when a significant minority
> of the real class, of the really existing workers, poor peasants, revolutionary youth,
> revolutionary women, revolutionary oppressed nationalities, recognizes it as their
> vanguard party, i.e., follows it in action. Whether that must be ten percent or fifteen
> percent, that does not matter, but it must be a real sector of the class. If it does not
> exist, then you have no real party, you have only the nucleus of a future party. What
> will happen to that nucleus will be shown by history. It remains an open question,
> not yet solved by history. You need a permanent struggle to transform that vanguard
> organization into a real revolutionary party rooted in the class, present in the work-
> ing class struggle, and accepted by at least a real fraction of the real class as such.[35]

According to this definition, as Mandel recognizes, the Bolsheviks did not constitute a vanguard party until 1912–1913. Notice too that Mandel refers to a *permanent* struggle to be a vanguard party. Such a party must be continually proving

itself in reality, testing itself, self-critically evaluating itself, continually developing. Nothing is constant except change. For a revolutionary party to remain true to itself, it must continue to evolve within the constantly changing social reality. If its cadres succumb to the temptation of seeing their party as a permanently revolutionary entity simply because it is the Party, and if they adhere to the perspectives of party leaders simply because these are The Leaders of the Revolutionary Party, they will be succumbing to what can be a fatal illusion.

Mandel makes a related point that speaks to one of the concerns raised by Sheila Rowbotham. Stressing the profound importance of the self-organization of the workers and the oppressed, he argues that "there is absolutely no contradiction between the separate organizations of revolutionary vanguard militants and their participation in the mass organizations of the working class." For members of a vanguard group to counterpose the interests of their group to the existence or interests of a broader working-class formation, he insists, is sectarian. Indeed, we have seen that it was just such sectarianism that had to be overcome among the Bolsheviks themselves before it was possible for their organization to move forward. "The only right you claim for yourself inside the unions, inside the mass parties, inside the soviets," he argues (and the list could be lengthened considerably), "is to be a more dedicated, a more courageous, a more lucid, a more self-denying *builder* of the mass parties, *builder* of the soviets, defenders of the general interests of the working class, without attributing to yourself any special privilege towards your fellow workers, except the right to try to convince them."[36]

The members of such a vanguard organization, however, have nothing to teach others unless they are at the same time continually learning: learning from experiences of the past by *critically* absorbing revolutionary theory; learning from their own experiences and those of their comrades (genuine democratic centralism plays a vital role here); learning from the new political, social, and economic developments of their own time; and, most important, learning from people outside of the vanguard group—especially the rich array of individuals who are the working class and who have the innumerable experiences and insights that will ultimately form the basis for a socialist revolution. Just as self-proclaimed "leaders" generally have few followers, "vanguardists" who already "know it all" have little of value that they are able to teach.

There is another way that one must "be careful," as C. Wright Mills put it. Nothing that we face is just as it was for Lenin and his comrades. Our 1903 and 1905 and 1912 and 1917 may not look at all like theirs, and the sequence of events may differ dramatically. We cannot allow our knowledge of their history to become an obstacle to understanding and making our own. This understood, it may be worth suggesting that we avoid thinking in terms appropriate to 1912 or 1917, when we—in a certain sense—have not even had our 1898 (when the Russian Social Democratic Labor party was formed). If we must transcend a romantic and uncritical adulation of Lenin and his ideas, which will prevent us from being alive to the realities of our own time, however, we must also transcend a narrow pragmatism that will keep us from what Rowbotham calls "a passionate and complex cultural tradition of revolutionary theory and practice on which we must certainly draw" if we hope to make socialism a living reality.

The revolutionary-internationalist underpinnings of Leninism have particular relevance for our own time, as the sectors of the world economy and world politics have become interconnected· more closely than ever before. The peoples of each country are affected by the levels of popular political consciousness and by the class struggles and liberation struggles in each of the other countries. Ultimately, capitalism as a global system can be overcome only through revolutionary efforts on an international scale.[37] Such an expansive triumph of freedom struggles is a precondition, too, for the development of a worldwide cooperative commonwealth that will overcome all vestiges of bureaucratic dictatorship, which cannot survive in a situation where there is enough for all and where all have a vital sense of their own dignity and self-worth. Workers and oppressed people in advanced capitalist countries, in the so-called underdeveloped capitalist countries, and also in the bureaucratically run postcapitalist countries are—more than they generally know—dependent on each other's struggles for freedom and for control over the institutions that shape their lives. What is more, the goals, strategies, and organizational norms that guided the Bolsheviks are in harmony with the aspirations of these contemporary and future struggles

There are many who are convinced, with an almost religious conviction, that revolutionary socialism has little relevance in such countries as the United States and that working people are incapable of thinking and acting in the way that the conscious workers of Russia did seventy-five years ago. And it is obvious that the American working class is not about to put socialism on the political agenda in the 1980s. But as Bertolt Brecht once commented, "because things are as they are, they will not stay as they are." What we begin to understand now, and what we begin to do now, can help to shape the future. In this context, there is much to learn from the actual ideas and experience of Lenin and the revolutionary party he led. And there is much to do.

Notes

Preface

1. Neil Harding, *Lenin's Political Thought*, vol. 1, p. 196; Marcel Liebman, *Leninism Under Lenin*, p. 26.
2. Roger Burbach and Orlando Núñez, *Fire in the Americas*, p. 26.
3. Additional material regarding the Leninist conception of organization, particularly for the period from 1924 (when Lenin died) to 1940, is gathered in Dianne Feeley, Paul Le Blanc, and Tom Twiss, *Leon Trotsky and the Organizational Principles of the Revolutionary Party*. Also see works cited in the final chapter of the present study.

Introduction by Ernest Mandel

1. "Basically, of course, their success was due to the fact that the working class, whose best representatives built the Social-Democratic Party, for objective economic reasons possesses a greater capacity for organisation than any other class in capitalist society. Without this condition an organisation of professional revolutionaries would be nothing more than a plaything, an adventure, a mere signboard. *What Is To Be Done?* repeatedly emphasizes this, pointing out that the organisation it advocates has no meaning apart from its connection with the 'genuine revolutionary class that is spontaneously rising to struggle'" (V.I. Lenin, *Collected Works* [Moscow: Foreign Languages Publishing House, 1962], vol. 13, pp. 103–104).
2. Marcel Liebman, *Le Léninisme sous Lénine*, 2 vols. (Paris: Le Seuil, 1973).
3. Ernest Mandel, *The Leninist Theory of Organization* (Baroda, India: Antar Rashtriya Prakashan, 1977).
4. This only occurs, however, if the function of that vanguard to embody the "historical memory of the working class" is constantly combined with intervention in living class struggle, and enriched with conclusions from new experiences.
5. Politically, however, the Russian working class, far from being backward, was among the most advanced in the world, as the revolution of 1905 clearly illustrated.
6. Note Shlyapnikov's only half-ironic interruption of a speech by Lenin, "I congratulate you, comrade Lenin, for exercising the dictatorship of the proletariat in the absence of a proletariat."
7. Leon Trotsky, *Nos Tâches Politiques* (Paris: Belond, 1970).
8. Isaac Deutscher, *The Prophet Armed* (the first volume of Deutscher's trilogy on Trotsky) (Oxford: Oxford University Press, 1954), chap. 14.

9. "But with the repression of political life in the land as a whole, life in the soviets must also become more and more crippled. Without general elections, without unrestricted freedom of press and assembly, without a free struggle of opinion, life dies out in every public institution, becomes a mere semblance of life, *in which only the bureaucracy remains as the active element*" [emphasis added] (Rosa Luxemburg, "The Russian Revolution," in Mary-Alice Waters, ed., *Rosa Luxemburg Speaks* [New York: Pathfinder Press, 1970], p. 391).

10. Christian Rakovsky, "The Professional Dangers of Power" (1928), in *Selected Writings in Opposition in the USSR 1923–30* (London: Allison & Busby, 1980), pp. 124–136.

11. "If we take Moscow with its 4,700 Communists in responsible positions, and if we take that huge bureaucratic machine, that gigantic heap, we must ask: who is directing whom? I doubt very much whether it can truthfully be said that the Communists are directing that heap. To tell the truth, they are not directing, they are being directed. Something analogous happened here to what we were told in our history lessons when we were children: sometimes one nation conquers another, the nation that conquers is the conqueror and the nation that is vanquished is the conquered nation. This is simple and intelligible to all. But what happens to the culture of these nations? Here things are not so simple. If the conquering nation is more cultured than the vanquished nation, the former imposes its culture upon the latter; but if the opposite is the case, the vanquished nation imposes its culture upon the conqueror. Has not something like this happened in the capital of the R.S.F.S.R.? Have the 4,700 Communists (nearly a whole army division, and all them the very best) come under the influence of an alien culture?" (V.I. Lenin, "Political Report of the Central Committee to the Eleventh Congress of the R.C.P. (B), March 27, 1922," in *Collected Works* [Moscow: Progress Publishers, 1966], vol. 33, p. 288).

12. Compare the end of Trotsky's *My Life* (New York: Pathfinder Press, 1970), p. 582: "I can only express my astonishment at the philistine attempt to establish a connection between mental balance and the present situation. I do not know, and I never have, of any such connection. In prison, with a book or a pen in my hand, I experienced the same sense of deep satisfaction that I did at the mass-meetings of the revolution. I felt the mechanics of power as an inescapable burden, rather than as a spiritual satisfaction."

13. V.I. Lenin, "The Question of Nationalities or 'Autonomisation'," in *Collected Works* (Moscow: Progress Publishers, 1971), vol. 36, p. 605. The English translation is tamer: "I have been very remiss with respect to the workers of Russia. . . ."

14. Moshe Lewin, *Lenin's Last Struggle* (New York: Vintage Books, 1970).

15. Recently an interesting study by V.V. Shuravlyov and A.P. Nenarokov, "The Georgian Affair," appeared in *Pravda*, August 12, 1988. It adds important new information about Lenin's intervention into this question and puts Trotsky's role in a much more positive light that has been the case until now.

16. See Lenin's "Letter to the Congress," in *Collected Works*, vol. 36, pp. 605–606, 609–610.

17. "The party is to a considerable extent ceasing to be that living independent collectivity which sensitively seizes living reality because it is bound to this reality with a thousand threads. Instead of this we observe the ever increasing, and now scarcely concealed, division of the party between a secretarial hierarchy and 'quiet folk', between professional party officials recruited from above and the general mass of the party which does not participate in the common life.

"This is a fact which is known to every member of the Party. Members of the party who are dissatisfied with this or that decision of the Central Committee or even of a provincial committee, who have this or that doubt in their minds, who privately note this or that error, irregularity or disorder, are afraid to speak about it at Party meetings, and are even afraid to talk about it in conversation, unless the partner in the conversation is thoroughly reliable from the point of view of 'discretion'; free discussion within the party has practically vanished, the public opinion of the party is stifled. Nowadays it is not the Party, not its broad masses, who promote and choose members of the provincial committees and the Central Committee of the RCP. On the contrary: the secretarial hierarchy of the Party to an ever greater extent recruits the membership of conferences and congresses, which are becoming to an ever greater extent the executive assemblies of this hierarchy" ("Platform of the 46, October 15, 1923," in Naomi Allen, ed., *The Challenge of the Left Opposition, 1923–25* [New York: Pathfinder Press, 1975), p. 399.

18. Mikhail Gefter, "Staline est mort hier," in Iuoi N. Afanasiev, ed., *Sakharov et 33 intellectels soviétiques en lutte pour la Perestroika: La Seule Issue* (Paris: Flammarion, 1989), p. 84. The sentence was attributed to Lenin by Jacques Sadoul in *Letters from Abroad to Lenin* (Moscow: Mysl Editions, 1966).

19. "In the beginning, the party had wished and hoped to preserve freedom of political struggle within the framework of the Soviets. The civil war introduced stern amendments into this calculation. The opposition parties were forbidden one after the other. This measure, obviously in conflict with the spirit of Soviet democracy, the leaders of Bolshevism regarded not as a principle, but as an episodic act of self-defence.... In March 1921, in the days of the Kronstadt revolt, which attracted into its ranks no small number of Bolsheviks, the tenth congress of the party thought it necessary to resort to the prohibition of factions, that is, to transfer the political regime prevailing in the state to the inner life of the party. This forbidding of factions was again regarded as an exceptional measure to be abandoned at the first serious improvement in the situation. . . . The prohibition of oppositional parties brought after it the prohibition of factions. The prohibition of factions ended in a prohibition to think otherwise than the infallible leaders. The police-manufactured monolithism of the party resulted in a bureaucratic impunity, which has become the source of all kinds of wantonness and corruption" (Leon Trotsky, *The Revolution Betrayed* [London: New Park Publications, 1967), pp. 96, 104–105.

20. Neil Harding, *Lenin's Political Thought* (London: Macmillan, 1983), vol. 2, p. 327.

21. The best account of the successive oppositions inside the Russian Communist party is still R.V. Daniels, *The Conscience of the Revolution, Communist Opposition in Soviet Russia* (Cambridge: Harvard University Press, 1960).

22. V.I. Lenin, *Collected Works*, vol. 32, p. 21.

23. This was especially the case with Zinoviev and Kamenev's coming out in public against insurrection on the eve of the October revolution. But it is typical of Lenin that, in his *Testament*, he explicitly asks the party not to reproach Zinoviev and Kamenev with that breach of discipline. Neither Stalin nor Bukharin heeded that advice once Zinoviev and Kamenev joined the United Opposition.

24. Lenin develops that theme in "Left-Wing Communism" and other writings and speeches.

25. This is the point where sectarians and factionalists depart from Marxism. Like the Gospel of St. John, they sincerely believe that in the beginning was the word. Therefore, a world of disaster will flow from what they consider a wrong sentence here, a wrong analysis there. The monster's name is "revisionism."

They do not understand that this is a retreat from historical materialism to fatalistic historical idealism. In the beginning, to paraphrase Goethe's *Faust*, is the deed, that is, the real, living class struggle. Any revisionism that has no practical effect on broad, real class struggle, because it is practiced by groups too small to influence events or because it has not been decisively translated into action, should be fought with arguments, not with splits. That is how Rosa Luxemburg, Lenin, Trotsky, and all other serious Marxists behaved in the Second International toward Bernstein's revisionism between 1898 and 1914—and correctly so. That is how Trotsky behaved inside the Comintern between 1923 and 1933—again, correctly so. You need momentous defeats in the class struggle—betrayals by the historic parties of the working class—to justify a split.

26. It is significant that the liberal Gorbachevite intellectuals who today promote "deepened" peaceful coexistence and cooperation with imperialism/capitalism base their argumentation on the impossibility of new socialist revolutions triumphing in a foreseeable future.

27. N. Bukharin, *Discours sur la Revolution prolétarienne et la Culture*, pp. 48, 50.

28. "Apart from public appeals too Aesopian to be effective, Bukharin, Rykov and Tomskii therefore colluded with Stalin in confining their fatal conflict to a small private arena, there to be 'strangled behind the back of the party'. And it is in this context that Stalin's decisive victory must be explained" (Stephen F. Cohen, *Bukharin and the Bolshevik Revolution* [Oxford: Oxford University Press, 1980], p. 325). See also Mikhail Gefter, "Staline est mort hier," p. 91: "Et le Boukharine de 1928? Qu'est-ce qui primait pour lui 'en derniere instance'? Defendre la NEP contre Staline, ou bien fût-ce au prix de sa propre capitulation, préserver l'unité du parti?"

1. Introduction: Authentic Leninism

1. Leon Trotsky, "Lenin," p. 697.

2. Karl Marx and Frederick Engels, *Selected Works*, vol. 1, p. 127.

3. James P. Cannon, "The Vanguard Party and the World Revolution," p. 349.

4. Karl Marx, *Early Writings*, p. 251.

5. J. Edgar Hoover, *Masters of Deceit*, pp. 26–27, 32. On Hoover and the FBI, see Frank J. Donner, *The Age of Surveillance*.

6. Bertram D. Wolfe, an ex-Communist employed by the U.S. State Department in various capacities, provides a more literate elaboration of the themes touched by Hoover; his posthumously published *Lenin and the Twentieth Century* concludes with this quote from an article by Max Beloff that appeared in *Encounter*: "The world has been a poorer and bleaker and more dangerous place because Lenin lived." A splendid collection of such anti-Leninist scholarship can be found in Jeane J. Kirkpatrick (ed.), *The Strategy of Deception*. A valuable discussion of CIA sponsorship and guidance for anticommunist intellectuals (including funding for such magazines as *Encounter*) can be found in Christopher Lasch, *The Agony of the American Left*, pp. 63–114. Alan Wald's *The New York Intellectuals* provides much rich background on this phenomenon. Also relevant are Noam Chomsky, *American Power and the New Mandarins*, pp. 323–366; G. William Domhoff, *The Higher Circles*, pp. 251–275; and Ralph Miliband, John Saville, and Marcel Liebman (eds.), *The Uses of Anti-Communism* (*Socialist Register 1984*).

7. Useful summaries of this phase of the Soviet Union's history can be found in Isaac Deutscher, *The Unfinished Revolution*, and E. H. Carr, *The Russian Revolution*.

8. Walter Duranty, *I Write as I Please*, pp. 262, 273, 274.

9. Stalin's oration is quoted in E. H. Carr, *The Interregnum*, pp. 354–355. A partial record of his "accomplishments" has been compiled in Roy Medvedev, *Let History Judge*. The positive estimates of Stalin are from N. Popov and his publishers, *Outline History of the Communist Party of the Soviet Union*, vol. 2, p. 435, and vol. 1, p. v.

10. V. Sorin. *Lenin's Teachings About the Party*, pp. 7, 30, 32, 37. The point about Bolshevism as "monolithic" can be found in Popov, vol. 2, p. 202.

11. Wolfgang Leonhard, *Three Faces of Marxism*, p. 57.

12. Michael Harrington, *Socialism*, p. 329; Norman Thomas, *America's Way Out*, pp. 70, 75–76; Norman Thomas, *A Socialist's Faith*, pp. 39, 41.

13. Sheila Fitzpatrick, *The Russian Revolution*, pp. 5, 76, 9.

14. Ibid., pp. 8, 3; Duranty, p. 274.

15. Fitzpatrick, pp. 25, 98, 81.

16. Stephen F. Cohen, "Bolshevism and Stalinism," p. 4.
17. E. H. Carr, "Marx-Lenin-Stalin," in Pipes (ed.), *Revolutionary Russia*, pp. 371–372, 373.
18. Moshe Lewin, *The Making of the Soviet System*, pp. 191–192.
19. For more on this point, see the concluding chapter of the present study.

2. The Context of Lenin's Early Organizational Perspectives

1. John M. Thompson, *Revolutionary Russia*, pp. 4–5. On working-class life in this period, see Victoria E. Bonnell (ed.), *The Russian Worker*, as well as Bonnell's *Roots of Rebellion*, pp. 20–72; also see Laura Engelstein, *Moscow, 1905*, pp. 1–72, and Iu. I. Kir'ianov, "On the Nature of the Russian Working Class."
2. Leon Trotsky, *Stalin*, pp. 53–54. Also see Maxim Gorky's *Mother* for a vivid fictional account of the early Russian Marxist movement at the grass-roots level.
3. N. K. Krupskaya, *Reminiscences of Lenin*, pp. 25, 26. A valuable study of Lenin's development leading up to this crucial period is Leon Trotsky's *The Young Lenin*.
4. Krupskaya, pp. 11–12.
5. V. I. Lenin, *Collected Works*, vol. 4, pp. 257, 217, 210–211.
6. Struve quoted in Leopold H. Haimson, *The Russian Marxists and the Origins of Bolshevism*, p. 53; on limitations of early Russian Marxism, see James D. White, "The First *Pravda* and the Russian Marxist Tradition," pp. 184–191; Trotsky, *1905*, p. 37. Useful for the historical emergence of this particular "ism" is Georges Haupt's penetrating discussion in *Aspects of International Socialism*, pp. 1–22. A brilliant discussion of Marxism can also be found in Ernest Mandel, *The Place of Marxism in History*, which offers a perspective that is essential for grasping issues touched on here.
7. Leon Trotsky, *The Young Lenin*, pp. 187, 188.
8. L. B. Kamenev, "The Literary Legacy of Ilyitch," p. 67. A similar point is suggested in Karl Korsch, *Marxism and Philosophy*, pp. 53–68.
9. V. I. Lenin, *Selected Works* (1930s ed.), vol. I, pp. 450, 451. Yet see note 20, below.
10. Ibid., pp. 451, 452.
11. Ibid., pp. 454–455.
12. Krupskaya, pp. 16, 18.
13. Allan K. Wildman, *The Making of a Worker's Revolution*, p. 36; Tony Cliff, *Lenin*, vol. 1, pp. 44–45.
14. Krupskaya, p. 18; Kremer and Martov, "On Agitation," in Neil Harding (ed.), *Marxism in Russia*, p. 199.
15. Krupskaya, pp. 19–20.
16. Ibid., p. 25.
17. Ibid., p. 22.
18. On "legal Marxism," see Richard Kindersley, *The First Revisionists*.
19. A sympathetic account of the Second International up to 1914 can be found in Julius Braunthal, *History of the International*, vol. 1. For an overview of the European workers' movement, see Wolfgang Abendroth, *A Brief History of the European Working Class*.
20. Krupskaya, p. 20. On Narodnaya Volya, see Franco Venturi, *Roots of Revolution*, pp. 633–708, and also Avraham Yarmolinsky, *Road to Revolution*, pp. 168–329. Although often exaggerated and distorted in the accounts of anti-Leninists, Russia's rich "pre-Marxist" revolutionary tradition had a significant impact on Lenin (and also on Marx)—and this is particularly true of the revolutionary populist current represented by N. G. Chernyshevsky and Narodnaya Volya. For valuable documentation (and a relatively balanced discussion by Derek Sayer and Philip Corrigan) of the impact on Marxism, see Teodor Shanin (ed.), *Late Marx and the Russian Road*.

21. Lenin, *Collected Works*, vol. 4, pp. 327–328.

22. Lenin, *Collected Works*, vol. 2, pp. 95–96.

23. Ibid., pp. 96, 108–109.

24. Ibid., p. 96, 119.

25. Gregory Zinoviev, *History of the Bolshevik Party*, p. 25; Lenin, *Collected Works*, vol. 4, p. 331.

26. Lenin, *Collected Works*, vol. 2, pp. 97, 96.

27. Ibid., pp. 112–113.

28. Ibid., pp. 116–117.

29. Ibid., p. 328.

30. Ibid., pp. 329–330.

31. Ibid., pp. 332, 334.

32. Ibid., pp. 335, 336.

33. Trotsky, "Lenin," p. 697; Neil Harding, *Marxism in Russia*, p. 16.

34. V.I. Lenin, *The Development of Capitalism in Russia*, pp. 563–567, 587–588, 602, 603, 604–605, 606. Of course, Lenin hardly offered the last word on the development of Russian capitalism. For a challenging recent work, see Teodor Shanin, *Russia as a 'Developing Society'*.

35. Lenin, *The Development of Capitalism in Russia*, pp. 588–589. Also see Joseph Freeman, *The Soviet Worker*, pp. 3–29 for a useful overview of the worker's general conditions.

36. Reginald Zelnik, "Russian Workers and the Revolutionary Movement", pp. 217, 218; Kir'ianov, p. 42.

37. S. I. Kanatchikov, "From the Story of My Life," in Bonnell, ed., *The Russian Worker*, pp. 39, 50. The whole of this fascinating and valuable memoir has been made available by Reginald Zelnik as *A Radical Worker in Tsarist Russia*.

38. Trotsky, *The Young Lenin*, pp. 149–150; Wildman, p. 35.

39. Reginald Zelnik, "Russian Bebels: An Introduction to the Memoirs of the Russian Workers Semen Kanatchikov and Matvei Fisher,"pt. 1, p. 264.

40. Ibid., pp. 265–266.

41. On the Socialist Revolutionaries, see Herbert J. Ellison, "The Socialist Revolutionaries"; Maureen Perrie, "The Social Composition and Structure of the Socialist-Revolutionary Party"; Oliver H. Radkey, *The Agrarian Foes of Bolshevism*. On workers' Marxism, see Zelnik, "Russian Bebels," pt. 2, p. 423.

42. Zelnik, "Russian Bebels," pt. 1, pp. 281, 271, 274.

43. Alexandra Kollontai, *Selected Writings*, pp. 41–42. For a superb account of female workers, see Rose L. Glickman, *Russian Factory Women*, which offers valuable data on the working class as a whole.

44. Zelnik, "Russian Bebels," pt. 1, pp. 277, 284; O. Piatnitsky, *Memoirs of a Bolshevik*, pp. 19, 20–21; David Mandel, *The Petrograd Workers and the Fall of the Old Regime*, pp. 13, 23–24, 26.

45. Bonnell, *The Russian Worker*, p. 11; Mandel, *The Petrograd Workers and the Fall of the Old Regime*, p. 17.

46. Zelnik, "Russian Bebels," pt. 2, pp. 435, 434, 436, 439; Engelstein, p. 58.

47. Zelnik, "Russian Bebels," pt. 2, p. 443.

48. Wildman focuses on the worker/intellectual conflict in *The Making of a Workers' Revolution*. On the Zubatov unions, see Solomon Schwarz, *The Russian Revolution of 1905*.

49. Engelstein, p. 58.

3. Revolutionary Program, Cohesive Organization

1. Leopold Haimson's *The Russian Marxists and the Origins of Bolshevism*, despite its pro-Menshevik bias, focuses informatively on this period. Neil Harding's *Lenin's Political Thought*, vol.

1, and Tony Cliff's *Lenin*, vol. 1, provide a useful counterbalance to aspects of Haimson's account.

2. V. I. Lenin, *Collected Works*, vol. 4, p. 222.
3. Ibid., pp. 323, 322.
4. Ibid., pp. 229, 230.
5. Ibid., pp. 230–231.
6. Ibid., pp. 211, 210.
7. This is the "Credo" written by E. S. Kuskova, quoted in its entirety in Lenin, *Collected Works*, vol. 4, pp. 172–174. A sympathetic account of the Economists is available in Allan K. Wildman, *The Making of a Workers' Revolution*. Also see the one-time leading Economist A. Martynov's reminiscenses and discussion of Lenin's fierce polemics against him, "The Great Proletarian Leader." On "Bernsteinism" see Peter Gay, *The Dilemma of Democratic Socialism*.
8. Lenin, *Collected Works*, vol. 4, pp. 366–367, 368.
9. Ibid., pp. 215–216.
10. Ibid., p. 216.
11. Ibid., pp. 216–217.
12. Ibid., p. 325.
13. Ibid., p. 213.
14. Ibid., pp. 280–281.
15. Ibid., p. 281.
16. Ibid., p. 282.
17. Ibid., pp. 279, 281, 282, 285.
18. Ibid., p. 231.
19. Ibid., p. 218.
20. Ibid., pp. 212, 219.
21. Ibid., pp. 217–218.
22. Ibid., p. 218.
23. Ibid., pp. 219–220.
24. Ibid., p. 219.
25. Ibid., pp. 221, 370–371.
26. V. I. Lenin, "What Is to Be Done?" in *Selected Works* (1967 ed.), vol. 1, pp. 209–210.
27. Ibid., pp. 211–212.
28. Ibid., p. 197.
29. Ibid., pp. 199–200.
30. Ibid., pp. 200–201.
31. Ibid., pp. 311–312.
32. Ibid., pp. 476–478.
33. Ibid., pp. 213–214.

4. The Birth of Leninism

1. V.I. Lenin, *Collected Works*, vol. 13, p. 102; Theodore Dan, *The Origins of Bolshevism*, pp. 236, 237–238; Allan K. Wildman, *The Making of a Workers' Revolution*, p. 234.
2. Marcel Liebman, *Leninism Under Lenin*, p. 29; Alfred Meyer, *Leninism*, p. 19.
3. V. I. Lenin, *Selected Works* (1967 ed.), vol. 1, pp. 121–122.
4. Ibid., p. 122.
5. Bertram D. Wolfe, *Three Who Made a Revolution*, p. 163; Wildman, p. 100; Meyer, pp. 31, 33, 21; Antonio Carlo, "Lenin on the Party," pp. 13, 12.
6. Neil Harding, *Lenin's Political Thought*, vol. 1, pp. 50, 51, 152–153, 154; Ernest Mandel, "The

Leninist Theory of Organization," p. 124; Lenin, *Selected Works*, vol. 1, p. 129; Liebman, *Leninism Under Lenin*, pp. 28, 29.

7. Lenin, *Collected Works*, vol. 4, p. 325; Lenin, *Selected Works*, vol. 1, pp. 131–132.
8. Lenin, *Selected Works*, vol. 1, pp. 131–132, 128–129.
9. Ibid., p. 123.
10. Leon Trotsky, *Stalin*, p. 58.
11. Samuel Baron, *Plekhanov*, pp. 250, 251.
12. Brian Pearce, 1903, pp. 169–170.
13. Ibid., pp. 158-159; Max Shachtman, "Lenin and Rosa Luxemburg," p. 143; Lenin, *Collected Works*, vol. 13, pp. 101–108.
14. Karl Radek, "On Lenin," p. 29.
15. Hal Draper, "The Myth of Lenin's Defeatism," pt. 2, pp. 313–314. The "bureaucracy vs. democracy" formulation can be found in Lenin's "One Step Forward, Two Steps Back," *Selected Works*, vol. 1, p. 424.
16. Lenin, *Selected Works*, vol. 1, p. 129.
17. Ibid., p. 130.
18. David Mandel, *The Petrograd Workers and the Fall of the Old Regime*, pp. 30, 31.
19. Lenin, *Selected Works*, vol. 1, pp. 206–207.
20. Ibid., pp. 154–155.
21. Ibid., pp. 155, 156.
22. Ibid., pp. 164, 166.
23. Tony Cliff, *Lenin*, vol. 1, p. 82.
24. Israel Getzler, *Martov*, p. 82.
25. Israel Getzler, "The Mensheviks," p. 15.
26. Bertram D. Wolfe, *Marxism*, p. 194.
27. Thornton Anderson, *Masters of Russian Marxism*, p. 101; E. H. Carr, *The Bolshevik Revolution*, vol. 1, p. 45; Dan, p. 245; Pearce, pp. 311, 312.
28. Lenin, *Selected Works*, vol. 1, pp. 312, 294, 306; Pearce, pp. 321, 322, 326–327.
29. Lenin, *Selected Works*, vol. 1, p. 214; Pearce, p. 328.
30. Richard N. Hunt, *German Social Democracy*, p. 59; Carl Schorske, *German Social Democracy*, p. 127.
31. Lenin, *Collected Works*, vol. 6, p. 501.
32. Trotsky, *Stalin*, p. 42; Lenin, *Collected Works*, vol. 34, pp. 164, 165, 161; Harding, *Lenin's Political Thought*, vol. 1, p. 195.
33. N.K. Krupskaya, *Reminiscences of Lenin*, p. 94; Lenin, *Collected Works*, vol. 34, pp. 161, 165, 162, 166.
34. Krupskaya, p. 89.
35. Harding, *Lenin's Political Thought*, vol. 1, pp. 193–194.
36. Leon Trotsky, *My Life*, p. 162; Krupskaya, p. 96.
37. Lenin, *Collected Works*, vol. 34, p. 161.
38. Getzler, *Martov*, pp. 88, 89, 83.
39. Lenin, *Collected Works*, vol. 7, p. 208.
40. Ibid., p. 137.
41. Ibid., p. 138; Lenin, *Collected Works*, vol. 34, p. 209.
42. Trotsky, *My Life*, p. 162.
43. Harding, *Lenin's Poltical Thought*, vol. 1, p. 196; David Lane, *The Roots of Russian Communism*, pp. 214–215.

5. Questions and Problems

1. Franz Borkenau, *World Communism*, pp. 45, 141.
2. Rosa Luxemburg, *Selected Political Writings*, p. 283.
3. Max Shachtman, "Lenin and Rosa Luxemburg," p. 143.
4. Rosa Luxemburg, *Rosa Luxemburg Speaks*, pp. 128–129.
5. Ibid.
6. Ibid., p. 116; V. I. Lenin, *Collected Works*, vol. 7, p. 472.
7. Luxemburg, *Rosa Luxemburg Speaks*, p. 116; Lenin, *Collected Works*, vol. 7, pp. 472–473.
8. Luxemburg, *Rosa Luxemburg Speaks*, p. 118; Lenin, *Collected Works*, vol. 7, pp. 473–474.
9. Luxemburg, *Rosa Luxemburg Speaks*, p. 119; Lenin, *Collected Works*, vol. 7, p. 474.
10. Luxemburg, *Rosa Luxemburg Speaks*, p. 119; Lenin, *Collected Works*, vol. 7, p. 474.
11. Luxemburg, *Rosa Luxemburg Speaks*, p. 117; Lenin, Collected Works, vol. 7, p. 475.
12. Luxemburg, *Rosa Luxemburg Speaks*, pp. 119, 112, 200.
13. Ibid., pp. 374, 375.
14. Ibid., pp. 119, 118, 129.
15. Ibid., pp. 129, 130.
16. Shachtman, "Lenin and Rosa Luxemburg," p. 144.
17. Michael Löwy, *Dialectique et Revolution*, p. 175. The critical coworker of Luxemburg was Karl Liebknecht. For a discussion of his criticism corroborating Löwy's interpretation, see Helmut Trotnow, *Karl Liebknecht*, pp. 165–168, 174. Luxemburg's general outlook on organization is even more complex than is indicated here. Several knowledgeable writers have raised serious questions: "The Social-Democracy of Poland and Lithuania, which she led, was, if anything, far more highly centralized and far more merciless towards those in its ranks who deviated from the party's line, than was the Bolshevik party under Lenin" (Shachtman, "Lenin and Luxemburg," p. 144). "And she was also hated by some prominent members of her own Polish Marxist Party whom she mercilessly expelled from the ranks of the organization when they dared to dissent from her views—even though it was known that the dissenters had behind them the majority of the underground membership" (Max Nomad, *Aspects of Revolt*, p. 264). More information can be found in Robert Blobaum, *Feliks Dzierzynski* and the *SDKPIL*, and is discussed in Paul Le Blanc, "Luxemburg and Lenin on the Organization Question."
18. For additional discussion of "Leninist" sectarianism in more recent times, see the concluding chapter of the present study.
19. James P. Cannon, "Engels and Lenin on the Party," pp. 29–30.
20. Bertram D. Wolfe, *Three Who Made a Revolution*, pp. 164–165.
21. See Robert Michels's classic study of the German Social Democracy, *Political Parties*, whose data is corroborated by Carl Schorske's *German Social Democracy*. On the problems (and absence) of genuine democracy in U.S. trade unions, see C. Wright Mills, *The New Men of Power*, pp. 62–65, 223–238; H. W. Benson, "Apathy and Other Axioms: Expelling the Union Dissenter from History"; William Serrin, *The Company and the Union*, pp. 115–154; and Charles Spencer, *Blue Collar*, pp. 117–133, 239–242.
22. Wolfe, *Three Who Made a Revolution*, p. 165.
23. V. I. Lenin, *Collected Works*, vol. 7; p. 237.
24. N. K. Krupskaya, *Reminiscences of Lenin*, pp. 124–125.
25. Leon Trotsky, *Stalin*, p. 61.
26. Leon Trotsky, *Our Political Tasks*, pp. 72, 46, 93.
27. N. K. Krupskaya, p. 125.
28. Cecilia Bobrovskaya, *Twenty Years in Underground Russia*, pp. 106–107.
29. Lenin, *Collected Works*, vol. 8, pp. 145–146.
30. Ernest Mandel, "The Debate Over the Character and Goals of the Russian Revolution," pp. 5, 7.

31. Doug Jenness, "Our Political Continuity with Bolshevism," pp. 3, 8.
32. Nikolai Bukharin and Eugen Preobrazhensky, *The ABC of Communism*, p. 373.
33. Ibid., p. 21.
34. Ibid., p. 22.
35. Lenin, *Collected Works*, vol. 8, pp. 145, 144.
36. Ibid., p. 144.
37. Theodore Dan, *The Origins of Bolshevism*, pp. 252, 255–256, 262.
38. Ibid., p. 262.
39. Ibid., p. 297.
40. V. I. Lenin, *Selected Works* (1930s ed.), vol. II, p. 477.
41. Ibid., pp. 489, 490.
42. Solomon Schwarz, *The Russian Revolution of 1905*, pp. 47-49.
43. Lenin, *Collected Works*, vol. 8, p. 195; Dan, p. 250.
44. Lenin, *Collected Works*, vol. 8, pp. 130, 194; Dan, p. 250.
45. Lenin, *Selected Works* (1930s ed.), vol. III, pp. 441-442.

6. The Test of Revolution

1. Leonard Schapiro, *The Communist Party of the Soviet Union* (1960 ed.), p. 73.
2. Ibid., pp. 73–74.
3. Theodore Dan, *The Origins of Bolshevism*, p. 340.
4. Abraham Ascher, *The Mensheviks in the Russian Revolution*, pp. 57–58.
5. Quoted in V. I. Lenin, *Collected Works*, vol. 8, pp. 282–283, 284.
6. Ibid., pp. 377, 24; V. I. Lenin, *Selected Works* (1967 ed.), vol. 1, pp. 463, 484, 486, 466.
7. Lenin, *Selected Works*, vol. 1, pp. 458, 487, 488, 489.
8. Ibid., p. 495.
9. George Lichtheim, *Marxism*, p. 333; Hamza Alavi, "Peasants and Revolution," p. 242; Esther Kingston-Mann, *Lenin and the Problem of Marxist Peasant Revolution*, pp. 109–110, 73. Also see Anna Rochester, *Lenin on the Agrarian Question*, for an uncritical but useful summary of his thinking; for a more recent and sophisticated discussion, see Athar Hussain and Keith Tribe, *Marxism and the Agrarian Question*, especially pp. 16–79. For a brief review of Trotsky's outlook on the peasantry, see Carlos Rossi, "Trotsky et les Paysans"; also see Leon Trotsky, *The Permanent Revolution*, pp. 69–74, 189–205, 276–277, as well as Leon Trotsky, 1905, pp. 24–35. In a rich and indispensable recent study, Russia, 1905–07, Teodor Shanin grapples with these and related questions in a manner that corroborates certain aspects of my interpretation while challenging others; the central thrust of his analysis of Lenin is compatible with that presented here.
10. See Michael Löwy, *The Politics of Combined and Uneven Development*, pp. 30–37, for a discussion of these and related matters.
11. Ascher, *The Mensheviks in the Russian Revolution*, pp. 56–58.
12. Solomon Schwarz, *The Russian Revolution of 1905*, p. 250.
13. Lenin, *Collected Works*, vol. 8, p. 289.
14. Trotsky, 1905, pp. 309, 310. For an excellent discussion of Trotsky's distinctive orientation, see Löwy, *The Politics of Combined and Uneven Development*. A remarkable critique of Trotsky's theory of permanent revolution and restatement of the "democratic dictatorship" formula can be found in Jack Barnes, "Their Trotsky and Ours: Communist Continuity Today." A critical analysis of Barnes's interpretation can be found in Dianne Feeley and Paul LeBlanc, *In Defense of Revolutionary Continuity*, which contains a lengthy and fully documented examination of Lenin's and Trotsky's views.

15. Schwarz, *The Russian Revolution of 1905*, pp. 14–15; Dan, p. 343; Israel Getzler, *Martov*, p. 110.

16. Lenin, *Collected Works*, vol. 10, pp. 251–252.

17. Trotsky, *1905*, p. 301; Dan, p. 348.

18. Trotsky, *1905*, pp. 300, 301. For an insightful historical critique of Menshevism, see Isaac Deutscher, "The Mensheviks," in *Ironies of History*.

19. Schwarz, *The Russian Revolution of 1905*, pp. 51–55.

20. Ibid., pp. 57–58, quoting P. A. Garvi.

21. Ibid., pp. 276, 281.

22. Ibid., pp. 276–300; Victoria Bonnell, *Roots of Rebellion*, pp. 80–93.

23. Schwarz, *The Russian Revolution of 1905*, pp. 281, 60. For a fine discussion of the Gapon movement, see Gerald D. Surh, "Petersburg's First Mass Labor Organization: The Assembly of Russian Workers and Father Gapon."

24. Trotsky, *1905*, p. 76.

25. Neil Harding, Marxism in Russia, p. 309; Bertram D. Wolfe, *Three Who Made a Revolution*, p. 285; Lenin, *Collected Works*, vol. 8, p. 98.

26. Schwarz, *The Russian Revolution of 1905*, p. 69, quoting N. Doroshenko.

27. Ibid., p. 69, quoting S. Somov.

28. Ibid., pp. 66, 69, 70.

29. Lenin, *Collected Works*, vol. 8, pp. 90, 91, 92–93.

30. Schwarz, *The Russian Revolution of 1905*, p. 67, quoting V. I. Nevskii.

31. Lenin, *Collected Works*, vol. 8, pp. 92, 97, 112, 106. On the phenomenon of "Christian Socialism" and revolutionary priests in Russia during this period, see William English Walling, *Russia's Message*, pp. 198–218.

32. Schwarz, *The Russian Revolution of 1905*, p. 66.

33. Ibid., pp. 153, 155, 156, 157.

34. Ibid., p. 158.

35. Ibid., pp. 131–132, 133, 134.

36. Trotsky, *1905*, pp. 104, 105, 253–254.

37. Schwarz, *The Russian Revolution of 1905*, pp. 183, 181.

38. Ibid., p. 191; Lenin, *Collected Works*, vol. 10, pp. 19, 20, 21.

39. Eva Broido, *Memoirs of a Revolutionary*, p. 90.

40. Lenin, *Collected Works*, vol. 34, p. 296.

41. Lenin, *Collected Works*, vol. 8, pp. 146, 218–219.

42. Lenin, *Collected Works*, vol. 10, pp. 29, 32, 33, 34–35, 33, 36.

43. Lenin, *Collected Works*, vol. 8, pp. 408, 411.

44. Tony Cliff, *Lenin*, vol. 1, pp. 181, 179; Lenin, *Collected Works*, vol. 8, p. 503. However, Ernest Mandel suggests that "the 1906–7 figures seem much inflated. Each historian copies them from the previous one, but the original source (presumably the figures submitted to the London party congress) is never checked. . . . Probably they include membership of unions and sickness benefit associations which put themselves collectively under party control, but are of course not identical with party militants in the strict sense of the word" (letter to author, May 14, 1986). Regardless of precise figures, the dramatic growth of RSDLP membership and influence is beyond dispute.

45. Lenin, *Collected Works*, vol. 10, p. 31. Valuable description of Bolshevik structure and functioning in 1905 and after can be found in O. Piatnitsky, *Memoirs of a Bolshevik*, pp. 76–79, 103–106.

46. Ibid., p. 35; Marcel Liebman, *Leninism Under Lenin*, p. 48.

47. Broido, pp. 133–134. Also see Bonnell, *Roots of Rebellion*, pp. 260–262, 328–334.

48. Lenin, *Collected Works* , vol. 10, pp. 33–34, 38–39, 32.

49. Lenin, *Collected Works*, vol. 8, pp. 163–164, 165.

50. Ibid., pp. 370, 373, 374; Lenin, *Collected Works*, vol. 9, pp. 201, 202.

51. Trotsky, *1905*, pp. 398, 396.

52. Lenin, *Collected Works*, vol. 9, pp. 344–345. An eyewitness account of reactionary violence supported by the government and of an unsuccessful attempt at working-class armed defense is provided in Piatnitsky, pp. 86–88.

53. Trotsky, *1905*, pp. 269, 247.

54. Gregory Zinoviev, *History of the Bolshevik Party*, p. 126; N. K. Krupskaya, *Reminiscences of Lenin*, p. 143; Lenin, *Collected Works*, vol. 10, 94.

55. Laura Engelstein, *Moscow, 1905*, pp. 1, 2, 6.

7. The Meaning of Democratic Centralism

1. Alfred Meyer, *Leninism*, pp. 92, 93, 100.

2. J. Peters, *The Communist Party*, pp. 23, 24; Philip Selznick, *The Organizational Weapon*, p. 62

3. Leonard Schapiro, *The Communist Party of the Soviet Union* (2nd ed.), p. 75.

4. Ralph Carter Elwood, *Resolutions and Decisions of the Communist Party of the Soviet Union*, p. 83.

5. Ibid., p. 87.

6. Axelrod and Trotsky quoted in Boris Sapir, "Notes and Reflections on the History of Menshevism," in Leopold H. Haimson (ed.), *The Mensheviks*, p. 354; V. I. Lenin, *Collected Works*, vol. 10, pp. 251–252.

7. Elwood, *Resolutions and Decisions*, pp. 93–94.

8. Michael Waller, *Democratic Centralism*, p. 30.

9. Lenin, *Collected Works*, vol. 10, pp. 310–311.

10. Ibid., pp. 442–443.

11. Lunacharsky's account quoted in Tony Cliff, *Lenin*, vol. 1, pp. 277–278.

12. Lenin, *Collected Works*, vol. 10, pp. 380–381.

13. Lenin, *Collected Works*, vol. 11, p. 434.

14. Lenin, *Collected Works*, vol. 10, p. 376; Lenin, *Collected Works*, vol. 11, p. 441.

15. Marcel Liebman, *Leninism Under Lenin*, pp. 61, 59, 55.

16. See, for example, Steve Zeluck, "The Evolution of Lenin's Views on the Party. Or, Lenin on Regroupment."

17. Lenin, *Collected Works*, vol. 20, p. 499.

18. Ibid., p. 319.

19. Ibid., pp. 320–321, 351.

20. Ibid., p. 528.

21. Ibid., pp. 528–529.

22. Ibid ., pp. 515–518, 521.

23. Ibid., pp. 518, 519.

24. Robert V. Daniels, *The Conscience of the Revolution*, pp. 12, 26.

25. K. D. Kristof Ladis, "B. I. Nicolaevski: The Formative Years," in Alexander Rabinowitch and Janet Rabinowitch, *Revolution and Politics in Russia*, p. 29; Anatoly V. Lunacharsky, *Revolutionary Silhouettes*, p. 41. Also see the account by W. S. Woytinsky, *Stormy Passage*, pp. 118–124. Like Nicolaevsky, he was a Bolshevik who turned Menshevik, but he remained impressed with Lenin's openness, flexibility, insight and great charm.

26. M. N. Pokrovskii, *Russia in World History*, p. 184; Lunacharsky, *Revolutionary Silhouettes*, p. 39; Leon Trotsky, *On Lenin*, pp. 193–194.

27. Pokrovskii, p. 189.
28. Ibid., pp. 195, 197.

8. Preparing for Revolution

1. Eva Broido, *Memoirs of a Revolutionary*, pp. 119–120, 136–137.
2. An informative account sympathetic to Krasin (but not Lenin) can be found in Michael Glenny, "Leonid Krasin: The Years Before 1917. An Outline."
3. Stephen F. Cohen, *Bukharin and the Bolshevik Revolution*, p. 15.
4. James D. White, "The First Pravda and the Russian Marxist Tradition," pp. 184, 186, 188, 191.
5. Maxim Gorky, *V. I. Lenin*, p. 26; Alexander Bogdanov, *Red Star*, p. 134; Anatoly Lunacharsky, *Revolutionary Silhouettes*, p. 48; N. K. Krupskaya, *Reminiscences of Lenin*, p. 193.
6. Bogdanov, pp. 24, 130.
7. Ibid., p. 130.
8. Ibid.; Gregory Zinoviev, *History of the Bolshevik Party*, p. 153.
9. Bogdanov, p. 131.
10. Gorky, p. 19.
11. V. I. Lenin, *Collected Works*, vol. 9, p. 346.
12. Leon Trotsky, *1905*, p. 196.
13. Iu. I. Kir'ianov, "On the Nature of Russian Working Class," p. 32.
14. Cecilia Bobrovskaya, *Twenty Years in Underground Russia*, pp. 151, 175–176; Leon Trotsky, *Stalin*, pp. 98–99.
15. Trotsky, *Stalin*, p. 110; Geoff Swain, "Editor's Introduction," pp. ix, viii.
16. Swain, "Editor's Introduction," pp. xii, xiii.
17. M. N. Pokrovskii, *Russia in World History*, p. 190.
18. Lenin, *Collected Works*, vol. 13, pp. 104–105; Zinoviev, *History of the Bolshevik Party*, pp. 153–154.
19. Avraham Yassour, "Lenin and Bogdanov," pp. 21, 14, 15; Richard Stites, "Fantasy and Revolution: Alexander Bogdanov and the Origins of Bolshevik Science Fiction," p. 10; Swain, "Editor's Introduction," pp. xxviii, xix–xx. A valuable study that I received too late to integrate into the present work is Robert C. Williams, *The Other Bolsheviks*, containing a wealth of information on Bogdanov and his cofactionalists and on the early history of Bolshevism, it nonetheless presents an interpretation of Lenin's politics that is inconsistent with the material presented here. Williams also constructs an argument in which he (unpersuasively) characterizes the Bogdanovites as "syndicalist" and (amazingly) insists that the philosophical orientation of the Bogdanovites surreptitiously triumphed, consequently propelling Bolshevik Russia along the path of totalitarianism. An older work worth consulting is Dan Levin's *Stormy Petrel*, a biography of Gorky which offers a sympathetic account of the writer's involvement with Bogdanov's faction on pp. 143–163.
20. Krupskaya, p. 167. Even in the period directly preceding the dispute with the ultra-lefts, this approach could be seen in Bolshevik work within the Petersburg unemployed movement— see Woytinsky, *Stormy Passage*, pp. 99–145, and Sergei Malyshev, *Unemployed Councils in St. Petersburg in 1906*.
21. Robert V. Daniels, *A Documentary History of Communism*, vol. 1, pp. 62, 63.
22. Lenin, *Collected Works*, vol. 15, pp. 458–459.
23. Solomon Schwarz, *The Russian Revolution of 1905*, pp. 154, 329–330.
24. Lenin, *Collected Works*, vol. 15, pp. 383–384.
25. Robert V. Daniels, *The Conscience of the Revolution*, p. 20; Swain, "Editor's Introduction," pp.

xvi, xvii, xix, xx; Yassour, pp. 10–14, 18–19.

26. Lenin, *Collected Works*, vol. 15, pp. 440, 458.

27. Ibid., p. 430.

28. Geoffrey Swain, *Russian Social Democracy and the Legal Labor Movement*, p. 93; Lenin, *Collected Works*, vol. 34, p. 406.

29. Bertram D: Wolfe, *Three Who Made a Revolution*, pp. 520–521.

30. Lenin, *Collected Works*, vol. 15, p. 458.

31. Daniels, *The Conscience of the Revolution*, p. 24; Yassour, pp. 23–24; Kendall Bailes, "Lenin and Bogdanov: The End of an Alliance," pp. 117–118.

32. Gorky, p. 27.

33. Ibid., pp. 26–27.

34. Carmen Sirianni, *Workers Control and Socialist Democracy*, p. 226; Leonard Schapiro, *The Communist Party of the Soviet Union* (1960 ed.), p. 111; Stites, pp. 10–11.

35. White, p. 190; James M. Edie, James P. Scanlon, Mary-Barbara Zeldin, and George L. Kline, *Russian Philosophy*, p. 404. In addition to other sources on Bogdanov cited in this section, the interested reader should consult a useful discussion (in a largely mediocre work) to be found in Leszek Kolakowski, *Main Currents of Marxism*, vol. 2, pp. 424–445.

36. G.V. Plekhanov, *Materialismus Militans*, pp. 8, 11, 77.

37. V. I. Lenin, *Materialism and Empirio-Criticism*, p. 336.

38. Nikolay Valentinov, *Encounters with Lenin*, pp. 169–189, 205–243; Wolfe, *Three Who Made a Revolution*, pp. 502–503.

39. Swain, "Editor's Introduction," p. xx; V. I. Lenin, *Selected Works* (1930s ed.), vol. 4, pp. 28, 29, 32.

40. Irving Howe, *Orwell's Nineteen Eighty-Four*, p. 95; David Riazanov, Karl Marx and Friedrich Engels, p. 210; Karl Marx, *Capital*, pp. 102–103; Engels, *Anti-Dühring*, pp. 27, 29. For expositions of dialectical materialism consistent with Lenin's approach, see Henri Lefebvre, *Dialectical Materialism*; Ernest Mandel, *Introduction to Marxism*, pp. 157–170; George Novack, *An Introduction to the Logic of Marxism*; Howard Selsam and Harry Martel, *Reader in Marxist Philosophy*.

The issue of the relationship of philosophy to politics arose in a fascinating later dispute among revolutionary socialists in 1939–1940, and specific references were made to the Lenin-Bogdanov debate. Certain American followers of Leon Trotsky—Max Shachtman (who was inclined to embrace dialectical materialism) and James Burnham (who rejected it in favor of pragmatism)—asserted that the practical partnership of Lenin and Bogdanov before 1907 demonstrated that philosophical agreement on dialectical materialism was not necessary for working out a correct revolutionary orientation. They publicly articulated this proposition in a 1939 polemic that urged deradicalizing intellectuals (many of whom argued that Marxism is too "Hegelian") not to abandon revolutionary politics, that an acceptance or rejection of dialectics is not essential for dealing with concrete political questions. Trotsky objected: "Lenin never declaimed for Bogdanov's profit that dialectical materialism is superfluous in solving 'concrete political questions.'" He elaborated: "The dialectic is not a magic master key for all questions. It does not replace concrete scientific analysis. But it directs this analysis along the correct road, securing it against sterile wanderings, in the deserts of subjectivism and scholasticism. . . . It is historical experience that the greatest revolution in all history was not led by the party which started out with bombs but by the part y which started out with dialectic materialism." (Trotsky, *In Defense of Marxism*, pp. 116, 52, 79).

There is no "iron law" in operation here; reality is too complex and fluid for that. There are examples of successful revolutionary organizations that have not started out with dialectical materialism (for example, the July 26 Movement in Cuba led by Fidel Castro). There are other examples of sterile left-wing sects that vigorously wave the banner of "dialectical materialism." Interestingly, however, the Shachtman-Burnham current was destined to abandon revolutionary politics—Shachtman within a decade and a half, Burnham in less than a year. There were more immediately practical questions involved in this dispute, particularly the complex issue of how to analyze the Soviet Union under Stalin; unlike those who agreed with Trotsky, Shachtman and Burnham ended up as Cold War anticommunists who saw U.S. foreign policy as a "bulwark against totalitarianism." (Another factor influencing them was the failure of the working class in the advanced capitalist countries to mobilize for a socialist revolution). Some critics of Shachtman and Burnham argue that their failure to utilize a dialectical methodology contributed to their political disorientation. And, returning to the focus of our study, the fact remains—as Trotsky suggests—that in the party of Lenin, the dialectical materialist worldview and method were taken seriously enough to become a live issue in inner-party disputes.

41. Pokrovskii, pp. 196–197.
42. Ibid.
43. Engels, *Anti-Dühring*.
44. Lenin, *Materialism and Empirio-Criticism*, p. 32; Michael Boll, "From Empirio-criticism to Empiriomonism," p. 43; Edie, et al., *Russian Philosophy*, pp. 396–397; Aileen Kelly, "Empiriocriticism: A Bolshevik Philosophy?" p. 112.
45. Boll, p. 51; Daniels, *Documentary History of Communism*, vol. 1, p. 49.
46. Boll, p. 52.
47. Boll, pp. 54, 52, 51.
48. Robert C. Williams, "Collective Immorality: The Syndicalist Origins of Proletarian Culture, 1905–1910," p. 393; White, p. 195; Kelly, pp. 100, 102.
49. Kelly, p. 99.
50. Williams, pp. 398–399.
51. Kelly, p. 107; David Joravsky *Soviet Marxism and Natural Science*, p. 34.
52. Lenin, *Materialism and Empirio-Criticism*, pp. 370, 334–335, 342–343.
53. Joravsky, pp. 41, 36, 34.
54. Carr's comment (made in Wolfe's presence) can be found in a summary of a scholars' discussion in Richard Pipes, *Revolutionary Russia*, p. 385.
55. Wolfe, *Three Who Made a Revolution*, pp. 511–512.
56. Lenin, *Materialism and Empirio-Criticism*, pp. 139, 190–191, 126.
57. Krupskaya, p. 195; Lenin, *Selected Works*, vol. 4, pp. 27–28, 33–34.
58. Joseph Stalin, *The Essential Stalin*, p. 300.
59. Joravsky, pp. 33, 41, 39, 43. Similar points are made in John Barber's admirable study *Soviet Historians in Crisis*, especially pp. 1–11.
60. Krupskaya, p. 147.
61. Lenin, *Collected Works*, vol. 2, pp. 361–362; William English Walling, *Russia's Message*, p. 187; O. Piatnitsky, *Memoirs of a Bolshevik*, pp. 165, 171–172. Also see Moira Donald, "Karl Kautsky and Russian Social Democracy, 1883–1917."
62. Swain, *Russian Social Democracy and the Legal Labor Movement*, pp. xiii, xiv, 54.
63. Ibid., p. 62.
64. Zinoviev, *History of the Bolshevik Party*, p. 165; Ralph Carter Elwood, *Russian Social Democracy in the Underground*, pp. 36, 35, 37.
65. Leon Trotsky, *History of the Russian Revolution*, vol. I, p. 50.
66. Trotsky, *Stalin*, pp. 110–111.
67. Abraham Ascher, *The Mensheviks in the Russian Revolution*, pp. 76, 77.
68. Leopold H. Haimson, "The Problem of Social Stability in Urban Russia, 1905–1917, 1," pp.

634–625.

69. Trotsky, *Stalin*, p. 111.

70. Ladis, K.D. Kristof, "B. I. Nicolaevsky: The Formative Years," in Alexander Rabinowitch and Janet Rabinowitch, *Revolution and Politics in Russia*, pp. 28–29.

71. Israel Getzler, *Martov*, pp. 125, 126.

72. Lenin, *Collected Works*, vol. 19, p. 398.

73. Lenin, *Collected Works*, vol. 15, pp. 432–433.

74. Zinoviev, *History of the Bolshevik Party*, p. 170.

75. Elwood, *Russian Social Democracy in the Underground*, p. 25.

76. Abraham Ascher, *Pavel Axelrod and the Development of Menshevism*, pp. 272, 273, 293.

77. Ascher, *The Mensheviks in the Russian Revolution*, pp. 72–73; Getzler, *Martov*, pp. 133, 134; Isaac Deutscher, *The Prophet Armed*, p. 201.

78. Lenin, *Selected Works*, vol. 4, p. 126; Lenin, *Collected Works*, vol. 20, p. 500.

79. Elwood, *Russian Social Democracy in the Underground*, p. 29.

80. Swain, *Russian Social Democracy and the Legal Labor Movement*, pp. 51–52, 89, 87.

81. Lenin, *Selected Works*, vol. 4, p. 129.

82. Tony Cliff, *Lenin*, vol. 1, pp. 309, 310; Krupskaya, pp. 205–206; Ascher, *Pavel Axelrod and the Development of Menshevism*, pp. 291-292; Zinoviev, *History of the Bolshevik Party*, pp. 166–167; Lenin, *Collected Works*, vol. 17, p. 481; Swain, *Russian Social Democracy and the Legal Labor Movement*, pp. 93–95.

83. Krupskaya, pp. 205–206.

84. Ibid., p. 206; Swain, *Russian Social Democracy and the Legal Labor Movement*, pp. 129–135; Ralph Carter Elwood, "Trotsky's Questionnaire," p. 300; Lenin, *Collected Works*, vol. 17, p. 258; Trotksy, *Stalin*, pp. 112, 131; Robert C. Tucker, *Stalin as Revolutionary*, pp. 149–150.

85. Krupskaya, p. 211; Swain, *Russian Social Democracy and the Legal Labor Movement*, pp. 178–179.

86. Trotsky, *Stalin*, p. 112.

87. Lenin, *Selected Works*, vol. 4, p. 41.

88. Ibid., pp. 43–44.

89. Elwood, *Russian Social Democracy in the Underground*, pp. 232–233; Zinoviev, *History of the Bolshevik Party*, p. 171; Swain, *Russian Social Democracy and the Legal Labor Movement*, p. 144.

90. Krupskaya, pp. 229–230, 231.

91. Elwood, *Russian Social Democracy in the Underground*, p. 234; Ascher, Pavel *Axelrod and the Development of Menshevism*, pp. 295–296; Trotsky, *My Life*, p. 225; Deutscher, *The Prophet Armed*, pp. 200–201. For a useful piece of scholarship on the Prague conference, which launched the Bolsheviks as a party, and the Vienna conference, which resulted in the ill-fated "August bloc," see R. Carter Elwood, "The Art of Calling a Party Conference."

92. Lenin *Collected Works*, vol. 20, pp. 336, 337.

93. Ibid., p. 500.

94. Ibid., pp. 500–501.

95. Ibid., 501.

96. Dan quoted in N. Popov, *Outline History of the Communist Party of the Soviet Union*, vol. 1, p. 283, and in R. Palme Dutt, *The Life and Teachings of V. I. Lenin*, p. 34.

9. The Almost-Revolution

1. Marcel Liebman, *Leninism Under Lenin*, p. 113.

2. Ralph Carter Elwood, *Russian Social Democracy in the Underground*, p. 61.

3. Ibid. .

4. Ibid., p. 62, quoting Haimson.
5. Ibid., pp. 64, 64.
6. Ibid., pp. 70, 63, 69.
7. Alexander Shlyapnikov, *On the Eve of 1917*, p. 6.
8. Leopold H. Haimson, "The Problem of Social Stability in Urban Russia, 1905–1917," pt. 1, pp. 630–631; N. K. Krupskaya, *Reminiscences of Lenin*, p. 242; V. I. Lenin *Collected Works*, vol. 20, p. 466. Also see Victoria E. Bonnell, *Roots of Rebellion*, pp. 410–417.
9. Leonard Schapiro, *The Communist Party of the Soviet Union*, (1960 ed.), pp. 136, 140.
10. Ralph Carter Elwood, "Lenin and Pravda, 1912-1914" pp. 361, 364, 367–368, 370.
11. Ibid., pp. 373, 374. The "anti-bodies" to police spies consisted of the dedication of loyal activists and the functioning of democratic centralism. A classic account, written in the early 1920s, of this phenomenon of tsarist provocateurs in the ranks of Russian revolutionaries is Victor Serge, *What Everyone Should Know About State Repression*. For more recent scholarship on police infiltration of the revolutionary movement, see Ralph Carter Elwood, *Roman Malinovsky*, and Bonnell, *Roots of Rebellion*, pp. 417–427.
12. Elwood, "Lenin and Pravda, 1912–1914," pp. 376–377, 378. Also see A. Badayev, *Bolsheviks in the Tsarist Duma*, pp. 178-184.
13. Badayev, pp. 103, 125–126.
14. Shlyapnikov, p. 2.
15. Badayev, p. 132. Also see Haimson, "The Problem of Social Stability in Urban Russian, 1905–1917," pt. 1, p. 632.
16. Leon Trotsky, *History of the Russian Revolution*, vol. 1, p. 50.
17. Haimson, "The Problem of Social Stability in Urban Russia, 1905-1917," pt. 1, pp. 631–632. Also see Victoria E. Bonnell, "Trade Unions, Parties and the State in Tsarist Russia," pp. 313-318, and Bonnell, *Roots of Rebellion*, pp. 393–408.
18. Haimson, "The Problem of Social Stability in Urban Russia, 1905-1917," pt. 1, pp. 634, 635, 632, 633.
19. Reginald Zelnik, "Russian Workers and the Revolutionary Movement," pp. 217, 218; Bonnell, "Trade Unions, Parties and the State in Tsarist Russia," p. 308; Leopold H. Haimson, "The Russian Workers Movement on the Eve of the First World War," p. 47; Haimson, "The Problem of Social Stability in Urban Russia, 1905–1917," pt. 1, p. 635.
20. Haimson, "The Problem of Social Stability in Urban Russia, 1905-1917," pt. 1, pp. 637, 638; William Chase and]. Arch Getty, "The Moscow Bolshevik Cadres of 1917," pp. 89–90.
21. Iu. I. Kir'ianov, "On the Nature of the Russian Working Class," p. 31; Haimson, "The Problem of Social Stability in Urban Russia, 1905–1917," pt. 2, p. 2; Bonnell, "Trade Unions, Parties and the State in Tsarist Russia," pp. 311, 318–319, 317; Zelnik, "Russian Workers and the Revolutionary Movement," p. 233. Also see Bonnell, *Roots of Rebellion*, pp. 427–434.
22. Haimson, "The Russian Workers Movement on the Eve of the First World War," pp. 85, 83–84.
23. Elwood, Russian *Social Democracy in the Underground*, pp. 66–67; Anne Bobroff, "The Bolsheviks and Working Women, 1905–1920," pp. 54–55, 58; Barbara Evans Clements, *Bolshevik Feminist*, pp. 75–81; Alexandra Kollontai, *The Autobiography of a Sexually Emancipated Communist Woman*, pp. 15–16, 19; Richard Stites, *The Women's Liberation in Soviet Society*, pp. 17–53; Rose L. Glickman, *Russian Factory Women*, pp. 156–280.
24. Kir'ianov, p. 41; Haimson, "The Russian Workers Movement on the Eve of the First World War," pp. 37–38, 95–96; Haimson, "The Problem of Social Stability in Urban Russia, 1905–1917," pt. 1, p. 637.
25. David Mandel, *The Petrograd Workers and the Fall of the Old Regime*, p. 16.
26. Trotsky, *History of the Russian Revolution*, vol. 3, p. 157; Trotsky, *The Challenge of the Left Op-*

position, p. 127.
27. Pierre Broué, *Le Parti Bolchevique*, p. 60.
28. Ibid., p. 61.
29. Haimson, "The Problem of Social Stability in Urban Russia, 1905–1917," pt. 1, pp. 628, 629.
30. Shlyapnikov, pp. 6–7.
31. Haimson, "The Problem of Social Stability in Urban Russia, 1905–1917," pt. 1, pp. 627–629; pt. 2, p. 17.
32. Ibid., pt. 1, p. 639.

10. Party and War

1. Antonio Gramsci, *Selections from Political Writings*, p. 34. Useful discussions of "Western Marxism," dealing with its relation to Leninism from counterposed perspectives, can be found in Russell Jacoby's *The Dialectic of Defeat* and Perry Anderson's particularly valuable *Considerations on Western Marxism*. For a suggestive comparison of Bogdanov with certain strands of Western Marxism, see Zenovia A. Sochor, "Was Bogdanov Russia's Answer to Gramsci?"
2. Steve Zeluck, "The Evolution of Lenin's Views on the Party. Or, Lenin on Regroupment," p. 14.
3. See Michael Löwy's "From the Great Logic of Hegel to the Finland Station in Petrograd," and Neil Harding's *Lenin's Political Thought*, vol. 2 for ample documentation.
4. William English Walling, *The Socialists and the War*, p. 12. On the other hand, see Georges Haupt, *Aspects of International Socialism*, pp. 101–131.
5. John Riddell, *Lenin's Struggle for a Revolutionary International*, p. 33.
6. Ibid., p. 35.
7. Ibid., pp. 10–11.
8. Ibid., p. 38.
9. Rosa Luxemburg, *Rosa Luxemburg Speaks*, p. 325.
10. Herman Gorter, "Imperialism, the World War, and Social Democracy," p. 650; Riddell, *Lenin's Struggle for a Revolutionary International*, p. 98.
11. Riddell, *Lenin's Struggle for a Revolutionary International*, p. 39.
12. All of these works are now available in English. Clear summaries of the debates of which they were a part can be found in Gerd Hardach, Deiter Karras and Ben Fine, *A Short History of Socialist Economic Thought*, pp. 38–50, and Paul Sweezy, *The Theory of Capitalist Development*, pp. 140–207, 239–328. Also see Harry Magdoff, *Imperialism*.
13. Riddell, *Lenin's Struggle for a Revolutionary International*, pp. 146, 147, 148; N.K. Krupskaya, *Reminiscences of Lenin*, pp. 285–286.
14. V. I. Lenin, *The Imperialist War*, pp. 68, 69.
15. Ibid., p. 63. For a lengthy examination of this question, see Hal Draper's three-part "The Myth of Lenin's Defeatism." Also see Brian Pearce, "Lenin Versus Trotsky on 'Revolutionary Defeatism.'"
16. Lenin, *The Imperialist War*, pp. 235, 236. Excellent discussions of this question can be found in Horace B. Davis, *Nationalism and Socialism*, and Michael Löwy, "Marxists and the National Question."
17. Georg Lukács, *Lenin*, pp. 11, 12; Robert C. Tucker, *Stalin as Revolutionary*, p. 40. Also see Haupt, *Aspects of International Socialism*, pp. 132–153.
18. V. I. Lenin, *Against Imperialist War*, pp. 181–182; Riddell, *Lenin's Struggle for a Revolutionary International*, p. 392.
19. Fritz Sternberg, *Capitalism and Socialism on Trial*, pp. 142, 144, 150, 155.
20. George Lichtheim, *Marxism*, p. 343.

21. Peter N. Stearns, *European Society in Upheaval*, pp. 303, 305–306; Michael R. Gordon, "Domestic Conflict and the Origins of the First World War," p. 198.

22. V. R. Berghahn, *Modem Germany*, pp. 8–9; also see Wolfgang Abendroth, *A Short History of the European Working Class*, pp. 55–56.

23. Luxemburg, *Rosa Luxemburg Speaks*, pp. 199–200.

24. Robert C. Williams, "Russians in Germany: 1900–14," p. 142; also see Mary Nolan, *Social Democracy and Society*, p. 151.

25. Wolfgang, J. Mommsen, "Domestic Factors in German Foreign Policy Before 1914," p. 26; Gordon, pp. 198–199; also see Nolan, pp. 240–245.

26. Luxemburg, *Theory and Practice*, pp. 146, 40–41, 45–46, 39.

27. Mommsen, p. 15; Gordon, p. 212; John Moody, "Did Capitalism Want the War?" p. 686. For scholarly surveys of interpretations explaining the causes of World War I, see the essays of Mommsen and Gordon, and also Keith Nelson and Spencer C. Olin, Jr., *Why War?*, pp. 92–132. Well worth looking at, too, is the stimulating chapter entitled "War or Revolution?" in Georges Haupt's *Socialism and the Great War*, pp. 216–249; also invaluable is the story documented in Nolan, pp. 246–250, which is especially relevant to the point made here. Nolan's work and also that of Vernon Lidtke in *The Alternative Culture* do much to counteract the all-too-easy latter-day assumption that the German Social Democracy's failure to pose a revolutionary challenge was inevitable.

28. For a detailed account of the case of the German Socialist Democratic party, see Dieter Groh, "The 'Unpatriotic Socialists' and the State." On the dynamic in the Second International, see Merle Fainsod, *International Socialism and the World War*, pp. 32–61.

29. Luxemburg, *Rosa Luxemburg Speaks*, pp. 271–272.

30. Ibid., pp. 326–327.

31. Ibid., pp. 330–331.

32. Alfred Erich Senn, *The Russian Revolution in Switzerland*, p. 30; Riddell, *Lenin's Struggle for a Revolutionary International*, p. 517.

33. Gregory Zinoviev, *History of the Bolshevik Party*, pp. 188–189; Senn, *The Russian Revolution in Switzerland*, p. 43.

34. A. Badayev, *The Bolsheviks in the Tsarist Duma*, p. 195; Shlyapnikov, *On the Eve of 1917*, pp. 13, 19.

35. Shlyapnikov, pp. 14, 17; Badayev, p. 195.

36. Shlyapnikov, p. 25.

37. Leon Trotsky, *History of the Russian Revolution*, vol. 1, pp. 51, 52.

38. Ronald G. Suny, "Toward a Social History of the October Revolution," p. 35.

39. Leonard Schapiro, *The Communist Party of the Soviet Union* (1960 ed.), pp. 152–153; David Mandel, *The Petrograd Workers and the Fall of The Old Regime*, pp. 74–75, 22.

40. Shlyapnikov, p. 26.

41. Ibid., p. 22.

42. Mandel, *The Petrograd Workers and the Fall of the Old Regime*, pp. 22–23.

43. Hal Draper, "The Myth of Lenin's Defeatism," pt. 3, p. 343; Krupskaya, p. 354. Also see Shlyapnikov, p. 97.

44. Tsuyoshi Hasegawa, *The February Revolution*, pp. 107, 108–109.

45. Schapiro, *The Communist Party of the Soviet Union* (1960 ed.) pp. 151, 152; Shlyapnikov, pp. 70, 91, 94–97, 88–91; Tony Cliff, *Lenin*, vol. 2, pp. 22–44.

46. Isaac Deutscher, *The Prophet Armed*, p. 233.

47. Hasegawa, *The February Revolution*, pp. 109–110.

48. Ibid., pp. 109, 106, 117, 119; Shlyapnikov, p. 103; P.V. Volobuev, "The Proletariat—Leader of the Socialist Revolution," pp. 67, 68.

49. Krupskaya, p. 286.

50. Stephen F. Cohen, *Bukharin and the Bolshevik Revolution*, pp. 22, 23–24, 39–43.

51. Krupskaya, pp. 296–297; Cohen, *Bukharin and the Bolshevik Revolution*, pp. 22–23, 24, 395; Senn, *The Russian Revolution in Switzerland*, pp. 38, 40.

52. Lenin, *Collected Works*, vol. 36, pp. 399, 401, 402, 404, 406. Cohen's interpretation of this conflict and, especially, that of Myron W. Hedlin in "Grigorii Zinoviev: The Myths of the Defeated" (in which Zinoviev is portrayed as rebelling against Lenin's "authoritarian" and "unfair" attitude toward Bukharin) seem not even to attempt to consider seriously the logic of Lenin's position. For more background on Lenin's position, see Lenin, *Collected Works*, vol. 35, pp. 393–396, and vol. 36, pp. 213–217, 218–222.

53. Cohen, *Bukharin and the Bolshevik Revolution*, pp. 36–41.

54. Hasegawa, *The February Revolution*, p. 103.

55. Ibid., pp. 120, 139–141, 573.

11. Party and Revolution

1. On the new wave of historians, see Ronald G. Suny, "Toward a Social History of the October Revolution." A valuable sampling is offered in Daniel H. Kaiser, *The Workers' Revolution in Russia, 1917*. Over the past three decades there have also been extremely important developments among and contributions from certain Soviet historians. Works by Iu. I. Kir'ianov and P. V. Volobuev have already been cited in this study, but also see E. N. Burdzhalov, "The Second Russian Revolution: The Uprising in Petrograd," as well as the introduction to that work by Donald J. Raleigh. Discussions of such Soviet historians can also be found in: Merle Fainsod, "Soviet Russian Historians," Tsuyoshi Hasegawa, "The Bolsheviks and the Formation of the Petrograd Soviet in the February Revolution," and Reginald Zelnik, "Russian Workers and the Revolutionary Movement." Recently, Raleigh has offered a translation of Burdzhalov's full-length 1967 study *Russia's Second Revolution: The February 1917 Uprising in Petrograd*, which is a landmark in Soviet historiography.

2. Richard Pipes, *Revolutionary Russia*, pp. 120, 282, 119. One of the earliest discussions of Lenin's alleged mental disorder can be found in the account by former Socialist Revolutionary Pitirim Sorokin, "Fanatic and Anti-Social Extremist." For a study written in this vein, also see Stefan T. Possony, *Lenin*.

3. Leonard Schapiro, *The Communist Party of the Soviet Union* (1960 ed.), pp. 175–177; Robert V. Daniels, *Red October*, pp. 39–40; Joel Carmichael, "On Lenin and Solzhenitsyn." Z. A. B. Zeman and W.B. Scharlau, in *The Merchant of Revolution*, offer one of the more sophisticated versions of the "German gold" thesis. Refutations of the myth can be found in Diane Koenker, *Moscow Workers and the 1917 Revolution*, p. 287; Alfred Erich Senn, "The Myth of German Money During the First World War"; and Boris Souvarine, "Solzhenitsyn and Lenin" (see also his brief response to Carmichael's "On Lenin and Solzhenitsyn").

4. The comments of Wolfe and Keep can be found in Stanley W. Page, *Lenin*, pp. 75, 59, 53. The assessment of Daniels is in *Red October*, pp. 19-20. Perhaps the most sophisticated and valuable work of scholarship written from this standpoint is John L.H. Keep's *The Russian Revolution*.

5. Koenker, p. 6.

6. Leon Trotsky, *History of the Russian Revolution*, vol. 1, p. 16.

7. Daniels, Red October, p. 9; Roy Medvedev, *The October Revolution*, pp. 42–44; N. K. Krupskaya, *Reminiscences of Lenin*, pp. 334–335.

8. John M. Thompson, *Revolutionary Russia*, pp. 9–16.

9. Ibid., p. 11; Medvedev, *The October Revolution*, p. 39.

10. Thompson, pp. 21, 11; William H. Chamberlin, *The Russian Revolution*, vol. 1, p. 73.
11. Tsuyoshi Hasegawa, *The February Revolution*, p. 140; Medvedev, *The October Revolution*, p. 40.
12. Zinoviev, *History of the Bolshevik Party*, pp. 192–193; Trotsky, *History of the Russian Revolution*, vol. 1, pp. 154, 153.
13. David Mandel, *The Petrograd Workers and the Fall of the Old Regime*, pp. 63–64.
14. Ibid., p. 64.
15. Ibid., p. 65.
16. Hasegawa, *The February Revolution*, p. 248.
17. Tsuyoshi Hasegawa, "The Bolsheviks and the Formation of the Petrograd Soviet in the February Revolution," p. 88.
18. Trotsky, *History of the Russian Revolution*, vol. 1, p. 125.
19. Hasegawa, *The February Revolution*, pp. 323, 258; also see pp. 117–118, 120, 228–229, 230–231, 239–240, 258–261.
20. Ibid., pp. 323, 341.
21. Mandel, *The Petrograd Workers and the Fall of the Old Regime*, p. 83.
22. Hasegawa, *The February Revolution*, p. 227; Marcel Liebman, *Leninism Under Lenin*, pp. 119–120; Mandel, *The Petrograd Workers and the Fall of the Old Regime*, pp. 85, 80.
23. Tony Cliff, *Lenin*, vol. 2, p. 97; Mandel, *The Petrograd Workers and the Fall of the Old Regime*, p. 86.
24. Liebman, *Leninism Under Lenin*, pp. 120–121.
25. D. A. Longley, "The Divisions in the Bolshevik Party in March 1917," p. 75.
26. N. K. Krupskaya, *Reminiscences of Lenin*, pp. 328, 329–330.
27. V. I. Lenin, *Collected Works*, vol. 21, pp. 372–373.
28. Leon Trotsky, *The Permanent Revolution*, p. 166; Riazanov, *Karl Marx and Friedrich Engels*, p. 100.
29. Karl Marx and Frederick Engels, *Selected Works*, vol. 1, pp. 177–179.
30. John Riddell, *Lenin's Struggle for a Revolutionary International*, p. 354.
31. V. I. Lenin, *Selected Works* (1967 ed.), vol 2, pp. 3, 8–9, 10.
32. Ibid., pp. 8–9.
33. Ibid., pp. 8, 9–10.
34. Lenin, *Selected Works* (1930 ed.), vol. VI, pp. 17, 18, 19.
35. C. Wright Mills, *The Marxists*, pp. 255, 256–257.
36. Victor Mustukov and Vadim Kruchina-Bogdanov, *Lenin and the Revolution*, p. 45.
37. Alexander Rabinowitch, *The Bolsheviks Come to Power*, pp. 331, xxi.
38. Ibid., pp. 311–312; P. V. Volobuev, "The Proletariat—Leader of the Socialist Revolution," pp. 67, 68.
39. Liebman, p. 129.
40. Longley, p. 64; Lenin, *On the Paris Commune*, p. 111.
41. Longley, pp. 65, 66.
42. Ibid., p. 69.
43. Ibid., pp. 71, 73, 70.
44. Robert C. Tucker, *Stalin as Revolutionary*, p. 165; Trotsky, *History of the Russian Revolution*, vol. 1, p. 306.
45. Tucker, pp. 154, 161, 167.
46. Zinoviev, *History of the Bolshevik Party*, pp. 177–178.
47. F. F. Raskolnikov, *Kronstadt and Petrograd in 1917*, p. 77; Trotsky, *History of the Russian Revolution*, vol. 1, pp. 302–303, 309.
48. Leon Trotsky, *The Stalin School of Falsification*, p. 239. This volume contains the minutes of the Bolshevik conference (pp. 231–301). Also see Trotsky, *History of the Russian Revolution*,

vol. 1, pp. 285–292.

49. Trotsky, *The Stalin School of Falsification*, pp. 261–262, 274.

50. Ibid., pp. 274, 275.

51. Ibid., p. 258.

52. Ibid., pp. 274, 275, 276.

53. Lenin, *Selected Works* (1967 ed.), vol. 2, pp. 15–16.

54. Liebman, *Leninism Under Lenin*, p. 132; Alexander Rabinowitch, *Prelude to Revolution*, pp. 36–41; Cliff, *Lenin*, vol. 2, pp. 119–131; Trotsky, *History of the Russian Revolution*, vol. 1, pp. 295, 301, 305.

55. Trotsky, *The Stalin School of Falsification*, p. 294; Lenin, *Selected Works* (1967 ed.), vol. 2, pp. 14–15; Lenin, *Selected Works* (1930s ed.), vol. VI, p. 42.

56. Lenin, *Selected Works* (1930s ed.), vol. VI, pp. 33, 34.

57. Trotsky, *History of the Russian Revolution*, vol. 1, p. 305.

58. Lenin, *Selected Works* (1930s ed.), vol. VI, pp. 35, 40.

59. Lenin, *On the Paris Commune*, p. 111.

60. Trotsky, *History of the Russian Revolution*, vol. 1, pp. 303, 304, 306.

61. Ibid., p. 304.

62. Rabinowitch, *Prelude to Revolution*, pp. 41, 46.

63. Mustukov and Kruchina-Bogdanov, p. 83.

64. John D. Basil, *The Mensheviks in the Revolution of 1917*, pp. 19–20, 25.

65. Rabinowitch, *The Bolsheviks Come to Power*, p. 312.

66. Ibid. For a vivid eyewitness account of events during this period, from a Bolshevik participant, see F. F. Raskolnikov, *Kronstadt and Petrograd in 1917*.

67. Basil, pp. 18, 15, 16, 179, 182.

68. Liebman, *Leninism Under Lenin*, pp. 152, 153.

69. Ibid., pp. 157, 149, 160, 161.

70. Pierre Broué, *Le Parti Bolchevique*, pp. 88–89.

71. Mustukov and Kruchina-Bogdanov, pp. 45–46.

72. Liebman, *Leninism Under Lenin*, pp. 150–151; Rabinowitch, *Prelude to Revolution*, pp. 44–45, 150–153. Important accounts of the July events can be found in Raskolnikov, pp. 141–209 and in Trotsky, *History of the Russian Revolution*, vol. 2, pp. 17–117.

73. Liebman, *Leninism Under Lenin*, pp. 154–155; Ann Bone, *The Bolsheviks and the October Revolution*, pp. 10, 22, 27–30, 38, 41.

74. Bone, pp. 90, 95, 107, 108, 121.

75. Ibid., pp. 117, 118, 119. For a defense of Zinoviev, see Myron W. Hedlin, "Zinoviev's Revolutionary Tactics in 1917."

76. Bone, pp. 120, 111, 112.

77. Trotsky, *History of the Russian Revolution*, vol. 3, p. 157; Trotsky, *The Revolution Betrayed*, p. 95.

78. Mills, *The Marxists*, pp. 142, 140.

79. Louise Bryant, *Six Red Months in Russia*, p. 55; John Reed, *Ten Days That Shook the World*, p. 292.

80. Lenin, *Selected Works* (1930s ed.), vol. 10, pp. 281, 285–286.

81. Trotsky, *History of the Russian Revolution*, vol. 3, p. 161.

82. Ibid., pp. 159, 161, 160, 168, 166.

83. Ibid., pp. 163, 169, 170.

84. Rabinowitch, *The Bolsheviks Come to Power*, p. xvii. Similar developments took place throughout Russia from Saratov to Siberia—as indicated, for example, in Donald J. Raleigh, *Revolution on the Volga*, and Russell E. Snow, *The Bolsheviks in Siberia*. Raleigh comments: "A vote

for Bolshevism in local terms stood for an all-soviet socialist government, but since only the Bolshevik party and splinter groups from the other parties advocated a transfer of power to the Soviets, it perhaps is not surprising that the new regime eventually turned into an exclusively Bolshevik one" (p. 325).

85. Rabinowitch, *The Bolsheviks Come to Power*, p. 62. The repressive policies were far less thoroughgoing than some would have liked, however. In this period the U.S. Ambassador to Russia, David R. Francis, complained strenuously to the provisional government over its failure to take sufficiently firm measures. "Had the Provisional Government arraigned Lenin and Trotsky and the other Bolshevik leaders," Francis explained a few years later, "tried them for treason and executed them, Russia would probably not have been compelled to go through another revolution." Not only were "Lenin and Trotsky and their fellow conspirators not shot as they should have been," but then Kerensky—"lacking the iron nerve of Cromwell"—made a second fatal blunder when facing the danger of a right-wing military coup: "During the Kornilov episode, he failed to seek to conciliate General Kornilov and instead turned to the Council of Workmen's and Soldiers' Deputies and distributed arms and ammunition among the workingmen of Petrograd." David R. Francis, *Russia From the American Embassy*, pp. 141, 143, 193–194. For a somewhat admiring evaluation of Francis by an influential U.S. diplomat of later years, see George F. Kennan, *Russia and the West Under Lenin and Stalin*, pp. 50–51.

86. Koenker, pp. 358, 361, 364.

87. David Mandel, *The Petrograd Workers and the Soviet Seizure of Power*, pp. 309, 318, 321.

88. Rex A. Wade, "Spontaneity in the Formation of the Workers' Militia and Red Guards, 1917," p. 39; Rex A. Wade, *Red Guards and Workers' Militias in the Russian Revolution*, pp. 295, 3, 302, 3–4, 5, 96, 99, 309.

89. Suny, pp. 51, 54.

90. Reed, pp. 363–364.

12. After Taking Power

1. This point is made, for example, in Carmen Sirianni, "Rereading Lenin," in response to a piece by Louis Menashe entitled "Vladimir Ilyich Bakunin: An Essay on Lenin." Menashe was stressing the libertarian element in Lenin's thinking. See also Louis Menashe, "The Methodology of Leninology: Reply to Carmen Sirianni."

The discussion offered in this chapter on changes in Lenin's party after taking power is only an initial approach to complex and, for revolutionary socialists, profoundly important problems. The crucial issues are the focus of a study in progress, which I hope to complete shortly, comparing the Russian and Nicaraguan revolutions.

2. Richard N. Hunt, *The Political Ideas of Marx and Engels*, vol. 1, pp. 341–342. Hunt's argument is presented throughout both volumes of his valuable study.

3. D. A. Smart, *Pannekoek and Gorter's Marxism*, pp. 100–101, 159, 161–162. For more on and by "council communists" see Noam Chomsky, *American Power and the New Mandarins*; Russell Jacoby, *Dialectic of Defeat*, pp. 76–81, 166–167; Paul Mattick, *Anti-Bolshevik Communism*; and Arthur Rosenberg, *A History of Bolshevism*.

4. For a different reading of the passage in question, which partially coincides with my own, see Ralph Miliband, "The State and Revolution," pp. 82–86.

5. V. I. Lenin, *Selected Works* (1967 ed.), vol. 1, p. 285.

6. Ibid., p. 284.

7. Eric Hobsbawm, "Lenin and the 'Aristocracy of Labor'." The "labor aristocracy" concept is a complex one. An examination of Marxist texts is offered in Steve Clark, "The Development of the Marxist Position on the Aristocracy of Labor," while more analytical efforts can be

found in Horace B. Davis, "Imperialism and Labor: An Analysis of Marxian Views"; Marc Linder, *European Labor Aristocracies*; and Gregor McLennan, "'The Labour Aristocracy' and 'Incorporation': Notes on Some Terms in the Social History of the Working Class." A vulgarized, pseudo-Leninist "orthodoxy"—fashioned out of pieces of Lenin's 1914–16 writings—advances the notion that only the least skilled and most impoverished sections of the proletariat can be reliably revolutionary, and that the better-off workers tend to evolve into a conservatized and corrupted "aristocracy of labor." This is inconsistent with the Russian experience and with Lenin's actual views. As a rounded examination of Lenin's works indicates, he believed the better-off workers can constitute a revolutionary vanguard sector of the working class—depending on whether they embrace revolutionary or reformist perspectives (which largely depends, in turn, on what socialist activists do or fail to do).

8. Lenin, *Selected Works* (1967 ed.), vol. 1, pp. 334, 335, 343–344.

9. Nikolai Bukharin and Eugen Preobrazhensky, *The ABC of Communism*, pp. 379, 380, 381.

10. Ernest J. Simmons, "The Origins of Literary Control"; Louise Bryant, *Six Red Months in Russia*, p. 224.

11. Roy Medvedev, *The October Revolution*, p. 115.

12. Jerry Hough and Merle Fainsod, *How the Soviet Union Is Governed*, pp. 79–80; John M. Thompson, *Revolutionary Russia*, pp. 175–177; E. H. Carr, *The Bolshevik Revolution*, vol. 2, pp. 119–129; Tony Cliff, *Lenin*, vol. 3, pp. 29–38.

13. Hough and Fainsod, pp. 78–79; Thompson, pp. 162–163; Carr, *The Bolshevik Revolution*, vol. 2, pp. 119–129; Cliff, *Lenin*, vol. 3, pp. 23–29; Medvedev, *The October Revolution*, p. 115.

14. Cliff, Lenin, vol. 3, p. 162; V. I. Lenin, *Collected Works*, vol. 25, p. 378; Bertram D. Wolfe, *Lenin and the Twentieth Century*, p. 179.

15. Max Shachtman, "Revolution and Counter-Revolution in Russia," p. 10; Lenin, *Collected Works*, vol. 26, p. 498; Cliff, *Lenin*, vol. 3, p. 10.

16. Victor Serge, *Year One of the Russian Revolution*, p. 243. A useful picture of Soviet democracy is found in the minutes of the All-Russian Central Executive Committee of Soviets from October 1917 to January 1918, available with anti-Leninist interpretations (in the introduction and notes) in John L. H. Keep, *The Debate on Soviet Power*. Important aspects of Bolshevik rule, especially the Council of People's Commissars established by the revolutionary soviets and the gradual blurring of distinctions between party and state, are explored in T. H. Rigby's scholarly and useful work *Lenin's Government*.

17. S. A. Smith, *Red Petrograd*, pp. 156, 150, 226.

18. Lenin's thinking on trade unions has been collected in the volume published under his name entitled *On Trade Unions*. Still valuable is Isaac Deutscher's *Soviet Trade Unions*; a more detailed and less-sympathetic survey of the early history can be found in Jay Sorenson's *The Life and Death of Soviet Trade Unionism*. A clear and early summary of the 1920 conflict between Lenin and Trotsky on trade unions can be found in Max Eastman, *Since Lenin Died*, pp. 135–137, though a more detailed and quite valuable discussion is offered in Richard B. Day, *Leon Trotsky and The Politics of Economic Isolation*, pp. 17–46. Among those criticizing the Bolsheviks, there is a tendency to champion one or another institution and to discount the others; thus Oskar Anweiler's *The Soviets* picks the soviets; Sorenson picks the trade unions; Carmen Sirianni, in *Workers Control and Socialist Democracy*, picks the factory committees. It seems to me that balanced judgments must flow from examining all of these, plus from taking more seriously the democratic goals and character of Bolshevism on the one hand, and the agony of civil war, foreign intervention, economic blockade, and the collapsing economy on the other. For a thoughtful review of Sirianni that raises some of the essential questions, see William Chase, "Workers Control and Socialist Democracy."

19. A fine sampling of Bolshevik discussion and debate on a wide variety of social and cultural

questions can be found in William G. Rosenberg, *Bolshevik Visions.*

20. Moshe Lewin, *Lenin's Last Struggle*, p. 17.

21. Bertrand Russell, *The Practice and Theory of Bolshevism*, pp. 54, 60–61, 21, 38, 10; Gorky's harsh criticisms can be found in *Untimely Thoughts.* This early account by Russell and anarchist Alexander Berkman's classic written in the same period, *The Bolshevik Myth*, stand as perhaps the most substantial critiques of Bolshevism ever written. They differ from the productions of later anticommunist ideologists (which add little to points they make) in that they were written by sensitive and honest radical observers who refused to become defenders of the capitalist status quo. At the same time, Berkman and even Russell are inclined, in their bitter disappointment, to judge the Bolsheviks without sufficiently taking into account what Isaac Deutscher has described in *Marxism in Our Time* as "the great tragedy of the isolation of the Russian Revolution; of its succumbing to incredible, unimaginable destruction, poverty, hunger and disease as a result of intervention, the civil wars, and of course the long and exhausting world war which was not of Bolshevik making. As a result of all this, terror was let loose in Russia. Men lost their balance. They lost, even the leaders, the clarity of their thinking and of their minds. They acted under overwhelming and inhuman pressures" (pp. 83–84). Also worth consulting is a fascinating "insider's" account of the Soviet government by a former Menshevik who, with critical sensibilities similar to those of Bertrand Russell, functioned as a highly placed non-party economic specialist from 1918 to 1925—Simon Liberman, *Building Lenin's Russia.*

22. Serge, *Year One of the Russian Revolution*, p. 370; Lenin, *Selected Works* (1930s ed.), vol. 6, p. 19.

23. Bertram D. Wolfe, *A Life in Two Centuries*, pp. 228–229.

24. Rosa Luxemburg, *Rosa Luxemburg Speaks*, p. 327.

25. Moshe Lewin, *The Making of the Soviet System*, p. 194.

26. Lenin, *Selected Works* (1967 ed.), vol. 2, pp. 678–679. One aspect of the dangerous international situation is reflected in the 1921 memoir by the U.S. Ambassador to Russia from 1916 up to November 1918, David R. Francis. As we've noted, Francis regretted the fact that "Lenin and Trotsky and their fellow conspirators had not been shot as traitors as they should have been" under the "bourgeois democracy" of the Kerensky regime; during the civil war period he "advocated the eradication of Bolshevism in Russia because it is a blot on the civilization of the Twentieth Century, and for the additional reason that it is in our interest to exterminate it in the land of its birth." Noting that high-level government figures in Britain, France and the U.S. were sympathetic to this policy, the Ambassador envisioned a substantial commitment of troops "which would have enabled the Allied Forces [already] in Northern Russia to depose the government of Lenin and Trotsky." (The two aspects of Bolshevik tyranny which Francis chose to stress are that "no man or woman is allowed to vote who does not perform manual labor" and that: "the decrees of Bolshevism made marriage and divorce so easy that they were to be had for the asking." He warned: "If Bolshevism is permitted to thrive in Russia it will promote unrest in all countries.") It should be noted that Francis felt compelled to add that "I do not mean that this Bolshevik Soviet Government should have been overthrown by any other power than the Russian people themselves," that the foreign intervention would only serve to "encourage the people to hold their differences in abeyance" until the Bolsheviks were exterminated. Even though the foreign intervention did not assume the size Francis would have liked, elements in Russia who favored the extermination policy were given aid and support by the governments in question. David R. Francis, *Russia From the American Embassy*, pp. 143, 335, 337, 333.

27. Serge, *Year One of the Russian Revolution*, p. 353. On the civil war and foreign intervention, see William H. Chamberlin, *The Russian Revolution*, vol. 2; Louis Fischer, *The Soviets in World*

Affairs, vol. 1, pp. 79–237; Evan Mawdsley, *The Russian Civil War*, William A. Williams, "American Intervention in Russia, 1917–1920"; and Erich Wollenberg, *The Red Army*. Also valuable for their probing examination of the ideological aspects of the confrontation of communism and liberal capitalism are N. Gordon Levin, *Woodrow Wilson and World Politics* and Arno J. Mayer, *Wilson vs. Lenin*, both of which provide insights into the impact of the Russian Revolution on U.S. foreign policy and contribute to an understanding of the later development of the Cold War. A fascinating Bolshevik memoir, A. F. Ilyin-Zhenevsky's *The Bolsheviks in Power*, provides a feel for 1918 realities in Russia, including the withering of Bolshevik democratic impulses under the impact of the civil war and of assassinations and armed revolts by the Left Socialist Revolutionaries (see pp. 102–116, 119–125). This phenomenon is also addressed in K. Sverdlova's memoir *Yakov Sverdlov*, pp. 119–128, and receives considerable attention in George Leggett's uncompromisingly anti-Leninist study *The Cheka*, pp. 70–83.

28. Stephen F. Cohen, *Bukharin and the Bolshevik Revolution*, p. 79. E. H. Carr, *The Bolshevik Revolution*, vol. 1 provides rich, if depressing, detail on much of this. Valuable fictional accounts that offer numerous insights can be found in Isaac Babel, *Collected Stories*, and Victor Serge, *Conquered City*. Also see Leggett, pp. 102–120.

29. On the Baku incident, which took place in the spring and early summer of 1918, see Roy Medvedev, *Leninism and Western Socialism*, pp. 92–93, and Ronald G. Suny, *The Baku Commune 1917–1918*, pp. 259–343. Karl Radek's comment is in his pamphlet *Proletarian Dictatorship and Terrorism*, p. 51; also see pp. 49–50 for his contrast of the relatively nonviolent early period with the growing violence of the civil war. The impact of the violence is also discussed in Russell E. Snow, *The Bolsheviks in Siberia*, pp. 228–229. Although many anticommunist commentators present the Bolsheviks as inherently violent and authoritarian, the weight of the evidence supports the contention of David J. Dallin and Boris I. Nicolaevsky (whose Menshevik background precludes a romanticization of Bolshevism) in the classic exposé *Forced Labor in Russia*: "The Communist party came to power as the great heir to an age-old revolutionary movement in which lofty ideals and humanitarian goals were the inspiring stimuli to self-sacrifice and devotion to the political cause. For 90 years thousands of revolutionists, the spiritual fathers and the prophets of the Revolution, passed through the prison gates of Russia, were subjected to the privations and diseases of Russian prison life, the cruelties of the Siberian katorga, and life-long deportation. The Communist leaders themselves had known all the dark sides of the old prison system. Humaneness was an intrinsic element of the expanding revolutionary movement, of which Bolshevism was but one part." In the violence of the civil war, the two authors noted, the Bolsheviks "resorted to terrorism and employed rigorous methods of coercion. . . . In the beginning terrorism could be considered a temporary phenomenon. The right to execute political opponents was abolished by Lenin in 1920. It was soon reintroduced, again abolished, and finally reintroduced, to become a permanent fixture of Sovietism to this day [1947]. At first political offenders, if jailed, were in many cases soon released. But eventually, in this struggle of two tendencies—humanitarianism and terrorism—the latter was the winner" (pp. 155–156).

Even a scholar as hostile to Bolshevism as George Leggett acknowledges that up to July–August 1918, the Cheka "was remarkably restrained" and "was not yet deeply involved in applying terror." He quotes a leading Chekist, M. Ia. Latsis, who protested: "Our people are shot in hundreds of thousands; we execute singly and after long deliberations and tribunals" (pp. 67, 104). By 1919, with the spread of large-scale executions during the "Red Terror," Latsis had less cause to complain. The consequences for workers' democracy were devastating. This general sequence of events also emerges in recent pro-Menshevik scholarship: Vera Broido, *Lenin and the Mensheviks* and Vladimir N. Brovkin, *The Mensheviks After October*. Whether or not, given the circumstances, this was an unavoidable tragedy has been hotly debated by revolutionaries as well as scholars from that time to the present.

30. Anweiler, p. 235. Also see Russell, pp. 140–146.

31. Lenin, *Selected Works* (1930s ed.), vol. ix, p. 261; Robert Service, *The Bolshevik Party in Revolution*, p. 166. In "Urbanization and Deurbanization in the Russian Revolution and Civil War," Diane Koenker effectively challenges the assertion that "the proletariat disappeared," which was Lenin's exaggerated formulation. Yet the data she offers suggests that there was an important element of truth in Lenin's comments (which Koenker too easily shrugs off)— a dramatic depletion of experienced revolutionary militants in the workplaces and communities, combined with no less dramatic disruptions and chaos, which severely diminished the political cohesion and vitality of the working class. It increasingly ceased to be the kind of active political force that it had been in 1917. Also see Lawrence E. Daxton, "Lenin and the Working Man," *Study Group on the Russian Revolution, SBORNIK* #1 1975.

32. Lenin, *Selected Works* (1967 ed.), vol. 3, p. 611.

33. Trotsky, *On the Paris Commune*, pp. 53, 56.

34. E. H. Carr, *The Bolshevik Revolution*, vol. 1, p. 204; Lenin, *Selected Works*, vol. 3, p. 547. Despite a somewhat flippant and sometimes hypercritical tone, Robert Service offers an informative discussion of changes in the Bolshevik Party in this period in *The Bolshevik Party in Revolution*. Service seems particularly sympathetic to the Workers' Opposition; because he is aware that the Bolshevik party was a democratic organization in 1917, he is able to trace developments to which many historians have been oblivious.

35. On Kronstadt, a quite valuable source is V. I. Lenin and Leon Trotsky, *Kronstadt*, which also offers a thoughtful and informative introductory essay by Pierre Frank (surveying recent scholarship), as well as critical pieces by Victor Serge and others. Also see Paul Avrich's more critical *Kronstadt 1921*.

36. Leon Trotsky, *Writings* 1935–36, pp. 185–186.

37. Lenin, *Selected Works* (1967 ed.), vol. 3, pp. 575–578.

38. Lenin, *Collected Works*, vol. 32, pp. 168, 253.

39. Shachtman, "Revolution and Counter-Revolution in Russia," p. 9; Lenin, *Collected Works*, vol. 32, p. 261. I am drawing from two different translations here.

40. Carr, *The Bolshevik Revolution*, vol. 1, p. 207; Bernie Taft, "The Leninist Party," p. 98. Also see Trotsky, *The Third International After Lenin*, pp. 149–150, 155.

41. Victor Serge, *Memoirs of a Revolutionary*, pp. 132–133.

42. Ibid., p. 119.

43. Victor Serge and Natalia Sedova, *The Life and Death of Leon Trotsky*, p. 103.

44. Among the best accounts are Eastman, *Since Lenin Died* and Lewin, *Lenin's Last Struggle*. Valuable documentation can be found in V. I. Lenin and Leon Trotsky, *Lenin's Fight Against Stalinism*.

45. This revolutionary internationalism, which was essential for the coherence of Lenin's views on the Russian revolution (and without which the libertarian vision that he projected in 1917 would have been almost criminally utopian), is given insufficient weight by too many intelligent commentators, including, for example, Roy Medvedev, *Leninism and Western Socialism*, pp. 167–200.

46. Three of the more useful volumes presently available are Tony Cliff, *Lenin*, vol. 4; Helmut Gruber, *International Communism in the Era of Lenin*; and Alix Holt and Barbara Holland, *Theses, Resolutions and Manifestos of the First Four Congresses of the Third International*. A superior account by Pierre Frank, *Histoire de l'Internationale Communiste*, has yet to be published in English translation. Perhaps the most thorough documentary collection in English will be the series edited by John Riddell, *The Communist International in Lenin's Time*, of which three substantial volumes have been published to date: *Lenin's Struggle for a Revolutionary*

International; The German Revolution and the Debate on Soviet Power, and *Founding the Communist International.*

47. Wolfe, *A Life in Two Centuries,* p. 564; Victor Serge, *From Lenin to Stalin,* pp. 36, 38.

48. Holt and Holland, pp. 27, 36. For a perceptive historian's discussion of the question of leadership within the three internationals, see Georges Haupt, *Aspects of International Socialism,* pp. 81–100.

49. Ibid., p. 124.

50. Lenin, *Collected Works,* vol. 21, p. 330.

51. Lenin, *Collected Works,* vol. 29, p. 307; Holt and Holland, pp. 125–126.

52. Cliff, *Lenin,* vol. 4, pp. 62, 63; James P. Cannon, *The First Ten Years of American Communism,* p. 65.

53. Isaac Deutscher, "Record of a Discussion with Heinrich Brandler," pp. 50–51.

54. Lenin, *Collected Works,* vol. 28, pp. 292–293.

55. For details on the negative impact of Zinoviev's policies on the German Communist Party, see Cliff, *Lenin,* vol. 4, pp. 72–77, 110–120, 161–187; and Rosa Leviné-Meyer, *Inside German Communism.*

56. Smith, p. 200; V. Mitzkovitch-Kapsukas, "Introduction," p. 22; Holt and Holland, p. 74. In the same period, in reference to the Russian Communist party, Lenin offered a narrowed definition, but it lacked the authoritarian bent of Zinoviev's: "Democratic centralism means only that representatives from the localities meet and elect a responsible body which must then govern. But how? That depends on how many suitable people, how many good administrators there are. Democratic centralism consists in the Congress checking on the Central Committee, removing it and electing a new one." (See Service, p. 131.)

57. Holt and Holland, p. 235.

58. Lenin, *Collected Works,* vol. 33, pp. 430, 431.

59. Lenin, *Collected Works,* vol. 31, pp. 21–22.

60. Les Evans, *James P. Cannon as We Knew Him,* pp. 203–204.

61. James P. Cannon, *The History of American Trotskyism,* pp. 14–15, 34; Cannon, *The First Ten Years of American Communism,* pp. 234, 317–318.

62. Wolfe, *A Life in Two Centuries,* pp. 373, 374, 375, 229. Wolfe implies that he was mistaken. If he had been, however, he and many of his comrades would have been expelled in the early 1920s under Lenin rather than in the late 1920s under Stalin. Especially from the early years of the Cold War onward, Wolfe read Stalinism back into the early period of Communism—and ultimately back into the mind of Karl Marx.

63. Lenin, *Collected Works,* vol. 29, p. 310; Ypsilon, *Pattern for World Revolution,* p. 38; Gregory Zinoviev, "The Fifth Anniversary of the Comintern," p. 108.

64. Gregory Zinoviev, "Nikolai Lenin," pp. 15–16.

65. Ibid., p. 14; Cliff, *Lenin,* vol. 4, p. 60; Service, p. 144; Trotsky, *The Third International After Lenin,* pp. 238, 155–156; Serge, *From Lenin to Stalin,* p. 43; Alfred Rosmer, *Moscow Under Lenin,* p. 54. Two attempts at a somewhat balanced evaluation of Zinoviev's career can be found in Myron W. Hedlin, "Gregorii Zinoviev: The Myths of the Defeated," and William Korey, "Gregori Yevseevich Zinoviev."

66. O. W. Kuusinen, "Under the Leadership of Russia," p. 134.

67. Theodore Draper, *The Roots of American Communism,* p. 281; Max Eastman, *Love and Revolution,* pp. 334, 335. For a useful review of much of the literature on Lenin's personality, see Paul N. Siegel, "Solzhenitsyn's Portrait of Lenin."

68. Ypsilon, pp. 54, 52. Ypsilon was the pseudonym for Karl Volk and Jules Humbert-Droz; these comments appear to have been written by the latter.

69. Robert C. Tucker, *Stalin as Revolutionary,* pp. 51, 53–54, 49.

70. Ypsilon, pp. 53, 54; Tamara Deutscher, *Not by Politics Alone*, pp. 88, 89.

71. Marx and Engels, *Selected Works*, vol. 1, p. 37; Trotsky, *The Revolution Betrayed*, p. 112.

72. Joseph Berger, *Shipwreck of a Generation*, pp. 89, 90.

73. Robert V. Daniels, *A Documentary History of Communism*, vol. 2, pp. 284, 286. For an intriguing eyewitness account of the situation in Russia at this time, by a left-wing civil libertarian striving to present a balanced picture, see Roger N. Baldwin, *Liberty Under the Soviets*. Unfortunately, it is impossible to explore the heroic struggle of the oppositionists here, though some of the organizational questions they raised are indicated in Diane Feeley, Paul Le Blanc, and Tom Twiss, *Leon Trotsky and the Organizational Principles of the Revolutionary Party*, pp. 6–32. Partial accounts of the opposition can be found in Serge, *Memoirs*, pp. 193–322, and Serge and Sedova, pp. 11–180. Two additional sources of great value are the fictional account by Victor Serge, *Midnight in the Century*, and the reminiscences of Mikhail Baitalsky, *Notebooks for the Grandchildren*.

74. Daniels, *A Documentary History of Communism*, vol. 2, pp. 289–290; Joseph Stalin, *Political Report of the Central Committee to the Fifteenth Congress of the C.P.S.U. (B)*, pp. 159, 132.

75. Leopold Trepper, *The Great Game*, pp. 44, 47.

76. Shachtman, "Revolution and Counter-Revolution in Russia," p. 9.

77. For data and additional detail, see Khrushchev's speech in Tariq Ali, *The Stalinist Legacy*, pp. 221–272; Roy Medvedev, *Let History Judge*; Solomon Schwarz, "Heads of Russian Factories," pp. 330–331; and Victor Serge, *Russia Twenty Years After*.

78. J. Arch Getty, *The Origins of the Great Purges*, pp. 206, 3, 6.

79. Ibid., pp. 37, 205, 203, 206. In Victor Serge's magnificent novel on the purges, *The Case of Comrade Tulayev*, these same insights are dramatically presented yet integrated into a superior political understanding.

80. Irving Howe, Orwell's *Nineteen Eighty-Four*, p. 135. On the other hand, the thoughtful Trotskyist writer and editor George Breitman, whose revolutionary activity spanned half a century, argues that Orwell's point "really has no substance. Hearing Comintern does not and never has had the effect on me, or millions of others, that Orwell says it has on him." (Letter to author, February 27, 1986.)

81. This is poignantly conveyed in such novels as André Malraux's *Days of Wrath, Man's Fate*, and *Man's Hope*, and even in Victor Serge's anti-Stalinist novel, *The Case of Comrade Tulayev*. It also comes through in Joseph Freeman's *An American Testament*, in which we see supporters of Stalin from various countries, as they seemed in the late 1920s, on pp. 499–668.

82. Leon Trotsky, *The Third International After Lenin*, pp. 160, 241, 238.

83. William Z. Foster, *Toward Soviet America*, pp. 258–259; Theodore Draper, *American Communism and Soviet Russia*, p. 166.

84. See Draper, *American Communism and Soviet Russia*, pp. 135–185; and Helmut Gruber, *Soviet Russia Masters the Comintern*.

85. Draper, *American Communism and Soviet Russia*, p. 141; Cannon, *The First Ten Years of American Communism*, p. 136; Wolfe, *A Life in Two Centuries*, pp. 368–369, 385. Gusev (whose actual name was Drabkin) was one of the original members of the early Bolshevik organization, at first quite closely associated with Lenin; described as being quite sociable, he had a fine baritone singing voice which he employed at social gatherings. His relative importance in the Bolshevik organization greatly declined after 1905. On this pre-1905 period, see: Krupskaya, pp. 88–89; L. Fotieva, *Pages from Lenin's Life*, pp. 12, 17; Nikolay Valentinov, *Encounters with Lenin*, pp. 44–45, 236. Gusev played a mixed role in the civil war period—see Ilyin-Zhenevsky, pp. 62–64, and Wollenberg, pp. 16, 45, 176, 179, 180, 184. On the savage role he played in the later struggle against the Left Opposition in the Soviet Union, see Victor Serge's eyewitness account in *Memoirs of a Revolutionary*, p. 212. Also see Rosa Leviné-Meyer's rather

friendly recollection in *Inside German Communism*, pp. 82, 140.

86. Draper, *American Communism and Soviet Russia*, p. 144.

87. Wolfe, *A Life in Two Centuries*, p. 385.

88. Ibid., pp. 573, 519; Cannon, *The First Ten Years of American Communism*, p. 13. Gusev died of natural causes in 1933 and was buried with military honors in Red Square. But he was posthumously declared an enemy of the people during the purges, resulting in the arrest of many friends and relatives. His daughter Yelizaveta Drabkina had in 1918–1919 been the last secretary to the late and highly respected party leader Sverdlov; it was Sverdlov's son— making a career for himself in the secret police—who brutally interrogated her and obtained a false confession. See Medvedev, *Let History Judge*, p. 202, and his essay on Sverdlov's son in Stephen Cohen, *An End to Silence*, pp. 119–123.

89. Georgi Dimitroff, *The United Front*, p. 110.

90. Discussions of some of the many developments in the world communist movement can be found in Tariq Ali, *The Stalinist Legacy*; Fernando Claudin, *The Communist Movement*; and Ernest Mandel, *From Stalinism to Eurocommunism*. Also important is a new study by Pierre Rousset, *The Chinese Revolution*. Most recently there has been a further (although uneven) erosion of Stalin's legacy in the Soviet Union. See Yuri Afanasyev, "Trotsky and Co."; Mikhail Gorbachev, October and Perestroika; but also Boris Kagarlitsky, "The Intelligentsia and the Changes," and Ernest Mandel, "The Significance of Gorbachev."

13. Conclusion

1. Victor Serge, "Marxism in Our Time," p. 32.

2. Sidney Hook, *Towards the Understanding of Karl Marx*, p. 43.

3. C. Wright Mills, *Power, Politics and People*, p. 259.

4. V.I. Lenin, *Selected Works* (1967 ed.), vol. 3, p. 340.

5. Ibid.

6. David Finkel makes this "let's wait for a revolutionary period" argument in his otherwise fairly clear-minded "Another Look at 'What Is to Be Done?'" in Mel Rothenberg, Steve Zeluck, and David Finkel, *The Problem of "The Party,"* pp. 24–26.

7. This point is elaborated in Paul Le Blanc, "Marx and Engels: Tough-Minded Democrats."

8. L. B. Kamenev, "The Literary Legacy of Ilyitch," pp. 68, 69.

9. Rosa Leviné-Meyer, *Leviné*, pp. 167–168.

10. Karl Marx and Frederick Engels, *Selected Works*, vol. 2, p. 14; vol. 1, pp. 119, 120, 137; Georg Lukacs, *Lenin*, p. 27.

11. Marx and Engels, *Selected Works*, vol. 1, p. 120. Also see Monty Johnstone, "Marx and Engels and the Concept of the Party."

12. Lukács, p. 33.

13. Leviné-Meyer, *Leviné*, pp. 168, 169.

14. Ernest Mandel, "The Leninist Theory of Organization," p. 78.

15. Ibid., pp. 78–79.

16. Leviné-Meyer, *Leviné*, p. 164; Lukacs, p. 35; James P. Cannon, "Engels and Lenin on the Party," pp. 29–30.

17. Ernest Mandel, "Vanguard Parties," pp. 6, 14–15. See also, Lukács, pp. 37–38.

18. Antonio Gramsci, *Selected Political Writings*, p. 210.

19. See John Molyneux, *Marxism and the Party*, pp. 141–161; Perry Anderson, "The Antinomies of Antonio Gramsci"; and Gramsci's *Selections from the Prison Notebooks*. Of related interest is Frank Rosengarten, "The Gramsci-Trotsky Question (1922–1932)." An excellent overview is offered in Livio Maitan, "The Revolutionary Marxism of Antonio Gramsci."

20. Norma Stoltz Chinchilla, "Class Struggle in Central America," pp. 19–20. Also see Paul Le Blanc, *Permanent Revolution in Nicaragua*.

21. Orlando Núñez, "The Third Force in National Liberation Struggles," p. 17.

22. James P. Cannon, *The First Ten Years of American Communism*, p. 38. One possible result of the "lyrical illusions" that frustrated Western radicals can develop about third world revolutions, has been a later, bitter disillusionment that contributes to an extreme rightward shift. For a fascinating analysis of how and why this happened in the 1960–1980 period, see Jean-Pierre Garnier and Roland Lew, "From the Wretched of the Earth to the Defense of the West; An Essay on Left Disenchantment in France," in Ralph Miliband, John Saville, and Marcel Liebman (eds.), *The Uses of Anti-Communism*, pp. 299–323. For a sad U.S. example, see Peter Collier and David Horowitz, "Goodbye to All That," and Frank Browning, "The Strange Journey of David Horowitz."

23. Leviné-Meyer, *Leviné*, pp. 170–171; James P. Cannon, *History of American Trotskyism*, pp. 80, 81.

24. Sheila Rowbotham, "The Women's Movement and Organizing for Socialism," pp. 14, 15.

25. Ibid., pp. 15, 19.

26. Ibid., p. 27.

27. Ibid.

28. Ibid.

29. An interesting self-portrait of the Communist Party, USA can be found in Philip Bart, *Highlights of a Fighting History*. Two of the more valuable memoir-analyses by former leaders of the Communist party are Cannon's *The First Ten Years of American Communism* and Steve Nelson's *American Radical*. My own attempt at analysis and a survey of some of the literature is offered in Paul Le Blanc, "The Tragedy of American Communism."

30. These are discussed with wicked humor in Max Shachtman, "Footnote for Historians," and in Daniel Bell, *Marxian Socialism in the United States*, pp. 153–157. Some people (particularly thoughtful ex-members) would argue that such utter contempt is unjust. See Sidney Lens's interesting comments in *Unrepentant Radical*, pp. 42–62.

31. For a useful brief survey up to 1978, see George Novack, "Fifty Years of American Trotskyism"; for a fine history of the Vietnam era antiwar movement and the nature of the Socialist Workers party's involvement, see Fred Halstead, *Out Now!* Cliff Connor's *Crisis in the Socialist Workers Party* discusses post-1979 developments, though for thoughtful discussions of certain pre-1979 problems, see George Breitman, "Don't 'Tighten' the SWP More, or You'll Strangle It to Death," and Evelyn Sell, "The Radicalization and the Socialist Workers Party." Also useful is the publications project of the Fourth Internationalist Tendency, "Materials for a History of Trotskyism in the United States," which has produced three volumes to date: Paul Le Blanc, *The Revolutionary Traditions of American Trotskyism*, and *Trotskyism in America, The First Fifty Years*; and Evelyn Sell, *Organizational Principles and Practices*.

32. Many of these and other groups are discussed in Jim O'Brien, American Leninism in the 1970s. Also see Guardian articles by John Trinkl listed in the bibliography, which discuss these developments and contain quotations from veterans of the party-building movement of the 1970s that appear in this section.

33. See Kirkpatrick Sale's substantial history, *SDS*, which provides much information and a lively narrative, despite some analytical limitations.

34. An interesting analysis can be found in Robert Brenner, "The Paradox of Social Democracy: The American Case."

35. Mandel, "Vanguard Parties," pp. 8–9.

36. Ibid., p. 11.

37. For a valuable and clearly written overview on developments in the world economy, which

lists additional relevant sources, see Carol McAllister, "Developments in the International Capitalist Economy." A rich analysis of some of the most recent developments is offered in Ernest Mandel, "A Profound Change in the World Situation." For useful discussions on the impact of economic developments for the working class, see Jeremy Brecher and David Montgomery, "Crisis Economy: Born-Again Labor Movement" and Peter Waterman, *For a New Labour Internationalism.*

Bibliography

The sources listed here are of varying quality and represent a broad range of political perspectives. I would not recommend each and every work as good reading for the general reader. They are listed here primarily because I made use of them in preparing this study. For the general reader who wants to gain a better understanding of Leninism, I would make several suggestions.

On Lenin himself, there are three fine books that—taken together—provide a fairly complete and reliable account of his political life: Leon Trotsky's *The Young Lenin*, N. K. Krupskaya's *Reminiscences of Lenin*, and Moshe Lewin's *Lenin's Last Struggle*.

The best way to understand Lenin's ideas is to read what he wrote. Some of the most important material is gathered together in the three-volume *Selected Works*, although a serious perusal of his *Collected Works* can also be quite fruitful. Three sympathetic broad surveys and analyses of his ideas are offered in the works by Marcel Liebman, Neil Harding, and Tony Cliff mentioned in the preface of this study. (Also worth mentioning is a difficult but intriguing study by Lennard Lundquist, *The Party and the Masses*, which offers a rigorously systematic discussion of Lenin's organizational concepts and a broad survey of secondary literature.) These studies have value but should be used with a critical mind and are no substitute for Lenin's own writings.

It is important to understand Lenin's ideas in their historical context. One short survey (focusing on 1917 and beyond) that is especially good is E. H. Carr, *The Russian Revolution*. Gregory Zinoviev's *History of the Bolshevik Party* has definite biases and imperfections but offers a very useful and concise overview of the period stretching from the 1880s to 1917. Two valuable works on 1905—which provide essential information on the social, economic, and political realities generating the revolutionary upsurge in Russia—are Leon Trotsky's *1905*, which concentrates on

Petersburg, and Laura Engelstein's *Moscow, 1905*. On the Bolshevik Revolution of 1917, see John Reed's classic *Ten Days That Shook the World* (which can be read profitably with Trotsky's essay "Lessons of October" in *Challenge of the Left Opposition*); Trotsky's three-volume *History of the Russian Revolution*; and Alexander Rabinowitch's *The Bolsheviks Come to Power*. An enormous amount of background and detail are offered in E. H. Carr's three-volume study *The Bolshevik Revolution*.

In the text and footnotes, I have indicated additional works I think are particularly valuable, but perhaps the foregoing suggestions will be helpful for those who may wonder where to begin.

Abendroth, Wolfgang. *A Short History of the European Working Class*. New York: Monthly Review Press, 1972.

Afanasyev, Yuri. "Trotsky and Co.," *Marxism Today* vol. 31, no. 11, November 1987.

Alavi, Hamza. "Peasants and Revolution," in *The Socialist Register 1965*, ed. Ralph Miliband and John Saville. New York: Monthly Review Press, 1965.

Ali, Tariq (ed.). *The Stalinist Legacy*. Harmondsworth, England: Penguin Books, 1984.

Anderson, Perry. *Considerations on Western Marxism*. London: Verso, 1979.

———. "The Antinomies of Antonio Gramsci," *New Left Review* November 1976/January 1977.

Anderson, Thornton (ed.). *Masters of Russian Marxism*. New York: Appleton Century Crofts, 1963.

Anweiler, Oskar. *The Soviets: The Russian Workers, Peasants, and Soldiers Councils, 1905–1921*. New York: Pantheon Books, 1974.

Ascher, Abraham. *Pavel Axelrod and the Development of Menshevism*. Cambridge: Harvard University Press, 1972.

———. (ed.). *The Mensheviks in the Russian Revolution*. Ithaca: Cornell University Press, 1976.

Avrich, Paul. *Kronstadt 1921*. New York: W. W. Norton, 1974.

Babel, Isaac. *Collected Stories*. New York: Meridian Books, 1971.

Badayev, A. *The Bolsheviks in the Tsarist Duma*. N.p.: Proletarian Publishers, n.d.

Bailes, Kendall E. "Lenin and Bogdanov: The End of an Alliance," in *Columbia Essays in International Affairs*, vol. 2, ed. Andrew W. Cordier. New York: Columbia University Press, 1967.

Baitalsky, Mikhail. *Notebooks for the Grandchildren*, translated by Marilyn Vogt-Downey; serialized in *Bulletin in Defense of Marxism* beginning no. 36, December 1986.

Baldwin, Roger N. *Liberty Under the Soviets*. New York: Vanguard Press, 1928.

Barber, John. *Soviet Historians in Crisis: 1928-1932*. New York: Holmes & Meier, 1981.

Barnes, Jack. "Their Trotsky and Ours: Communist Continuity Today," vol. 1, no. 1, *New International* Fall 1983.

Baron, Samuel. *Plekhanov: The Father of Russian Marxism*. Stanford: Stanford University Press, 1963.

Bart, Philip (ed.). *Highlights of a Fighting History: 60 Years of the Communist Party, USA*. New York: International Publishers, 1979.

Basil, John D. *The Mensheviks in the Revolution of 1917*. Columbus: Slavica Publishers, 1984.

Bell, Daniel. *Marxian Socialism in the United States*. Princeton: Princeton University Press, 1967.

Benson, H. W. "Apathy and Other Axioms: Expelling the Union Dissenter from History," *Dissent* Winter 1972.

Berger, Joseph. *Shipwreck of a Generation*. London: Harvill Press, 1971.

Berghahn, V. R. *Modern Germany*. Cambridge: Cambridge University Press, 1982.

Berkman, Alexander. *The Bolshevik Myth*. New York: Boni and Liveright, 1925.

Blobaum, Robert. *Feliks Dzierzynski and the SDKPIL: A Study of the Origins of Polish Communism*.

New York: Columbia University Press, 1984.

Bobroff, Anne. "The Bolsheviks and Working Women, 1905–1920," *Radical America* vol. 10, no. 3 May/June 1976.

Bobrovskaya, Cecilia. *Twenty Years in Underground Russia: Memoirs of a Rank-and-File Bolshevik.* Chicago: Proletarian Publishers, 1976.

Bogdanov, Alexander. *Red Star.* Bloomington: Indiana University Press, 1984.

Boll, Michael M. "From Empiriocriticism to Empiriomonism: The Marxist Phenomenology of Aleksandr Bogdanov," *Slavonic and East European Review* vol. 59, no. 1, January 1981.

Bone, Ann (trans.). *The Bolsheviks and the October Revolution: Central Committee Minutes of the Russian Social Democratic Labor Party (Bolsheviks). August 1917–February 1918.* London: Pluto Press, 1974.

Bonnell, Victoria E. "Radical Politics and Organized Labor in Pre-Revolutionary Moscow , 1905–1914," *Journal of Social History* vol. 12, no. 2, Winter 1978.

———. *Roots of Rebellion: Workers' Politics and Organizations in St. Petersburg and Moscow, 1900–1914.* Berkeley: University of California Press, 1983.

———. (ed.). *The Russian Worker: Life and Labor Under the Tsarist Regime.* Berkeley: University of California Press, 1983.

———. "Trade Unions, Parties and the State in Tsarist Russia: A Study of Labor Politics in St. Petersburg and Moscow," *Politics and Society* vol. 9, no. 3, 1980.

———. "Urban Working Class Life in Early Twentieth Century Russia: Some Problems and Patterns," *Russian History / Histoire Russe* vol. 8, pt. 3, 1981.

Borkenau, Franz. *World Communism.* Ann Arbor: University of Michigan Press, 1962.

Braunthal, Julius. *History of the International: 1864-1914.* New York: Frederick A. Praeger, 1967.

Brecher, Jeremy, and David Montgomery. "Crisis Economy: Born-Again Labor Movement," *Monthly Review* vol. 35, no. 10, March 1984.

Breitman, George. "Don't 'Tighten' the SWP More, or You 'll Strangle It to Death: Introduction to a New Pamphlet by James P. Cannon," *Bulletin in Defense of Marxism* no. 20, July 1985.

Brenner, Robert. "The Paradox of Social Democracy: The American Case," in *The Year Left: An American Socialist Year Book*, vol. 1, ed. Mike Davis, Fred Pfeil, and Michael Sprinker. London: Verso, 1985.

Broido, Eva. *Memoirs of a Revolutionary.* London: Oxford University Press, 1967.

Broido, Vera. *Lenin and the Mensheviks, The Persecution of Socialists Under Bolshevism.* Boulder: Westview Press, 1987.

Broué, Pierre. *Le Parti Bolchevique.* Paris: Les Editions de Minuit, 1963.

Brovkin, Vladimir. *The Mensheviks After October, Socialist Opposition and the Rise of the Bolshevik Dictatorship.* Ithaca: Cornell University Press, 1987.

Browning, Frank. "The Strange Journey of David Horowitz," *Mother Jones* vol. 12, no. 4, May 1987.

Bryant, Louise. *Six Red Months in Russia.* London: Journeyman Press, 1982.

Bukharin, Nikolai, and Eugen Preobrazhensky. *The ABC of Communism.* Ann Arbor: University of Michigan Press, 1966.

Burbach, Roger, and Orlando Núñez. *Fire in the Americas: Forging a Revolutionary Agenda.* London: Verso, 1987.

Burdzhalov, E. N. *Russia's Second Revolution: The February 1917 Uprising in Petrograd.* Bloomington: Indiana University Press, 1987.

———. "The Second Russian Revolution: The Uprising in Petrograd," *Soviet Studies in History* vol. 8, no. 1, Summer 1979.

Cannon, James P. "Engels and Lenin on the Party," *Bulletin in Defense of Marxism* no. 19, June 1985.

————. *The First Ten Years of American Communism*. New York: Lyle Stuart, 1962.

————. *The History of American Trotskyism*. New York: Pathfinder Press, 1972.

————. "The Vanguard Party and the World Revolution," in *Fifty Years of World Revolution: An International Symposium*, ed. Ernest Mandel. New York: Pathfinder Press, 1971.

Carlo, Antonio. "Lenin on the Party," *Telos* no. 17, Fall 1973.

Carmichael, Joel. "On Lenin and Solzhenitsyn," *Dissent* vol. 25, no. 1, Winter 1978.

Carr, E. H. *The Bolshevik Revolution: 1917–1923*, 3 vols. Baltimore: Penguin Books, 1966.

————. *The Interregnum: 1923–24*. Baltimore: Penguin Books, 1969.

————. *The Russian Revolution: From Lenin to Stalin*. New York: The Free Press, 1979.

Chamberlin, William H. *The Russian Revolution: 1917–1921*, 2 vols. New York: Grossett & Dunlap, 1963.

Chase, William. "Workers Control and Socialist Democracy." *Science & Society* vol. 50, no. 2, Summer 1986.

Chase, William, and J. Arch Getty. "The Moscow Bolshevik Cadres of 1917," *Russian History/Histoire Russe* vol. 5, pt. 1, 1978.

Chinchilla, Norma Stoltz. "Class Struggle in Central America: Background and Overview," *Latin American Perspectives* vol. 7, nos. 2–3, Spring 1980.

Chomsky, Noam. *American Power and the New Mandarins*. New York: Vintage Books, 1969.

Clark; Steve. "The Development of the Marxist Position on the Aristocracy of Labor," *New International* vol. 1, no. 2, Winter 1983/1984.

Claudin, Fernando. *The Communist Movement: From Comintern to Cominform*, 2 vols. New York: Monthly Review Press, 1975.

Clements, Barbara Evans. *Bolshevik Feminist: The Life of Aleksandra Kollontai*. Bloomington: Indiana University Press, 1979.

Cliff, Tony, *Lenin. Volume 1: Building the Party*. London: Pluto Press, 1975.

————. *Lenin. Volume 2: All Power to the Soviets*. London: Pluto Press, 1976.

————. *Lenin. Volume 3: Revolution Besieged*. London: Pluto Press, 1978.

————. *Lenin. Volume 4: The Bolsheviks and World Revolution*. London: Pluto Press, 1979.

Cohen, Stephen F., ed. *An End to Silence: Uncensored Opinion in the Soviet Union*. New York: W. W. Norton, 1982.

Cohen, Stephen F. "Bolshevism and Stalinism," in *Stalinism: Essays in Historical Interpretation*, ed. Robert C. Tucker. New York: W. W. Norton, 1977.

————. *Bukharin and the Bolshevik Revolution: A Political Biography, 1888–1938*. New York: Vintage Books, 1975.

Collier, Peter, and David Horowitz. "Goodbye to All That," *Contentions* May 1985; reprinted from the *Washington Post Magazine* March 17, 1985.

Connor, Cliff. *Crisis in the Socialist Workers Party*. New York: Fourth Internationalist Tendency, 1984.

Dallin, David J., and Boris I. Nicolaevsky. *Forced Labor in Soviet Russia*. New Haven: Yale University Press, 1947.

Dan, Theodore. *The Origins of Bolshevism*. New York: Schocken Books, 1970.

Daniels, Robert V. (ed.). *A Documentary History of Communism*, 2 vols. New York: Vintage Books, 1962.

————. *Red October: The Bolshevik Revolution of 1917*. New York: Charles Scribner's Sons, 1967.

————. *The Conscience of the Revolution: Communist Opposition in Soviet Russia*. New York: Simon and Schuster, 1969.

Davis, Horace B. "Imperialism and Labor: An Analysis of Marxian Views," *Science & Society* vol. 26, no. 1, Winter 1962.

————. *Nationalism and Socialism: Marxist and Labor Theories of Nationalism to 1917*. New York:

Monthly Review Press, 1967.

Daxton, Lawrence E. "Lenin and the Working Man," *Study Group on the Russian Revolution, SBORNIK* #1, 1975.

Day, Richard B. *Leon Trotsky and the Politics of Economic Isolation.* Cambridge: Cambridge University Press, 1973.

Deutscher, Isaac. *Ironies of History: Essays on Contemporary Communism.* Berkeley: Ramparts Press, 1971.

———. *Marxism in Our Time.* Berkeley: Ramparts Press, 1971.

———. "Record of a Discussion with Heinrich Brandler," *New Left Review* no. 105, September/October 1977.

———. *Soviet Trade Unions.* London: Royal Institute of International Affairs, 1950.

———. *The Prophet Armed: Trotsky, 1879–1921.* New York: Vintage Books, 1965.

———. *The Unfinished Revolution: Russia 1917–1967.* London: Oxford University Press, 1967.

Deutscher, Tamara (ed.). *Not by Politics Alone: The Other Lenin.* London: George Allen & Unwin, 1973.

Dimitroff, Georgi. *The United Front.* New York: International Publishers, 1938.

Domhoff, G. William. *The Higher Circles: The Governing Class in America.* New York: Vintage Books, 1971.

Donald, Moira. "Karl Kautsky and Russian Social Democracy, 1883–1917," *Study Group on the Russian Revolution, SBORNIK* #11, 1985.

Donner, Frank J. *The Age of Surveillance: The Aims and Methods of America's Political Intelligence System.* New York: Vintage Books, 1981.

Draper, Hal. "The Myth of Lenin's Defeatism," 3 pts., *New International* vol. 19, no. 5, September/October 1953, vol. 19, no. 6, November/December 1953, and vol. 20, no. 1, January/February 1954.

Draper, Theodore. *American Communism and Soviet Russia.* New York: Viking Press, 1963.

———. *The Roots of American Communism.* New York: Viking Press, 1963.

Duranty, Walter. *I Write as I Please.* New York: Halcyon House, 1935.

Dutt, R. Palme. *The Life and Teachings of V. I. Lenin.* New York: International Publishers, 1934.

Eastman, Max. *Love and Revolution: My Journey Through an Epoch.* New York: Random House, 1964.

———. *Since Lenin Died.* London: Labour Publishing, 1925.

Edie, James M., James P. Scanlon, Mary-Barbara Zeldin, and George L. Kline (eds.). *Russian Philosophy*, vol. 3. Chicago: Quadrangle Books, 1965.

Ellison, Herbert J. "The Socialist Revolutionaries," *Problems of Communism* vol. 16, no. 6, November/December 1967.

Elwood, Ralph Carter. "Lenin and *Pravda*, 1912–1914," *Slavic Review* vol. 31, no. 2, June 1972.

———. "Lenin and the Social Democratic Schools for Underground Party Workers, 1909–11," *Political Science Quarterly* vol. 81, no. 3, September 1966.

———. (ed.). *Resolutions and Decisions of the Communist Party of the Soviet Union. Vol. 1: The Russian Social Democratic Labor Party*, 1898–October 1917. Toronto: University of Toronto, 1974.

———. *Roman Malinovsky: A Life Without a Cause.* Newtonville, Mass.: Oriental Research Partners, 1977.

———. *Russian Social Democracy in the Underground.* Assen, the Netherlands: Van Gorcum & Co., 1974.

———. "The Art of Calling a Party Conference," editor's introduction to *Vserossiiskaya Konferentsia Ros. Sots.-Dem. Rab. Partii 1912 goda (All-Russian Conference of the Russian Social-Democratic Labour Party 1912) together with Izveschenie o Konferentsii Organiizatsii RSDRP (Account of a Conference of RSDLP Organizations).* Milwood, N.Y.: Kraus International Publications, 1982.

———. "Trotsky's Questionnaire," *Slavic Review* vol. 29, no. 2, June 1970.

Engels, Frederick. *Herr Dühring's Revolution in Science (Anti-Dühring)*. New York: International Publishers, 1966.

Engelstein, Laura. *Moscow, 1905: Working-Class Organization and Political Conflict*. Stanford: Stanford University Press, 1982.

Evans, Les (ed.). *James P. Cannon as We Knew Him*. New York: Pathfinder Press, 1976.

Fainsod, Merle. *International Socialism and the World War*. Garden City: Anchor Books, 1969.

———. "Soviet Russian Historians," *Encounter* vol. 18, no. 3, March 1962.

Feeley, Dianne, and Paul Le Blanc. *In Defense of Revolutionary Continuity*. San Francisco: Socialist Action, n.d.

Feeley, Dianne, Paul LeBlanc, and Tom Twiss. *Leon Trotsky and the Organizational Principles of the Revolutionary Party*. New York: Fourth Internationalist Tendency, 1984.

Fischer, Louis. *The Soviets in World Affairs*, 2 vols. Princeton: Princeton University Press, 1951.

Fitzpatrick, Sheila. *The Russian Revolution: 1917–1932*. Oxford: Oxford University Press, 1984.

Footman, David. *Civil War in Russia*. London: Faber and Faber, 1961.

Foster, William Z. *Toward Soviet America*. New York: Coward-McCann, 1932.

Fotieva, L. *Pages from Lenin's Life*. Moscow: Foreign Language Publishing House, 1960.

Francis, David R. *Russia from the American Embassy*. New York: Charles Scribners Sons, 1921.

Frank, Pierre. *Histoire de l'Internationale Communiste*, 2 vols. Paris: Editiones Ia Breche, 1979.

Freeman, Joseph. *An American Testament*. New York: Farrar and Rinehart, 1936.

———. *The Soviet Worker: An Account of the Economic, Social and Cultural Status of Labor in the U.S.S.R.* New York: Liveright, 1932.

Gay, Peter. *The Dilemma of Democratic Socialism: Eduard Bernstein's Challenge to Marx*. New York: Collier Books, 1962.

Geras, Norman. *The Legacy of Rosa Luxemburg*. London: Verso, 1983.

Getty, J. Arch. *The Origins of the Great Purges*. Cambridge: Cambridge University Press, 1985.

Getzler, Israel. *Martov: A Political Biography of a Russian Social Democrat*. Cambridge: Cambridge University Press, 1967.

———. "The Mensheviks," *Problems of Communism* vol. 16, no. 6, November/December 1967.

Glenny, Michael. "Leonid Krasin: The Years Before 1917. An Outline," *Soviet Studies* vol. 22, no. 2, October 1970.

Glickman, Rose L. *Russian Factory Women: Workplace and Society, 1880–1914*. Berkeley: University of California, 1984.

Gorbachev, Mikhail. *October and Perestroika: The Revolution Continues*. Moscow: Novosti Press Agency Publishing House, 1987.

Gordon, Michael R. "Domestic Conflict and the Origins of the First World War: The British and the German Cases," *Journal of Modern History* vol. 46, no. 2, June 1974.

Gorky, Maxim. *Mother*. New York: Collier Books, 1962.

———. *Untimely Thoughts: Essays on Revolution, Culture and the Bolsheviks, 1917–1918*. New York: Paul S. Erikson, 1968.

———. *V. I. Lenin*. Moscow: Novosti Press Agency Publishing House, 1973.

Gorter, Herman. "Imperialism, the World War, and Social Democracy," *International Socialist Review* vol. 15, no. 11, May 1915.

Gramsci, Antonio. *Selections from Political Writings: 1910–1920*. New York: International Publishers, 1977.

———. *Selections from Political Writings: 1921–1926*. New York: International Publishers, 1978.

———. *Selections from the Prison Notebooks*. New York: International Publishers, 1973.

Groh, Dieter. "'The Unpatriotic Socialists' and the State," *Journal of Contemporary History* vol. 1, no. 4, October 1966.

Gruber, Helmut (ed.). *International Communism in the Era of Lenin*. Greenwich, Conn.: Fawcett, 1967.

———. (ed .). *Soviet Russia Masters the Comintern: International Communism in the Era of Stalin's Ascendancy*. Garden City, N.Y.: Anchor Books, 1974.

Haimson, Leopold H. (ed.). *The Mensheviks*. Chicago: University of Chicago Press, 1974.

———. "The Problem of Social Stability in Urban Russia, 1905–1917," 2 pts., *Slavic Review* vol. 23, no. 4, December 1964 and vol 24 no. 1, March 1965.

———. *The Russian Marxists and the Origins of Bolshevism*. Boston: Beacon Press, 1966.

———. "The Russian Workers Movement on the Eve of the First World War." Paper presented at annual meeting of American Historical Association, December 1971.

Halstead, Fred. *Out Now! A Participant's Account of the American Movement Against the Vietnam War*. New York: Monad Press, 1978.

Hardach, Gerd, Dieter Karras, and Ben Fine. *A Short History of Socialist Economic Thought*. New York: St. Martin's Press, 1979.

Harding, Neil. *Lenin's Political Thought. Volume 1: Theory and Practice in the Democratic Revolution*. New York: St. Martin's Press, 1975.

———. *Lenin's Political Thought. Volume 2: Theory and Practice in the Socialist Revolution*. New York: St. Martin's Press, 1981.

———. (ed.). *Marxism in Russia: Key Documents 1879–1906*. Cambridge: Cambridge University Press, 1983.

Harrington, Michael. *Socialism*. New York: Bantam Books, 1973.

Hasegawa, Tsuyoshi. "The Bolsheviks and the Formation of the Petrograd Soviet in the February Revolution," *Soviet Studies* vol. 29, no. 1, January 1977.

———. *The February Revolution: Petrograd, 1917*. Seattle: University of Washington Press, 1981.

Haupt, Georges. *Aspects of International Socialism: 1871–1914*. Cambridge: Cambridge University Press, 1986.

———. *Socialism and the Great War: The Collapse of the Second International*. London: Oxford University Press, 1972.

Hedlin, Myron W. "Grigorii Zinoviev: The Myths of the Defeated," in *Reconsiderations on the Russian Revolution*, ed. Ralph Carter Elwood. Cambridge, Mass.: Slavica Publishers, 1976.

———. "Zinoviev's Revolutionary Tactics in 1917." *Slavic Review* vol. 34, no. 1, March 1975.

Hobsbawm, Eric. "Lenin and the 'Aristocracy of Labor,'" *Monthly Review* vol. 21, no. 11, April 1970.

Holt, Alix, and Barbara Holland (trans.). *Theses, Resolutions and Manifestos of the First Four Congresses of the Third International*. London: Ink Links, 1980.

Hook, Sidney. *Towards the Understanding of Karl Marx: A Revolutionary Interpretation*. New York: John Day, 1933.

Hoover, J. Edgar. *Masters of Deceit*. New York: Pocket Books, 1964.

Hough, Jerry, and Merle Fainsod. *How the Soviet Union Is Governed*. Cambridge: Harvard University Press, 1980.

Howe, Irving (ed.). *Orwell's Nineteen Eighty-Four: Text, Sources, Criticism*. New York: Harcourt, Brace & World, 1963.

Hunt, Richard N. *German Social Democracy: 1918–1933*. Chicago: Quadrangle Books, 1970.

———. *The Political Ideas of Marx and Engels. Volume 1: Marxism and Totalitarian Democracy, 1818–1850*. Pittsburgh: University of Pittsburgh Press, 1974.

———. *The Political Ideas of Marx and Engels. Volume 2: Classical Marxism, 1850–1895*. Pittsburgh: University of Pittsburgh Press, 1984.

Hussain, Athar, and Keith Tribe. *Marxism and the Agrarian Question. Volume 2: Russian Marxism and the Peasantry, 1861–1930.* Atlantic Highlands, N.J.: Humanities Press, 1981.

Ilyin-Zhenevsky, A. F. T*he Bolsheviks in Power: Reminiscences of the Year 1918.* London: New Park, 1984.

Jacoby, Russell. *Dialectic of Defeat: Contours of Western Marxism.* Cambridge: Cambridge University Press, 1981.

Jenness, Doug. "Our Political Continuity with Bolshevism," *International Socialist Review* June 1982.

Johnstone, Monty. "Marx and Engels and the Concept of the Party," in *Socialist Register* 1967, ed. Ralph Miliband and John Saville. London: Merlin Press, 1967.

———. "Socialism, Democracy and the One-Party System," 3 pts., *Marxism Today* August, September, and November 1970. ·

Joravsky, David. *Soviet Marxism and Natural Science: 1917–1932.* New York: Columbia University Press, 1961.

Kagarlitsky, Boris. "The Intelligentsia and the Changes," *New Left Review* no. 164, July/August 1987.

Kaiser, Daniel H. (ed.). *The Workers' Revolution in Russia, 1917: The View from Below.* Cambridge University Press, 1987.

Kamenev, L. B. "The Literary Legacy of Ilyitch," *Communist International* no. 1 in 1924.

Kanatchikov, Semen. *A Radical Worker in Tsarist Russia: The Autobiography of Semen Kanatchikov.* Stanford: Stanford University Press, 1986.

Keep John L. H. ed. *The Debate on Soviet Power: Minutes of the All-Russian Central Executive Committee of Soviets, Second Convocation, October 1917-January 1918.* Oxford: Clarendon Press, 1979.

———. *The Russian Revolution: A Study in Mass Mobilization.* New York: W. W. Norton, 1976.

Kelly, Aileen. "Empiriocriticism: A Bolshevik Philosophy?" *Cahiers du Monde Russe et Sovietique* vol. 22, no. 1, January/March 1981.

Kennan, George F. *Russia and the West Under Lenin and Stalin.* Boston: Little, Brown and Company, 1961.

Kindersley, Richard. *The First Russian Revisionists: A Study of "Legal Marxism" in Russia.* Oxford: Clarendon Press, 1962. ·

Kingston-Mann, Esther. *Lenin and the Problem of Marxist Peasant Revolution.* New York: Oxford University Press, 1983.

Kir'ianov, Iu. I. "On the Nature of the Russian Working Class," Soviet Studies in *History* vol. 22, no. 3, Winter 1983/1984.

Kirkpatrick Jeane J. (ed.). *The Strategy of Deception: A Study in World-Wide Communist Tactics.* New York: Farrar, Strauss and Co., 1963.

Koenker, Diane. *Moscow Workers and the 1917 Revolution.* Princeton: Princeton University Press, 1981.

———. "Urbanization and Deurbanization in the Russian Revolution and Civil War," *Journal of Modern History* vol. 57, no. 3, September 1985.

Kolakowski, Leszek. *Main Currents of Marxism, Volume 2: The Golden Age.* Oxford: Clarendon Press, 1981.

Kollontai, Alexandra. *Selected Writings,* ed. Alix Holt. New York: W. W. Norton 1980.

———. *The Autobiography of a Sexually Emancipated Communist Woman.* New York: Schocken Books, 1975.

Korey, William. "Grigori Yevseevich Zinoviev," *Problems of Communism* vol. 16, no. 6 November/December 1967.

Korsch, Karl. *Marxism and Philosophy.* New York: Monthly Review Press, 1971.

Krupskaya, N. K. *Reminiscences of Lenin.* New York: International Publishers, 1970.

Kuusinen, O. W. "Under the Leadership of Russia," Communist International no. 1 in 1924.

Lane, David. *The Roots of Russian Communism: A Social and Historical Study of Russian Social-Democracy, 1898–1907.* Assen, the Netherlands: Van Gorcum & Co., 1969.

Lapidus, Gail Warshofsky. *Women in Soviet Society: Equality, Development and Social Change.* Berkeley: University of California Press, 1978.

Lasch, Christopher. *The Agony of the American Left.* New York: Vintage Books, 1969.

Le Blanc, Paul. "Luxemburg and Lenin on the Organization Question," *International Marxist Review* vol. 2, no. 3, Summer 1987.

———. "Marx and Engels: Tough-Minded Democrats," *Monthly Review* vol. 38, no. 2, June 1986.

———. *Permanent Revolution in Nicaragua.* New York: Fourth Internationalist Tendency, 1984.

———. (ed.). *The Revolutionary Traditions of American Trotskyism.* New York: Fourth Internationalist Tendency, 1987.

———. "The Tragedy of American Communism," *Michigan Quarterly Review* vol. 21, no. 3, Summer 1982.

———. *Trotskyism in America: The First Fifty Years.* New York: Fourth Internationalist Tendency, 1987.

Lefebvre, Henri. *Dialectical Materialism.* London: Jonathan Cape, 1968.

Leggett, George. *The Cheka: Lenin's Political Police.* Oxford: Clarendon Press, 1981.

Lenin, V. I. *Against Imperialist War.* Moscow: Progress Publishers, 1974.

———. *Collected Works,* 45 vols. Moscow: Progress Publishers, 1960–1970.

———. *Materialism and Empirio-Criticism: Critical Comments on a Reactionary Philosophy.* New York: International Publishers, 1970.

———. *On the Paris Commune.* Moscow: Progress Publishers, 1970.

———. *On Trade Unions.* Moscow: Progress Publishers, 1970.

———. *Selected Works,* 12 vols. New York: International Publishers, 1934–38.

———. *Selected Works,* 3 vols. New York: International Publishers, 1967.

———. *The Development of Capitalism in Russia.* Moscow: Progress Publishers, 1967.

———. *The Imperialist War.* New York: International Publishers, 1930. Lenin, V. I., and Leon Trotsky. Kronstadt. New York: Monad Press, 1979.

———. *Lenin's Fight Against Stalinism.* New York: Pathfinder Press, 1975.

Lens, Sidney. *Unrepentant Radical.* Boston: Beacon Press, 1980.

Leonhard, Wolfgang. *Three Faces of Marxism: The Political Concepts of Soviet Ideology, Maoism and Humanist Marxism.* New York: Holt, Rinehart and Winston, 1974.

Levin, Dan. *Stormy Petrel: The Life and Work of Maxim Gorky.* New York: Appleton-Century, 1965.

Levin, N. Gordon. *Woodrow Wilson and World Politics: America's Response to War and Revolution.* London: Oxford University Press, 1973.

Leviné-Meyer, Rosa. *Inside German Communism.* London: Pluto Press, 1977.

———. *Leviné: The Life of a Revolutionary.* Farnsborough, England: Saxon House, 1973.

Lewin, Moshe. *Lenin's Last Struggle.* New York: Vintage Books, 1970.

———. *The Making of the Soviet System: Essays in the Social History of Interwar Russia.* New York: Pantheon Books, 1985..

Liberman, Simon. *Building Lenin's Russia.* Chicago: University of Chicago Press, 1945.

Lichtheim, George. *Marxism: An Historical and Critical Study.* New York: Frederick A. Praeger, 1967.

Lidtke, Vernon L. *The Alternative Culture: Socialist Labor in Imperial Germany.* New York: Oxford University Press, 1985.

Liebman, Marcel. "Lenin in 1905: A Revolution That Shook a Doctrine," *Monthly Review* vol. 21, no. 11, April 1970.

———. *Leninism Under Lenin*. London: Merlin Press, 1980.

Linder, Marc. *European Labor Aristocracies*. Frankfurt: Campus Verlag, 1985.

Longley, D. A. "The Divisions in the Bolshevik Party in March 1917," *Soviet Studies* vol. 24, no. 1, July 1972.

Löwy, Michael. *Dialectique et Revolution: Essais de Sociologie et d'Histoire du Marxisme*. Paris: Editions Anthropos, 1973.

———. "From the Great Logic of Hegel to the Finland Station in Petrograd," *Critique* no. 6, Spring 1976.

———. "Marxists and the National Question," *New Left Review* no. 96, March/April 1976.

———. *The Politics of Combined and Uneven Development: The Theory of Permanent Revolution*. London: Verso, 1981.

Lukács, Georg. *Lenin: A Study of the Unity of His Thought*. Cambridge: MIT Press, 1971.

Lunacharsky, Anatoly V. *Revolutionary Silhouettes*. New York: Hill and Wang, 1968.

Lundquist, Lennart. *The Party and the Masses: An Interorganizational Analysis of Lenin's Model for the Bolshevik Movement*. Stockholm: Almqvist & Wiksell International, 1982.

Luxemburg, Rosa. *Rosa Luxemburg Speaks*, ed. Mary-Alice Waters. New York: Pathfinder Press, 1970.

———. *Selected Political Writings*, ed. Dick Howard. New York: Monthly Review Press, 1971.

———. *Theory and Practice*. Detroit: News & Letters, 1980.

Magdoff, Harry. *Imperialism: From the Colonial Age to the Present*. New York: Monthly Review Press, 1978.

Maitan, Livio. "The Revolutionary Marxism of Antonio Gramsci," *International Marxist Review* vol. 2, no. 3, Summer 1987.

Malyshev, Sergei. *Unemployed Councils in St. Petersburg in 1906*. San Francisco: Proletarian Publishers, 1976.

Malraux, André. *Days of Wrath*. New York: Random House, 1936.

———. *Man's Fate*. New York: Vintage Books, 1969.

———. *Man's Hope*. New York: Bantam Books, 1968.

Mandel, David. *The Petrograd Workers and the Fall of the Old Regime*. New York: St. Martin's Press, 1984.

———. *The Petrograd Workers and the Soviet Seizure of Power*. New York: St. Martin's Press, 1984.

Mandel, Ernest. "A Profound Change in the World Situation," *International Viewpoint* no. 130, November 23, 1987.

———. *From Stalinism to Eurocommunism*. London: New Left Books, 1978.

———. *Introduction to Marxism*. London: Ink Links, 1979.

———. "Liebman and Leninism," *The Socialist Register* 1975. ed. Ralph Miliband and John Saville. London: Merlin Press, 1975.

———. "The Debate over the Character and Goals of the Russian Revolution," *International Socialist Review* April 1982.

———. "The Leninist Theory of Organization," in *Revolution and Class Struggle: A Reader in Marxist Politics*, ed. Robin Blackburn. Glasgow: Fontana, 1977.

———. *The Place of Marxism in History*. Montreuil, France: International Institute for Research and Education, 1987.

———. "The Significance of Gorbachev," *International Marxist Review* vol. 3, no. 4, Winter 1987.

———. "Vanguard Parties," *Mid-American Review of Sociology* no. 2 in 1983.

Martynov, A. "The Great Proletarian Leader," *Communist International* no. 1 in 1924.

Marx, Karl. *Capital*, vol. 1. New York: Vintage Books, 1977.

———. *Early Writings*. New York: Vintage Books, 1975.

Marx, Karl, and Frederick Engels. *Selected Works*, 3 vols. Moscow: Progress Publishers, 1973.

Mattick, Paul. *Anti-Bolshevik Communism*. White Plains, N.Y.: M. E. Sharpe, 1978.

Mawdsley, Evan. *The Russian Civil War*. Boston: Allen & Unwin, 1987.

Mayer, Arno J. *Wilson vs. Lenin: Political Origins of the New Diplomacy, 1917–1918*. Cleveland: World Publishing, 1964.

McAllister, Carol J. "Developments in the International Capitalist Economy," *Bulletin in Defense of Marxism* no. 48, January 1988.

McLennan, Gregor. "'The Labour Aristocracy' and 'Incorporation': Notes on Some Terms in the Social History of the Working Class," *Social History* vol. 6, no. 1, January 1981.

Medvedev, Roy A. *Leninism and Western Socialism*. London: Verso, 1981.

———. *Let History Judge: The Origins and Consequences of Stalinism*. New York: Vintage Books, 1973.

———. *The October Revolution*. New York: Columbia University Press, 1979.

Menashe, Louis. "The Methodology of Leninology: Reply to Carmen Sirianni," *Socialist Revolution* vol. 5, no. 1, April 1975.

———. "Vladimir Ilyich Bakunin: An Essay on Lenin," *Socialist Revolution* vol. 3, no. 6, November/December 1973.

Meyer, Alfred G. *Leninism*. New York: Frederick A. Praeger, 1967.

Michels, Robert. *Political Parties: A Sociological Study of the Oligarchical Tendencies of Modern Democracy*. New York: Collier Books, 1962.

Miliband, Ralph. "The State and Revolution," *Monthly Review* vol. 21, no. 11, April 1970.

Miliband, Ralph, John Saville, and Marcel Liebman (eds.) *The Uses of Anti-Communism* (*Socialist Register 1984*). New York: Monthly Review Press, 1984.

Mills, C. Wright. *Power, Politics and People: Collected Essays*. New York: Ballantine Books, n.d.

———. *The Marxists*. New York: Dell, 1962.

———. *The New Men of Power: America's Labor Leaders*. New York: Harcourt, Brace and Co., 1948.

Mitzkovitch-Kapsukas, V. "Introduction" in *Lenin on Organization*. New York: Workers Library Publishers, 1926.

Molyneux, John. *Marxism and the Party*. London: Pluto Press, 1978.

Mommsen, Wolfgang J. "Domestic Factors in German Foreign Policy Before 1914," *Central European History* vol. 6, no. 1, March 1973.

Moody, John. "Did Capitalism Want the War?" *New Review* vol. 2, no. 12, December 1914.

Mustukov, Victor, and Vadim Kruchina-Bogdanov. *Lenin and the Revolution*. Moscow: Novosti Press Agency Publishing House, n.d.

Nelson, Keith L., and Spencer C. Olin, Jr. *Why War? Ideology, Theory and History*. Berkeley: University of California Press, 1980.

Nelson, Steve, with James R. Barrett and Rob Ruck. *Steve Nelson: American Radical*. Pittsburgh: University of Pittsburgh Press, 1981.

Nettl, Peter. *Rosa Luxemburg*. London: Oxford University Press, 1969.

Nolan, Mary. *Social Democracy and Society: Working-Class Radicalism in Dusseldorf, 1890–1920*. Cambridge: Cambridge University Press, 1981.

Nomad, Max. *Aspects of Revolt*. New York: Noonday Press: 1961.

Novack, George. *An Introduction to the Logic of Marxism*. Merit Publishers, 1969.

———. "Fifty Years of American Trotskyism," *International Socialist Review* June 1978.

Núñez, Orlando. "The Third Force in National Liberation Struggles," *Latin American Perspectives* Spring 1981.

O'Brien, Jim. *American Leninism in the 1970s*. Somerville, Mass.: New England Free Press, n.d.; reprinted from *Radical America* November 1977/February 1978.

Page, Stanley W. (ed.). *Lenin: Dedicated Marxist or Revolutionary Pragmatist?* Lexington Mass.:

D. C. Heath and Co., 1970.

Pannekoek, Anton. "The Downfall of the International," *New Review* vol. 2, no. 11, November 1914.

———. "The Great European War and Socialism," *International Socialist Review* vol. 15, no. 4, October 1914.

Pearce, Brian. "Lenin Versus Trotsky on 'Revolutionary Defeatism," *Study Group on the Russian Revolution, SBORNIK* #13, 1987.

Pearce, Brian (ed.). *1903: Second Congress of the Russian Social Democratic Labor Party, Complete Text of the Minutes*. London: New Park, 1978.

Perrie, Maureen. "The Social Composition and Structure of the Socialist-Revolutionary Party Before 1917," *Soviet Studies* vol. 24, no. 2, October 1972.

Peters, J. *The Communist Party: A Manual on Organization*. New York: Workers Library Publishers, 1935.

Piatnitsky, O. *Memoirs of a Bolshevik*. New York: International Publishers, 1931.

Pipes, Richard (ed.), *Revolutionary Russia: A Symposium*. Garden City, N.Y.: Anchor Books. 1969.

Plekhanov, G. V. *Materialismus Militans: Reply to Mr. Bogdanov*. Moscow: Progress Publishers, 1973.

Pokrovskii, M. N. *Russia in World History: Selected Essays*. Ann Arbor: University of Michigan Press, 1970.

Popov, N. *Outline History of the Communist Party of the Soviet Union*, 2 vols. Moscow-Leningrad: Co-Operative Publishing Society of Foreign Workers in the USSR, 1934.

Possony, Stefan T. *Lenin: The Compulsive Revolutionary*. Chicago: Henry Regenery, 1964.

Rabinowitch, Alexander. *Prelude to Revolution: The Petrograd Bolsheviks and the July 1917 Uprising*. Bloomington: Indiana University Press, 1968.

———. *The Bolsheviks Come to Power: The Revolution of 1917 in Petrograd*. New York: W. W. Norton, 1976.

Rabinowitch, Alexander, Janet Rabinowitch, and Ladis K. D. Kristof (eds.). *Revolution and Politics in Russia: Essays in Memory of B. I. Nicolaevsky*. Bloomington: Indiana University Press, 1972.

Radek, Karl. "On Lenin," *International Socialist Review* vol. 34, no. 10, November 1973.

———. *Proletarian Dictatorship and Terrorism*. Detroit: Marxian Educational Society, 1921.

Radkey, Oliver H. *The Agrarian Foes of Bolshevism*. New York: Columbia University Press, 1958.

Raleigh, Donald J. "Introduction," in *Soviet Studies in History* vol. 22, no. 3, Winter 1983/1984.

———. *Revolution on the Volga: 1917 in Saratov*. Ithaca: Cornell University Press, 1985.

Raskolnikov, F. F. *Kronstadt and Petrograd in 1917*. London: New Park, 1985.

Reed, John. *Ten Days That Shook the World*. New York: International Publishers, 1926.

Riazanov, David. *Karl Marx and Friedrich Engels: An Introduction to Their Lives and Work*. New York: Monthly Review Press, 1973.

Riddell, John (ed.). *Founding the Communist International. Proceedings and Documents of the First Congress: March 1919*. New York: Pathfinder Press, 1987.

———. *Lenin's Struggle for a Revolutionary International: Documents, 1907–1916*. New York: Monad Press, 1984.

———. *The German Revolution and the Debate on Soviet Power: Documents, 1918–1919*. New York: Pathfinder Press, 1986.

Rigby, T. H. *Lenin's Government: Sovnarkom, 1917–1922*. Cambridge: Cambridge University Press, 1979.

Rochester, Anna. *Lenin on the Agrarian Question*. New York: International Publishers, 1942.

Rosenberg, Arthur. *A History of Bolshevism*. Garden City, N.Y.: Anchor Books, 1967.

Rosenberg, William G. (ed.). *Bolshevik Visions: First Phase of the Cultural Revolution in Soviet Russia*. Ann Arbor: Ardis, 1984.

Rosengarten, Frank. "The Gramsci-Trotsky Question (1922–1932)" *Social Text* no. 11, Winter 1984/1985.

Rosmer, Alfred. *Moscow Under Lenin*. New York: Monthly Review Press, 1972.

Rossi, Carlos. "Trotsky et les Paysans," *Critique Communiste* no. 25, November 1978.

Rothenberg, Mel, Steve Zeluck, and David Finkel. *The Problem of "the Party": Contributions to a Discussion*. n.p. , n.d.

Rousset, Pierre. *The Chinese Revolution. Volume 1: The Second Chinese Revolution and the Shaping of the Maoist Outlook*. Montreuil, France: International Institute for Research and Education, 1987.

———. *The Chinese Revolution. Volume 2: The Maoist Project Tested in the Struggle for Power*. Montreuil, France: International Institute for Research and Education, 1987.

Rowbotham, Sheila. "The Women's Movement and Organizing for Socialism," *Radical America* vol. 13, no. 5, September/October 1979.

Russell, Bertrand. *The Practice and Theory of Bolshevism*. London: George Allen & Unwin, 1949.

Sale, Kirkpatrick. *SDS*. New York: Vintage Books, 1974.

Schapiro, Leonard. *The Communist Party of the Soviet Union*. New York: Vintage Books, 1960.

———. *The Communist Party of the Soviet Union*, 2nd ed., rev. and enlarged. London: Eyre & Spottiswoode, 1970.

Schorske, Carl. *German Social Democracy: 1905–1917*. New York: John Wiley & Sons, n.d.

Schwarz, Solomon. "Heads of Russian Factories," *Social Research* vol. 9, no. 2, September 1942.

———. *The Russian Revolution of 1905: The Workers' Movement and the Formation of Bolshevism and Menshevism*. Chicago: University of Chicago Press, 1967.

Sell, Evelyn (ed.). *Organization al Principles and Practices*. New York: Fourth Internationalist Tendency, 1987.

———. "The Radicalization and the Socialist Workers Party," *Bulletin in Defense of Marxism* no. 8, June 1984.

Selsam, Howard, and Harry Martel (eds.). *Reader in Marxist Philosophy*. New York: International Publishers, 1963.

Selznick, Philip. *The Organizational Weapon: A Study of Bolshevik Strategy and Tactics*. New York: McGraw-Hill, 1952.

Senn, Alfred Erich. "The Myth of German Money During the First World War," *Soviet Studies* vol. 28, no. 1, January 1976.

———. *The Russian Revolution in Switzerland: 1914–1917*. Madison: University of Wisconsin Press, 1971.

Serge, Victor. *Conquered City*. London: Writers and Readers Publishing Cooperative, 1978.

———. *From Lenin to Stalin*. New York: Monad Press, 1980.

———. "Marxism in Our Time," *Partisan Review* vol. 5, no. 3, August/September 1938.

———. *Memoirs of a Revolutionary*. London: Writers and Readers Publishing Cooperative, 1984.

———. *Midnight in the Century*. London: Writers and Readers Publishing Cooperative, 1982.

———. *Russia Twenty Years After*. New York: Hillman-Curl, 1937.

———. *The Case of Comrade Tulayev*. Garden City, N.Y.: Anchor Books, 1963.

———. *What Everyone Should Know About Repression*. London: New Park, 1979.

———. *Year One of the Russian Revolution*. Chicago: Holt, Rinehart and Winston, 1972.

Serge, Victor, and Natalia Sedova. *The Life and Death of Leon Trotsky*. New York: Basic Books, 1975.

Serrin, William. *The Company and the Union: The "Civilized Relationship" of the General Motors Corporation and the United Automobile Workers*. New York: Vintage Books, 1974.

Service, Robert. *The Bolshevik Party in Revolution: A Study in Organizational Change, 1917–1923*. New York: Barnes & Noble Books, 1979.

Shachtman, Max. "Footnote for Historians," *New International* vol. 4, no. 12, December 1938.

——. "Lenin and Rosa Luxemburg," *New International* vol. 4, no. 5, May 1938.

——. "Revolution and Counter-Revolution in Russia," *New International* vol. 4, no. 1, January 1938.

Shanin, Teodor. (ed.). *Late Marx and the Russian Road: Marx and "The Peripheries of Capitalism".* New York: Monthly Review Press, 1983.

——. *Russia as a 'Developing Society'.* New Haven: Yale University Press, 1986.

——. *Russia, 1905–07: Revolution as a Moment of Truth.* New Haven: Yale University Press, 1986.

Shlyapnikov, Alexander. *On the Eve of 1917.* London: Allison & Busby, 1982.

Siegel, Paul N. "Solzhenitsyn's Portrait of Lenin," *Clio* vol. 14, no. 1, 1984.

Simmons, Ernest. "The Origins of Literary Control," *Survey* no. 36, April/June 1961.

Sirianni, Carmen. "Rereading Lenin," *Socialist Revolution* vol. 5, no. 1, April 1975.

——. *Workers Control and Socialist Democracy: The Soviet Experience.* London: Verso, 1982.

Smart, D. A. (ed.). *Pannekoek and Gorter's Marxism.* London: Pluto Press, 1978.

Smith, S. A. *Red Petrograd: Revolution in the Factories, 1917–18.* Cambridge: Cambridge University Press, 1985.

Snow, Russell E. *The Bolsheviks in Siberia: 1917–1918.* London: Associated University Presses, 1977.

Sochor, Zenovia A. "Was Bogdanov Russia's Answer to Gramsci?" *Studies in Soviet Thought* vol. 22, no. 1, February 1981.

Sorenson, Jay B. *The Life and Death of Soviet Trade Unionism.* New York: Atherton Press, 1969.

Sorin, V. *Lenin's Teachings About the Party.* Bell Gardens, Calif.: October League, 1973; reprinted from *The Party Organizer*, May, June, and July 1931.

Sorokin, Pitirim. "Fanatic and Anti-Social Extremist," *Current History* vol. 19, no. 6, March 1924.

Souvarine, Boris. "Solzhenitsyn and Lenin," *Dissent* vol. 24, no. 3, Summer 1977.

Spencer, Charles. *Blue Collar: An Internal Examination of the Workplace.* Chicago: Lakeside Charter Books, 1977.

Stalin, Joseph. *Political Report of the Central Committee to the Fifteenth Congress of the C.P.S.U.* (B). Moscow: Foreign Languages Publishing House, 1950.

——. *The Essential Stalin: Major Theoretical Writings, 1905–52,* ed. Bruce Franklin. Garden City, N.Y.: Anchor Books, 1972.

Stearns, Peter N. *European Society in Upheaval: Social History Since 1800.* London: Macmillan, 1970.

Sternberg, Fritz. *Capitalism and Socialism on Trial.* London: Victor Gollancz, 1951.

Stites, Richard. "Fantasy and Revolution: Alexander Bogdanov and the Origins of Bolshevik Science Fiction," in *Red Star,* ed. Alexander Bogdanov. Bloomington: Indiana University Press, 1984.

——. *The Women's Liberation Movement in Russia: Feminism, Nihilism and Bolshevism, 1860–1930.* Princeton: Princeton University Press, 1978.

Suny, Ronald Grigor. *The Baku Commune 1917–1918: Class and Nationality in the Russian Revolution.* Princeton: Princeton University Press, 1972.

——. "Toward a Social History of the October Revolution," *American Historical Review* vol. 88, no. 1, February 1983.

Surh, Gerald D. "Petersburg's First Mass Labor Organization: The Assembly of Russian Workers and Father Gapon," 2 pts., *Russian Review* vol. 40, no. 3, July and vol. 40, no. 4, October 1981.

Sverdlova, K. *Yakov Sverdlov.* Moscow: Progress Publishers, 1981.

Swain, Geoffrey. "Editor's Introduction," in *Protokoly Soveshaniya Rasshirennoi Redaktsil "Proletariya" Iyun' 1909 (Proceedings of the Meeting of the Expanded Editorial Board of Proletarii June*

1909). Milwood, N.Y.: Kraus International Publications, 1982.

———. *Russian Social Democracy and the Legal Labor Movement: 1906–14*. London: Macmillan, 1983.

Sweezy, Paul. *The Theory of Capitalist Development*. New York: Monthly Review Press, 1968.

Taft, Bernie. "The Leninist Party," *Socialist Revolution* vol. 5, no. 1, January 1975.

Thomas, Norman. A*merica's Way Out: A Program for Democracy*. New York: Rand School Press, 1931.

———. *A Socialist's Faith*. New York: W. W. Norton, 1951.

Thompson, John M. *Revolutionary Russia: 1917*. New York: Charles Scribner's Sons, 1981.

Trepper, Leopold. *The Great Game*. New York: MacGraw-Hill, 1977.

Trinkl, John. "Amid Partybuilding's Ruins: What Went Wrong?" *Guardian* September 4, 1985.

———. "Not the Time for a Leninist Party?" *Guardian* September 11, 1985.

———. "We Don't Need Another Vanguard," *Guardian* December 11, 1985.

———. "Where Have all the Party-builders Gone?" *Guardian* August 21, 1985.

Trotnow, Helmut. *Karl Liebknecht: A Political Biography*. Hamden, Conn: Archon Books, 1984.

Trotsky, Leon. *History of the Russian Revolution*, 3 vols. London: Sphere Books, 1967.

———. *In Defense of Marxism*. New York: Pathfinder Press, 1970.

———. "Lenin," in *Encyclopedia Britannica*, 13th ed., vol. 30. London: Encyclopedia Britannica, 1926.

———. *My Life: An Attempt at an Autobiography*. New York: Pathfinder Press, 1970.

———. *1905*. New York: Vintage Books, 1972.

———. *On Lenin: Notes Towards a Biography*. London: George G. Harrap, 1971.

———. *On the Paris Commune*. New York: Pathfinder Press, 1970.

———. *Our Political Tasks (1904)*. London: New Park. n.d.

———. *Stalin: An Appraisal of the Man and His Influence*. New York: Stein and Day, 1967.

———. *The Challenge of the Left Opposition: 1923–25*. New York: Pathfinder Press, 1975.

The Permanent Revolution and Results and Prospects. New York: Pathfinder Press, 1978.

The Stalin School of Falsification. New York: Pathfinder Press, 1972.

The Third International After Lenin. New York: Pathfinder Press, 1970.

The Revolution Betrayed. New York: Merit Publishers, 1965.

The Young Lenin. Garden City, N.Y.: Doubleday & Co., 1972.

Writings: 1935–36. New York: Pathfinder Press, 1977.

Tucker, Robert C. *Stalin as Revolutionary: 1879–1929*. New York: W. W. Norton, 1974.

Valentinov, Nikolay. *Encounters with Lenin*. Oxford: Oxford University Press, 1968.

Venturi, Franco. *Roots of Revolution: A History of the Populist and Socialist Movements in 19th Century Russia*. New York: Grossett & Dunlap, 1966.

Volobuev, P. V. "The Proletariat—Leader of the Socialist Revolution," *Soviet Studies in History* vol. 22, no. 3, Winter 1983/1984.

Wade, Rex A. *Red Guards and Workers' Militias in the Russian Revolution*. Stanford: Stanford University Press, 1984.

———. "Spontaneity in the Formation of the Workers' Militia and Red Guards, 1917," in *Reconsiderations on the Russian Revolution*, ed. Ralph Carter Elwood. Cambridge, Mass.: Slavica Publishers, 1976.

Wald, Alan. *The New York Intellectuals: The Rise and Decline of the Anti-Stalinist Left from the 1930s to the 1980s*. Chapel Hill: University of North Carolina Press, 1987.

Waller, Michael. *Democratic Centralism: An Historical Commentary*. New York: St. Martin's Press, 1981.

Walling, William English. *Russia's Message: The People Against the Czar*. New York: Alfred A. Knopf, 1917.

————. *The Socialists and the War*. New York: Henry Holt and Co., 1915.

Waterman, Peter (ed.). *For a New Labour Internationalism: A Set of Reprints and Working Papers*. The Hague: International Labor Education Research and Information Foundation, 1984.

White, James D. "The First *Pravda* and the Russian Marxist Tradition," *Soviet Studies* vol. 26, no. 2, April 1974.

Wildman, Allan K. *The Making of a Workers' Revolution: Russian Social Democracy, 1891–1903*. Chicago: University of Chicago Press, 1967.

Williams, Robert, C. "Collective Immortality: The Syndicalist Origins of Proletarian Culture, 1905-1910," *Slavic Review* vol. 39, no. 3, September 1980.

————. "Russians in Germany: 1900–14," *Journal of Contemporary History* vol. 4, no. 1, October 1966.

————. *The Other Bolsheviks: Lenin and His Critics, 1904–1914*. Bloomington: Indiana University Press, 1986.

Williams, William A. "American Intervention in Russia, 1917–1920," 2 pts., *Studies on the Left* vol. 3, no. 4, Fall 1963 and vol. 4, no. 1 Winter 1964.

Wolfe, Bertram D. *A Life in Two Centuries: An Autobiography*. New York: Stein and Day, 1981.

————. *Lenin and the Twentieth Century: A Bertram D. Wolfe Retrospective*, ed. Lennard D. Gerson. Stanford: Hoover Institution, 1984.

————. *Marxism: One Hundred Years in the Life of a Doctrine*. New York: Dell, 1967.

————. *Three Who Made a Revolution*. New York: Dell, 1964.

Wollenberg, Erich. *The Red Army*. London: New Park, 1978.

Woytinsky, W. S. *Stormy Passage, A Personal History Through Two Russian Revolutions to Democracy and Freedom: 1905–1960*. New York: Vanguard Press, 1961.

Yarmolinsky, Avrahm. *Road to Revolution: A Century of Russian Radicalism*. New York: Collier Books, 1962.

Yassour, Avraham. "Lenin and Bogdanov: Protagonists in the 'Bolshevik Center,'" *Studies in Soviet Thought* vol. 22, no. 1, February 1981.

Ypsilon. *Pattern for World Revolution*. Chicago: Ziff-Davis, 1947.

Zelnik, Reginald E. "Russian Bebels: An Introduction to the Memoirs of the Russian Workers Semen Kantachikov and Matvei Fisher," 2 pts, *Russian Review* vol. 35, no. 3, July 1976 and vol. 35, no. 4, October 1976.

————. "Russian Workers and the Revolutionary Movement," *Journal of Social History* vol. 6, no. 2, Winter 1972/1973.

Zeluck, Steve. "The Evolution of Lenin's Views on the Party. Or, Lenin on Regroupment," *Against the Current* vol. 3, no. 4, Winter 1985.

Zeman, Z. A. B., and W. B. Scharlau. *The Merchant of Revolution: The Life of Alexander Israel Helphand (Parvus), 1867–1924*. New York: Oxford University Press, 1965.

Zinoviev, Gregory. *History of the Bolshevik Party: A Popular Outline*. London: New Park, 1973.

————. "Nikolai Lenin," *Communist International* no. 1 in 1924.

————. "The Fifth Anniversary of the Comintern," *Communist International* no. 1 in 1924.

Index